Alessandro Novembre
Young Schopenhauer

Alessandro Novembre

Young Schopenhauer

The Origin of the Metaphysics of Will and its Aporias

Translated by
Sarah De Sanctis

DE GRUYTER

The translation of this work has been funded by SEPS

Segretariato Europeo per le Pubblicazioni Scientifiche
Via Val d'Aposa 7 – 40123 Bologna – Italy
seps@seps.it – www.seps.it

This work was originally published in Italian as *Il giovane Schopenhauer. L'origine della metafisica della volontà* by Alessandro Novembre.
© 2018 Mim Edizioni srl (Milan-Udine).   http://www.mimesisedizioni.it

ISBN 978-3-11-066559-8
e-ISBN (PDF) 978-3-11-066869-8
e-ISBN (EPUB) 978-3-11-066546-8

Library of Congress Control Number: 2023939903

Bibliographic information published by the Deutsche Nationalbibliothek
The Deutsche Nationalbibliothek lists this publication in the Deutsche Nationalbibliografie; detailed bibliographic data are available on the internet at http://dnb.dnb.de.

© 2025 Walter de Gruyter GmbH, Berlin/Boston
This volume is text- and page-identical with the hardback published in 2023.
Cover image: rarinlada / iStock / Getty Images Plus
Printing and binding: CPI books GmbH, Leck

www.degruyter.com

Acknowledgments

I would like to first thank De Gruyter, specifically the Philosophy Editor Christoph Schirmer, and my Italian publisher Mimesis, especially Editorial Director Roberto Revello, for making this project possible. I also wish to express my sincere gratitude to the SEPS (European Secretariat for Scientific Publications) for their financial help with the translation costs.

I am particularly grateful to the translator, Sarah De Sanctis, for the intelligence, professionalism, and kindness with which she carried out this work.

The English translation gave me the opportunity to make some improvements to the text and update the secondary literature. There are many scholars with whom I had the privilege to discuss individual points of my research; in particular, I would like to thank Stephan Atzert, Márcio Benchimol Barros, Dieter Birnbacher, Maria Lúcia Mello e Oliveira Cacciola, Flamarion Caldeira Ramos, Simone Cavallini, Michał Dobrzański, Sossio Giametta, Oswaldo Giacóia Júnior, Fabio Grigenti, Giovanni Gurisatti, Philipp Höfele, Lore Hühn, Giuseppe Invernizzi, Christopher Janaway, Yasuo Kamata, Matthias Koßler, Jens Lemanski, Thomas Regehly, Alexander Sattar, Daniel Schubbe, Marco Segala and Sandra Shapshay, for the valuable and generous insights I received from them after the publication of the Italian version.

Finally, I wish to thank my wonderful big family for their love, without which my endeavors would be meaningless. No words can express how grateful I am to you all.

Grosseto, December 2022

Contents

Notes on Text and Translation —— XVII

Abbreviations and Short Citations —— XIX

Introduction —— 1

Part 1 The Manuscripts of the Years 1804–1811: From a Pietist Education to the Study of Philosophy

1 Schopenhauer's Early Understanding of the World: The Dualism between Temporality and Eternity —— 9
1.1 Introduction —— 9
1.2 The Translation of Milton's *On Time* —— 10
1.3 From Eternity to Time —— 12
1.4 The "Direct Echo of Eternity": Music —— 14
1.5 "Corporeal World" and "Spiritual World". Philosophy, Contemplation and Remembrance —— 16
1.6 Time and Immortality —— 19
1.7 The Idea of Evil and Tragedy. The Possibility of an Evil Divine Principle —— 21
1.8 Cognition of the Supersensible through Interiority. Religion and Art —— 25
1.9 Schopenhauer's Early Understanding of the Will. Θέλημα and βούλησις —— 29

2 Attending G. E. Schulze's Lectures and Reading Plato, Schelling and Kant —— 34
2.1 Introduction —— 34
2.2 Schulze: The Human Tension towards the Absolute and the Eternal. Philosophy and Metaphysics —— 35
2.3 "On Plato": The Difference between Platonic Idea and Abstract Concept. The Ideas "of the Forms of Nature" —— 37
2.4 "On Plato": "Those Ideas that Reside within Us without Having an Object in the Material World of Sense" —— 40
2.5 Art and Philosophy as the Expression of the Supersensible through Sense Objects. The Basis of the Metaphysical Predilection for Music —— 42

2.6 Kant's (Anti-)Copernican Revolution: The Distinction between "Appearance" and "Thing-in-Itself" —— 45
2.7 Reading Tennemann's *Geschichte der Philosophie*. Kant and Plato, or, *Erscheinung* and φαινόμενον —— 49
2.8 The "Nightmare" of Critical Philosophy —— 56
2.9 Yearning for Eternity and the Transcendental Ideality of Time —— 57
2.10 Truth and Life. The Philosopher and the Philistine —— 58
2.11 The Philosophies of Fichte and Schelling according to Schulze —— 60
2.12 Moral Sentiment and Hope for Greater Happiness —— 61
2.13 Conclusion. The Platonic Vector and the Kantian Vector —— 64

Part 2 The Critical Confrontation with Fichte and Schelling (1811/12): From Initial Enthusiasm to Complete Rejection

3 Appearance and Thing-in-Itself —— 69
3.1 Introduction —— 69
3.2 The Intuition of Things-in-Themselves: Genius and Madness —— 69
3.3 Genius and Knowledge of the Absolute. Schelling's Response to Plato —— 74
3.4 The *Besonnenheit* of Genius according to E. T. A. Hoffmann and Jean Paul —— 76
3.5 The "Flash of Evidence" and "True Knowledge" "Beyond All Experience" —— 79
3.6 Kant's Appearance and Plato's Cave. The Determination of Phenomenal Knowledge as Non-Truth —— 82
3.7 Schulze's Presentation of Kantian Philosophy at Göttingen: The Reduction of "Appearance" to "Representation" —— 86
3.8 The Skeptical Interpretation of Kantian Criticism: The Determination of the "Thing-in-Itself" as "Truth" —— 89
3.9 Conclusion. Critical Dualism and Ontological Dualism —— 92

4 Will and World. The Will as ὄντως ὄν —— 96
4.1 Nothingness of the World and Reality of the Will in Moral Consideration —— 96
4.2 Meaning of This Early Relevance of the Term "Will". A First False Precedent of the System —— 98
4.3 "Being" as "the Product of the Operation of the Categories". Schopenhauer's Early Theory of Cognition —— 99

4.4 The Will, "as a Thing-in-Itself, Stands beyond All Time". A Second False Precedent of the System —— 106
4.5 Conclusion —— 111

5 Fichte: Empirical Consciousness and *Consciousness* of Empirical Consciousness. The Philosophical *Besonnenheit* —— 112

5.1 Introduction —— 112
5.2 Fichte: Philosophy as Knowledge of Knowledge —— 112
5.3 Fichte: "Higher Consciousness" or *absolute Besonnenheit* —— 114
5.4 Interlude: *Absolute Besonnenheit* and σωφροσύνη. The Knowledge of Knowledge in Socrates and Fichte —— 116
5.5 Schopenhauer: The Difference between the "Understanding's Concept" and the "Thing Itself" of the "Perception of Perception". The World as the Totality of the Perceivable —— 119
5.6 *Absolute Besonnenheit* as Metempirical Consciousness —— 122
5.7 The Contradictory Nature of Naive Realism —— 125
5.8 In Perspective: The *philosophische Besonnenheit* in *The World as Will and Representation* —— 127
5.9 Conclusion —— 132

6 The "Transcendent Use of the Understanding": The Illegitimacy of Fichte's and Schelling's Philosophies from the Perspective of Kantian Criticism —— 133

6.1 Introduction —— 133
6.2 "Cause" vs. "Supersensible Ground". The Scope of the Sciences and the Meaning of the Question "Why" —— 135
6.3 The Illegitimate Use of the Category of Causality as the Foundation of Fichtean Idealism —— 138
6.4 In Perspective: Man's Endless *Streben* in Fichte's Idealism and Schopehauer's Metaphysics of Will —— 142
6.5 Schelling's Concept of the "Absolute" as a "Product of the Transcendent Understanding" —— 146
6.6 The Impossible Identity of the Different and the Disguised Trinitarian Dogma: Criticism of Schelling's "Intellectual Intuition" —— 150
6.7 The Irreducible Subject-Object Polarity and the Consequent Impossibility of the Subject's Self-Cognition —— 154
6.8 From the Eternal to Time. The Transcendent Use of Causality in Schelling's Cosmogony and Anthropogony —— 157

6.9   The Reduction of the Ideas of Reason to Concepts of the Understanding. The Cognizability of the Supersensible and the Project of a "True Criticism" —— **161**
6.10 Conclusion —— **165**

Part 3 A First Attempt at a Post-Kantian Metaphysics: The Theory of the "Better Consciousness"

7   Schopenhauer's Original Thought in the Manuscripts of 1812: The Project of a "True Criticism" and the Figure of the "Better Consciousness" —— 171
7.1   After Kant: The Program of a "True, Thorough and Pure Criticism" —— **171**
7.2   "World of Semblance" and "True World". Difference between Transcendent and Figurative Use of Empirical Determinations. The Essence of Religion —— **173**
7.3   Religion and Philosophy. "True Criticism" as the "Ultimate System" of Thought —— **174**
7.4   The Identity between Understanding and Theoretical Reason and the Inadequacy of the Term "Practical Reason" for the Moral Faculty —— **177**
7.5   The Absolute Incompatibility of Moral Law and Practical Reason —— **182**
7.6   The Cornerstone of "True Criticism": The "Better Consciousness" —— **186**
7.7   Some Remarks on the Expression "Better Consciousness". Fichte's Probable Influence —— **188**
7.8   Art as a Stimulus to Better Consciousness: "Out of What Appeared to Be Nothing a World Springs Up and the Prodigious Vanishes into Nothing" —— **191**
7.9   The Moral Law as a "Higher Faculty of Cognition". The Annihilation of One's Own Will in the Notes to Fichte's *System der Sittenlehre*: A Third False Precedent of the System —— **193**
7.10 Dualism of Things and Duplicity of Man. Philosophical Astonishment —— **197**
7.11 The Will as a Faculty of Choice between Empirical Consciousness and Better Consciousness: The Root of Schopenhauer's 'Voluntarism' —— **202**
7.12 Nature as a Will-to-Life and Well-Being: A Fourth False Precedent of the System. The Duplicity of Man and the Consequent Ambiguity of the Term "Nature" —— **204**
7.13 Γνῶτι σεαυτόν: Man's "Supersensible Self-Consciousness". Better Consciousness and Intellectual Intuition —— **207**
7.14 Conclusion: The Contradictory Attempt to Positively Express the Absolutely Opposite Realm to the Empirical One —— **210**

8 The Theory of the Better Consciousness in the Manuscripts of 1813. A First Attempt at a System —— 213

- 8.1 "Being" and "Nothingness" in Young Schopenhauer's Reflections before 1813 —— 213
- 8.2 The Concept of "Nothing" as a "Mere Concept of Relation". From the Ontological to the Gnoseological Sense of the Opposition between "Being" and "Nothing" —— 214
- 8.3 The Freedom of the I as a Capacity for Self-Positing. *Esse sequitur operari* —— 218
- 8.4 Duplicity and the Experience of Contradiction. The "Residue" of Individuality and the Impossibility of Suppressing Original Duplicity —— 223
- 8.5 The Role of the Concept of "Nothing" within "True Criticism" —— 224
- 8.6 The Impossibility of a Personal God. The Term "God" as a Symbolic Expression of the Better Consciousness —— 227
- 8.7 Practical Affirmation and Negation of Temporality or Eternity. The Salvific Power of Pain —— 230
- 8.8 Freedom in the Negative Sense: "Breaking Away" from the World, i.e. from Empirical Consciousness. Virtue and Asceticism as the Possible "Return Journey" —— 232
- 8.9 Reason as a Necessary Condition of Negative Freedom: The Difference between Man and Animal —— 234
- 8.10 The Analogy between Man and Animal: The Intelligible Character as a Ground for Existence —— 238
- 8.11 Life and Death, or: The Dream and Awakening of an "Eternal Spirit". More on the Indeterminate Residue of Individuality —— 239
- 8.12 The Aesthetic Phenomenon of the Sublime as a Manifestation of the Duplicity of Human Consciousness —— 243
- 8.13 Beauty as Theoretical Affirmation of the Eternal World and Theoretical Negation of the Temporal World. The Contemplation of the Platonic Idea —— 246
- 8.14 The Platonic Idea as an Object of Cognition of the Better Consciousness —— 253
- 8.15 "The Magic of the Past". Memory and Contemplation —— 255
- 8.16 The Better Consciousness and Music. The Lost Essay *On the Gradation of the Arts* —— 256
- 8.17 The Peak of Humanity: Genius and Sainthood —— 258
- 8.18 The Mysterious "Connexion" between Empirical Consciousness and Better Consciousness and the Primacy of the Will —— 260

8.19 The "Transcendental Illusion" of the Relationship between Empirical and Better Consciousness and the Dogma of Original Sin as Its Mythical Representation —— 264
8.20 The Fundamental Aporia: The Better Consciousness "Does Not Think and Cognize, Since It Lies beyond Subject and Object". Absolute and Non-absolute Opposition —— 268
8.21 Conclusion. The Unfinished Project of a Work on the Better Consciousness —— 270

Part 4 The Abandonment of the Theory of the Better Consciousness and the Origin of the Metaphysics of Will

9 Will and Intelligible Character in the Dissertation of 1813: Between Fichte's *System der Sittenlehre* and Schelling's *Freiheitsschrift* —— 277
9.1 Introduction: A Short Biographical Outline —— 277
9.2 Some Preliminary Reflections: The Four Basic Laws of the Understanding and the Principle of the Unalterability of a Concept —— 279
9.3 Purpose and Structure of the Dissertation *On the Fourfold Root of the Principle of Sufficient Reason*. The Identity of "Appearance" and "Representation" and the First Three Forms of the Principle of Reason —— 283
9.4 First Retrospective Digression: The Study of Fichte's *System der Sittenlehre* in 1812. The Will as the Second Predicate of the I and the Possibility of the Subject's Self-Cognition —— 289
9.5 The "Miracle *Par Excellence*": The Identity, in One and the Same I, of Subject of Cognition and Subject of Will. Comparison of Some Passages from the *System der Sittenlehre* and the Dissertation —— 292
9.6 The Lived-Body (*Leib*) as the Immediate Object of Cognition and Willing. Echoes of Fichte and Schelling —— 295
9.7 The Fourth Form of the Principle of Reason: The *principium rationis sufficientis agendi*. Motive and Determination of the Will —— 298
9.8 The Intelligible Character: "A Universal Act of Will Lying Outside of Time", a "Willing, Which by Its Nature Is Free to the Greatest Degree, Indeed, Which Is the Innermost Essence of the Human Being" —— 299
9.9 Some Fundamental Differences between Kant's and Schopenhauer's Doctrines of the Intelligible Character. The Meaning of the Explicit Reference to Schelling's *Freiheitsschrift* —— 304

9.10 Second Retrospective Digression: The Study of Schelling's *Freiheitsschrift* in 1811. The "Will" as "Original Being" and Young Schopenhauer's Criticism —— 308
9.11 Schelling: Man's "Intelligible Being" as a Free Act of Self-Position Based on a Primal Willing. Comparison with Some Passages from the Dissertation —— 313
9.12 The Immanent Metaphysics Contained *in nuce* in the Dissertation. Difference between Schelling's and Schopenhauer's Metaphysics of Will —— 316
9.13 The Function of the Dissertation within "True Criticism" and the Announced Project of a "Larger Work". The Hidden References to the Better Consciousness and Some Consequent Changes in the Second Edition —— 319
9.14 Conclusion: The Treatment of "Will" as a Link between the Discourse on Empirical Consciousness and the Discourse on Better Consciousness —— 327

10 The Manuscripts of 1814: The Development of the Doctrine of Intelligible Character. The Prodromes of the Metaphysics of Will —— 330

10.1 The Crucial Year —— 330
10.2 Identity and Difference between Religion and Philosophy. The Superiority of Philosophy —— 331
10.3 "The Main Problem of Philosophy": The Origin of Empirical Consciousness —— 333
10.4 The "Fall of Adam" and the "Expiatory Death of Jesus": Original Sin and Redemption —— 335
10.5 The Better Consciousness as the "Nothing" and "Annihilation" of the Empirical Consciousness. The Extinction of the Self —— 337
10.6 "Willing-Happiness Is the Opposite of Willing-Life". Life in Time as a "Practical Error" —— 339
10.7 Intelligible Character, Temporal Existence and the Body: The Shadow of Schelling. The 'Deduction' of an Individual and Metaphysical "Willing-Life" —— 340
10.8 The Pure Subject as the Antithesis of Will and Body. *Kshetra* and *Kshetrajna* —— 345
10.9 The Doctrine of Intelligible Character as the Solution to the "Main Problem of Philosophy". The Fulfillment of the Voluntarist Position: *esse sequitur velle* —— 348
10.10 "We Are Sanctified Not by Works, But by Faith". Irrelevance of *operari* and Decisiveness of *esse* —— 353

10.11 Looking at the Mirror of Life: Pain, Better Cognition and Redemption. The Rejection of the Intelligible Character —— **356**

10.12 Beyond the Principle of Reason: Art and Philosophy. Knowledge of the "Idea of Being in Time" and the Consequent "Will-Not-to-Be". The Double Nature of Human Consciousness and Will —— **361**

10.13 Voluntarism or Intellectualism? The Subordination of the Will-in-Itself to the Law of Motivation —— **364**

10.14 The Vanity of Suicide —— **370**

10.15 Will as the Origin of Pain. The Infinity of Will —— **372**

11 The Study of *Oupnekhat* and the Elaboration of the Concept of a Universal "Will-To-Life". The Abandonment of the Theory of the Better Consciousness and the Birth of the System —— 375

11.1 The Encounter with Indian Wisdom —— **375**

11.2 The Reading of the *Oupnekhat*: Maya as Universal *voluntas aeterna* and Individual *appetitus existentiae. Cognitio, nolitio* and *annihilatio* —— **376**

11.3 The First Occurrence of the Term *Maya* in the Manuscripts of 1814 and the New Concept of a Universal Metaphysical Will, of Which the Whole World Is the Appearance —— **381**

11.4 A Few Reasons for Young Schopenhauer's Sensitivity to Oriental Wisdom. The Meaning of His Ambiguous Retrospective Reflections —— **385**

11.5 Starting from the Subject: The Method of the "Wiser Indians" as the Only Possible Alternative to Transcendent Dogmatism —— **388**

11.6 The Original Analogical Inference of Manuscripts: From the Concept of Intelligible Character to the Concept of a Universal Will-to-Life —— **390**

11.7 Meaning and Consequences of the Analogical Argument. Fidelity to "True Criticism" and Following Differences between the Will-to-Life and the Maya of the *Oupnekhat* —— **395**

11.8 The Pure Subject of Cognition: Suspension of the Will and Intuition of the Idea. The *Besonnenheit* of Genius —— **400**

11.9 The Secret Concordance between Plato and Kant: The Identity of Plato's Idea and the Thing-in-Itself —— **404**

11.10 Coincidence and Opposition of Better Consciousness and Cognition of the Idea. The Better Consciousness Is Not "Consciousness": The Breaking Point of the Theory and the Abandonment of the Expression "Better Consciousness" —— **409**

11.11 Affinities and Differences between Better Consciousness and the Pure Subject of Cognition. Cognition of the Idea as a Result of "Disengaging Oneself" from the Will —— **414**

11.12 "The World as Thing-in-Itself Is a Great Will". The Identification of Thing-in-Itself, Platonic Idea and Will —— **420**
11.13 Self-Cognition and Self-Denial of the Will-to-Life —— **423**
11.14 Univocity of Human Consciousness, Cognition and Will. 'Positivity' of Pain and 'Negativity' of Pleasure. Turning Back from Existence: Nothing and Nirvana —— **427**
11.15 Conclusion. Absolute and Non-absolute Opposition: The Splitting of Contradictory Determinations That Constituted the Figure of the Better Consciousness —— **433**

12 From the Early Manuscripts to *The World as Will and Representation*. Origin and Meaning of the Aporias in Schopenhauer's Mature System —— 436
12.1 Introduction —— **436**
12.2 The Analogical Argument in *The World as Will and Representation:* The Silent Foundational Role of the Doctrine of the Intelligible Character —— **437**
12.3 Denomination from the Superior Term, Genus and Species. Observational or 'Inductive' Confirmation of the Analogical Inference and the Difference between Science and Philosophy —— **449**
12.4 Terminological Analysis: The 'Platonizing' Description of the Distinction between Appearance and Thing-in-Itself —— **456**
12.5 Platonic Idea and Thing-in-Itself —— **464**
12.6 Cognizability and Uncognizability of the Thing-in-Itself. The Original Identification of Platonic Idea and Thing-in-Itself and the Subsequent Correction in the Light of Criticism —— **467**
12.7 The Intelligible Character as a Platonic Idea of the Individual. The Intuitive Cognition of the Thing-in-Itself and the 'Consequent' Denial of the Will-to-Life —— **476**
12.8 Intuitive Cognition or Uncognizability of the Thing-in-Itself? Primacy of the Will or Primacy of Cognition? Explanation of These Aporias in the Light of the Genetic Perspective —— **482**
12.9 From the Youthful Dualism between Time and Eternity to the Mature Dualism between Appearance and Thing-in-Itself: The Paradigm Shift and Ambiguity of the Platonic Idea —— **498**
12.10 Man's Transcendental Freedom and the Summit of Philosophy: Epilogue into "Nothing" —— **508**

Bibliography of Works Cited —— 517
1 Schopenhauer's Works —— **517**
2 English Translations of Schopenhauer's Works —— **517**
3 Primary Literature —— **518**
4 Secondary Literature —— **523**

Index —— 541

Notes on Text and Translation

The present book refers to the *Cambridge Edition of the Works of Schopenhauer* whenever quoting Schopenhauer's works. The only exception is Schopenhauer's manuscript legacy, which is only available in the edition partially translated and edited by E. F. J. Payne (*Manuscript Remains in Four Volumes*, Oxford 1988). For the passages not included in the latter volume, we will use our own translation.

In some cases, Payne and the translators of the Cambridge edition made different and incompatible choices, so it was necessary for the internal coherence of the present text to standardize the translation of Schopenhauer's main technical terms. Therefore, we decided to modify Payne's translation according to the translation choices of the Cambridge edition for the terms reported below.

Furthermore, in most English translations of Schopenhauer the distinction between *Leib* (the body as lived or experienced by the subject) and *Körper* (the body as a physical, anatomical object) is largely ignored. We report the difference either in translation or by noting the German in brackets.

More broadly, in our citations of primary literature texts, we occasionally chose to correct the English translations used and indicated the changes in a footnote. We only did this when we believed the original text's sense was compromised.

In addition to these purely terminological choices, we also standardized typographical usage across the various reference editions. In this vein, we always capitalized the term "idea" when referring to the Platonic Idea, capitalized "Absolute" when intended in the philosophical sense, and used lowercase for the adjective "philistine" to emphasize its figurative meaning. We used hyphens in "will-to-life" and "thing-in-itself" to facilitate reading and, for the same reason, we adopted the English spelling of terms coming from Indian texts. Finally, we standardized the spelling of Wolff's surname to include two effs, instead of one as in Payne's texts.

Unless otherwise stated, biblical quotations come from the New International Version of the Bible.

Alessandro Novembre and Sarah De Sanctis

Translation Choices:

Anschauen:	to intuit	*Verstand:*	understanding
Anschauung:	intuition	*Wahn:*	delusion
Bekehrung:	conversion	*Wahrhaft seyend,*	
Erkennen:	cognize	ὄντως ὄν:	truly being
Erkenntnis:	cognition	*Wahrnehmung:*	perception
Erlösung:	redemption	*Wendung:*	turning, turning around
Erscheinung:	appearance[1]	*sich wenden:*	reverse course, turn around
Heil:	salvation	*Wille zum Leben:*	will-to-life
Nichtig:	null, vacuous	*Wissen:*	knowledge, to know
Nichtigkeit:	nothingness		
Objektität:	objecthood		
Objektivation:	objectivation		
Objektivirung:	objectification		
Quietiv:	tranquillizer		
Schein:	semblance		
Trieb:	drive		
Übereinstimmung:	agreement, accordance		
(Über)Sinnlich:	(super)sensible (sensuous is only used with a sensual connotation, e.g. "sensuous pleasure")		

---

1 As is well known, *Erscheinung* is a key term in Kantian and post-Kantian philosophy. It must therefore be considered a technical term, at least whenever it is (implicitly or explicitly) opposed to *Ding an sich* (thing-in-itself). Payne mostly renders *Erscheinung* with "phenomenon", while the translators of the Cambridge edition mostly use "appearance". This inconsistency is also present in the Italian language: most Italian translators render *Erscheinung* with "fenomeno"; others, however, primarily use "apparenza". In the Italian version of the present book (pp. 31–34), I defend, for various reasons, the term "phenomenon", which I used there to standardize the translation of *Erscheinung*. The semantic spectrum of the English "appearance" does not entirely match that of the Italian word "apparenza", so some of my observations regarding the latter term are not applicable to the first. Furthermore, I had to take into account the preference given by most English translators of Kant and Schopenhauer to the word "appearance". The alternate use of "phenomenon" and "appearance" for *Erscheinung* was not practical because these two terms, strictly speaking, are not semantically equivalent; it was therefore necessary to standardize the translation. To make the text more accessible to the English-speaking audience, it seemed appropriate to adhere to the most accredited English translations, opting for "appearance" in Schopenhauer's texts, at least when the term is intended as opposed to *Ding an sich* (thing-in-itself).

Abbreviations and Short Citations

HN	Schopenhauer, Arthur. 1985. *Der handschriftliche Nachlaß*, edited by Arthur Hübscher, 5 vols. Munich: Deutscher Taschenbuch Verlag:
HN I:	Vol. I: *Frühe Manuskripte (1804–1818)*;
HN II:	Vol. II: *Kritische Auseinandersetzungen (1809–1818)*;
HN III:	Vol. III: *Berliner Manuskripte (1818–1830)*;
HN IV/1:	Vol. IV/1: *Die Manuskriptbücher der Jahre 1830–1852*;
HN V:	Vol. V: *Randschriften zu Büchern*).
MR 1	Schopenhauer, Arthur. 1988a. *Manuscript Remains*, vol. 1: *Early Manuscripts (1804–1818)*, edited by Arthur Hübscher, translated by E. F. J. Payne. Oxford/New York/Hamburg: Berg.
MR 2	Schopenhauer, Arthur. 1988b. *Manuscript Remains*, vol. 2: *Critical Debates (1809–1818)*, edited by Arthur Hübscher, translated by E. F. J. Payne. Oxford/New York/Hamburg: Berg.
MR 3	Schopenhauer, Arthur. 1989. *Manuscript Remains*, vol. 3: *Berlin Manuscripts (1818–1830)*, edited by Arthur Hübscher, translated by E. F. J. Payne. Oxford/New York/Munich: Berg.
WWV 1844	Schopenhauer, Arthur. 1844. *Die Welt als Wille und Vorstellung. Zweite, durchgängig verbessert und sehr vermehrte Auflage*, 2 vols. Leipzig: Brockhaus.
WWV 1859	Schopenhauer, Arthur. 1859. *Die Welt als Wille und Vorstellung. Dritte, verbesserte und beträchtlich vermehrte Auflage*, 2 vols. Leipzig: Brockhaus.

Introduction

> Philosophy is a high mountain road which is reached only by a steep path covered with sharp stones and prickly thorns. It is an isolated road and becomes ever more desolate, the higher we ascend. Whoever pursues this path must show no fear, but must leave everything behind and confidently make his own way in the wintry snow. Often he suddenly comes to a precifice and looks down upon the verdant valley. A violent attack of dizziness draws him over the edge, but he must control himself and cling to the rocks with might and main. In return for this, he soon sees the world beneath him; its sandy deserts and morasses vanish from his view, its uneven spots are levelled out, its jarring sounds no longer reach his ear, and its roundness is revealed to him. He himself is always in the pure cool mountain air and now beholds the sun when all below is still engulfed in dead of night. [1]

One of the questions that authors of philosophical monographs hear most often is: "What does this philosopher still have to say to us?" Or else: "How is this philosopher's thought still relevant today?" In the present study, the thinker at issue is Arthur Schopenhauer (1788–1860). Since questions of this kind are asked rather often, at times with a claim to genuine criticism, it is worth considering them briefly. In order to try to seriously answer such questions (which in this case would sound like: "What can Schopenhauer still teach us today?" or: "How is Schopenhauer's thought still relevant?"),[2] I would propose to invert them and ask: "What could we really teach Schopenhauer today?", i.e., "From a strictly and purely philosophical point of view, what about today's world would be relevant and 'new' in Schopenhauer's eyes?"

The question of what a certain philosopher of the past might have to say usually implies that the answer is nothing at all, unless proven otherwise. This assumption, more than unfounded, is partial: it can only be truthfully assumed in relation to properly historical elements – the 'facts' that occurred after the death of said philosopher – and the progress of natural science (and technology).

---

[1] Schopenhauer 1988a (henceforth MR 1), p. 14.
[2] R. Malter addressed this question very seriously. Cf. Malter 1996.

With regard to *everything else* – for example, to the meaning of those 'facts' and the general consequences to be drawn from them – it is certainly possible that a given philosopher is 'outdated' and no longer has anything to say; possible, indeed, but not clear-cut or obvious. This is something to discuss, and indeed, we should talk about it, justifying and substantiating each thesis in an adequate manner.

The point is, however, that the strictly philosophical contribution of a thinker concerns precisely all that escapes the non-problematic nature of that assumption – namely, *all those things* about which no thesis or antithesis can be taken for granted. To use approximative (and abused) terms, that philosophical contribution lies in trying to decipher the 'meaning' and 'reason' of 'facts' – above all, of the complex set of facts we call life or existence; or even asking *whether* facts and existence do or should have, in general, some 'sense' or 'reason' at all. Well, in relation to problems of this kind (and of this magnitude), I would venture to doubt, beyond the rhetoric of any explicit or implicit post-philosophy, that we, today, would have much to say to thinkers like Schopenhauer, Schelling or Plato.

Young Schopenhauer's philosophical vocation arose, as we shall see, along with his conviction that no knowledge of his time – not even scientific knowledge – was capable of adequately answering the fundamental questions of life. At first he enrolled in the faculty of Medicine; however, he later decided to devote himself to philosophy, because he realized he wanted to investigate the world and existence not (only) by focusing on some particular 'regions' of it, but life as such and as a whole, so he could in no way be satisfied by the kind of knowledge offered by science. In particular (as his very first annotations testify), Schopenhauer was violently shaken by the transience of all things, namely by the disconcerting but certain fact that this existence, together with everything included in it, is ultimately destined to end.

Very early on, he realized that in the face of this inescapable fact, as well as the overall question of 'meaning' that follows, science as such can do or say nothing. Yet the traditional answers provided by religion seemed to him equally incapable of bearing the theoretical and, at the same time, personal or 'existential' weight of his questions. Indeed, his meditation on these themes became so radical and overwhelming that it soon subordinated every other occupation or project: as he confided to the poet Wieland in 1811 (at the age of 23), he intended to spend his whole life reflecting on life itself.[3]

Dissatisfaction with the answers provided by science and general human knowledge was a *topos* of the time, one of which Goethe's *Faust* is probably the

---

[3] Cf. Cartwright 2010, p. 149.

most complex and powerful literary example. But Faust, in his abysmal and superhuman thirst for knowledge, was also disillusioned with philosophy (as such), not just all the sciences;[4] this is why he decided to turn to the occult arts and, ultimately, made a pact with Mephistopheles. Young Schopenhauer, on the other hand, never abandoned his 'faith' in the possibility of a strictly *philosophical* solution to the "riddle of the world" – so much so that, having ascertained (like Faust) its absence, he decided to commit himself fully to its search. The articulated unfolding of this research is the subject of the present work.

Through the analysis of Schopenhauer's youthful notebooks, I will try to reconstruct in detail the long and intricate course of Schopenhauer's speculation which led him to conceive his original philosophical system. A preliminary remark should be made here. In a testamentary disposition dated 26 June 1852, Schopenhauer decided to leave his entire manuscript legacy to his pupil and friend Julius Frauenstädt.[5] It consists of a large number of mostly unpublished texts written by the philosopher between 1804 and his death in 1860. The fact that he bequeathed them to a pupil, rather than hiding or destroying them, clearly indicates his desire to make them available for investigation. The analysis of this material, therefore, does not violate Schopenhauer's intentions or last wishes, but fulfills them; anyone who engages in the reading and study of these manuscripts does so with the permission and approval of their author.

The contribution that this volume intends to offer to the study of Schopenhauer's philosophy is structured along four main lines. The first concerns the reconstruction of young Schopenhauer's philosophical training and the identification of the texts that most stimulated – and at the same time conditioned – his precocious speculative vivacity. Some of the authors I will examine have been hitherto underestimated by the critical literature (such as W. G. Tennemann), others have already been extensively discussed and studied, but I will clarify their influence in a new or more detailed way (this is the case especially with G. E. Schulze, Fichte and Schelling; but also with Indian wisdom).

Secondly, following on from the first point, I will focus on the heterodox and essentially insubordinate way in which Schopenhauer used these authors' thought (in some individual traits). Indeed, the aforementioned conditioning should not be understood as a purely passive reception and thus, ultimately, as a lack of real autonomy or originality on Schopenhauer's part. On the contrary, he appropriated the reflections of others only to twist them and subordinate them to his own speculative aims, thus showing from the outset a very marked and assertive philosoph-

---

4 Cf. J. W. Goethe, *Faust* I, v. 354–360, in Goethe 2014, p. 13.
5 Cf. Schopenhauer 1911–1942, vol. XVI, p. 173, p. 13.

ical personality. In relation to every author or doctrine that may have influenced Schopenhauer's thought, I will therefore always try to account for the substantial transformations he brought about.

Thirdly, and more generally, I will illustrate the evolution and internal development of Schopenhauer's philosophy, highlighting the fundamental objectives and the constant effort of consequentiality on the part of the young philosopher – which led him, at times, to immediately discard certain theoretical solutions, or, in other cases, to abandon previously embraced speculative paths, in order to try new and more fruitful ones. The construction of the metaphysics of will, in its definitive physiognomy, came after numerous failed theoretical attempts, to which I will try to give due attention here. To this end, the manuscript legacy of the years 1804–1814 will be analyzed with particular attention. The definition of this *terminus ad quem* is due to the fact that, as Schopenhauer himself wrote, it was precisely in 1814 (in his 27th year of age) that "all the dogmas [...], even the unimportant ones", of his "thinking"[6] took shape – that same "one thought" set out four years later in *The World as Will and Representation*.[7]

Finally, in the last chapter I shall try to make heuristic (hermeneutically fruitful) use of the findings from the previous chapters. Critics have long emphasized the importance of studying the early manuscripts for an adequate understanding of Schopenhauer's philosophy: the themes peculiar to the published works can be observed here in their primitive directness or 'informality', and throughout the slow and complex process of their evolution. The manuscripts thus offer a formidable key to read Schopenhauer's speculative traits that, in the printed works, appear in such a perfect stylistic and formal balance that they generate considerable resistance to analysis.

In particular, I will examine some of the aporias into which Schopenhauer's mature philosophy seems to inevitably fall: they concern the compatibility, within the system, between the theory of cognition and the metaphysics of will. The attitude taken so far by critics with regard to these aporias (when they have been dis-

---

[6] Schopenhauer 1988a, fn to n. 207, p. 122. For the original, my edition of reference is Schopenhauer 1985, vol. I: *Frühe Manuskripte (1804–1818)* (henceforth HN I), to which the English translation refers.

[7] The first edition of *Die Welt als Wille und Vorstellung* was published at the end of 1818, bearing the date of the following year (1819). Cf. Schopenhauer 1819. English translation: Schopenhauer 2010b. As pointed out by the editors, the English translation is based on the text edited by Arthur Hübscher, *Arthur Schopenhauers Sämtliche Werke* (Schopenhauer 1988), which essentially follows the third edition (Schopenhauer 1859, vol. 1), "though with later editorial changes introduced by Julius Frauenstädt in the first complete edition of Schopenhauer's works (1873), and by subsequent editors" (p. 567).

cussed at all) has roughly been of three kinds: either they have been ignored as negligible, if not non-existent; or they have been emphasized to the point of concluding that the system is contradictory and therefore inconsistent; or, again, interpretations or solutions have been devised that nevertheless, however refined and ingenious, are based on a conceptuality and terminology that are in fact *foreign* to Schopenhauer's thought.[8]

My genetic analysis will be able to avoid all three of these outcomes. Indeed, by recognizing the effectiveness and scope of the aporetic elements, I will offer an explanation that is conceptually and terminologically intrinsic to Schopenhauer's thought, considered not only 'synchronically', but in the whole process of its evolution. In addition to the early notebooks, I will examine some significant variants of the three editions of *The World as Will and Representation* that Schopenhauer published during his lifetime. In any case, no attempt will be made here to 're-solve', in the sense of eliminating, the aporias; in fact, even such an elimination would produce a result extrinsic to Schopenhauer's philosophy: the latter does unquestionably give rise to aporias. My aim is to explain them by tracing them back to the specific genetic circumstances in virtue of which they were inevitable: *propositions formulated by Schopenhauer himself* will serve as explanatory principles in this sense.

Given the breadth of the research, I have structured the text according to a very analytical paragraphing, also inserting numerous internal cross-references between the single sections. This should allow the volume to be also read thematically as an alternative (or in addition) to the strictly sequential reading.

These, in short, are the fundamental and very general coordinates of this volume – which, however, do not exclude the possibility of further, collateral or secondary dimensions. For example, it has been rightly observed that the genetic reconstruction of a philosophical system can also constitute, at the same time, the most suitable and natural introduction to it.[9] In learning how a philosophical theory originated, one is introduced to it as it takes shape, and thus, so to speak, discovers it along with its author. In this sense, in the following pages we will get ac-

---

8 Here I take up, modifying it, the classification proposed by M. Booms in *Aporie und Subjekt* (2003, p. 23–25). In addition to the first two groups enumerated here, Booms identifies a third one (which in his list appears as the first), including all attempts to present the aporetic nature of Schopenhauer's thought as a mark of value of the system. I believe that the contributions in this third group can only be successful if they are ultimately based on concepts and terms that cannot be found in Schopenhauer's works. More precise bibliographical indications will be given in the last chapter. For an overview of the issue, cf. Lemanski and Schubbe 2018.
9 Cf. App 2011, p. 7.

quainted, step by step, with Schopenhauer's mature philosophy, in the company of young Schopenhauer himself.

Now, a question closely related to the two mentioned at the beginning – which is also, unfortunately, asked with great frequency to those who write about philosophy – is the following: "What is philosophy for?" (Aristotle already warned of the need to take this into consideration).[10] It is clear that the question is whether philosophy can be an effective means in relation, or in subordination, to certain ends. That question therefore means, properly: "What are the ends in relation to which philosophy can be an effective means?" That philosophy serves no purpose or is useless simply means that it is (presumably) an ineffective means in relation to the purposes that are being pursued. Which leads to the truly essential question: "What are the purposes that one should in principle pursue?"

It is extremely unfortunate that those who ask that question ("What is philosophy for?") completely lose sight of the very important fact that philosophy aims and has always aimed precisely at establishing *what are the most worthy purposes* – those in relation to which it is necessary to seek the most effective means. Whoever asks this question, on the other hand, basically presumes to already know what these ends are (and they are almost always the most immediate ones, or at least the most generally shared), because it is only in relation to them that they can doubt or contest the usefulness of philosophy. But philosophy is not something that serves something else; it is rather the critical and radical search for *that* 'something' in relation to which alone one can – and indeed should – ask about any other thing, "What is it for?", that is, precisely, "What value does it have?"

Schopenhauer's passionate and tormented intellectual, or (broadly speaking) 'spiritual' quest is an eminent attempt to solve that vital question. Witnessing the way in which a great young spirit conducted this research – even regardless of the specific results it historically led to – may 'be useful', perhaps, to emancipate our thinking from the persuasion (or illusion) of already knowing what is 'useful' and what isn't. Perhaps it will free us from the very immodest conviction of already knowing what aims are to be pursued (whereby supposedly there would really be nothing left for us to do but calculate and arrange the most effective means to achieve them). The invitation not to passively and unreflectively presuppose such knowledge is indeed the very least that Schopenhauer – like every true philosopher of every age – still has to say to us.

Is there anything more 'relevant' *today* than the need to heed this invitation?

---

10 Aristotle, *Metaphysics*, A 2, 982 a–b, Aristotle 1926 ff., vol. 17, pp. 12–13.

Part 1 **The Manuscripts of the Years 1804–1811: From a Pietist Education to the Study of Philosophy**

1 Schopenhauer's Early Understanding of the World: The Dualism between Temporality and Eternity

1.1 Introduction

In a letter of 1851, Schopenhauer says that he was "awakened [*auferweckt*]" to philosophy by Gottlob Ernst Schulze, his professor at the University of Göttingen in the winter semester of 1810–1811.[1] This chapter will analyze the fragments written by Schopenhauer prior to this "awakening". They convey Schopenhauer's understanding of the world *before* he dedicated himself fully to the study of philosophy – that is, before he started turning his worldview and its assumptions into a constant and programmatic object of reflection. As we will see, the leitmotif of the first manuscripts – the element that gives them univocal coherence, beyond their apparently rhapsodic nature – is the dualism between time and eternity, combined with an energetic yearning for the latter. In relation to this theme and the intensity with which it is felt, one can plausibly detect the influence of the pietist religiosity to which Schopenhauer, at his father's behest, had been educated in Hamburg, at the school of Johann Heinrich Christian Runge, from 1799 to 1803.

In this context, a very significant reading was undoubtedly Matthias Claudius's short essay *An meinen Sohn H.* (To My Son H.), published anonymously in 1799,[2] which Schopenhauer received as a gift from his father and which he treasured until his death. It stated that man is fundamentally alien to this life and this world, in which "all things" vanish (*dahingehen*): in truth, he belongs to a higher order of things.[3]

---

[1] Cf. Schopenhauer 1911–1942, vol. XV, p. 55.
[2] Anonymous 1799 (now in Claudius 1990, pp. 290–295, under the title *An meinen Sohn Johannes*).
[3] Anonymous 1799 pp. 5–6. On Schopenhauer and pietism, cf. Hübscher 1969; Siebke 1970; Hübscher 1973 (En. tr. Hübscher 1989); Safranski 1987 (En. tr. Safranski 1990); De Cian 2002, pp. 21–31. At Runge's school, which was to initiate Arthur to a career as a merchant, as intended by his father Heinrich Floris, pupils were required to attend church services and follow religious teaching for four hours a week. The content of the religious classes, as documented in the diaries of one of Schopenhauer's classmates, Lorenz Meyer, did not concern theological matters: theoretical speculation was left aside in favor of more concrete moral teachings (cf. Marchtaler 1968; Hübscher 1965). Against the tendency to overestimate the influence of Claudius' text on Schopenhauer, R. Siebke argued, on the basis of textual evidence, that Schopenhauer's explicit reference to Claudius occurred only in his mature period and in relation to other works of his. On the other

1.2 The Translation of Milton's *On Time*

In 1803–1804 Schopenhauer and his parents undertook a long journey through Europe. Arthur's father Heinrich Floris only allowed him to join them on condition that he gave up his classical studies to devote himself entirely to the family business. Heinrich's untimely death (perhaps by suicide) in 1805 freed young Arthur from this onerous promise.[4]

The first of Schopenhauer's fragments we have is a German translation of a poem by John Milton, *On Time*.[5] Hübscher,[6] following Grisebach, dates this translation to the 1803–1804 journey period. There, according to his travel diaries, Schopenhauer had the opportunity to study the English language and to visit the graves of John Gay and Milton himself in Westminster Abbey on 14 June 1803.[7]

In *On Time*,[8] the poet, addressing the "envious Time" that consumes everything, reminds it that it can only devour "what is false and vain [*das Eitle, Falsche*] and merely mortal dross; So little is our loss".[9] In the end, then, time will entomb "each thing bad [*alles Böse*]" – precisely "what is false and vain and merely mortal dross" – including itself ("thy greedy self consumed");[10] for it lives on the death of things, so that, by destroying them all, it will eventually destroy itself too.

Consequently, precisely through this terrible and inevitable process of dissolution and death, "long Eternity shall greet our bliss With an individual kiss, And joy shall overtake us as a flood".[11] When all that is perishable will *finally* be gone, "every thing that is sincerely good and perfectly divine, with Truth, and Peace, and Love shall ever shine".[12] To the "supreme throne" of God, says the text,

> When once our heavenly-guided soul shall climb,
> Then, all this earthy grossness quit,

---

hand, it must also be said that the explicit reference could not have been made until Schopenhauer knew the author's name.

4 Cf. Safranski 1990, pp. 54–56. Cf. also Cartwright 2018.
5 Schopenhauer owned Milton's *Poetical Works*, London 1731, in two volumes (cf. Schopenhauer 1985, vol. V: *Randschriften zu Büchern*; henceforth HN V, p. 461). The poem is found on p. 186 of the second volume.
6 HN I, p. 492.
7 Cf. Lütkehaus 1988, p. 69.
8 On the poetic value of Schopenhauer's translation, indicated between square brackets, cf. Lütkehaus 1984, pp. 260–264.
9 MR 1, n. 1, p. 1.
10 MR 1, n. 1, p. 1.
11 MR 1, n. 1, p. 1.
12 MR 1, n. 1, p. 1.

> Attired with stars we shall for ever sit,
> Triumphing over Death, and Chance, and thee, o Time![13]

The "we" of the text forcefully asserts its own vocation to eternity.

This poem very clearly presupposes an ontological dualism. On the one hand there is the realm of things over which the womb of time has power (expressed in the prevalence of chance and, ultimately, death): "each thing bad", "what is false and vain", "earthy grossness". On the other hand, there is the realm of things over which time has no power: "bliss", "joy", "every thing that is sincerely good", "Truth, and Peace, and Love". The most relevant theoretical feature of this discourse is the (broadly Platonic)[14] identity between truth, good and eternity, on the one hand, and falsity, vanity, evil and temporality, on the other. Only that which is false, evil and vain is prey to time; conversely, all that is not prey to time is necessarily true and good.

The "we" of the text is not, *at the moment*, experiencing "joy" or "bliss", "attired with stars", "triumphing over Death, and Chance, and [...] Time": this condition is described in the future tense ("we *shall* [italics mine] for ever sit"). *At the moment*, the "we" of the text is subject to time; and yet this subjection is not eternal, but is itself subject to time, as it were, because it will eventually give way to the blissful condition of eternity. In the text, therefore, it is assumed that the "we" is twofold: at present, it is the union of *two different and opposite natures*, one subject to time and destined to perish, the other eternal.

On the one hand, "Eternity shall greet our bliss"; on the other, the "we" of the text "shall climb" to the "supreme throne" of divinity. This is not some contradictory beginning of eternity (that which is eternal cannot begin, because it always is), but the remaining of those elements over which time has no hold, once everything over which it *does* have a hold has been consumed. This reciprocal approaching of "we" and eternity is the very fulfillment of time: the consumption of what, first and foremost in "us", is subject to time.

It is important to clarify an essential point implicit in the text: given that everything subject to time is false, evil and vain, and given that a part of "us" is subject to time, then this part of "us" is necessarily false, evil and vain. Conversely, and specularly, since in eternity "every thing that is sincerely good" will triumph ("Truth, and Peace, and Love"), and since the "we" is (also) destined to eternity, the true and good "we" is the eternal "we" (the part or nature of "us" that is not subject to time).

---

13 MR 1, n. 1, p. 1.
14 On the importance of Platonic references in Milton's work, cf. Agar 1928; Samuel 1947.

All of Schopenhauer's fragments prior to 1810 can be said to dwell within the fundamental theoretical framework that governs Milton's poem: *the dualism between the temporal and the eternal.* This dualism is one of the most recurrent themes of pietist religiosity, so it cannot be a coincidence that young Schopenhauer, within Milton's vast poetic oeuvre, chose to translate this very poem.[15] The topic of the transience of human existence is already evident, for example, in some pages of his travel diaries.[16]

For Milton, the triadic identity of Eternity, Truth and Good applies not only in relation to the human being (to "us"), but also and above all in relation to the objective order of things. As we shall see, Schopenhauer would soon deny this identity in the latter respect.

1.3 From Eternity to Time

In a poem written by Schopenhauer around 1806, the dualism between time and eternity corresponds (as in Milton's poem) to the dualism between "earth" and "heaven":

> Voluptuous pleasure [*Wollust*], infernal delight,
> Love [*Liebe*] insatiable and invincible!
> From the heights of heaven
> Thou hast dragged me down
> And cast me in fetters
> Into the dust of this earth.
> How shall I aspire and soar
> To the throne of the eternal,
> Or be reflected in the imprint
> Of the thought supreme [...]
> Yet, bond of weakness,
> Thou draggest me down and
> Thy threads and webs
> Hold me firmly in their grasp.
> All my efforts [*Streben*] to rise [*nach oben*]
> Are abortive and vain.[17]

---

15 Cf. Hübscher 1989, pp. 2–3.
16 Cf. Lütkehaus 1988, pp. 52, 133.
17 MR 1, n. 2, pp. 1–2.

The "love" spoken of here ("Voluptuous pleasure, infernal delight, Love") is not the "Love" of Milton's poem ("Truth, and Peace, and Love [...] shall ever shine"): that one was close to the "supreme throne" of divinity, in eternity and peace, this one is "infernal" and *opposed* to the "throne of the eternal"; that one, to use the apostle Paul's term, is love as ἀγάπη (*caritas*),[18] this one instead, being voluptuous pleasure (*Wollust*), is love as ἔρως.

It is clear that the "efforts to rise" coexist, in the same individual, with the "bond of weakness". In this perspective, then, it is "fine" to "wander through the wastes of life on earth, Our feet untrammelled by its dust, Our gaze unaverted from heaven".[19] That is – beyond the metaphor, or rather continuing it – it is desirable to live *free* from the "bond of weakness" and "voluptuous pleasure", only embracing our *Streben nach oben.*

In his innermost nature, man strives towards the Eternal, and this tension or aspiration takes the form of a "yearning [*Sehnsucht*]" that "breaks our hearts".[20] Not time, but eternity is man's true home, the place from which he comes or, in some way, has fallen (his voluptuousness has "dragged" him "down" (*gezogen*) and "cast" (*hingeworfen*) him "from the heights of heaven" "into the dust of this earth"), and to which he must finally return. In a letter to his mother from this period, Schopenhauer mentions "the exile of the eternal soul in the body".[21]

The same assumption of man's irreducibility to the "earthly" world can be found in a note probably written in Gotha in 1807:

> The degree on the scale of minds is determined entirely by the way in which a man looks at the external world, how deeply and how superficially. The ordinary European's gaze is often almost like the animal's, and he would never suspect the invisible in the visible, if he were not told about it by others. Therefore he is as little able as the animal to think seriously beyond the external world [*Er kann also so wenig wie das Thier ernsthaft über die Außenwelt hinweg*] or even to think of himself outside of it through his own intuition [*oder auch nur mit einer eigenen Anschauung sich aus derselben hinausdenken*].[22]

The conjunction "therefore [*also*]" opening the clause ("Therefore he is as little able as the animal [...]") indicates that it is to be understood as a consequence of the preceding proposition. The meaning of the text is thus as follows: *since* he

---

[18] Cf. Corinthians 1:13. All Biblical quotations in this book will refer to the New International Version. For the Greek text of the New Testament, reference is made to *Nuovo Testamento Interlineare. Greco-Latino-Italiano* (Beretta 1998).
[19] MR 1, n. 2, pp. 2–3.
[20] MR 1, n. 2, pp. 2–3.
[21] Schopenhauer 1978a, p. 2. For Schopenhauer family's epistolary, cf. Lütkehaus 1991.
[22] MR 1, n. 6, p. 4. Translation modified.

is unable to grasp the "invisible in the visible", the common man, like the animal, is unable to think of anything that transcends the world of the senses, and therefore cannot think or imagine himself (his own consciousness) as existing beyond it. On page 6 of his copy of *An meinen Sohn H.*, Schopenhauer could read: "This world is too little for him [man], and he neither sees nor knows the invisible world".[23]

On the other hand, an individual who is able to think himself "beyond the external world" perceives in himself something that *exceeds* the dimension of that world (man is in fact "the noblest and sublimest [creature] in nature").[24] The content of this transcendence is thus what constitutes "the invisible in the visible". However, Schopenhauer does not specify which *organ* or faculty enables man to "suspect [*ahnden*]" this "invisible" element (which certainly does not belong to the world of the senses).

1.4 The "Direct Echo of Eternity": Music

From 1803 onwards, Schopenhauer devoted himself to intense and passionate reading (including various works by Schiller, Boileau, Racine, Voltaire, Rousseau, and Sulzer's *General Theory of the Fine Arts*).[25] Around 1806, he came to appreciate Wackenroder's collection of writings, *Fantasies on Art for Friends of Art* (1799).[26] Its author was identified by many, including Schopenhauer, as the volume's editor, Ludwig Tieck (Wackenroder had died in 1798, aged only 25).

Several critics have emphasized the importance that this text had in young Schopenhauer's education, in relation not only to his general aesthetic theory, but also to his metaphysics of music.[27] For Wackenroder, the art of music has a unique characteristic compared to all other arts: "in the effect of the tone" "lies hidden" something "dark" and "indescribable", "which is to be found in no other art"; "no other [art] is capable of fusing these qualities of profundity, of sensual power, and of a dark, visionary significance in such an enigmatical way".[28]

---

23 Anonymous 1799, p. 6.
24 MR 1, n. 7, p. 5.
25 The edition found in Schopenhauer's library is J. G. Sulzer, *Allgemeine Theorie der schönen Künste in einzeln, nach alphabetischer Ordnung der Kunstwörter auf einander folgenden Artikeln abgehandelt*, Leipzig: Weidmanns Erben und Reich, 1778–1779 (cf. HN V, n. 550, p. 176). These readings can be reconstructed from his correspondence. Cf. Hübscher 1989, pp. 38–39.
26 Tieck 1799 (cf. HN V, n. 1582, p. 435); En. tr. Wackenroder 1971a.
27 Cf. Benz 1939; Pfeiffer-Belli 1948; Hübscher 1952, pp. 1–17; Hübscher 1989, pp. 42–43; Safranski 1990, pp. 61–65; De Cian 2002, pp. 54–73; App 2011, pp. 23–28; Fauth 2018.
28 Wackenroder 1971b, pp. 188–189.

One of the writings in the collection is *A Wondrous Oriental Tale of a Naked Saint*. It is about one of the hermit saints of the desert considered by the "oriental mind" "as the wondrous receptacles of a higher spirit which strayed away from the realm of the firmament into a human form".[29] This saint "had no rest", "day and night", because he was incessantly tormented by the tremendous uproar of the "wheel of time".[30] On "a beautiful, moonlit summer night", listening to the "ethereal music" sung by two lovers ("these were the first harmonies which had drifted into this desolate place"), he finally found liberation: "the lost spirit [was] released from its earthly shell" and, in the form of "an angelically beautiful phantom", he "flew around between the stars in serpentine turns", losing himself in "the infinite firmament".[31] The art of music, by reducing the "wheel of time" to silence, allowed the saint (or, more properly, the "higher spirit" of which the saint's body was a "receptacle") to return to his true home.

In the essay *The Marvels of the Musical Art* (*Die Wunder der Tonkunst*) it is similarly said that "music" is "like a child lying dead in the grave; – one reddish sunbeam from heaven gently draws its soul away and, transplanted into the heavenly aether, it enjoys golden drops of eternity and embraces the original images of the most beautiful human dreams".[32] Music gives man a taste of eternity, as it "speaks a language which we do not know in our ordinary life", "and which one would consider to be the language of angels".[33]

This text must have made a strong impression on Schopenhauer. In a letter to his mother dated 8 November 1806, he comments on it as follows:

> [...] Nothing is bound to hold fast in a transitory life; no unending pain, no eternal joy, no enduring sensation, no lasting enthusiasm, no higher decision that could hold good for life. Everything is annulled by the passage of time [*Alles löst sich auf im Strohm der Zeit*]. The minutes, the countless atoms of small details into which every action decays, are the worms that consume everything great and bold. The monster, ordinary life, pushes down everything that strives upwards. There is nothing serious in life, because the dust is not worth the trouble.[34]

In a letter to his mother written shortly afterwards, Schopenhuer said that, as consolation from this terrible spectacle of disintegration, a "compassionate angel has pleaded on our behalf for the heavenly flower", which, despite being "rooted in the soil of wretchedness", "rises tall in full magnificence": the "pulsations of divine

---

29 Wackenroder 1971b, p. 175.
30 Wackenroder 1971b, p. 175.
31 Wackenroder 1971b, pp. 176–178.
32 Wackenroder 1971b, p. 178.
33 Wackenroder 1971b, p. 180.
34 Cf. Lütkehaus 1991, p. 116. Translation from Cartwright 2010, p. 108.

music [*Tonkunst*] have not ceased beating through the centuries of barbarism, and a direct echo of eternity [*ein unmittelbarer Widerhall des Ewigen*] has remained with us as a result of it".[35]

Music, as a "direct echo of eternity", breaks the misery of "transitory life" and offers man a remedy against the anguish of the inexorable "passage of time", which devours everything.

1.5 "Corporeal World" and "Spiritual World". Philosophy, Contemplation and Remembrance

In a fragment written in Weimar in 1809, Schopenhauer outlined the possibility of a "new life", where "Man's planless and boundless hopes, The stern and steely passage of time" can be replaced by a "flow of melodious notes [*Wohllaut*]".[36] This harmonious oasis is described with greater detail in another fragment from the same period:

> All philosophy and all the consolation it affords go to show that there is a spiritual world and that in it we are separated from all the phenomena [*Erscheinungen*] of the external world and from an exalted seat can view [*zusehen*] these with the greatest calm [*Ruhe*] and unconcern, although that part of us, belonging to the corporeal world, is still pulled and swung around so much in it.[37]

Being able to "view" the "phenomena of the external world" while being "separated" from them – that is, "from an exalted seat", "with the greatest calm and unconcern" – is evidently the same ideal as the ability "lightly and softly to wander" through life (fragment 2).

In pietist circles, with reference to the Lutheran translation of Psalm 35, those who practiced the ideal of *Stille* ("silence", "stillness", "serenity", "meekness") were called the *Stillen im Lande*. *Stille* was an attitude of serene acceptance of the divine will, which entailed a fundamental detachment from the events of the world and an intensification of 'inner' life,[38] according to Augustine's admonition: *Noli foras ire, in te ipsum redi* ("Do not go abroad. Return within yourself").[39] Indeed,

---

35 Lütkehaus 1991, pp. 125–126. Translation from Cartwright 2010, p. 111.
36 MR 1, n. 9, p. 6.
37 MR 1, n. 12 [i], p. 8.
38 This ideal is expressed in several parts of the works of Gerhard Tersteegen (1697–1769) and Nikolaus Ludwig Graf von Zinzendorf (1700–1760). See Mittner 2002, vol. 1, pp. 45–48. For the key concepts of German Pietism, see also Lange 1968².
39 Augustine, *De vera religione*, xxxix, 72. En. tr. Augustine 1964, p. 69.

Schopenhauer explicitly contrasts the "spiritual world" with the "external world [Außenwelt]" (or "corporeal world [Körperwelt]"): the former, in his intentions, can therefore only be accessed inwardly.

The text assumes that the subject ("we") has both a spiritual nature (by virtue of which it can take refuge in a "spiritual world") and a bodily nature (by virtue of which it cannot avoid being "pulled and swung around" in the "corporeal world"). There are thus *two distinct natures in the single "we"*, corresponding to two different worlds. The subject's belonging to the "spiritual world" emerges through the possibility of a purely *contemplative* relationship with the outside world: in other words, separation "from all the phenomena [*Erscheinungen*] of the external world", being able to *"view* [italics mine]" them "with the greatest calm and unconcern" "from an exalted seat".

The use of the term *Erscheinung* is unlikely to be an allusion to Kant, as there is no evidence that Schopenhauer was familiar with Kant's works at this time. The term *Erscheinung*, indicating the external world, could rather be a reference to Plato's texts in Friedrich Schleiermacher's (then) very recent translation.[40] In it, in fact, the verb *erscheinen* is often used to render the Greek verb φαίνομαι, which in Plato denotes both the appearing of empirical things to the senses,[41] and the appearing of the Idea in them (the beautiful in itself "appears" in all beautiful things).[42] Even the noun φαντασία is rendered by Schleiermacher as *Erscheinung*.[43] In his introduction to the *Gorgias*, Schleiermacher uses the terms *Erscheinung* and *Schein* in reference to sensible or phenomenal reality, understood as opposed to the truth of the Idea.[44] If this interpretative hypothesis is correct, Schopenhauer must have begun reading Plato's works as early as 1808–09. The analysis of fragment 12 [vi], as we shall see, also points in this direction.

Now, according to Schopenhauer, "all philosophy" consists in looking with unconcern at "the phenomena of the external world". This notion is reminiscent of the definition given, according to an ancient anecdote, by Pythagoras: the "philosopher" is the one who attends the big and noisy "fair" of life (compared to the great games of Olympia) not in order to engage in activities that may procure him personal gain (glory, prizes, profit), as all other men do, but only to watch, as a simple spectator.[45]

---

40 Cf. *Platons Werke*, edited by F. Schleiermacher, Berlin 1804–1828 (henceforth: Plato 1804 ff.). This was the first complete German translation of Plato's works.
41 Cf. the translation of *Theaetetus* in Plato 1804 ff., II.1, pp. 205–206 (152 a–b).
42 Cf. the translation of *Hippias Major* in Plato 1804 ff., II.3, p. 419 (289 c).
43 Cf. *Theaetetus*, 152 b, Plato 1804 ff., II.1, p. 206.
44 Plato 1804 ff., II.1, pp. 6–10.
45 Cf. Cicero, *Tusculanae disputationes*, V 3, 9. En. tr. Cicero 1927, pp. 432–433.

For Schopenhauer, the pure contemplation of external "phenomena" is free from the worries connected with them;[46] it is, however, disturbed by the fact that our belonging to the "spiritual world" is not exclusive, but conflictingly *coexists* with our belonging to the "corporeal world", so that "part of us, belonging to the corporeal world", during contemplation, "is still pulled and swung around".

This miraculous ability to view events in the external world with "unconcern" also occurs in the activity of recollection:

> Why does there lie over the memory [*Andenken*] of former times such a delightful tranquillity [*Ruhe*]? Why are we seized with wistful and melancholy feelings at the mere mention of old times? Why do we see their forms and figures in so soft and faint a light, and thus without a tinge of the crude and gaudy? Is it because death has levelled them all, because their cares and sorrows no longer exist and time has taught us that these were delusions [*Täuschungen*] and we now smile at them as at the misfortunes of children?[47]

Figures from the past, when recalled, are devoid of the "crude and gaudy" that came with them: "*time* [italics mine]", consuming them, "has taught us that these were delusions" – they were not eternal. *What is not eternal is a delusion* (according to Milton's poem, time can only grasp what is "vain" and "false"). But the sorrows linked to delusions are necessarily delusions, too, so once they have revealed themselves as such, it is possible to "smile" at them as childish worries.

In remembrance, therefore, even an ordinary person, despite remaining within the world of phenomena, can look at them without concern, entertaining the same relationship with past events that the philosopher, from the "spiritual world", entertains with present ones. For ordinary people, the present is in relation to the past what, for philosophers, the "spiritual world" is in relation to the "external world": an "exalted seat", a viewpoint outside of phenomena, from which to realize that they are but delusions.

Schopenhauer's text is not really assertive, but answers the question ("Why does there lie over the memory of former times such a delightful tranquillity?" etc.) with another question ("Is it because [...]?"). The solution to the problem is therefore only hypothetical here; nevertheless, it will be presented affirmatively in the same terms in *The World as Will and Representation* (albeit in the context of the metaphysics of will, which is absent here).[48]

---

46 See also Schopenhauer 2010b, I 230–231, § 38, pp. 219–220.
47 MR 1, n. 12 [iv], p. 8.
48 "Finally, it is also the blessing of a will-less intuition that, through an act of self-deception, it casts such a wonderful spell over things in the past or far away, presenting them to us in a so much rosier light. [...] Now objective intuition operates in memory just as intuition of the present

1.6 Time and Immortality

Still in 1809, Schopenhauer made this mysterious remark:

> Deep down in man there lies the confident belief that something outside him is conscious of him as he is of himself [*daß etwas außer ihm sich seiner bewußt ist wie er selbst*]. The opposite vividly presented, together with boundless infinity, is a terrible thought [*ein schrecklicher Gedanke*].[49]

For man it is "terrible" to think that *nothing* "outside him is conscious of [...] him as he is of himself". It is very likely that the implicit basis of this statement was the opposition between exteriority and interiority (made explicit in the following fragment).[50] Indeed, what has the *same* consciousness of man as he has of himself, despite being "outside" man, must clearly also know his (man's) 'inner' self. But if this is so, this "something" cannot be another person. In fact, one can only access one's own interiority, and not that of others, so that each individual, knowing only the 'externality' of another, is *less*, and not equally, conscious of the other than he (the other) is of himself. It is therefore highly probable that this "something" is God (to whose existence the term "confident belief [*Vertrauen*]" would then refer).[51]

Schopenhauer does not specify why the idea of the *non-existence* of this "something" is "a terrible thought". The reason is perhaps the consequence of such an idea, namely that each individual would then be the sole witness to his inner life, his most authentic and precious thoughts and feelings. It was probably the sense of such immense solitude that terrified Schopenhauer in his early youth.

On the other hand, and following from what we have just said, the "confident belief" in something that, outside of man, "is conscious of him as he is of himself" could also represent faith in some form of immortality: the consciousness of this "something" would in fact be a safe place in which the individual, with his entire interiority, is already forever contained and enclosed and therefore, in some way, saved from the danger of annihilation.

---

would operate if we were able to free ourselves from the will and surrender ourselves to intuition" (Schopenhauer 2010b, I 234, § 38, pp. 222).
49 MR 1, n. 12 [ii], p. 8. Translation modified.
50 MR 1, n. 12 [iii].
51 The identity between this "something" and God has always been implied but never justified by critics. Cf.: Zint 1921, p. 8–9; Zint 1930, p. 3; Aler 1970, p. 52; Hübscher 1989, p. 10; Kamata 1988, p. 114; De Cian 2002, p. 65; Berg 2003, p. 354.

> We are not meant to thrive and flourish like the plants of the earth; every tragedy tells us this. Indeed, there must be something better, as the spectator says to himself, who finds relish in seeing the destruction of all those things which often seemed to him the most desirable.[52]

The pleasure with which the tragedy's spectator sees everything that seemed "most desirable" go to "destruction" is due to the fact that he discovers, through this spectacle, that he is destined for "something better". This last expression is to be understood both in relation to what he considered "most desirable", which is destined to be destroyed, and in relation to the condition of thriving and flourishing "like the plants of the earth". But then, what the spectator (wrongly) considers as the highest good is, according to the text, precisely such a condition: that is, in the final analysis, (prosperous) existence in time, growth, becoming, whose inexorable consequence is fading, "destruction" – *dying*.

In a poem, possibly from 1808,[53] Schopenhauer expresses this awareness with anguish:

> In the depth of a tempestuous night
> I awoke in great alarm.
> I heard it sough and heard it rage [...].
> How far away lay yestereve
> With all its mirth and pomp! [...]
> But now all this had passed away
> In the witching-hours of the midnight storm.
> So remote it lay, pale and faint as in a dream.
> 'Twas hard to believe it could have been. [...][54]

Tragedy shows this terrible spectacle of death because it reveals how all the joys experienced and hoped for (day) will ultimately be no more, becoming nothingness (night). In this way, however, tragedy drives the spectator to understand that he is destined for something higher – something that does *not* go to "destruction", that does *not* come to end.

---

52 MR 1, n. 12 [v], p. 8.
53 Cf. HN I, 493. Hübscher notes that these verses evidently arose from the same frame of mind as the sonnet that Schopenhauer took up in *Parerga and Paralipomena*, vol. 2. Cf. Schopenhauer 2015, henceforth *Parerga and Paralipomena* II, pp. 586–587, "Weimar, 1808".
54 MR 1, n. 8, pp. 5–6.

1.7 The Idea of Evil and Tragedy. The Possibility of an Evil Divine Principle

The following fragment clarifies what was presupposed in the one just quoted: *tragedy provides the spectator with "an awareness of eternity"*. This thesis, however, is now expressed in a theoretical context that drastically breaks with the Platonic perspective present in Milton's poem, according to which truth, goodness and eternity coincide.

> Not only the faculty of reason from the belvedere of speculation, which it has climbed through syllogisms, but also a lively yet sober feeling, much closer to us, tells us that all our afflictions, even the most fearful, are not so at all, for they are positively only conditioned and can easily be surmounted (at least always by death). Indeed it tells us that they are only an image *of an actual evil existing in eternity* [*in der Ewigkeit vorhandenen wirklichen Uebels*] and not in time (like the image itself). We cognize [*erkennen*] or *recall* this evil through inner intuition [*durch die innere Anschauung*] *vulgo* imagination [*Phantasie*]. But if we are gripped by earthly afflictions, we as our own executioners are actively engaged in falsely attributing to them the image *of that real and terrible evil*, and then we feel an urge to grumble and fly into a rage. Training of the faculty of reason enables us to cognize and avoid this delusion; indeed this is what the Stoics had in mind. And as all poetry is the image of the eternal in time, the *Idea of that real, indissoluble* [*unauflösbaren*] *and unconditioned evil* is also awakened by images of earthly misfortune, and an awareness of eternity is thus brought home to us. This is the tragedy.[55]

The "afflictions" that man finds so fearful, insofar as they are in time, "are not so at all", because they are only an image of the *"actual evil existing in eternity"*, which, as such – i.e. as eternal – is *"real, indissoluble and unconditioned"*. There is such a thing as *metaphysical evil*.

Here it is still the case that on the side of eternity there is truth, and on the side of temporality there is "delusion", i.e. falsehood. By attributing to his own pain the *"real and terrible evil"*, man attributes to the former the "insurmountability" that properly belongs only to the latter. The awareness of the distinction between temporal and eternal evil, provided by tragedy, is then consolatory insofar as it shows man that his pain, his evil, unlike the eternal one, is "conditioned and can easily be surmounted (at least always by death)"; this awareness, as said at the beginning of this fragment, does not only come from "the faculty of reason" but also from a "lively [...] feeling".

It is remarkable that, for Schopenhauer, eternal evil can be known through "inner intuition" (commonly known as "imagination"), namely that it can be *"re-*

---

[55] MR 1, n. 12 [vi], p. 9. Translation modified.

called". This term seems to be a reference to the Platonic theory of anamnesis. For Plato, the Idea is necessarily the object of a recollection (ἀνάμνησις),[56] i.e., of prior metaphysical knowledge (προειδέναι)[57] of the soul, because this knowledge cannot originate in experience. That the "inner intuition" mentioned by Schopenhauer has precisely this meaning is revealed by the equivalence, set out in the text, between this "inner intuition" and what the people improperly call "imagination" (which is precisely the subject's capacity to represent to himself what, as such – i.e. as a whole – is not and has never been a content of experience). At the end of the passage, Schopenhauer writes: "the *Idea of that real, indissoluble and unconditioned evil* is also awakened [*erweckt*] by images of earthly misfortune, and an awareness of eternity is thus brought home to us."

It should therefore be noted that the relationship between eternal evil (the content of the Idea) and temporal evil expressed in the text is similar to the relationship Plato posited between the Idea and the thing of which the Idea is the essence. The thing is, "in time", an "image" (Plato uses the term εἰκών, from which the word "icon" derives)[58] of the Idea, and, when perceived in the world of the senses, awakens the Idea to consciousness (causes it to be "recalled").

The implication of the text, which can be determined through these hidden references to Plato, is then that the eternal evil mentioned by Schopenhauer is the Idea (in the Platonic sense) of temporal evils: that is, *there is an Idea of evil*. The term "Idea" in the fragment is thus not to be understood in the Cartesian sense of "representation present to consciousness", as is commonly done today and as it might seem at first reading. Rather, it should be interpreted in the specifically *Platonic* sense of "eternal essence", the knowledge of which does not originate in experience (even if Schopenhauer, unlike Plato, does not here determine the origin of such knowledge). Tragedy, then, is properly the consciousness of the Idea of evil, that is to say of metaphysical evil – which, being eternal ("existing in eternity"), is "indissoluble".

If this interpretation is correct, it is necessary to assume that Schopenhauer already had some knowledge, albeit indirect, of Platonic thought in 1808–09. Indeed, a degree of familiarity with ancient philosophy is testified to in the text by the explicit mention of the "Stoics". It is possible that Schopenhauer's knowledge of ancient philosophy came from his secondary school studies in Gotha and Weimar in 1807–1808 in preparation for university.[59]

---

56 Cf. Plato, *Meno*, 81 d, Plato 1914 ff., vol. 3, pp. 302–303.
57 Cf. Plato, *Phaedo*, 74 d–e, Plato 1914 ff., vol. 1, pp. 362–363.
58 Cf. Plato, *Phaedrus*, 250 b, Plato 1914 ff., vol. 9, pp. 484–485.
59 Cf. Riconda 1969, pp. 45–49.

1.7 The Idea of Evil and Tragedy. The Possibility of an Evil Divine Principle

In any case, on the one hand this passage maintains the identity between "eternal" and "true"; on the other, it contradicts the necessity of the identity both between "eternal" and "good" and between "good" and "true". In fact, there is an Idea of evil, that is, a true and eternal evil, of which finite (temporal) evils are the "image". The negation of these necessities, however, does not concern man's being, but rather *the objective order of things*. In other words, the fragment does not say that the eternal part of man is evil; rather, it says that there is such a thing as eternal evil.

Now, the existence of eternal evil seems to be related to the possibility, which Schopenhauer admits, of a malignant divinity:

> Either all things are perfect [...]: Or else (and who in view of this world could then abide by that assumption?) two other cases only are possible; either we must, unless we assume everything to be for an evil purpose, concede power to the good will as well as to the bad, [...] *or* we must attribute this power only to chance and hence a want of perfection to the will that guides and directs in the arrangement or control of things.[60]

Here Schopenhauer raises the question of how the existence of evil in the world is compatible with the existence of a good and omnipotent divinity. He categorically denies this compatibility: provided that evil exists (i.e., assuming the falsity of the assertion "all things are perfect"), and provided, however, that evil is not the only thing that exists (i.e., assuming the falsity of the assertion "everything [is] for an evil purpose"), the "good will" cannot be the sole "power" that "guides" the "arrangement" of things; next to it one must admit, as the cause of evil in the world, either "chance" or even, like the Manichees, the existence of a "bad" will.

Just as he excludes the existence of an omnipotent and good God, Schopenhauer also rules out the existence of an omnipotent and evil God. The two possible solutions to the problem of evil (the existence of an evil power or of chance alongside a good power,) are introduced by the concessive clause: "unless we assume everything to be for an evil purpose". Since there is *also* some good, there must be an adequate cause for it.

However, based on this very assumption (that there is not only evil or only good, but that there are both evil and good), and excluding the hypothesis that chance alone governs the fate of the world, *a third solution* would still be possible. The two powers to be admitted would be a non-omnipotent evil principle and chance – the result of whose conflict with the divinity would be, however, not evil, but *good*. Schopenhauer did not consider this third possibility, because he did not doubt that good is the effect of a good divinity. In other words, young

---

[60] MR 1, n. 12 [vii], p. 9.

Schopenhauer did not (yet) question the existence of a good God; that is why he only considered *two* possible cases, instead of three.

Now, if one admits that the "power" and "will" that govern the world are eternal, then the possibility of a "bad" will is, in the final analysis, the possibility of the synthesis of eternity and evil. Once again, this disproves the necessity of a synthesis of eternity and goodness, though, again, not in relation to man's being, but in relation to a divine being.

The two previous quotations clearly show that young Schopenhauer's 'Platonism' did not apply to the Idea of evil and the hypothesis of an evil divinity. Or, rather, his Platonism was very heterodox: while holding firm to the dualism between "temporal" and "eternal" and the identity between "true" and "eternal" (along with the terminology – "Idea" – and the relationship between the Idea and the thing), it dropped the necessity of the identity between "true" and "good" and between "good" and "eternal". That is to say, in the trinity of "eternal", "true" and "good", Schopenhauer suppressed the term "good".

In *Cholerabuch* (1832), Schopenhauer says:

> At age seventeen, without any advanced schooling, I was as overwhelmed by the *wretchedness of life* as the Buddha in his youth when he saw illness, old age, pain, and death. Soon enough, the truth, proclaimed loudly and clearly by the world, overcame the Jewish dogmas that I had also been indoctrinated with, and the result for me was that this world cannot be the work of an all-good being but rather of a devil, who had brought creatures into existence in order to gloat over the sight of their anguish. This is what the data indicated; and my belief that this is the case gained the upper hand.[61]

The two fragments analyzed above were written in the 1808–1809 period; Schopenhauer was in his early twenties. Indeed, in affirming an Idea of evil and denying the existence of a good *and* omnipotent God, "the truth", i.e. the existence of evil ("who in view of this world could then abide by that assumption [that all is perfect]?"), has the better of the "Jewish dogmas". In the passage from the *Cholerabuch*, Schopenhauer mentions his belief in a single evil divinity, whereas in the fragment analyzed earlier, the existence of a good (albeit not omnipotent) divinity, as we have seen, is not questioned at all. We must therefore note this difference

---

[61] Cf. Schopenhauer 1985, vol. IV/1: *Die Manuskriptbücher der Jahre 1830–1852* (henceforth HN IV/1), *Cholerabuch* [36], p. 96. Translation from Wicks 2020, p. 98. Cf. De Cian 2002, pp. 33–34. This passage has been used by some critics as a key to interpreting the diaries written by Schopenhauer during his long journey through Europe, in particular with reference to the episodes concerning the poverty of the inhabitants of Westphalia (cf. Lütkehaus 1988, p. 48) and the Bagne of Toulon (cf. Lütkehaus 1988, pp. 144–145). For a questioning of the legitimacy of such a use of this passage from *Cholerabuch*, cf. De Cian 2002, pp. 33–47.

between the youthful fragment and Schopenhauer's later recollection. In the latter, Schopenhauer either remembers inaccurately, or refers to something that, out of *partial* reverence for the "Jewish dogmas", he never wrote down despite having thought of it (by affirming the existence of a good but not omnipotent divinity, the "Jewish dogmas" are only partially denied, i.e., as to the non-omnipotence, and are maintained instead as to the goodness of the divinity).

1.8 Cognition of the Supersensible through Interiority. Religion and Art

In his travel diaries, written between 1803 and 1804, Schopenhauer displays great sensitivity to works of art: he was very impressed, among other things, by St Paul's Cathedral in London,[62] and visited the Louvre several times, where he was able to admire some of the works later mentioned in *The World as Will and Representation*.[63]

Around 1807, his most significant readings were Zacharias Werner's play *Martin Luther, oder Die Weihe der Kraft* (Martin Luther or the Consecration of Strength),[64] Lafontaine's novel *Quinctius Heymeran de Flaming*,[65] Shakespeare's *Hamlet*, Goethe's *Wilhelm Meister's Apprenticeship* and *Hermann and Dorothea*, and a collection by Jean Paul.[66]

Explicit reflections on art, however, only appear in the manuscripts from 1808–09 onwards. Fragment 12 [iii], with regard to poetry, mentions the dualism between the "external world" and "interiority":

> The objective poet cannot become anything more than an accomplished depicter and can portray only the external world. For everything supernatural [*jedes Uebersinnliche*], everything lying outside the earthly sphere [*jedes außerhalb des Erdenkreises Liegende*] is known to him [*kennt er*] only from his own nature [*nur aus seinem Innern*], and with this he would at once become subjective. The external world presents itself most faithfully, – but the poet crystallizes the essential [*das Wesentliche*] and characteristic [*Charakteristische*], and separates the adventitious and accidental [*Zufällige*].[67]

---

62 Cf. Lütkehaus 1988, p. 84.
63 These include the Laocoon (cf. Lütkehaus 1988, pp. 96–97; cf. Schopenhauer 2010b, I 268, § 46, p. 252) and the works of Correggio and Carracci (cf. Lütkehaus 1988, pp. 95–96, 115; cf. Schopenhauer 2010b, I 274, § 48, p. 258; I 280–282, § 50, pp. 263–266; I 486, § 71, p. 439).
64 Werner 1807.
65 Cf. Lafontaine 1798; cf. HN V, p. IX.
66 Cf. Jean Paul 1801–1804. Cf. Hübscher 1989, pp. 38–39.
67 MR 1, n. 12 [iii], p. 8. Translation modified.

Interiority is a privileged gateway to knowledge: through it, the supersensible (*das Übersinnliche*) can be known. Schopenhauer was operating in a still pre-critical (pre-Kantian) horizon. It should be remembered that in fragment 12 [i] the "spiritual world" was also set against the external world.

Commenting on the final lines of Schiller's poem *The Pilgrim*, Schopenhauer notes:

> Cognize [*erkenne*] the truth in yourself, cognize yourself in the truth, and behold, at the same moment you will cognize to your astonishment the heaven and home, so long and vainly sought and wistfully dreamt of, in the sum-total and in every individual in the very place that surrounds you; *it is there that the heavens reach down to earth*.[68]

Here there seems to be an echo of Augustine's famous words: *In interiore homine habitat veritas* ("in the inward man dwells truth").[69] The superiority of internal over external knowledge had been emphatically praised a few years earlier by Novalis:

> We dream of a journey through the universe. But is the universe then not in us? We do not know [*kennen ... nicht*] the depths of our spirit. Inward [*Nach Innen*] goes the secret path. Eternity with its worlds, the past and future, is in us or nowhere. The external world is the shadow world, casting its shadows into the world of light.[70]

In *Henry of Ofterdingen*, Novalis openly celebrated the poets' inner and metaphysical knowledge.[71] Another famous fragment of his reads: "In the beginning poets and priests were one, and only later times have separated them. The genuine poet, however, is always a priest, just as the genuine priest has always been a poet. And should not the future again re-establish the old state of things?"[72]

Now, according to Schopenhauer, the poet, in order to be "objective", must leave aside his own inner cognition of the supersensible and concern himself only with the "earthly sphere", separating the "accidental" from the "essential"

---

[68] MR 1, n. 26, p. 17. Translation modified.
[69] Augustine, *De vera religione*, xxxix, 72; En. tr. Augustine 1964, p. 69.
[70] Novalis, *Pollen*, fragment n. 16 (Novalis 1996, p. 11). Cf. Pikulik 2005.
[71] Cf. Novalis 1842. This issue emerges immediately. Already in the second chapter, "the way of experience [*Erfahrung*]", which is "laborious and boundless", is set against the way of internal reflection (*innerer Betrachtung*), which is "but one leap" and is typical of poets: "The wanderer of the first must find out one thing from another by wearisome reckoning; the wanderer of the second perceives the nature of everything and occurrence directly by their very essence [...]". (cf. Novalis 1842, p. 50).
[72] Novalis, *Pollen*, fragment n. 71 (Novalis 1996, pp. 21–22).

and only describing the latter. However, this "essential" (as well as the "accidental") is still part of the external or sensible world, not the supersensible one, as here the question only concerns the "objective poet".

Schopenhauer warns that this solution risks diminishing the meaning of poetry and the role of the poet: "But is this the pinnacle of poetry? Is this more divine than the image of inner intuitive divination? Must the world, created by the poet, be a mosaic of stones already existing?"[73] Recall that, in fragment 6, Schopenhauer had spoken of "suspecting" (*ahnden*) the "invisible in the visible".

In fragment 12 [vi], which deals with eternal evil (the Idea of evil), Schopenhauer conceives of poetry in a different way: "*all* [italics mine] poetry is the image of the eternal in time".[74] But the eternal is certainly outside "the earthly sphere" and is part of the supersensible world, so *no* poetry is "objective", that is, a simple description of the external world. Therefore, every poet must necessarily make use of his own interiority (*das Innere*), his "inner intuitive divination" (*die innere Ahndung*). In fact, according to Schopenhauer, what the poet represents in tragedy, namely eternal evil, is known or recalled by the spectator through inner intuition (*durch die innere Anschauung*).

Except for "the few moments of religion, art and pure love [*der reinen Liebe*]", life is nothing but "a number of trivial thoughts".[75] A "thinking person" cannot help but notice with horror the "hazards and uncertainties" of life, where there is "nothing "solid, secure, and beyond dispute on to which he can hold".[76] The only hope in the face of this horror is "the knowledge of the eternal truth [*das Wissen der ewigen Wahrheit*]", which, having "receded into the background" in everyday life, gives rise to art and science if it "comes to the fore".[77]

In his *Fantasies on Art for Friends of Art*, Wackenroder claimed that "this constant monotonous succession of thousands of days and nights", this "endless, strange game on a board of black and white fields, whereby in the end no one wins but cursed Death", "could drive one crazy at many an hour"; the only solution is to cling to "art, which reaches beyond everything into eternity, – which offers us its radiant hand from heaven".[78] "Religion and art" are the "two grand, divine realities" which reveal "the true nature of all things [*den wahren Geist aller Dinge*]".[79] To the "nothingness [*Nichtigkeit*] and transience [*Vergänglichkeit*] of all things",

---

73 MR 1, n. 12 [iii], p. 8.
74 MR 1, n. 12 [vi], p. 9.
75 MR 1, n. 12 [viii], p. 9.
76 MR 1, n. 14, p. 10.
77 MR 1, n. 14, p. 10.
78 Wackenroder 1971b, p. 187.
79 Wackenroder 1971b, p. 170.

Wackenroder opposed the "eternity of art [*Ewigkeit der Kunst*]" – or, specifically, of the *content* of art – and "the supreme and purest love [*höchste und reinste Liebe*]".[80] Every work of art contains the "trace" of a "heavenly spark".[81]

The similarity of these passages to fragment 14 of the manuscripts, quoted above, is undeniable. As for Wackenroder, so for Schopenhauer art has as its content not the temporal, but the Eternal, i.e. "the knowledge of the eternal truth". Hence, art offers man the remedy against the horrific sight of the impermanence of everything. Insofar as it addresses the Eternal, art is something exceptional, totally different from the "monster" of everyday life, in which "everything is annulled by the passage of time" (cf. *supra*, 1.4) and there is nothing "solid, secure, and beyond dispute on to which he can hold". The "moments of religion, art and pure love" are "few", because the "knowledge of the eternal truth", in everyday life, passes "into the background".

Now, if art has the Eternal (i.e. the truth) as its content, then *it has the same content as religion.* This is evidently the basis of their juxtaposition ("the few moments of religion, art and pure love"), that is, of a form of "art religion"[82] in young Schopenhauer. In this sense, Schopenhauer's appreciation of art is not in contradiction with, but entirely sympathetic to, the religious drive, while at the same time heralding his emancipation from a strictly pietist formation, i.e. from "his father's religion", alien in principle to any openness to the Romantic conception of art.[83]

In the *Outpourings of an Art Loving Friar*[84] by the same author (a work of 1797 which, according to some critics, marks the beginning of German literary Romanticism),[85] the affinity between religion and art – apart from being embodied by the

---

[80] These passages belong to an essay entitled "Eternity of Art [Ewigkeit der Kunst]", included in the collection *Fantasies on Art for Friends of Art* (Wackenroder 1971b) but not translated in the cited English edition. Cf. Wackenroder 1984, pp. 299–303.
[81] Cf. Wackenroder 1971a, p. 109: "in each work of art" there is "the trace of the heavenly spark which, having animated from Him [the Creator], passed over through the breast of the individual into his little creation [the work of art], from which it then glows back again to the great Creator".
[82] Cf. Safranski 1990, p. 63; App 2011, p. 25.
[83] Cf. Safranski 1990, p. 63. Safranski does not seem to detect this solidarity between art and religion (both containing the Eternal) as the basis of young Schopenhauer's "art religion".
[84] Anonymous, *Herzensergießungen eines kunstliebenden Klosterbruders*, Unger, Berlin 1797. Tieck then merged this text with the *Phantasien über die Kunst für Freunde der Kunst* in the book *Phantasien über die Kunst von einem kunstliebenden Klosterbruder* (Berlin 1814), indicating in the preface exactly which parts of the two works were to be attributed to him and which to Wackenroder. On Tieck's epistolary novel *William Lovell* (Tieck 1795/1796), which seems to anticipate the 'pessimism' of Schopenhauer's mature system in some respects, cf. Pikulik 2005; Fauth 2018.
[85] Cf. Mittner 2002, p. 737.

(fictitious) author referred to in the title (the "art loving friar") – is affirmed on almost every page. The "appreciation of sublime artworks is akin to prayer";[86] "Artworks are by their very name as little part of the common flow of life as is the thought of God".[87] There is a "divine element" in art: the "greatest artists" reached their excellence only by "divine inspiration"[88] or by the "direct intermediation of God".[89]

For instance, the "heavenly Raphael"[90] was greatly devoted to the Mother of God: the "incomparable beauty"[91] of his Holy Virgins did not come from the world, but from a miraculous "vision [that] was imprinted forever on his soul".[92] Hence his statement: "I cling to a certain image which dwells within me".[93] The text also opposes Raphael and Michelangelo: the first is "the painter of the New Testament", the second "of the Old Testament"; "on the first there reposes the divine and tranquil spirit of Christ [...] while on the second there reposes the spirit of the inspired prophets, of Moses and the other poets of the Orient".[94]

In *The World as Will and Representation*, Schopenhauer wrote that Raphael's works (which he admired on several occasions in 1803–1804, during his long trip with his family)[95] constitute, together with those of Correggio, "the summit of all art".[96]

1.9 Schopenhauer's Early Understanding of the Will. Θέλημα and βούλησις

As we have seen, in relation to the problem of evil, like the Manichees, Schopenhauer admits the possibility that a good divine power (whose "will" is "good") may coexist with an evil one (whose "will" is "bad").[97] This discourse evidently presupposes that the determining ground of the will as such can be both good and evil, and that the will acquires the same character as its ground: it is "good" if and in-

---

86 Wackenroder 1975, p. 70.
87 Wackenroder 1975, p. 71.
88 Wackenroder 1975, p. 6.
89 Wackenroder 1975, p. 9.
90 Wackenroder 1975, p. 18.
91 Wackenroder 1975, p. 18.
92 Wackenroder 1975, p. 9.
93 Wackenroder 1975, p. 9.
94 Wackenroder 1975, pp. 76–77.
95 Cf. Lütkehaus 1988, pp. 29, 68, 104, 113.
96 Schopenhauer 2010b, § 48, p. 259, I, 275.
97 MR 1, n. 12 [vii], p. 9.

sofar as it is determined by good, and "bad" if and insofar as it is determined by evil. However, in that text, good and evil do not determine the same will, but two different (divine) wills: respectively, the will of the good power and the will of the evil power.

In fragment 13 Schopenhauer writes:

> Can this life awaken wisdom indeed only for this life? In other words, do the changes, which my will undergoes through the παίδευσις of life in its innermost depths whether for good or for evil, really determine my will only to the extent that this material world of the senses is its sphere? Or does the whole of my endless existence participate in feeling those changes and consequently finiteness becomes causal for infinity, just as conversely, with every virtuous action, infinity becomes causal for finiteness? If we do not assume this, we must ask: what is the point of the mockery and sham of the world?[98]

The presupposition here is man's participation in "this life" (relating to the "world of the senses") and, at the same time, in an "endless existence".

Schopenhauer asks whether the παίδευσις (teaching) of life can "determine" the human will only in relation to the "world of the senses" (i.e., solely in relation to man's finite existence) or also in relation to man's "endless existence" (i.e., beyond the "world of the senses"). This question evidently presupposes – as something unquestionable – the *reality* of this παίδευσις. The latter consists in the "changes [*Änderungen*]" of the will towards both evil and good (*gleichviel ob zum Bösen oder zum Gute*). In contrast to the fragment on the problem of evil, here it is the *same* (human) will that can determine itself according to both evil and good. In this sense, the human will is *free*.

The assumption that the determining ground of the will can be both good and evil (as Schopenhauer supposes) would have been absurd for ancient Greek philosophers. According to Plato (or rather, according to Plato's Socrates), no one does evil "willingly".[99] The Greek word for "willingly" (or similar expressions, e.g. "of one's own free will") is ἑκών, i.e. "voluntarily" (*sua sponte*), "wittingly". Every person is naturally oriented towards goodness, so that they only do evil because they mistake it for something good. The 'unintentionality' of evil deeds lies precisely in this cognitive error: the *ignorance* of what is really good. This is the coercion undergone by those who unwittingly commit evil.

This Socratic doctrine has been called "ethical intellectualism", because in it the will follows (from) the cognitive judgment: the individual wants what, *prior to* the act of will, they consider and evaluate as "good". In the *Laws* (the last dia-

---

[98] MR 1, n. 13, p. 10.
[99] Plato, *Protagoras*, 358 c–d, Plato 1914 ff., vol. 3, pp. 244–245.

logue written by Plato, in which Socrates is absent) it is clearly stated that "the unjust man [ὁ μὲν ἄδικος] is, indeed, bad [κακός], but the bad man is unwillingly [ἄκων] bad": α-ἐκών, i.e. "not-willingly".[100]

The orientation towards goodness, which is inherent in every person, is called βούλησις in Platonic texts; the corresponding verb is βούλομαι. These two words are usually translated as "will" or "wish". According to this translation choice, in *Gorgias* it is said that evil men, like tyrants, actually "do nothing that they wish [βούλονται] to do, practically speaking, though they do whatever they think to be best" (though even just for themselves), but are mistaken about it.[101] Real βούλησις is in fact the orientation towards what is good *objectively*, and in all respects.

Referring to this dimension of objectivity (which presupposes an adequate evaluation), Aristotle defines βούλησις as rational desire (ὄρεξις λογιστική), which as such is necessarily aimed at the good (ἀγαθοῦ).[102] However, according to Aristotle it is still possible to do evil consciously, contrary to what Socrates claimed.[103]

A striking example of this can be found in Greek mythology itself: Medea killed her own children, even though she knew perfectly well that she was committing an evil deed (one could even say that she did it precisely *because* of the wickedness of such an act). In Euripides' tragedy, she openly recognizes that what she is about to do is the most unholy deed (ἔργον ἀνοσιώτατον),[104] but this awareness is of no use to her: "I know well [μανθάνω] what evil [κακά] I am about to do, but my wrath overbears my calculation [βουλεύματα], wrath that brings mortal men their gravest hurt."[105] Likewise, in Ovid's version of the story, Medea says: *video meliora proboque, deteriora sequor* ("The better course I see and do I approve, the worse I follow").[106]

From Aristotle's perspective, however, "following" the "worse" (that which is contrary even to one's *own* advantage), despite knowing "the better course", does not depend on some orientation towards evil ("for no one wishes for anything unless he thinks it is good"),[107] but rather on the fact that the orientation towards the good – βούλησις – is not translated into action, and does not find a correspond-

---

100 Plato, *Laws*, 860 d, Plato 1914 ff., vol. 11, pp. 222–223.
101 Plato, *Gorgias*, 466 d6–e2, Plato 1914 ff., vol. 3, pp. 324–325.
102 Aristotle, *Rhetoric*, I 10, 1369 a2, Aristotle 1926 ff., vol. 22, pp. 106–107.
103 Aristotle, *Nicomachean Ethics*, III 1111 b-1112 a, Aristotle 1926 ff., vol. 19, pp. 128–133.
104 Euripides, *Medea*, v. 796, Euripides 1994, pp. 356–357.
105 Euripides, *Medea*, vv. 1077–1080, Euripides 1994, pp. 382–383. Translation modified.
106 Ovid, *Metamorphosis*, VII 20–21. En. tr. Ovid 1998, p. 144.
107 Aristotle, *Rhetoric*, I 10, 1369 a, Aristotle 1926 ff., vol. 22, pp. 106–107.

ing choice or decision (προαίρεσις). This *failure to act* is called ἀκρασία (*incontinentia*).[108] Indeed, even in Euripides' text it is assumed that the content of βουλεύματα is something good. The notion of βούλησις as "rational desire" then passed into Stoicism,[109] and one can see why Cicero, translating (probably for the first time)[110] the Greek word with *voluntas*, defines the latter as *quae quid cum ratione desiderat* ("a rational longing for anything").[111]

According to the Judeo-Christian tradition, on the other hand, man can *also* want evil (as such). Only in this perspective can the Ten Commandments (Ex 20), for example, make sense: they are certainly not theoretical or descriptive theses about what, being good, is necessarily willed; rather, precisely because they are "commandments", they have an expressly prescriptive (imperative) value with regard to what is good.

In the New Testament, the verb θέλω and the noun θέλημα – which in the Vulgate are rendered respectively as *volo* and *voluntas*, and in Luther's version as *wollen* and *Wille* – indicate both the divine "will"(cf. e.g. Rev 4:11; Mt 6:10; Mk 3:31–35) and the human "will", which may or may not conform to the divine will (cf. e.g. Mt 21:29; Lk 22:42), thus determining itself towards either good or evil.[112] This dualistic understanding of the human *voluntas* was developed and 'canonized' by Augustine (especially in *De civitate Dei*),[113] to the point that some scholars have credited him with the "invention of the will" – that is, the *meaning* that has been attributed to this term ever since.[114]

It would thus seem that, according to the Gospels, the circumstance mentioned by Ovid and excluded by Socrates – the ability to "see" what the "better course" is and yet consciously follow the "worse" – constitutes *sin* (ἁμαρτία) in the proper sense: "If you were blind, you would not be guilty of sin; but now that you claim you can see, your guilt remains" (Jn 9:41; cf. also Lk 12:47). Those who crucified Jesus, on the other hand, can be forgiven because they did not "see": they "do not know [οὐ γάρ οἴδασιν] what they are doing" (Lk 23:35).

---

108 Cf. Aristotle, *Nicomachean Ethics*, VII (H) 1146 b 8, Aristotle 1926 ff., vol. 19, pp. 380–381.
109 Cf. von Arnim 2016, 463–464, pp. 115–116.
110 Cf. entry "Wille" in Ritter, Gründer and Gabriel 1971–2007, vol. XII, pp. 763–766.
111 Cicero, *Tusculanae disputationes*, IV, 6, 12. En. tr. Cicero 1927, pp. 340–341.
112 For Luther's translation, cf. Luther 1883–2009, vol. 6–7.
113 Cf. Augustine 1998, XII, 6–8, pp. 504–509; XIV, 6, pp. 590–591. On the prominence of the concept of *voluntas* in Seneca, who seems to depart radically from Greek intellectualism, cf. Pohlenz 1959. On the lack of a Greek equivalent for what we call "will" today, cf. Pohlenz 1992⁷, pp. 319–321. Cf. also E. Severino, "Socrate, il sileno e la virtù", in Severino 1992, pp. 119–133.
114 Cf. Wetzel 2010, pp. 44–52; Koßler 2009a.

1.9 Schopenhauer's Early Understanding of the Will. Θέλημα and βούλησις

In sum, if we accept the translation of βούλομαι and θέλω as "to will", we can say that according to ancient Greek philosophy – with reference to man – the good is what "must" be willed in the sense of *Muss* (unavoidable necessity); according to the Judaeo-Christian tradition, instead, it is what "ought to" be willed in the sense of *Soll* (ethical duty). The will as βούλησις must necessarily (*muss*) aim at the good; the will as θέλημα, on the other hand, ought to (*soll*) aim at the good only ethically, because, unlike βούλησις, it can also aim at evil.

In an annotation from 1825, six years after the publication of *The World as Will and Representation*, Schopenhauer complains that two Greek terms with such different meanings – βούλησις and θέλημα – are translated into German with the same word, *Wille* ("will"), and ascribes the misunderstanding of his philosophy to this insufficiency of the German language.[115] (The same insufficiency can be attributed to English). What he properly means when speaking of the "will" as a "thing-in-itself" is not βούλησις (the reflective will, *der überlegte Wille*), but θέλημα: "the will proper [*der eigentliche Wille*]", not guided by reason, because it is prior to, and more original than, any knowledge.[116] The *Wille* that lies at the heart of Schopenhauer's masterpiece is a "blind impulse [*blinder Drang*]", a "striving in the absence of cognition [*erkenntnißloses Streben*]".[117] For these reasons, Schopenhauer's mature philosophy has been regarded as a form of "voluntarism" in antithesis to the old "ethical intellectualism".[118] We shall see how and within what framework such voluntarism is to be understood (cf. *infra*, 9.13; 12.7 and 12.8).

Already in the manuscripts of 1808–09, however, the human will, insofar as it can be generally determined as both evil and good, is certainly θέλημα, not βούλησις. This specific conception of the *Wille*, which certainly conforms more to the Judeo-Christian tradition than to ancient Greek philosophy, was Schopenhauer's early understanding of the will. As we shall see, and as is already confirmed by the annotation of 1825 mentioned above, Schopenhauer would largely retain this view, albeit with remarkable theoretical elaborations, which we shall deal with in the following chapters.

---

115 Schopenhauer 1985, vol. III: *Berliner Manuskripte (1818–1830)* (henceforth HN III), Quartant [64], pp. 213–214; En. tr. in Schopenhauer 1989 (henceforth MR 3), p. 234.
116 MR 3, p. 234.
117 Schopenhauer 2010b, I 178, § 27, p. 174. Translation modified. Cf. Schopenhauer 2020, p. 116.
118 Cf. Berg 2003, pp. 38–52.

2 Attending G. E. Schulze's Lectures and Reading Plato, Schelling and Kant

2.1 Introduction

In October 1809, Schopenhauer enrolled in the medical faculty of the University of Göttingen, renowned for its scientific department. Here, among other things, he attended the Natural history and Mineralogy course held by the famous Johann Friedrich Blumenbach,[1] as well as Arnold Hermann Ludwig Heeren's ethnography lectures, part of which were devoted to Indian religion and culture.[2] Fragments 13 and 14, analyzed in the previous chapter, were written in this first year of university, and it is possible that the mention of science, alongside art, as the guardian of "eternal truth" (fragment 14) was due to young Schopenhauer's enthusiasm for the course of study he had just undertaken.

Between July and October 1810, Schopenhauer borrowed Schelling's *On the World Soul* and *Ideas for a Philosophy of Nature* from the university library, as well as Plato's *Dialogues*, both in Schleiermacher's then brand new translation and in the traditional Bipontine edition.[3] The choice to read such texts must have been motivated by a desire for a broader (that is, not only scientific, but also philosophical) understanding of natural phenomena.[4]

As we have seen, Schopenhauer already showed some knowledge of philosophical literature in a few fragments of the years 1808–1809 (cf. *supra*, 1.5 and 1.7). Now, however, with the reading of Schelling and Plato, young Arthur's interest in philosophy intensified: it was during this period that he began to consider interrupting his medical studies to enroll in the Department of Philosophy. In the winter semester of 1810–1811, he attended courses in Metaphysics and Psychology

---

[1] Cf. Stollberg and Böker 2013. On Schopenhauer's overall scientific education, cf. Segala 2009, p. 200–214.
[2] A few pages of Schopenhauer's notes from this course are transcribed and analyzed in App 2003. On the relationship between the genesis of Schopenhauer's philosophy and the sacred texts of India, see *infra*, Chapter 11.
[3] *Platonis philosophi quae exstant Graece ed editionem Henrici Stephani accurate expressa cum Marsilii Ficini interpretatione. Praemittitur L. III Laertii de vita et dogmatibus Platonis cum notitia literaria. Accedit varietas lectionis*, Stud. Soc. Bip. Biponti, ex Typographia Societatis, I–XII, 1781–1787. On the books borrowed from the library of the University of Göttingen, cf. Schopenhauer 1911–1942, vol. XVI, pp. 105–106.
[4] On the connections between natural science and philosophy and literature in the Romantic Age, cf. Poggi 2000.

given by Gottlob Ernst Schulze – the author who, eighteen years earlier, had caused such a stir among Kant's supporters with his famous *Aenesidemus*[5] that the young Fichte was prompted to develop a new version of transcendental philosophy: the *Wissenschaftslehre*.[6] Schopenhauer must have been very positively impressed by Schulze: in the summer semester of 1811, he also attended his lectures on Logic.[7]

To this fine and powerful critic of Kantian philosophy, capable of extraordinary clarity and expositional efficiency, Schopenhauer would ascribe, as mentioned, the merit of having "awakened him to philosophy".[8] It is therefore worth looking into how Schulze defined "philosophy" in his lectures.

2.2 Schulze: The Human Tension towards the Absolute and the Eternal. Philosophy and Metaphysics

In the Introduction to the Metaphysics course, entitled "Of Philosophy in General and of the Peculiar Purpose of Metaphysics", Schulze states that every art and science arise from particular human "predispositions" and "needs [*Bedürfnisse*]".[9] This is also true of philosophy: it originates from the "dissatisfaction of the human spirit" with empirical knowledge and the consequent attempt to achieve a more complete and profound knowledge of the world through "speculation".[10] For philosophers, the world itself is therefore "a problem" that, as such, "requires a solution"; however, according to Schulze, all philosophers have failed in their search for one.[11]

---

5 Cf. G. E. Schulze, *Aenesidemus, oder über die Fundamente der von dem Herrn Professor Reinhold in Jena gelieferten Elementar-Philosophie. Nebst einer Vertheidigung des Skeptizismus gegen die Anmaßungen der Vernunftkritik* (Schulze 1792). An excerpt in English, translated by G. de Giovanni, can be found in Di Giovanni and Harris 2000, pp. 104–135.
6 Cf. J. G. Fichte, *Zur Rezension Aenesidemus*, in Fichte 1962ff., vol. II, 2, p. 295.
7 Cf. D'Alfonso 2008, p. 11. On the topics covered by Schulze in these two courses, see M. d'Alfonso, "Schopenhauer als Schüler Schulzes: Die Vorlesungen zur Metaphysik und Psychologie in Göttingen 1810–11", in D'Alfonso 2008, pp. 7–34.
8 Cf. Schopenhauer 1911–1942, vol. XV, pp. 260–261.
9 D'Alfonso 2008, p. 47. This text is partly translated in Schopenhauer 1988b (henceforth MR 2), pp. 5–16. Wherever possible, I will refer to MR 2 for the translation, in line with the rest of the present work. Where Payne's is not available, I will use my own translation.
10 D'Alfonso 2008, p. 47.
11 D'Alfonso 2008, pp. 48–49; cf. also p. 113. Cf. MR 2, p. 6.

> To proceed from the worldly to the otherworldly, from the transient and conditioned of existence to the eternal and unconditioned, and to do so precisely according to clear and certain principles: this is the original and peculiar tendency of metaphysics.[12]
>
> Thus in its searches for the grounds of being, our faculty of reason does not meet with satisfaction until it has arrived at the unconditioned, which is not to be found either in the external world or in the internal.[13]

In these words (which, with regard to the "dissatisfaction" of human reason with the knowledge of the conditioned, seem to evoke the Introduction to the Transcendental Dialectic of the *Critique of Pure Reason*),[14] Schopenhauer could certainly sense his own heart-breaking yearning (*Sehnsucht*) for eternity (fragment 2), that is, his rejection of "transitory life"[15] and his longing for a "knowledge of the eternal truth", which alone can save man from the "horror" of the hazards of life (fragment 14) (cf. *supra*, 1.3; 1.8). In other words, it is possible that Schopenhauer, hearing and transcribing Schulze's lecture, identified his own passionate yearning for the Eternal with the particular "predisposition" of the human spirit that, according to Schulze, originates philosophy.

However, unlike Schulze, young Arthur thought that the supersensible *could* be known, precisely from one's own interiority (fragment 12 [iii]). Indeed, referring precisely to the passage of the lecture just quoted, Schopenhauer objected that the unconditioned (in the New Testament terms of the "peace of God, which transcends all understanding") is indeed given in the inner world.[16] But this remark contains nothing new with respect to the annotations of the years 1808–09 (except for the quotation from the Letter to the Philippians): it is therefore irrelevant whether it was written at the same time, or rather (as the handwriting seems to suggest) a little later than the transcription of the lecture.[17] Moreover, from a passage of the Psychology course, Schopenhauer drew the conclusion that Schulze did not understand the meaning of Plato's discourse on divinity in the *Philebus*.[18] These two references alone show that Schopenhauer, from the very be-

---

12 MR 2, p. 6.
13 D'Alfonso 2008, pp. 50–51.
14 Kant 1998, B 349–366, pp. 384–393.
15 Lütkehaus 1991, p. 116. Translation from Cartwright 2010, p. 108.
16 MR 2, p. 6. The quotation from Paul, which Schopenhauer reports in Greek, is taken from the Letter to the Philippians 4:7. On the first page of his notes for the Metaphysics course, Schopenhauer remarks: "The continuous text are Schulze's dictations; what is enclosed in brackets he has said but not dictated; that which has 'ego' written over it are my observations)" (MR 2, p. 5). However, this indication is not always observed (cf. e.g. MR 2, p. 7).
17 Cf. De Cian 2002, p. 84, n. 22.
18 D'Alfonso 2008, p. 152.

ginning, was far from Schulze's radical skepticism. As if to express his general feeling, on the first page of his notes to Schulze he marked this quote from Goethe's *Faust*: "[*Zweifel*] Doubt's the Devil's [*Teufel*] boon companion".[19]

Driven (also) by this tension towards the supersensible and the divine, in the second half of 1810 Schopenhauer devoted himself with passion and commitment to reading the works of Plato and Schelling. Indeed, the former titles a fragment of the manuscripts that we now need to analyze, and which appears to derive from the young medical student's combined philosophical and naturalistic interests.

2.3 "On Plato": The Difference between Platonic Idea and Abstract Concept. The Ideas "of the Forms of Nature"

In fragment 15, entitled "On Plato" (October 1810), Schopenhauer addressed for the first time the subject of the Platonic Idea explicitly and programmatically. Given the wealth and variety of issues tackled in this fragment, for explanatory reasons, I will divide the analysis of its content into this and the following paragraph.

Firstly, Schopenhauer raises the problem of the "difference, denied by many, between Platonic Idea and abstract general concept":

> [...] We can abstract general concepts from things having their existence merely in relation and from artificial products, and hence from things, whose concept springs originally from human understanding, so that this again perceives in them its own creation; for it [the human understanding] assembles [*zusammenstellt*] those elements in a thing that are essential for a purpose, and abstracts [*abstrahirt*] from the contingent and unessential of all the things of this species. But it has Ideas only of the forms of nature in addition to those residing in it without any sense-object. Of course, it sets about abstracting the unessential and assembling the essential [*Die Abstraktion vom Unwesentlichen und Zusammenstellung des Wesentlichen nimmt er zwar auch*] even when forming [*bei Bildung*] the Ideas of natural objects. But the difference is that, although incomparably more perfect and only as parts of a greater Idea, these Ideas in the same way must have resided in the Deity at the creation of the species, and in this way the Deity conveys its Idea to man through the organ of nature, which is to be regarded as its language.[20]

To fully grasp this passage, it is necessary to render its content in a more systematic form than that adopted by Schopenhauer himself. First of all, the English translation cited above renders quite well the derivation of the nouns *Abstraktion*

---

[19] MR 2, p. 5. The quotation comes from *Faust* I, v. 4361 (En. tr. in Goethe 2014, p. 111). Payne uses Bayard Taylor's translation, which reads "But Devil rhymes with Doubt alone".
[20] MR 1, n. 15, pp. 10–11.

and *Zusammenstellung* from the verb *abstrahiren* and *zusammenstellen* found in the German text, conveying their perfect identity of meaning, which is essential to understand what Schopenhauer means. Both in the German text and in the English translation, in fact, it is immediately clear that both Ideas *of natural objects* and concepts have as their content the essence of things or objects of experience, and are, in this sense, the product of abstraction (*Abstraktion*) and assembling (*Zusammenstellung*) on man's part. It is precisely with respect to this double commonality that the problem of the *difference* between Idea and general concept arises. Schopenhauer places this difference in the origin and content of the two terms.

As for their *origin*, all Ideas (therefore also Ideas of natural objects) "must have resided in the Deity at the creation of the species"; on the contrary, the "concept springs originally from human understanding". As for their *content*, man can have Ideas either "of the forms of nature" (these are the Ideas that man "forms"), or of things that do not correspond to any "sense-object". Concepts, on the other hand, can be either of artificial things (*Artefakte*), whose origin is the human understanding, or of things "having their existence merely in relation", that is, of relations between things (where the positing of these relations is again the work of human understanding).

Schopenhauer thus seems to presuppose that in God and in man, respectively, the Idea and the concept *precede*, as a 'project', the creation or realization of their content (Ideas existed in the Deity "at the creation of the species [*bei der Schöpfung der Gattung*]"; human understanding, forming the concept of an artificial object, "*again* [italics added] perceives in [it] its own creation [*Geschöpf*]", or rather, to be more faithful to the German text, its "creature"). For this reason, what is created by God is the content of Ideas, while what is created by man is the content of concepts.

In the text, however, there does not seem to be a perfect analogy between man and God: the relationship between human understanding and concept is not entirely equal to the relationship between divine intellect and Idea. Indeed, Schopenhauer writes that the concept is a product [*Geschöpf*] of human understanding, but not that the Idea is, in the same way, a product or creation of God or of the divine intellect. This is probably because Schopenhauer assumes (with Plato) the eternity and therefore non-generation of Ideas.

Now, the assertion that Ideas reside in the Deity from the beginning of creation *does not contradict* the assertion that they are, like concepts, a product of man's abstract and compositional activity (so that they only come into existence after creation). In fact, the Ideas of natural objects that man "forms" *are not the same* as the Ideas already existing in the Deity at the origin of the world: the latter are "incomparably more perfect" than the former and "parts of a greater Idea" (they are parts of the whole creative project, which man, according to Schopenhauer, cannot fully know). God does not communicate the Ideas of natural objects to man directly, but "through the organ of nature", on which man exercises his faculty of abstraction and assembly. This mediation means that human knowledge of these Ideas is necessarily imperfect or "less clear".

What has been said so far involves a third difference between Ideas and concepts, which is only implicit in the text: the latter exist only for and in human understanding, while the former also exist in God. In other words, Ideas have *absolute truth and existence*, independent of man.

In this regard, it can also be noted that the "essential" that man "assembles" in the concept is such, according to Schopenhauer, "for a purpose [*zu einem Behuf*]". The content of concepts, which is made up of artificial things, is in fact functional to man's needs and desires. This limitation ("for a purpose") is not attributed to the "essential" that constitutes the content of Ideas. In relation to this point, too, therefore, one can detect the third difference just mentioned: the Idea, unlike the concept, expresses the absolute – i.e., absolutely true – essence of its object (and not only true in relation to man and his purposes).

With regard to this last point, it has been justifiably suggested that Schopenhauer here was influenced by Schelling, in particular the *Aphorismen zur Einleitung in die Naturphilosophie* (Aphorisms as an Introduction to the Philosophy of Nature).[21] But even Schulze – when discussing Schelling's *Bruno* – had recalled that "the ancients" called the individual "essence of things" an "Idea" insofar as it is "dissolved in God".[22] In other words, the Idea "is not the general concept or the species, but the particular, since it constitutes an eternal truth in God. To consider things according to Ideas is thus to consider them [...] as they are in God, in themselves, without any relation to one another, that is, according to their eternal life".[23]

In commenting on Schelling's *Bruno* – in which it is said that the "eternal concepts [*ewige Begriffe*]" of things, present in the divine intellect, express the true nature of things beyond their accidental temporal vicissitudes[24] – Schopenhauer writes:

'eternal concepts' are [...] impossible; only in finiteness are there concepts. What underlies all original concepts [*Urbegriffe*] or images [*Urbilder*] (for these are one and the same) is the eternally beautiful and true, the divine Idea [*die göttliche Idee*]. But this is just expressed by every

---

21 Cf. Kamata 1988, p. 117.
22 D'Alfonso 2008, p. 105.
23 D'Alfonso 2008, p. 105: "Das in Gott aufgelöste Wesen der Dinge haben die Alten *Idee* genannt".
24 Schelling 1984, pp. 123–129.

> original concept or image only one-sidedly and hence imperfectly, just as again every individual thing expresses only imperfectly the original concept.[25]

Here Schopenhauer seems to understand the different "original concepts" of things as a kind of middle term between the *one* super-essential "divine Idea" – which coincides with the beautiful and the true in itself – and individual finite things.

Now, it is quite surprising that Schopenhauer does not mention here the question of evil in the world (openly admitted in fragment 12 [vi]), and therefore neither metaphysical Evil or the Idea of Evil (mentioned in fragment 12 [vii]; cf. *supra*, 1.7). The Ideas present in God, from which finite things are derived, are "perfect". However, provided that everything in the world was created from an Idea present in God, and provided that evil, too, exists – as is explicitly acknowledged in fragment 12 [vi] – then the Idea of Evil must also have "resided in the Deity at the creation of the species". In this way (assuming the coherence of Schopenhauer's discourse), it is *once again* questioned whether the good God – in whom "good" Ideas reside – is omnipotent, or whether he is the sole Creator: he would rather appear to share his lordship over the world with the "power" that, bearing the Idea of Evil in itself, used it as a creative model.

2.4 "On Plato": "Those Ideas that Reside within Us without Having an Object in the Material World of Sense"

In addition to Ideas of natural objects, according to Schopenhauer, there is a second type of Idea:

> But those Ideas that reside within us without having an object in the material world of sense have been conveyed to us by God directly, so to speak, and not like those first Ideas through the language of nature. But as we are so involved in the material world of sense that what is expressed in this seems to us, at least for the greater part of our lives, to be more palpable than those indwelling Ideas [*jene inwohnenden Ideen*]; further, as we can convey to one another only sensible objects or expressions for these and for their relations, we imitate the Deity and attempt to express our indwelling Ideas likewise through the language of nature. But since we lack the power of creation, we cannot create new objects that would be wholly conformable to the inner Ideas [*den innern Ideen*]; we therefore try do this by assembling [*durch die Zusammenstellung*] the already existing objects of nature, These necessarily imperfect attempts are philosophy, poetry and arts.[26]

---

[25] Schopenhauer 1985, vol. II: *Kritische Auseinandersetzungen (1809–1818)* (henceforth HN II), p. 304. En. tr. MR 2, p. 339.
[26] MR 1, n. 15, p. 11. Translation modified.

In his consciousness, man finds Ideas that do not correspond to any "object in the material world of sense". These Ideas cannot be a human product, they cannot have been formed by an abstract and compositional process, seeing as experience (the world of sense) is the starting point for any such formation (*Bildung*). In this second type of Idea, therefore, the twofold commonality with concepts, as mentioned above in relation to Ideas of natural objects, does not apply, so Schopenhauer does not even raise the question of the difference between the two terms.

Ideas to which no sense object corresponds are "inner" ones, in the sense that their knowledge does not derive from external experience but is found within: they are communicated by God "directly [*unmittelbar*]" and not "through the language of nature". As the object of immediate knowledge (communication), these Ideas are "more palpable [*offenbarer*]" than the others, which correspond to sensible objects and arise by abstraction and composition. But, on the contrary, we regard the latter as more evident than the former because we are almost always "involved [*befangen*] in the material world of sense". The object or *content* of this second type of Idea is not determined in the text, but it is certainly something *supersensible*, since there are no corresponding "sensible objects".

For man, therefore, what is supersensible is in truth more manifest than what is sensible. The supersensible is the object of the "inner Ideas", therefore it is revealed in man's interiority (as in fragment 12 [iii]) and is the object of poetry (as in fragment 12 [vii]), art (as implicit in fragment 14) and philosophy. With these activities, man seeks to express or represent inner Ideas through sense objects. In this way he *completes* God's creative process, because he manifests the Ideas of the divine intellect that would otherwise have no counterpart in the sensible world (nature).

In general, it can be noted that Schopenhauer here develops a theory of Ideas in which, in relation to gnoseology, an empiricist component[27] (the human spirit "forms" universals by "abstraction" from experience: this applies to concepts and Ideas of natural objects) coexists with a Platonic or innatist component[28] (regarding Ideas that have no correspondence in the sensible world). On the other hand, the ontological aspect seems to be broadly Augustinian: the fact that Ideas "resided in the *Deity* [italics mine] at the *creation* [italics mine] of the species" means that they are the forms *quae in divina intelligentia continentur,*[29] used by God as models for the creation of finite things.[30]

---

27 Cf. e.g. Locke 1975, Book II, chap. 11, § 9, p. 159.
28 Cf. Plato, *Phaedo*, 73e-76a, Plato 1914ff., vol. 1, pp. 358–365.
29 Cf. Augustine 1975, q. 46.2, cols. 29–31.
30 In view of these considerations, one can assume that Schopenhauer drafted fragment 15 under the influence of the monumental work of J. J. Brucker, *Historia philosophica doctrinae de ideis*

2.5 Art and Philosophy as the Expression of the Supersensible through Sense Objects. The Basis of the Metaphysical Predilection for Music

In the essay *Of Two Wonderful Languages and Their Mysterious Power*, contained in the volume *Outpourings of an Art Loving Friar*, Wackenroder wrote:

> The language of words is a precious gift of Heaven, and it was to our everlasting benefit that the Creator loosed the tongue of our first ancestor so that he might name all the things which the Almighty had put in the world around him [...] Yet words cannot call down into our hearts the invisible spirit which reigns above us.
>
> Yet I know of two wonderful languages through which the Creator has granted man the means of grasping and comprehending the Divine in all its force [...]. They are: Nature and Art. [...]
>
> Art is a language [*Sprache*] quite different from nature [...]. Art speaks through pictorial representations of men; that is, it employs a hieroglyphic language whose signs we recognize and understand on sight. But in the figures which it presents, the spiritual and the sensuous are merged [...].
>
> Art, [...] which by the meaningful combination [*Zusammensetzungen*] of colored earth and a little moisture recreates the human shape in ideal form within a narrow, limited sphere (a kind of creative power which was vouchsafed to mortals) – art reveals to us the treasures of the human breast, turns our gaze inward, and shows us the Invisible, I mean all that is noble, sublime, and divine in human form.[31]

Here Wackenroder picks up on some of Hamann's suggestions, who, drawing on the Cabbalistic tradition, understood reality as the "language" with which God speaks, or reveals himself, to man.[32] Young Schopenhauer agreed that "the Deity conveys its Idea to man through the organ of nature, which is to be regarded as its language [*Sprache*]".[33] For him, in fact, nature was the expression of the Ideas present in God.

Now, for Wackenroder, the language of words is not capable of expressing the invisible: there are ineffable contents that concern "the Divine" (*arcana verba*,

---

(Brucker 1723) (cf. Hübscher 1989, p. 171). The latter, in fact, reconstructed the history of the term "Idea" up to the most recent debate (Locke and Leibniz). On the "eclecticism" of 18th-century philosophical historiography and on Brucker, see Bottin, Longo and Piaia 1979, pp. 329–551.
31 Wackenroder 1975, pp. 59, 61.
32 Cf. Hamann 2002, pp. 1–24. The first edition of this work appeared anonymously in Königsberg in 1762 in the collection *Kreuzzüge der Philologen* (pp. 159–220). Cf. also the entry "Hamann" in Jens 1988, vol. 7, p. 202.
33 MR 1, n. 15, p. 11.

quae non licet homini loqui).³⁴ These contents, however, can be expressed in the very special 'languages' of nature and art. The latter, unlike nature, is the product of man: "in the figures which it [art] presents, the spiritual and the sensuous are merged", insofar sensible things or their images are used as terms of a "hieroglyphic language" to denote spiritual ones. Art is "a kind of creative power which was vouchsafed to mortals [*eine Art von Schöpfung, wie sie sterblichen Wesen hervorzubringen vergönnt ward*]": from a material point of view, in fact, a work of art is nothing more than an ingenious *Zusammensetzung* of "colored earth and a little moisture".

In the same way, according to Schopenhauer, through art (as well as poetry and philosophy) humans try to "express" (*ausdrücken*) the Ideas that lie within them "without having an object in the material world of sense" (i.e. whose content is something supersensible). However, man does not have the same "power of creation [*Schöpfungskraft*]" as the divinity, so he can only realize this expression through the *Zusammenstellung* of "already existing objects of nature".³⁵

For both Wackenroder and Schopenhauer, God relates to nature as man relates to art: both – the former by creating, the latter only by "assembling" – express the supersensible in them through sense objects. Schopenhauer, however, also includes poetry and philosophy in this (imperfect) analogy: unlike Wackenroder, he does not exclude that words, too, can express the supersensible, albeit inadequately (like the figurative arts). Schopenhauer, therefore, assumes that *philosophy and art have the same content: the supersensible*. This corresponds precisely to Platonic Ideas contained in the divine intellect, which have no counterpart in nature, and are conveyed to man directly by God. In this sense, art and philosophy complement nature (understood as the manifestation or revelation of divine Ideas).

By defining the supersensible as the true content of *art*, Schopenhauer followed not so much Plato (according to whom art reproduces or imitates sensible objects) but rather Plotinus.³⁶ For Schelling, too, the object of art is the eternal models of things.³⁷ On the other hand, Schopenhauer's determination of the supersensible as the content of *philosophy* might have been influenced both by the read-

---

34 Cf. 2 Corinthians 12:4: "inexpressible things, things that no one is permitted to tell".
35 MR 1, n. 15, pp. 10–11.
36 Cf. Plotinus, *Ennead* 5.8.1, in Plotinus 2018, p. 610. In this respect, see also the considerations by Berg 2003, pp. 242–262.
37 Cf. Schelling 1984, pp. 125–127. German editions of Schelling's complete works: F. W. J. Schelling, *Sämtliche Werke*, edited by K. F. A. Schelling, Stuttgart: Cotta, 1856–1861; F. W. J. Schelling, *Historisch-Kritische Ausgabe*, edited by T. Buchheim, J. Hennigfeld, W. G. Jacobs, J. Jantzen, and S. Peetz, Stuttgart-Bad Cannstatt: Frommann-Holzboog, 1976 ff.

ing of Plato (to whom fragment 15 is dedicated) and, in no small measure, by Schulze's courses (according to which philosophy and metaphysics arise from the yearning for the Eternal and the unconditioned).[38] But it should also be recalled that Schelling, in his *Bruno*, spoke at length about the eternal archetypes (*ewige Urbilder*) or eternal concepts (*ewige Begriffe*) of finite things, according to which "productive nature" is said to have formed all species and all individuals.[39] These metaphysical archetypes, according to Schelling, realize the "supreme identity of Truth and Beauty"; this necessarily entails the perfect identity of their respective disciplines, namely "philosophy and poetry".[40]

Fragment 15 presents for the first time the theoretical problem of the expression of supersensible content through sense objects. In fact, we can generally only communicate through "sensible objects or expressions for these and for their relations". This entails the *impossibility* of adequately rendering any content that transcends sensibility: the attempts to do so, which we call "philosophy, poetry and arts", are "*necessarily* [italics mine] imperfect".[41]

These considerations, concerning the necessity of using experiential determinations to express metempirical or supersensible determinations, might well have had a decisive role in shaping Wackenroder's and Schopenhauer's preference for music (cf. *supra*, 1.4; *infra*, 8.16). This metaphysical, rather than aesthetic, predilection was due to the view that musical art is the most adequate (or least inadequate) expression of the supersensible. Music, in fact, with regard to its constituent elements (sounds), seems to be the art form that is least compromised by material sense objects.

However, according to young Schopenhauer, Plato was naively mistaken by thinking that metaphysical truths could "be attained by numbers and quantities" (the reference here is perhaps to *Timaeus*):[42] metaphysical truths, "[…] just because they are so, i.e. lie outside space and time, cannot be reached by any mathematical consideration".[43] The relation, implicit in the text, between space and time on the one hand, and mathematical sciences on the other, seems to presuppose some knowledge of the Transcendental Aesthetics of the *Critique of Pure Reason*.[44]

In any case, the problem of the expression of supersensible contents through sense objects would become extremely significant in the subsequent development

---

[38] Cf. D'Alfonso 2008, pp. 50–51.
[39] Schelling 1984, p. 123–127.
[40] Schelling 1984, p. 128.
[41] MR 1, n. 15, p. 12.
[42] Cf. Plato, *Timaeus*, 29 e–43 a, Plato 1914 ff., vol. 9, pp. 54–95.
[43] MR 1, n. 15, p. 12.
[44] Cf. Kant 1998, B 40–42, p. 176; B 55–56, p. 183.

of Schopenhauer's thought, precisely in relation to Kant's interdiction of a "transcendent use" of the determinations of experience.

2.6 Kant's (Anti-)Copernican Revolution: The Distinction between "Appearance" and "Thing-in-Itself"

In the Preface to the second edition of the *Critique of Pure Reason* (the first edition remained unknown to Schopenhauer until 1826: cf. *infra*, 9.2), Kant starts from what he sees as an unquestionable assumption: the reality of Newton's science of nature (*Naturwissenschaft*).[45] If, as common *realism* believes, our representations simply adapt to the objects of experience in a purely passive sense, then it would be completely impossible to know anything about them *a priori*, i.e. prior to experience itself.[46] Any definite cognition of experience would only be possible *a posteriori*, i.e. *after* the actual encounter with the object. Yet "*mathematics* and *physics* [Mathematik und Physik]", on the contrary, are able to "determine their objects *a priori*": both express necessary connections about them in advance, formulating effective *predictions* (laws).[47]

According to Kant, the correctness of these predictions indicates, beyond any doubt, that the very general or *formal* (with respect to the accidentiality of the content) determinations presupposed by the mathematical science of nature – such as "space", "time", "cause", "substance" – have an 'objective' value: that is, they belong not only to the way science speaks of the objects *of experience*, but also and above all to these objects *as such*. The point is that all (human) cognition of experience takes place precisely according to the same determinations or – in a broad sense – cognitive 'categories' presupposed by Newtonian physics. Thus, in the final analysis, the reality of the science of nature – as evidenced by the efficacy of its predictions – attests, for Kant, to the validity of our natural or common cognition of experience (in terms of its purely formal or categorical dimension).[48]

In order to explain all this, Kant puts forward a revolutionary theoretical proposal, destined to mark a point of no return for the history of Western philosophy: that is, to *invert* the realist gnoseology of common sense, assuming that it is not our "cognition" that conforms (*sich … richten*) to the "objects [*Gegenständen*]", but, rather, these objects conform to our cognition (*nach unserem Erkenntnis*).[49] In

---

[45] Cf. Kant 1998, B X, p. 107.
[46] Cf. Kant 1998, B XVI, p. 110.
[47] Kant 1998, B X, p. 107.
[48] Cf. Kant 1998, B 116–118, pp. 219–220.
[49] Cf. Kant 1998, B XVI, p. 110.

other words, for Kant, it might be that the object does not determine cognition, but, on the contrary, cognition determines the object (in terms of its form). The truth of this "hypothesis [*Hypothese*]"[50] would imply that "we can cognize of things *a priori*" precisely "what we ourselves have put [*legen*] into them".[51]

Simplifying, and using a less rigorous terminology, Kant's complex reasoning can be summarized as follows. The reality of the mathematical science of nature – its being a 'science', or exact knowledge – implies the *correspondence* between the given form of 'thought' or knowledge, in which it consists, and every 'being' of experience in general – even those not yet experienced. The *necessity* of this correspondence (the impossibility of its denial) can only be affirmed by admitting that it is not 'being', always appearing in unpredictable forms, that determines the 'thought' of being time after time, in an equally unpredictable way. *Conversely* it is 'thought' – in the form presupposed by science – that determines or structures every 'being' in general.

This surprising reversal of the relationship between (cognized) object and cognition (of the object), that is to say between the subject and the object of cognition, is compared by Kant to the Copernican revolution. In an attempt to explain "the motion of the heavenly bodies", Copernicus had tried to redefine the relationship between the Earth (the seat of the observer) and the Sun (the observed).[52] In this successful metaphor, the datum that Copernicus wished to account for (the motions of celestial bodies) corresponds in Kant to the reality of the science of nature, or, in general, to the possibility of *a priori* cognition about experience. The theory that, according to Copernicus, can and must be overturned (geocentrism), because it does not provide a satisfactory explanation of the datum in question, corresponds in Kant to the naive realism of common sense.[53]

---

[50] Cf. Kant 1998, B XXII, p. 113.

[51] Cf. Kant 1998, B XVIII, p. 111.

[52] Kant 1998, B XVIII, p. 111. Cf. also B XXII, p. 113: "[...] the central laws of the motion of the heavenly bodies established with certainty what Copernicus assumed at the beginning only as a hypothesis, and at the same time they proved the invisible force (of Newtonian attraction) that binds the universal which would have remained forever undiscovered if Copernicus had not ventured, in a manner contradictory to the senses yet true, to seek for the observed movements not in the objects of the heavens but in their observer. In this Preface I propose the transformation in our way of thinking presented in criticism merely as a hypothesis [*Hypothese*], analogous to that other hypothesis, only in order to draw our notice to the first attempts at such a transformation, which are always hypothetical, even though in the treatise itself it will be proved not hypothetically but rather apodictically from the constitution of our representations of space and time and from the elementary concepts of the understanding."

[53] On the problematic nature of this traditional reading of Kantian text and the more recent positions in the Kant-Forschung, cf. Lemanski 2012; Carl 2013.

Kant warns that, as a consequence of his 'revolutionary' hypothesis, "the object [*Objekt*] should be taken in *a twofold meaning*", i.e. as "phenomenon" or "appearance" (*Erscheinung*) and as "thing-in-itself [*Ding an sich*]".[54] The first term denotes the *inter-subjective* content of (possible) experience, as regulated or structured according to our cognitive faculty (the latter, for Kant, is identical in all rational beings). The second term, instead, indicates that which exists 'prior to' and, in general, outside and independently of all cognition.[55] The "thing-in-itself", by "affecting"[56] the sense organs, would provide the "matter" of experience, thus initiating the (cognitive) process of 'structuring' and 'informing' this "matter", from which the object as "appearance" would finally result.[57]

According to this perspective, therefore, the thing-in-itself is "what appears" in the "appearing" (*erscheinen*) of the appearance (*Erscheinung*), i.e. what is phenomenized in the phenomenon.[58] Given the concept of "appearance", i.e. the phenomenon *as such*, the thing-in-itself must therefore be thought of as necessarily existing, even though by definition it lies outside any possible "experience" – or, for Kant, "cognition". It is, indeed, "in itself": irretrievably closed off and inaccessible to (human) cognition.[59]

If we take Kant's metaphor to a slightly higher level compared to Kant's explicit text, we can observe the following. Just as, according to Copernicus, the observer (from Earth) ascribes to the Sun *his own motion*, and yet cannot escape the appearance that it is the Sun that is moving, so for Kant the empirical subject ascribes to objects (in themselves) determinations that belong only to *his way of cognizing them*, and yet cannot escape the appearance that it is they, the objects, that determine his representations.[60] The process of 'structuring' or 'informing' the "matter" of experience takes place, according to Kant, 'unbeknownst' to the empirical cognitive subject, who finds himself, in fact, *already* immersed in a world that is regulated or oriented according to his cognitive faculty (the world of experience).[61] This is because the aforementioned process is not to be referred to the particular individual or empirical subjectivity (which, precisely as such, is itself a 'result' of that

---

54 Kant 1998, B XXVII, p. 116.
55 Kant 1998, B XXVII, p. 116.
56 Cf. Kant 2012, Note III in § 13 and § 32 and pp. 41 and 66; Kant 1998, A 358–359, pp. 420–421; B 521–523, pp. 512–513.
57 Kant 1998, B 33, p. 155.
58 Kant 1998, B XXVII, p. 115; B 305–306, pp. 360–361.
59 Kant 1998, B XXVII, p. 115. B 305–306, pp. 360–361.
60 Kant 1998, B XXII n., p. 113.
61 According to some critics, this would indicate Kant's implicit recognition of the "unconscious". Cf. Giordanetti, Pozzo and Sgarbi 2012.

structuring, i.e. an "appearance"), but to a deeper and impersonal subjectivity. The latter constitutes the "form" or fundamental "logical" structure of *any* empirical subjectivity – Kant calls it *"I think"*, or *"original apperception"*.[62] Consequently, just as the observer, from within his own reference system (Earth), cannot directly observe the planet's revolution around the Sun, so the empirical cognitive subject, being *already* inside experience, cannot directly witness the constitution of experience itself.

Now, in this new gnoseology, the formal determinations of experience, which the science of nature presupposes, have a purely 'ideal' character. They only exist in our (collective) cognition of objects: they pertain to the "object" only as known or regulated by our cognitive faculty (as an "appearance"), and not to the "object" *per se*, as external and independent of cognition (as a "thing-in-itself"). Kant calls this theoretical position "formal" or "transcendental" idealism.[63] The first adjective ("formal") means that the 'ideality' of the objects of experience concerns, as said, only their "form", not their "matter" (this would in fact result from the action of the "thing-in-itself" on the senses). The second adjective ("transcendental") indicates that the 'ideality' of the objects of experience – the fact that they are *only* "appearances" – solely applies from the point of view of critical reflection on knowledge. This approach alone, in fact, highlights the twofold meaning of the word "object" and therefore identifies a thing-in-itself as absolutely opposed to "what appears". From the point of view of experience ("in perception"), appearances remain perfectly "real [*wirklich*]", existing externally and independently of individual (empirical) self-consciousness.[64] Kant's "transcendental idealism" is thus, at the same time, an "empirical realism".[65]

First of all, the *Critique of Pure Reason* offers a detailed articulation of this complex theoretical framework (regarding the various 'structuring' phases of the "matter" of experience); secondly, it represents the attempt to corroborate or *confirm* it through a decisive "experiment" on "concepts".[66] More precisely, Kant intends to show the *conclusive* consequences of his proposal with regard to the major problems of metaphysics concerning the "unconditioned" (whose concept is articulated in the three terms of "soul", "world" as a totality, and "God").[67] Unlike the problems of natural science, Kant laments, the problems of

---

[62] Cf. Kant 1998, B 131–142, pp. 246–252.
[63] Kant 1998, B 519, p. 511.
[64] Kant 1998, B 519, p. 511.
[65] Kant 1998, B 519, p. 511.
[66] Cf. Kant 1998, B XVIII–XIX, p. 111 (footnote).
[67] Cf. Kant 1998, B 390-396, pp. 405–408.

metaphysics still have no universally recognized solution.⁶⁸ A terrible "conflict of reason with itself" has always reigned over these three main questions, generating the greatest disagreement among philosophers and hindering the establishment of metaphysics as a "science".⁶⁹

According to Kant, this regrettable "conflict" ceases to be "unavoidable" only if one embraces his 'Copernican' (or rather Anti-Copernican)⁷⁰ revolution in the theory of cognition and the consequent distinction between "appearance" and "thing-in-itself".⁷¹ In fact, the *inevitable* contradictions into which the various metaphysical systems have fallen would ultimately derive from the attribution to the "unconditioned" of *empirical* determinations, which belong to the world of experience alone. The "unconditioned", on the other hand, can only be thought of *"without contradiction"* as a "thing-in-itself", as constitutively *outside* all possible (human) knowledge, and therefore as *devoid* of all the formal determinations that only pertain to our way of cognizing objects.⁷² If, and to the extent that, this thesis is demonstrated, the conceptual "experiment" will be proven successful and Kant's revolutionary hypothesis will be "apodictically" confirmed.

2.7 Reading Tennemann's *Geschichte der Philosophie*. Kant and Plato, or, *Erscheinung* and φαινόμενον

In the same letter in which he praises Schulze as the one who awakened him to philosophy, Schopenhauer adds, as a further reason for praise, that Schulze also

---

68 Cf. Kant 1998, B XII-XV, pp. 109–110.
69 Kant 1998, B XVIII, p. 111 (footnote).
70 It could be argued that Kant actually achieved an Anti-Copernican revolution, because, from a gnoseological point of view, he seems to have put man (with his cognitive faculties) at the 'center' and made 'reality' 'revolve' around him. Cf. Russell 1948, p. 9. Cf. on that Gerhardt 1988.
71 Kant 1998, B XVIII, p. 111 (footnote).
72 Cf. Kant 1998, B XX, p. 112: "Now if we find that on the assumption that our cognition from experience conforms to the objects as things-in-themselves, the unconditioned cannot be thought *at all without contradiction*, but that on the contrary, if we assume that our representation of things as they are given to us does not conform to these things as they are in themselves but rather that these objects as appearances conform to our way of representing, then *the contradiction disappears*; and consequently that the unconditioned must not be present in things insofar as we are acquainted with them (insofar as they are given to us), but rather in things insofar as we are not acquainted with them, as things-in-themselves: then this would show that what we initially assumed only as an experiment [the distinction between appearance and thing-in-itself] is well grounded." Cf. in this regard the title of section VI of chap. II: "Transcendental Idealism as the Key to Solving the Cosmological Dialectic" (Kant 1998, B 518, p. 511).

gave him the "wise advice" to devote himself, "first and foremost [*fürs Erste*]", "exclusively [*ausschließlich*]" to the study of Plato and Kant, and not to consider any other philosopher before becoming thoroughly acquainted with their thought.[73]

On 16 October 1810, Schopenhauer borrowed from the library of the University of Göttingen the *Prolegomena to Any Future Metaphysics that Will Be Able to Come Forward as Science*, a work in which Kant had attempted to give a more agile and concise exposition of the results of his critical investigation.

In fragment 17 of the manuscripts (from late 1810), probably after receiving the "wise advice" mentioned above, Schopenhauer attempts a comparison between Plato and Kant:

> The *Critique of Pure Reason* might be called the suicide of the understanding (that is to say in philosophy). Epicurus is the Kant of practical philosophy, just as Kant is the Epicurus of speculative philosophy. Kant's regulative use of reason [*Vernunft*] is perhaps the worst miscarriage of the human mind. It is perhaps the best way to express Kant's defects [*Mangel*] if we say that he was not acquainted with contemplation. One person tells a lie; another who knows the truth says this is a pack of lies and here you have the truth. A third person who does *not* know the truth, but is very acute and clever, points out the contradictions and impossible statements in that lie and says that it is therefore fraud and falsehood. The lie is life, the acute and clever person, however, is only Kant; the truth has been brought to us by many a person, by Plato for example.[74]

This short text reveals a fatal step taken by Schopenhauer in his understanding of Kantianism, one that would condition the entire subsequent development of his thought.

Life (*Leben*) is a lie (*Lüge*). Now, "only Kant" has revealed the lie as such, yet without knowing the "truth"; some, including Plato, instead, have held this truth first-hand. Schopenhauer understood the term "life" in a very broad sense, as what both Kant and Plato referred to in their theories. Secondly, Schopenhauer also understood the term "truth" in a very broad, indeed unambiguous way: *the truth, which Kant did not know, is the same truth which Plato did know.* If one admits that the "truth" that Kant did not know is the thing-in-itself, and that the "truth" that Plato did know is the Idea, then the implicit – perhaps the "unconscious" – meaning of this passage is that *Plato's Idea is Kant's thing-in-itself.* In the manuscripts of 1814 Schopenhauer would explicitly argue for this identity (cf. *infra*, 11.9).[75]

---

[73] Schopenhauer 1978a, p. 261.
[74] MR 1, n. 17, pp. 12–13.
[75] MR 1, n. 228, pp. 143–144.

Wilhelm Gottlieb Tennemann, in his *History of Philosophy*[76] (which Schulze strongly recommended reading in his lecture),[77] had used the Kantian terms of "appearance" and "thing-in-itself" as universal categories of thought. The central paragraph of his exposition of Plato in the second volume of the work (which Schopenhauer borrowed on 14 October 1810) is entitled: *Dinge an sich und Erscheinungen*.[78] The importance of this early reading seems to have been given little consideration in Schopenhauerian research. Tennemann – like Schopenhauer himself in *Parerga and Paralipomena*[79] – states that the philosophers of the Eleatic School were the first to distinguish *Erscheinungen* from *Dinge an sich* as φαινόμενα and ὄντα respectively.[80] This distinction, Tenemman goes on to say, was then taken to a level of greater theoretical coherence by Plato,[81] who set out to rigorously separate "appearances", as that which *becomes*, from "things-in-themselves", which *are* always.[82] In Plato, the *Erscheinung*, i. e. the φαινόμενον, is the reality that can be perceived with the senses; the "thing-in-itself", on the other hand, is "the object of a concept of reason [*Vernunftbegriff*]", a "noumenon", i. e. an "Idea".[83] (Tennemann renders the Greek term νόησις as "reason [*Vernunft*]"). Whereas the appearance exists only in space and time, and is therefore changeable and impermanent, the thing-in-itself, on the contrary, "is neither in space, nor composed, nor changeable, nor destructible".[84]

According to Tennemann, Plato considered Ideas as "original, innate concepts", placed by God in human reason:[85] they would be "principles of all cognition [*Principien aller Erkenntniß*]" of things, since God shaped things in accordance with them.[86] Platonic Ideas, therefore, are both the primordial form of things

---

76 Tennemann 1798–1819. On Tennemann, cf. Bianco, Longo, Micheli, Santinello and Steindler 1995, pp. 25–153. Tennemann himself mentioned Schopenhauer's *The World as Will and Representation* in the fourth edition of his *Grundriße der Geschichte der Philosophie für den akademischen Unterricht* (Tennemann 1825, p. 516). Cf. Hübscher 1966, pp. 64–65.
77 D'Alfonso 2008, p. 101 (footnote). A. Sattar (2019, p. 39) correctly points out that this annotation is probably later than October 1810, and dates from the end of the winter semester 1810/11, thus January or February 1811. This does not exclude the possibility that Schopenhauer knew of this recommendation by Schulze even before he jotted it down in his notebook.
78 Tennemann 1798–1819, II, pp. 363.
79 Schopenhauer 2014.
80 Tennemann 1798–1819, II, p. 363.
81 Tennemann 1798–1819, II, pp. 363–364.
82 Tennemann 1798–1819, II, pp. 365–366.
83 Tennemann 1798–1819, II, p. 366.
84 Tennemann 1798–1819, II, pp. 369–370.
85 Tennemann 1798–1819, II, p. 370.
86 Tennemann 1798–1819, II, p. 371. Sattar (2019, pp. 40–42) argues that Schopenhauer already considered Tennemann's exposition in the fragment "On Plato" to contest the identity between

and the apriori form of their cognition. "Things-in-themselves, that is, the divine Ideas [*Die Dinge an sich, d. i. die göttlichen Ideen*], constitute the intelligible region (νοητος τοπος), the archetype of the real world".[87] The identity between "Ideas" and "things-in-themselves" is reiterated several times by Tennemann.

Nevertheless, it would be a serious misunderstanding to think that Tennemann maintained this identity himself. In the earlier paragraphs of his book, in fact, he complains that Plato failed to realize a "critique [*Kritik*]" of "the faculty of thought [*Denkvermögen*]" and to "divide [*scheiden*], according to a given criterion, empirical cognition from pure cognition".[88] Plato's main mistake was to believe that the "Ideas", the "concepts of reason", were "things-in-themselves",[89] and so he confused "the logical essence [*das logische Wesen*] with the real essence [*Realwesen*]".[90] Tennemann, therefore, interpreted and even *judged* Plato's philosophy from the point of view of Kantian criticism. Kant himself, critically discussing Plato's doctrine of Ideas, had written: "when we compare the thoughts that an author expresses about a subject [...], it is not at all unusual to find that we understand him even better than he understood himself".[91]

It is clear, then, that by using the terms "Ideas" and "things-in-themselves" as synonyms, Tennemann did not indicate his own position at all, but only *Plato's*, with which he disagreed. And yet, the fact that the latter is in fact expounded with Kantian terminology (which obviously could not belong to Plato) often blurs the difference between the historian's point of view and the philosopher's perspective. It is not known whether Schopenhauer fully grasped this difference, but it is certainly possible that he took the equivalence of "Idea" and "thing-in-itself" at face value. However, compared to the letter of Kant's texts, this equivalence is a serious misunderstanding. An affinity between Kant's *Erscheinung* and the φαινόμενον as understood by Plato can perhaps be ascribed to Kant's pre-critical writings (in particular to the dissertation *De mundi sensibilis atque intelligibilis for-*

---

concepts of reason and Platonic Ideas (which Tennemann instead affirmed from his 'Kantian' point of view). This is certainly possible, but would imply that Schopenhauer had not adequately understood Tennemann's position. Indeed, the concepts that Tennemann identified with Platonic Ideas are the "innate" ones (*a priori*), whereas the type of concept that Schopenhauer intends to distinguish from Platonic Ideas is primarily the abstract universal concept (*a posteriori*).

87 Tennemann 1798–1819, II, p. 371. Tennemann does not indicate the spirits and accents of the Greek words.
88 Tennemann 1798–1819, II, pp. 264–265.
89 Tennemann 1798–1819, II, pp. 264–265.
90 Tennemann 1798–1819, II, pp. 264–265,
91 Kant 1998, B 370, p. 396.

mae et principiis).⁹² But, if referred to later works, presuming such a double affinity means overlooking an essential difference between the philosophies of the two authors – or rather, it means positing an illegitimate identity.

According to Plato's Socrates, in the *Republic*, what appears or shows itself to the senses, the φαινόμενον, while not being absolute nothingness, but something intermediate between being and non-being (i. e. becoming),⁹³ is nevertheless something illusory⁹⁴ compared to the true being of the Ideas. That is, the φαινόμενον is explicitly opposed to the truth (ἀλήθεια) of the Idea.⁹⁵ As exemplified in the famous allegory of the cave, the sensible world is a world of "shadows" as opposed to the world of Ideas,⁹⁶ so the knowledge contained in the former is only opinion, δόξα, while the knowledge contained in the latter is true science, ἐπιστήμη.⁹⁷

In Kant's critical philosophy, on the other hand, the *Erscheinung* (the empirical, sensible object) is not something illusory: "truth [*Wahrheit*] and illusion [*Schein*] [...] are not in the object, insofar as it is intuited" – i. e. insofar as it is perceived by the senses – but only "in the judgment about it insofar as it [the object] is thought".⁹⁸ Truth and non-truth (or illusion) concern the relationship – respectively, of correspondence or non-correspondence – between the judgment of the understanding and the object of perception, so that they are *internal* to the realm of experience (or appearances) and do not concern this realm itself as a whole in relation to something else. This is because, in Kant's view, the knowledge whose content is the appearance can relate to no other, truer knowledge with respect to which it can be illusion (non-truth): the thing-in-itself is in fact, by definition, absolutely inaccessible to (human) knowledge. It is the unknown and unknowable.

---

92 Here Kant argues that, through the senses, we cognize things in their phenomenal form, while through the understanding we cognize them in their truth, i.e. as they are in themselves: "Obiectum sensualitatis est sensibile; quod autem nihil continet, nisi per intelligentiam cognoscendum, est intelligibile. Prius scholis veterum *phaenomenon*, posterius *noumenon* audiebat. Cognitio, quatenus subiecta est legibus sensualitatis, est *sensitiva*, intelligentiae, est *intellectualis* s. rationalis. [...] Sensitiva cogitata esse rerum repraesentationes, *uti apparent*, intellectualia autem, *sicuti sunt*" (*De mundi sensibilis atque intelligibilis formae et principiis*, Sectio II, §§ 3–4, in Kant 1900 ff., vol. 2, p. 392).
93 Cf. Plato, *Republic*, 477 a, Plato 1914 ff., vol. 5, pp. 552–553.
94 Plato, *Republic*, 596 e–598 b, Plato 1914 ff., vol. 6, pp. 392–403.
95 Plato, *Republic*, 596 e–598 b, Plato 1914 ff., vol. 6, pp. 392–403.
96 Plato, *Republic*, 514 a–517 b, Plato 1914 ff., vol. 6, pp. 106–107.
97 Cf. Plato 1914 ff., vol. 5, 476 d–477 c, pp. 550–555; vol. 6, 509 d–511 e, pp. 94–103. Cf. also *Protagoras*, 356 d, Plato 1914 ff., vol. 3, pp. 238–239; *Theaetetus*, 210 a, Plato 1914 ff., vol. 12, pp. 254–255.
98 Cf. Kant 1998, B 350, p. 384. Cf. also Kant 2012, pp. 41–45.

This is the essential difference between the philosophies of Kant and Plato, which is dismissed by identifying Kant's *Erscheinung* with Plato's φαινόμενον. Kant peremptorily rules out what Plato's Socrates admits: reality, indeed even the possibility of (human) knowledge about something that transcends the world of experience, and in relation to which knowledge about experience can be determined as untrue. For this reason, the further identification (expressly formulated by Schopenhauer in 1814) of the terms respectively opposed to φαινόμενον and *Erscheinung*, that is, the identification of the Platonic Idea and the Kantian thing-in-itself, is ultimately *the identification of the object of knowledge (and, specifically, of epistemic knowledge) with that which cannot be the object of any knowledge.*[99]

By defining "life" as a "lie" and by considering Kant as the one who showed this lie to be such, Schopenhauer evidently meant to refer to the overall sense of the critical enterprise, which showed the world of experience to be only an "appearance", and not a "thing-in-itself". Schopenhauer thus viewed the former as the content of untrue knowledge: *contra* Kant, the *Erscheinung* is understood as untruth, and the thing-in-itself, i.e. what Kant did not cognize, as "truth" (Kant "does not know the truth"). This is the fatal step taken by Schopenhauer in his understanding of Kantianism, which is revealed in the implications of this fragment. This interpretative choice must be regarded not so much, or not only, as a misunderstanding of Kant's words, but mainly as the direct consequence of the fact that Schopenhauer – like Plato and unlike Kant – admitted the possibility, and indeed the reality, of knowing what transcends the world of experience: this knowledge is accessible by looking inward (*das Innere:* fragments 12 [iii] and 15; cf. also the reference to Schulze containing the quotation from Paul).

Only based on this understanding can Schopenhauer define Kant's critical philosophy, which had limited human cognition to the world's phenomena, as "the suicide of the understanding", i.e. as the understanding's demonstration of the untruthfulness of its own cognition (of its own inability to know the truth). Here it is clear that "understanding" stands for what Kant called, broadly speaking, "pure reason" (cf. *infra*, 7.4), which in the first *Critique* raised itself to its own "court of justice"[100] and ultimately – to take Schopenhauer's metaphor further – sentenced itself to death.

According to Schopenhauer, "the best way to express Kant's defects" is to say that "he was not acquainted with contemplation". If we assume that Schopenhauer

---

99 Kant himself reiterates this difference with respect to Plato: cf. Kant 1998, B 9, p. 140. On Kant's reception of Plato, cf. Siani 2007.
100 Kant 1998, A XI, p. 101.

refers to fragment 12 [i], in which he mentions "a spiritual world" from which it is possible to look at the "phenomena of the external world" with "unconcern" (cf. *supra*, 1.5), we can conclude that, for young Schopenhauer, Kant did not know contemplation because he only knew the *Erscheinungen* and not this "spiritual world".

According to Kant, the "unconditioned" as such, being thinkable without contradiction only as a "thing-in-itself", is beyond all possible human knowledge.[101] However, Kant had theorized a "regulative use" of the three ideas of "reason" (soul, world, God) – producing, according to Schopenhauer, "the worst miscarriage of the human mind". In his lecture, Schulze presented this point as follows: "without any use or benefit and without any special definition [*Bestimmung*], these concepts and principles" – i.e. the three ideas of reason, to which no possible knowledge corresponds – "cannot even exist. But their real destiny is to promote a completeness of the use of the understanding in the continuity of experience".[102] In other words, they are there to serve as an (unattainable) cognitive ideal, which prompts man to expand his knowledge of the empirical world indefinitely. Schopenhauer adds: "In Italy a rip of hay is tied to a stick and fastened to a donkey's saddle so that the animal sees the hay in front of it and goes the faster in order to reach it."[103]

The meaning and consequences of Schopenhauer's understanding of the terms "appearance" and "thing-in-itself", also in relation to Schulze's exposition of Kant's philosophy, requires further discussion (cf. *infra*, 3.2, 3.5 – 3.9). For now it should be noted once more that, according to Schopenhauer, Plato is not the only one who knew the truth that Kant missed ("the truth has been brought to us by many a person, by Plato for example"). This means that, between the lines of fragment 17 (1810), Kant's thing-in-itself is not identified exclusively with the Platonic Idea (as opposed to the fragments of 1814), but with a broader and more unique dimension of truth, of which the Platonic doctrine of Ideas is only one expression among others.[104]

---

101 Kant 1998, B XX, p. 112.
102 MR 2, p. 11.
103 MR 2, p. 11.
104 Regarding the closeness between the concepts of "Platonic Idea" and "thing-in-itself", R. J. Berg (2003, p. 364) hypothesizes the influence of Schelling's *Abhandlungen zur Erläuterung des Idealismus der Wissenschaftslehre*, where Schelling asserts indeed the identity between "Idea" and "thing-in-itself". However, Schopenhauer did not read this text until a year after he read Tennemann's exposition, i.e. not until 1811, in the reprint published in the first volume of the *Philosophische Schriften* (Schelling 1809, pp. 115 – 200).

2.8 The "Nightmare" of Critical Philosophy

In the continuation of fragment 17, Schopenhauer writes:

> If Goethe had not been sent into the world simultaneously with Kant in order to counterbalance him, so to speak, in the spirit of the age, the latter would have haunted like a nightmare many an aspiring mind [*auf manchem strebenden Gemüth*] and would have oppressed it under a great affliction. But now the two from opposite directions have an infinitely wholesome effect and will possibly raise the German spirit to a height surpassing even that of antiquity.[105]

Having imperatively limited human knowledge to the phenomenal world alone (to the "lie"), Kant could have been an oppressive "nightmare" and a "great affliction" for all "aspiring minds", that is, for all those who yearn for an absolute and transcendent truth. The fact that Goethe intervened to "counterbalance" Kant may mean, in general, that art, at its highest level (Schopenhauer had a sort of veneration for Goethe in those years), allows one to break through the cognitive limits (im)posed by criticism. This interpretation is confirmed by fragment 14, according to which art preserves "the knowledge of the eternal truth"; fragment 15 also states that art, together with philosophy, (imperfectly) expresses the Ideas that have no corresponding sense object and result from direct communication between God and man. In 1811, Schopenhauer would explicitly attribute to the genius (and the madman) the ability to intuit (*anschauen*) things-in-themselves (cf. *infra*, 3.2).[106]

For young Schopenhauer, Kantian criticism was something that, although of inestimable value, needed to be *completed* and *remedied*. This conviction was the natural consequence, on the one hand, of the identification between phenomenal knowledge and untrue knowledge and, on the other hand, of the assumption that man's supreme interest and the very task of philosophy are, indeed, the knowledge of truth. It is certainly with reference to this line of reasoning that, for Schopenhauer, "Epicurus is the Kant of practical philosophy, just as Kant is the Epicurus of speculative philosophy."[107] Just as Epicurus did in the practical sphere, so Kant drastically rejected any discussion of the divine and the supersensible in the theoretical sphere.

From 1812 onwards, Schopenhauer sought to develop a "true criticism" that, while remaining faithful to Kant's intentions, could at the same time give voice

---

[105] MR 1, n. 17 pp. 12–13.
[106] Cf. MR 2, pp. 18–19.
[107] MR 1, n. 17, p. 12.

and – mainly – theoretical (epistemological) legitimacy to the yearning for an absolute truth of all "aspiring minds".

2.9 Yearning for Eternity and the Transcendental Ideality of Time

The qualification of phenomenal knowledge as non-truth, implied in fragment 17, is not a purely and coldly 'theoretical' operation. The illusory nature of what is in time and the necessary relationship between truth and eternity can be found in Schopenhauer's very first notes; as already noted, this is a theme dear to the pietist tradition in which Schopenhauer was educated. Young Schopenhauer combined his early knowledge of Kant's texts with a religious element that, for him, was still present and explicit in these years. In this respect, a significant reference is the comment on Schulze containing the quotation from Paul, according to which the unconditioned is *given* in the inner world (cf. *supra*, 2.2). Fragment 15 also states that God conveys the eternal Ideas directly to man. Such statements contradict not only Schulze's skepticism, but also Kant's own philosophy, according to which even the "inner sense" is subject to the "form" of all appearances: "time".[108] For Kant, not only "external" but also "internal" cognition reveals a merely phenomenal reality.

Of course, it may be excessive to describe the translation of Milton's *On Time*, and in particular the opposition between time and eternity, as a sign or anticipation of Schopenhauer's mature philosophy, based on the distinction between appearance and thing-in-itself.[109] However, one can justifiably assume that this early *Weltanschauung* – centered on the (broadly Platonic) dualism between time (illusion) and eternity (truth), and accompanied by an energetic yearning for the latter – predisposed young Schopenhauer to welcome the Kantian thesis of the "transcendental ideality" of time and space, *interpreting it, however, in continuity with that dualism* – namely, as a confirmation or even as the apodictic demonstration of the illusoriness (non-truth) of what is in space and time.

Indeed, in the Appendix to *The World as Will and Representation,* Schopenhauer argues precisely for this interpretation of Kantian philosophy: Kant is said to have expressed "the same truth that Plato tirelessly repeats", according to which "this world that appears to the senses does not have true being, but is in-

---
108 Kant 1998, B 49–50, p. 163.
109 Cf. Lütkehaus 1984. For a criticism of the radical nature of this position, see De Cian 2002, p. 52.

stead only an incessant becoming, it is and it is not, and apprehending it does not involve cognition so much as delusion [*Wahn*]". However, Kant "made it into an established and incontrovertible truth [*machte sie ... zur erwiesenen und unstreitigen Wahrheit*]" (cf. *infra*, 3.6).[110]

Nevertheless, according to fragment 17 (from 1810), Kant was the one who "pointed out" the "lie" of "life". A note on Fichte (1811), which I will analyze later (cf. *infra*, 3.5), states even more clearly that Kant, by showing the "nothingness [*Nichtigkeit*] of space and time", generated the awareness (*Bewußtsein*) that all "knowledge within the limits of experience" (knowledge about the "appearance") is "error".[111]

2.10 Truth and Life. The Philosopher and the Philistine

In fragment 16, Plato is referred to as "the divine [*der göttliche*]" because, unlike Aristotle, he was able to consider the things of the world as "letters" in which one could read the "divine Ideas".[112] The predicate "divine" seems to imply that – as stated in fragment 15 – the Ideas existed in the Divinity when the human species was created. Also according to Tennemann's exposition of Platonic philosophy, as we have seen, the "divine Ideas", i.e. "things-in-themselves", are the "archetype" of the real world.[113]

In line with fragment 6 (cf. *supra*, 1.3), Schopenhauer thus assumes that "the degree on the scale of minds" is determined by the ability to see "the invisible" (the divine Ideas) "in the visible" (the things of the world): that is, by the awareness that *what is visible, the external world, is not all*.

The "philistine" lacks this awareness:

> The simple philistine tries to attach to life a kind of infinity or eternity, a positive and absolute state, and he attempts to consider it and to get through it as though there were nothing more left to desire. The learned philistine does the same thing with principles and methods; to some of these he attaches absolute perfection and objective force and authority [...]. But here happiness and truth should and can never be seized. Only their phantoms are sent to us [...].[114]

---

110 Cf. Schopenhauer 2010b, I 496–497, pp. 445–446. Cf. Schopenhauer 2020, pp. 302–304.
111 MR 2, pp. 24–25. Translation modified.
112 MR 1, n. 16, p. 12.
113 Tennemann 1798–1819, II, p. 368.
114 MR 1, n. 18, pp. 17–18.

The philistine, whether "simple" or "learned", makes the specular mistake to that of attributing the absoluteness and insurmountability of eternal evil to temporal evil (fragment 12 [vi]). In fact, he ascribes to his own temporal good (to his own life) the absolute values of happiness and truth.[115]

But finite life, which takes place "here", can only accommodate the "phantoms [*Schattenbilder*]" of absolute truth and happiness; in this way, however, it awakens the consciousness of the latter (just as, in tragedy, the "images [*Bilder*] of earthly misfortune" awaken the memory of true and eternal evil, i.e. of the Idea of Evil). Life in time, therefore, has value not in itself, but only insofar as it gives man a teaching (a παίδευσις, cf. fragment 13) about the eternal truth that transcends life itself, and of which the latter is only an image: "if this doctrine could be brought home to us in any other way, we would not live".[116] Life teaches each of us something different: it is "like the Apostles preaching on the day of Pentecost who, teaching the multitude, seem to speak to each in his own tongue".[117]

Man, and especially the philosopher, must necessarily raise his consciousness above the sensible world in order to find the truth:

> Philosophy is a high mountain road which is reached only by a steep path covered with sharp stones and prickly thorns. It is an isolated road and becomes ever more desolate, the higher we ascend. Whoever pursues this path must show no fear, but must leave everything behind and confidently make his own way in the wintry snow. Often he suddenly comes to a precipice and looks down upon the verdant valley. A violent attack of dizziness draws him over the edge, but he must control himself and cling to the rocks with might and main. In return for this, he soon sees the world beneath him; its sandy deserts and morasses vanish from his view, its uneven spots are levelled out, its jarring sounds no longer reach his ear, and its roundness is revealed to him. He himself is always in the pure cool mountain air and now beholds the sun when all below is still engulfed in dead of night.[118]

---

115 Arthur Hübscher is of the opinion that Schopenhauer became acquainted with the Romantic struggle against philistinism through the works of Tieck, which he read already during the Hamburg period (cf. Hübscher 1989, pp. 128–130). Novalis also wrote: "Philistines lead only a daily life [...]. They do everything for the sake of their early life" (Novalis 1996, p. 24).
116 MR 1, n. 18, p. 13.
117 MR 1, n. 18, p. 14.
118 MR 1, n. 20, p. 14. According to Gwinner, this fragment was written on 8 September 1811, on the occasion of a pleasure trip to the Harz mountain range (cf. Gwinner 1878, p. 87; HN I, p. 494). With regard to the metaphor of philosophy as a "high mountain road" that offers a view from "an exalted seat", one can also mention the three mountain climbs Schopenhauer made during his long journey through Europe in 1803–1804. The descriptions of these climbs are found in his diaries (cf. Lütkehaus 1988, pp. 163–171, 194–200, 246–251). In particular, with regard to the second ascent, which took place on Mount Pilatus, Schopenhauer notes: "To see the world in this way from above is such a singular spectacle that I think it must be of great comfort to those who are burdened by worries" (Lütkehaus 1988, p. 196).

The metaphorical significance of the description of philosophy as a "high mountain road", which leaves the world "beneath", is evident – in this respect, it is reminiscent of the "spiritual world" of fragment 12 [i], from which the philosopher looks at the *Erscheinungen* with "unconcern", as if "from an exalted seat". All this betrays a very aristocratic conception of philosophy: only those who reach so high can see the "sun" of truth, while the multitudes below are "still engulfed in dead of night".

2.11 The Philosophies of Fichte and Schelling according to Schulze

In his Metaphysics course, Schulze devoted a chapter to "the attempt, by means of an intellectual intuition of the Absolute [*vermittelst einer intellektuellen Anschauung des Absoluten*], to attain the goal of metaphysics and solve the riddle of the world [*das Rätsel der Welt*]": that is, to "Fichte's science of knowledge [*Wissenschaftslehre*]" and "Schelling's philosophy of nature".[119]

The aim of metaphysics, as Schulze had said in his introduction to the course, is to "proceed from the worldly to the otherworldly, from the transient and conditioned of existence to the eternal and unconditioned, and to do so precisely according to clear and certain principles".[120] Now, Kantian philosophy had decreed the necessary failure of any metaphysics, and in general of any attempt to theoretically determine the relationship between what is "finite and transient (the world of experience)" and a possible "infinite" and "eternal" reality.[121] This is why it is surprising, according to Schulze, that this very philosophy gave rise to the construction of "two metaphysical systems".[122]

The authors of these two systems, namely Fichte and Schelling, accepted "the result of the critique of reason", according to which "our natural cognition in the sensible world" is conditioned by the senses and the understanding (*Verstand*) and thus consists of "mere appearances [*bloßen Erscheinungen*]".[123] Nevertheless, they claimed to solve the "riddle of the world" in a metaphysical way, maintaining that "our spirit is capable of rising to cognition of all things as they are in themselves [*Erkenntniß aller Dinge wie sie an sich selbst ... sind*]", i.e. "as they are made in truth [*wahrhaft beschaffen*]".[124] These two philosophers therefore had to posit an-

---

[119] D'Alfonso 2008, p. 100.
[120] D'Alfonso 2008, pp. 50–51.
[121] D'Alfonso 2008, p. 100.
[122] D'Alfonso 2008, p. 100.
[123] D'Alfonso 2008, p. 100.
[124] D'Alfonso 2008, p. 100.

other cognitive faculty or power (*Erkenntniẞkraft*) in addition to those recognized by Kant (with which it is indeed impossible to know things-in-themselves or the Absolute): that is, "intellectual intuition".[125] (On the implicit determination of the thing-in-itself as "truth", see *infra*, 3.7 and 3.8).

Now, the affirmation of a possible immediate access to the Absolute was typical of mysticism in general, and was also to be found in the philosophers of the "neo-Platonic school".[126] However, Fichte's and Schelling's systems, due to their peculiarity and their departure from Kant, could not be classified simply as "a new edition [*eine neue Auflage*]" of Neo-Platonism.[127] Schulze presented the peculiar theses of Fichte's and Schelling's philosophies by dividing both into two phases.[128] In particular, according to Schulze, the second phase of Fichte's philosophy, namely "the brand new presentation of the science of knowledge" (which Schopenhauer would hear in Berlin a few months later), focused on the concept of God as the only truly existing reality, of which everything else is a manifestation (*Aeuẞerung*), namely an image (*Bild*) or scheme (*Schema*).[129]

Beyond the specific individual tenets of the two philosophers, what clearly emerges from Schulze's lecture is that Fichte and Schelling, while taking Kant's philosophy into full account, did not exclude the possibility of an epistemologically legitimate discourse on the supersensible. In other words, both sought to build *a metaphysics that would break down the Kantian interdiction*. This presentation must have greatly impressed young Schopenhauer, who, for his part, was convinced of the extraordinary relevance of Kant's philosophy, but at the same time had no intention of renouncing his conviction that man can access knowledge of the supersensible.

2.12 Moral Sentiment and Hope for Greater Happiness

During the Easter holidays of 1811, Schopenhauer visited the poet Christoph Martin Wieland (1733–1813) in Weimar and told him about his decision to devote his life to philosophy. When the poet warned him against such an impractical field of study, Schopenhauer promptly replied that life is a troubling matter, and he intended to spend his own reflecting on it. Wieland, positively impressed, immediately

---

125 D'Alfonso 2008, p. 100.
126 D'Alfonso 2008, pp. 101–102.
127 D'Alfonso 2008, pp. 101–102.
128 D'Alfonso 2008, pp. 102–108.
129 D'Alfonso 2008, pp. 102–103.

changed his mind: "Young man, I now understand your nature. Stick to philosophy."[130]

On 3 August 1811, Schopenhauer borrowed the *Critique of Practical Reason* and the *Critique of Judgment* from the library of the University of Göttingen. In the former, Kant had admitted not only man's freedom, but also the immortality of the soul and the existence of God as "postulates" for moral action.[131] According to Kant, the "moral law", which in itself is an unquestionable *"fact* [italics mine] of pure reason",[132] necessarily implies the "supreme good", understood as the perfect correspondence between virtue and happiness ("happiness distributed in exact proportion to morality").[133] Now, the conditions of possibility of such a correspondence, according to Kant, are moral perfection or holiness, which can be attained by man only in an *infinite life,* and *the existence of a perfect Being* who, having power over all things, grants people happiness according to their conduct.[134]

As we have seen, based on the *Critique of Pure Reason*, human knowledge is necessarily limited to the world of experience or phenomena. Instead, through those three postulates, the moral sphere – "pure practical reason" – opens up to the consideration of metempirical terms ("freedom" as uncaused causality, "soul", "God"). For Kant, this determines a "primacy of pure practical reason" over purely speculative reason.[135]

However, those postulates "are not theoretical dogmas" because they do not extend speculative knowledge but only justify "concepts even the possibility of which it could not otherwise [based on the *Critique of Pure Reason*] presume to affirm".[136] Contrary to what Schulze stated in his lecture, it is not a matter of "a practical-dogmatic cognition [*praktisch-dogmatische Erkenntniß*] of God and of the immortality of the soul",[137] but, much more modestly, it is the explication of the *"presuppositions* [Voraussetzungen]" that necessarily underlie every truly moral action.[138]

In his Metaphysics course, Schulze sought to refute this Kantian doctrine by showing the *contradictory* nature of its fundamental assumption, namely the union of virtue and happiness: the former would necessarily exclude the satisfac-

---

130 Cartwright 2010, p. 149.
131 Kant 1996a, p. 246.
132 Kant 1996a, pp. 177–178.
133 Kant 1996a, p. 266.
134 Cf. Kant 1996a, pp. 166–205.
135 Kant 1996a, p. 236.
136 Kant 1996a, p. 246.
137 D'Alfonso 2008, p. 96.
138 Kant 1996a, p. 246.

tion of sensual appetites, while the latter would necessarily include them.[139] Young Schopenhauer scornfully remarked that Schulze, in this definition, reduced human happiness to that of pigs.[140]

In September, Schopenhauer moved from Göttingen to Berlin with the intention of attending Fichte's lectures. Probably during the journey, he jotted down the following fragment:

> There is a consolation, a sure hope, and these we experience *from moral feeling*. If it speaks to us so clearly, if in our hearts [*im Inneren*] we feel so strong an incentive even to make the greatest sacrifice that is wholly opposed to our apparent well-being, then we realize in a lively manner that ours is a different well-being; that accordingly we should act in opposition to all earthly grounds and reasons; that heavy duty and responsibility point to an exalted happiness in keeping with them; and that the voice we faintly hear comes from a bright place. – However, no promise lends force to God's commandments, but his commandment is instead of the promise ...[141]

One can interpret this text as meaning that Schopenhauer's hope in a different kind of well-being from the earthly one (an "exalted happiness") is *only* ensured by "moral feeling". If so, he would be attempting to rework in his own way (by relating the sphere of morality to feeling rather than reason) the "primacy" of moral consideration over purely theoretical or cognitive reason. Indeed, for Kant, the question that ethics must answer through these "postulates" is precisely: "*What may I hope?* [Was darf ich hoffen]?"[142]

According to Schopenhauer, moral sentiment demands that we "act in opposition to *all* [italics mine] earthly grounds and reasons" – in other words, we should completely sacrifice our sensory well-being. This thesis may contain an implicit reference to Kant's rigorism, according to which moral action is absolutely incompatible with any sensory or (in a very broad sense) material motivation.

On the other hand, for Schopenhauer, moral sentiment attests to man's destination to a higher happiness precisely *because* it requires such a sacrifice. But the link between morality (or virtue) and happiness is merely presupposed, not justified or argued for, so that, granting philosophical depth rather than a purely religious interest to these words, here too Schopenhauer seems to be implying the results of Kant's investigation.

In any case, the overall sense of the text is as follows: moral feeling, by revealing man's destination for a higher happiness than that of the senses (we "are not

---

139 D'Alfonso 2008, pp. 98–99.
140 D'Alfonso 2008, p. 99. Cf. MR 2, p. 12.
141 MR 1, n. 20, pp. 14–15.
142 Kant 1998, B 833, p. 677.

meant to thrive and flourish like the plants of the earth", cf. fragment 12 [v]), testifies "in a lively manner" that man *exceeds* the sensory world.

2.13 Conclusion. The Platonic Vector and the Kantian Vector

As mentioned above, young Schopenhauer began to devote himself entirely to philosophy at a time when the religious dimension was still very much a part of his life: it was not until 1812 that he stopped going to church regularly.[143] This yearning towards transcendence, on the one hand, led him to feel great affinity with Plato's thought, and on the other hand, obliged him to engage with Kant's philosophy. Of the latter he recognized both the revolutionary character ("only Kant" pointed out that life is a "lie", cf. fragment 17) and the destructive potential towards man's metaphysical needs (criticism, taken in itself, is a "nightmare").

Plato, unlike Kant, knew the "truth" (fragment 17). Schopenhauer, like the former and unlike the latter, is certain that man *can* cognize transcendent or supersensible reality, and can do so precisely through interiority (in addition to fragments 12 [iii] and 15 and the comment on Schulze, note that, according to fragment 20, hope in otherworldly well-being resides "in our hearts [*im Inneren*]", in the form of a "moral feeling"). At the same time, however, Schopenhauer – like Kant and unlike Plato – feels the need to ask an epistemological question about the possibility of metaphysics in general. In other words, he senses the need to abandon 'naive' metaphysics (Plato mistakenly believed that metaphysical truths could be "attained by numbers and quantities", cf. fragment 15).

In this sense, according to young Schopenhauer, it is necessary to correct or rather *integrate* Kant through Plato and, at the same time, Plato through Kant. Tennemann, in his *Geschichte der Philosophie*, judged the specific results of Plato's philosophy through the lens of Kant's philosophy (cf. *supra*, 2.7). Young Schopenhauer, instead, corrected and integrated *one philosopher by means of the other*, trying to overcome their opposite one-sidednesses ('positive' for Plato, 'negative' for Kant). In fact, Schopenhauer sought a *non-naive metaphysics*, one that could withstand Kant's criticism and successfully hold its own.

This overall need for a post-Kantian metaphysics explains Schopenhauer's close attention to the work of Schelling (who, at this time, had momentarily retired from academia), and the enthusiasm with which he decided to move to Berlin in

---

143 Cf. A. Hübscher 1989, pp. 8–10.

the summer of 1811, "in the hope of finding in Fichte a true philosopher and a great mind".[144]

In the following chapters, through textual analysis, I will show that the entire subsequent development of Schopenhauer's thought, right up to the first elaboration of his mature system, was the problematic result of these two opposing forces: the Platonic vector (in the broad sense, as the affirmation of the *possibility* of cognizing absolute reality) and the Kantian vector (in the narrow sense, as the affirmation of the limits of the human cognitive faculty, i.e., the *impossibility* of cognizing absolute reality).

---

[144] Schopenhauer 1978a, p. 261.

Part 2 **The Critical Confrontation with Fichte and Schelling (1811/12): From Initial Enthusiasm to Complete Rejection**

3 Appearance and Thing-in-Itself

3.1 Introduction

In Berlin, Schopenhauer attended the lectures of famous scholars, including the zoologist Martin Heinrich Lichtenstein, the chemist Martin Heinrich Klaproth, the physicist Paul Erman, the antiquarian Friedrich August Wolf, and the theologian and philosopher Friedrich Schleiermacher. This in-depth study of the science of the time formed the basis of his 1813 dissertation *On the Fourfold Root of the Principle of Sufficient Reason*, which is also (but not only) a philosophical reflection on science (cf. *infra*, 9.2 – 9.3).[1]

The main purpose of Schopenhauer's move to Berlin, however, was to personally attend the lectures given by Fichte (then rector of the university). Schopenhauer took a short introductory course on Fichte's "On the Study of Philosophy" (held the week before the start of the winter semester of the 1811–1812 academic year), the course "On the Facts of Consciousness" (21 October–20 December 1811) and the course "On the Science of Knowledge [*Wissenschaftslehre*]" (6 January– 20 March 1812). In his notebook, Schopenhauer recorded not only Fichte's arguments but also his own (mostly critical) notes and comments.[2]

In this chapter, I will analyze three of these notes, in which Schopenhauer uses the Kantian concepts of "appearance" and "thing-in-itself" but with an essentially different meaning. I will investigate the theoretical and historical presuppositions of this very first understanding of Kantian criticism, which would have a decisive influence on the development of Schopenhauer's thought.

3.2 The Intuition of Things-in-Themselves: Genius and Madness

In the first lecture "On the Study of Philosophy", Fichte outlines the two possible types of "knowledge": historical knowledge (*das historische Wissen*) and scientific

---

[1] Cf. Segala 2009, pp. 222 – 228.
[2] On the philological issues related to Schopenhauer's notes, cf. Novembre 2018a, pp. 249 – 257. Parallel to the analysis and commentary on Fichte's exposition, in this book I discuss the notes that young Schopenhauer took while attending the course "On the Facts of Consciousness". Those in which Schopenhauer attempts to develop some fundamental theoretical issues are analyzed on pp. 257– 298.

knowledge (*das wissenschaftliche Wissen*).³ Historical knowledge, unlike scientific knowledge, is not based on one's own, but on someone else's "perception [*Wahrnehmung*]"; it is therefore "not knowledge", but only "a semblance, an impression" of it⁴ (which implies that true knowledge is based on one's own perception). Historical knowledge is of two types, depending on whether its content can no longer be perceived (as in history, *Geschichte*), or whether it can (as in zoology and botany): in the latter case, this content can be attested; in the former, it cannot.⁵ Fichte specifies that each I is *in principle* equal to all other Is and "must be capable of experiencing the same modifications": that is, the different Is must be able to perceive the same thing in the same way.⁶ Clearly, only based on this assumption can a kind of historical knowledge be accepted as valid even by those who have not perceived, and never will perceive, its content.

Against this uniformity of different Is, Fichte goes on to say, some have pointed out the instances of originality (*Originalität*) and genius (*Genie*), which are "specially modified Egos or Is".⁷ To this objection he replies that dissimilarity of perception is often madness (*Wahnsinn*), and only rarely genius.⁸ Certainly, genius and madness both depart from the common human perspective (and in this sense are precisely two kinds of "originality"), but in opposite directions: "genius or poetry is divine and is far above that point of view, but madness is animal and is below that point".⁹

> Many a man who feels in himself originality considers this to be poetry and himself to be a genius, whereas he is a fool [*Narr*]. The criterion on which every eccentric can test to which of two originalities he belongs is as follows. Before he makes his appearance as such, the genius must first have been a human being, a rational [*vernünftiger*] and ethical man; let everyone first become this, and then we will speak of genius and poetry.¹⁰

Fichte's presumed relationship between morality and genius is very clear here. Indeed, the moral predisposition is a condition of genius.

Young Schopenhauer completely disagreed with Fichte and wrote down a note that seems to partially anticipate what he would argue in *The World as Will and*

---

3 MR 2, pp. 17–22.
4 MR 2, p. 17.
5 MR 2, p. 17.
6 MR 2, p. 18.
7 MR 2, p. 18.
8 MR 2, p. 18.
9 MR 2, p. 18.
10 MR 2, p. 20.

Representation (albeit with reference to the Platonic Idea and in the context of the metaphysics of will: two elements still absent here).[11]

First of all, Schopenhauer resolutely denied that "the madman [*der Wahnsinnige*] closely approximates to the animal" – as Fichte instead claimed – and that "sound common sense" is at an equal distance (albeit in opposite directions) between genius and madness. Indeed, the latter two, "although widely different", are much *closer* to each other than the former is to the common intellect and the latter to the animal.[12] Against the affinity between madness and animality, Schopenhauer pointed out that "The clever dog is to be compared to the ordinary man of demureness and intelligence [*dem gemeinen gesezten verständigen Menschen*] rather than to the man of unsound mind (not weakness of mind)".[13] Secondly, against the radical difference, posited by Fichte, between genius and madness, Schopenhauer objected: "the lives of great geniuses show that in life they often behave almost like insane men and, according to Seneca, Aristotle says: *Nullum magnum ingenium sine mixtura dementiae fuit.*"[14]

Schopenhauer then tried to determine what it is about the *affinity between genius and madman* that makes them different from the common man. The latter is firmly and irrevocably "encased in the bodily conditions of our consciousness and thinking" represented by space, time and the concepts of the understanding ("they fit closely to his body [...] and cover him like a well-cut garment"). Instead, the genius and the madman both have the capacity to look at what lies beyond the appearance: the former "cognizes [*erkennt*] his own essence-in-itself and that of things [*sein Eignes und der Dinge Wesen an sich*]" by virtue of "a power [*Kraft*] which, as something entirely supernatural, cannot be further defined" (so that, as it were, "he is too big for his garment and looks out of it and upwards"). The latter, on the other hand, can cognize things beyond or without the conditions of experience, because his empirical cognitive powers are impaired or worn out ("his garment is torn, but for this very reason his I or ego, which is not subject to any derangement, at times sees through it [his garment]").[15]

---

11 Cf. Schopenhauer 2010b, § 36 and § 37, I 217–230, pp. 207–219 (cf. Schopenhauer 2020, pp. 141–149). On this, see D'Alfonso 2006, pp. 203–206.
12 MR 2, p. 18. The text of this quotation, which Schopenhauer reports incorrectly (cf. HN II, p. 18: "nullum magnum ingenium sine insaniae mixtura"; correction made by the English translator) is found in Seneca's *De tranquillitate animi*, though not in XV, 16, as reported in *The World as Will and Representation* (Schopenhauer 2010b, § 36, p. 214), but in XVII, 10. The (spurious) Aristotelian text to which Seneca refers is *Problemata*, XXX, 1.
13 MR 2, p. 18.
14 "There has been no great mind without an admixture of madness": cf. MR 2, p. 18.
15 MR 2, pp. 19–20. Translation modified.

This fundamental difference between the common man, on the one hand, and the genius and the madman, on the other, results in a *further* difference: the former is completely at ease in the world of experience, he "knows his way" around it; the latter, on the other hand, are not "at home" in it:

> On the other hand, in his actions the genius often resembles the madman because by intuition of the things-in-themselves [*durch Anschauung der Dinge an Sich*], he dwells less in the world of experience [*Erfahrungswelt*] and is less at home in this. Just like the madman he also confuses appearances [*Erscheinungen*] by simultaneously cognizing things-in-themselves [*indem es zugleich die Dinge an sich erkennt*].[16]

Here we find an implicit reference to the genius's fundamental unhappiness.

For Schopenhauer, by attesting to the possibility of a knowledge that does not take place according to the usual conditions of experience, madness shows that these "do not belong", i.e. are not inherent, to things-in-themselves.[17] Indeed, Schopenhauer defines the "conditions of our consciousness and thinking" as "bodily" (*körperlich*). It is not clear whether this is to be understood in the sense that, through these conditions, one can only cognize the bodily world, or in the sense that they are closely linked to having a body, so that, without one, it would be possible to cognize things *beyond* these conditions (in this case, Schopenhauer's statement could contain an implicit reference to Plato's *Phaedo*).[18]

Schopenhauer also describes the *difference* between genius and madness:

> Insane persons utter maxims of genius, or at any rate they would do so did they not lack that lofty thoughtfulness [*hohe Besonnenheit*], which is the characteristic [*Charakter*] of the man of genius and by virtue of which he is able to express what he cognizes [*kennt*] beyond all experience [*über alle Erfahrung*] in concepts, pictures and works of art, and these again have objects of experience as their material. For this the madman has something of the first condition, but lacks the second, namely soundness of conditions for the world of experience.[19]

"Lofty thoughtfulness [*hohe Besonnenheit*]" is the peculiar "characteristic" of the genius and entails the ability to express (*ausdrücken*) and communicate (*mittheilen*) metempirical knowledge.[20] But two conditions are necessary for this expressive activity of the genius: firstly, access to such knowledge; secondly, "soundness of conditions for the world of experience". In fact, the expression of metempirical

---

16 MR 2, p. 19. Translation modified.
17 MR 2, p. 18.
18 Cf. Plato, *Phaedo*, 65 a–66 b, Plato 1914 ff., vol. 1, pp. 320–321.
19 MR 2, p. 19. Translation modified.
20 MR 2, p. 19.

knowledge necessarily takes place through empirical matter (through "objects of experience"), and therefore presupposes a sound knowledge of experience.

The madman has "something of the first condition" of the genius (access to metempirical knowledge), "but lacks the second", namely adequate knowledge of the empirical world.[21] It should be noted, however, that Fichte also implicitly admits a degree of identity between genius and madness: both are "specially modified Egos or Is", in that both perceive things differently from the ordinary man. The problem of their distinction arises in Fichte precisely because of this identity, which tends to confuse them. Schopenhauer, unlike Fichte, emphasizes this identity and tries to specify it.

Finally, Schopenhauer clarifies the distinction between the "weak-minded imbecile [*der Blödsinnige*]" and the "worldly wise [man] [*der Weltkluge*]" using the garment metaphor. While the genius and the madman wear the "garment" of the conditions of experience too small (out of metaphor: their understanding exceeds their experience), the fool "does not fill out his garment which hangs on him like a sack" (out of metaphor: experience exceeds his understanding). The intelligent man, on the other hand, is just the opposite: his garment "fits" perfectly, "as a *tricot*".[22]

There are at least three points worthy of attention in this remark on Fichte. Firstly, for young Schopenhauer, *cognition of things-in-themselves is possible*, if only for exceptional individuals (the madman and the genius). For them, the thing-in-itself is not a negative *"boundary concept* [Grenzbegriff]",[23] to use Kant's words, but has a positive gnoseological reality: it is positively cognizable. In this sense, the figure of the genius (exemplified by Goethe in fragment 17) can act as a "counterbalance" to the "nightmare" of criticism, because it attests that the cognitive limits universalized by Kant are surmountable (cf. *supra*, 2.8).[24] The genius cognizes (or is aware of) *two distinct worlds:* the supersensible world, of things-in-themselves, and the world of experience, the sensible world, in which he achieves the "expression" of the former.

Secondly, the *cognition of things-in-themselves is called "intuition"* (*Anschauung*). According to Schulze's explanation, the intuition theorized by Fichte

---

21 A few lines earlier Schopenhauer had already indicated, albeit implicitly, this difference between the genius and the madman, providing *another* justification for their ability to cognize things-in-themselves: for the genius, it depends on a metaphysical force or capacity; for the madman, on the other hand, it depends on the fact that the conditions of the knowledge of experience are "torn" in him.
22 MR 2, p. 20.
23 Kant 1998, B 310–311, p. 350.
24 Cf. MR 1, n. 17, p. 13.

and Schelling consists precisely in the "cognition of all things as they are in themselves" (cf. *supra*, 2.11).[25]

Thirdly, the intuition of things-in-themselves *can be expressed through objects of experience*. As we have seen, Wackenroder affirms the necessity of using empirical determinations to express metempirical or supersensible determinations in his essay *Of Two Wonderful Languages and Their Mysterious Power* (cf. *supra*, 2.5). In fragment 15 of his manuscripts ("On Plato") Schopenhauer related this necessity to the Platonic Ideas that are present in man but do not correspond to any sensory object; now he relates it to the Kantian concept of "thing-in-itself". Evidently, what's at stake is the theoretical problem concerning the possibility of referring in general to a metaphenomenal reality, provided that such a reference can only be made in phenomenal terms. The genius is precisely one who can 'force' the appearance to express that which is not an appearance. A similar act of 'forcing' the appearance would occur in § 22 of *The World as Will and Representation*, where the thing-in-itself would be determined, according to a denomination from the superior term, as "will" (cf. *infra*, 12.2–12.4).[26]

However, something similar was already in place in Schopenhauer's youthful note to Fichte: the "garment" (something that belongs to experience) is used there as a metaphor for the conditions of experience (which as such, aside from the empirical matter with which they appear, cannot be experienced), and looking out of the garment is a metaphor for knowledge that goes beyond these conditions. In this passage, then, Schopenhauer uses an empirical term to express not the *content* of metempirical knowledge – as the genius does – but the very *act* of such knowledge. Schopenhauer here does not speak about its content at all; he does not express it, but rather theorizes this expression as the peculiar act of the genius.

3.3 Genius and Knowledge of the Absolute. Schelling's Response to Plato

The idea that the unconditioned, or absolute reality, is revealed in works of art appears in various ways in several of Schelling's works, which Schopenhauer read between late 1811 and early 1812. These include, notably, *Bruno*, the *System of Transcendental Idealism*, *Über das Verhältnis der bildenden Künste zur Natur* (On the Relationship of the Fine Arts to Nature), and *On University Studies*.

---

25 D'Alfonso 2008, p. 100.
26 Cf. Schopenhauer 2010b, I 132, § 22, p. 135.

In particular, the fourteenth lecture of the *Studies* (borrowed by Schopenhauer on 23 August 1811 in Göttingen) is entitled: "The Science of Art".[27] Here Schelling states that he is not interested in art "whose sole purpose is to produce visible beauty and whose products are either merely *deceptive images* [italics mine] of truth". Indeed, truth is "accessible only to the mind's eye, not to the eye of sense" and philosophers know it by "intellectual intuition".[28] Rather, he wishes to "speak of art in a more sacred sense", that is, "of the art which, in the words of the ancients, is an instrument of the gods, herald of divine mysteries, unveiler of the Ideas".[29] His object is "preternatural beauty whose inviolate light illumines only pure souls, which is as hidden and inaccessible to the sensible eye as pure truth itself".[30] The only kind of art that interests the philosopher is that which expresses, albeit in a different form from philosophy, the *same content* as "intellectual intuition". All this presupposes that the creator of art – the *genius* – is driven, albeit unconsciously, by "the same principle" that is found "in the philosopher as a subjective reflection".[31] "The forms of art are the forms of the things-in-themselves [*Dinge an sich*]."[32] The similarity between this text and Schopenhauer's comment on Fichte is undeniable.

In the same lecture, Schelling also addresses the great condemnation that the "divine Plato" uttered against art and artists in the *Republic*. According to the latter text, artists and poets do not reproduce ideal realities, but sensible realities, which in turn are merely images or copies of the former and thus are ontologically and axiologically inferior to them.[33] Schelling argues that this assumption, and thus also the resulting condemnation of art, could in no way be applied to "Christian poetry": indeed, the latter "as a whole expresses the infinite as unmistakably as ancient poetry expressed the finite".[34] However, Plato is in no way contradicted by this: his judgment of ancient art remains absolutely valid, and should even be regarded as the prophetic feeling of a "longing" that only the Christian era would be able to fulfill:[35] "The Christian religion, and with it the longing for spiri-

---

27 F. W. J. Schelling, "The Science of Art", in Schelling 1966, p. 143.
28 Schelling 1966, p. 144.
29 Schelling 1966, p. 144.
30 Schelling 1966, p. 144.
31 Schelling 1966, p. 147.
32 Schelling 1966, p. 149.
33 Cf. Plato, *Republic*, 597 d-598 d, Plato 1914 ff., vol. 6, pp. 400–402.
34 Schelling 1966, p. 146.
35 Schelling 1966, p. 146.

tuality which ancient poetry could not fully gratify or express, has created its own poetry and art."[36]

Young Schopenhauer, by describing the object of art as eternal reality, also disagreed (albeit only implicitly) with Plato's assumption. And indeed, in commenting on the passages from the *Republic* mentioned above, Schopenhauer noted: "clear expression of *Plato's great error* on art".[37]

3.4 The *Besonnenheit* of Genius according to E. T. A. Hoffmann and Jean Paul

We have seen that, for Schopenhauer, the peculiar "characteristic [*Charakter*]" of the genius is a *hohe Besonnenheit*, thanks to which he is able to express the knowledge of the supersensible through sense-objects (works of art).

In reviewing Beethoven's Fifth Symphony for the *Allgemeine Musikalische Zeitung* in Leipzig (July 1810),[38] the writer Ernst Theodor Amadeus Hoffmann (1766–1822) took a stand against some critics who found Beethoven's creativity to be extraordinarily powerful, but undisciplined: his works would merely be "products of a genius who ignores form and discrimination of thought and surrenders to his creative fervour and the passing dictates of his imagination".[39] Hoffmann objected:

> He is nevertheless fully the equal of Haydn and Mozart in rational awareness [*Besonnenheit*], his controlling self detached from the inner realm of sounds and ruling it in absolute authority. Just as our aesthetic overseers have often complained of a total lack of real unity and inner coherence in Shakespeare, when only profounder contemplation shows the splendid tree, buds and leaves, blossom and fruit as springing from the same seed, so only the most penetrating study of the inner structure of Beethoven's music can reveal its high level of rational awareness [*Besonnenheit*], which is inseparable from true genius and nourished by continuing study of the art. Beethoven bears the romanticism of music, which he expresses with such originality and authority in his works, in the depths of his spirit.[40]

To sum up "in a few words" his opinion on the symphony, Hoffmann writes that "it is conceived of genius and executed with profound awareness [*mit tiefer Besonnen-*

---

36 Schelling 1966, p. 146.
37 MR 2, p. 436.
38 Cf. Hoffmann 1810, col. 652–659. En. tr. in Hoffmann 1989, pp. 234–251.
39 Hoffmann 1989, p. 238.
40 Hoffmann 1989, pp. 238–239.

heit], and that it expresses the romanticism of music to a very high degree".⁴¹ The *Besonnenheit*, "which is inseparable from true genius", consists in his ability to master his own creative forces by inwardly distinguishing and detaching himself from them. By describing and celebrating the *hohe Besonnenheit* that shines through the Fifth Symphony, Hoffmann thus intends to assert, against the aforementioned critics, Beethoven's absolute formal control over his own compositional art.⁴²

In any case, the concept of *Besonnenheit* had already been the subject of an important paragraph in Jean Paul's *Vorschule der Ästhetik*, first published in 1804.⁴³ According to Jean Paul (who would later become the editor of Hoffmann's posthumous works), *Besonnenheit* as such "presupposes, in every degree, a mutual balancing and conflict between activity and passivity, between subject and object [*ein Gleichgewicht und einen Wechselstreit zwischen Tun und Leiden, zwischen Sub- und Objekt*]". In general, it consists in "balancing [*Äquilibrieren*]",⁴⁴ through mediation, "the outer world and the inner world", preventing one of the two from impairing or suppressing the perception of the other ("in animals" the first usually "devours [*verschlingt*]" the second, while "in moved men [*im bewegten Menschen*]" it is often the second that devours the first).⁴⁵

There is, however, also a higher (*höhere*) *Besonnenheit*, characteristic of the poetic and philosophical genius, which is inward-looking; by virtue of this, the genius splits or divides the inner world itself into an inner and an outer world – that is to say, into "an I and in its realm", or "a creator [*Schöpfer*] and in his world".⁴⁶ The common *Besonnenheit*, on the other hand, is directed exclusively outwards (*nach außen*), so that it is always, so to speak, outside itself (*außer sich*), and never at itself (*bei sich*); ordinary people therefore have far more consciousness (*Bewußtsein*) than self-consciousness (*Selbstbewußtsein*).⁴⁷ The latter is connected rather with the higher type of *Besonnenheit* and is akin to seeing oneself (*Sichselbersehen*) simultaneously in two different mirrors, reflecting the same head movement from two different viewpoints and thus in two entirely different ways: one as turning to look, the other as turning away.⁴⁸

---

41 Hoffmann 1989, p. 251.
42 On this point, see Segala 2000.
43 Jean Paul 1990.
44 Jean Paul 1990, pp. 56–57.
45 Jean Paul 1990, p. 57.
46 Jean Paul 1990, p. 57.
47 Jean Paul 1990, p. 57.
48 Jean Paul 1990, p. 57.

The "divine" and inner *Besonnenheit* of the genius is so superior to the ordinary *Besonnenheit* that it often presents itself as its opposite, namely as an *imbalance* between the inner world – which thus takes over – and the outer world.[49] However, within the confines of the former, the genius always maintains the balance and equilibrium of his spiritual forces: none of them ever overpowers the others to the point of becoming the whole or a new pseudo-self; the genius is always in a position to unleash or appease them all at will ("the creator never loses himself in his own creation").[50] For Jean Paul, therefore, as well as for Hoffmann, the *Besonnenheit* of the genius consists in the absolute mastery of all inner energies or faculties; the power of genius ("the best that Earth has to offer") always presupposes the concordant cooperation of several forces of the spirit, and cannot therefore be confused with the "instinctive" or wild exercise of a single faculty (which should rather be ascribed to mere virtuosity).[51]

In his note to Fichte, Schopenhauer does not give an explicit definition of *Besonnenheit:* he merely says that, by virtue of it, the genius is able to to express his metempirical knowledge through objects of experience. Since, for young Arthur, metempirical knowledge is only accessible inwardly (cf. *supra*, 1.8), its communication through sense objects clearly presupposes the ability to "balance the outer world and the inner world" (according to Jean Paul's laconic definition). In other words, it entails the ability to "project" outwardly, through the technical and formal mastery of the means of expression (as Hoffmann would have it), the knowledge drawn from within. The hypothesis that Schopenhauer was already familiar with Hoffmann's and Jean Paul's writings at this time therefore finds consistent confirmation in this commentary on Fichte.[52]

Indeed, Jean Paul also acknowledged a certain affinity between genius and madness: the *Besonnenheit* of genius in some ways resembles the opposite of common *Besonnenheit*, i. e. the *Unbesonnenheit*, which is the "oblivion" of relations with the outside world;[53] precisely for this reason, in dream (*Traum*) and in madness (*Wahnsinn*), where this oblivion reaches its highest level, reflection (*Reflektieren*) and poetic activity (*Dichten*) frequently take over.[54] In Chapter 31 of the Supplements to *The World as Will and Representation*, Schopenhauer would identify the peculiarity of the genius precisely in his *Besonnenheit*, expressly referring to

---

[49] Jean Paul 1990, p. 57.
[50] Jean Paul 1990, p. 57.
[51] Jean Paul 1990, pp. 55–56.
[52] Cf. Hübscher 1989, pp. 81–83.
[53] Jean Paul 1990, p. 57, fn.
[54] Jean Paul 1990, p. 57, fn.

the terminology (rather than the content) of Jean Paul's *Vorschule der Ästhetik* (cf. *infra*, 5.8);[55] furthermore, in Chapter 39, he would offer an interpretation of Beethoven's music that is extremely close to that proposed by Hoffmann.[56]

3.5 The "Flash of Evidence" and "True Knowledge" "Beyond All Experience"

In the first lecture "On the Study of Philosophy", after having dealt with "historical knowledge", Fichte moves on to consider the second type of knowledge, namely "scientific knowledge". Its characteristic feature is "the statement of the *reason or ground* of the perceptions, from which full and positive evidence follows and the establishment of a law for all possible perceptions of this kind", so that these can be determined *a priori* in the future.[57] While the content of historical knowledge is perception (its content is or has been perceptible), "science rises entirely above the individual perception" and deals with its ground, which is something entirely "separate" from it, "higher" than it, and supersensible (*etwas ... ganz getrenntes, höheres, übersinnliches*).[58] Anyone who wants to "go deeply into some branch of science must raise himself", with his own strength, to the "the region of reasons or grounds [*Region der Gründe*]", which is supersensible and "spiritual [*geistlich*]", and therefore completely different from the one in which we are all born, namely the region of perceptions.[59] The passage from the latter to the former – that is, the discovery of the reason or ground – takes place by means of "an evidence [*Evidenz*] hitherto quite unknown to him [to the seeker] and instantly illuminating his soul like a flash", so that he recognizes "what he now thinks" as eternal truth.[60]

Now, since the truth of a hypothesis consists in its accordance (*Übereinstimmen*) with *all* possible perceptions of the same type, and since, on the other hand, this accordance can only be experimentally verified for a limited number of cases, the *criterion* of truth is not experimental confirmation (which is still necessary), but rather a "flash of evidence": it is on this basis that the truth of a hy-

---

55 Cf. Schopenhauer 2018, II 436–437, chap. 31, pp. 398–399. On the meaning of *Besonnenheit* in Schopenhauer, cf.: Koßler 1990, 2002b, 2006a.
56 Cf. Schopenhauer 2018, II 514–515, chap. 39, p. 467. On this, cf. Pikulik 2005.
57 MR 2, pp. 20–21.
58 MR 2, p. 20. Translation modified.
59 MR 2, p. 21.
60 MR 2, pp. 22–23.

pothesis is affirmed.⁶¹ In fact, Fichte goes on to say that some knowledge, such as mathematical knowledge, is scientific even though it does not require any perception, and is demonstrated precisely and exclusively through this kind of evidence.⁶²

Schopenhauer disputes that the flash of evidence is always an infallible criterion for the truth of a hypothesis, and raises the *problem of error*. How is it possible, for example, that the phlogiston theory has long been held to be true by people who, possessing "other knowledge of mathematics and physics", must necessarily [*müssen*] "have felt and therefore known the flash of evidence"?⁶³ In other words, how is it possible that such individuals were capable and at the same time incapable of distinguishing truth from error? Schopenhauer then proposes his *own* theory of error:

> In general I regard all knowledge [*alles Wissen*] within the limits of experience [*innerhalb der Gränzen der Erfahrung*] as conditioned by the senses and as valid only in experience, indeed I regard it as null [*nichtig*], [...]. Indeed I take it to be error [*Irrthum*], just because the reality [*Realität*] of experience is error and to every *therefore* [*Darum*] remaining within experience there appears a new *wherefore* [*Warum*], and all our truth is always only the ultimate error. Within the limits of experience we cannot go further than becoming aware that the most solid, ultimate and fundamental truth, the basic pillar of all experience, is simply error. This is what Kant achieved when he demonstrated the nothingness [*Nichtigkeit*] of space and time and reduced the understanding to suicide.⁶⁴

If "all knowledge within the limits of experience" is "error", the flash of evidence, in order to concern truth in the full sense, as Fichte claims, must concern a knowledge that stands beyond experience (different, therefore, from the knowledge of the "ground" or rather *cause* of which, in Schopenhauer's view, Fichte actually speaks: cf. *infra*, 6.2). And indeed, only in this specific sense does Schopenhauer admit the flash of evidence:

> There is that flash of evidence, but only where the domain of true knowledge [*das Gebiet des wahren Wissens*] rises beyond all experience [*über alle Erfahrung*]. There comes a moment when the entire world of appearance [*Welt der Erscheinung*] fades, outshone and eclipsed by the ego or I which cognizes [*erkennt*] its reality [*Realität*] and that of a supersensible [*übersinnlichen*] world; like a shadow-show it vanishes when a light is kindled. The moment may come to a few, to the genuine philosophers. Therefore Plato says: Πολλοι μεν ναρθηκοφοροι, βακχοι δε γε παυροι.⁶⁵

---

61 MR 2, p. 23.
62 MR 2, p. 24.
63 MR 2, p. 24.
64 MR 2, pp. 24–25. Translation modified.
65 MR 2, p. 25. Translation modified. Schopenhauer does not usually write the spirits and accents of Greek words.

3.5 The "Flash of Evidence" and "True Knowledge" "Beyond All Experience" — 81

The flash of evidence (which Fichte also calls "intimate phenomenon [*innere Erscheinung*]")[66] concerns the cognition of "a supersensible world": the cognition of the latter is linked to the cognition that the self has of "*its own* [italics mine] reality".

In late 1811, Schopenhauer read the first volume of Schelling's *Philosophische Schriften*, in which the *Philosophical Letters on Dogmatism and Criticism* were republished along with other works. Here Schelling stated:

> We all have a secret and wondrous capacity [*Vermögen*] of withdrawing from temporal change into our innermost self, which we divest of every exterior accretion. There, in the form of immutability, we intuit the eternal in us. This intuition is the innermost and in the strictest sense our own experience [*die innerste, eigenste Erfahrung*], upon which depends everything we know and believe of a supersensible [*übersinnlichen*] world. It is this intuition which first convinces us that anything *is*, strictly speaking, while everything else merely appears [*erscheint*].[67]

As Schelling says later in the text, this intuition, unlike sensory intuition, is an "intellectual intuition [*intellectuale Anschauung*]".[68] The similarity between this passage and Schopenhauer's note is evident: both affirm that the supersensible world can be cognized through an exceptional inner experience, and both describe the latter as accessible only to a chosen few. Commenting on this passage from Schelling, young Schopenhauer wrote enthusiastically that it contained a "great and genuine truth".[69] In *Bruno*, too, Schelling had described the I as that "concept [*Begriff*] that makes the world disclose its riches, as if responding to some magic blow".[70]

One can imagine that, in those last months of 1811, Schopenhauer viewed Schelling's concept of intellectual intuition as aligned with his own conviction that reality in itself can be cognized through interiority. To show the extraordinary relevance that this theme would have in the development of Schopenhauer's philosophy, it is sufficient to recall that, in *The World as Will and Representation*, the identification of the thing-in-itself with the "will" is carried out based on the content of "self-consciousness".[71] However, Schopenhauer would never present the latter as actual or exhaustive cognition of the thing-in-itself (cf. *infra*, 12.2).[72]

---

66 MR 2, p. 22.
67 Schelling 1980, Eighth Letter, p. 180. Translation modified.
68 MR 2, p. 181.
69 MR 2, p. 347.
70 Schelling 1984, p. 186.
71 Cf. Schopenhauer 2018, II 736, chap. 50, p. 659.
72 Cf. Schopenhauer 2010b, I 121, § 18, p. 186.

3.6 Kant's Appearance and Plato's Cave. The Determination of Phenomenal Knowledge as Non-Truth

In the above-mentioned note on Fichte, the equivalence between *error* and *phenomenal knowledge* ("all knowledge within the limits of experience") is clear: "to every *therefore* remaining within experience there appears a new *wherefore*, and all our truth is always only the ultimate error".[73] The possible infinite regress of natural causes – which for young Schopenhauer implies the infinite recursiveness of the question "Warum"[74] – was dealt with by Kant in the Third Antinomy.[75]

By demonstrating "the nothingness [*Nichtigkeit*] of space and time", which are necessary determinations of all experience, Kant would have demonstrated, according to Schopenhauer, that "all knowledge within the limits of experience" is "error". In a further comment on the same Fichtean lecture, Schopenhauer reiterates this position, stating that in experience "nothing is false [*irrig*] except the reality [*Realität*] of space and time".[76]

Schopenhauer thus interpreted Kant's thesis of the "transcendental ideality" of space and time[77] as a negation of their reality, or as an affirmation of their nothingness (cf. *supra*, 2.9). This interpretation seems to completely miss the point of Kant's scrupulous warnings about the "empirical", even if not "absolute", reality of space and time.[78] Starting from the non-absoluteness of space and time, Schelling also argued for the nothingness (*Nichtigkeit*) "of all merely finite knowledge" in *On University Studies*.[79] "Absolute" knowledge or "primordial knowledge [*Urwissen*]", is rather constituted by "Ideas", i.e., by the "eternal archetypes of [finite] things", which the philosopher accesses through intellectual intuition.[80] "Without intellectual intuition [there is] no philosophy!".[81]

It is precisely around this time, and in relation to this kind of consideration, that the theme of the world and life as a "dream" first appears in Schopenhauer's manuscripts: "We have woken and we shall wake again. Life is a night filled by a long dream that often becomes a nightmare."[82] Empirical, finite life is only a brief

---

73 Cf. MR 2, p. 24.
74 MR 2, pp. 21–22.
75 Cf. Kant 1998, B 473–479, pp. 485–489.
76 MR 2, p. 25.
77 Kant 1998, B 44–53, pp. 160–165.
78 Kant 1998, B 44–53, pp. 160–165.
79 Schelling 1966, Lecture IV, p. 49.
80 Schelling 1966, Lecture IV, p. 49.
81 Schelling 1966, Lecture IV, p. 49.
82 MR 1, n. 23, p. 15.

parenthesis of illusion, a dark nightmare, preceded and followed by bright 'wakefulness'. According to fragment 26, truth does not dwell in the world, but in man's innermost self.[83] In this sense, philosophers, insofar as they turn to that truth and seek to spread it, are for many people like "night-birds who disturb their sleep".[84]

In his first note on Fichte, Schopenhauer quotes a passage from Plato in Greek, whose translation is: "the thyrsus-bearers are many, but the mystics few".[85] According to this Orphic saying (quoted in the *Phaedo*), many people carry the thyrsus during sacred ceremonies, but very few know how to make this external gesture correspond to the (internal) realization of union with God. The first Christian thinkers already noted the similarity of this passage with Matthew 22:14: "Many are invited, but few are the chosen". According to Schopenhauer, too, only few are capable of achieving the "flash of evidence". ("The moment may come to a few, to the genuine philosophers.")

The same note on Fichte contains a further reference to Plato, which is implicit but much more significant from a theoretical point of view. Schopenhauer writes that "the entire world of appearance [*die ganze Welt der Erscheinung*]" disappears before the knowledge of the supersensible world, just "like a shadow-show [*Schattenspiel*] [...] vanishes when a light is kindled". The knowledge of the phenomenal world is to that of the supersensible world what the knowledge of shadows is to that of light; this means that the phenomenal world is to the supersensible world what shadows are to light.

In the allegory of the cave, Plato – through Socrates – explicitly sets the shadows (σκίαι) of the objects (the only thing the prisoners can see) against the truth (τὸ ἀληθές, τἀληθῆ).[86] On the other hand, when explaining the myth, he says that one should understand the cave as a metaphor of the world being revealed through sight (τὴν μὲν δι' ὄψεως φαινομένην ἕδραν), that is, in general, through the senses.[87] The shadows are therefore, in turn, a metaphor for sense objects. Human life is thus compared by Socrates to a dream (ὄναρ) from which one should awaken as soon as possible.[88]

In the note on Fichte, Schopenhauer opposes the Kantian appearance to a "supersensible world" that would constitute the realm of "true knowledge", which

---

83 MR 1, n. 26, p. 17.
84 MR 1, n. 24, p. 16.
85 Plato, *Phaedo*, 69 c–d: ναρθηκοφόροι μὲν πολλοί, βάκχοι δέ τε παῦροι, Plato 1914 ff., vol. 1, pp. 240–241. The quotation is also found in Schopenhauer 2010b, I 204–225, § 31, pp. 195–197.
86 Plato, *Republic*, 515 c, 520 c, Plato 1914 ff., vol. 6, pp. 108–109 and pp. 126–127.
87 Plato, *Republic*, 517b, Plato 1914 ff., vol. 6, pp. 112–113.
88 Plato, *Republic*, 520c, Plato 1914 ff., vol. 6, pp. 126–127. Cf. also Plato, *Republic*, 476 c–d, Plato 1914 ff., vol. 5, pp. 550–551.

Plato is said to have already spoken of. ("The moment may come to a few, to the genuine philosophers. Therefore Plato says: Πολλοι μεν ναρθηκοφοροι, βακχοι δε γε παυροι.") But Plato opposed true knowledge, namely the knowledge of the supersensible, to the knowledge of the φαινόμενα. The implication of the note is thus the equivalence between Kant's *Erscheinung* and Plato's φαινόμενον (cf. *supra*, 2.7). This equivalence would remain forever part of Schopenhauer's thought: in the Appendix to *The World as Will and Representation* he states that Kant, through the distinction between appearance and thing-in-itself (his "greatest merit"), has presented, albeit "in yet another, completely different way",

> the same truth that Plato tirelessly repeats, usually expressing himself, in his own language, as follows: this world that appears to the senses [*diese, den Sinnen erscheinende Welt*] does not have true being, but is instead only an incessant becoming, [...] and apprehending it does not involve cognition so much as delusion [*Wahn*]. Plato also expresses this mythologically at the beginning of the seventh book of the *Republic*, which I already mentioned in the Third Book of the present text as the most important passage in all Plato's works; there he says that the people who are chained firmly in a dark cave would not see either the true, original light or real things [*die wirklichen Dinge*], but rather only the dim light of the fire in the cave and the shadows of real things that pass by this fire behind their backs: they would think that shadows were reality [*Realität*] and true wisdom consisted of determining the succession of the shadows.[89]

Kant's *Erscheinung* and Plato's φαινόμενον both denote "this world that appears to the senses", which "does not have true being [*Seyn*]", but is a delusion (*Wahn*) and a dream (*Traum*).[90] By distinguishing the appearance from the thing-in-itself, Kant would have done no more than *demonstrate* "the same truth" that Plato and the Indians had already expressed in mythical form.[91] In fact, even according to the very ancient authors of the *Vedas*, this "visible world" is nothing more than "a magic trick, an insubstantial, an intrinsically inessential semblance [*wesenloser Schein*] comparable to an optical illusion or a dream, a veil wrapped around human consciousness, something that can be said both to be and not to be with equal truth and equal falsity".[92] The Maya of the Indians, like Plato's φαινόμενον, is nothing other than Kant's *Erscheinung*.[93]

---

[89] Schopenhauer 2010b, I 494–497, pp. 443–447 (cf. Schopenhauer 2020, pp. 302–303).
[90] Schopenhauer 2010b, I, p. 445.
[91] Schopenhauer 2010b, I, p. 446.
[92] Schopenhauer 2010b, I, p. 446.
[93] Schopenhauer 2010b, I, p. 446.

The 'mythical' doctrine offered by Plato and the Indians would thus have become, with Kant's criticism, "an established and incontrovertible truth".[94] "In this respect", Schopenhauer continues (taking up the metaphor of the Copernican revolution, and in fact probably intending to extend its meaning), Kant is to Plato and the Indians what Copernicus is to "the Pythagoreans, Hicetas, Philolaus and Aristarchus" – who already in antiquity had supported the heliocentric theory, though more for mythical-religious reasons than for scientific ones in the modern sense.[95]

However, in several passages across his works, Kant expressly denies that the world of the senses is to be considered as semblance (*Schein*),[96] delusion (*Wahn*),[97] a dream (*Traum*),[98] an error (*Irrtum*)[99] or, in general, anything that is opposed to the truth; on the contrary, experience (external perception) is for him precisely the criterion for the truth of subjective representation. Those 'negative' terms, in Kant, concern only the relationship of *non*-correspondence, *within* the world of phenomena, between subjective or individual representation and the (intersubjective) object of perception. In fact, in 'positive' terms, "truth" is precisely correspondence, or the "agreement [*Übereinstimmung*] of cognition with the object[s] [*Objekten*]" of experience.[100]

Yet, according to young Schopenhauer, the theoretical result of Kant's criticism is the identity between "knowledge within the limits of experience" and "error". Based on the text, he seems to attribute the postulation of this identity to Kant's real intentions, that is, not to the 'spirit' but the 'letter' of Kant's thought. At this point, it is therefore necessary to consider very carefully the terminology with which Schulze, in his Metaphysics course, had expounded Kant's philosophy.

---

94 Cf. Schopenhauer 2010b, I, p. 446: "Kant not only expressed this same doctrine [as Plato and the Indians] in a completely new and original manner, but also made it into an established and incontrovertible truth through the calmest and most sober presentation, while both Plato and the Indians only grounded their claims in a general world-view, articulating these claims as direct expressions of their consciousness, and presenting them more mythically and poetically than clearly and philosophically."
95 Schopenhauer 2010b, I, p. 446.
96 Cf. Kant 1998, B 349–350, p. 384.
97 Kant 1998, B 297, p. 340; B 525, p. 514.
98 Cf. Kant 2012, p. 42; Kant 1998, B 247, p. 312; B 520–521, pp. 511–512. However, cf. also Kant 1998, B 807–808, pp. 663–664, in which the determination of "life" as a dream acquires the dignity of a "transcendental hypothesis".
99 Cf. Kant 2012, p. 43.
100 Kant 1998, B 236, p. 306.

3.7 Schulze's Presentation of Kantian Philosophy at Göttingen: The Reduction of "Appearance" to "Representation"

Young Schopenhauer's determination of the Kantian appearance as "non-truth", and therefore of the thing-in-itself as "truth", was not only due to Tennemann's influence or to the admission of knowledge of the supersensible (with respect to which the knowledge of the sensible is "error"); indeed, it received essential support also and above all from a third element, namely a specific understanding of Kant's philosophy. In fact, it should be noted that the same relationship that Kant posited between *subjective (or individual) representation* and *appearance* – a relationship whereby the former can be determined as untrue (namely, as "semblance", "delusion", "dream" or "error") – was posited by young Schopenhauer between *appearances* and *things-in-themselves*. According to this analogy (equality of relations), the problem of a criterion of truth, which for Kant only held for subjective or individual representations, was shifted by Schopenhauer to a higher level in relation to the *Erscheinung* itself.

The theoretical presupposition for this shift was clearly *the reduction of appearances to representations* – something that was very likely due to Gottlob Ernst Schulze's lectures. If this is the case, then Schopenhauer (unintentionally) shared with Fichte and Schelling – but also with Hegel – Schulze's decisive influence on his own interpretation of Kantian philosophy.[101]

Kant distinguished between "representation [*Vorstellung*]" on the one hand, and "appearance [*Erscheinung*]" (understood as "object of experience") on the other, by describing the latter as the *content* of the former.[102] Of course, Kant also insisted that the appearance is nothing but representation;[103] but this identity

---

[101] Cf. Fincham 2000. According to Daniel Elon (2018), *The World as Will and Representation* is an attempt to overcome Schulze's skepticism, i.e., to answer the questions that, according to Schulze, Kant had left unresolved. These are, in particular, the unproven unknowability of the thing-in-itself, the unproven impossibility of a universally valid philosophical system, and the precise definition of the field of the principle of causality. In what follows, I will focus on the possible influence of Schulze's Göttingen lectures on Schopenhauer's early understanding of Kantian philosophy. On the theoretical and historical relationship between Schopenhauer and Schulze, cf. Fischer 1901; Schröder 1911; Kamata 2006.

[102] Cf. e.g. Kant 1998, B 59, p. 168 ("all our intuition is nothing but the representation of appearance [*Vorstellung von Erscheinung*]"); B 61, p. 169 ("The representation of a *body* in intuition, on the contrary, contains [*enthält*] nothing at all that could pertain to an object in itself, but merely the appearance [*die Erscheinung*] of something and the way in which we are affected by it [...]").

[103] Cf. e.g. Kant 1998, B 521–522, p. 512.

held for him only from the transcendental point of view, in relation to the critical investigation of cognition, which alone legitimizes the admissibility of a "thing-in-itself" as absolutely opposed to "appearance". On the other hand, from the empirical point of view ("in perception"), the content of experience, the *Erscheinung*, is necessarily something real (*wirklich*).[104]

Kant's position therefore consisted, as said, in a transcendental idealism that is, at the same time, an empirical realism (cf. *supra*, 2.6).[105] From a transcendental point of view, the thing that appears (that presents itself to the senses) is only a representation, but from an empirical point of view it is rather the "object [*Objekt*]" (the objective reference) of representations – understood, strictly speaking, as "internal determinations of our mind [*innere Bestimmungen unseres Gemüts*]".[106] Only in virtue of this "relation to an object [*Gegenstand*]" do our representations acquire an objective "reality [*Realität*]", in addition to the merely subjective one.[107] In the Transcendental Deduction of the Categories, Kant tried to demonstrate – against Hume's skepticism – the necessary validity of our knowledge of experience as regards its purely formal or categorial dimension (in the strict sense): that is, the "necessary agreement [*notwendige Übereinstimmung*]" between the "synthetic representation" and *"its* [italics mine] objects [*ihre Gegenstände*]"*,* which are objects of experience, that is, precisely, *Erscheinungen.*[108]

Introducing Kant's philosophy in his Metaphysics course, Schulze called things-in-themselves "real things [*wirkliche Dinge*]" and said first that they are "outside our representations [*außer unsren Vorstellungen*]", and then that they are set against sense objects (*Sinnenobjekte*) as appearances (*Erscheinungen*).[109] The terms *Vorstellung, Sinnenobjekt* and *Erscheinung* were thus implicitly equated, as opposed to things-in-themselves. Compared to Kant's wording, the fundamental distinction between the empirical and the transcendental point of view takes a back seat here.

Thus, in Schulze's exposition, the Kantian *Erscheinung* is identified, through the term *Vorstellung*, with what in pre-Kantian modern philosophy – i.e. in Descartes, Locke, Berkeley and Hume – was considered the immediate content of consciousness.[110] In the same way, and consequently, the thing-in-itself is identified, through the terms *Ding* and *wirklich*, with what those same philosophers consid-

---

104 Cf. Kant 1998, B 520–525, pp. 511–514.
105 Kant 1998, A 370–371, pp. 426–427.
106 Kant 1998, B 242, p. 309.
107 Kant 1998, B 242, p. 309.
108 Kant 1998, B 124, p. 223; B 167, p. 264.
109 D'Alfonso 2008, p. 70.
110 Cf. D'Alfonso 2008, pp. 63–68.

ered a possible and problematic reality external to consciousness.[111] A similar, very general use of the terms *Vorstellung* and *Ding* was adopted by Schulze in his *Kritik der theoretischen Philosophie*, which Schopenhauer read in Göttingen in early 1811.[112]

Regarding the inappropriateness of this drastic terminological uniformization with respect to Kant's texts, it is sufficient here to recall a single but decisive passage. In the second edition of the *Critique of Pure Reason*, Kant examines the doubt – raised by Descartes and Berkeley – concerning the existence of a reality outside of our "representations" (external to consciousness), and expressly refers this doubt to the existence of "objects in space outside us".[113] But the latter, in his terminology, are "appearances", certainly not "things-in-themselves", which are devoid of spatial determinations. This is the famous Refutation of Idealism (understood as "material" idealism).[114] This circumstance indicates very clearly that, for Kant, the immediate content of consciousness addressed by Descartes and Berkeley corresponds not to the appearance, but to the individual (private or subjective) representation, while the "objective" or (spatially) external reality of consciousness, questioned by these two philosophers, corresponds not to the "thing-in-itself", but to the "appearance", understood as the intersubjective object of experience (of perception).

Now, according to Schulze, all philosophers who preceded Kant held the general principle that "a representation [*Vorstellung*] can be granted reality [*Realität*] only insofar as something corresponding [*entsprechendes*] and fully conforming [*angemeßenes*] to it can be indicated in external or internal perception [*Wahrnehmung*]".[115]

On the basis of all these premises, then, it is natural that the same relationship should arise between appearance and thing-in-itself as the one occurring between subjective representation and appearance (as the intersubjective object of experience) in Kant's texts. With respect to appearances, things-in-themselves acquire the predicate of "reality" (*Wirklichkeit*). Reciprocally, appearances (understood as "representations"), insofar as they are opposed – or rather, necessarily do not conform or correspond – to things-in-themselves, are deprived of the predicate of "reality" (*Realität*).

---

111 D'Alfonso 2008, pp. 63–68.
112 Schulze 1801–1802; on Locke, cf. vol. 1, pp. 113–141; on Kant, vol. 1, pp. 172–582. Schopenhauer borrowed this book from the library of the University of Gothenburg on 4 May 1811.
113 Kant 1998, B 274, p. 326; cf. also Kant 2012, pp. 40–41, 126.
114 Kant 1998, B 274, p. 326.
115 D'Alfonso 2008, p. 63.

According to the letter of Kant's texts, however, reality as *Wirklichkeit* (in the sense of *Dasein*, existence) is not a property of things-in-themselves, but of the objects of experience (appearances); and reality as *Realität* is not a property of the things of experience (or appearances), but of their "concept", i.e. of the subjective representation corresponding to a possible perception.[116]

Schulze goes on to say that, "from the point of view of experience", "sense objects" are for Kant "real things [*wirkliche Dinge*]", as opposed to imaginations (*Einbildungen*).[117]

So, to sum up the overall sense of this interpretation of Kant: just as sense objects (appearances) are, literally, *wirkliche Dinge* with respect to imaginations, so things-in-themselves are *wirkliche Dinge* with respect to sense objects. That is, insofar as the "appearance" is analogous to what Kant calls (strictly speaking) "representation", the "thing-in-itself" is analogous to what Kant calls "appearance". Things-in-themselves are thus understood as the actual "reality" (*Wirklichkeit*) – that is, as the only content of a knowledge (or "representation") to which the predicate of "reality" (*Realität*) can be correspondingly attributed.[118]

3.8 The Skeptical Interpretation of Kantian Criticism: The Determination of the "Thing-in-Itself" as "Truth"

From a theoretical point of view, all these presuppositions trigger a series of very relevant consequences. Indeed, given that things-in-themselves are unknowable[119] and, at the same time, they are what is "real", Schulze's interpretation of Kantianism is inevitably a skeptical one. In it, as in dogmatic or ideal-typical skepticism, what is real (i.e., what would constitute the content of true knowledge) is at the same time defined as unknowable.[120] Based on this interpretation, in fragment

---

116 Cf. Kant 1998, B 266–274, pp. 321–326; B 182, p. 274.
117 D'Alfonso 2008, p. 70.
118 Through careful text analysis, Adickes (1924) tried to show that this is the actual implication of Kant's discourse.
119 D'Alfonso 2008, p. 70. On the importance of Schulze's course for Schopenhauer's philosophical development (though not with regard to the identity of appearance and representation), cf. D'Alfonso 2009; De Cian 2009, p. L–LXVI.
120 This interpretation of Kantian philosophy is most evident in a passage from the *Kritik der theoretischen Philosophie* (Schulze 1801–1802, vol. 2, p. 230). On the failure of Reinhold's attempt, in the *Versuch einer neuen Theorie des menschlichen Vorstellungsvermögens* (1789, in Reinhold 2013), to avoid this particular form of skepticism, and, in general, on skepticism as a historical consequence of Kant's criticism, cf. Hoyos 2008 (esp. pp. 93–98).

17 of the manuscripts and in the comment to Fichte, Schopenhauer wrote that criticism is the "suicide" of the understanding.[121]

As mentioned, Schulze stated that, according to "the result of the critique of reason", "our natural cognition in the sensible world" is conditioned by "senses and understanding" and therefore consists of "mere appearances" (*bloßen Erscheinungen*), while Fichte and Schelling admitted the possibility of a "cognition of all things as they are in themselves" (*Erkenntniß aller Dinge wie sie an sich selbst ... sind*), i.e. "as they are made, in truth [*wahrhaft beschaffen*]" (cf. *supra*, 2.11).[122] The thing-in-itself, as opposed to the appearance, is the true reality. In fragment 17, from the same time as Schulze's lectures, Schopenhauer describes what Kant did not know, namely the thing-in-itself, as "truth" (cf. *supra*, 2.7).[123]

However, in the very delicate conceptual balance devised by Kant, the "Copernican revolution" implied that the criterion of a truthful (*realistic*) accordance (*Übereinstimmung*) between cognition and cognized object *only applies from the empirical point of view*. In other words, it only holds in the relationship between subjective – private or individual – representation and the intersubjective object of perception (appearance), and not also in the relationship between the object of perception – which is "representation" only from the transcendental point of view – and "thing-in-itself". In this sense, once again, Kant's realism is empirical, not transcendental (and, conversely, his idealism is transcendental, not empirical).

Now, if, as Aristotle maintains[124] (taking up Plato),[125] "truth" is properly a predicate not of things, but of *cognition* about things (i.e. of things not as such, but *as cognized*), then the very determination of the thing-in-itself as "truth" analytically presupposes – despite, and indeed precisely because of, any possible skeptical intention – that the thing-in-itself lies, at least potentially, *within* the horizon of cognition. It is not by chance that Kant reserved the predicate of "truth" and the opposite predicate of "error" for the object of experience as "thought", and not as "perceived": only the judgment of the understanding can be properly true or untrue.[126] This is because for Kant truth is "the agreement [*Übereinstimmung*] of cog-

---

121 MR 1, n. 17, p. 12; MR 2, p. 25.
122 D'Alfonso 2008, pp. 100–101.
123 MR 1, n. 17, p. 13.
124 Cf. Aristotle, *Metaphysics*, E 4, 1027 b 25, Aristotle 1926ff., vol. 17, pp. 304–305.
125 In *Parmenides* (134a), Plato had argued for a necessary relation between ἀλήθεια ('truth') and ἐπιστήμη ('science'): (true) knowledge, i.e. science, is knowledge of truth, and, on the other hand, truth is the object of (true) knowledge. See also *Republic*, 508 d; *Sophist*, 263 b–d. Cf. respectively Plato 1914ff., vol. 9, pp. 224–225; vol. 5, pp. 90–91 and vol. 12, pp. 438–439.
126 Kant 1998, B 236, p. 306.

nition with the object" of experience – more precisely, the accordance between the judgment of the understanding and what the judgment is about.[127]

If this is the case, the skeptical interpretation of Kant's criticism, according to which the thing-in-itself is "truth", necessarily implies that the thing-in-itself is, at the same time, not knowable (as "in-itself") and knowable (as "truth"). The contradiction that has been traditionally contested in all forms of dogmatic skepticism lies precisely in the determination of truth as both knowable and unknowable (the definition of *all* knowledge as "non-truth" would necessarily presuppose, *in actu exercito*, i.e. in the effective dimensions of discourse, what is denied *in actu signato*, i.e. nominally or explicitly: the knowledge of what is "truth"). Thus, this heresy against the letter of Kantianism – the reduction of the appearance to representation and the consequent determination of the thing-in-itself as truth – fundamentally implies the ultimate heresy: the knowability of the thing-in-itself.

This whole set of historical and theoretical assumptions is what underlies Schopenhauer's two notes to Fichte. Schopenhauer openly admits the intuition (*Anschauung*) of things-in-themselves (cf. *supra*, 3.2), even though he reserves it only for the genius and the madman. And in the second comment, the determination of knowledge about the appearance as "error" presupposes the existence of "true knowledge", "beyond all experience", with respect to which the former can (and must) be characterized as non-truth (cf. *supra*, 3.5). In his published texts, Schopenhauer understood Kant's "appearance" precisely as "representation". Paragraph 18 of the dissertation on the principle of sufficient reason (1813) states that "complete" representations are so called because "they contain not merely what is formal, but also what is material in appearances".[128] "Appearance [*Erscheinung*] means representation [*Vorstellung*], and nothing more".[129] On the other hand, this identity is magnificently revealed in the incipit ("The world is my representation") and in the very title of Schopenhauer's masterpiece: *The World as Will and Representation* – that is, "The World as Thing-in-itself and Appearance".

Consider that the ultimate outcome of Schopenhauer's thought, as presented in the Epiphilosophy (at the end of the second volume of *The World as Will and*

---

127 Kant 1998, p. 197 (B 82). It should be noted, however, that in a passage in the first edition of the *Critique of Pure Reason*, omitted from the second, things-in-themselves are called "true things [*wahre Dinge*]" (cf. Kant 1998, A 392, p. 437).
128 Schopenhauer 2012, § 18 in the first edition of 1813 (corresponding to § 17 of the second edition of 1847), p. 33. The Cambridge edition contains the second edition's text and then, in the Appendix, the passages from the first edition that were later expunged or modified. Here, as well as in the following, I will refer mostly to the first edition, recomposing what in the Cambridge translation is divided between the body of the text and the Appendix.
129 Schopenhauer 2010b, I 131, § 21, p. 134. Cf. Schopenhauer 2020, pp. 89, 162.

Representation), in perfect analogy with Schulze's interpretation of Kantianism, is a largely skeptical one. Its basis is precisely the otherness – non-accordance – between what is knowable (the appearance) and the thing-in-itself. But this presupposes, once again, the determination of the Kantian thing-in-itself – which, as "in itself", is unknowable – as "truth" (and therefore as knowable, or known).[130]

This fundamental (contradictory) presupposition, which induced young Schopenhauer to consider Kant's critical project unfinished, must be regarded as the 'archetype' of the contradiction noted by various interpreters (starting from Karl Ludwig Michelet)[131] in Schopenhauer's mature system, between the affirmation of the unknowability of the thing-in-itself and its positive – or, in a broader sense, cognitive – determination as "will". This point will have to be explored further (cf. *infra*, 12.4–12.6).

3.9 Conclusion. Critical Dualism and Ontological Dualism

The skeptical interpretation of Kantian criticism is not the form of skepticism that Schulze himself advocates. The latter, in fact, is more radical than the former, since, even before the knowability of things-in-themselves, it denies the possibility of establishing their very existence – even within Kant's criticism. In fact, as already noted by Jacobi,[132] Kant had admitted the thing-in-itself as the *cause* of sensations,[133] thus violating his own prohibition of attributing determinations of the appearance to the thing-in-itself.[134]

With reference to Schulze's assertion that the "being" with which philosophy is concerned is, on the one hand, given through cognition and, on the other hand, independent of all cognition, Schopenhauer polemically deduces the unthinkability of such a "being".[135] But after all, in this deduction, he does no more than prema-

---

130 The identity between *Ding an sich* and ἀλήθεια is also implied in Schopenhauer 2014, p. 32, in relation to Eleatic philosophy.
131 Cf. Hübscher 1989, p. 353–355. For a discussion of this point also in relation to the genesis of Schopenhauer's metaphysics, see the essay by M. Segala and N. De Cian, *What Is Will?* (2002).
132 Cf. Jacobi 1787, now in Jacobi 1998ff., vol. 2.1, p. 109.
133 Appearances are "effects [*Wirkungen*]" of the thing-in-itself (Kant 2012, p. 96). Cf. Kant 1998, B 522–523, pp. 512–513.
134 D'Alfonso 2008, p. 76. Cf. also Schulze 1792, pp. 259–264.
135 Cf. D'Alfonso 2008, p. 59: "Our concept of 'being' is twofold: 1) Consciousness, i.e., the capacity to receive impressions and 2) the capacity to produce impressions, i.e., to be represented and cognized. Now, if we do not attribute the first capacity (that which we know only in ourselves) to a thing, but neither do we attribute the second, i.e. we posit the thing-in-itself, according to Schulze's expression, as 'independent of our representation and cognition (i.e. [of the representation and

turely develop the coherence of the argument, unwittingly anticipating the professor's skeptical conclusions.

Schopenhauer, for his part, is deeply convinced of the existence and knowability of an absolute reality, i.e. of a supersensible world, which he identifies with what Kant calls the "thing-in-itself" (as opposed to the empirical or finite world). In this sense, for Schopenhauer *the thing-in-itself exists and can be cognized* (by the genius and the madman), so that all of Schulze's objections to the Kantian concept of the thing-in-itself are only valid, for him, as arguments *ad hominem*, not *ad rem*: they correctly refute the legitimacy of the specific way in which Kant introduced the concept of the thing-in-itself, not the legitimacy of the concept itself.[136] Space and time, with everything they contain, are nothingness (*Nichtigkeit*); only the supersensible world is "reality [*Realität*]" and therefore, as such, the object of "true knowledge".[137] The Kantian *critical dualism* between appearance and thing-in-itself is thus converted, by young Schopenhauer, into an *ontological type of dualism* (in line with the very first fragments of the years 1804–1809: cf. *supra*, Chapters 1 and 2).

This point becomes very clear when looking at the different ways in which Kant and young Schopenhauer admit the thing-in-itself. The former (Kant) does so by *remaining within the point of view of experience* – i.e. starting from sensations, of which things-in-themselves would be the cause – or by analyzing the concept of *Erscheinung* ("appearance"), which would necessarily imply the existence of something that, in this appearance, appears.[138] Schopenhauer, on the other hand, admits the thing-in-itself or metempirical reality (as something positively cognizable) *from a point of view that is explicitly external to what Kant calls "experience"* (it is the "knowledge of the eternal truth", which takes place in the inner self;[139] the intuition of things-in-themselves, that the genius and the madman can achieve; the "true knowledge" that originates from the "flash of evidence").

Young Schopenhauer unlike Kant, is not at all concerned with justifying or grounding the distinction between appearance and thing-in-itself (which for him coincides with the distinction between sensible and supersensible world), nor does he consider, in these texts, the development and coherence of Kant's complex arguments, but only their *result*. This is precisely because for Schopenhauer, *contra*

---

cognition] of every cognizing being)', then we have something manifestly unthinkable; indeed, I ask: how do we distinguish such a 'being' from non-being?"
136 This point is made explicit in Schopenhauer 2014, p. 83. Cf. also Schopenhauer 2010b, I 516, pp. 462–463; MR 3, pp. 711–721. (Adversaria [302]). Cf. Meattini 2013.
137 MR 2, p. 24.
138 Cf. Kant 1998, B XXVI–XXVII, p. 115.
139 Cf. MR 1, n. 14, p. 10.

Kant, both terms of the distinction are given – albeit in a different way – so that their distinction or difference is also given; as such, it does not require any ground or justification (and therefore is not to be considered, properly speaking, as the result of some chain of argumentation).

There are at least three elements that, in a singular combination of circumstances, led young Schopenhauer towards an ontological understanding of Kant's critical dualism – that is, ultimately, of the term "thing-in-itself". First of all, the religious longing for the Eternal, understood as "truth" (knowable in one's innermost self), and the determination of what is in time as "illusion". Secondly, the parallel between Kant's *Erscheinung* and Plato's φαινόμενον and, consequently, between the "thing-in-itself" and "the Idea" as ὄντως ὄν[140] (the latter identification would come to light in the manuscripts of 1814:[141] cf. *infra*, 11.9); in this respect, Tennemann's *History of Philosophy* is very likely to have played a significant role. Recall also that Schleiermacher, introducing his translation of Plato's dialogues (read by Schopenhauer), used *Erscheinung* and *Schein* as semantically equivalent terms to indicate what is opposed to the truth of the Idea (cf. *supra*, 1.5).[142] Thirdly, but most importantly from a theoretical standpoint, the skeptical interpretation of Kantian philosophy, based on the reduction of the concept of "appearance [*Erscheinung*]" to that of "representation [*Vorstellung*]" and on the consequent determination of the thing-in-itself as "truth" and "reality"; this was probably due to Schulze's influence. The compatibility or solidarity between the last two elements, however, might not be coincidental, since the "wise advice" to read Plato and Kant in parallel came to Schopenhauer from Schulze (who, moreover, as mentioned, advised his students to consult Tennemann's work).

In all of this, however, one should not underestimate the importance of Schelling, who in some of his early works (in accordance with Schulze's presentation of his philosophy) had expressly admitted the knowability, on the part of exceptional individuals, of absolute reality or things-in-themselves.

In spite of the undoubted importance of all these themes in Schopenhauer's mature philosophy, one should not lose sight of the fact that the complex and articulated speculative path that would lead to the future system, in the texts cited here, was still taking shape. Nevertheless, it is precisely with reference to the aforementioned dualism and, more precisely, to the "nothingness" of the empirical

---

[140] Cf. e.g. Plato, *Republic* 490 b; *Philebus*, 58 a. Cf. Plato 1914ff., vol. 6, pp. 26–27 and vol. 9, pp. 366–367.
[141] Cf. MR 1, n. 250, p. 163: "The *Platonic Idea* is *Kant's thing-in-itself* [...] free from time and space, and thus from plurality, change, beginning and end. It alone is the ὄντως ὄν or [*oder*] *thing-in-itself*".
[142] Plato 1804ff., II.1, pp. 6–10.

world that young Schopenhauer, in his 1811/12 notes, began to attribute a very special, indeed even exclusive, importance to the term "will" – in a sense that, however, was still far away from, or at least partial compared to, the key role it would play in *The World as Will and Representation*. It is now necessary to determine the proper meaning of this relevance.

4 Will and World. The Will as ὄντως ὄν

4.1 Nothingness of the World and Reality of the Will in Moral Consideration

In morality, young Schopenhauer believed he glimpsed a vision that was perfectly in line with his own theoretical (ontological) considerations. In fact, in his view, the fundamental premise of morality was the nothingness or unreality of the external world:

> Morality is concerned solely and exclusively with the *will*; it is quite immaterial whether an external force hampers the will's action. For morality the external world has reality [*Realität*] only to the extent that it can or cannot determine the will. Once the will is determined, that is to say a decision [*Entschluß*] exists, then the external world and its events are null [*nichtig*] and do not exist at all.[1]

The "moral law" or "inner law", which concerns the Kingdom of God, is opposed to the "outer law" or positive law, which concerns the external world and the state.[2] Moral consideration, in fact, concerns the *intention* with which an action is carried out: the essential thing is not what the acting subject actually achieves, but what they *want* or *wanted* to achieve. The realization of the intention can be prevented by events in the external world that the subject cannot control and for which he is therefore in no way responsible. Therefore, "whether an external force hampers the will's action" – whether the intention is or isn't realized – is completely irrelevant from a moral point of view (*given* the intention, i.e., given the determination of the will); "once the will is determined", the external world loses all importance, it no longer exists.[3]

This world is nothing but "the kingdom of chance and error";[4] as Greek tragedy teaches, "even the man who wants to do his best commits crimes in spite of his will!"[5] But all this just goes to show that "it is a question not of what is *done*, but of

---

[1] MR 1, n. 25, p. 16. Translation modified.
[2] MR 1, n. 25, p. 16. On the concepts of state and law in young Schopenhauer, cf. Durante 2014.
[3] Cf. MR 2, p. 352 (note to Schelling's *Philosophical Investigations into the Essence of Human Freedom and Related Objects*): "Can there be conceived anything more real [*etwas Realeres*] than the moral? Must you not regard as null [*nichtig*] everything that usually seems real to you, the moment it collides with this?" Translation modified.
[4] MR 1, fn to n. 25, p. 16.
[5] MR 2, p. 348.

4.1 Nothingness of the World and Reality of the Will in Moral Consideration

what is *willed*".[6] These considerations have an evidently consolatory function: the chance and error of the world, over which man has no power, have no reality, after all.[7]

In the *Critique of Practical Reason*, Kant had attributed an almost absolute moral value to the intention (*Gesinnung*) of the acting subject: "Of every action that conforms to the law but is not done for the sake of the law [*um des Gesetzes willen*], one can say that it is morally good only in accordance with the *letter* but not the *spirit* (the disposition)."[8] Indeed, Kant had distinguished between mere "legality" and full "morality" of action.[9] Schopenhauer's contraposition between moral law (or "inner" law) and the state (or outer law) seems to allude to this page of the *Critique of Practical Reason*. According to Schopenhauer, however, intention (the will of the acting subject) is not only what determines the moral value of an action, as for Kant, but also what gives "the external world and its events" meaning (*Bedeutung*) or reality (*Realität*). This thesis, radicalized and transposed to a more properly theoretical (transcendental) level, could be understood as the expression of a moral '(Anti-)Copernican revolution'.[10]

Now, if the events of the external world acquire some reality only through their relation to the human will, then the latter is what is real or essential in the full sense. And indeed, in challenging Schelling's theory of history and providence, Schopenhauer expressly states that the real element (*das Reale*) of life is the "will in every individual"; the events of the world – which constitute history – are its null or empty side (*das Nichtige*).[11]

> Only one thing do we see outside the power of fate, namely the will itself [*der Wille selbst*], and in the consciousness of the spectator [of the tragedy] it breaks forth out of the night so that not an object of the will but the will itself is truly being [*wahrhaft seyend*].[12]

It is interesting that the same expression that Schopenhauer refers to the *Wille* (*wahrhaft seyend*) was used by Schleiermacher to translate the Greek expression that Plato refers to the Idea: ὄντως ὄν.[13]

---

6 MR 2, p. 388. Note to Schelling's *System of Transcendental Idealism*.
7 Cf. MR 1, n. 20, p. 15.
8 Kant 1996a, p. 198.
9 Kant 1996a, p. 198.
10 Cf. Atwell 1995, p. 98.
11 MR 2, pp. 388–389. Note to Schelling's *System of Transcendental Idealism*.
12 MR 2, p. 348. Translation modified.
13 Schleiermacher thus translates *Philebus* 58a, 59d (cf. Plato 1804ff., II.3, pp. 225, 228). Schopenhauer translates it in the same way in *Parerga and Paralipomena* I (Schopenhauer 2014, p. 32) and in *The World as Will and Representation* (Schopenhauer 2010b, I 202, p. 194).

4.2 Meaning of This Early Relevance of the Term "Will". A First False Precedent of the System

One must resist the hermeneutical temptation to see Schopenhauer's statements here as a direct prelude or anticipation of his later metaphysics of will. In fact, the theoretical elements that would underpin the latter (cf. *infra*, Chapter 11) are still completely absent in these texts.[14] The fundamental presupposition at this stage was simply the *freedom* of the human will; the latter being the only thing "outside the power of fate". Only under this assumption is ethics possible: "the moral law [...] wants everyone *to do* the right thing".[15] In fact, however, not everyone "wants to do his best".[16] The human will (*Wille*), insofar as it is free, can, but must (*muss*) not necessarily seek the good or what's best. That is, it certainly ought to (*soll*) seek the good, but only in a moral sense. The *Wille* of these texts is to be understood as θέλημα, absolutely not as βούλησις (cf. *supra*, 1.9).

In fragment 13 (1810), Schopenhauer had written that the only possible meaning of the "mockery and sham of the world" is the education (παίδευσις) of the will: the changes that the will undergoes "whether for good or for evil", in relation not so much or not only to this life, but first and foremost to the "endless existence" of the acting subject.[17] Finite (temporal) life has meaning or value only as a dimension in which man's infinite existence is determined, and, in particular, in the sense of an eternal reward or punishment (depending on whether the will has undergone more "changes", respectively, "for good" or "for evil").

This meaning can also be attributed to the identity, implied in fragment 25 of the manuscripts, between the "inner law" (or moral law) and the "Kingdom of God":[18] the verdict of the divine tribunal, unlike that of a civil or state court, does not depend in any way on the actions that man has actually carried out, but exclusively on what he has willed. Not what happens, but man's free will, as such, is the only relevant, "real", "truly being [*wahrhaft seyend*]" thing from the divine point of view on the world. Everything else, i.e. the external world, is just "smoke" destined to "vanish into nothing" after forming "strange shapes".[19] This is precisely why life is just a farce.[20]

---

14 On this, I agree with Gjellerup 1919, pp. 501–502.
15 MR 1, n. 25, p. 16.
16 MR 2, p. 348.
17 MR 1, n. 13, p. 10.
18 MR 1, n. 25, p. 16.
19 MR 2, p. 389.
20 MR 2, p. 348.

All this would seem to fundamentally presuppose the immortality of the individual soul, understood as the center or subject of will (the participation of the *willing* subject in an infinite existence is also clearly implied in fragment 13). If this is so, the general sense of this entire discourse recalls once again Schopenhauer's repeated assertions, quoted in the previous chapters, that what is in time ("events") is an illusion; the truth is to be found in the innermost (*im Inneren*; in this case, in acting subject's relation with the inner law, i.e., in his intention or will). The external world, on the other hand, is the "kingdom of chance and error". The significance of the will in these notes from the years 1811–12 is thus directed more backwards than forwards – more to the past than to the future of Schopenhauer's theoretical elaboration.

Nevertheless, commenting on Fichte's thirty-third lecture "On the Facts of Consciousness" (given on 5 December 1811),[21] young Schopenhauer wrote that the will, "as a thing-in-itself, stands beyond all time [*als ein Ding an sich, über alle Zeit steht*]".[22] The color of the ink seems to suggest that this note was taken roughly at the same time as the transcription of Fichte's lecture.[23] In order to determine with certainty the exact time before which it must have been written, it is necessary to momentarily interrupt the main thread of the present discourse and devote a paragraph to the theory of cognition that young Schopenhauer had elaborated before writing his dissertation on the principle of sufficient reason.

4.3 "Being" as "the Product of the Operation of the Categories". Schopenhauer's Early Theory of Cognition

A number of passages in Schopenhauer's *Nachlass* written in the years 1811–1813 document an early theory of empirical cognition that left no trace in the printed works. The reconstruction and analysis of this theory are not only of historical or philological relevance, but also and mainly offer an indispensable hermeneutic key for other texts, as will become clear in the next section of this chapter.

Commenting on Fichte's first lecture "On the Study of Philosophy", Schopenhauer tackles the problem of concept formation, which he had already discussed in fragment 15, entitled "On Plato", in 1810 (cf. *supra*, 2.3).

---

21 Cf. Fichte 1962 ff., vol. IV, 4, pp. 73–74.
22 MR 2, p. 60.
23 Schopenhauer's *Nachlass* is available on the website of the Schopenhauer-Archiv. The text of this note can be found in the 6th volume, pp. 23v–24r.

> [...] perception [...] is assuredly not the mere *work of the senses*. With the senses we do not cognize [*erkennen*] anything; only through the categories of the understanding and to these the senses give the material. The understanding alone forms every concept and hence also the concept of resting and falling; and gravity is one concept abstracted from many (which just constitute perception). From what is seen the categories form concepts and through them we cognize [*erkennen*] all things in *relation* and hence also by means of the concept of *causality* [...]. Pure sensibility gives us space and time and only in these two is movement possible. The eye perceives them, and the understanding unites this perception into a concept of *falling* after previously uniting the stone and the earth each into a concept.[24]

In this note, Schopenhauer also addresses the problem of the relationship between "cause" and "supernatural reason or ground". For the sake of systematic exposition, I have omitted the passages on this subject here; they will be analyzed separately later (cf. *infra*, 6.2).

Compared to fragment 15 (which deals with the difference between general concepts and Platonic Ideas), Schopenhauer here uses terms that unmistakably belong to Kant's theoretical apparatus: "understanding", "categories", "manifold". Empirical concepts (such as "resting" and "falling") are the work of the understanding and originate from the action of the categories (pure concepts) on "what is seen", i.e. on the empirical, perceived objects.[25] The understanding is therefore, in Kantian terms, the faculty relating to both.[26] Again in a commentary on Fichte – specifically, on the twenty-sixth lecture "On the Facts of Consciousness", given on 26 November 1811[27] – Schopenhauer noted:

> The concept is the product of the act of the categories, [an act] which is to unite the manifold given in perception into a thing, an *ens*, a substance. Thus they unite the given extension, impenetrability, figure, red colour into a concept of a thing, and memory is the repetition of this concept which through practice has become dexterity or proficiency. In this concept it therefore retains all the accidents of the thing, one of which is the red colour. Thus in a similar manner the understanding makes for itself several concepts. Now if it (the understanding that is the sum of the categories) finds in several things, or in its concepts of them already

---

24 MR 2, p. 21. Translation modified.
25 Causality is first defined as a "concept" ("From what is seen the categories form concepts and through them we perceive and know all things in *relation* and hence also by means of the concept of *causality* [...]"), and then as a "category" ("the category of causality is for ever and always asking why"). In order to attempt to harmonize these two points, while at the same time maintaining their relation to the rest of the text, it can be assumed that Schopenhauer, when referring to causality as a concept, doesn't mean pure causality (the category), but causality as already empirically defined as gravity (the cause of the fall), in line with the example chosen in Fichte's lecture (cf. MR 2, p. 21).
26 Cf. Kant 1998, B 33–34, p. 155; B 90–116, pp. 202–218.
27 Cf. Fichte 1962 ff., vol. IV, 4, p. 209.

taken into memory, the same accident, e.g. the red colour, then it once more unites these manifolds thus given to it into a whole, which is then the concept *red*.²⁸

The act of the categories consists above all in the unification of "the manifold given in perception" into "a thing, an *ens*, a substance". In the *Critique of Pure Reason*, Kant had admitted a "manifold of sensibility [...] *a priori*" that provides "the pure concepts of the understanding with a matter, without which they would be without any content, thus completely empty".²⁹ It is probable that Schopenhauer intended the "manifold given in perception", from whose unification by the categories the thing or *ens* arises, to correspond to Kant's "manifold of sensibility".

The result of the application of categories to the immediate content of perception is thus the thing, the *ens*. In an 1813 commentary on the *Critique of Pure Reason*, Schopenhauer expressly wrote: "Through the word *being* [*Seyn*] we really indicate the product of the operation of the categories. As soon as they have combined perceptions (given by sensibility), we say *it is*".³⁰ Being as a "product of the categories" is also mentioned in the notes on Schelling's *Philosophy and Religion*.³¹ Young Schopenhauer attempts to explain the origin of the world of experience from the cognitive faculties of the cognizing subject, and does so in terms of transcendental idealism (broadly understood). He uses the term "being" (*Seyn, ens*) to denote empirical reality, i.e., what appears to "be" within the standpoint of experience. Here this word does not denote what, for him, constitutes "being" in the absolute sense (ὄντως ὄν; cf. *supra*, 3.9). The ambiguity of the concept "being", implicit in these annotations, will be explicitly thematized in the fragments of 1813 (cf. *infra*, 8.2).

Now, a further act of the categories – this time applied not to the manifold of perception, but to this manifold as *already* unified in the "thing" – results in the *concept of the thing:* "thus [as the categories unify "the manifold given in perception" into "a thing, an *ens*, a substance"], they unite the given extension, impenetrability, figure, and red colour into a concept of a thing".

Given the concept of a thing, the origin of *the concept of an accident of the thing* is easily explained through a *third* unifying act of the understanding. The concept of the thing contains "all the accidents of the thing"; when the occurrences of the same accident (the color red), perceived in several things and recorded in several concepts, are unified by the understanding, the concept of that accident (the concept of the color red) arises. Consequently, in the concept of a thing the

---

28 MR 2, pp. 51–52. Translation modified.
29 Kant 1998, B 102, p. 210.
30 MR 2, p. 310.
31 MR 2, p. 371.

accidents are indeed unified, but *not yet as concepts:* each of them becomes a concept only if it is "united" with the same accident as repeatedly perceived in other things and registered in the corresponding concepts (of things). Precisely for this reason, the accident is initially memorized only as an element of the concept of the thing (substance) to which it is inherent.

Schopenhauer admits two types of concepts: the concept of the "thing, *ens*, substance", in which all the accidents of the thing are united ("extension, impenetrability, figure, red colour"), and the concept of "red", which is the concept of an accident (*Accidenz*). It is not clear how these two types of concepts relate to one another; furthermore, Schopenhauer does not specify the relation between the "manifold given in perception" – from whose unification (by the categories) the *thing* arises – and the manifold of the "given extension, impenetrability, and red colour" from whose unification (also by the categories) the *concept of the thing* arises.[32]

But the main problem lies in the "concept of the thing", the formation of which is preliminary to the formation of the concept of the accident. If one understands the "concept of the thing" as a universal concept, namely as the concept of the species of the thing, at least three problems arise.

1) The categories "unify the given extension, impenetrability, figure, and red colour in a concept of a thing". In this sense, it is problematic that the concept of the species of the thing, which is supposed to express its essence, also contains the *accidents* of the thing ("it [memory] thus retains all the accidents of the thing").

---

[32] If these two manifolds were identical, the results of their unification – the thing and the concept of the thing – would also be identical; but this latter identity is denied by the text, according to which the concept is not the thing, but is, in fact, the concept of the thing. Moreover, even according to Schopenhauer's later transcendental idealism, the thing is a "representation", not a "concept": (the concepts of) "concept" and "representation" are to be distinguished, for Schopenhauer. Assuming, then, that the two manifolds are different, only the manifold whose unification gives the concept of the thing ("the given extension, impenetrability, figure, and red colour") is determined – probably incompletely – and not also "the given manifold" whose unification produces the thing. Nor is it possible to assume that, according to Schopenhauer, the elements of the manifold, whose unification gives rise to the concept of the thing, are in turn the concepts of the elements of the manifold (of perception) whose unification gives rise to the thing. The former, in fact ("the given extension, impenetrability, figure, and red colour", which Schopenhauer considers "accidents" of the thing), as "given", cannot be "concepts" (the result of an act of the categories). Furthermore, according to this interpretative hypothesis, the concept of the thing would result from the unification of the concepts of its accidents; but this would contradict what follows in the text, i.e., that the formation of the concept of the thing is prior to the formation of the concept of the accident.

2) The concept of the thing arises in a different way from the concept of the accident. The latter is formed through the unification of multiple experiences (of the thing itself); instead, in the case of the concept of the thing, Schopenhauer does not speak of multiple experiences at all. Or rather, in the case of the concept of the thing, the unification does not concern the manifold experiences of the thing, but its accidents. Now, the concept of the color red is undoubtedly an abstract or general concept; if the concept of the thing is also understood in this latter sense, it is difficult to justify how the same kind of concept (the same result) can derive from two different formation processes.
3) Furthermore, referring to the concept of the thing, Schopenhauer writes that "memory is the repetition, become skill [*Fertigkeit*] through exercise, of this concept". If we understand "concept" as an abstract representation or concept of species, it follows that memory is the repetition of abstract representations. Moreover, what is repeated must first have been perceived; so, if the concepts, which are repeated, were concepts of species, then Schopenhauer would imply that the species (as the content of such concepts) have been perceived.

This entire anomaly dissipates if one understands "concept of the thing" as *representation of the single, concrete thing*. In a note to the *Critique of Pure Reason*, written no later than spring 1813 (i.e., about a year and a half after the lecture in which Fichte spoke of the concept of quality),[33] Schopenhauer addresses the Kantian notion of "schema":

> I deny that the schema [*Schema*] is different from the image [*Bild*]. –
>
> An image or schema I call the reproduction of a sensible intuition through the imaginative faculty; its content is therefore always an individual object [...] I therefore call image or schema an *immediate representation* [*unmittelbare Vorstellung*], to whatever sphere the intuition of actual objects of the senses may belong.
>
> A *concept* I call the representation of a representation or an *indirect representation* [*mittelbare Vorstellung*]. In the combinations of the understanding the concept acts as a substitute for the immediate representations and with advantage because it is easier to handle, just as in algebra letters are a substitute for numbers. By its nature it [the concept] can have for its content individual things as well as genera and species, but the latter are its exclusive property and exist only in the concept.[34]

"By its nature" the concept "can have for its content individual things as well as genera and species". The "genera", insofar as they "exist only in the concept"

---

33 MR 2, p. XXIX.
34 MR 2, p. 298. Translation modified.

and are "its exclusive property", are here implicitly opposed to the "individual things" that also exist outside the concept. Since the class of immediate representations includes both "intuitions of actual objects of the senses" (or "sensible intuitions") and images or schemas, the fact that the concept is an "indirect representation" means that it is a *representation* of a sensible intuition or a *representation* of an image or schema (which are themselves representations). The determination of the concept as the "representation of a representation", also found in Schopenhauer's mature texts, may have been regarded by the young philosopher as the implicit content of a passage in the *Critique of Pure Reason*.[35]

The concept of an individual thing differs in the text from the "image or schema", i.e. the "reproduction" of "sensible intuition" (of which the concept is the representation). This difference, however, is not specified in the text. The latter only says that the concept "is easier to handle [*leichter zu handhaben*]" than the immediate representations (the class that includes the "image or schema"). The same expression would be repeated in the treatise on the principle of sufficient reason and in *The World as Will and Representation*.[36] In any case, this passage in the *Nachlass* testifies beyond doubt that young Schopenhauer admitted concepts of individual things.

Now, if in the fragment relating to Fichte's course, "concept of the thing" is interpreted not as "concept of the species of the thing" but as "concept of the individual thing", the difficulties encountered in relation to the previous interpretative hypothesis disappear.

1) The *concept* of the "thing" is the concept of an *ens*, of a "first substance" (according to Aristotelian terminology) which, unlike the color red (which is an accident), cannot be predicated of anything else. In this way, it is no longer problematic, but natural, that the concept of the thing should include its accidental notes.
2) Memory is "the repetition, become skill", of calling to mind the representation of the individual thing and not, counter-intuitively, of its species.
3) Finally, it is justified that Schopenhauer does not speak of many experiences of the "same" thing as a condition of the concept of the thing, which he would have to do if by "concept of the thing" he meant the concept of the species of the thing. We can then explain the difference between the two processes of concept formation, depending on whether we are dealing with the concept

---

[35] Cf. Kant 1998, B 93–94, p. 205. Schopenhauer would explicitly refer to this passage in 1816 (MR 2, p. 464).
[36] Cf. Schopenhauer 2010b, I § 28, p. 177; Schopenhauer 2018, II 89, p. 88 ("easier to manage").

of the thing (single or individual) or the concept of the accident (which is a general concept).

The content that, as a whole, formed this primitive theory of concepts can also be found elsewhere in the *Nachlass*. The origin of the concept from the act of categories is stated again in a note on the *Critique of Pure Reason*.[37] The meaning of the word "concept" as concept of an individual thing, which can be repeated, is presupposed in a further note on Fichte, which will be analyzed in the next section of this chapter, as well as in a commentary on the first volume of Schelling's *Philosophische Schriften*.[38] In fragment 46 of the manuscripts, written in 1812, the distinction (left undefined in the text) between "abstract concept" and "concrete concept"[39] is presupposed, so it can be assumed that Schopenhauer meant by the former "general concept" and by the latter "concept of the individual thing".

This theory of cognition is very different from the one that Schopenhauer would present in his published writings. In his dissertation of 1813, the faculty of concepts is no longer the understanding (*Verstand*), but reason (*Vernunft*), and concepts are defined as "abstract representations":

> *Concepts*, however, are always general because, as mere representations of representations, they cannot contain everything contained by the representation; *i.e.* they are not so thoroughly determined.[40]

In the dissertation, the concept is never a concept of a single thing, but always and only general. As such, it is not to be "confused", on the one hand, "as often occurs, with the category of unity, which unifies the manifold of all sensible intuition", nor, on the other hand, with the "repetitions spontaneously recalled" of real objects "(i.e. mental images [*Phantasmen*])", wich "are always particular representations".[41] However, before settling on this definitive position, Schopenhauer would devote several more reflections to the subject of the "concept" (cf. *infra*, 6.9; 7.4).

It is interesting that in these passages of the dissertation Schopenhauer seems to warn the reader against his own earlier "confusion". In fact, if the concept is not to be mistaken for "the category of unity, which unifies the manifold of all sensible intuition", this seems to exclude that the concept may be the unity of the accidental

---

37 Cf. MR 2, p. 310.
38 Cf. MR 2, p. 349.
39 MR 1, n. 46, p. 27.
40 Schopenhauer 2012 [1813], § 27, p. 176; cf. Schopenhauer 2012 [1847], § 26, p. 94.
41 Schopenhauer 2012 [1813], § 27, p. 176.

determinations of the thing. In other words, contrary to what he said in the note to Fichte, here Schopenhauer denies that the categories "unify the given extension, impenetrability, figure, and red color in a *concept* of a thing [italics mine]". On the other hand, the fact that the concept, as a general representation, is not to be confused with the "mental image" as a "particular representation" certainly excludes that a concept might have "individual things" as its content.

In his dissertation, Schopenhauer would no longer speak of the concept of a single thing, but only of an abstract representation (general concept) or of a mental image; nor would he resort to the act of categories to explain the origin of concepts, since the faculty of concepts would there no longer be the understanding (which is the faculty of categories), but reason.[42] It can be assumed that Schopenhauer abandoned the notion of concepts of individual things (retaining only general concepts) in order to eliminate the ambiguity of the term "concept" and thus safeguard its specificity with respect to the term "mental image" (as a reproduction of what has been perceived).

4.4 The Will, "as a Thing-in-Itself, Stands beyond All Time". A Second False Precedent of the System

We now come to the commentary on Fichte in which Schopenhauer wrote that the will, "as a thing-in-itself, stands beyond all time".

> According to Kant's teaching Fichte's reproduction is, I think, very simple to explain as the activity of the understanding by means of its categories and the forms of pure sensibility carried on in concepts to which matter taken from sensibility is not given at this moment, but is given earlier [...]. Purpose is a concept that becomes causal; [...] It could be said that the decision is outside all time in so far as it is an act of the will which, as a thing-in-itself, stands beyond all time [*daß der Entschluß außer aller Zeit stehe, ließe sich sagen insofern er ein Akt des Willens ist, der als ein Ding an sich, über alle Zeit steht*].[43]

It is evident that, here too, the "concepts" to which Schopenhauer refers are concepts of individual things, not general concepts. Reproduction, in fact, consists in the series of these concepts: their content, before it can be reproduced, must have been perceived, so that, as such, it cannot consist in an (abstract) species. In the last sentence of the quotation, Schopenhauer also writes that "purpose is

---

[42] On the systematic function of the theory of concepts in Schopenhauer's thought, cf. Dobrzański 2017.
[43] MR 2, p. 60.

a concept that becomes causal". Here, too, it is very unlikely that "concept" means "general concept": this would only be appropriate in the case of "ideal" purposes, such as goodness, virtue, etc. Schopenhauer, on the other hand, was speaking of a determinate and concrete purpose, which is the concept of a single thing (to be realized or achieved), certainly not a concept of a species. If this is the case, even at the end of the passage "concept" means "concept of a single thing".

Since the concepts referred to here are therefore concepts of individual things, and since in the dissertation of 1813 concepts of individual things are no longer admitted ("concepts [...] are always general"), then this note must have been written entirely *before the dissertation*. In the early notebooks, the first fragment in which the thing-in-itself is connected to the will is from 1814.[44] Based on the available documents, this is therefore the first annotation in which Schopenhauer related the concepts of will and thing-in-itself.

At this point, however, it is essential to determine the meaning of this relation, expressed by the term *als: der [Wille], als ein Ding an sich*. In the final analysis, it is essential to establish the grammatical and logical meaning of the term *als*. This question requires some consideration. In fact, this meaning has already been specified, in the present text, by the translation of the passage: the will "*as* [italics mine] a thing-in-itself". It is therefore a matter of justifying the appropriateness of this translation choice.

According to the Grimm Dictionary, the term *als* can have three meanings: it can be comparative (*vergleichend*), demonstrative (*demonstrativ*) or consecutive (*konsekutiv*).[45] Now, the consecutive *als* expresses a consequentiality relating more to the "whole discourse" than to its individual components.[46] It follows that in the proposition *der Wille, als ein Ding an sich, steht über alle Zeit*, insofar as it relates the term *Wille* to the expression *ein Ding an sich*, *als* can only be either demonstrative or comparative.

Let us assume as a first hypothesis that *als* is demonstrative. Schopenhauer's proposition would mean: "the will, insofar[47] as it is a thing-in-itself, stands beyond

---

44 MR 1, n. 278, pp. 184–186.
45 J. Grimm and W. Grimm 1854–1971, vol. 1, p. 247.
46 J. Grimm and W. Grimm 1854–1971, vol. 1, p. 257.
47 On the demonstrative *als* referring to a noun in nominative case: "*bei vielen verbis hebt sich das im nom. stehende praedicat durch ein als hervor. die mhd. und ahd. sprache, gleich den klassischen, ja den meisten übrigen enthielt sich hier noch ganz der partikel und setzte den reinen nominativ:* des starb er mensche und starb niht got; si gebar in maget; ich scheide iuwer gevangen hin, *d. h.* mensche wesende, maget wesende, gevangen wesende; er wart gekorn künec, gewîhet bischof, genant Artûs. *wir sagen noch heute:* er ward Artus genannt, aber zum könig erwählt, zum bischof geweiht und für mensch wesend *sagen wir* als mensch" (J. Grimm and W. Grimm 1854–1971, vol. 1,

all time". In this case, the proposition "the will is a thing-in-itself" would be the fundamental statement, because it would be the ground of the proposition "the will stands beyond all time": that is, the will standing "beyond all time" would be the consequence of the will being a thing-in-itself. In contrast to the manuscripts of 1814[48] and *The World as Will and Representation*,[49] the will would be determined not as *the* thing-in-itself, but as *a* thing-in-itself. This would imply the admission of a plurality of things-in-themselves.

Indeed, the use of the plural form (*Dinge an sich*), present both in Kant's texts[50] and in Schulze's lectures,[51] was recurrent in Schopenhauer's annotations until 1814 (cf. *supra*, 3.2; *infra*, 11.9). Later, this term would be definitively abandoned, as Schopenhauer would come to affirm that the thing-in-itself "lies outside of time and space, outside the *principium individuationis*, i. e. the possibility of multiplicity".[52] But, in any case, Schopenhauer always seemed to assume that the concept of the thing-in-itself is *univocal*, i. e., that things-in-themselves are not essentially different from one another.

In his commentary on Fichte's first lecture "On the Study of Philosophy", Schopenhauer uses precisely the plural form: the genius and the madman can intuit the "things-in-themselves".[53] However, they are here unambiguously determined as that which is cognized outside "the conditions of the cognition of experience".[54] In 1814, things-in-themselves were generally determined as something that cannot be represented;[55] later they would be identified with Platonic Ideas.[56] The latter certainly constitute a plurality; but, even in this case, the concept of thing-in-itself has only one meaning – that is, precisely, "Platonic Idea". The unambiguousness of this concept was always maintained by Schopenhauer – and in this sense the principle that the thing-in-itself "lies outside [...] the possibility of multiplicity" was already posited in the manuscripts.

---

pp. 254–255). Thus, if in *"Der Wille, als ein Ding an sich"* als were demonstrative, it would mean *wesend* or *seiend*: *"Der ein Ding an sich seiende Wille"*.
48 MR 1, n. 305, pp. 205–206.
49 Schopenhauer 2010b, I 134, § 23, p. 137.
50 Cf. e.g. Kant 1998, B 62, p. 169; B 327, p. 372; B 526, p. 514.
51 Cf. D'Alfonso 2008, p. 70.
52 Schopenhauer 2010b, I 134, § 23, p. 138.
53 MR 2, p. 19.
54 MR 2, p. 19.
55 MR 1, n. 171, p. 104. See also MR 1, n. 263, p. 175 ("time appertains not to things-in-themselves"); n. 287, p. 193 ("*time* and *space* do not belong to *things-in-themselves*").
56 MR 1, n. 228, p. 143; n. 301, p. 203; n. 352, p. 240; n. 363, p. 248; n. 462, p. 332; n. 467, p. 335; n. 473, p. 346; n. 488, p. 359.

4.4 The Will, "as a Thing-in-Itself, Stands beyond All Time"

So, if *als* were demonstrative, Schopenhauer would mean to say that the will is *a* thing-in-itself; this would imply the possibility of other things-in-themselves that are not the will. In other words, things-in-themselves could vary in essence. But this clearly contradicts the univocality of the concept of "thing-in-itself", which Schopenhauer always seems to presuppose.

In order to preserve the demonstrative value of *als* and the unambiguousness of the concept of thing-in-itself, one can only assume that Schopenhauer meant to say that *every individual will* is a thing-in-itself. But in the annotations prior to 1814 (according to the available documents) Schopenhauer never attributed the determinations of things-in-themselves (being cognized only outside "the conditions of the cognition of experience", not being able to be "represented") to the will, nor did he ever relate the two concepts, except for this note. The color of the ink, as we have seen, suggests that this commentary is coeval with the transcription of Fichte's course, which took place at the end of 1811; if, then, one attributes a demonstrative value to *als*, one must conclude that Schopenhauer set aside this thought of great theoretical relevance (every will *is* a thing-in-itself) for a long time, suddenly recovering it only two and a half years later, in 1814, without any reference to this previous note to Fichte and, moreover, in a profoundly different theoretical context and formulation (affirming that the will is not *a*, but *the* thing-in-itself: cf. *infra*, 11.12). All this is very unlikely.

Let us therefore consider the second hypothesis, according to which *als* is comparative. The proposition *Der Wille, als ein Ding an sich, steht über alle Zeit* would mean: "the will, like a thing-in-itself, stands beyond all time".[57] *Als* would thus mean *wie*. In this case, the proposition "the will is above time" would represent the fundamental thought, because it would be the ground of the proposition "the will is like a thing-in-itself". As can be seen, with this interpretation, the two difficulties produced by the previous one disappear. First of all, the univocality of the concept of thing-in-itself is not lost, because the will is not *a* thing-in-itself, but *as* or *like* a thing-in-itself (since it too stands outside of time). Secondly, this

---

57 About the comparative (*vergleichend*) *als*, the Grimm Dictionary states: "*neben dem subst. verhält es* [das 'Als'] *sich ebenso, da überall ein verbum hinzu kann gedacht werden:* glauben als ein senfkorn. *Matth.* 17, 20; äste oder reben als arm oder schenkel. Frank *weltb.* 6a; einen weg als den andern. *Simplic.* 1, 239; nun überlegen sie, was für schwierigkeiten dieses genie in einem lande als Deutschland zu übersteigen habe. Lessing 4, 444. *auch hier bald mit über-wiegendem wie:* tausend jahre sind vor dir wie der tag, der gestern vergangen ist. ps. 90, 5; seine gestalt war wie der blitz. *Matth.* 28, 23; die zeiten sind als wie ein rad. Logau 3, 109, 46. *heute stets wie:* worte wie ein schwert; kinder wie die orgelpfeifen; einfälle wie ein alt haus" (J. Grimm and W. Grimm 1854–1971, vol. 1, p. 249).

claim is in line with Schopenhauer's contemporary annotations, according to which the will determines the individual's eternal destiny and thus constitutes, with respect to the nothingness of temporal and contingent events, what is *wahrhaft seyend* (cf. supra, 4.1–4.2).

For these reasons, it is highly probable that *als* here means "as" or "like", not "insofar as". If this is true, in the note to Fichte Schopenhauer did not identify the will with a thing-in-itself, but only juxtaposed the two terms on the basis of their common characteristic of being beyond time.[58] For the purposes of research, consequently, it is extremely important to establish why Schopenhauer describes the will as something that is "beyond all time". Two hypotheses can be made in this respect.

In his lecture, Fichte described decision as "something timeless [*ein Zeitloses*]",[59] without referring to the "will". Schopenhauer writes: "decision is outside all time in so far as it is an act of the will which, as [*als*] a thing-in-itself, stands beyond all time". With this statement, Schopenhauer intends to clarify the *ground* of Fichte's assertion: decision is "something timeless" because the organ or faculty of which it is an act (the will), "stands beyond all time". Now, the fact that Schopenhauer presents his own determination of the will ("beyond all time") as the *ratio essendi* of the Fichtean determination of decision ("outside all time"), does not exclude that he saw the latter as the *ratio cognoscendi* of the former. It is therefore possible that Schopenhauer deduced the determination of the organ (the will) from Fichte's determination of the act (the decision).

However, the juxtaposition of will and thing-in-itself – based on their common characteristic of being outside or beyond time – could also depend on his reading of Schelling. Between late 1811 and early 1812 (partly at the same time as he was attending Fichte's lectures "On the Facts of Consciousness"), Schopenhauer read the first volume of Schelling's *Philosophische Schriften*,[60] in which the *Philosophical Investigations into the Essence of Human Freedom* appeared for the first time. Here Schelling states that "Will is primal Being", so that its predicates include: "groundlessness, eternality, independence from time, self-affirmation";[61] he then claims that Kant "distinguished things-in-themselves from appearances only negatively through their independence from time".[62] The implication here is that the

---

58 On this specific point I understand the text differently from M. d'Alfonso (2006, p. 209), who interprets *als* in the sense of an identification between the terms it connects: namely "will" and "thing-in-itself".
59 MR 2, p. 59.
60 Schelling 1809, pp. 399–511.
61 Schelling 2006, p. 21.
62 Schelling 2006, p. 22.

will, like a thing-in-itself, is independent of time; moreover, the plural form *Dinge an sich* implies the possibility of a plurality of things-in-themselves (just as in Schopenhauer's note). It is therefore possible that Schopenhauer's assertion – the will, "as a thing-in-itself, stands beyond all time" – was affected by Schelling's influence, without, however, constituting or grounding an actual theoretical thesis.

As will be seen later, Schopenhauer's theory of intelligible character presented in his 1813 dissertation – according to which intelligible character is "a universal act of will lying outside of time"[63] – undeniably betrays the influence of the *Philosophical Investigations on the Essence of Human Freedom* (cf. *infra*, 9.8 – 9.11).

4.5 Conclusion

The relevance of the term "will" in the 1811/1812 notes is essentially the *consequence* of its preliminary understanding as θέλημα: the human will (as presupposed in the commentary on Fichte) is generally the faculty of "decision [*Entschluß*]". More specifically, it is that which – insofar as it is "outside the power of fate"[64] – allows for the free choice between good and evil, which man's *eternal* destiny depends on.[65] The centrality of the *Wille* is thus ultimately a reflection of the extraordinary importance Schopenhauer attaches to this eternal fate.

In fact, however, this kind of considerations led young Schopenhauer to attribute for the first time to the *will* the characteristics that, according to Tennemann,[66] belong to the *thing-in-itself* and to the *Platonic Idea:* being ὄντως ὄν (*wahrhaft seyend*), standing "beyond all time". After this sudden rapprochement, which was largely fortuitous and implicit, the orbits of these three fundamental concepts – "will", "Platonic Idea", and "thing-in-itself" – would again diverge, but would eventually meet again and even coincide in 1814, this time explicitly (and based on further theoretical presuppositions, cf. *infra*, 11.12).

---

63 Schopenhauer 2012 [1813], § 46, pp. 187–188.
64 MR 2, p. 348.
65 MR 1, n. 13, p. 10.
66 Cf. Tennemann 1798–1819, II, pp. 363–364.

5 Fichte: Empirical Consciousness and *Consciousness* of Empirical Consciousness. The Philosophical *Besonnenheit*

5.1 Introduction

In this chapter, I will analyze the only one of Fichte's theoretical theses which Schopenhauer openly agreed with in his notes.[1] As I will try to show here, this tenet would have a far-reaching influence on Schopenhauer's thought, especially in relation to his understanding of the general sense of criticism and the determination of the *starting point* of his philosophical investigation.

5.2 Fichte: Philosophy as Knowledge of Knowledge

The "purpose" of Fichte's four introductory lectures "On the Study of Philosophy" was "to determine the way in which philosophy can and should be *communicated* [mitgetheilt]".[2] This task required first answering the question, "What *is* philosophy?"[3] Now, to provide a concrete and comprehensive answer to this question, Fichte argued, it would be necessary to set forth the philosophical investigation in its entirety.[4] In the "few hours" of these lectures, however, nothing more could be offered than a general explicative concept of philosophy.[5]

> When anyone asks me what philosophy is, I say: You want to *know* [wissen] what philosophy is, thus you *know* something in general. Now after having said *what* he knew, I would limit this more and more by combining it under general points of view until I arrived at an *x* whose place is to be filled by philosophy. First of all, then, the concept of knowledge [*Wissen*] must be determined because philosophy ought to be *knowledge*.[6]

Whoever asks what philosophy is wants to *know* what philosophy is, and therefore presupposes the moment (or the notion) of knowledge: that is, he reveals that he already knows "something in general". Philosophy thus begins *at the end point* of

---

1 Cf. MR 2, pp. 28, 32, 78.
2 MR 2, p. 17. Translation modified.
3 MR 2, p. 17.
4 MR 2, p. 17.
5 MR 2, p. 17.
6 MR 2, p. 17.

the process in which the initial content of knowledge (what the asking person knew) is progressively "limited" and "combined" "under general points of view". The position x occupied by philosophy is the most general point of view, where the initial content of knowledge has disappeared and only its form – knowledge *as such* – remains. Through this line of reasoning, Fichte sought to demonstrate that, in order to answer the question about philosophy, it is first necessary to answer the question about knowledge (*Wissen*). "*First of all* [italics mine], then, the concept of knowledge must be determined."[7]

The implication of these short lines anticipates the main point of Fichte's entire discourse: the definition of philosophy as "knowledge of knowledge". In the third lecture, in fact, Fichte affirms that all sciences address a particular phenomenon (*Phänomen*) that constitutes their field and of which they investigate the ground (*Grund*) by asking the question "why" (*Warum*).[8] For example, mechanics deals with the resting and falling of bodies. "Now as philosophy is also a knowledge, the question arises what phenomenon it undertakes to establish, Answer: knowledge."[9]

> But in order to understand merely the *definition* of philosophy, we must have arrived at the consciousness of knowledge [*Bewußtseyn des Wissens*]. Whoever looks at the stove here, is conscious of the stove; the focus of his knowledge is the stove and he says: the stove is. But if he communes with himself and grasps that he is conscious of the stove, then the focus of his knowledge is no longer the stove, but his being conscious of the stove. Now if he likewise becomes conscious of his consciousness of all perceptions and of all his knowledge of their reasons or grounds, and he makes precisely this the focus of his knowledge, then he has the phenomenon of knowledge, the establishment of which is the object of philosophy.[10]

Philosophy provides the ground of all scientific knowledge (or: of scientific knowledge *as such*) and is, therefore, "knowledge of knowledge" or science of science, i.e. *Wissenschaftslehre* "in the strict sense of the term".[11] The "natural" human point of view, says Fichte, is the simple consciousness of objects; the point of view of philosophy is instead the consciousness of knowledge, or the consciousness of the consciousness of objects.[12] Man has to rise on his own to the latter point of view and, until this happens, no philosophy is possible. Many do not reach it because they

---

7 On Fichte's later philosophy, cf. Lauth 1999; Furlani 2004; Radrizzani 2012; Zöller 2016.
8 MR 2, p. 23.
9 MR 2, p. 27. Translation modified.
10 MR 2, p. 27.
11 MR 2, p. 28.
12 MR 2, p. 26.

expect it to be given to them from outside, like a "dig in the ribs": either they are completely blind in spirit, or they fear that, if they admit they have such a point of view, it may result in adverse consequences for them.[13]

Schopenhauer notes: "This means to be *stubborn and impenitent*, like Gottlob Ernst Schulze, professor of misosophy at Göttingen, for instance".[14] The term "misosophy" is the etymological opposite of the term "philosophy", because μῖσος (enmity, hatred), in ancient Greek, is the opposite of φιλία (friendship, love). Schulze is said to teach the "hatred of wisdom". One can clearly see the negative connotation of this reference, as well as Schopenhauer's dissatisfaction with the skeptical outcome of Schulze's reflections.

Schopenhauer seems to be deeply convinced that the point of view of "knowledge of knowledge" exists and is evident (as not wanting to admit it "means to be stubborn"). Here one can see a fundamental – if implicit – *agreement* between the student Schopenhauer and professor Fichte. Up to this point, Arthur's annotations had only expressed dissent (cf. *infra*, 6.1–6.3).

5.3 Fichte: "Higher Consciousness" or *absolute Besonnenheit*

In the fourth and last introductory lecture "On the Study of Philosophy", Fichte announces that the following classes "On the Facts of Consciousness" should help the pupil to achieve the point of view of "knowledge of knowledge", or rather of absolute reflectiveness (*absolute Besonnenheit*). In other words, these lectures should show "the phenomenon that has to establish the science of knowledge",[15] namely knowledge (*Wissen*) as such. They are therefore a necessary preliminary step to come to *Wissenschaftslehre*.

Consistent with this programmatic statement, in the first lecture of the course "On the Facts of Consciousness" Fichte declares: "In this investigation we are concerned with the pure observation, namely […] that of the perception of perception [*Wahrnehmung der Wahrnehmung*]."[16] While the external world is a *"factum"* accessible to everyone through the external senses, the "perception of perception" can only occur through *an inner sense*, so that "philosophy is not for the man to whom this sense is not open [*offen*]", that is, available to investigation.[17] "Here then is the boundary of philosophy; the perception of perception is its province

---

13 MR 2, p. 28.
14 MR 2, p. 28.
15 MR 2, p. 28. Translation modified.
16 MR 2, p. 32.
17 MR 2, p. 32.

in which we shall always remain and which in every lecture I shall try to enlarge and extend for you."[18]

According to this method, it is illegitimate to speak of an object that, through its impression on the senses, produces perception.[19] Such an object would in fact be *eo ipso* external to perception, so that its admission would constitute an "opinion about perception" and violate the limit defined by the scope of research.[20] An object that, by definition, cannot be perceived by consciousness cannot be included among the "facts of consciousness".

This investigation "shall therefore stick to the evident perception of perception", from whose perspective one contemplates not a single perception, but "the whole world of perceptions [*die gesammte Welt der Wahrnehmungen*]", "the whole world of experience [*die ganze Welt der Erfahrung*]", "as in a picture [*wie in einem Bilde*]".[21] Fichte provides an example:

> If I see a stove, feel it and soon, I am conscious of the stove, my knowledge is absorbed in it [*mein Wissen geht in ihm auf*]. But if I arrive at the higher consciousness of my perception of the stove, then my knowledge is absorbed in this [higher consciousness]. The perceiving of appearing objects is natural to man; he then perceives all things singly and separately, stove, window, bench, trees, and sky, and, unless he attains to that higher consciousness [*höherem Bewußtsein*], he will never keep the bond whereby they are all tied together, namely perception.[22]

The point of view of perception of perception, which is characteristic of a "higher consciousness", considers things as perceptions (insofar as they are perceived), and therefore allows us to grasp what all things have in common: precisely, their being perceived.[23]

Fichte points out that, according to common sense, on the one hand, the thing is perceived exactly as it is in itself, on the other, it is separate and distinct from the perception that concerns it: it would exist, as it is perceived, even if it were not perceived.[24] The common point of view, therefore, posits the perception of the thing as identical and at the same time not identical with the thing perceived. "If we now raise ourselves above this and consider the whole of perception as a *factum* which we again perceive, then we are at the standpoint of absolute reflec-

---

18 MR 2, p. 32.
19 MR 2, p. 32.
20 MR 2, p. 32.
21 MR 2, p. 32.
22 MR 2, p. 32.
23 MR 2, p. 32.
24 MR 2, pp. 33–34.

tiveness which, I hope, each one of us has now reached."²⁵ Such a standpoint is devoid of the contradictory nature of common sense, since it rejects on principle the admission of an external reality that is independent of perception.

Fichte's concept of "perception of perception" involves a double way of looking at things: from the common point of view, they appear indeed as "things"; from the philosopher's point of view, they appear as perceptions, that is, as perceived, represented things. *Two different consciousnesses* correspond to this twofold aspect of things: the common consciousness, whose "focus" is things as such, and the *consciousness* of the common consciousness, i.e. the "higher" consciousness, characteristic of the philosopher, whose "focus" is knowledge, the perception of things.²⁶

5.4 Interlude: *Absolute Besonnenheit* and σωφροσύνη. The Knowledge of Knowledge in Socrates and Fichte

Fichte's concept of *Besonnenheit* has been seen as the explicit and radical thematization of the *intentio obliqua* – that is, addressed not to things, but to cognition or knowledge of things – which, according to a shared historiographic interpretation, has characterized almost all of modern philosophy, from Descartes to Kant.²⁷ In this sense, the concept of *Besonnenheit* has been called "the historical-philosophical locus of Fichte's late philosophy".²⁸

The term *Besonnenheit*, however, traditionally belongs not to the theoretical sphere, but to the ethical one: in the German translations of Plato, it renders the Greek σωφροσύνη,²⁹ by which the ancient Greeks designated man's ability to dominate his senses, his impulses towards pleasure; by virtue of this ability, writes Antiphon, for example, man can defeat himself (νικᾶν ἡδυνήθη αὐτὸς ἑαυτόν) and thus master himself (αὐτὸς ἑαυτὸν κρατεῖν).³⁰

In the *Republic*, Plato defines σωφροσύνη as the virtue of the soul which consists in the mastery of its rational part over the irrational one (passions, appetites).³¹ Only in this sense, for Plato, can one actually affirm – without contradicting oneself or being ridiculous – that he who exercises σωφροσύνη is "master of

---

25 MR 2, p. 34.
26 See also MR 2, p. 27 (third of the four introductory lessons to the study of philosophy).
27 Cf. Janke 2000.
28 Janke 2000, pp. 1–2.
29 Cf. Schleiermacher himself.
30 Cf. Antiphon, fragment D55 (B58), Laks and Most 2016, pp. 74–75.
31 Cf. Plato, *Republic*, 430 e, Plato 1914 ff., vol. 5, p. 384.

himself [ἑαυτοῦ κρείττων]".³² The Greek term σωφροσύνη was then rendered in Latin by the word *temperantia*, which in Scholasticism indicates one of the four cardinal Christian virtues (together with "prudence", "justice", and "fortitude") – the same virtues enumerated by Plato, in the *Republic*, as necessary for the moral perfection of both the individual and the city as a whole.³³

However, in the *Charmides*, the concept of σωφροσύνη undergoes an (unresolved) attempt at *theoretical* bending. In the course of the dialogue, in fact, Critias identifies σωφροσύνη with the self-knowledge (τὸ γιγνώσκειν ἑαυτόν) prescribed in the inscription of the temple of Delphi.³⁴

In order to better determine the meaning of the Apollonian warning, and therefore of the concept of σωφροσύνη, Critias defines the latter as the only "science [ἐπιστήμη] of the other sciences [ἐπιστημῶν] and of its own self": the σωφροσύνη would consist in "knowing oneself", in the specific sense "that one should know what one knows and what one does not know".³⁵ Thus, "only the temperate person [Ὁ σοφρῶν] will know himself, and be able to discern what he really knows and does not know, and have the power of judging what other people likewise know and think they know, in cases where they do know, and again, what they think they know, without knowing it".³⁶ To know oneself would therefore be equivalent to knowing exactly what one knows and what one does not know.

Socrates, however, has serious reservations about the possibility of such a "science of science [ἐπιστήμης ἐπιστήμην]"³⁷ (i.e. of "a science which knows itself [ἐπιστήμην ἥ αὐτὴ αὐτὴν γιγνώσκει]").³⁸ As a polemic example of such a thing, he mentions the very counterintuitive idea of "a sort of vision which is not the vision of things that we see in the ordinary way, but a vision of itself and of the other sorts of vision"; or of "a sort of hearing which hears not a single sound, but hears itself and the other sorts of hearing"; or, in general, of some sense (αἴσθησις) that is "sense of the senses [αἰσθήσεων] and of itself, but insensible of any of the things of which the other senses are sensible".³⁹ But, in spite of all these perplexities, Socrates declares himself unable to peremptorily deny the possibility of such a sci-

---

32 Plato, *Republic*, 430 e, Plato 1914ff., vol. 5, pp. 384–385.
33 Cf. Plato, *Republic*, 428 b–434 d, 441 d–444 e, Plato 1914ff., vol. 5, 374–399, 426–439.
34 Plato, *Charmides*, 164 d, Plato 1914ff., vol. 8, pp. 46–47.
35 Plato, *Charmides*, 166 c–167 a, Plato 1914ff., vol. 8, p. 52–57.
36 Plato, *Charmides*, 166 e–167 a, Plato 1914ff., vol. 8, p. 54–57.
37 Cf. Plato, *Charmides*, 169 b–170 c, Plato 1914ff., vol. 8, pp. 64–69.
38 Plato, *Charmides*, 169 e, Plato 1914ff., vol. 8, pp. 66–67.
39 Plato, *Charmides*, 167 d, Plato 1914ff., vol. 8, p. 58–59.

ence; the dialogue therefore closes in an aporetic way, with the intention of continuing the discussion on what σωφροσύνη is at another time.[40]

In the German translation of this dialogue, published by Schleiermacher in 1805, the term σωφροσύνη is rendered as *Besonnenheit*, the term ἐπιστήμη as *Erkenntnis* and the term αἴσθησις as *Empfindung*. Consequently, the defining locutions that Critias refers to σωφροσύνη (i. e., in translation, to *Besonnenheit*), namely αἴσθησις αἰσθήσεων and ἐπιστήμης ἐπιστήμην, are rendered by Schleiermacher, respectively, as *Empfindung der Empfindungen* (sensation of sensations)[41] and *Erkenntnis der Erkenntnis* (cognition of cognition).[42] Moreover, the expression "science which cognizes itself [ἐπιστήμην ἥ αὐτὴ αὑτὴν γιγνώσκει]" corresponds, in Schleiermacher, to the German: *Erkenntnis, welche sich selbst erkennt* (cognition that cognizes itself).[43]

These passages of the Platonic dialogue in Schleiermacher's translation, from a terminological point of view, might have constituted a significant precedent for the theoretical-transcendental shape that the term *Besonnenheit* assumed in later Fichte, denoting, precisely, the "perception of perception [*Wahrnehmung der Wahrnehmung*]", or, more generally, the knowledge of knowledge. It should be noted, however, that, in Plato's *Charmides*, the "knowledge" expressed by the term σωφροσύνη concerns the *content* of known knowledge: σωφροσύνη would in fact be equivalent, as we have seen, to knowing "*what* one knows and *what* one does not know [italics mine]". In Fichte, on the other hand, the "knowledge" expressed by the term *absolute Besonnenheit* primarily concerns the *form* of the known "knowledge": that is, *the fact that* one knows what one knows.[44]

The determination of the unitary meaning of the term σωφροσύνη in Platonic texts is beyond the scope of this work. Here it is mainly important to note that the *Besonnenheit* of which Fichte speaks seems to have at least *two elements in common* with the σωφροσύνη mentioned by Plato, respectively, in *Charmides* and the *Republic:* the identification with a knowledge that has knowledge itself as its object, and the prerogative of making the person who has it "master of himself"

---

40 Cf. Plato, *Charmides*, 175 a–end, Plato 1914 ff., vol. 8, pp. 84–91.
41 Cf. Plato 1804 ff., I.2, p. 34.
42 Plato 1804 ff., I.2, pp. 37–38.
43 Plato 1804 ff., I.2, p. 38.
44 However, the hypothesis that σωφροσύνη consists in knowing not *what* one knows, but *that* one knows what one knows, is also considered by Socrates in the *Charmides:* see especially 170 d, Plato 1914 ff., vol. 8, pp. 68–69: "Then being temperate, or temperance [σωφροσύνη], will not be this knowledge of what one knows or does not know, but, it would seem, merely knowing that one knows or does not know."

– indeed, superior to that part of himself that is bound to the senses. The *absolute Besonnenheit* consists, in fact, in the awareness of knowing or perceiving as such; precisely for this reason, it represents a higher consciousness (*höheres Bewusstsein*) than that which is reduced to mere sensible perception, and therefore expresses, according to Fichte, a rising (*sich erheben*) of man above himself (as identified with factual or merely perceptual consciousness).[45]

5.5 Schopenhauer: The Difference between the "Understanding's Concept" and the "Thing Itself" of the "Perception of Perception". The World as the Totality of the Perceivable

Schopenhauer wrote a long and impassioned commentary on Fichte's notion of *absolute Besonnenheit*. This commentary deserves very special attention. Its relevance to the genetic process of Schopenhauer's philosophy has already been emphasized by Hübscher:[46] it is here, in fact, that Arthur spoke explicitly for the first time of two distinct consciousnesses in man, thus anticipating the theory of the "better consciousness" which he developed from 1812 onwards (cf. *infra*, 7.6 – 7.7).

Now, this note contains both features that relate to Fichte's lecture and features that belong to Schopenhauer's own theoretical reflections (although he took his cue from Fichte's words). The analysis of this note will occupy, correspondingly, the present and the next section.

> The bond which for common sense ties objects together is the concept *world*, that is to say the totality of possible objects of perception. On the other hand, in this perception alone does it [common sense] become conscious *of itself*. The *understanding's* mere concept of the perception of perception at which the esteemed hearers have for the most part stopped, gives hardly more than just that concept of *world*. The point of absolute reflectiveness, to which Fichte wants to guide them, is, as it seems to me, that of a consciousness which exists by itself, is not dependent on perception, is not given through this […]. […] Fichte quite rightly calls [the point of absolute reflectiveness] "a *perceiving* of perceiving". 'This word (underlined the first time) is used figuratively [*bildlich*], because the thing itself [*die Sache selbst*] like everything that is not taken from perception or from the world of experience, cannot have a

---

45 Cf. MR 2, p. 41 ("On the Facts of Consciousness"). Cf. also the lectures "On the Science of Knowledge", in particular MR 2, pp. 89 – 97; on p. 104 there is a mention of an "inner reflectiveness" (*innige Besonnenheit*), which consists in the consciousness of thinking or acting as such.
46 Hübscher 1989, p. 186. Cf. also p. 27. Cf. Novembre 2013.

name. Now if the hearer does not already know the thing, then I believe that he stops and, as usual, finds himself at the figure [*Bild*] or simile (or concept of the understanding).[47]

According to Schopenhauer, the "*understanding's* mere concept of the perception of perception [...] gives hardly more" compared to the "concept of *world*" typical of common sense, understood as "the totality of possible objects of perception". Schopenhauer also distinguishes between the perception of perception (the "thing itself [*die Sache selbst*]") from the "understanding's mere concept" of it. At the end of the passage, he specifies that the perception of perception can only be called "perception" "figuratively" (*bildlich*), and equates such a "figure" with the intellectual concept: "the figure [*Bild*] (or [...] concept of the understanding)". The *perception* of perception is "perception" not *formaliter*, but *metaphorice*. The figurative use concerns the first occurrence of the term "perception" (*perception* of perception), not the second, since the "perception" that is perceived is common, empirical perception.

Now, through this distinction between the "thing itself" of the "perception of perception" and its figure "or" its intellectual concept Schopenhauer limits the effectiveness of the lecture: the hearer, if he does not already know the "thing itself" of the perception of perception, cannot but remain stuck on its figure (i.e. its concept). Schopenhauer is evidently implying that he already knows for himself "the thing itself" of the perception of perception. But Fichte himself had clearly stated in his lecture that man must arrive at the viewpoint of the "consciousness of knowledge" *by himself* (this cannot be given to him "from outside", like "a dig in the ribs"[48]).

It is interesting that Schopenhauer, on the one hand, admits the "understanding's [...] concept of the perception of perception", and on the other hand states that the "thing itself" of the perception of perception "is not taken [...] from the world of experience". According to the theory of concepts enunciated in the note to Fichte's first introductory lecture (cf. *supra*, 4.3), "from what is seen the categories form concepts".[49] But the concept of "perception of perception" cannot be drawn "from what is seen", because "the thing itself" "is not taken from the world of experience". The possibility of such a concept, which, if it cannot be empirical, is not even a pure concept (category) in the Kantian sense, is therefore problematic.

This point can be clarified in relation to Schopenhauer's equating the *figure* with the *concept* of the perception of perception. The figure (*Bild*) of the perception

---

47 MR 2, pp. 32–33.
48 MR 2, p. 28.
49 MR 2, p. 21.

of perception consists in the fact that the name of something that belongs to experience (the *"perception* [italics mine] of perception") is used figuratively (*bildlich*), to designate something "that is not taken from experience" (the "thing itself" of the perception of perception). It is evidently this *reference to experience* that acts as a link between the figure and the concept (which is constructed precisely from "what is seen") and thus allows Schopenhauer to identify the two terms, as well as to speak, in general, of the "understanding's concept" of the perception of perception. But, if this is so, there can only be an intellectual concept of the perception of perception insofar as, to designate it, one makes figurative use of an element coming from experience (perception): that is to say, there can only be a "concept" of the latter. Consequently, stopping at the figure or the intellectual concept of the perception of perception means exclusively understanding this figurative reference to empirics (in relation to the first occurrence), without grasping that which, despite being denoted by the name of an empirical reality, is not empirical at all. The general problem involved here, concerning the possibility of a concept (*Begriff*) of something metempirical, would be one of the main themes of Schopenhauer's further reflections (cf. *infra*, 5.5 – 5.6).

A second interesting point concerns the definition of the world as "the totality of possible objects of perception", which implies that there is nothing in the world that cannot be perceived. Such a definition of the world (which Schopenhauer attributes to common sense) presupposes that perception is the "bond [...] which ties objects together". In other words, it presupposes what for Fichte can be grasped not from the common point of view, but from the point of view of absolute consciousness. For this reason, for Schopenhauer, the Fichtean concept of "perception of perception" "gives hardly more than just the concept of *world*".

However, the perception that is implied by this concept of the world is *possible* perception (the *possibility* of being perceived: "possible objects of perception"). In contrast, when speaking of the perception that must be perceived, Fichte clearly means *actual* perception, i.e. the *fact*, not the mere possibility of being perceived.[50]

---

[50] Talking about something that can be perceived but is not, indeed, would not have the character of "evidence" (one might say: of immanence to consciousness) that Fichte holds dear, and would "overstep the limit of our investigation", because it "is concerned merely with perception" (not with "opinion about perception"). The perception which Fichte speaks of must be *perceived* in actuality, and only a real (actual) object can be perceived in actuality, certainly not a merely possible object (this also applies in the case where, as in Fichte's discourse, the object of perception is perception itself, or, more precisely, perception as such). Fichte also states that one must consider "the whole of perception as a *factum*, which we *again* [italics mine] perceive" (cf. *supra*, 5.2 – 5.3). If and insofar as one perceives in actuality, one can perceive perception. The *reality* of perception, as opposed to its bare *possibility*, is thus perhaps that something "more" that, according to Schopen-

In any case, Schopenhauer's definition of the world is consistent with the identity (which he explicitly posits in this period) between "being" and "being able to be cognized" (cf. *infra*, 6.5) and presupposes a profession of transcendental idealism that is not further specified.

5.6 *Absolute Besonnenheit* as Metempirical Consciousness

We now come to the main point, which is also the clearest: Schopenhauer's understanding of *absolute Besonnenheit*.

> The point of absolute reflectiveness, to which Fichte wants to guide them, is, as it seems to me, that of a consciousness which exists by itself, is not dependent on perception, is not given through this [...], and from which there arises *philosophical astonishment* [*das* Philosophische Befremden] at the world, in other words at that second consciousness in perception (which for common sense is the only one). This astonishment makes the philosopher and the philosopher is a man who endeavours to unite those two quite different consciousnesses. Failure has induced some to deny the consciousness that is not given through perception; they are called realists and materialists. Others went so far as to deny the consciousness that is given in perception; these are idealists. According as a man with some philosophical talent inclines more to the realists or the idealists, he asks: "how does there run into my consciousness through perception that which is not in perception?" or "how do I arrive at the consciousness of perception?"[51]

Schopenhauer shared with Fichte both the designation as "a *perceiving* of perceiving" ("[...] the point of absolute reflectiveness, which of course *Fichte* quite rightly calls 'a *perceiving* of perceiving'"), and the inability of common sense to achieve such a point of view (the "consciousness in perception [...] for common sense is the only one"). It is worth noting that, in this respect, Schopenhauer admits the "*perceiving* of perceiving"; however, shortly afterwards, with critical reference to Fichte and Schelling, he begins to radically question the possibility of the subject's self-cognition as well as the possibility of cognition of cognition (cf. *infra*, 6.7; 7.13; 9.4).[52]

For Schopenhauer, *absolute Besonnenheit* is a consciousness outside or extraneous to the realm of perception (that is, to the empirical or sensible world) and opposed to the "consciousness in perception". He thus seems to attribute to *absolute Besonnenheit* a quality of 'transcendence' that is absent from Fichte's dis-

---

hauer, the Fichtean concept of perception gives compared to the concept of "world" as "the totality of possible objects of perception". This point, however, is not made explicit in the note.
51 MR 2, pp. 32–33.
52 Schopenhauer 2012 [1813], § 42, p. 182; Schopenhauer 2012 [1847], § 41, p. 201.

course. Consequently, and more importantly, Schopenhauer assumes that, within the same human individual, there is fundamental *duplicity* between a consciousness "given" and a consciousness *not* "given" in or through perception.

According to Plato and Aristotle, philosophy arises from wonder (τὸ θαυμάζειν) at the things of the world.[53] Schopenhauer writes that the properly philosophical *Befremden* about the world arises from the point of view of absolute reflectiveness;[54] so he agrees with Fichte also on a third point, which is probably the most important: *absolute Besonnenheit* constitutes the *peculiar point of view of philosophy.*[55]

Now, a philosopher is one who looks at the world from the point of view of absolute reflectiveness, is "astonished" by it and "endeavours [*strebt*] to unite [*vereinigen*]" the two consciousnesses. It seems, then, that *uniting the two consciousnesses*, being the object of the philosopher's effort, is *the purpose of philosophy.* In any case, for Schopenhauer, realism and materialism, on the one hand, and idealism, on the other, are the opposite and specular outcomes of the failed attempt to unite the two consciousnesses.

Schopenhauer then addresses the questions posed, respectively, by those who tend more towards realism or idealism: "how does there run into my consciousness through perception that which is not in perception?" or "how do I arrive at the consciousness of perception?" Note that Schopenhauer does not write: the questions posed by "the realist" and "the idealist". And indeed, the difference between these two pairs of terms emerges from the text itself. Those who ask these two questions, in fact, problematize the relationship between the two consciousnesses – beyond the specificity of each question – and therefore admit both consciousnesses; the realist and the idealist, instead, *deny* one of the two ("Failure [to unite those two consciousnesses] has induced some to deny", etc.).

Incidentally: given that the philosopher is one who strives to unite the two consciousnesses, and given that the realist and the idealist, by denying one of the two consciousnesses, cannot undertake such an endeavor, the necessary consequence – which Schopenhauer does not seem to draw – would be that the realist and the idealist are not philosophers. In any case, the one who "inclines more to the realists" is not yet a realist, and the one who "inclines more to the idealists" is not yet an idealist. Asking these questions, however, means having already reached *absolute Besonnenheit.*

---

53 Cf. Plato, *Theaetetus*, 155 d, Plato 1914 ff., vol. 12, pp. 54–55; Aristotle, *Metaphysics*, Aristotle 1926 ff., vol. 17, A 2, 982 b 10–13, pp. 12–13.
54 For a discussion of this point in relation to Schopenhauer's mature philosophy, cf. Giametta 2012, pp. 88–91; Giametta 2013, pp. 26–28.
55 Schopenhauer 2012 [1813], § 42, p. 182.

Certainly, the *difference* between the two questions consists in the fact that one who tends more towards realism asserts the consciousness given through perception, problematizing the other consciousness, not given in perception; one who tends more towards idealism, instead, asserts the second consciousness, problematizing the first. According to Schopenhauer, the tendency or inclination (*hinneigen*) towards realism or idealism, which the difference between the two questions depends on, is due to the personal "philosophical talent [*philosophische Anlage*]" of the questioner. This statement seems to recall the famous Fichtean motif of the choice between "idealism" and "dogmatism" (or realism), which, also according to Fichte, depends on the person's inclination (*Neigung*) and interest (*Interesse*).[56] The *identity* between the two questions, instead, lies in the fact that each of them is asked from the point of view of *absolute Besonnenheit* and only asserts one of the two consciousnesses, problematizing the other.

Schopenhauer does not explain the difference between *leaning* towards realists or idealists (asking those questions) and actually *being* a realist or idealist. However, considering that the two questions both admit consciousnesses, and that realism and idealism originate from the failure to unite the two consciousnesses and from the consequent negation of one of them, we can hypothesize the following. One who is predisposed to realism and achieves the point of view of *absolute Besonnenheit* becomes a realist when, having failed to solve the problem ("how does there run into my consciousness [given] through perception that which is not in perception?") one ends up denying the term of the problem (consciousness not given in perception). Similarly (but in reverse), one who is predisposed to idealism and reaches the point of view of *absolute Besonnenheit* becomes an idealist when, not finding a solution to the problem, ("how do I arrive at the consciousness of perception?"), and thus equally failing to unite the two consciousnesses, one ends up denying the term of the problem (the consciousness given in perception).

Interpreting the text in this way, however, means identifying the effort to unite the two consciousnesses, whose failure gives rise to realism and idealism, with the search for the answer to those questions: in other words, it means understanding this effort as purely theoretical. It would essentially amount to an attempt to justify the possibility of the relationship between "those two quite different consciousnesses". Schopenhauer does not clarify the key point here: *whether the effort to unite the two consciousnesses, which is proper to the philosopher, is of a theoretical or practical (moral) nature, or both theoretical and practical.* The nature of this unification, and thus of this effort, is left unexplained.

---

56 Cf. Fichte 1994, p. 18. Cf. also Schelling 1980, pp. 156–158 (Sixth Letter).

It is clear, however, that Schopenhauer admits the existence in man of "a consciousness which exists by itself, is not dependent on perception, is not given through it". As such, it is necessarily situated in – it is *consciousness of* – a world other than that of perceptions (i.e., of experience). Recall that, in his commentary on the first lecture "On the Study of Philosophy", Schopenhauer stated that the genius is aware of *both* the world of experience *and* that which transcends all experience ("he dwells less in the world of experience and is less at home in this", by "*simultaneously* [italics mine] cognizing things-in-themselves [*indem es zugleich die Dinge an sich erkennt*]").[57] On the other hand, unlike the genius, the *madman* intuits things-in-themselves but cognizes the world of experience only in an altered way, because he lacks the "soundness of conditions for the world of experience" ("for him the laws of experience are abolished": cf. *supra*, 3.2).[58]

The theorization of this cognitive dualism, namely, of a duplicity of consciousness that is only found in superior individuals ("consciousness in perception [...] for common sense is the only one"), was to engage young Schopenhauer's reflections intensely between 1812 and 1814, constituting his first attempt at developing a system.

5.7 The Contradictory Nature of Naive Realism

Concerning the point where Fichte notes the inconsistency of the common view, according to which the perception of the thing is both identical and not identical with the thing perceived (cf. *supra*, 5.3), Schopenhauer writes:

> There is, however, still the question whether common sense yet conceives the object as something separate from man's feeling [*Gefühl*] of the object; and perhaps this applies only to sight, hearing and smell. If the rough and uncultured man perceives objects through these, then he assumes the object as something still existing outside this perception. But if he feels [*fühlt*] the object, then he no longer separates his feeling from the object; what he has in his hands is the object, and he has of it just as much perception as he has of his own body. Yet he naturally assumes the object as something that *is*, granting also that he did not feel it; but he also assumes his body as something that *is*, although he will no longer feel [*fühlen*] it.[59]

In this rather non-linear passage, Schopenhauer probably means to say that, for the senses of sight, hearing and smell, which perceive at a distance, the *distinction*

---

57 MR 2, p. 19. Translation modified.
58 MR 2, p. 19.
59 MR 2, p. 19, pp. 33–34.

between the perception of the object and the perceived object already arises in the actuality of perception, whereas in the case of touch, which perceives only through direct contact, this distinction only arises in the absence of perception itself. All this, however, only concerns the common point of view: the perceiver, in the text, is the "rough and uncultured man" (*der rohe Mensch*). Schopenhauer thus seems to share Fichte's view that common sense – whether in the case of sight, hearing and smell, or touch – contradictorily distinguishes the perception of the object from the perceived object.[60]

In the second volume of *The World as Will and Representation*, the contradictory nature of realist dualism is described by Schopenhauer in terms very similar to Fichte's: the two worlds distinguished by realism (the "represented" one and the supposedly "objective" one) are in reality perfectly identical: that is, they are identical – insofar as the second "resemble[s] the first down to the smallest hair" – and non-identical, insofar as for realism the objective world would exist, as we know it, even independently of its being cognized.[61] For Schopenhauer, too, this contradiction between identity and non-identity is a sufficient reason to reject the realistic dualism of common sense.

But if "that absolutely *objective* world" of which realism speaks "is none other than the second, the *subjectively* cognized world, the world of representation [last italics mine]",[62] then "representation and object are the same thing".[63] Against naive realism one must therefore say: "The world is my representation" – a principle that, according to the famous opening of Schopenhauer's masterpiece, expresses "*philosophische Besonnenheit*".[64]

---

60 According to Schopenhauer, one's own body (*Körper*), like the objects (*Gegenstände*) of perception, is also understood by the common man as something that is, even if it is not 'felt'. It is not clear whether Schopenhauer is referring to sleep or death when he speaks of the body no longer being felt; it is more likely that he is referring to latter, given his use of the future tense and the adverb "no longer", which together give a sense of finality ("he will *no longer* [italics mine] feel it"). With regard to this parallelism between *Körper* and *Gegenstand*, the analogy between human body and object – however, respectively, in the more specific terms of *Leib* ("lived-body") and *Objekt* ("object", as specifically opposed to a knowing subject) – will be of decisive importance in Schopenhauer's mature philosophy (cf. *infra*, 12.2).
61 Schopenhauer 2018, II 11–12, chap. 1, pp. 12–13.
62 Schopenhauer 2018, II 11–12, chap. 1, p. 13.
63 Schopenhauer 2010b, I 17, § 5, p. 35.
64 Schopenhauer 2010b, I 3, § 1, p. 23.

5.8 In Perspective: The *philosophische Besonnenheit* in *The World as Will and Representation*

In *The World as Will and Representation*, the term *Besonnenheit* takes on a very similar value to that found in Fichte's discourse – although it is transfigured by the different theoretical context in which it is used. The incipit of Schopenhauer's masterpiece is very famous:

> 'The world is my representation' [*Die Welt ist meine Vorstellung*]: – this holds true for every living, cognitive being, although only a human being can bring it to abstract, reflective consciousness: and if he actually does so philosophical reflection [*die philosophische Besonnenheit*] has begun [*eingetreten*] in him. It immediately becomes clear and certain to him that he is not acquainted with either the sun or the earth, but rather only with an eye that sees a sun, with a hand that feels an earth, and that the surrounding world exists only as representation, that is, exclusively in relation to something else, the representing being that he himself is [...]. Thus, no truth is more certain, no truth is more independent of all others and no truth is less in need of proof than this one: that everything there is for cognition (i.e. the whole world) is only an object in relation to a subject, an intuition of a beholder, is, in a word, representation.[65]

Here Schopenhauer calls *philosophische Besonnenheit* the point of view from which "everything" of the "world" is grasped as "representation". More precisely, the *philosophical Besonnenheit* consists in "immediately" or intuitively knowing the represented (perceived) *as represented* (perceived) and hence, by generalization (i.e., through abstraction of reason), the representation in its totality *as such*; it is therefore, ultimately, the awareness that "*everything* [italics mine] there is for cognition (the whole world) is *only* [italics mine] an object in relation to a subject, an intuition of a beholder, is, in a word, representation". This philosophical *Besonnenheit* thus involves a first intuitive moment and a second abstract one.

The text evidently presupposes that those who are deprived of this peculiarly philosophical consciousness take *represented* things to be *things-in-themselves* (external and independent of their being represented). In other words, those who do not rise to the point of view of philosophy mistake representation as a whole for non-representation, i.e., for reality in itself. The difference between these two terms is necessarily implied by the word "only [*nur*]", which indicates the *defective* nature of representation (as such) – where the 'defect' or 'flaw' consists precisely in *not being* the thing-in-itself.

---

[65] Schopenhauer 2010b, I 3, § 1, pp. 23–24. Slightly modified translation.

According to Schopenhauer, this very general concept of "representation" unifies *all* the objects of the world ("sun", "earth") and thereby unambiguously characterizes the world as such and as a whole. The principle "The world is my representation" expresses precisely this unification and is the fundamental premise of Schopenhauer's entire discourse – so much so that it is used as the incipit of his major work.

Through these considerations, Schopenhauer intends to refer to the fundamental turning point of modern philosophy, inaugurated by Descartes and taken to its extreme consequences by Kant.

> This truth ["the world is my representation"] is not at all new. It was already present in the sceptical considerations that served as Descartes' point of departure. Berkeley however was the first to express it definitely.[66]

For Schopenhauer, the principle "The world is my representation" has been valid not only since Descartes or Berkeley, but always and universally; in terms of its evidence, it can even be compared to a Euclidean axiom.[67] "Thus, no truth is more certain, no truth is more independent of all others and no truth is less in need of proof than this one".[68] The prominent role played by Descartes and Berkeley only concerns Western (European) philosophy: this truth was the "fundamental tenet" of Indian philosophy a few millennia before.[69]

We have seen that Fichte's *absolute Besonnenheit* is the consciousness of "knowledge" *as such*, that is, of the so-called 'things' as primarily and essentially something known or perceived. In two other transcriptions of the same course, this same awareness is called precisely *philosophische Besonnenheit*.[70]

Now, although he does not explicitly mention "perception", Schopenhauer exemplifies the fact that things are "representation" by stating that we do not really know objects, but *sensations of objects:* we are "not acquainted with either the sun or the earth, but rather only with an eye that sees [*sieht*] a sun, with a hand that feels [*fühlt*] an earth". But the sensory "apprehension [*Apprehension*]" of external objects is nothing other than "perception [*Wahrnehmung*]".[71]

---

[66] Schopenhauer 2010b, I 4, § 1, p. 24. On Kant's contribution, cf. Schopenhauer 2010b, I 8–10., § 3, pp. 27–28.
[67] Schopenhauer 2018, II 4, chap. 1, p. 6.
[68] Schopenhauer 2010b, I 3, § 1, p. 23.
[69] Schopenhauer 2010b, I 4, p. 24.
[70] Cf. Fichte 1962ff., vol. IV, 4, pp. 88 and 133.
[71] Schopenhauer 2010a, § 1, p. 48.

5.8 The *philosophische Besonnenheit* in *The World as Will and Representation* — 129

For Fichte, whoever attains the point of view of *absolute Besonnenheit* passes from the consciousness of the perceived (seen, touched) stove to the consciousness of (one's own) perceiving – seeing, touching – the stove, and then extends this consciousness to all perceived things, so as to include in it the "whole world of perceptions", the "whole world of experience" (cf. *supra*, 5.2).[72] In the same way, for Schopenhauer, one who achieves *philosophische Besonnenheit* shifts from the consciousness of the sun and the earth to the consciousness of (one's own) feeling or perceiving them – through one's eye and hand respectively – that is, to the consciousness of (one's own) *representing* them, and then extends this same consciousness to "[e]verything that can or does belong in any way to the world", thus to the world itself in its entirety.[73]

The very first conceptual and terminological precedent for this passage can be found in a critical note to Schelling's *Ideas for a Philosophy of Nature*, from 1811–1812. Here Schopenhauer identifies philosophical reflection (*das philosophische Besinnen*) with the knowledge that the "being [*Seyn*]" of the so-called "external things" "is nothing but a being-represented [*Vorgestelltwerden*]": against the common understanding (*der gemeine Verstand*), philosophy refutes the distinction between these two moments and, with it, any assertion about the "reality [*Realität*] of external things".[74] But this "reality" of empirical objects that, according to young Schopenhauer, is denied by philosophy, is to be clearly equated with what Kant calls "transcendental": a reality that is absolutely external to and independent of all possible (human) knowledge. It is certainly not the negation of the "empirical reality" of things that Schopenhauer intends to attribute to philosophy here.

In any case, both for mature Schopenhauer and for Fichte, the acquisition of this uncommon consciousness – respectively of the world of experience as something perceived or represented – is indispensable and, indeed, strictly *propaedeutic* for philosophical investigation proper (it is not by chance – I repeat – that this is the opening line of Schopenhauer's masterpiece). It should also be noted that the verbs of perception mentioned by Schopenhauer in relation to the sun and the earth are exactly the same as the ones Fichte, in his example, refers to the stove: *sehen* ("to see") and *fühlen* ("to feel" in the sense of "touch").[75]

In sum, just as the determination of "*Wahrnehmung*" (or, in a broader sense, "*Wissen*") for Fichte, so too the determination of "*Vorstellung*" for Schopenhauer

---

72 MR 2, p. 32.
73 Schopenhauer 2010b, I 3, § 1, p. 24.
74 MR 2, p. 356.
75 Cf. MR 2, p. 32: "If I see [*sehe*] a stove, feel [*fühle*] it and soon, I am conscious of the stove, my knowledge is absorbed in it. But if I arrive at the higher consciousness of my perception of the stove, then my knowledge is absorbed in this [higher consciousness]".

constitutes, within the world of experience, the *identity of the different*, that is, what all things in the world have and will always have in common, however different and opposite they may be. The *Besonnenheit* is thus peculiarly "philosophical" because, by thematizing and determining this identity of the different, it allows for the consideration of the totality of things – a consideration that has always been a feature of philosophy.[76]

It should be noted that the consciousness of the world as representation, which Schopenhauer admits, does not contradict the *impossibility* of cognizing cognition, which he himself affirms.[77] In fact, unlike Fichte, Schopenhauer excludes the possibility of cognizing *cognition as cognition*, that is, cognizing *cognition in actuality:* this is a necessarily contradictory supposition, because then the cognition being cognized would be, at the same time, in actuality (as cognizing) and not in actuality (as cognized; cf. *infra*, 9.3 – 9.5). The *philosophische Besonnenheit* consists instead in the consciousness of *the cognized as cognized*, or of the represented as (precisely) represented; which does not produce the above contradiction.

This theoretical or gnoseological value of the term *Besonnenheit* would recur in several other places in Schopenhauer's work.[78] It would also acquire a specific value in the ethics and aesthetics of his mature system, but always starting from the gnoseological meaning explained above.

In the first two books of *The World as Will and Representation*, *Besonnenheit* is defined as the ability, derived from reason (the faculty of abstract concepts), to survey the future and the past, i. e. to raise one's consciousness to a broader perspective than that comprised of immediate circumstances alone and to achieve "the panoramic view of life as a whole".[79] In this sense, *Besonnenheit* is the individual's capacity to focus on, and thus go beyond, his immediate or 'present' (in a specifically temporal sense) consciousness. This *cognitive* act gives man "the ability to act in a premeditated manner, abstracted from the present" (something of which animals are not capable) – an ability that is described precisely as acting with *Besonnenheit*.[80] Here the English translator renders *Besonnenheit* no longer as "reflection" (as he does at the beginning of the work) but as "circumspection" and

---

76 Cf. Plato, *Republic*, 533 b, Plato 1914ff., vol. 6, pp. 172–173.
77 Schopenhauer 2012 [1813], § 42, p. 182; Schopenhauer 2012 [1847], § 41, p. 201.
78 Cf. e.g. *Parerga and Paralipomena* I, pp. 7–8, where Schopenhauer writes that "the problem of the ideal and the real, i.e. the question what in our cognition is objective and what subjective" – became "the characteristic theme of *modern* philosophy, after the necessary reflectiveness [*Besonnenheit*] had first been awakened in Descartes": "Closely considered, his famous proposition [*cogito ergo sum*] is the equivalent of that from which I started, namely: 'The world is my representation'".
79 Schopenhauer 2010b, I 121, § 18, p. 111.
80 Schopenhauer 2010b, I 180, § 27, p. 176.

"soundness of mind".⁸¹ This difference corresponds perfectly to the shift in meaning of the term from the theoretical, or gnoseological, to the practical sphere. The German term thus recovers the ancient connotation of σωφροσύνη (*temperantia*), indicating man's capacity to disregard his instinct and direct his actions even *in contrast to it* (and according to reason).⁸²

But even in the aesthetic sphere, in relation to which Schopenhauer explicitly refers to Jean Paul's terminology, the term *Besonnenheit* retains a certain Fichtean connotation. For Schopenhauer, the *Besonnenheit* of the genius is the capacity to retain cognition of the Platonic Idea long enough to reproduce or represent it through objects of the sensible world (cf. *supra*, 3.4).⁸³ This presupposes that the consciousness of the genius is not reduced to the immediate (intuitive) cognition of the Idea, but *exceeds* it enough for the realization of the poietic activity. Here too, therefore, *Besonnenheit* denotes a degree of awareness that exceeds, by distancing and focusing it, the immediate (immediately cognizing) consciousness.

Finally, in the fourth book of *The World*, Schopenhauer states that the *Besonnenheit* – as the ability to rise to the view of life in its entirety – makes human freedom possible (cf. *infra*, 8.9).⁸⁴

In the early manuscripts, the *Besonnenheit* of the genius is expressly identified with the consciousness of the world as representation. Referring to Goethe's *Lied Willkommen und Abschied* (Welcome and Farewell, the first lines of which read "When on my mount my heart did throb apace"), Schopenhauer notes:

> Here willing is satisfied; it is joy and happy love, and yet this does not fill his fine broad mind [*seinen weiten schönen Geist*] so that he still did not view profoundly with the greatest energy of cognition [*Erkenntnis*] the world as representation, the evening landscape around him. This is the reflectiveness [*Besonnenheit*] of genius.⁸⁵

---

81 Schopenhauer 2010b, I 43, § 8, p. 59; 180, § 27, p. 156.
82 See also Schopenhauer 2018, II 64–65, chap. 5, pp. 66–67. Here *Besonnenheit* is rendered as "deliberation".
83 Cf. Schopenhauer 2010b, I 219, § 36, p. 209; I 229, § 37, p. 218.
84 Cf. Schopenhauer 2010b, I 478, § 70, p. 431 ("The possibility of a freedom that expresses itself in this way is the greatest advantage of being human, and one that animals will always lack because it requires a careful and deliberate reason [*Besonnenheit der Vernunft*] that can survey the whole of life, abstracted from any present impression").
85 The German reads: "*Es schlug mein Herz, geschwind zu Pferde*". MR 1, fn. to n. 266, p. 179. Translation modified.

This close relationship between the gnoseological and aesthetic connotations of the term *Besonnenheit* is described at great length in the second volume of *The World*.[86]

5.9 Conclusion

Of the 119 comments that Schopenhauer made on Fichte's lectures, only three express agreement.[87] Two of them have been analyzed in this chapter (cf. *supra*, 5.2, 5.5 and 5.6); the third will be mentioned later (cf. *infra*, 7.7). Schopenhauer's notes otherwise denote a strong and radical dissent. Within the whole of Fichte's discourse, Schopenhauer only accepts the statement concerning *the existence of a superior point of view to the common one;* indeed, it is this section of the lectures – involving the meaning of the term *Besonnenheit* – that produced the richest developments in Schopenhauer's later reflections.

At this point it is necessary to determine the theoretical reasons that led young Schopenhauer to distance himself not only from Fichte, but also from another great philosophical personality of the time: Schelling.

---

[86] Cf. Schopenhauer 2018, II 436–438, chap. 31, pp. 398–400.
[87] Cf. MR 2, pp. 28, 32–33, 80 (HN II, pp. 26, 30, 74).

6 The "Transcendent Use of the Understanding": The Illegitimacy of Fichte's and Schelling's Philosophies from the Perspective of Kantian Criticism

6.1 Introduction

We have seen that young Schopenhauer understood the Kantian critical dualism of appearance and thing-in-itself as an ontological dualism, thus determining the sensible world (in space and time) as nothingness (*Nichtigkeit*), or existing in only a relative sense, and the supersensible world as truly being or true "reality" (cf. *supra*, 3.9). This, however, does not mean that Schopenhauer simply wanted to recover or re-propose a pre-Kantian metaphysics; rather, he sought a *new* (post-Kantian) *metaphysics*, which, while taking into account the momentous achievements of criticism, would complement and correct its oppressive negative one-sidedness.

According to Schulze, Fichte and Schelling had claimed to build such a metaphysics themselves, and it was probably this expectation that led young Arthur to move to Berlin, "in the hope of finding in Fichte a true philosopher and a great mind".[1] His enthusiasm and hope, however, were short-lived: this *"a priori* veneration soon turned", *a posteriori* (after his actual acquaintance with Fichte), "into contempt and scorn".[2]

Against Kant and Schulze, Schopenhauer openly admitted the possibility and, indeed, the reality of human knowledge of the supersensible. At this point, however, he was faced with the crucial question of how the expression of such knowledge, namely *philosophy*, should be terminologically configured. This problem emerged for the first time in fragment 15 of the manuscripts, in particular in relation to the "Ideas" whose object or content is supersensible reality.[3] In fact, since we "can convey to one another only sense objects or expressions for these and for their relations", knowledge of those Ideas can only be expressed through terms belonging to the sensible world.[4] All attempts that man makes to achieve this expres-

---

1 Schopenhauer 1978a, p. 261.
2 Schopenhauer 1978a, p. 261.
3 MR 1, n. 15, p. 11.
4 MR 1, n. 15, p. 11. Translation modified.

sion – i.e. "philosophy, poetry and the arts" – are therefore "necessarily imperfect" (cf. *supra*, 2.5).[5]

In the commentary on Fichte's first lecture "On the Study of Philosophy", the same problem is related to Kant's concept of the "thing-in-itself": the genius, who is capable of the "intuition [*Anschauung*] of the things-in-themselves", "is able to express what he knows about all experience in concepts, pictures and works of art, and these again have objects of experience as their material" (cf. *supra*, 3.2).[6]

Between the end of 1811 and the beginning of 1812, in further notes to Fichte and Schelling, the terms of the question – originally dependent, perhaps, on Wackenroder's text *Of Two Wonderful Languages and Their Mysterious Power* – took on a more technical and rigorous theoretical connotation, linking themselves to Kant's interdiction of the "transcendent use of the understanding". Kant had in fact declared that it is epistemologically illegitimate to use the categories of the understanding – and, in general, empirical or phenomenal determinations – to denote or describe what is beyond all possible experience. Schulze, in his lectures, had dealt at length with this subject,[7] noting that Kant himself seemed to have violated his own principle by determining the thing-in-itself as the "cause" of sensations.[8]

Now, a *new* metaphysics (such as the one young Schopenhauer was looking for), insofar as it intends to be legitimate from the point of view of criticism, inevitably undertakes to respect that fundamental Kantian interdiction. In the following pages, it will be shown that, precisely in relation to this specific expectation, Schopenhauer saw the great hopes he had placed in Fichte and Schelling as profoundly and irrevocably dashed.

This crucial disappointment, however, would have the *positive* effect of inducing Schopenhauer to finally embark on the solitary and grand undertaking of constructing a new, ultimate metaphysics (fraudulently promised, in his opinion, by Fichte and Schelling). It was precisely from this fundamental ambition that, in 1812 (immediately after attending Fichte's courses), Schopenhauer started the long and articulated speculative process that would lead, six years later, to *The World as Will and Representation*.

---

[5] MR 1, n. 15, p. 11.
[6] MR 2, p. 19. Translation modified.
[7] Cf. D'Alfonso 2008, p. 93.
[8] Cf. D'Alfonso 2008, p. 76.

6.2 "Cause" vs. "Supersensible Ground". The Scope of the Sciences and the Meaning of the Question "Why"

A particularly emblematic passage – perhaps, in chronological order, even the first – in which Schopenhauer accuses Fichte of making transcendent use of the categories can be found in his Berlin course notes. In the first lecture "On the Study of Philosophy", Fichte classifies all possible knowledge (*Wissen*) into forms of either "historical knowledge" – i.e., recording of perceptions – or of "scientific knowledge" (*supra*, 3.2).[9] The latter indicates firstly the reason or ground (*Grund*) of a certain class of perceptions; secondly, it deduces from it the "law" concerning "all possible perceptions" of that type, in such a way that they can be determined or established "*a priori*".[10] "Therefore science rises [...] above the individual perception" and deals with its "reason or ground", which is "something quite separate from that, something higher and supernatural".[11]

The question of the supersensible reason properly asks the "why or wherefore [*Warum*]" of things, whereas experience attests to or contains only their "that" (*daß*), i.e. their factual being; consequently, the concept of ground is not "abstracted" from perception, it does not come from it.[12] People see that some bodies fall, while others are "at rest", but this does not lead them to ask the question "why?": experience only contains the fact *that* some bodies fall, *that* others are at rest.[13]

Questions such as "Where is gravity in bodies?" or "Where is the soul in man?" are fallacious: if the ground of perceptions were somewhere in space, it would be something perceptible, and thus would not be the ground of perception, but only a further perception, which would in turn need to be grounded.[14] "The law of gravity is something supernatural, spiritual, directly divine, although the lowest of its kind [*das niedrigste der Art*]": "Every force [*Kraft*] is just the same".[15] Every natural force is thus the lowest degree of the manifestation of the supersensible.

Fichte exemplifies the group of *perceptions of the same type* as the phenomenon of falling bodies, their *supersensible ground* as gravity and the *law* that follows from it as the law of gravitation.[16] Schopenhauer makes a long dissenting comment.

---

9 MR 2, p. 17.
10 MR 2, p. 20.
11 MR 2, p. 20.
12 MR 2, p. 20.
13 MR 2, p. 20.
14 MR 2, p. 22.
15 MR 2, p. 22.
16 MR 2, pp. 20–21.

> In accordance with Kant I explain our asking about the *cause* [*Ursache*]. Thus it certainly springs from perception, for this is assuredly not the mere *work of the senses*, as Fichte seems to think. [...] causality is the great bond [*Band*] which holds together the scattered cognition of experience and gives this some unity [...] and if the establishment of the *reason or ground*, that is to say of the *causal connexion*, makes every piece of *knowledge scientific*, then I ask what scullery-maid is without scientific knowledge; indeed to my dog I cannot deny this. [...] The supernatural reason or ground [*Der übersinnliche Grund*] of the fall remains unknown; but from all perceived falling the understanding abstracts for itself the law of gravitation which is certainly not the cognized supernatural reason of falling, but only the universally perceived and cognized phenomenon [*Phänomen*], and which for experience takes the place of the reason or ground. The same holds good of all forces; but perceiving and uniting them into concepts does not raise us above the world of perceptions, and so not even the study of the branches of ordinary science does this.[17]

I have already analyzed the passages in this note concerning the formation of empirical concepts (*Begriffe*) (cf. *supra*, 4.3). In this section I will examine how Schopenhauer tries to determine the difference between "cause" and "supernatural ground".

Schopenhauer begins by mentioning the question of the cause (*Ursache*); but Fichte had spoken of the question of the supersensible reason or ground (*Grund*) of phenomena. Schopenhauer would therefore seem to identify the latter with the cause; and indeed, a little further on, he writes: "the establishment of the *reason or ground*, that is to say [*das heißt*] of the *causal connexion*". At the same time, however, he speaks of a supersensible ground that is different from the cause: "the supernatural reason or ground of the fall remains unknown", even if its cause has been determined. The difference between them, though, remains undefined, as does the question answered by the supersensible ground: it cannot be the question "why?", which concerns the cause.

All this does not mean that Schopenhauer contradicts himself. The supersensible ground that he *identifies* with the cause is the one of which (in his opinion) Fichte spoke improperly; the supersensible ground that he *distinguishes* from the cause is instead the real one. In other words, Schopenhauer believed that the supersensible ground mentioned by Fichte was actually the cause of perceptions (i.e. a *non*-supersensible ground), insofar as Fichte's description of it (as the answer to the question "why"), as well as the example he chose (the law of gravitation), pertain to causality.

Now, causality, according to Kant, is a determination of appearance alone; the implication of Schopenhauer's note, then, is that *the question "why" concerns only*

---

17 MR 2, pp. 21–22. Translation modified.

the world of appearances. This point becomes explicit in a further commentary on Fichte's lecture:

> *Ego.* (I think that the question *Why* does not aim at the supernatural reason or ground, but at the connexion of one appearance [*Erscheinung*] with other appearances. But if through this question I try to find the *supernatural* reason or ground, then in a wrong-headed way (as Kant has shown) I am simply making a *transcendent use of the understanding*.)[18]

Insofar as the question "why" is exclusively concerned with the connection between appearances, the sciences, which investigate the world essentially through that question, do not at all "raise us above the world of perceptions".

Schopenhauer states that Fichte's definition of the supersensible ground is, from the point of view of criticism, necessarily illegitimate, because it presupposes the use of a category (causality) to determine what, being supersensible, does not and cannot belong to the realm of the understanding. Fichte would therefore be guilty of a transcendent use of the category of causality – according to Schulze and Jacobi, Kant did the same in relation to the thing-in-itself.

It is difficult to reconstruct the philosophical references that young Schopenhauer presupposes in his reflections on the distinction between supersensible ground and cause. In a few rare passages, Kant had indicated the "thing-in-itself"[19] and the "transcendental object"[20] as the ground (*Grund*) of appearances (*Erscheinungen*); in the *Critique of the Power of Judgment* he had spoken, in passing and rather vaguely, of a "supersensible real ground [*übersinnlicher Realgrund*]" of appearances.[21] But Schelling too, in his *Abhandlungen zur Erläuterung des Idealismus der Wissenschaftslehre* (Essays in Explanation of the Idealism of the Science of Knowledge, 1796), had written:

> "The principle of the sensible cannot lie again in the sensible, it must lie in the supersensible"; this is what Kant said, as all true philosophers before him, and at the same time, no one said it more clearly and excellently than Jacobi. – Therein lies the character of all the sensible, that it is conditioned, that it does not have its ground [*Grund*] in itself.
>
> Kant symbolised the supersensible ground [*den übersinnlichen Grund*] of all sensual things by the expression: things-in-themselves [...].[22]

---

18 MR 2, p. 22. Translation modified.
19 Kant 2012, p. 107: "if we view the objects of the senses as mere appearances, as is fitting, then we thereby admit at the very same time that a thing in itself underlies them [*ihnen ... zum Grunde liege*]". Cf. also Kant 1998, B 66, p. 66.
20 Kant 1998, B 333, p. 375.
21 Kant 2000, p. 278.
22 Schelling 1809, p. 276. On the general problem of the distinction between ground and cause, cf. Hammacher 1994; Sandkaulen 2000; Jacobs 2021.

The principle whereby the question "why" only concerns appearances would be the fundamental premise of the 1813 dissertation *On the Fourfold Root of the Principle of Sufficient Reason*. In fact, the stated aim of this work is to determine the four different answers to the question "why" – that is, the four different forms of the necessary connection between appearances.[23] In contrast to the dissertation, however, "why" has only one meaning in the 1811 note: the causal one. Moreover, in the dissertation Schopenhauer would clearly formulate the distinction – which here begins to emerge implicitly as a problem – between *Grund* as *ratio cognoscendi* and *Grund* as cause or *ratio fiendi*, and would no longer speak of any "supersensible reason or ground" (cf. *infra*, 9.3).

From the point of view of Schopenhauer's mature texts, even to speak of a metempirical ground of appearances,[24] or of anything supersensible,[25] would mean making transcendent use of the principle of reason. In 1811, however, Schopenhauer (generally) admitted a "supersensible ground", but not the specific way in which Fichte determines it. And indeed, in relation to metempirical knowledge, young Schopenhauer recognized the reality of the "flash of evidence", which Fichte refers to the supersensible ground (cf. *supra*, 3.5).

6.3 The Illegitimate Use of the Category of Causality as the Foundation of Fichtean Idealism

Between late 1811 and early 1812, Schopenhauer did not just attend Fichte's lectures; he also read and commented on some of Fichte's most famous works, such as the *Foundations of the Entire Science of Knowledge*,[26] *The Way Towards the Blessed Life*,[27] *The System of Ethics*,[28] and *The Characteristics of the Present Age*.[29]

The core of Schopenhauer's objections to Fichte is expressed most clearly in a commentary on the *Foundations of the Entire Science of Knowledge*:

---

23 Schopenhauer 2012 [1813], §§ 3–4, pp. 8–10.
24 Schopenhauer 2012 [1813], § 59, pp. 150–151.
25 Schopenhauer 2010b, I 321, § 53, pp. 298–299.
26 Cf. J. G. Fichte, *Grundlage der gesammten Wissenschaftslehre*, Leipzig: Gabler, 1794. I indicate here the German editions owned and commented on by Schopenhauer.
27 Cf. J. G. Fichte, *Die Anweisung zum seeligen Leben oder auch die Religionslehre*, Berlin: Reimer, 1806.
28 Cf. J. G. Fichte, *Das System der Sittenlehre nach den Principien der Wissenschaftslehre*, Jena/Leipzig: Gabler, 1798.
29 Cf. J. G. Fichte, *Die Grundzüge des gegenwärtigen Zeitalters*, Berlin: Realschulbuchhandlung, 1806.

> It seems to me that Fichte contrasts with each other consciousness (I) and what occurs in consciousness (not-I), and determines their reaction and relation to each other according to laws that hold good only within experience, according to causality and reciprocal effect, according to quantitative relations (space), whereas the I and not-I are indeed the factors [*Factoren*] of experience, are that within which the realm of experience lies and hence to which the laws valid within *this* experience cannot apply.[30]

In fact, there are some passages in which Fichte explicitly states that the I must be thought of as the cause (*Ursache*) of the not-I.[31] For Schopenhauer this statement is illegitimate, because it refers a law that is valid only within experience – the law of causality – to the relationship existing between two terms that, instead, do not belong to experience at all, being rather the "factors", the prime conditions of it: that is, precisely, subject (or "I") and object (or "not-I").

The same critical remark is also formulated by Schopenhauer with reference to Fichte's 36th lecture "On the Facts of Consciousness".[32] Here Fichte speaks of a fundamental drive (*Trieb*) of the I, which would constitute the immediate expression of superfactual being (*der unmittelbare Ausdruck des überfaktischen Seyns*) in consciousness.[33] This drive is "shapeless [*gestaltlos*]", "absolute shapelessness [*Gestaltlosigkeit*]", since in the mere feeling (*Gefühl*) of the drive there is nothing but the drive itself: bare, indeterminate, it simply strives (*strebt*), without knowing what for (*wohin*).[34] In order for the I, by acting, to be able to achieve the satisfaction (*Befriedigung*) of the drive, it is therefore necessary that the latter *first* acquire a "shape", a form; that is, it must be translated into a concrete concept of purpose (*Zweckbegriff*) which, having a determined content, can be realized.[35] This concept of purpose, continues Fichte, is constructed or elaborated by the I on the basis of the configuration of the world, i.e. of what is available in the world at that given moment.[36]

At this point, however, an antinomy arises between the (now admitted) *possibility* of the fulfillment (*Erfüllung*) of the drive and the *impossibility* of its suppression (*Aufhebung*):[37] in fact, this impossibility must also necessarily be admitted, be-

---

30 MR 2, p. 392.
31 Cf. Fichte 2003, p. 221: "The absolute self [*das absolute Ich*] must therefore be *cause* [*Ursache*] of the not-self [*das Nicht-Ich*] [...] and the not-self [*das Nicht-Ich*] must to that extent be its *effect* [*Bewirktes*]."
32 Schopenhauer records this lecture under the title "First Protocol". For the correspondence between Schopenhauer's notes and the number of the lecture, see Fichte 1962 ff., vol. IV, 4, pp. 73–74.
33 MR 2, p. 63 (cf. HN II, p. 59).
34 MR 2, p. 63.
35 MR 2, pp. 62–63.
36 MR 2, p. 63.
37 MR 2, p. 63.

cause the drive is the expression of the superfactual being, so that it is "eternal" and "everlasting [*unvergänglich*]" like the latter.³⁸ This antinomy can only be resolved by positing the fulfillment of the drive as always only *provisional*, that is, as always only relative to *that* particular and contingent concept of purpose into which the drive itself has previously been translated.³⁹

Consequently, the new configuration of the world, which *results* from the I acting in accordance with that concept of purpose, becomes in turn, due to the lasting nature of the drive, the *starting point* for the formation of a second, further concept of purpose, and thus for a new, further action. The attainment of this second goal (i.e., the realization of the corresponding purpose) will also satisfy the drive only provisionally; the respective configuration of the world will therefore be the starting point for the formation of a third, further concept of purpose; and so on *ad infinitum*. The impossibility of the "abolition" – or, for Fichte, of a definitive "fulfillment" – of the drive thus gives rise to an "endless series of actions of the I", aimed at satisfying the drive itself.⁴⁰

Referring to these passages in Fichte's exposition, Schopenhauer makes a very interesting comment:

> Ego. I shall attempt to explain how this whole fairy-tale developed in Fichte's brain. He wants *idealism!* That he wants it is a consequence of his individual failure to understand Kant's teaching, and again such misunderstanding is possibly due to a defect in Kant's doctrine. Therefore he [Fichte] wants the I to be the *principle* [Princip] of all its representations, in other words of the entire world of experience. (He does not say *cause*, since this concept, as being immanent, is banished by Kant from metaphysics proper; but the use of the word *principle* is a paper raincoat and shows that Fichte does not scorn to employ such feeble defences.) Now the soul (more politely and exclusively called the I, also knowledge, or even being, after it appears more or less *in pontificalibus* lest we again make the acquaintance of the Paralogism of Pure Reason shown [*überwiesenen*] by Kant to be false) must be, in consequence of the Paralogism of Pure Reason, entirely one, unchangeable, incapable of any modification and all-sufficient. But we see that the world, its derivative [*Principiat*] (instead of effect) is thoroughly manifold, changeable, and a strange and odd thing. To explain this, he gives the soul a drive which is just as strange and odd, always wills something and, when it has this, again wills something else; and so [this drive] sets the world in motion.⁴¹

First of all, it is important to underline the essential reasoning that supports Schopenhauer's reflection here: Fichte "wants idealism", i.e. he wants to place "the I" as the "principle" of the "entire world of experience"; and since the world of experi-

---

38 MR 2, p. 63.
39 MR 2, p. 64.
40 MR 2, p. 64. On the Fichtean concept of *"Trieb"*, cf. De Pascale 1994.
41 MR 2, p. 64. Translation modified.

ence is "a strange" and "changeable" "thing", he is compelled to place in the I the same oddness and changeability that characterize the world. That is why Fichte ascribes to the I "a drive which is *just as* [italics mine] strange and odd, always wills something and, when it has this, again wills something else": in other words, in order to remedy the discrepancy that would otherwise be created between what he posits as cause and what he posits as effect. Fichte would be obliged to do this by the principle according to which all the determinations of the effect must in some way already be contained in the cause, since it is precisely the latter that produces the effect with all its determinations.

According to Schopenhauer's transcription, however, Fichte never mentions any causality of the I in relation to the world (the not-I), in the entire course "On the Facts of Consciousness". Arthur therefore interprets Fichte's lecture on the basis of his own acquired understanding of Fichte's thought and works – probably *Foundations of the Entire Science of Knowledge* in particular.

It should also be noted that Schopenhauer reproaches Fichte for wishing to set up "feeble defences" against the theoretical results of Kant's critical enterprise. In fact, on the one hand Kant unmasked the sophism underlying any psychology or doctrine of the soul – and therefore Fichte would not use the term "soul", despite meaning the same concept, but the terms "I", "knowledge" and "even being".[42] On the other hand, Kant has "banished" the concept of "cause", "as being immanent" "from metaphysics proper", which is instead the science of the transcendent; therefore Fichte, referring to the "I", would not use the term "cause", despite meaning the same concept, but the term "principle".

The fundamental content of this note is therefore an accusation of intellectual dishonesty against Fichte: the latter would do nothing more than re-propose a pre-Kantian type of metaphysics – that is, a metaphysics based on determinations (such as "cause") that Kant sought to definitively expel from it – while fraudulently presenting it as post-Kantian. This same accusation – also implied in Schopenhauer's amusing parody of Fichte's courses[43] – would be reiterated in later works,

---

[42] It is not possible here to specify what parts of Fichte's exposition make Schopenhauer's interpretation necessarily inadequate. Cf. Novembre 2018a, pp. 155–157, 173–176, 213–216, 268–269.
[43] The text is entitled "Fichte's leaden and lumpish fairy-tale *in nuce*": cf. MR 2, pp. 392–393. G. Zöller has rightly pointed out that the terminology here does not refer to *Foundations of the Entire Science of Knowledge*, but to Fichte's Berlin lectures (cf. Zöller 2006, p. 375). The text starts as follows: "There is a *being* (Sein). This is formed out of the superlative of consciousness, for to us consciousness is the most real thing, but being should be even many thousand times more real" (MR 2, p. 392). The fact that Being is nothing more than a superlative, i.e. a superfetation, of man's common consciousness (the "better consciousness" is certainly not at issue here: cf. *infra*, 7.6–7.7), means that Fichte claims to be doing metaphysics by hypostatizing the determinations of finite consciousness, and thus making an implicit transcendent use of these determinations. Moreover,

as Arthur's main (and perhaps, in the end, also only) theoretical objection to Fichte (cf. *infra*, 6.10).

6.4 In Perspective: Man's Endless *Streben* in Fichte's Idealism and Schopehauer's Metaphysics of Will

In the above-mentioned note (probably written towards the end of 1811), Schopenhauer ascribes to Fichte the idea that the I "always wills something and, when it has this, again wills something else [*immer etwas will und wenn ers hat, wieder etwas andres will*]". But in his lectures "On the Facts of Consciousness", Fichte does not mention the "will", but the "drive [*Trieb*]". Schopenhauer therefore interprets Fichte's concept of "drive" as completely equivalent to that of "will".

In reformulating Fichte's doctrine on the basis of this presupposed equivalence, Schopenhauer ends up attributing to Fichte the same thesis that he himself would later argue for in *The World as Will and Representation:* namely that man, as a subject of will, is destined to eternal dissatisfaction.

> All *willing* springs from need, and thus from lack, and thus from suffering. Fulfilment [*Erfüllung*] brings this to an end; but for every wish that is fulfilled [*erfüllt*], at least ten are left denied: moreover, desired lasts a long time and demands go on forever [*ins Unendliche*]; fulfilment is brief and sparsely meted out. But even final satisfaction [*Befriedigung*] itself is only illusory: the fulfilled wish quickly gives way to a new one: the former is known to be a mistake, the latter is not yet known to be one [...].[44]

The will is "an endless stream";[45] the subject of willing is "the eternally yearning Tantalus".[46]

Now, reading the commentary on Fichte's lecture, one gets the impression that Schopenhauer is quoting a thought that sounds foreign and completely implausible to him: Fichte would attribute such a "strange" "drive" to the "I" solely and exclusively in order to establish his own idealist position. Schopenhauer seems to consider this characterization of the I not only new or unprecedented, but also and

---

Schopenhauer's terminology seems to be partially contaminated by Schelling's *Philosophical Inquiries into the Essence of Human Freedom*, insofar as the derivation of finite realities from "Being" is traced back to the concepts of *Lust* ("desire") of Being itself and *gebären* ("to give birth"; cf. *infra*, 9.10).

44 Schopenhauer 2010b, I 230–231, § 38, p. 219. Cf. Schopenhauer 2020, p. 149.
45 Schopenhauer 2010b, I, p. 220.
46 Schopenhauer 2010b, I, p. 220.

above all biased – that is, purely instrumental to the specific theoretical position that Fichte intends to defend.

However, in a note to Schelling a few months later (spring-summer 1812), Schopenhauer seems to be arguing something very similar himself:

> Do you not see the spirit of the earth [*der Erdgeist*] on his throne? In his eyes one man has the same value as another, or rather no value, but only the whole race has. This spirit wills merely the interminable tumult, the inexhaustible flow of generations. There is to be no rest or repose; in moments when you look up to a better existence [*zu einem besseren Seyn*], you must first purloin his sceptre. He drives [*treibt*] incessantly [*unablässig*] from need [*Bedürfnis*] to its fulfilment [*Erfüllung*], from fulfilment to a fresh need in order that you may feed, grow, propagate and die.[47]

Human existence is a continuous passage from "need" to "fulfilment", and from the latter to a further and renewed "need". It is difficult not to notice the similarity between these statements and the very famous ones in *The World as Will and Representation*, according to which human life "swings back and forth like a pendulum between pain and boredom" – that is, respectively, between the discomfort caused by "need [*Bedürftigkeit*]" or "lack [*Mangel*]", and the dissatisfaction that inevitably follows every fulfillment.[48] Since no object of the will, once attained, provides lasting satisfaction, man's essence consists in "a continual striving [*Streben*], without goal and without rest", which is comparable to an "unquenchable thirst".[49] The will is, essentially, "an endless yearning [*ein endloses Streben*]".[50]

It must be observed that the Fichtean theory of the infinite "drive" – which Schopenhauer interpreted as a synonym for "will" – pushed Schopenhauer to his first formulation of the infinity of the will (albeit through an initial attribution to Fichte).[51] However, as in the other passage of the lecture "On the Facts of Consciousness" – in reference to which Schopenhauer stated that the will, "as a thing-in-itself, stands above all time" (cf. *supra*, 4.4) – here too Fichte does not speak of "will". Once again, Schopenhauer's original 'addition' amounts to the latter term;

---

47 MR 2, p. 391.
48 Schopenhauer 2010b, I 367–368, § 57, pp. 337–338.
49 Schopenhauer 2010b, I, p. 338.
50 Schopenhauer 2010b, I 195, § 29, p. 188.
51 C. Fortlage, in his *Genetische Geschichte der Philosophie seit Kant* (1852, pp. 407–423), begins his discussion of Schopenhauer from the consideration that the latter, like Fichte, determined the concept of "thing-in-itself" as a striving (*Streben*) or will (*Wille*), and regarded the term *Trieb* as a synonym of *Wille*. But Schopenhauer, strictly speaking, did not consider the two concepts identical, because he subordinated the *Trieb* to the *Wille*, indicating with the former the movement (tension) through which the latter is expressed or manifested (cf. e.g. Schopenhauer 2010b, I 179, § 27, p. 175).

nevertheless, he did not (yet) realize the originality of this addition, because he believed he was merely reporting Fichte's thought.

The idea of man's infinite striving (*Streben*) – infinite because it is a striving for infinity itself – is certainly one of the great themes of German Romanticism, which Goethe rendered in dramatic form, with all its tragic and grandiose meanings, in his *Faust*. In this work, God himself states that man, as long as he is alive (*lebt*), strives (*strebt*); and as long as he strives, he errs (*irrt*).[52] The "spirit of the earth", mentioned by Schopenhauer in the note on Schelling, appears in the first scene of *Faust* and presides over the turbulent becoming and perpetual dissatisfaction of all living creatures.[53] The authors of early Romanticism, especially F. Schlegel and Novalis, had also given artistic form to this infinity of the human *Streben*.[54] The strictly *philosophical* foundation of this idea, however, was provided by Fichte himself: it has been said that "early Romanticism was a spiritual fire lit by Fichte", because "it was primarily the result of a poetic and fantastic use of the Fichtean way of thinking".[55]

In the third section of *Foundations of the Entire Science of Knowledge* (entitled "Foundation of Knowledge of the Practical"), Fichte developed the discourse on the not-I from a practical-ethical point of view. The essential basis for his reflections was the indisputable *fact* that every finite I necessarily faces an otherness, a not-I, which appears to it as a limit, as something external and independent. However, as soon as the I "reflects [*reflektiert*]" on the not-I in front of it – that is, as soon as the I thinks or represents the not-I *as such* – the latter ceases *eo ipso* to be such (external to and independent of the I), becoming rather a "product [*Produkt*]" of the I and of its thinking activity.[56] Insofar as it is thought of by the I and in the I, the not-I can no longer be such; it is therefore removed or absorbed into the I, but *only* "insofar as it [the not-I] is to exist for the self (in the concept thereof) [*insofern es für das Ich (im Begriff davon) da sein soll*]".[57]

The I's act of reflection does not suppress the not-I as such, but only insofar as it is determined in that particular element or term on which the I has exercised its reflective activity. Consequently, "that very thing, which was initially posited as in-

---

52 Cf. J. W. Goethe, *Faust* I, v. 317, Goethe 2014, p. 10; cf. also *Faust* II, v. 11936, Goethe 2014, p. 301.
53 Cf. J. W. Goethe, *Faust* I, I, vv. 501–509, Goethe 2014, p. 16: "In the tides of life, in action's storm, I surge and ebb, move to and fro! As cradle and grave, as unending sea, as constant change, as life's incandescence, I work at the whirring loom of time and fashion the living garment of God".
54 For a reconstruction of Fichte's influence on his time see the classic study by X. Léon, *Fichte et son temps* (1922–1924).
55 Cf. Pareyson 2014, p. 106. Cf. also Vercellone 1999.
56 Fichte 2003, p. 247.
57 Fichte 2003, p. 247.

dependent, has become dependent on the thinking of the self, it is not thereby abolished [*gehoben*], but merely posited further out [*nur weiter hinausgesetzt*]".⁵⁸ The not-I does not disappear completely, but presents itself again in a new form or determination, immediately placing itself beyond the limit reached by the I's reflection. The I will be able to reflect on this further determination of the not-I, but this, again, will produce nothing but a further displacement or deferral of the not-I; and so on *ad infinitum*. "This fact", writes Fichte, "is that circle [*Zirkel*] which [the spirit] is able to extend into infinity [*in das Unendliche*], but can never escape".⁵⁹ The "activity of the self" is therefore, essentially, *"an infinite striving* [*ein unendliches Streben*]" – the ethical endeavor to become infinite and thus realize absolute and complete *unity*.⁶⁰ The influence that this specific trait of Fichte's philosophy exerted on the literary production and aesthetic reflection of the early Romantic period has been well documented.⁶¹

Coming to the question that is of primary interest here, the dialectic (in the broad sense) which, in Fichte's lectures, concerns the object of drive and, in *The World as Will and Representation*, the object of will, is similar to the dialectic (in the narrow sense) which, in the third section of *Foundations of the Entire Science of Knowledge*, concerns the "not-I" (i.e., that which is presented to the I as a "thing-in-itself").⁶² Firstly, these three terms are essentially related to the human *Streben*. Secondly, they are in fact unattainable, because time after time, all that can be obtained is, properly speaking, only a particular configuration or determination of these three terms, the achievement of which recursively produces their perpetual reappearance under a new and further determination. This generates, in all three cases, an infinite process – hence the substantial and constitutive inexhaustibility of the *Streben* itself.

Precisely in relation to this last point, it is very significant that the metaphor with which Schopenhauer describes the condition of the subject of will – being an "eternally yearning Tantalus"⁶³ – was used in a critical key by the 19th-century philosopher and historian of philosophy Jakob Sengler, to characterize the condition of the finite Fichtean I in the *Foundations of the Entire Science of Knowledge*. Sengler writes, in fact, that in virtue of the "permanent duty [*permanentes Sollen*]" to eliminate the not-I – which, on the other hand, can never be eliminated except in

---

58 Fichte 2003, p. 247.
59 Fichte 2003, p. 247.
60 Fichte 2003, p. 231.
61 Cf. Pareyson 2014, p. 106; X. Léon (1922–1924, p. 449–450) attributed even the Romantic concept of 'irony' to the effects of Fichte's thought.
62 Cf. Fichte 2003, p. 249.
63 Schopenhauer 2010b, I 231, § 38, p. 219.

an infinite or asymptotic process – the finite I "condemns itself to the torment of Tantalus".[64]

However, it must be borne in mind that, while for Fichte this infinite process has an essentially *ethical* destination, for mature Schopenhauer, on the contrary, the ethical purpose is to *escape* the infinite striving of the will. In the remainder of this work, I shall explore this aspect in more detail, but I shall also show how Schopenhauer's first formulations on the infinity of the will in 1814 closely resemble (even from a terminological point of view) Fichte's lectures on the drive of the I (cf. *infra*, 10.15).

We must now turn our attention to Schopenhauer's criticism of another great star of classical German idealism: Friedrich Schelling.

6.5 Schelling's Concept of the "Absolute" as a "Product of the Transcendent Understanding"

In the 1809–1811 period, Schopenhauer carefully read many of Schelling's works, including: *Bruno, or On the Natural and the Divine Principle of Things*,[65] *Ideas for a Philosophy of Nature*,[66] and *On the World Soul*,[67] the first volume of *Philosophische Schriften* (1809).[68] In addition to new editions of previous works – *Of the I as Principle of Philosophy* (1795),[69] *Philosophical Letters on Dogmatism and Criticism* (1795),[70] *Essays in Explanation of the Idealism of the Science of Knowledge* (1796),[71] *On the Relationship of the Fine Arts to Nature* (1807)[72] – the first volume of *Philosophische Schriften* included the previously unpublished *Philosophical Investigations into the Essence of Human Freedom*.[73] In 1812 Schopenhauer read *System of Transcendental Idealism*[74] and *Philosophy and Religion*.[75]

---

64 Sengler 1834; cf. vol. 2: Sengler 1837, p. 95.
65 Cf. F. W. J. Schelling, *Bruno oder über das göttliche und natürliche Princip der Dinge. Ein Gespräch*, Berlin: Unger, 1802. I indicate here the editions owned by Schopenhauer.
66 Cf. F. W. J. Schelling, *Ideen zu einer Philosophie der Natur*, Landshut: Krüll, 1803.
67 F. W. J. Schelling, *Von der Weltseele. Eine Hypothese der höheren Physik zur Erklärung des allgemeinen Organismus*, Hamburg: Perthes, 1798.
68 Schelling 1809.
69 Cf. Schelling 1809, pp. 1–114.
70 Cf. Schelling 1809, pp. 115–200.
71 Cf. Schelling 1809, pp. 201–340.
72 Cf. Schelling 1809, pp. 341–396.
73 Cf. Schelling 1809, pp. 397–511.
74 F. W. J. Schelling, *System des transzendentalen Idealismus*, Tübingen: Cotta, 1800.

6.5 Schelling's Concept of the "Absolute"

In his lectures on metaphysics, Schulze had strongly criticized the arbitrariness with which, in his view, Fichte and Schelling used the concepts of "existence" and "Absolute". In particular, with regard to the first concept he said:

> They want to theorize a pure and general existence [*Existenz*], and for this purpose they abstract from that which is given in our consciousness and which always constitutes an individual existence. Now, if one abstracts from this individual existence, e.g. from that of my own self, or from that of an object different from it, then, of course, the word existence remains, but it is quite uncertain whether anything real [*reelles*] is posited with it.[76]

Furthermore, in relation to Fichte, Schulze explicitly noted "an illegitimate use [*unstatthafter Gebrauch*] of the word 'absolute'" in reference to the I's self-cognition.[77]

Schopenhauer was so impressed by Schulze's fleeting remarks that he tried to find them directly in the writings of the two philosophers in question. Examining the concept of the Absolute set out by Schelling in *Of the I as Principle of Philosophy* Schopenhauer wrote:

> It is a product of the transcendent understanding just as are God, chaos, creation and all the theology and demonology of all times. It is *the absolute resting point* which our understanding compels us to conceive. [...] if we consistently and logically follow up its concept, we are left with nothing pure and simple. Apart from the Absolute there cannot be anything, namely in the sense in which the Absolute *is*; and hence in reference to it, for it, and against it there is nothing. We are then incapable of any concept of an existence [*Existenz*] which is not a representer and a represented (a subject and object) and, in order to conceive any being [*Seyn*] at all, we always need plurality or at any rate a dualism. [...]. But if we want to abolish dualism, then we no longer conceive anything at all [...].[78]

The concept of the Absolute is inadmissible because with it – as happens with every concept as such – one either thinks of something *in line with* empirical realities (and therefore something that is not at all "absolute"), or one thinks of *nothing*. The presupposition of this radical alternative is the identity between what is concretely *thinkable* and what is *empirical*. The Absolute is "a product of the transcendent understanding" because with it (if, in general, one thinks of something) one thinks of something as non-empirical. Yet this something has precisely – and necessarily, since it is thought of – the same characteristics as what is *empirical*. That is to say, in the *concept* of the Absolute (provided it is not an empty or null

---

75 F. W. J. Schelling, *Philosophie und Religion*, Tübingen: Cotta, 1804. On the importance of these readings, cf. Segala 2001.
76 D'Alfonso 2008, p. 107.
77 D'Alfonso 2008, p. 107.
78 MR 2, p. 342.

concept), the determinations of what belongs to experience are surreptitiously referred to what does not and cannot belong to experience.

The exact same considerations must be made, according to Schopenhauer, in relation to the concept of "existence" attributed to such an Absolute. In his commentary on the *Philosophical Letters on Dogmatism and Criticism*, he again notes that the concept of the Absolute ("as the name already indicates") is merely "negative", because it results from the negation of *all* the determinations inherent in what is cognizable by us.[79] The only possibility of attributing a 'positive' consistency to this concept, i.e. of legitimately giving it a true and proper content, depends on the difference between "being [*Seyn*]" (which, in this case, would be precisely the being of the Absolute, considered as inaccessible to human cognition) and "being-able-to-be-cognized [*Erkanntwerden-können*]" (i.e. the being of what is cognizable by us); but this difference is, according to Schopenhauer, dubious to say the least.[80]

Even in commenting on *Philosophy and Religion*, Schopenhauer states that Schelling's Absolute is a "being" that "lacks the conditions of being" as such.[81] "Being [*Seyn*]" and "being-represented [*Vorgestelltwerden*]" coincide:[82] "being, used of the object, means nothing more than *appearing* [*Erscheinen*]".[83] "Being is a product of the categories" (cf. *supra*, 4.3); each being as such must therefore have the determinations of the appearance (*Erscheinung*), including those of "cause" and/or "effect".[84] But the Absolute, being original, must be causeless. Its concept is therefore necessarily either *empty* (the Absolute "vanishes" as soon as one thinks one has grasped it)[85] or *transcendent* (like the "God of the deists").[86]

The fundamental presupposition of all these considerations, namely the necessary extraneousness of the Absolute to the dimension of "knowledge", emerges in a critical note to Schelling's *Ideas for a Philosophy of Nature*. Here Schopenhauer, prompted by Schelling's definition of philosophy as "absolute science" (absolute knowledge of things), expressly states:

---

79 MR 2, p. 346.
80 MR 2, p. 347: "Therefore the question is whether there is a difference between *being* and *being-able-to-be-cognized*, whether after the removal of all cognizability there would still be left a *being*, whether beyond *subject* and *object* there still *is* something for us." Translation modified.
81 MR 2. p. 371.
82 MR 2, p. 356.
83 MR 2. p. 381.
84 MR 2. p. 381.
85 MR 2. p. 381.
86 MR 2, p. 372.

> I say that philosophy is the conditioned knowledge [*Wissen*] of the Absolute. Proof: If it were not conditioned, it would be absolute and the Absolute is according to its concept only one thing, a being, not a knowledge, also not in need of a knowledge. Thus where knowledge is necessary, there is conditionality. There is knowledge only for the understanding and for the faculty of reason, [...] and hence these are conditioned. They are the faculty of concepts and of the creation of new concepts from those already existing.[87]

For Schopenhauer, the fact that the Absolute is "only one thing" means it cannot be knowledge; this is because he evidently assumes that knowledge necessarily implies duality (between knower and known, i.e. between the subject and object of knowledge). He therefore limits the possibilities of human knowledge, to the point of declaring adequate knowledge of the Absolute to be impossible in principle. Knowledge is by its nature something non-absolute, so adequate (absolute) knowledge of the Absolute would be knowledge that is not knowledge, or an Absolute that is not absolute. The "knowledge" in question here is that which occurs through "reason" and "understanding" and implies the duality between subject and object.

Now, philosophy too is a form of knowledge: it is precisely the least imperfect or inadequate knowledge of the Absolute.

> The highest knowledge is that of the Absolute, in other words philosophy; yet, according to the foregoing, even this as knowledge necessarily remains conditioned and hence is a conditioned knowledge of the Absolute.
>
> In so far as man unconditionally approaches the Absolute (as he can and should) he does not *know* about the Absolute but *is* the Absolute itself; but in so far as he philosophizes he does not do this.[88]

If absolute knowledge (of the Absolute) is impossible because it is contradictory, on the other hand it is possible for man to *be* the Absolute, or at least 'come close' to being it. As long as one practices philosophy, i.e. as long as one 'knows', in a non-absolute way, the Absolute, one is not the Absolute; vice versa, insofar as one *is* it, one knows (and needs to know) nothing about it. This alternative is necessary in virtue of the *unitary* character of the Absolute, which excludes the presence of any duality in it (even that which arises between knower and known).

In support of the latter thesis Schopenhauer quotes Plato, according to whom "the man who has eternal truth [Schopenhauer means: he who *is* the Absolute] as little philosophizes as does the one who does not look for it".[89] Schopenhauer

---

[87] MR 2, p. 358.
[88] MR 2, p. 359.
[89] MR 2, p. 359.

writes that he does not remember in which dialogue Plato put forward this thesis ("perhaps in the *Theaetetus* or *Philebus*");⁹⁰ in fact, it is expounded in the *Symposium:* since love is a *conscious* lack of what is loved (Eros is the son of Poros and Penia, "Resource" and "Poverty"), and since philosophy is, literally, "love of wisdom", then only he who *consciously* lacks wisdom philosophizes.⁹¹

But all this means that Schopenhauer, by challenging the legitimacy of Schelling's concept of the Absolute, does not at all intend to deny the 'existence' of something absolute, but only the possibility of constructing a *conceptual* knowledge of it.

6.6 The Impossible Identity of the Different and the Disguised Trinitarian Dogma: Criticism of Schelling's "Intellectual Intuition"

Reading Schelling's works, young Schopenhauer repeatedly came across the expression "intellectual intuition". By this, Kant had meant a type of intuition "through which the existence of the object of intuition is itself given": an intuition which is itself the origin of its object.⁹² According to Kant, man is not capable of such an intuition: it belongs "only to the original being [*nur dem Urwesen*]".⁹³

In the *System of Transcendental Idealism*, Schelling defines "intellectual intuition" as a type of knowledge that is, indeed, the "production" of its own object. Linking up with Fichte,⁹⁴ he believes that its effectiveness or reality is found in the I's self-relation:

> The *self* is such an intuition, since it is *through the self's own knowledge of itself* that that *very self* (the object) first comes into being. For since the self (as object) is nothing else but the very

---

90 MR 2, p. 359.
91 Cf. Plato, *Symposium*, 203 a–204 b: "[...] no gods ensue wisdom or desire to be made wise; such they are already; nor does anyone else that is wise ensue it. Neither do the ignorant ensue wisdom, nor desire to be made wise: in this very point is ignorance distressing, when a person who is not comely or worthy or intelligent is satisfied with himself. The man who does not feel himself defective has no desire for that whereof he feels no defect." Cf. Plato 1914 ff., vol. 9, pp. 178–183. Schopenhauer had borrowed the *Symposium* from the library in Weimar on 1 November 1810 (cf. Schopenhauer 1911–1942, vol. XVI, p. 105).
92 Kant 1998, B 71–72, pp. 191–192.
93 Kant 1998, B 71–72, p. 192.
94 Cf. the passage from the *Second Introduction to the* Wissenschaftslehre, in Fichte 1994, pp. 46–51.

6.6 The Impossible Identity of the Different and the Disguised Trinitarian Dogma — 151

knowledge of itself, it arises simply out of the fact *that* it knows of itself; the *self itself* is thus a knowing that simultaneously produces itself (as object).[95]

Schopenhauer's judgment of the concept of "intellectual intuition" appeared to be relatively positive at first. Consider fragment 45 of the manuscripts:

> The *standpoint of the philosophers of nature* is that we picture to ourselves the entire objective world [...]. Then suddenly we pause and say that everything conceived simply as existing is not thought of as being unless there is an intelligence perceiving it, a subject for this world of objects; for *to be* [seyn] (and this the natural philosophers never clearly state) is simply to be object for a subject or a subject for objects [*Objekt für ein Subjekt oder Subjekt für Objekte seyn*]. [...] Does the subject create the object or the object the subject? Neither the one nor the other, but the two are *one*. This we grasp [*Dies begreift man*] only through intellectual intuition, for it is contrary to, and *consequently beyond*, all understanding, since it upsets the principle of identity and that of contradiction, precisely as was done formerly by the doctrine of the Trinity.[96]

Since the content of intellectual intuition is something that the understanding is unable to comprehend – namely the (contradictory) identity of two non-identical terms: subject and object –, this intuition is "contrary to, and *consequently beyond*, all understanding [*gegen* mithin über *allen Verstand*]". Just as the content of the trinitarian dogma is constituted by the inconceivable identity of three different terms (the three divine Persons), so, according to Schopenhauer, the content of intellectual intuition is made up of the inconceivable identity of subject and object. In a footnote to the fragment, Schopenhauer refers to Schelling's *System of Transcendental Idealism*.[97]

In his commentary on the *Ideas for a Philosophy of Nature*, Schopenhauer further analyzes the concept of the "unity of the subjective and objective", which Schelling posits as the origin and first principle of all reality (characterized by the *division* of these two moments).[98] This unity, according to Schopenhauer, is already a contradiction as such, and therefore is not admissible.[99] Schopenhauer explains the reasons for this contradiction in his commentary on the *System of Transcendental Idealism* (cf. *infra*, 6.7).

Moreover, as "absolute", the "unity of the subjective and objective" should have nothing outside itself, so that it should necessarily "embrace [*umfassen*]"

---

95 Schelling 2001, p. 27.
96 MR 1, n. 45, pp. 26–27.
97 MR 1, n. 45, p. 27.
98 Cf. Schelling 1803, p. 71; MR 2, p. 360.
99 MR 2, p. 360.

the "world" in itself.¹⁰⁰ But if one asks what kind of relation there is between this unity and the world, one inevitably falls into further contradictions. The world, in fact, cannot be a "part [*Theil*]" of that unity, precisely because it is an "absolute unity", without parts. On the other hand, the world cannot even be one of its "effects [*Wirkung*]", because every cause has its effect outside itself, while that unity, as "absolute", cannot have anything outside itself.¹⁰¹ The unity of subject and object, therefore, is indeed absolutely "one" and "identical", but, including the world in itself, it is also "eternal change", "eternal becoming".¹⁰² All this, Schopenhauer concludes, is completely inconceivable for the understanding: it can be "grasped [*erfassen*]" "only through lofty intellectual intuition [*die hohe intellektuale Anschauung*]".¹⁰³

As one can easily notice, in these two passages Schopenhauer does not express his own position, but the stance taken by Schelling and the other "natural philosophers" from whom he resolutely distances himself (the adjective "lofty [*hohe*]" is therefore to be understood as ironic). Fragment 45 begins with a warning: "The *standpoint of the philosophers of nature* is that"; and ends with a comparison between "intellectual intuition" and the "doctrine of the Trinity". That this comparison carries a critical intention is evident from the following commentary on the *Ideas for a Philosophy of Nature*, quoted above.¹⁰⁴ Here, in fact, Schopenhauer, continuing to illustrate the (contradictory) relationship between the "unity of the subjective and objective" and the world, writes that the "absolutely One" in which this unity consists has three fundamental aspects: it "(1) passes perpetually as the infinite into the finite (i.e. it becomes "world", which is the sphere characterized by the division of those two aspects); "2) at the same time [it] passes as the finite back into the infinite" (i.e. the division is gradually raised to unity); "and (3) nevertheless remains eternal identity and absolute unity".¹⁰⁵

The absolute identity of subject and object is, therefore, one and three; indeed, the first aspect (the infinite becoming finite) is equated by Schopenhauer with "God the Son"; the second (the finite becoming infinite again) with "the Holy Ghost"; the third (absolute identity and unity), finally, with "God the Father".¹⁰⁶ "The philosophy of nature considers God the Son; the science of knowledge [*Wis-*

---

100 MR 2, p. 360.
101 MR 2, p. 360.
102 MR 2, p. 360.
103 MR 2, p. 360.
104 R. J. Berg (2003, p. 359), instead, seems to interpret fragment 45 as containing Schopenhauer's theoretical consideration of the concept of "intellectual intuition".
105 MR 2, p. 360.
106 MR 2, p. 361.

senschaftslehre] considers the Holy Ghost, and yet every philosophy that is not one-sided must embrace the entire Trinity [*Dreyeinigkeit*]. In each of the three all three are again found *in effigie*".[107]

Apart from the irony that is undoubtedly present in these considerations, Schopenhauer first of all intends to detect in Schelling a sort of underground theological or dogmatic scheme that, although concealed by a non-theological terminology, fatally undermines his discourse's claim to novelty (in the 'post-Kantian' sense). Secondly, Schopenhauer notes that the content of intellectual intuition is presented by Schelling (but also by Fichte)[108] precisely as a dogma, that is, as something absolutely incommunicable and indemonstrable, which escapes, in principle, any possible intersubjective investigation or verification. From the "shameless arrogance" with which Schelling self-referentially affirms that what he writes about "is given to him in intellectual intuition", it is clear, according to Schopenhauer, that his theses are nothing more than "an impudent lie", and that his whole system is nothing more than a "fairy-tale, a day-dream".[109]

Nevertheless, Schopenhauer is prepared to recognize a fundamental kernel of truth in Schelling's speculations, namely that

> if we commune deeply with ourselves, we find that [in our empirical existence] we are not in an absolute state and that time (which philosophers and mystics long before Kant expressed through the concept of an eternity) is to us immaterial, likewise the division of our consciousness into object and subject. We even feel a longing for liberation [*Befreiung*] from all these determinations.[110]

Time and the duality of subject and object are immaterial determinations for us: they do not belong to our true being, that is, to our "absolute state". This note by Schopenhauer seems to echo a passage from Schelling's *Philosophical Letters on Dogmatism and Criticism*, which deals precisely with "intellectual intuition" (cf. *supra*, 3.5).[111]

In the annotation quoted above, Schopenhauer states that the reason for all genuine philosophical endeavour is the sense of extraneousness to temporal and cognitive determinations (subject-object) and the consequent yearning to free oneself from them.

---

107 MR 2, p. 361. Translation modified.
108 Cf. MR 2, p. 381.
109 MR 2, p. 359.
110 MR 2, p. 360.
111 Schelling 1980, pp. 180–181 (Eighth Letter).

Schelling therefore establishes his absolute unity as identical through and through, that is to say without any determinations, as the unity of subjective and objective. (This as a contradiction cannot be accepted at all; according to the above, we can go only so far as to say that there must be a state in which there are no subject and object, but therefore also nothing analogous to my existing consciousness; and although there is to be found in this a tendency [*Streben*] and presentiment [*Vorgefühl*] of them, there can never be specified a concept of it just because it is above and beyond all understanding.)[112]

The *understanding's concept* of the unity of subjective and objective cannot be admitted, because it is contradictory, i. e. it violates a law of the understanding itself – the principle of identity and non-contradiction. What Schelling wishes to denote with this concept, on the other hand, is admissible, but only as the term of a mere non-conceptual "presentiment" or "tendency". Schopenhauer therefore rejects the absence of subject-object polarity not *simpliciter*, but *secundum quid*, i. e. only insofar as it is expressed conceptually. By generally admitting (knowledge of) something that can in no way be referred to concepts, Schopenhauer betrays that he presupposes a cognitive faculty that is *further and irreducible* to that of concepts – in the human being in general or, at least, in himself. This assumption is made explicit in another comment on Schelling (cf. *infra*, 6.9).

But the point is that Schelling, according to Schopenhauer, posits the culture of the understanding (*Verstandeskultur, Verstandesbildung*) as the "condition [*Bedingung*]" of the intellectual *Anschauung*.[113] This, in the final analysis, is the essential reason why Schopenhauer rejects Schelling's "intellectual intuition": it is based on the use of concepts, i. e. of the understanding's determinations ("unity", "identity", "subject" and "object"), to denote and describe what instead lies essentially "above and beyond all understanding".[114]

6.7 The Irreducible Subject-Object Polarity and the Consequent Impossibility of the Subject's Self-Cognition

As we have seen, Schopenhauer's criticism of the "intellectual intuition" is essentially based on the *contradictory nature of its content*, i. e. on the inconsistency of

---

[112] MR 2, p. 360.
[113] MR 2, p. 351. On the subject of intellectual intuition, and Schopenhauer's understanding of Schelling in general, cf. Norman and Welchman 2020. Cf. also Kerkmann 2021.
[114] Schopenhauer seems to assume that Schelling regards the relationship between the finite and the infinite as something perfectly explicable or demonstrable. However, Schelling, as evident from his earliest writings, was perfectly aware of the problematic nature of any possible attempt to determine or define this relationship. Cf. Loer 1974.

the identity between subject and object. In the *System of Transcendental Idealism*, Schelling asks whether, given "the coincidence [*Übereinstimmung*] of an objective with a subjective" that grounds all knowledge, it is the former that conditions the latter, or vice versa[115] (this is more or less the same question that Kant asked in the *Critique of Pure Reason*, just before the Transcendental Deduction of the Categories).[116] In other words, Schelling asks which is "primary" between the terms "subjective" and "objective".[117] But for Schopenhauer this is an illegitimate question:

> And here I surmise the πρωτον ψευδος of the Philosophy of Nature.
>
> The basis of our consciousness, its falling apart into subjective and objective, is *"explained"* by that philosophy trying to *refer it to laws* according to which it must be so and not otherwise. But where do these come from? From the understanding! That philosophy does not understand that, when Kant says: "The laws of the understanding and of pure sensibility do not concern *things-in-themselves*'", – this means that they are not *absolute* laws, but *conditioned*, and that their condition is our empirical consciousness; but then the condition of our empirical consciousness is its falling apart into subject and object. [...]. If this is admitted, then the question whether the subjective precedes the objective as its cause or vice versa (the question Schelling makes the principal problem of philosophy) is – *nonsense*. For *prius* and *posterius*, cause and effect already presuppose as their condition an empirical consciousness and hence subject and object.[118]

The question posed by Schelling already presupposes, necessarily, what is supposed to be thematized in the question itself: the polarity of subject and object. Consequently, any answer cannot but presume what should instead be explained in it; this is precisely the πρῶτον ψεῦδος, the vicious circle.

For Schopenhauer, the subject-object polarity is something that cannot be transcended by empirical consciousness. This assumption corresponds perfectly to Reinhold's "principle of consciousness", which Schulze had mentioned in his lecture ("through the subject, the representation is distinguished from the object, and yet it is related to both by the subject itself").[119] Moreover, Schopenhauer had personally met Reinhold in Weimar in 1809. According to the aforementioned

---

115 Schelling 2001, pp. 5–6.
116 Cf. Kant 1998, B 124–125, pp. 223–224: "There are only two possible cases in which synthetic representation and its objects can come together, necessarily relate to each other, and, as it were, meet each other: Either if the object alone makes the representation possible, or if the representation alone makes the object possible."
117 Schelling 2001, pp. 5–6.
118 MR 2, pp. 378–379.
119 D'Alfonso 2008, p. 101. Cf. K. L. Reinhold, *Neue Darstellung der Hauptmomente der Elementarphilosophie*, in Reinhold 1790–1794, vol. 1, p. 267.

principle, *every* "representation", as such and in general, always implies two sides, which cannot be thought of separately: "subject" and "object". From Schopenhauer's point of view, asking which of these two sides has priority over the other means presupposing the possibility that one of them (i.e. the one that would be determined as primary) can exist without the other; but this contradicts their necessary reciprocity.

On the other hand, Schopenhauer interprets this priority sought by Schelling in terms of *causality* ("*prius* and *posterius*, cause and effect, already presuppose as their condition an empirical consciousness and hence subject and object"). In the passage under consideration, however, Schelling does not mention the causal relationship between subjective and objective at all. Schopenhauer thus traces Schelling's alternative back to his own general interpretation of Fichte's idealism, according to which (as stated in the above-mentioned note to the *Foundations of the Entire Science of Knowledge:* cf. *supra*, 6.3) Fichte posits a causal relation between subject and object, i.e. between I and not-I. For this reason, too, Schopenhauer judges Schelling's exposition as irretrievably flawed by an illegitimate use of the categories.[120]

The necessary polarity of subject and object has an important and radical consequence for Schopenhauer: *the impossibility of the subject's self-cognition.* This self-cognition – indicated by Schelling as the content of intellectual intuition – would entail, according to Schopenhauer, the suppression of that original polarity or duality. "That the subject itself becomes object is the most monstrous contradiction that was ever concocted, for object and subject are conceivable only as the one in reference to the other".[121] Since these two terms can only be thought of in relation to each other (but, precisely, each *as* "other" than the other, and therefore both in their reciprocal otherness), their coincidence or identity is contradictory; yet this very coincidence would occur if the subject knew itself: in this case, in fact, the subject would become its own object.

In other words, the determinations of "subject" and "object", falling within the sphere of the understanding, are necessarily subordinate to the latter's fundamental law, namely the principle of non-contradiction. Consequently, Schopenhauer concludes, the subject's self-cognition (the identity of subject and object), being contradictory, is impossible. This observation is repeated in several places in the *Nachlass*.[122] However, following his reading of Fichte's *System der Sittenlehre*,

---

120 Cf. Reinhold 1790–1794, vol. 1, pp. 376, 380.
121 Reinhold 1790–1794, vol. 1, p. 381.
122 Cf. Reinhold 1790–1794, vol. 1, pp. 383–385, 360–361.

Schopenhauer would admit the possibility of the subject's self-cognition, though understood as the knowing subject's knowledge of his own will (cf. *infra*, 9.4–9.5).

Now, "knowledge *of myself*", or "self-consciousness", constitutes for Schelling the first and primary knowledge, which precedes and grounds all other knowledge: it is "the lamp of the whole system of knowledge".[123] The self's knowledge of itself is therefore the true "principle" of transcendental philosophy (which is the science of knowledge as such).[124] By contesting the possibility of the subject's self-cognition, Schopenhauer rejects what Schelling expressly indicates as the *foundation* and starting point of his entire investigation.

6.8 From the Eternal to Time. The Transcendent Use of Causality in Schelling's Cosmogony and Anthropogony

Schelling's *Philosophy and Religion*, which Schopenhauer probably read in early 1812, addresses the problem of the origin of finite things from the Absolute. Since only the Absolute properly *is*, the basis of existence of finite things can only consist in a "fall" from the Absolute itself.[125] The starting point of Schelling's argument is the "*pure absoluteness, without any further determination*", which is accessible to the philosopher exclusively through "intellectual intuition".[126]

> Just as the nature of intellectual intuition – which is simple by definition and for which no other expression is available to us than that of absoluteness – is absoluteness, it cannot have being other than by its very notion (because if this were not the case, it would have to be determined by something other, outside of itself, which is impossible). It is therefore not *real* at all; rather, it is in itself only *ideal*. Equally eternal as the ideal-per-se [*schlechthin-Ideale*] is the *eternal form:* the ideal-per-se is not subjected to this form, for it is *itself* without all form, as surely as it is absolute; rather, this form is subjected to it, for it precedes it, not temporally but notionally. This form is such that the ideal-per-se is *immediately* also a *real* — *without egressing from its ideality.*
>
> This real is now only a mere effect of the form, just as the form is an unmoving and calm [*stille und ruhige*] effect of the ideal, the simple-per-se.[127]

In the idea of the Absolute, Schelling thus distinguishes three elements: the ideal-per-se, the real-per-se and the mediating term of both, namely the form. The "*real-*

---

[123] Schelling 2001, p. 18.
[124] Schelling 2001, p. 18.
[125] Schelling 2010, p. 28.
[126] Schelling 2010, p. 18.
[127] Schelling 2010, pp. 18–19. Translation modified.

per-se" cannot be the "true real" of the "ideal-per-se" "without becoming *another absolute*, only under a different guise", i.e. a "counter-image" of the "ideal-per-se", in which this recognizes itself without going out of itself.[128] This "self-recognition [*Selbsterkennen*]"[129] of the ideal-per-se coincides with its becoming "objectified in the real as an autonomous counter-image".[130]

Now, the Absolute would not be truly objectified in the real, if the latter did not have, like the Absolute itself, the faculty of transforming ideality into reality and, therefore, of objectifying itself in particular forms.[131] This second self-objectification of the real produces the universal "Ideas", in which all of nature archetypically rests; strictly speaking, however, "all Ideas", as a whole, "are but one Idea".[132] The Ideas are themselves productive in the same way: they too generate further absoluteness, thus only Ideas, and every unity that proceeds from them stands to them as they stand to the original unity. "This is the true transcendental theogony".[133]

> "He who formed the universe was good, and no envy can ever come out of goodness; being free from envy he desired that all things should be like himself as much as possible," as it is written in the figurative language of the *Timaeus*. – The exclusive particularity of the Absolute lies in the fact that when it bestows its essentiality upon its counter-image [*Gegenbild*], it also bestows upon it its self-dependence. This being-in-and-for-itself, this particular and true reality of the first-intuited, is *freedom* [...] The counter-image, as an absolute entity and having all its attributes in common with the originary image, would not truly be in itself and absolute if it could not grasp [*ergreifen*] itself in its selfhood [*Selbstheit*], in order to have true being as the *other* absolute. But it cannot be as the *other* absolute unless it separates itself or falls away from the true Absolute.[134]

The counter-image of the Absolute can only be truly such if it is *itself*, in its own way, something absolute. But absoluteness is, also etymologically speaking, the negation of any relationship of dependence – even that which arises with regard to the Absolute itself. The relationship of 'similarity' with the Absolute therefore implies that the counter-image must be able to "grasp" itself as distinct from the Absolute, that is, "in its [own] selfhood". This *possibility*, however, entails the further

---

128 Schelling 2010, 19–20.
129 Schelling 2010, p. 20.
130 Schelling 2010, p. 20.
131 Schelling 2010, pp. 22–23.
132 Schelling 2010, p. 22.
133 Schelling 2010, p. 24.
134 Schelling 2010, pp. 27–28. Translation modified.

and fatal possibility of the *fall*, that is, of the conscious and intentional separation from the Absolute. Precisely through this extreme act of freedom, which is at the same time the radical expression of its own (derived) absoluteness, the counter-image ends up losing its own absoluteness and, therefore, freedom itself.[135] In fact, in order to be as "absolute" as the Absolute, that is, to be unconditionally *free*, the counter-image *must* remain united to the Absolute; vice versa, if detached from the Absolute, that is, "separate from necessity, it ceases to be free and becomes entangled in that necessity, which is the negation of absolute necessity, ergo purely finite".[136]

> The producing agent [*Producirende*] continues to be the idea, which is the *soul* insofar as it is destined to produce finiteness and to intuit itself in it. That wherein it becomes objective is no longer the real but rather a pseudo-image [*Scheinbild*] – a produced reality that is not in itself real but real in relation to the soul and even then only insofar as it has fallen away from the originary image [*Urbild*].[137]

The sensible universe is the "consequence" of this eternal and timeless fall.[138] The "ultimate goal of the universe and its history is nothing other than the complete reconciliation with and reabsorption [of finite things, and thus of the universe itself] into the Absolute".[139] In other words, the aim of the universe is its own dissolution. Through these reflections, Schelling believes he has raised the ancient and venerable doctrine of the "Fall of Man" to the status of philosophical truth.[140]

It is extremely interesting that, according to Schelling, only Fichte fully understood these truths among modern philosophers. Fichte stated that "the principle of finite consciousness in an *active* deed [*Thathandlung*] rather than a matter *of fact* [*Thatsache*]". Schelling identified this deed with the act of separating the counter-image from the Absolute.[141]

> On its pass through finitude, the being-for-itself of the counter-image [*Gegenbild*] expresses itself most potently as "I-ness" [...]. The I-ness is the general principle of finitude. [...]. Fichte says that the I-ness is *its own deed* [die Ichheit ist nur *ihre eigene That*], its own action [*Handeln*]; *it is nothing* apart from this activity, and it is merely *for-itself* [für sich selbst], *not in-*

---

135 Schelling 2010, p. 28: "For it [the counter-image] is *truly* in itself and absolute only in the self-objectification of the Absolute, i.e., only insofar as it is simultaneously in the latter; this very relationship to the Absolute is one of *necessity*." Translation modified.
136 Schelling 2010, p. 28.
137 Schelling 2010, p. 29.
138 Schelling 2010, p. 30.
139 Schelling 2010, p. 31.
140 Schelling 2010, p 31.
141 Schelling 2010, p. 30.

> *itself* [nicht an sich selbst]. That the cause of all of finite things is merely residing in finitude and not in the Absolute could not have been expressed in clearer words. How purely the ancient doctrine of true philosophy [i.e. the doctrine of the original sin] argues for the nothingness of the I-ness [posited by Fichte] as the principle of the world [...].[142]

The self's act (*Tathandlung*) of self-position described by Fichte[143] coincides, in Schelling's view, with original sin, i.e. the act by which the counter-image of the Absolute posits itself *as* something separate from the Absolute itself. Schelling believes that in this way he has unveiled the "secret doctrine" of the ancient Greek mysteries, as well as the authentic meaning of the Platonic myths concerning the soul's otherworldly destiny.[144] On the basis of these assumptions, Schelling also elaborates a soteriology.

> Just as a planet in its orbit no sooner reaches its farthest distance from the center than it returns to its closest proximity, so the point of the farthest distance from God, the I-ness, is also the moment of its return to the Absolute, of the re-absorption into the ideal. [...]. The soul, becoming aware of its falling-away, nonetheless strives to become another absolute and thus to produce absoluteness. [...] Only by surrendering its selfness [*Ablegung der Selbstheit*] and returning to its ideal oneness will it once again arrive at intuiting the divine and producing absoluteness.[145]

In order to return to the Absolute, and thus to become absolute itself, the soul must lay down its "selfness", revoking or neutralizing, by an equal and opposite act, the original act by which it posited itself.

Now, Schopenhauer had a fundamental objection against this whole argument of Schelling's. Thinking in general of any process of "becoming" in the Absolute, which would result in the world, means presupposing in the Absolute the conditions of becoming itself, namely "time" and "the category of causality", which, however, only concern phenomenal reality.[146] Moreover,

---

142 Schelling 2010, pp. 31–32.
143 Cf. Fichte 2003, pp. 97–99.
144 Cf. Schelling 2010, p. 35 and esp. pp. 36–37, in which Schelling also recalls the "old, sacred doctrine" according to which the soul, as a consequence of that original guilt, would be incarcerated into the prison [*Kerker*] of the physical body [*Leib*], while retaining within itself the "memory [*Erinnerung*] of the unison and harmony of the one *true* universe" – a memory that, in the sensible world, is obscured and clouded. This is a clear reference to Plato's *Phaedo*. *Phaedrus* and the *Republic* are expressly mentioned on p. 25.
145 Schelling 2010, pp. 30–33.
146 MR 2, p. 376.

> That the I or ego is its own *action* [*seine eigne* Handlung] lies (1) again in the realm of time and causality and is (2) even in this realm not to be thought as a contradiction [...] and nonsense. Therefore the entire fall of man is also a transcendent hypothesis, and moreover cannot possibly be conceived as an *action prior to all individuality.*
>
> Schelling's whole doctrine is therefore to be rejected for the same reason as is Wolff's dogmatics, namely because of *the transcendent use of the categories and of the laws of pure sensibility.*[147]

It has been rightly observed that in *Philosophy and Religion* (1804) Schelling's "philosophy of identity" gradually begins to turn into a metaphysics of will, and that this process finds completion in the *Philosophical Inquiries into the Essence of Human Freedom* of 1809.[148]

Despite young Arthur's criticism of *Philosophy and Religion*, this work, together with the aforementioned *Philosophical Inquiries into the Essence of Human Freedom*, was to have a strong influence on Schopenhauer, especially in relation to the doctrine of "intelligible character" (cf. *infra*, 9.8 – 9.11; 10.3, 10.7 and 10.9).

6.9 The Reduction of the Ideas of Reason to Concepts of the Understanding. The Cognizability of the Supersensible and the Project of a "True Criticism"

Young Schopenhauer's criticism of Fichte and Schelling consists almost entirely in the detection of a transcendent use of the understanding, i.e. the explicit or surreptitious attribution of the understanding's determinations to terms that do not belong to the latter's realm. More precisely, Schopenhauer believed that Fichte and Schelling attempted to construct "concepts" of supersensible realities. But since the faculty of concepts (the understanding) is exactly the same as that which is in charge of – and thus also limited to – the cognition of sensible reality, the (concept of the) concept of a supersensible reality is, in itself, a *contradiction* – which then inevitably leads to a myriad of further contradictions.[149]

---

147 MR 2, p. 376.
148 Cf. Berg 2003, pp. 173 – 176.
149 The violation of the principle of non-contradiction as a consequence of the transcendent use of the understanding is noted by Schopenhauer in several places in Schelling's works: cf. MR 2, pp. 340, 345, 346, 358, 360, 361, 371, 372, 373, 374, 379 (HN II, pp. 305, 308, 315, 316, 318, 319, 326, 327, 328, 334, 336).

However, Schopenhauer did not seem to have ruled out the possibility of a concept of a supersensible reality from the outset. Commenting on Schelling's *Philosophical Letters on Dogmatism and Criticism*, he wrote:

> We must not record if it should be found that the *concept* of a *being* [Seyn] that is neither reality [*Wirklichkeit*] nor existence [*Daseyn*] might be hyperbolical [*überschwänglicher*], that is to say a null [*nichtiger*] concept. For if this should follow from the *Critique of Pure Reason*, then it also follows from this that we have a faculty other than that of concepts.[150]

We shall soon see how this last statement concerning the *Critique of Pure Reason* is to be understood in concrete terms (cf. *infra*, 7.1). What is of interest here is that the nothingness of *any* concept concerning a transcendent reality appears within a purely hypothetical proposition.

Again in a note to Schelling, specifically to the *Philosophical Inquiries into the Essence of Human Freedom*, Schopenhauer states:

> [...] underlying [*zum Grunde*] the appearance in time of a human being [*der Erscheinung des Menschen in der Zeit*], there is something outside all time as well as outside all the conditions of the appearance. If we try to adapt these conditions to the otherwise correct concept of that something, then we get *monstra*.[151]

When writing these two passages, Schopenhauer still seemed to leave open the possibility of a 'correct' concept of extra-phenomenal or supersensible reality.

Later on, however, he developed (or made explicit) the coherence of his previous assumptions, according to which every concept as such is a product of the understanding, realized starting from "what is seen [*aus dem Gesehenen*]",[152] i.e. from sensible experience (cf. *supra*, 4.3),[153] which exhausts the scope of the understanding itself as a cognitive faculty. From this it necessarily follows that every concept of a supersensible reality – turning Schopenhauer's hypothetical expressions into an assertion – is "hyperbolic" or "null", because it is impossible for its condition of legitimacy to be fulfilled: that is, it is impossible for the "conditions of the appearance" *not* to be "adapted" to this concept.

Every concept of an extra-phenomenal reality is illegitimate, a *monstrum* – where this monstrous nature consists, literally, in its being composed of heterogeneous limbs: the conditions of the appearance or *Erscheinung* (which cannot but be presupposed in every concept, as a product of the understanding) and the *neg-*

---

150 MR 2, p. 347. Translation modified.
151 MR 2, p. 353. Translation modified.
152 MR 2, p. 21.
153 MR 2, p. 21.

ation of these same conditions (since, with such a concept, one would refer to something *non*-phenomenal). More concretely: Fichte and Schelling relate the violation of the laws of the understanding – in particular, of the principle of non-contradiction – to terms that belong to the realm of the understanding itself, acting "like a man who paints buildings which can never stand up according to the law of gravity".[154]

According to Schopenhauer, the "transcendental ideas" of pure reason which Kant spoke of – that is, the "pure concepts of reason", in relation to which "no congruent object can be given in the senses"[155] (soul, world as totality and God)[156] – are nothing but concepts of the understanding. Criticizing Schelling's claim that dogmatism brings about an "admixture [*Vermischung*] of ideas with concepts of finitude",[157] he writes:

> it says that dogmatism mixes the ideas of reason with the concepts of finiteness. – I (and Kant also) are of the opinion that the ideas of reason which are expressed by dogmatism are simply nothing but concepts of the understanding and through their being without object, they are inferior to the others [...].[158]

The identification of the concepts of the understanding with the ideas of reason makes it clear that Schopenhauer began to problematize the terms in which Kant distinguished between "reason" and "understanding" already at this early stage of his reflections. This point would be fully addressed by Schopenhauer in 1812 (cf. *infra*, 7.4 – 7.6).

In any case, all this talk about the illegitimacy of a transcendent *concept* did not lead young Arthur's metaphysical spirit to resignation or despair. In other words, it did not cause him to believe that access to a transcendent reality was irretrievably precluded. Indeed, he believed that, in addition to the understanding and reason, *man possesses a further cognitive faculty*, i.e. "a faculty other than that of concepts".[159] Only through this faculty can man actually relate to the supersensible. The fundamental fallacy found in Fichte and Schelling – as well as every dogmatist – consists in constructing a discourse on supersensible reality using the understanding, rather than that other faculty. See this emblematic note to *Philosophy and Religion:*

---

154 MR 2, p. 374.
155 Kant 1998, B 383, p. 402.
156 Cf. Kant 1998, B 391–392, pp. 405–406.
157 Cf. Schelling 2010, p. 31.
158 MR 2, p. 374.
159 MR 2, p. 347.

Every word must denote a concept of the understanding. According to Schelling's own statement the Absolute cannot possibly be incognizable [*unerkennbar*] to the understanding and for a cognition [*Erkenntniß*] of it philosophy can do nothing "but show the nothingness [*Nichtigkeit*] of all finite contrasts." Good and entirely my opinion! But then let philosophy content itself with showing the limited nature of the understanding, as Kant has done, and add that in us there is a faculty quite different from the understanding, and let it point out to the understanding the expressions of this faculty, empirically and historically, for there is nothing else for the understanding. But do not let it posit an Absolute as concept and give for its explanation nothing but logical impossibilities, do not let it require of the understanding *to imagine itself as one* through whose separation *it itself only becomes possible*, do not let it demand the abolition of the principle of contradiction […]; and do not let it put causality outside all time […] and so forth. In short, do not let it turn the understanding into madness for the very reason that it is just the understanding and nothing else.

I argue against your Absolute precisely as I do against the God of the deists. However, I do not say to either of the two that their concepts (the Absolute and God) are as groundless as that of the hippocentaur, but that such concept is a work of the transcendent understanding. It has arisen through man's not wanting to separate [*trennen*] his supreme innermost essence and faculty [*sein höchstes innerstes Wesen und Vermögen*] from the understanding (and genuine criticism should be just this); through his making this into the only and unconditioned cognitive faculty, believing he has reached all cognition through it, and seeking for it a point of suspension and repose.[160]

Through "his supreme innermost essence and faculty" man is capable of a "better cognition [*beßre Erkenntniß*]", which the true critical philosopher must "separate", i.e. rigorously distinguish from "empirical cognition" of the understanding.[161] When these two modes of cognition (and, therefore, also the two human faculties that make them possible) will be perfectly distinct, their respective *objects* – the sensible world and the supersensible world – will also be distinct. This is precisely the task of "true criticism", understood as an exhaustive treatment of the human cognitive faculties and their respective spheres.

Schopenhauer, therefore (in accordance with what I have already pointed out with regard to the concepts of "intellectual intuition" and "Absolute"), did not intend to deny the *content* of the "hyperbolic" concepts – supersensible reality – or even its cognizability, but only the possibility that such a content can actually be expressed through concepts of the understanding; that is, he did deny this content, though not as such, but only as conceptually expressed (i.e., through the determinations of the phenomenal or sensible word). It is precisely in this sense that his

---

160 MR 2, pp. 371–372.Translation modified
161 MR 2, p. 376. Translation modified. Contrary to what I. Vecchiotti (1989, p. 162) posits, this further faculty of *cognition* is in no way identifiable – neither conceptually nor genetically – with the "will-to-life" of Schopenhauer's mature system.

criticism of the concepts of "God" and "Absolute" differs from the (general) criticism that can be made of the concept of "hippocentaur".

In another note to Schelling, Schopenhauer clearly wrote:

> I positively deny such an intellectual intuition that depends [...] on the formation of the understanding [*Verstandesbildung*], though not [...] that which the dreamers have called illumination from above and Plato (*Respublica* VII) called rising to the spiritual sun. This does not depend [...] on the development of the understanding [...].[162]

This vision "has been as little capable of pure presentation in a concept of the understanding as is light locked up in a vessel".[163] Even with reference to Fichte, Schopenhauer certainly admitted the "thing itself [*die Sache selbst*]" of the "perception of perception" and the "flash of evidence", but not the 'intellectualistic' way in which Fichte describes and determines them (cf. *supra*, 5.5; 3.5).[164]

"True criticism", like Kant's, will have to give sensibility, understanding and reason their own legitimate sphere of application; but for Schopenhauer this comes with the priority aim, which is absolutely foreign to Kant's project, of guaranteeing the exercise of another, "supreme faculty", which allows for "better cognition" and is also the "supreme essence" of the human being. "I maintain that my essential nature is still something different from my thinking through categories."[165] The theory of "better consciousness" will represent this attempt to separate man's "supreme innermost essence and faculty"[166] from his empirical cognitive faculty, in order to build an epistemologically legitimate discourse on the supersensible.

6.10 Conclusion

During his youthful study of the works of Fichte and Schelling, Schopenhauer came to formulate a theoretical objection to them that he would maintain throughout his life. If, in fact, one reads his mature writings disregarding his frequent sarcasm and hostility and rather focuses on the strictly *theoretical* reasons for his criticism of Fichte and Schelling (but also of Hegel), one will always find the same objection:

---

162 MR 2, p. 351.
163 MR 2, p. 351.
164 MR 2, pp. 24, 32.
165 MR 2, p. 390.
166 MR 2, p. 372.

the transcendent use of the understanding.[167] The radicalism and, one might say, the hastiness with which young Schopenhauer raises this fundamental theoretical objection seem to have prejudiced his in-depth understanding of the two philosophers' texts.

This is why, when referring to these three philosophers and their followers, Arthur sometimes uses the expression "the *so-called* [italics mine] post-Kantian school"[168] and characterizes them as dishonest.[169] In his view, the "post-Kantian" philosophers are not such at all; or rather, they are such ("*post*-Kantian") in a merely chronological sense. In a strictly philosophical sense, however, they would be covertly (and fraudulently) re-proposing the same kind of speculations that Kant, in the *Critique of Pure Reason*, had proven to be illegitimate.

In this regard, it is particularly significant that, for Schopenhauer, "Schelling's whole doctrine is [...] to be rejected for the same reason as is Wolff's dogmatics, namely because of *the transcendent use of the categories and of the laws of pure sensibility*" (cf. *supra*, 6.8). Wolff – who, according to Kant, was "the greatest among all dogmatic philosophers"[170] – is the main *explicit* polemical target of Kant's criticism.[171] Even in a note to the course "On the Science of Knowledge", in which Fichte speaks of the "Absolute" and the "being of the Absolute", Schopenhauer objects: "I ask in what way does this differ from Ontotheology? And how generally does its entire concept of being stand up to the *Critique of Pure Reason*?"[172]

Schulze had stated in his lecture that

> Fichte and Schelling, while taking their cue from Kant in certain points, depart so much from him that they claim to have achieved, in the knowledge of the world, what he, according to the determination of the human cognitive faculty, considers absolutely unattainable; and yet, they never seriously show *that* [italics mine] and *where* [italics mine] Kant was mistaken in his demonstration of human ignorance about supersensible things.[173]

While agreeing with this, unlike Schulze, Schopenhauer unreservedly admitted the object or topic of Fichte's and Schelling's philosophies, namely "supersensible things" (and their cognizability).[174] After all, Schulze himself maintained in his lecture that the metaphysical question was still open because no philosophical system

---

[167] Cf. e.g. Schopenhauer 2010b, I 16–18, § 5, pp. 34–37; I 31, § 7, p. 48.
[168] Cf. Schopenhauer 2014, I, p. 25 (cf. also p. 30: "the so-called post-Kantian philosophy").
[169] Schopenhauer 2014 I, p. 25.
[170] Kant 1998, B XXXVI, p. 119.
[171] Cf. Kant 1998, B 61–62, p. 168–169.
[172] MR 2, p. 111.
[173] D'Alfonso 2008, p. 107.
[174] Here I agree with De Cian 2002, pp. 121–122.

had succeeded in demonstrating, according to certain and irrefutable principles, either the nature of supersensible reality or, as in the case of Kantian philosophy, its absolute incognizability.

This set of circumstances must have been perceived by young Schopenhauer's "aspiring mind"[175] as an irresistible invitation, indeed as a real challenge to fully embark on the supreme enterprise of philosophy: to finally solve – on the basis of Kant's interdiction – the "secret of the world" that had been hitherto left shrouded in mystery. His combative and passionate response to this challenge will take up the remainder of this book.

---

175 MR 1, n. 17, p. 13.

Part 3 **A First Attempt at a Post-Kantian Metaphysics: The Theory of the "Better Consciousness"**

7 Schopenhauer's Original Thought in the Manuscripts of 1812: The Project of a "True Criticism" and the Figure of the "Better Consciousness"

7.1 After Kant: The Program of a "True, Thorough and Pure Criticism"

In the previous chapters we have seen that, for Schopenhauer, the epochal value of Kantian philosophy was the demonstration that "life" is a "lie" and that all knowledge concerning experience is an "error". As already pointed out, these statements presuppose a skeptical interpretation of Kantian criticism (conveyed by Schulze), in which the opposition thing-in-itself/appearance is made to correspond to the opposition truth/error. That is why young Arthur, while acknowledging Kant's greatness, described criticism – which has limited human cognition to the "appearance" – as "the suicide of the understanding" and Kant himself as an oppressive nightmare for all "aspiring minds" (cf. *supra*, 2.7–2.8; 3.5–3.8). Against Kant (and against Schulze himself), young Schopenhauer was deeply convinced of the cognizability of supersensible reality: in addition to the understanding and reason, he admitted the existence of a further cognitive faculty in man, one that Kant would have ignored (cf. *supra*, 6.9).

On the basis of all these assumptions, in 1812 Schopenhauer began to devise an autonomous philosophical system that aimed to be, at the same time, the true and definitive completion of Kant's philosophy. In this way, he fully took part in the extraordinarily rich chapter in the history of Western philosophy characterized by the struggle over Kant's legacy. In Fichte and Schelling young Schopenhauer saw, so to speak, illegitimate heirs, who had ended up betraying, rather than furthering, the fundamental and genuine inspiration of Kant's doctrine. In essential opposition to idealist philosophy, he therefore sought to build a "true criticism" which, recovering the authentic core of Kant's criticism, would nourish and expand it to the point of overcoming its negative one-sidedness (represented by the declared impossibility of any cognizability of the supersensible). Truly post-Kantian philosophy must not abandon Kant's epochal acquisitions, but maintain them and, at the same time, overcome them.

In the fragment "On Fichte as a Whole", written in early 1812, all this is expressed in a programmatic way:

> Fichte did not perceive from Kant's great discoveries that the world of the understanding is one existing by itself and enclosed in the cage of the sensible world [*Sinnenwelt*]; that there is a totally Other world [*eine ganz andre Welt*] which *among other things manifests itself* in the categorical imperative (although Kant observed only this one manifestation), that is to say comes within the orbit of the understanding as a phenomenon foreign to this; that further from now all true philosophy, instead of uniting the two heterogeneous worlds into *monstra* as did ancient philosophy, will always try to separate them more completely and consequently be true, thorough and pure criticism, and will show where that higher world sends still more rays into the dungeon-night of the understanding, so that its existence may also be revealed [*sich ... offenbare*] as clearly as possible to the understanding, since only for this do we philosophize (Plato), the other world itself needs no philosophy in order to cognize itself. Instead of seeing all this, Fichte as usual considered the understanding and its laws as absolute [...].[1]

The content of Kant's "great discoveries" is that the human understanding can only cognize empirical reality ("the world of the understanding" is "enclosed in the cage of the sensible world") and that there is a "higher world", "totally Other" from that of the senses and the understanding. This second world, however, has been indicated by Kant in a partial or incomplete way, i.e. only in relation to one particular manifestation of it: "the categorical imperative" (the reference here evidently involves the three "postulates of practical reason").

After Kant, philosophy must therefore continue its critical investigation of this "totally Other" world, first of all by determining it and describing it exhaustively, but without erasing its irreducible difference or heterogeneity with respect to the world of the senses and thus falling back, like Fichte and Schelling, into a pre-Kantian kind of philosophy (which achieves nothing more than "uniting the two heterogeneous worlds into *monstra*").[2] This illegitimate act of unification, which philosophy must avoid, consists in attributing to these two distinct worlds the *same* determinations – that is, it consists in the transcendent use of the understanding. Secondly, and consequently, philosophy has to *indicate the 'places' where the light of that higher world breaks through the sensible world*, revealing itself to the understanding. Only when these two tasks are fulfilled will there be "true, thorough and pure criticism" – which is what young Schopenhauer set out to achieve at this point.

---

[1] MR 2, pp. 411–412. Translation modified.
[2] It should be noted that, in *Philosophy and Religion* (Schelling 2010, p. 38), Schelling also "demanded 'the absolute separation of the phenomenal world from reality-per-se' as an essential condition for the cognition of true philosophy".

7.2 "World of Semblance" and "True World". Difference between Transcendent and Figurative Use of Empirical Determinations. The Essence of Religion

As early as 1810, Schopenhauer began to thematize the difficulty of expressing or communicating knowledge about the supersensible (cf. *supra*, 2.5). This is problematic because, although it concerns metempirical content, this knowledge can only be expressed through empirical terms (or objects). In particular, philosophy makes use of language, and "every word must denote a concept of the understanding", which is the faculty of cognition of the sensible world alone.[3]

In 1811, in two commentaries on Fichte's lectures, Schopenhauer had admitted the possibility of a figurative – i. e. positive, but improper – use of empirical terms. Regarding Fichte's definition of the philosopher's point of view as "*perceiving* of perceiving", he observes that the word "perceiving" in the first occurrence "is used figuratively [*bildlich*], because the thing itself [*die Sache selbst*], like everything that is not taken from perception or from the world of experience, cannot have a name" (cf. *supra*, 5.5).[4] The genius, thanks to his "lofty thoughtfulness [*hohe Besonnenheit*]", "is able to express what he cognizes beyond all experience in concepts, pictures and works of art, and these again have objects of experience as their material"[5] (cf. *supra*, 3.2).

Well, this figurative use of empirical determinations to denote metempirical reality now constitutes, for Schopenhauer, the peculiarity of the religious discourse:

> *Religion* is an arbitrarily assumed and figuratively [*bildlich*] represented (the one follows from the other and the two are inseparable) connexion [*Zusammenhang*] of the world of semblance [*Scheinwelt*] with the true [*wahren*] world (of the sensible world with the supersensible).[6]

In the years 1808–1809 Schopenhauer had already set the "external world", which can be cognized through the (external) senses, against the supersensible one (cf. *supra*, 1.8).[7] In 1812 he described the sensible world as the "world of semblance", i.e. as the untrue world, and the supersensible world as the "true world". If we

---

3 MR 2, pp. 371–372.
4 MR 2, p. 33.
5 MR 2, p. 19. Translation modified.
6 MR 1, n. 32, p. 20. Translation modified.
7 Cf. MR 1, n. 12 [iii], p. 8.

assume that the sensible world that Schopenhauer referred to corresponds to the Kantian "world of experience", then we have to conclude once again that he understood Kant's *Erscheinung* as *Schein* (cf. *supra*, 1.5; 3.6).[8]

The *arbitrariness* of the connection established by religion between the world of semblance and the true world is "inseparable" from the fact that this connection is expressed "figuratively". Schopenhauer here is evidently referring to the arbitrary – i.e. unfounded – semantic connection between terms belonging to the world of semblance, used figuratively as *signifiers*, and terms belonging to the true world, understood as *signified*. The "essence" of religion – and, therefore, what differentiates it from dogmatic philosophy – consists precisely in the figurative character (*Bildlichkeit*) of its contents.[9] It is perhaps this structural figurativeness that makes Schopenhauer say that religion, just like art, is the "work of genius".[10] Such a semantic connection, precisely because of its arbitrariness, is not admissible in philosophy.

Schopenhauer thus seems to assume that when the *figurative sense* of the linguistic expressions used to denote the supersensible (typical of art and religious discourse) is affirmed or understood as its *proper sense* – that is, when the determinations of what is sensible are attributed *simpliciter* or *as such* to the supersensible – then the figurative use of those expressions and the terms they contain becomes a transcendent use (typical of dogmatic philosophy).

7.3 Religion and Philosophy. "True Criticism" as the "Ultimate System" of Thought

In fragment 32, Schopenhauer goes on to write that the "progressive cultivation of the understanding" is destined to disjoint the arbitrary and figurative connection created by religion.[11] This is because the progressive cognition of the sensible world and its determinations shows that the latter cannot be inherent in the supersensible, and thereby invalidates the value of that connection, revealing it precisely as arbitrary, "as a mere fictum".[12] The result is the awareness that the sensible world and the supersensible world "are not a *continuum*", but are on the

---

8 Cf. also MR 1, n. 33, p. 21, where it is said that "the concrete and individual of the appearance [*Erscheinung*]" and "the variety and diversity of experience" have only a "semblance of reality [*Schein von Realität*]". Translation modified.
9 MR 1, n. 32, p. 20.
10 MR 1, n. 31, p. 19.
11 MR 1, n. 32, p. 20.
12 MR 1, n. 32, p. 20.

7.3 Religion and Philosophy. "True Criticism" as the "Ultimate System" of Thought — 175

contrary completely "separate [*getrennt*]" from each other.[13] As we have seen, the essence of religion consists precisely in (implicitly) treating these two worlds as a continuum, placing them in "connexion" with each other. Consequently, the development of the understanding will inevitably lead to the disappearance of religion (*die Religion* [...] *muss* [...] *ganz fallen*).[14]

Now, if man had only the understanding at his disposal, cognition of the supersensible world would be hopelessly precluded to him. But man cognizes (*erkennt*) the supersensible "through other powers [*durch andre Kräfte*]".[15]

> The separation [*Sonderung*] of these powers from the understanding; the communication of what is cognized through them to the understanding according to its nature (in an immanent way), which is susceptible possibly only to a negative communication; on the other hand, what communication will forever confine the understanding to its limits so that its progress will no longer impair the at present pure cognition of the supersensible [*Erkenntniß des Uebersinnlichen*], as it previously did the figurative cognition [of religion]; – all this is philosophy. The upshot of this conception is that philosophy can be only one thing and that there will be a final system which will be genuine criticism.[16]

Recall Schopenhauer's statement, in a note to Fichte, that the genius "cognizes [*erkennt*] his own essence-in-itself and that of things [*sein Eignes und der Dinge Wesen an sich*]" through a "power [*Kraft*] which, as something entirely supernatural, cannot be further determined" (cf. *supra*, 3.2). The task of philosophy, then, is primarily to determine the boundaries between the understanding, which presides over the cognition of the sensible world, and these "other powers" ("other" than the understanding), which allow man to cognize the supersensible. Secondly, the task of philosophy is "the communication of what is cognized through them to the understanding". "But the divine, which is above all understanding and is revealed to man, should be deposited by philosophy in the understanding."[17]

Such communication, however, can only take place "according to the rule of its [the understanding's] nature". Philosophy must therefore seek to express, through the terms of the understanding, the truths learned through those other powers. But the realm of the latter is diametrically opposed to the realm of the understanding (the two do not form a continuum), so that this cognition can "perhaps" be communicated (to the understanding) in a purely negative way – that is, through the *negation* of the determinations proper to the understanding itself. The under-

---

13 MR 1, n. 32, p. 20.
14 MR 1, n. 32, p. 20.
15 MR 1, n. 32, p. 20.
16 MR 1, n. 32, pp. 20–21. Translation modified.
17 MR 1, n. 31, p. 20.

standing, for Schopenhauer, is thus in explicit opposition to dogmatic philosophy, the organ of reception (and possibly of expression), and not of acquisition, of supersensible knowledge. The enigmatic statement at the end of fragment 31 should be understood in this sense: "The dogmatists investigated and inquired through [*durch*] the understanding; we will do so for [*für*] it."[18]

When these tasks are fulfilled, the ultimate system of philosophy, namely, "true criticism", will be realized. While its advent will inevitably entail the disappearance of religion as such (that is, of every religion), it will also definitively safeguard the true and proper *content* of religion itself – the supersensible – from any possible refutation of the understanding. In fact, since the sensible and the supersensible world are utterly opposed to each other, the positive formulation (by the understanding) of truths concerning the former cannot but clash with the positive formulation (by the understanding) of truths concerning the latter. On the other hand, the *negative* formulation of the latter will remove the very possibility of such a conflict, so that the progress of the understanding "will no longer impair the at present pure cognition of the supersensible".[19]

In 1812, Schopenhauer attended Schleiermacher's course on *The History of Philosophy at the Time of Christianity* in Berlin. In his notebook, he commented:

> Genuine philosophy (as something much loftier than any possible religion) will give religion its due (which it [philosophy] must grasp and see through) and will know that what religion calls God [...] is the same as what philosophy cognizes [*erkennt*] with greater abstraction and purity and irrefutably (as being free from all addition).[20]

---

[18] MR 1, n. 31, p. 20. Cf. also MR 2, p. 412: "[...] the understanding, since only for this do we philosophize".

[19] In relation to this project by young Schopenhauer, one can perhaps attribute a retrospective and autobiographical value to the following passage from Schopenhauer 2014, p. 133: "Its [pure philososphy's] lofty goal is to satisfy that noble necessity, which I call the *metaphysical*, which makes itself profoundly and vividly felt by humankind at all times, but in particular when, as at the present time, the esteem of religious doctrine has been declining more and more. This doctrine, intended and adequate for the great mass of humanity, can only comprise *allegorical* truth, which, however, it must pass off as true in the literal sense. For that reason, with the ever wider dissemination of all sorts of historical, physical, and even philosophical *knowledge*, the number of people for whom this kind of truth does not suffice any longer grows ever larger, and they will increasingly insist on truth in the proper sense." On Schopenhauer's theory of religion, cf. Deussen 1915, pp. 8–16; Zint 1930; Schmidt 1986.

[20] MR 2, p. 241. Translation modified. On the content of Schleiermacher's course, cf. Regehly 1990. Schopenhauer's notes on this course are still unpublished, apart from some notes that can be found in Hübscher (cf. MR 2, pp. 240–246).

Philosophy and religion are two profoundly different ways of relating to the supersensible: "No one who is religious attains to philosophy; he does not need it. No one who really philosophizes is religious: he walks without leading-strings, perilously, but freely."[21] "True philosophy" ("true criticism"), like religion and unlike Kant's criticism, will express the cognition of the supersensible; in doing so, however, it will avoid both the figurative and the transcendent use of empirical determinations, thus differentiating itself, respectively, from religion itself and from dogmatic philosophy, both old (pre-Kantian) and new (Fichte and Schelling).[22]

In Schulze's words, Fichte and Schelling could only claim to go beyond the cognitive limits set by Kant by attributing to man a cognitive faculty or power (*Erkenntnißkraft*) beyond those admitted by Kant himself (the "intellectual intuition").[23] It is easy to see that young Schopenhauer's reflections were pointing in the same direction; he seemed to want to realize what Fichte and Schelling had, in his opinion, had only promised but not fulfilled (Fichte also wanted to build, with his science of knowledge, the "truly thorough-going criticism [*echter durchgeführter Kritizismus*]").[24]

7.4 The Identity between Understanding and Theoretical Reason and the Inadequacy of the Term "Practical Reason" for the Moral Faculty

All these premises inevitably entailed a radical departure from Kant, not only in the articulation and general aims of the discourse, but also in relation to more specific and technical features. In order to realize his philosophical project, Schopenhauer first had to integrate and correct all those elements of Kant's criticism that structurally hinder its refinement or completion.

In March 1812, in a fragment entitled *Zu Kant*, Schopenhauer criticized Kant's definitions of "reason [*Vernunft*]" and "understanding [*Verstand*]".

> The faculty of determining something *a priori* is called by Kant the faculty of reason, and here he commits the great error [...] of making an unessential characteristic the basic character of a *genus* and of dealing with the most heterogeneous things under one heading. Thus, on the

---

21 MR 2, p. 243.
22 A. Schmidt (1986, p. 312) has argued that Schopenhauer's distancing from institutional religion was conditioned by Schleiermacher's philosophy. Here, however, I argue that this distancing was mainly due to his need for consistency with the fundamental principles of Kantian criticism.
23 Cf. *supra*, 2.11.
24 Fichte 2003, p. 92.

one hand, he deals with the faculty of syllogisms and the predetermination of experience according to the conditions of our sensible nature and, on the other, with that which constitutes the innermost ground of our absolute essence [*unsres absoluten ... Wesens*] that is superior to all experience and to sensible nature and treats these as utterly null and void [*als ganz nichtig*].[25]

For Kant, "pure reason" is, in a broad sense, "that which contains the principles for cognizing something absolutely *a priori*".[26] By "reason" in the strict sense, however, he means "the faculty of inferring [*das Vermögen zu schließen*]", i.e. of logically deriving (deducing) non-given judgments from given judgments.[27] Schopenhauer refers respectively to these two meanings of the term when he writes that in Kant reason is both "the predetermination of experience according to the conditions of our sensible nature" and "the faculty of syllogisms". The combination of these two potentialities or capacities constitutes *"theoretical reason"*.[28]

On the other hand, Kant also spoke of a "practical reason", which would contain the moral law, again as an *a priori* (practical) principle.[29] In relation to the latter, as we have seen, Kant admits the three postulates of pure practical reason (human freedom, immortality of the soul and the existence of God). Schopenhauer refers to this part of the argument when he writes that for Kant reason is also "that which constitutes the innermost ground of our absolute essence that is superior to all experience and to sensible nature and treats these as utterly null and void". According to Kant, in fact, the moral law is "the fundamental law of a supersensible nature".[30]

But then the term "reason" (understood as the faculty of *a priori* principles), for Kant, unites the faculty with which man relates to the sensible world with the faculty with which man relates to the supersensible world. His first great error, according to Schopenhauer, consists in this fallacious unification of heterogeneous things. "Genuine criticism", on the contrary, should "separate [man's] supreme innermost essence and faculty"[31] – that is, those "other powers" that enable him to know the supersensible – from the understanding.[32] (At first, though, as document-

---

[25] MR 2, p. 336. Translation modified.
[26] Kant 1998, B24, p. 132.
[27] Kant 1998, B 386, p. 403.
[28] MR 2, p. 336.
[29] MR 2, p. 336.
[30] Kant 1996a, p. 174.
[31] MR 2, p. 372.
[32] MR 1, n. 32, p. 20.

ed in the notes to Fichte's *The Guidance to the Blissful Life*, Schopenhauer had admitted reason as a faculty of moral law and cognition of the "supreme good").[33]

Now, the fact that Schopenhauer contrasts these "other powers" with the understanding reveals that, by the latter terms, he *generally* means the faculty of cognition of the sensible world – what Kant calls "reason" in the broad sense. And in fact, Kant's second "great error" (opposite and specular to the first) consisted, in his opinion, in "separating [*trennen*]" what is instead *one:* that is, precisely, "understanding" and "theoretical reason".[34]

For example, Schopenhauer argues, the deductive capacity, which Kant ascribes to reason, can only depend on the faculty of judgments – which, however, according to Kant himself, is the understanding.[35] Or again, for Kant reason is a specifically human faculty; but this – assuming reason to be a deductive faculty – is contradicted by experience: "Even animals draw conclusions, otherwise the dog would not be afraid if we held him outside a window; he knows *a priori* that gravity will be the *cause* of his fall and the fall will be the *cause* of his being dashed to pieces."[36] In other words, the dog knows very well "what *must* [*muß*] be".[37] Recall what Schopenhauer had written in 1811, against the similarity between madness and animality maintained by Fichte: "the clever dog is to be compared to the ordinary man of demureness and intelligence [*dem gemeinen gesezten verständigen Menschen*] rather than to the man of unsound mind", because, like the common man and unlike the madman, he has adequate cognition of experience (cf. *supra*, 3.2).[38] This cognition is indeed attributed here to dogs and, more generally, to animals.

Young Schopenhauer thus wanted to point out that theoretical reason and understanding coincide with the faculty of cognition of the sensible world; consequently, they are one and the same thing and must not be separated. These considerations represent an initial but important stage of reflection on the meaning of the terms "reason" and "understanding".[39] In his 1813 dissertation Schopenhauer would differentiate, *within cognition of experience itself,* the "intuitive cognition" and "abstract cognition", and would distinguish once more, but in a new way, be-

---

[33] Cf. MR 2, pp. 397–399.
[34] MR 2, p. 337.
[35] MR 2, p. 337.
[36] MR 2, p. 337.
[37] MR 2, p. 337.
[38] MR 2, p. 18; cf. also MR 2, p. 21, where the dog is attributed knowledge of causation through the same example of falling bodies.
[39] On the propulsive value of these reflections in relation to Schopenhauer's mature position, cf. Hübscher 1966, pp. 29–71; Koßler 2012, pp. 467–471; Koßler and Ruffing 2018.

tween the understanding and (theoretical) reason, attributing to the former the *intuitive* cognition of external objects as the "cause" of sensations and to the latter abstract, conceptual and deductive knowledge (cf. *infra*, 9.3). The cognition of "causes" would be understood here as intuitive (intellectual), not deductive (rational); animals would consequently be granted understanding, but not reason.

Returning to the dog example, it is evident that the latter has the faculty of cognition of the sensible world (i.e., for young Arthur, "theoretical reason" or "understanding"), so that it has some representation of what must (*muß*) necessarily happen in experience following a certain event (e.g. its fall). Nevertheless, it knows absolutely nothing about the "unconditioned *ought* [von *unbedingtem* Sollen]".[40] But then – and here we come back to the refutation of Kant's first error – the faculty of cognition relating to the general *necessity* of experience and its laws (which Kant calls, broadly speaking, "theoretical reason") has nothing to do with that which invests moral *freedom* (which Kant calls "practical reason"); otherwise, having the former would *eo ipso* mean having the latter as well.

In the Transcendental Dialectic of the *Critique of Pure Reason*, Kant had defined reason in yet another way, namely as the "faculty of principles": it aims to bend the *entire* given manifold to the "highest unity of thinking".[41] The three "pure concepts" of reason – the "transcendental ideas" of soul, world, and God – correspond precisely to this extreme unification: the first (the soul) represents "the absolute (unconditioned) *unity* of the *thinking subject*", i.e. of the I, and is therefore "the object of *psychology*". The second (the world as totality) represents "the absolute *unity* of the *series* of *conditions of appearance*", i.e. of 'external' reality, and is therefore "the object of *cosmology*". The third (God), finally, represents "the absolute *unity* of the *condition of all objects of thought* in general", that is, of "all beings", and constitutes "the object of *theology*".[42] No object of the senses, and therefore no possible (human) cognition, can *ever* correspond to these three terms.[43] The intention announced in the title, namely the "Critique of Pure Reason", is thus realized in this section of the work (cf. *supra*, 2.6).

Now, for Schopenhauer, as we have seen, the three "ideas of reason" are "nothing but concepts of the understanding".[44] At first Schopenhauer also attributed this view to Kant (cf. *supra*, 6.9),[45] but it is clear that such an identity *contradicts* the

---

40 MR 2, p. 337.
41 Kant 1998, B 355, p. 387.
42 Kant 1998, B 391–392, p. 406.
43 Kant 1998, B 391–392, p. 406.
44 MR 2, p. 374.
45 MR 2, p. 374.

Kantian distinction between understanding and reason.[46] In the fragment entitled *Zu Kant* Schopenhauer becomes aware of the divergence or peculiarity of his own position compared to Kant's. As a consequence, he has to explain, against Kant, how the ideas of reason are ascribable to the *understanding*, and he does so – coherently – by putting them down to the high "degree of *clearness*" that "sensible consciousness and consciousness of the understanding" achieve in human beings.[47] In other words, it is because of a purely *quantitative* difference in the understanding that the ideas of reason arise only in humans and not also in animals.[48]

The conclusion Schopenhauer draws from all these considerations is the following:

> The name *reason* (*Vernunft*) must therefore belong *solely* to [what Kant calls] theoretical or to [what Kant calls] practical reason. German usage has at all times given it to theoretical reason and with it has described a greater clearness and proficiency of the understanding. Indeed Kant at first spoke of practical reason (in this sense). – It must have a different name.[49]

In "true criticism", the faculty of cognition of the sensible world must be distinguished from the faculty of cognition of the supersensible world: what Kant mistakenly put together under the single name of "reason" must therefore also be distinguished from a terminological point of view. But the term "reason" commonly denotes the faculty of cognition of the sensible world; consequently, what Kant called "practical reason" will have to be called something else.[50] It is then a question of finding an adequate denomination.

---

46 Cf. Kant 2000, pp. 217–218: "Since in transcendental philosophy we so frequently find occasion to distinguish ideas from concepts of the understanding, it may be of use to introduce terms of art appropriate to their difference [...]. Ideas in the most general meaning are representations related to an object in accordance with a certain (subjective or objective) principle, insofar as they can nevertheless never become a cognition of that object. They are either related to an intuition in accordance with a merely subjective principle of the correspondence of the faculties of cognition with each other (of imagination and of understanding), and in this case they are called aesthetic; or they are related to a concept in accordance with an objective principle, yet can never yield a cognition of the object, and are called ideas of reason, in which case the concept is a *transcendent* concept, which is distinct from the concept of the understanding, to which an adequately corresponding experience can always be ascribed, and which is therefore called *immanent*."
47 MR 2, p. 338.
48 MR 2, p. 338.
49 MR 2, p. 338. On young Schopenhauer's reflections on the Kantian concept of "practical reason", cf. also D'Alfonso 2020. Here and in the following quotations, the word *Vernunft* between round brackets appears as such in the English translation of the text.
50 Cf. MR 2, p. 284, where Schopenhauer states that he cannot bear the expression "practical reason".

7.5 The Absolute Incompatibility of Moral Law and Practical Reason

For Schopenhauer, "Kant observed only [...] one manifestation [*Aeußerung*]" of what he calls "quite a different world" from that of the understanding: the "categorical imperative".[51] However, Kant traced the latter back to practical (pure) reason; indeed, as we have just seen, what he called "practical reason" is in fact not "reason" at all, but "the innermost ground of our absolute essence".[52] It is extremely significant in this regard that Schopenhauer identifies the "rising to the spiritual sun" (i.e. the knowledge of the Idea of Good) of which Plato speaks in the *Republic* with the "pure will".[53] In Kant, this is precisely the will determined by the categorical imperative.[54]

In the remainder of the fragment *Zu Kant*, Schopenhauer argues that theology – whose object, namely God, is for Kant the content of the third idea of theoretical pure reason, as well as the third postulate of practical pure reason – has a threefold origin: firstly, the "fear, hope, happiness, gratitude" essentially associated with human existence; secondly, the need to answer the questions posed "by theoretical reason (*Vernunft*) or the understanding"; finally, the truly transcendent dimension, the ineffable:

> The inexpressible [*das Unnennbare*], of which Kant's practical reason is *one* kind of revelation [eine Art der Offenbarung], prevails in genuine Christianity, in the doctrine of I or individuality, in theosophy, in enthusiasm [*Schwärmerey*].[55]

In all these expressions, however, the revelation of the ineffable has been "contaminated" by contact "with those [two] other sources" of theology, "just as some bodies are oxidized as soon as they come in contact with air or water".[56]

> It [the revelation of the ineffable] has never yet been presented in complete purity [*ganz rein*] [...]. When this is done, we shall then have the genuine and final philosophy which cannot be anything but a separation [*Sonderung*] of the three sources [of theology] and their precise delineation, a spiritual [*geistige*] chemistry, *true criticism*.[57]

---

51 MR 2, p. 411.
52 MR 2, p. 336.
53 MR 2, p. 351.
54 Cf. Kant 1996a, p. 164.
55 MR 2, p. 338. Translation modified.
56 MR 2, p. 338.
57 MR 2, p. 338. Translation modified.

7.5 The Absolute Incompatibility of Moral Law and Practical Reason

In fragment 35 Schopenhauer elaborates on the meaning of all these annotations, in order to determine the difference between reason, on the one hand, and the faculty with which man relates to the supersensible, on the other

> [...] there are three kinds of data *a priori.*
> (1) Theoretical reason (*Vernunft*), i.e. the conditions for the possibility of all experience, i.e. of all concepts.
> (2) Instinct, rule for the attainment of an unknown purpose that favours my sensible existence.
> (3) The moral law. The rule for an action without purpose.[58]

In a note to the fragment, Schopenhauer states that the true meaning of Plato's doctrine of anamnesis is the *a priori* nature of these three elements: "all learning is for him [Plato] a recollection; he simply has no other word for expressing the notion of being *a priori* given prior to all experience".[59] Now, in correspondence with these three *a priori* elements, action is also threefold:

> (1) The rational or judicious action is done according to a rule that is laid down in conformity with a concept of purpose.
> (2) The instinctive action according to a rule without a concept of purpose.
> (3) The moral action according to a rule without purpose.[60]

Theoretical reason is the transcendental condition of experience – that which, in the fragment *Zu Kant*, is identified with the understanding; it corresponds to "rational or [*oder*] judicious action". The latter in fact consists in the *application* of theoretical reason itself – i.e. knowledge of the necessary connections of experience – to calculate the most effective means in relation to a given purpose, which is pursued consciously (i.e. according to its "concept").

Instinct, on the other hand, concerns the *unconscious* pursuit of a purpose "that favours [...] sensible existence" of the agent. The fact that the aim is unknown, or that there is no concept of it, means that it is nevertheless pursued, even though it is not represented or known *as such.*

> Now just as *theoretical reason* (Vernunft) is the aggregate of rules according to which all my cognizing [Erkennen], i.e. the entire world of experience, must eventuate, so is *instinct* the aggregate of rules according to which all my conduct must eventuate, unless an interruption

---

[58] MR 1, n. 35, p. 23.
[59] MR 1, n. 35, p. 23.
[60] MR 1, n. 35, p. 23.

occurs. Therefore the name *Practical Reason* seems to me to be the most appropriate for *instinct, for it* [instinct] *determines like theoretical reason the MUST for all EXPERIENCE.*[61]

Both the rational action of humans and the instinctive action of animals presuppose a "purpose" that favors "sensible existence" (although only humans are capable of representing the purpose *as such*). Instinct too, therefore, consists in the application – albeit unconscious – of cognition of the laws governing the world of experience, because these laws determine what does or does not favor "sensible existence" – that is, the individual aims that an animal must pursue in order to survive, and the means necessary to achieve them. For this reason, Schopenhauer writes that the instinct *"determines like theoretical reason the must for all experience"* – that is to say, being bound to act in a certain way, given certain purposes (and, first of all, given the fundamental purpose of maintaining and promoting "sensible existence"). Consisting, therefore, in the practical (albeit unconscious) application of the cognition of experience, which indeed belongs to reason (as the cognitive faculty of the sensible world), instinct can rightly be called "practical reason".

The essential point of all these reflections is that practical reason (in the strict sense) – i.e., theoretical reason *consciously* applied to action, with a view to aims that favor the agent's sensible existence – is only a particularly evolved and enhanced form of instinct; and instinct, in turn, is only a still undeveloped and embryonic form of practical reason (in the broad sense). In the fragment *Zu Kant*, the difference between man and animal in relation to the cognition of experience is determined as purely quantitative: it concerns only the "degree of *clearness*" of "sensible consciousness and consciousness of the understanding".[62] Well, from a practical point of view, even between the rational action of humans and the instinctive action of animals there is only a quantitative difference, concerning the degree of consciousness with which the cognition of experience is applied.

The moral law, which represents the third *a priori* element, is instead, unlike practical reason, *qualitatively* different from instinct (and therefore from practical reason itself): it is a "rule for an action without purpose". In moral action, therefore, purpose is totally absent, not only (as in instinct) in its purely conceptual dimension. This total absence is precisely what underlies the qualitative character of the aforementioned difference. Schopenhauer here presupposes certain Kantian considerations, which it is worth recalling briefly here.

---

[61] MR 1, n. 35, p. 23. Translation modified.
[62] MR 2, p. 338.

In the Introduction to the *Critique of Practical Reason*, Kant presented the capital issue discussed in the work in the following terms: "whether pure reason of itself alone suffices to determine the will or whether it can be a determining ground of the will only as empirically conditioned".[63] The question is whether reason can autonomously direct human activity independently of sensory impulses and inclinations, or only insofar as it is determined by them. Only in the first case can there be *freedom*; in the second case, man's conduct would be determined solely by his sensory nature – and nature is governed by blind determinism. Kant thus distinguished between *pure* practical reason (which directs action *a priori*, irrespective of sensory inclinations and thus of experience) and *empirical* practical reason, i.e. "empirically conditioned" (determined by experience and sensibility). Further on in his investigation, he noted that the moral law is present in man as "a fact of reason": by determining the human will *a priori* and thus excluding any perceptible motive or purpose,[64] it constitutes "the fundamental law of a supersensible nature".[65]

Schopenhauer, like Kant, relates the moral law to action without purpose; but unlike Kant, he resolutely *opposes* it to "practical reason". This is because, in his view, "pure practical reason" does not exist; what Kant calls "empirical practical reason" is practical reason *tout court* (theoretical reason applied to action, with a view to attaining certain ends). In fact, just as for Kant "empirical practical reason" produces only "empirical practical principles" (rules for the attainment of a particular aim),[66] so for Schopenhauer "rational action" *tout court* takes place according to "a rule that is laid down in conformity with a concept of purpose".

> The so-called moral law, on the other hand, is only a one-sided [*einseitige*] view [*Ansicht*] of the *better consciousness* [*des* bessern Bewußtseyns] taken from the standpoint of instinct. This consciousness lies beyond all experience and thus beyond all reason, both theoretical and practical (instinct). It is not concerned with reason except that, by virtue of its mysterious connexion with this in one individual, it meets with experience, and here for the individual there then arises the choice whether he wants to be *reason* or *better consciousness*.[67]

---

63 Kant 1996a, p. 148.
64 Kant 1996a, p. 164.
65 Kant 1996a, p. 174.
66 Cf. Kant 1996a, p. 155: "All practical principles that presuppose an object (matter) of the faculty of desire as the determining ground of the will are, without exception, empirical and can furnish no practical laws."
67 MR 1, n. 35, p. 23. Translation modified.

The moral law is the way in which the better consciousness manifests itself in the sphere of practical reason. But the most significant element of this fragment is the sudden appearance of a new theoretical figure: the "better consciousness".

7.6 The Cornerstone of "True Criticism": The "Better Consciousness"

In the quote above, Schopenhauer states that the moral law "is only a *one-sided* [italics mine] view of the *better consciousness*", which "lies beyond all experience". As already mentioned, the categorical imperative constitutes for Schopenhauer a mode of "manifestation" or "revelation" of the supersensible world, or of the "inexpressible" (cf. *supra*, 7.1). It would seem, therefore, that the better consciousness – only partially manifested in the moral law – denotes here precisely the ineffable that "true criticism" is meant to expose in an epistemologically legitimate way. This interpretative hypothesis is fully confirmed in the remainder of the fragment:

> If [the individual] wants to be *reason*, then as theoretical reason he will be a philistine and as practical reason a scoundrel [*Bösewicht*]. If he wants to be *better consciousness*, then we positively [*positiv*] cannot say anything more about him, for what we say lies in the province of reason. Therefore we can only say what happens in this sphere, and in this way we speak only negatively [*negativ*] of the better consciousness.[68]

Since theoretical reason is the faculty of cognition of the sensible world alone, the individual, as theoretical reason, can only be a *philistine* (one who grasps no reality other than the empirical kind). Similarly, since practical reason is the application of theoretical reason to selfish ends (i.e., serving the agent's sensible existence), the individual, as practical reason, is necessarily a *scoundrel*.

The better consciousness is absolutely opposed to reason, both theoretical and practical, and consequently can only be described in negative terms (words only designate concepts of the understanding);[69] that is, it is absolutely "inexpressible", unless we use *negative* linguistic formulations, where the determinations of reason and its sphere are grammatically negated. The very denomination of inexpressible or ineffable (*unnennbar*) is purely negative.

In an addition to the fragment, Schopenhauer writes: "In Jacobi's divine things, p. 18, we find a mixture of better consciousness with instinct through a syn-

---

68 MR 1, pp. 23–24.
69 MR 1, n. 32, p. 20.

cretism of which only so unphilosophical a mind as Jacobi's is capable."[70] Jacobi certainly does not use the expression "better consciousness", but he does speak of a human "instinct" that is superior, even if analogous, to that of animals: just as the lower instinct drives animals towards something of which they have no knowledge, but which they need all the same, namely nourishment, so the higher instinct pushes humans to search for an "invisible" entity, namely God, whom we can never have complete knowledge of, but whom we constitutively need.[71] The fact that the instinct is "mixed" with the better consciousness in this text evidently means that, for Schopenhauer, what Jacobi attributes to the former – the immediate relationship with the divine – is proper only to the latter.

Now, the fundamental task of "true criticism" is to separate the faculty of "better cognition" (*beßre Erkenntnis*) i.e. the cognition of the supersensible, from the "empirical cognition" of the understanding (cf. *supra*, 6.9).[72] In his commentary on Fichte's *Attempt at a Critique of All Revelation* Schopenhauer reformulates this same intention using the term "better consciousness":

> Thus genuine criticism will separate [*wird ... trennen*] the better consciousness [*das beßre Bewußtseyn*] from the empirical [*vom empirischen*], like gold from ore, will present it in its purity without any admixture of sensibility or understanding. It will set it out completely, gather everything by which it [the better consciousness] is revealed in [empirical] consciousness, and combine all this into a unity. It will then also preserve the empirical and classify it according to its differences.[73]

The conditions of the "empirical cognition", i.e. the *a priori* laws of the understanding and pure sensibility, are exactly the same as the conditions of the "empirical consciousness". Schopenhauer radically contrasts this pair of terms with the other pair, consisting of "better cognition" and "better consciousness". By "better consciousness" Schopenhauer therefore means to denote those *powers other than the understanding* that enable man to cognize the supersensible (cf. *supra*, 7.3): like the understanding, the better consciousness has its own peculiar "province [*Gebiet*]".[74]

All this means that man is *empirical consciousness*, insofar as he cognizes the sensible world; but he is also *better consciousness* insofar as he cognizes (or can

---

70 MR 1, fn. to n. 35, p. 23.
71 Jacobi 1811, p. 18.
72 MR 2, pp. 376–377.
73 MR 2, p. 416.
74 MR 2, p. 374.

cognize) the supersensible reality.[75] In other words, empirical consciousness is the consciousness of the empirical world; the better consciousness, on the other hand, is the consciousness of the metempirical world.

7.7 Some Remarks on the Expression "Better Consciousness". Fichte's Probable Influence

At this point it is worth making a few considerations on the meaning and origin of the expression "better consciousness". First of all, the use of the noun "consciousness" is extremely significant, as it implies a gnoseological connotation – and in fact, as we have seen, the better consciousness is the consciousness of the supersensible world. But another interesting fact is that this noun is specified by means of an *adjective in comparative form* ("better"): this evidently presupposes, as a term of comparison, a second consciousness, namely man's habitual or ordinary consciousness, which Schopenhauer calls "empirical consciousness".

In the years when Schopenhauer was writing, the adjective 'better' was used quite frequently – both in literature and in philosophy – to indicate what in humans exceeds the purely empirical or material dimension. For example, in the *Groundwork of the Metaphysics of Morals*, Kant wrote that man, insofar as he fulfills the categorical imperative and thinks of himself as a "member of the world of understanding", feels that he is a "better person [*bessere Person*]".[76] In *On Divine Things and Their Revelation*, referring to the supersensible nature of man, Jacobi had spoken of man's "nobler and better part [*edlern und bessern Theil*]" and (quoting Herder) of man's "supreme self [*höchste Selbst*]".[77] Goethe's *Faust* also mentions man's "better soul".[78] Similarly, in his *Philosophical Investigations into the Essence of Human Freedom*, Schelling spoke of "the inner voice of his [man's] own better nature [*seines eignen besseren Wesens*]".[79] In *Philosophical Letters on Dogmatism and Criticism*, Schelling mentioned the "better selves [*besseres Selbst*]" of all true philosophers, which makes them aspire to the re-establishment of an orig-

---

75 This point seems to be underestimated by R. Safranski (1990, pp. 132–133), according to whom "the 'better consciousness' is not consciousness of *something*', but a pure "unrelatable" inner "experience": it "has the world before it", but it's "a world which [...] ceases, in a certain sense, to be 'actual'".
76 Kant 1996b, p. 101.
77 Cf. Jacobi 1811, pp. 164, 185; Chenet 1997.
78 J. W. Goethe, *Faust*, I 1181, Goethe 2014, p. 32.
79 Schelling 2006, p. 54.

7.7 Some Remarks on the Expression "Better Consciousness"

inal and lost "absolute state".[80] The very expression *besseres Bewußtsein* (or *besseres Bewußtseyn*) is found in the works of two German writers contemporary with Schopenhauer, namely Therese Huber[81] and Benedikte Naubert.[82]

However, the combination of the noun "consciousness" with an adjective in comparative form ("better") – and thus the assumption of a second consciousness within the same individual as a term of comparison – undoubtedly came to Schopenhauer from Fichte. It is in fact when commenting on Fichte's first lecture "On the Facts of Consciousness" that Schopenhauer spoke for the first time of two different consciousnesses in man (cf. *supra*, 5.6). In that note, Schopenhauer names the higher consciousness using Fichte's terminology (i.e. as "a perceiving of perceiving"), thus revealing that he had not yet developed his own original lexicon ("better consciousness").

Indeed, in 1812 Schopenhauer attributed to the better consciousness the same predicates that, a few months earlier, he had referred to the "thing itself [*die Sache selbst*]" of the "perceiving of perceiving" (cf. *supra*, 5.6): just as the latter "cannot have a name" because "it is not taken from the world of experience",[83] so too the former can only be expressed "negatively [*negativ*]", as it "lies beyond all experience".[84] Moreover, just as the "thing itself" of the "perceiving of perceiving" was opposed to the "*understanding*'s [...] concept",[85] so now the better consciousness is opposed to "reason" (theoretical reason and understanding, for young Arthur, are one and the same thing: cf. *supra*, 7.4). Finally, the "mysterious connexion" between better consciousness[86] and reason in the same individual seems to thematize precisely the *foundation* of the two questions posed by those who reach the *absolute Besonnenheit*:[87] in fragment 35, too, the relationship in the self between a "consciousness that is given in perception" and a "consciousness that is not given through perception" is extremely problematic.[88] In the light of these considerations, it is likely that Schopenhauer took the fundamental idea of two opposing

---

80 Schelling 1980, p. 182.
81 Cf. T. Huber 1800 (cf. V. A. Huber 1830–1833, vol. 5, p. 133).
82 Cf. Naubert 1793–1797, part 5, p. 9.
83 MR 2, p. 33.
84 MR 1, n. 35, p. 23.
85 MR 2, pp. 33.
86 MR 1, n. 35, p. 23.
87 MR 2, pp. 33.
88 MR 2, pp. 33.

consciousnesses in man from Fichte (even if he then determined them differently from Fichte).[89] But there are further elements that reinforce this thesis.

In the last lectures "On the Facts of Consciousness", Fichte speaks of a "higher intuition [*höhere Anschauung*]",[90] a "higher knowledge [*höheres Wissen*]",[91] a "higher consciousness [*höheres Bewußtseyn*]",[92] and a "higher view [*höhere Ansicht*]".[93] And, at the beginning of his course "On the *Wissenschaftslehre*", he contrasts the "factual consciousness [*faktisches Bewußtseyn*]" with a "higher consciousness [*höheres Bewußtseyn*]", understood as consciousness (or awareness) of the former.[94] Fichte also characterizes factual consciousness as "empirical consciousness [*empirisches Bewußtseyn*]".[95]

Moreover, Fichte intentionally speaks of the "higher intuition" in a *negative* way: the "seeing" in which this intuition consists is a "seeing of nothing" (*ihr Sehen ist ein Sehen von Nichts*), because it is the 'nothingness' of factual intuition.[96] Similarly, for Schopenhauer, the negative form of any possible discourse on better consciousness consists in the negation of empirical determinations.[97] Finally, Fichte's "higher intuition" is closely connected to moral consciousness (it "appears [...] in reference to the factual I as an absolute law of its action, an ought [*Soll*]"),[98] just like the better consciousness (the latter appears to reason as a moral duty, as *Soll*).[99]

Schopenhauer expressed unequivocal agreement with all these aspects of Fichte's exposition (cf. *supra*, 5.2–5.5). Commenting on the remarks about "higher intuition", he even let out a burst of enthusiasm: "Truly spoken [*"Wahr gesprochen*]!".[100] Listening to Fichte's lectures thus probably had an extraordinarily propulsive effect on Schopenhauer, urging him to elaborate his *own* (original) theory

---

89 On the possibility that the expression "better consciousness" originated under the influence of Fichte's courses, cf. Kamata 1988, pp. 120–121; Chenet 1997, p. 107; Barbera 1998, pp. 70–71; Barbera 2004, p. 24; De Cian 2002, p. 152; App 2011, p. 57.
90 MR 2, p. 78. Translation modified.
91 MR 2, p. 75.
92 MR 2, p. 80.
93 MR 2, p. 78.
94 Cf. MR 2, p. 89.
95 Cf. MR 2, p. 84.
96 MR 2, p. 89.
97 Schopenhauer certainly heard about Plotinus and negative theology in Schleiermacher's lectures; but these were given in the summer semester of 1812, after Fichte's lectures. Cf. MR2, pp. 240–243.
98 MR 2, p. 85.
99 MR 1, n. 35, p. 23.
100 MR 2, p. 80.

7.8 Art as a Stimulus to Better Consciousness: "Out of What Appeared to Be Nothing a World Springs Up and the Prodigious Vanishes into Nothing"

of twofold consciousness – without prejudice to the above-mentioned substantial theoretical differences that Schopenhauer intended to imprint on his own theoretical project as opposed to the philosophies of Fichte and Schelling (cf. *supra*, 6.10; *infra*, 7.13).

Trying to further define and ground the opposition between reason – both practical and theoretical – and better consciousness, Schopenhauer wrote:

> Thus *reason* [...] undergoes a disturbance; as *theoretical* reason we see it supplanted and in its place *genius*, as *practical* we see it supplanted and in its place *virtue*. – The *better consciousness* is neither practical nor theoretical, for these are merely divisions of *reason*. – But if the individual is still at the standpoint of choice, then the better consciousness appears to him from the side where it supplants practical reason (*vulgo* instinct) as a *commanding law*, as *an ought* [*Soll*]. It *appears* to him, I say, in other words obtains this form in theoretical reason which makes objects and concepts of everything. But to the extent that the better consciousness tries to supplant theoretical reason, it does not appear to this at all [...].[101]

Nothing positive can be predicated about the better consciousness; it can only be described in negative terms, and in this sense it is "neither practical nor theoretical", because these two determinations also belong to reason. However, the better consciousness makes itself visible through the very rare phenomena of "genius" and "virtue" (understood as compliance with the moral law: cf. *supra*, 7.5 – 7.6).

Immediately before, Schopenhauer had stated that "as theoretical *reason* [the individual] will be a philistine and as practical reason a scoundrel". Now he writes that theoretical reason is supplanted by genius and practical reason by virtue. This implies the opposition of the terms genius / philistine (or theoretical reason), on the one hand, and virtue / scoundrel (or practical reason), on the other.

For Schopenhauer, a "philistine" is anyone who limits their horizon to the sensible sphere (cf. *supra*, 2.10). The fact that the genius supplants theoretical reason and stands in opposition to the philistine therefore means that he is capable of cognizing the supersensible world. This implication is perfectly consistent with other annotations I have already examined. In particular, in the note to Fichte's first lecture "On the Study of Philosophy", Schopenhauer had affirmed that the genius cog-

---

[101] MR 1, n. 35, p. 24.

nizes (*erkennt*) not only appearances, but also things-in-themselves;[102] and, in his commentary on Schelling's *Essays in Explanation of the Idealism of the Science of Knowledge*, he wrote that what the mystics call "illumination" and Plato, in the *Republic*, "rising to the spiritual sun" constitutes "the inner essence of genius".[103] I have already noted the Romantic origins of this conception of genius and art (cf. *supra*, 1.8; 3.2 – 3.4).[104]

Precisely because of this essential relation to the better consciousness, which is inexpressible and incomprehensible to reason, genius can never explain the origin and functioning of its creative process (it "can never give an account of its own works").[105] The mention of this characteristic of genius and the attempt to offer a justification for it reveal Schopenhauer's familiarity with some fundamental pages of Kant and Schelling.[106]

The connection between *art* and *cognition of the supersensible* is explicitly emphasized in fragment 46. Here Schopenhauer writes that "In fairy-tales, Arabesques and the *Parmenides* of Plato the attractive and the aesthetic are to be found in the fact that in them the impossible appears as the possible": for example, in arabesques the law of gravity is abolished, in the Parmenides the laws of logic are suppressed.[107] Hence

> an entirely new course of things has come about; at every step we are surprised afresh by the otherwise impossible. The heavy has become light and the light heavy; out of what appeared to be nothing a world springs up and the prodigious vanishes into nothing.
>
> That all this affects us aesthetically, that is to say arouses the better consciousness, is due to our perceiving how conditioned this world of the senses and its laws are, how unessential and adventitious. On the other hand, we recognize [*erkennen*] the more clearly the contrast [*den Gegensatz*], that with which we cannot trifle, the unconditioned [*das Unbedingte*], the essential, the necessary.[108]

The representation of what is logically or physically "impossible" in the realm of experience makes the subject aware of the finiteness and transience of the sensory world (and its laws), i.e. of the fact that the latter – contrary to what the philistine

---

102 MR 2, pp. 18 – 19.
103 MR 2, p. 351.
104 See also Hübscher 1989, pp. 35 – 36.
105 MR 1, n. 35, p. 24.
106 This problem, addressed by Kant in the *Critique of the Power of Judgment*, Kant 2000, §§ 46 – 47, pp. 186 – 189, had found a radical speculative development in Schelling (cf. Schelling 2001, p. 219 – 228).
107 MR 1, n. 46, p. 27.
108 MR 1, n. 46, p. 27.

believes – *is not everything.* By presenting what is impossible (in the world of the senses) as possible, fairy tales, Arabesques and Plato's *Parmenides* hint at the sphere in which the impossible is, in fact, possible; the reader of these works thus opens up, albeit indirectly, to the "unconditioned", in the face of which the world and the understanding appear as a contingent nothingness (*zufälliges Nichtiges*).[109] This is why the aesthetic effect of a work of art is to stimulate the better consciousness, which is precisely the consciousness of the unconditioned. The verb used by Schopenhauer here, as in fragment 32, is *erkennen:* the unconditioned can be *cognized.*

Conversely, the violation of the "moral and aesthetic forms and rules", which fall within the realm of the unconditional, would produce "the entirely opposite effect": by hinting at the domain in which those rules can be (and in fact are) violated, it would focus the reader's attention on the world of the senses.[110] This, according to Schopenhauer, cannot happen in any fairy tale or arabesque, because it contradicts their didascalic intent.

Along with cognition of the unconditioned, brought about by the enjoyment of works of art, the entire sensory world, which the common man views as something "prodigious", "vanishes into nothing [*verschwindet in Nichts*]"; at the same time, from what until then "appeared to be nothing" – the sphere of the supersensible – "a world springs up". Here, once again, we find Schopenhauer's radical dualism: the unconditioned (the supersensible) is the opposite (*Gegensatz*) of the world of the senses, because the "laws" or "rules" that apply in the former are perfectly opposed to those that apply in the latter, and vice versa. By virtue of this total opposition, for those who only cognize the sensory world, the sphere of the supersensible is "nothing"; and vice versa, for those who come to cognize the latter, it is the former that becomes "nothing". These considerations, only sketched out here, would soon be significantly developed (cf. *infra,* 8.2).

7.9 The Moral Law as a "Higher Faculty of Cognition". The Annihilation of One's Own Will in the Notes to Fichte's *System der Sittenlehre:* A Third False Precedent of the System

In some notes on Fichte's *System der Sittenlehre,* the idea that the moral law is a special place for the manifestation or revelation of the supersensible is taken to

---

[109] MR 1, n. 46, p. 27.
[110] MR 1, n. 46, p. 27.

theoretical extremes, which even seem to anticipate the mature doctrine of the "negation of the will". In this work, the concept of "will" takes on an extraordinary relevance from the very first pages, in which the "theorem" is enunciated (and then demonstrated): "I find myself as myself only as willing".[111] This theorem would have an enormous and decisive influence on Schopenhauer (cf. *infra*, 9.4 – 9.6, 9.12).

For Fichte "the will is always a power of choosing [...]. There is no will [*Wille*] without arbitrary choice [*Willkür*]".[112] He distinguishes *material freedom* from the *formal freedom* of the will. The former coincides with the "arbitrary choice" itself, i.e., the faculty to choose either between "several possible satisfactions" of a given natural drive or between "the satisfaction of a selfish drive (namely, the natural drive) and an unselfish one (the ethical drive)"; the "formal freedom" of the will, which makes the former possible (in both versions), is "the power to postpone" or suspend "natural satisfaction" and reflect on what to do.[113]

Schopenhauer comments that the *Willkür* – which he understands as the "choice with reflectiveness [*Besonnenheit*] among objects of desire [*Gegenständen des Begehrens*]" – implies a *calculation* of the ratio between means and ends, and thus also of present and future pleasures; it is thus essentially free from the "limitation through time" and constitutes a peculiarity of the human being: animals only live in the present.[114] Consisting in this careful choice between different objects of desire, the *Willkür* ultimately coincides with "practical reason" – "however loudly Kantians may shout".[115] It is clear that this statement presupposes the considerations made in the fragment *Zu Kant* and fragment 35 concerning the concept of "reason" (cf. *supra*, 7.4 – 7.5).

On the possibility that the will may choose between ethical and selfish actions, Schopenhauer observes:

> The freedom of the will could be called a freedom of *not-willing* [*Freyheit des* Nichtwollens]. [...] But the freedom of the will is the ability of annihilation [*Vernichtung*] of the whole of one's own will [*des ganzen Eigenwillens*], and its supreme law is "thou shalt will nothing" [*Du sollst nichts wollen*].[116]

---

111 Fichte 2005, p. 24.
112 Fichte 2005, p. 151.
113 Fichte 2005, p. 153.
114 MR 2, p. 402.
115 MR 2, p. 402.
116 MR 2, p. 402. Translation modified.

While *arbitrary choice* presupposes a will directed towards certain objects (those that are in fact favored in the choice), the *true freedom of the will* consists, for Schopenhauer, in not willing at all, or in the "annihilation" of "one's own will". In the first case, the will is free only in relation to certain objects (those that are discarded in the choice); in the second case, on the other hand, the will is free in relation to *all* possible objects, because nothing is willed.

After annihilating one's own will, Schopenhauer continues, "all individuality has ceased", so that all those who have achieved such destruction act in the same way.[117] This is why Kant called the moral law "objective": because acting according to it is regulated not by the subject, but by the object of the action.[118]

> Now although in this case all willing has ceased, my action nevertheless appears as the consequence of a willing, but only so does it appear. I act as though the object were my concept of purpose, for the moment of acting I even make it for this, because this is the condition of all acting (just as one tells a story that a spirit or God assumes human form in order to act on human beings). However, I do not act as I *will* but as I *ought*, and this *ought* [Soll] abolishes *willing*.[119]

Ought (*Soll*) suppresses (*hebt ... auf*) willing (*Wollen*). Consequently, writes Schopenhauer, "I, my *self*, my individuality, no longer acts at all, but it is the instrument of something inexpressible [*eines Unnennbaren*], of an eternal law".[120] In enabling a relationship with this "inexpressible", the moral law is actually *"a higher faculty of cognition* [ein höheres Erkenntnisvermögen]".[121] Recall that Schulze, in his lecture, had described the postulates of practical reason as a form of "cognition" of their objects (cf. *supra*, 2.12). In fragment 60 Schopenhauer states that "the motive of a purely moral resolve is a supersensible one"[122] – which therefore, if only as a "motive" for action, must be known in some way. This allows him to refer expressly to Plato, according to whom virtue is *episteme* and vice is error.[123]

Now, the fact that chance prevents one from carrying out what this eternal law (the moral law) prescribes is irrelevant: the aim of ethical action is not the object (which is only taken as a *"pro forma"* purpose), but the action itself ("therefore Kant calls the moral law a *formal* law"), i.e. the *proposition* to act.[124]

---

117 MR 2, p. 402.
118 MR 2, p. 403.
119 MR 2, p. 402.
120 MR 2, pp. 402–403.
121 MR 2, p. 404. Translation modified.
122 MR 1, n. 60, p. 34.
123 MR 2, p. 404.
124 MR 2, p. 403.

> [...] instead of my will, the relation between object and subject (the deed) should be determined by something different (the inexpressible).
>
> The virtuous man acts as though he *willed*, but he no longer *wills*.[125]

For the moral law to be truly and purely "objective", "my individuality, i.e. my own will [*Eigenwille*] should [...] be annihilated [*vernichtet*]".[126] The Kantian moral law ("So act that the maxim of your will could always hold at the same time as a principle in a giving of universal law"),[127] in fact, prescribes a universal action: that is, an action in which the individuality of the agent is not relevant, since their specific personal interests (i.e. any kind of interest) are eliminated. Kant himself had stated that the moral law does not belong "to the element to which he [man] is naturally accustomed", but instead "it constrains him to leave this element, often not without self-denial [*Selbstverleugnung*], and to go to a higher element in which he can maintain himself only with effort and with unceasing apprehension of relapsing".[128]

Schopenhauer identifies *the fulfillment of the moral law* with the *negation of one's "own will"*. Similarly, in fragment 28, he contrasts the fulfillment of the moral law with the affirmation (*behaupten*) of one's "own will", which is aimed at "selfhood" (*den Eigenwillen seiner Selbstheit*).[129]

In these passages of the *Nachlass*, we might see an anticipation of the "negation of the will-to-life [*Verneinung des Willens zum Leben*]",[130] which would be one of the central themes of Schopenhauer's mature system.[131] But Schopenhauer's concept of "will" was destined to become much more complex before acquiring the meaning it would take on in the mature system; and, after all, one can legitimately refer the logically dependent concept of "negation of the will" only to this meaning (cf. *infra*, 10.7–10.13; 11.3, 11.12–11.13). For now, let's only note that the "will" mentioned in the comment to the *System der Sittenlehre* is not yet the *will-to-life*, nor is it the *thing-in-itself*, of which the whole world is the appearance; consequently, its negation cannot yet mean what in *The World as Will and Representation* will be called, precisely, "negation of the will-to-life".

Rather, it is likely that young Schopenhauer was referring to the writings of Jakob Böhme and Schelling. The term *Eigenwille* had been used in German mysti-

---

[125] MR 2, p. 403.
[126] MR 2, p. 403. Translation modified.
[127] Kant 1996a, p. 164.
[128] Kant 1996a, p. 266.
[129] Cf. MR 1, n.28, p. 18. Translation modified.
[130] Cf. Schopenhauer 2010b, I 363–487, § 56–71, pp. 334–439.
[131] Cf. G. Zöller 2006, pp. 382–386.

cism – especially by Meister Eckhart and Johannes Tauler – to indicate the perverse and intentional 'bending back' of the creature on itself (the *natura in se ipsa recurva* described by Aquinas):[132] the will to selfhood rather than will to God.[133] In the *Philosophical Investigations into the Essence of Human Freedom* (which Arthur read in 1811), developing the reflections made in *Philosophy and Religion*, Schelling had taken up this terminology, following a passionate theoretical exchange with the works of Böhme.[134]

In 1812, Schopenhauer was already familiar with Böhme's work: he said of Schelling's *Philosophical Investigations* that "It is almost only a recasting of Jacob Böhme's *Mysterium magnum*, in which practically every sentence and every expression can be identified" (cf. *infra*, 9.10).[135] Thus, when he identified the content of Kant's moral law with the *Vernichtung* of the *Eigenwille*, Schopenhauer was probably thinking of something similar to the mystical annihilation of one's own individuality (the description and celebration of which could also be found in Zacharias Werner's plays).[136] But this, in itself, is not enough to anticipate the peculiarity of his mature discourse, concerning the "negation of the will-to-life".

On the other hand, one should not underestimate the importance of the first theorem of Fichte's *System of Ethics*, according to which "I find *myself* [italics mine] as myself only as *willing* [italics mine]". Indeed, Schopenhauer could identify the annihilation of *oneself* with that of *one's will* based on that theorem, which identifies precisely the individual's self (as known by the individual) with his will.

7.10 Dualism of Things and Duplicity of Man. Philosophical Astonishment

In 1808 Schopenhauer expressly contrasted the "external", "corporeal" world with a "spiritual world" (cf. *supra*, 1.5). Although these are two absolutely and mutually opposed realms, man participates in both.[137] In 1812 Schopenhauer similarly distinguished between a sensible and a supersensible world: they are completely separate from each other, i.e. they "are not a *continuum*" (cf. *supra*, 7.3). In the human

---

132 Cf. Thomas Aquinas, *Quaestiones quodlibetales*, I, q. 4, 3; Thomas Aquinas 2019, p. 195.
133 Cf. Eckhart 2009, pp. 108–111.
134 Cf. Berg 2003, pp. 173–176. On Schopenhauer and Böhme, cf. Weeks 1992; Hübscher 1969, p. 22; Rätze 1820; Garewicz 1987. Cf. also Bonheim and Regehly 2008.
135 MR 2, p. 353.
136 Cf. App 2011, p. 33.
137 MR 1, n. 12, p. 8.

individual, however, the subjective correlates of these two worlds (reason and better consciousness, respectively) lie in a "mysterious connexion [*geheimnißvolle Verbindung*]" – so much so that one can switch from one to the other, choosing whether to "be *reason* or *better consciousness*".[138] This connection is "mysterious" precisely because it unites two realms which in themselves, as they do not form a continuum, are (or should be) irretrievably separate.

Every 'thing' – any entity other than man – belongs exclusively and necessarily to only one of the two realms; the human subject, on the other hand, is unique within them, because, unlike a 'thing' (*any* 'thing'), he is simultaneously a member of both. A distinction must therefore be made between *dualism*, which concerns things, and *duplicity*, which concerns the subject. The inexplicability of that connection concerns precisely the possibility of a *relation* (and thus of a middle term) between two *absolutely opposite* realms. Schopenhauer admits such a connection not on the basis of any deduction (what can be deduced is by no means mysterious), but by virtue of direct (inner) experience, i.e. as a *fact*.[139]

> From time to time there arises in me the most vivid awareness of having existed from time immemorial, and the effect on me is one of great elation and of renewed vigour.
>
> Again there is sometimes forced on me an astonishment at the present moment, and I have to ask: why is this Now right now?
>
> I have tried to stimulate this thought in others by saying that *the future like the past is not real and actual* [wirklich]; Socrates and Julius Caesar, Shakespeare and Rousseau, are nothing *real* and all these have merely *been*. The present alone is *real and actual* and we are the ones made happy by it. – But this present is in time exactly what the mathematical line is in space; it is nothing but the boundary between past and future. Therefore our something real and actual is merely the boundary between two non-existences, and as a boundary it is without extension.
>
> That awareness of a beginningless past and this astonishment at the present, at that one thing which I can never for one moment lose sight of, these two are an illusion [*Täuschung*], or rather they are the temporal expression of my supertemporal being.[140]

The terms with which the passage opens, "awareness [*Bewußtseyn*]" and "astonishment [*Verwundern*]", are repeated at the end: "*that* [italics mine] awareness", "*this* [italics mine] astonishment". This means that the "awareness of having existed from time immemorial" mentioned at the beginning is identical with the "awareness of a beginningless past" mentioned at the end. It is therefore the subject's

---

138 MR 1, n. 35, p. 23.
139 Contrary to F. Decher (1996, p. 68), I therefore fully agree with H. Zint (1921, p. 22), according to whom Schopenhauer's early philosophy is also an expression of his direct inner 'experience'.
140 MR 1, n. 22, p. 15. Translation modified.

awareness of his *own* infinite past. The "astonishment at the present" arises from the consideration that, with respect to an infinite past and future, the 'being-now' of the actual "Now" seems accidental; that is, the *link* between a precise temporal coordinate (the "Now") and its being present seems fortuitous and therefore inexplicable: any other coordinate of this infinite time could have been "now".[141]

However, Schopenhauer goes on to say that both of these things – the awareness of one's own infinite past and the astonishment at the present – are nothing but an "illusion" or, more precisely, "the temporal expression of my supertemporal being", because they concern the way in which the subject, through time relations, represents his own being outside of time. In more general terms, an empirical determination (time) is here used figuratively (cf. *supra*, 7.2) to express what is beyond all possible empiricism (the subject's own "supertemporal being").

Schopenhauer feels that he is part of both a temporal existence and a "supertemporal being", but it is only the latter that he considers to be his true essence: "if we commune deeply with ourselves, we find that [...] time (which philosophers and mystics long before Kant expressed through the concept of an eternity) is to us immaterial, likewise the division of our consciousness into object and subject".[142] He feels his eternal nature so strongly that he is *surprised* that he exists in time, as a finite subjectivity:

> I wonder how I have become a subject, and that is why I philosophize: driven by the consciousness that subject-objectivity is not my absolute state or condition, but a state from which I long for redemption [*Erlösung*].[143]

The "motive of all genuine philosophical endeavour" is precisely the "yearning [*Sehnsucht*]" to free oneself from all determinations of finiteness.[144] In analyzing Fichte's concept of *absolute Besonnenheit*, Schopenhauer wrote, in a very similar sense, that "philosophical astonishment at the world, *in other words* [italics mine] at that second consciousness in perception (which for common sense is the only one)", arises when man rises to "a consciousness which exists by itself,

---

141 This thought is taken up in fragment 263, pp. 174–175: "The question, for ever unanswerable, is why the Now is precisely now, it arises from the fact that we regard time as independent of our existence and this existence as thrown into time, We assume two Nows, one belonging to the object and one to the subject, and marvel at their coincidence. But the NOW is simply this coincidence, this contact of object and subject; (again both these exist only in this contact and nowhere else). For naturally it must be identical with itself, Now = Now, the Now is always just now". Translation modified.
142 MR 2, p. 360.
143 MR 2, pp. 364–365. Translation modified.
144 MR 2, pp. 364–365.

is not dependent on perception, is not given through this"[145] (cf. *supra*, 5.6). If and insofar as he is aware of his own absoluteness, man wonders at being confined to the narrow contingency and imperfection of the empirical world. The famous passage from the *Life of Plotinus*, in which Porphyry recounts that Plotinus seemed to be ashamed to be in a body, comes to mind here.[146] But young Schopenhauer did not attribute man's duplicity to body-soul dualism, because for him the "soul" – together with the other two "transcendental ideas" of reason – is a transcendent concept of the understanding:[147] any discussion of the "soul" is therefore a "paralogism" of pure reason (cf. *supra*, 6.3 and 6.9).[148]

In fragment 58, probably taking up a passage from Schelling's *Philosophical Letters*,[149] Schopenhauer admits man's "better self", situated above all the events of empirical or finite life:

> *Against suicide* it could be said that man ought to rise above life, ought to recognize that al happenings and events, pleasures and pains, do not touch his better and inner self [*sein bessres und Innres Selbst*] and that therefore the whole thing is a game, an ignominious tournament, and not a struggle in earnest, and consequently he ought not to introduce into it any seriousness. But this he could do in two different ways: either by vice, which is nothing but an action contrary to that inner and better self, whereby he thus makes this self an object of mockery and fun, the game, however, being played in earnest. Or he could do it by suicide, and here he shows that he cannot take a joke, but takes this as something serious. [...].[150]

Vice and *suicide* result from taking the *pleasures* and *pains* of the "game" of life seriously, as if they were real.

Now, attaining cognition of supersensible reality (i.e. the "better cognition"), man recognizes the "duplicity of his being [*Die Duplicität seines Seyns*]", or rather its "two kinds [*Arten*]".[151] The spectacle of "tragedy" can have a didascalic value in this respect: "In Oedipus Rex, Hamlet, The Steadfast Prince, Egmont, Lear and oth-

---

145 MR 2, p. 33.
146 Plotinus 1969, p. 3.
147 MR 2, p. 378.
148 MR 2, p. 342.
149 Schelling 1980, p. 182: "All philosophers, even those of the earliest antiquity, seem to have felt, at least, that there must be an absolute state in which we, —present to ourselves alone", fully content, and not in need of any objective world and therefore free from its limitations—live a higher life [*ein höheres Leben*]. This state of intellectual being they all located outside of their selves. They felt that their better selves [*ihr besseres Selbst*] were unceasingly striving for that state yet could never fully attain it. Consequently, they conceived of it as the final goal desired by what was best in them" (Eighth Letter).
150 MR 1, n. 58, p. 33.
151 MR 2, p. 377. Translation modified.

ers, the innocent, the noble and the very virtuous are overthrown and vice triumphs and mocks". Consequently, "the spectator is forced to rise to a loftier world [*in eine höhere Welt*], from which the events of this world (that which is knowable through the understanding) are seen as semblance and nothingness [*Schein und Nichtigkeit*]: he feels his true being – οντως ον – and obtains an imperturbable and absolute satisfaction".[152] In 1813, Schopenhauer would similarly write that "Just as the chord of the seventh requires the next full chord, as red demands green and even produces this in the eye, so does every *tragedy* call for another world",[153] in which the 'dissonance' presented by the triumph of evil and pain is resolved once and for all.

"True criticism" will have to recognize and legitimately expose the essential duplicity of the human being; to the extent that it explains it fully, it will solve the original mystery from which philosophical astonishment springs, and by doing so, it will bring about the end – or perfect fulfillment – of philosophy itself.[154]

The idea that philosophizing is the theoretical and practical *separation* of man's two heterogeneous natures (irrespective of how they are defined or determined: as "body" and "soul", or as "empirical consciousness" and "better consciousness"), and thus of his two different and respective modes of cognition, is set out most clearly in Plato's *Phaedo*.[155] It is likely that young Schopenhauer kept these pages very much in mind – though many years later, he would criticize these very passages as the paradigm of "false dianoiology" with a metaphysical purpose, definitively refuted by Kant.[156]

In two notes to Fichte, Schopenhauer describes in extremely dramatic tones the disagreement that man, once aware of his own duplicity, feels between his "fictitious I [*scheinbares Ich*]", confined to the sensible world, and his "true I [*wahres Ich*]": "the serene and sublime hour", in which the "highest attainment" of the "true I" prevails, is rare; life, even "of the best man", consists mostly of "hours of gloom, dreariness and brutishness", marked by the consciousness of the "fictitious I", so that they are a "long, constant and restless struggle without a victory".[157] The "toil and labour of life" consists precisely in lighting up the dark mo-

---

[152] MR 2, p. 416. Translation modified.
[153] MR 1, n.124, p. 85.
[154] Cf. MR 2, p. 377.
[155] Cf. Plato, *Phaedo*, 80 c–83 c, Plato 1914 ff., vol, 1, pp. 384–389.
[156] Cf. Schopenhauer 2014, p. 42.
[157] MR 2, pp. 396–397.

ments of existence with the awareness of those supreme moments of cognition (*Erkenntniß*) of the truth.[158]

Like Plato (and Plotinus), Schopenhauer excludes that this painful "contradiction" between man's two natures can be resolved before death.[159] This implies that only death (of the body) will bring about their total separation. If, therefore, Schopenhauer rejects the term "soul" to denote man's *supersensible nature*, he implicitly maintains the opposition between the latter and the "body" (considered precisely as man's *sensible nature*).

7.11 The Will as a Faculty of Choice between Empirical Consciousness and Better Consciousness: The Root of Schopenhauer's 'Voluntarism'

The duplicity of the human being consists of the opposition between an empirical consciousness and a better consciousness in every individual. For the person who becomes aware of these two natures, "arises the choice whether he wants to be *reason* or *better consciousness* [*die Wahl* [...] *ob es* Vernunft *oder* bessres Bewußtseyn *seyn will*]".[160]

The will is what enables man to choose *what to* be: "if he *wants* [italics mine] to be *reason* [*Will es* Vernunft seyn]", then he *will be* reason; "if he *wants* [italics mine] to be *better consciousness*", then he *will be* better consciousness.[161] This implies the existence of an area or dimension of the individual which, outside of this act of will, is originally and essentially indeterminate, and thus must be determined on the basis of free choice (cf. *infra*, 8.4 and 8.11).

Besides a "better consciousness" and "better cognition", Schopenhauer also posits a "better will" in man:

> [...] the genuine, that is to say the critical, philosopher should do theoretically what the virtuous man does practically. Thus the latter does not make the desire [*Begehren*] attaching to him through his sensible nature into an absolute desire, but follows the better will [*dem bessern Willen*] in him without associating it with that desire, as for example with a reward [...]. In just the same way, the genuine critical philosopher separates his better cognizing [*sein*

---

[158] MR 2, pp. 396–397. The importance of this note to Fichte's *Grundzüge des gegenwärtigen Zeitalters* has rightly been underlined by N. De Cian (2002, pp. 114–117).
[159] Cf. MR 2, p. 399: "no blissful life, as Fichte wants, is possible before death" (note to Fichte's *Anweisung zum Seligen Leben*).
[160] MR 1, n. 35, p. 23. Translation modified.
[161] MR 1, n. 35, p. 23.

beßres Erkennen] from the conditions of empirical cognizing and does not carry these over into the former (as does the sensible man his sensible pleasures into paradise [...]) [...]. On the contrary, he coldly and imperturbably leaves behind the conditions of his empirical cognition, content to have clearly separated the better cognition from that other, and to have recognized the duplicity of his being.[162]

The virtuous man separates his "better will" from his "desire [*Begehren*]" for finite things, just as the critical philosopher separates his "better consciousness" from empirical consciousness. Elsewhere Schopenhauer contrasted man's "empirical will" with the illumination of the mystics and the spiritual sun mentioned in Plato's *Republic*, which in his view coincide with the "pure will"[163] (Kant's term for the will as determined by moral law; cf. *supra*, 7.5). The empirical will is determined by material purposes (Kant spoke of "the empirically affected will");[164] the better will is instead the yearning for the metempirical world. Goethe, in his *Faust*, gave a paradigmatic expression to the dissonance between these two opposing human tensions: "Two souls, alas! Reside within my breast [*Zwei Seelen wohnen, ach! In meiner Brust*], / and each is eager for separation [*sich ... trennen*]: / In throes of coarse desire, one grips / the earth with all its senses; / the other struggles from the dust / to rise to high ancestral spheres."[165]

Now, in Schopenhauer's above-mentioned reflections, the will is the main element, because only on the basis of the will can the individual determine himself as reason (in the broad sense, i.e. empirical consciousness) or as better consciousness. This already presupposes a radical, albeit as yet unexpressed, form of 'voluntarism': *the will is more original than reason and better consciousness*, because the latter are only the two possible objects of "choice" for the former, so that they are essentially and inevitably subordinate to it.[166]

The development of this part of the discourse, still confined here to the implicit dimension of the texts, would decisively condition the evolution of Schopenhauer's thought (cf. *infra*, 8.3, 8.18 and 8.19; 10.7–10.13; 11.11; 12.7–12.10).

Arthur posited in all human beings the duplicity of empirical consciousness and better consciousness, as well as the possibility of determining oneself, through the will, as one or the other: this presupposed an unexpressed 'analogical argu-

---

162 MR 2, pp. 376–377. Translation modified.
163 MR 2, p. 351.
164 Kant 1996a, p. 214.
165 J. W. Goethe, *Faust* I, vv. 1112–1117, Goethe 2014, p. 30.
166 Therefore, I cannot agree with R. Malter (1988, p. 24), according to whom the "will" as such is neglected in the philosophy of the better consciousness; on the contrary, it holds a place of primary, albeit implicit, importance.

ment', through which Schopenhauer extended to other human beings what he could only experience in himself.

7.12 Nature as a Will-to-Life and Well-Being: A Fourth False Precedent of the System. The Duplicity of Man and the Consequent Ambiguity of the Term "Nature"

The affirmation of the duplicity of the human being has very important consequences for Schopenhauer's understanding of *nature*. Fragment 34, entitled "A little system [*Ein Systemchen*]", reads:

> Everywhere nature has only one purpose, namely to provide life and well-being [*Leben und Wohlseyn*] as much as possible, for possibility has its limits. [...]. Nature wills life and well-being as complete and for as long as possible, and the many different species of creatures are only many different paths to enjoyment [...].[167]

The teleology of nature consists in its wanting life and well-being for all the different species of living things. Now, man's *Soll*, his moral duty, is to want (and try to foster) what nature wants: the life and well-being of *all* living creatures, not just his own.

> The highest degree of self-consciousness manifests itself in man, a degree so high that he ought [*soll*] to do with consciousness what all other creatures do without it, namely promote life and well-being. This *ought* [*Soll*] that declares itself in his consciousness is the Categorical Imperative – he ought to will what nature wills – this is the meaning of the Peripatetics' *secundum naturam vivere*. [...] Just as nature sacrifices the smaller and less important in order to preserve the greater and more important, so does the Categorical Imperative require a man to sacrifice himself for the whole, for his country, and for the many. [...] our innermost being is concerned only with serving the purpose of nature [...].[168]

Compared to Kant's dictate, here the individual is not an "end in itself", but a simple means that nature predisposes and uses in view of the well-being of the Whole[169] (an idea that was destined to be retained in Schopenhauer's mature thought).[170]

---

[167] MR 1, n. 34, pp. 21–22.
[168] MR 1, p. 22.
[169] A. Sattar relates the content of this fragment to Herder's organicistic conception, conjecturing a potential influence of the latter's *Ideas for the Philosophy of the History of Humanity* (cf. Sattar 2016).
[170] Cf. Schopenhauer 2010b, I 325–337, § 54, pp. 301–312.

Schopenhauer's title for this fragment – "A little system" – can perhaps be explained by reference to the dualism between the temporal and the supertemporal realms (cf. *supra*, 7.1–7.2 and 7.10). The investigation of the sensible world, even if exhaustive and correct, can never constitute a true system, because it will only ever concern *a part* of reality (and, moreover, from young Schopenhauer's point of view, the part of least value). This title is probably intended in a sense that is not only slightly self-mocking (with respect to the reflections in the same fragment 34), but also, and above all, *critical* of those who believe the great task of philosophy can be completed through the investigation of nature.

"Now nature is a very fine thing, [...] but she remains a thing, albeit the greatest."[171] The fundamental error made by the philosophers of nature is to assume that cognition of nature is cognition "of the Absolute and not of the conditioned, of being [*des Seyns*] and not of semblance [*des Scheins*]".[172] This clearly implies that nature is semblance, not being.

> Nature is indeed that which alone is positively right and true and necessary, just the opposite of the will must be able to go wrong [*Irren können muß*]. She is the fixed point, the core, of life, the eternally, reliable, innocent like children who are still incapable of sinning. But try once to be entirely nature [*ganz Natur zu seyn*]; it is terrible to contemplate. You cannot have peace of mind unless you are resolved, if need be, to destroy yourself, and that means all of nature for yourself.[173]

If, on the one hand, imitating and supporting nature in its desire for "life and well-being" for the Whole means fulfilling the categorical imperative, on the other hand, the thought of "being entirely nature" is "terrible" for the individual. Now, Schopenhauer certainly does not mean that fulfilling the categorical imperative is terrible. And again: nature alone is truly untainted and innocent; nevertheless, man cannot attain "peace of mind" unless he first destroys the nature he finds within himself (unless he destroys himself *as* a natural being). Once again, Schopenhauer certainly does not intend to argue that the individual, in order to achieve "peace of mind", must destroy all righteousness and innocence in himself.

This fundamental ambiguity of the term "nature" does not denote inconsistency or contradiction in Schopenhauer's writings, but is the direct consequence of the duplicity of the human being, which is the basic premise of all these reflections. As a sensible being, man is part of nature; as a supersensible being, he is

---

171 MR 1, n. 47, p. 28.
172 MR 1, n. 30, p. 19. Translation modified.
173 MR 1, n. 47, p. 28. Translation modified.

not part of nature. Consequently, nature is – or rather, the term "nature" means – *what man is* and, at the same time, *what man is not*.

In this light, it seems very likely that by the expression "be entirely nature" Schopenhauer means man's loss of all participation in the supersensible world; and that by the expression "destroy all of nature for yourself" he means, on the contrary, man's loss of all participation in the sensible world. If this is so, what is "terrible" is, in fact, the thought of losing all participation in the supersensible world; while "peace of mind" is, conversely, the loss of all participation in the sensible world (that is, exclusive belonging to the supersensible world). If this interpretation is correct, the above-mentioned texts (as well as in fragment 2: cf. *supra*, 1.3) reveal an implicit desire on young Arthur's part to abolish or "annihilate" his sensible nature.

According to fragment 34, nature "wills life and well-being" for all creatures; the fact that man must destroy all nature for himself means that he must destroy all will (or desire) for life and well-being in himself. These youthful reflections should not be misunderstood as an anticipation of the mature system and, in particular, of the doctrine of the negation of the *Wille zum Leben*.[174] Nature's desire for life and well-being, which man must destroy, cannot be traced back to *The World*'s "will-to-life", which man must negate: unlike the latter, the former has no overtly metaphysical significance, coinciding rather with the will to self-preservation inscribed in every being. The mature system's "will-to-life" would be something much more radical than a mere, 'horizontal' will to self-preservation (cf. *infra*, 10.9).

These fragments are therefore more backward-looking than forward-looking, so to speak, in the sense that rather than anticipating something truly and radically new, they clarify the consequences of previously formulated thoughts. Take fragment 12 [v] (cf. *supra*, 1.6):

> We are not meant to thrive and flourish like the plants of the earth; every tragedy tells us this. Indeed, there must be something better [*etwas Besseres*], as the spectator says to himself, who finds relish in seeing the destruction of all those things which often seemed to him the most desirable.[175]

To think of "being entirely nature" is to reduce one's destiny to "thriving and flourishing like the plants of the earth". But the dreadful spectacle, offered by every

---

174 This interpretation is supported by A. Deligne (1991), who consequently believes that the title "A little system" does not have a parodic sense, because it would rather mean "a system in a nutshell" (cf. Deligne 1991, p. 31).
175 MR 1, n. 12, p. 8.

tragedy, of the disintegration that inevitably follows every "thriving" arouses in the spectator the *salvific* awareness of not "being entirely nature", that is, – in a positive sense – of having a supernatural, supersensible being.

7.13 Γνῶτι σεαυτόν: Man's "Supersensible Self-Consciousness". Better Consciousness and Intellectual Intuition

According to Schopenhauer, "genuine criticism", by fully differentiating the better consciousness (and its manifestations) from the empirical consciousness, will lead humankind to "supreme self-consciousness [*höchsten Selbstbewußtseyn*]": the commandment of the temple of Delphi, "know thyself", will finally be attained and the history of philosophy will come to an end (i.e. to its fulfillment).[176] The achievement of true criticism will in fact be to reveal and demonstrate the two different natures that constitute every human being: indeed, "empirical consciousness" and "better consciousness".[177] On the other hand, for Schopenhauer only the latter constitutes the "supreme innermost essence" of man;[178] the "I" that belongs to the world of the senses is only "fictitious", it is not the "true I" of the individual.[179] Man's true "supreme self-consciousness" consists in his self-cognition as a supersensible being.

In his lectures on the "History of Philosophy in the Time of Christianity", Schleiermacher contested Porphyry's testimony that Plotinus had only intuited God at exceptional moments and not constantly. For Schleiermacher, in fact, "a man must always have the intuition [*Anschauung*] of God, or he never has it."[180] Schopenhauer comments:

> *Nego ac pernego*. Either I do not admit at all the concept "intuition of God", or it must mean *"man's supreme self-consciousness, that is in the highest possible degree independent of his sensible nature."* In this sense I also take the sublime Jacob Boehme's illumination; we are informed that he was illuminated for the first time when he was an apprentice, for the second time in his twenty-fifth year, and for the third time in his thirty-fifth year. The [time] intervals are admittedly long, but everyone capable of supersensible self-consciousness knows that it is not always open to him; on the contrary, only rarely does it break through.[181]

---

176 MR 2, p. 416.
177 MR 2, p. 416.
178 MR 2. p. 372.
179 MR 2, p. 396.
180 MR 2, p. 242. Translation modified.
181 MR 2, p. 242. Translation modified.

Schopenhauer here identifies the "intuition of God" with man's "supreme self-consciousness" (or "supersensible self-consciousness"). This implies that the content of the intuition of God – i.e. God – is identical with the content of this self-consciousness – man's self (*Selbst*). Man's supersensible self-consciousness, therefore, is none other than his consciousness of himself as divine (i.e. his divine Self). It is "independent of his sensible nature" in the sense that, unlike the empirical one – which is the subject's self-consciousness as an empirical cognizing subject[182] – is not acquired in reference or in relation to external objects. According to Schopenhauer, man does not have this self-consciousness either "always" or "never", as Schleiermacher claims, but only rarely: the "serene hour", in which the "highest attainment" of man's "true I" prevails, is in fact only the smallest part of life (cf. *supra*, 7.10).[183]

The fundamental presupposition of Schopenhauer's remark is therefore the identity between God (the Absolute) and man's supersensible Self. On this point, recall the note on Schelling's *Ideas for a Philosophy of Nature*, cited earlier: "In so far as man unconditionally approaches the Absolute (as he can and should) he does not know about the Absolute but *is* the Absolute itself; but in so far as he philosophizes he does not do this" (cf. *supra*, 6.5).[184]

Contra Fichte and Schelling, Schopenhauer peremptorily excludes the possibility of the subject's actual self-cognition (cf. *supra*, 6.7). The splitting into subject and object is for him "the basis" and "the condition of our consciousness";[185] it can never fail, which means that the subject's self-cognition – understood as the *coincidence* of subject and object – is impossible.[186] Furthermore, in the wake of Kant's *Metaphysics of Morals*, Schopenhauer distinguishes between man "as thing-in-itself, *homo noumenon*", and man as phenomenon, "*homo phaenomenon*"; also (again in accordance with Kant), he explicitly states that one can only know oneself as *Erscheinung*, never as a thing-in-itself.[187]

At the same time, however, Schopenhauer feels the "presentiment [*Vorgefühl*]" of his own "absolute state", "in which there are no subject and object",[188] and thus admits man's "supersensible self-consciousness", i.e. man's knowledge of his own "better self".[189] How do these two sets of statements relate to each other?

---

182 MR 2, p. 383.
183 MR 2. p. 396.
184 MR 2, p. 359.
185 MR 2, pp. 378–379.
186 Cf. MR 2, pp. 380–381.
187 MR 1, n. 52, p. 30.
188 MR 2, p. 360.
189 MR 1, n. 58, p. 33.

The *subject's self-cognition* that Schopenhauer *excludes* is certainly not the same as the one he *admits*. The subject (and object) of the first is the empirical self of the individual, i.e. the empirical consciousness; the second one, on the other hand, concerns man's metempirical nature. The split into subject and object – the *impossibility* of their coincidence and therefore, in general, of any self-cognition – is neither the "basis" nor the "condition" of man's metempirical consciousness. This difference, however, seems rather weak, especially in view of the fact that Schelling, too, used the expression "intellectual intuition" to denote the self-cognition of man's eternal and divine nature (cf. *supra*, 3.5).[190] Schopenhauer's "better consciousness", just like Schelling's "intellectual intuition", is a cognitive "faculty [*Vermögen*]" that enables man to access the supersensible reality – first and foremost, *his own* supersensible reality. Both (better consciousness and intellectual intuition) relate to what "is contrary to, and *consequently beyond*, all understanding".[191]

Despite these important similarities, Schopenhauer understands his own discourse as profoundly different from that of Fichte and Schelling:

> Schelling's intellectual intuition is yet [*doch*] something different from the *better consciousness* which I attribute to man. The reader should always keep it in mind, and this can be done only through a concept of the understanding; what I mean is outside time and is not within our arbitrary choice in accordance with concepts.[192]

If *doch* indicates refutation here, it means Schopenhauer thought, albeit for a short time, that Schelling's intellectual intuition was *not* something different from the *better consciousness*. In that case, the identification of the two terms only fell apart when Schopenhauer interpreted "intellectual intuition" as necessarily related to the understanding (and its products: the "concepts").

The difference that Schopenhauer explicitly underlines between his discourse and that of Fichte and Schelling is that in the former, in contrast to the latter, the terms of the understanding are not used.[193] For Schopenhauer, Fichte's and Schelling's "doctrine of the I" – as well as "Kant's practical reason", "genuine Christianity", "theosophy" and mystical "ecstasy" – is an attempt to express that same "ineffable" which true criticism must present fully and in complete purity.[194]

---

190 Cf. esp. Schelling 1980, pp. 179–181.
191 MR 1, n. 45, p. 27. Remember that, according to fragment 35, the better consciousness "lies beyond all reason", and that "theoretical reason" and "understanding" are to be considered synonymous in such cases.
192 MR 2, p. 373.
193 Cf. MR 2, p. 375.
194 MR 2, p. 338.

But at this point we must ask ourselves whether this purity of expression (perfect independence from the terms of the understanding), which young Schopenhauer set out to achieve, was actually attained by him. This question requires further and more general reflections.

7.14 Conclusion: The Contradictory Attempt to Positively Express the Absolutely Opposite Realm to the Empirical One

The philosophical challenge that young Schopenhauer took on himself – or rather, the challenge that his 'Platonic soul' took on against his 'Kantian soul' – consisted in the attempt to *positively* express a reality that is *absolutely opposed* to the sensible one. But this attempt, based on Schopenhauer's own theoretical assumptions, was doomed to failure. Indeed, as he himself wrote in a note to Schelling's *Philosophy and Religion*, "every word must [*muß*] denote a concept of the understanding",[195] and the latter – i.e., "theoretical reason"[196] – is the cognitive faculty of the sensible world alone. Consequently, there can be no "word" capable of effectively indicating or denoting a supersensible reality. It is based on these considerations that Schopenhauer considers the metempirical sphere to be "the inexpressible [*das Unnennbare*]".

According to fragment 32, between the sensible and the supersensible world there is no "connexion [*Zusammenhang*]" and no "bond [*Verbindung*]": they have absolutely nothing in common, they are irrevocably "separate [*getrennt*]" from each other.[197] The latter (the supersensible world) can only be expressed and communicated, "possibly", in a negative form – that is, through the *negation* of the determinations of the former.[198] In fragment 35, any possible uncertainty in this regard disappears, and the tone becomes completely assertive: since "what we say lies in the province of reason", "we speak only negatively [*negativ*] of the better consciousness".[199]

Nevertheless, young Schopenhauer did not immediately resign himself to the impossibility of a *positive* expression of the supersensible. Indeed, he spoke of a "better cognition" (as opposed to "empirical cognition"), of a "better self", of

---

195 MR 2, pp. 371–372.
196 MR 2, p. 338.
197 MR 1, n. 32, p. 20.
198 MR 1, n. 32, p. 20.
199 MR 1, n. 35, pp. 23–24.

man's "true being" and "true I", of his "supreme innermost essence and faculty", of a "supersensible self-consciousness", of a "higher faculty of cognition", of a "supersensible ground" of appearances and even of a "sphere" of better consciousness. In all these expressions, the noun – "cognition", "being", "self", "I", "essence", "faculty", "self-consciousness", "ground", "sphere" – indicates a determination belonging to the realm of the understanding, i. e. to the sensory or phenomenal world (recall that the term "being" itself, for Schopenhauer, means nothing other than "being represented": *supra*, 6.5), so that the expression of the absolute opposition to the realm of the understanding is left entirely to the predicates ("better", "true", "superior", "higher", "supreme", "supersensible").

This does not alter the fact, however, that Schopenhauer referred these nouns *sensu proprio* to the supersensible world – for if this were a conscious figurative use, Schopenhauer could not distinguish his own discourse from the religious one, as he claimed to do (cf. *supra*, 7.3).[200] Each of these determinations thus inevitably constitutes a *common trait* of the two worlds, achieving precisely that "connexion" between them which Schopenhauer peremptorily denies. The use of attributes in comparative form ("better", "superior"), implying the 'comparison' of these two spheres (which, however, insofar as they are absolutely opposed, should be beyond any mutual commensurability), only makes sense under the surreptitious assumption of such a common trait.

All this means that Schopenhauer's discourse, in each of these points, is vitiated by a *transcendent use of the understanding* – the same use that he implacably condemned in the philosophers of his time: positive determinations, originally belonging to the understanding and its realm (experience), are attributed to the metempirical sphere. This is also and above all true in relation to the main theoretical figure of all these texts: the "better consciousness". Schopenhauer writes that it is only possible to speak of it "negatively"; but "consciousness" is a *positive* denomination.[201] This aporia is what would ultimately undermine the theory of the better consciousness (cf. *infra*, 8.20 – 8.21; 11.10).

More generally, the contradiction between the *theoretical or programmatic assertion*, concerning the impossible positive formulation of cognition of the supersensible, and the *actual use* of positive terms, which can be found in all the texts examined so far, constitutes the fundamental (implicit) element of tension within young Schopenhauer's reflections. In spite of his best intentions and best efforts to

---

200 MR 1, n. 32, p. 20.
201 In his commentary on Jacobi's *David Hume on Belief*, Schopenhauer writes that if it is possible to have consciousness of oneself as something other than as an appearance, then this consciousness is not a subject, and therefore has no objects set against it (cf. MR 2, p. 426). It is nevertheless "consciousness".

the contrary, Schopenhauer ended up committing the same illegitimacy he reproached Schelling, Fichte and Jacobi with. It was clearly the – still partial – awareness of this point that led him to abandon almost all of the above-mentioned theoretical figures, which must be considered essentially as terminological experiments. In fact, as early as 1813, he only retained the "better consciousness" and (in rare occurrences) the "better cognition" and the "better will".

After 1812, Schopenhauer focused much less on cognition of the supersensible, or the supersensible *as such,* and more on the particular ways in which the latter manifests itself or exceptionally 'breaks into' the sensible world. Of the two tasks he assigned in 1812 to "true criticism" – to present "the inexpressible" "in complete purity [*ganz rein*]"[202] and to indicate where it breaks into the realm of the understanding (cf. *supra,* 7.1)[203] – the fragments of 1813 focus mainly on the latter. They thus give great prominence to the relationship between the better consciousness and the *aesthetic* and *moral* spheres (which in 1812 were only dealt with secondarily and in passing).[204]

The radicalization of the 'critical' position, relating to the necessity to *negatively* express the cognition of the supersensible, would give rise to a fundamental reflection on the concept of "nothingness", which not surprisingly, as we shall see in a moment, opens the fragments of 1813 – a powerful anticipation, moreover, of the concluding considerations of *The World as Will and Representation.*

---

202 MR 2, p. 338.
203 MR 2, p. 412.
204 Cf. MR 1, n. 35, pp. 23–24 ("The so-called moral law, on the other hand, is only a one-sided view of the better consciousness"; the "genius" is in some kind of unspecified relationship with the better consciousness); n. 46, p. 27 (what "affects us aesthetically" is equated with what "arouses the better consciousness").

8 The Theory of the Better Consciousness in the Manuscripts of 1813. A First Attempt at a System

8.1 "Being" and "Nothingness" in Young Schopenhauer's Reflections before 1813

As we saw in detail in the first chapter, the initial fragments of Schopenhauer's manuscripts, written between 1804 and 1806, are almost all marked by the opposition between time and eternity. In the years 1808–1809, Schopenhauer described what is in time as an illusion (*Täuschung*):[1] only what is eternal is truly real[2] (*wirklich*: cf. *supra*, 1.5, 1.8 and 1.9). Later, this antithesis took the form of a real ontological dualism (of Platonic matrix), according to which what exists in space and time is nothingness (*Nichtigkeit*): only the supersensible world truly *is*, as it ultimately constitutes true reality (*Realität*; cf. *supra*, 3.9).

At the bottom of the moral consideration of events – which only focuses on the will (i.e. the intention) of the acting subject and completely disregards the actual outcome of actions – young Schopenhauer saw the presupposition of the "nothingness" of the external world (cf. *supra*, 4.1). The moral subject 'practices' or applies, so to speak, this nothingness.

In 1812, Schopenhauer still characterized "this world" as "semblance and nothingness" as opposed to the "true being [*wahres Seyn*] – οντως ον" of a "loftier world".[3] According to fragment 32, the sensible, phenomenal world is the world of semblance (*Scheinwelt*): only the supersensible world is the true world (cf. *supra*, 7.2). In accordance with this dualism, Schopenhauer posited the duplicity of man, that is, his belonging to both worlds (cf. *supra*, 7.10). I have already pointed out how the identification of Kant's *Erscheinung* with Plato's φαινόμενον – and thus with a dimension of pure semblance, which is set against true being, the ὄντως ὄν – came to Schopenhauer from Tennemann (cf. *supra*, 2.7).

---

1 MR 1, n. 12 [iv], p. 8.
2 Cf. MR 1, n. 12 [vi], p. 9. Here Schopenhauer states that earthly evils that man suffers have no reality; only the *"actual evil existing in eternity"* (i.e. the Idea of Evil), which the former are an "image" of, is truly "real" (*wirklich*).
3 MR 2, p. 416. Translation modified. Cf. also MR 2, p. 336: "our absolute essence [...] is superior to all experience and to sensible nature and treats these as utterly null and void [*ganz nichtig*]".

Well, even in several of Schelling's writings, which Schopenhauer read in 1811, the phenomenal world is explicitly described as *Nichtigkeit*. Consider, for instance, the following passage from *Philosophy and Religion:*

> [...] it is the Philosophy of Nature that has demonstrated most clearly the absolute nonreality of all apparitions [*Erscheinungen*] and stated the laws that, according to Kant, articulate its possibility "that they are instead genuine expressions of their absolute nullity [*Nichtigkeit*] and nonessentiality by testifying to a being outside of absolute oneness, a being that is in itself a nothing".[4]

Like Schelling, Schopenhauer considers empirical reality to be *Nichtigkeit* in itself, so that within the "two kinds [*zwei Arten*]"[5] that make up man's being, only the one belonging to the metempirical sphere constitutes his true being, his true essence.

8.2 The Concept of "Nothing" as a "Mere Concept of Relation". From the Ontological to the Gnoseological Sense of the Opposition between "Being" and "Nothing"

However, still in 1812, while delving into Kantian philosophy, Schopenhauer began to drastically relativize the very concept of being – that is, he began to properly understand it in a gnoseological sense. "Being", referring to an object, means nothing other than "being represented [*Vorgestellt werden*]", i.e. "appearing [*Erscheinen*]".[6] "*Being* is a product of the categories" of the understanding:[7] it is they who unify "the manifold given in perception" into "a thing, an *ens*, a substance".[8] The term "being [*Seyn*]" indicates for Schopenhauer either the subject or the object of cognition, thus only an "appearance [*Erscheinung*]":[9] thus it means nothing other than "being cognized" (or cognizable) when conjugated to the second and third person, or "cognizing" when conjugated to the first person (cf. *supra*, 4.3; 6.5).

In fragment 66 of the manuscripts (the first dated 1813), Schopenhauer draws the necessary and radical consequence that this special understanding of the term "being" has on the definition of the concept of "nothing":

---

[4] Schelling 2010, pp. 37–38.
[5] MR 2, p. 377.
[6] MR 2, p. 381. Cf. also MR 2, pp. 346–347.
[7] MR 2, p. 371.
[8] MR 2, p. 51.
[9] MR 2, p. 384.

8.2 The Concept of "Nothing" as a "Mere Concept of Relation" — 215

> *"Nothing"* [Nichts] *is a mere concept of relation* [ein bloßer Verhältnißbegriff], namely that which *is in no kind of relation* to another thing, is called *nothing* by that other thing, and again also calls [*nennt*] this other thing *nothing*.[10]

These reflections on the relativity of the concept of nothing seem to recall Plato's *Sophist*. Here the main character of the dialogue, the Stranger, states that "When we say not-being, we speak [...] not of something that is the opposite [ἐναντίον] of being, but only of something different [ἕτερον]" – where "being" is to be understood as being in itself, the Idea of being.[11] Based on this assumption, the Stranger surprisingly comes to admit that even non-being *is* – meaning "non-being" as "different from being", which includes both other Ideas and the empirical world. Non-being as the "opposite" of being is absolute nothingness, which can neither be thought of nor said to be; it is impossible even simply to speak or think of it in general. Non-being as "different" from being, on the other hand, consists of everything that is not absolute being (and in this sense is 'nothing') but *is* – and in this sense is only relative, not absolute nothing.[12]

Young Schopenhauer, unlike Plato, did not admit an absolute sense of the term "being". The notion of a being in itself, existing independently of its being cognized (and of all the conditions of empirical cognizability), was contradictory for him. Therefore he rejected the Schellingian concept of "Absolute", which he believed designated precisely such a "being".[13] He also made a similar objection to Fichte.[14] If "being" means nothing but "being cognized" (or "being able to be cognized"), the term "non-being" can only have a relative meaning, consisting in the *negation of everything that is cognized or cognizable*.

> For instance, if we consider ourselves [*betrachten wir uns*] as existing in space and time, then we call [*nennen*] everything that is outside space and outside time – *nothing*, or say [*sagen*] that it does not exist at all [*es ist gar nicht*]. We also rightly say that "as soon as we cease to be in space and time (obviously as organic aggregates, for only these say We), we shall no longer be at all. Our being (the opposite [*Gegentheil*] of nothing) therefore ceases with death; *we*, i.e. living beings, *are* only as long as we live; for us, as *living* beings, *living* and *being* are one, death and not-being are also one." On the other hand, if we become conscious of ourselves as not in time and space, then we rightly call [*nennen*] *nothing* just that which is in these; and as beginning and end are only in time, then these words, as referring merely to nothing, have no meaning for us. [...]. As it is with *something* and with *nothing*, so also is it with the terms subordinate to them, *many* and *few*. What for us, as temporal and spatial beings, is

---

10 MR 1, n. 66, p. 36.
11 Plato, *Sophist*, 257 b 3–4, Plato 1914 ff., vol. 12, pp. 414–415.
12 Cf. Plato, *Sophist*, 256 e–259 d, Plato 1914 ff., vol. 12, pp. 412–425.
13 Cf. MR 2, p. 371; cf. also MR 2, pp. 342–343.
14 Cf. MR 2, p. 111.

much and of much value is for us from another point of view [*auf dem andern Standpunkt*] nothing and without value; and conversely the value we as extratemporal beings have stands for *nothing* in space and time. [...][15]

"Nothing" as a "mere concept of relation" is not equivalent to Plato's relative nothing (which is "different [ἕτερον]" from, but not "opposite" to being). Indeed, between Schopenhauer's relative *nothing* and *being* there is a relation of absolute opposition, not one of simple difference or 'diversity': insofar as the latter *is*, the former *is not* and cannot be, and vice versa. In this sense, Schopenhauer's relative nothing corresponds rather to non-being as the "opposite [ἐναντίον]" of being, because it is absolutely opposed to the concept of being. Schopenhauer uses precisely the term *Gegentheil*, "opposite".

On the other hand, for Schopenhauer, the (extent of the) concept of "being" is not determinable in absolute terms and once and for all, as it depends on what is (or can be) cognized: i.e., it is *relative* to what the subject can cognize. So, not even the concept resulting from its negation – namely the concept of nothing – is determinable in absolute terms and once and for all. In this exact sense, the concept of nothing is always and only relative, as it is defined through the mere relationship (*Verhältnis*) of negation with the concept of "being" thus understood.

For both Schopenhauer and Plato, relative nothing consists of *what is not*, although it does not coincide with absolute nothing; that is, it consists of *what is*, although it does not coincide with absolute being. However, unlike Schopenhauer, Plato accepts an absolute sense of "being", i.e. an absolute being in itself, which cannot not be or be "nothing". This produces a radical difference between the positions of the two philosophers. Plato's relative nothing – not-being as "different" from being – is relative insofar as it is the *partial or non-absolute negation of absolute being* (in fact, even relative nothing *is*, in that it shares with absolute being the non-coincidence with absolute nothing). Schopenhauer's "nothing", on the other hand, is relative insofar as it results from the *total or absolute negation of the relative "being"*. In Plato, the relativity of relative nothing concerns the nature of its opposition to absolute being (it is, in fact, a partial, non-absolute opposition); in Schopenhauer, the relativity of the concept of nothing follows from the relativity of the concept of being, to which that first concept (nothing) is absolutely opposed. I will go deeper into these considerations in relation to the last paragraph of *The World as Will and Representation* (cf. *infra*, 12.10).

In the *Critique of Pure Reason*, Kant distinguished four meanings of the term *Nichts*, namely: *ens rationis*, understood as "the object of a concept to which no intuition that can be given corresponds", although the concept itself is not contra-

---

[15] MR 1, n. 66, p. 36.

dictory, "like the *noumena*"; *nihil privativum*, understood as the object or content of the "concept of the absence [or deprivation] of an object, such as a shadow or cold"; *ens imaginarium*, as the "merely formal condition" of any object of empirical intuition (which is not itself the object of empirical intuition), "like pure space and pure time"; and *nihil negativum*, as the extent of a self-contradictory concept, "like a rectilinear figure with two sides".[16]

At the time of writing the fragment quoted above, Schopenhauer was certainly aware of Kant's fourfold distinction: it is quoted in Schulze's lectures on metaphysics.[17] One can imagine, then, that by affirming the relativity of *any* concept of nothing (i.e., of the concept of nothing as such), he believed he could bring the other three meanings enumerated by Kant back to the *nihil privativum*. Indeed, the *ens rationis* could be defined as the nothing (or negation) of every possible object of intuition; the *ens imaginarium* as the nothing of every material element within empirical intuition; and the *nihil negativum* as the nothing of every non-contradictory content (or meaning). This last point is made explicit in *The World as Will and Representation*.[18]

Now, Schopenhauer's nothing is closer to Kant's *nihil privativum* than to Plato's relative nothing: it is in fact a determined nothing – namely, the *determined negation* of what, constituting the general (possible) content of cognition, takes on the meaning of "being". This is why the determination of the concepts of being and nothing depends on the point of view (*Standpunkt*) one takes: if man regards (or cognizes) himself as a temporal nature, this constitutes "being" for him, so that the extratemporal (or non-temporal) sphere is non-being, "nothing" for him; but if he becomes aware of himself as a extratemporal nature, it is rather the latter that will constitute "being", whereas the temporal sphere will be "nothing" for him. In the fragment, this dependence of the concept of being on the subject's point of view is unequivocally expressed by the repeated use of the verb *nennen* (depending on our perspective, "we call … nothing […]" what is in time or what is eternal).

A potential anticipation of this point may be found in fragment 46: here Schopenhauer writes that in aesthetic experience, in which the supersensible is revealed, "out of what appeared to be nothing a world springs up and the prodigious vanishes into nothing" (cf. *supra*, 7.8).[19]

In his *Philosophical Letters on Dogmatism and Criticism*, Schelling had stated that "the supreme moment of being [*Der höchste Moment des Seyns*]" – i.e. union

---

16 Kant 1998, B 347–348, pp. 382–383.
17 D'Alfonso 2008, p. 60.
18 Cf. Schopenhauer 2010b, I 484, § 71, p. 436.
19 MR 1, n. 46, p. 27.

with the Absolute – "is, for us", insofar as we belong to the "phenomenal reality", "transition to non-being [*Uebergang zum Nicht-Seyn*], the moment of annihilation [*Vernichtung*]".[20] That is, the highest dimension of "being" is implicitly identified with the nothing (negation) of the sensible world (which, however, from the point of view of intellectual intuition, is nothingness[21]): the nothing of nothing. Furthermore, referring to a passage in Kant's *The End of All Things*, which expressly mentions Lao-tzu,[22] Schelling referred to some "Chinese sages" for whom "the supreme good" and "the absolute bliss [*Seligkeit*], consist of nothingness [*Nichts*]".[23]

> For if this nothing [*Nichts*] signifies [*heißt*] what is absolutely not an object, then this nothing must certainly occur wherever a nonobject is supposed, nevertheless, to be intuited objectively, that is, wherever all thought and understanding cease.[24]

While speaking of a non-being that is such only "for us", Schelling did not go so far as to explicitly assert the relativity of the concepts of being and nothing.

Now, if he carried out his considerations on a strictly ontological (or 'Platonic') level, Schopenhauer could not affirm the relativity of the two concepts. In a strictly ontological sense, in fact, being is always and only "being", it cannot not be or be nothing; and likewise nothing (as the opposite of being) is always and only "nothing", it cannot in any way be. Schopenhauer could support the dependence of the above-mentioned concepts from the point of view of the subject only on an essentially gnoseological level. In this sense, he achieves here an '(Anti-)Copernican revolution' in the definition of the concepts of being and nothing.

8.3 The Freedom of the I as a Capacity for Self-Positing. *Esse sequitur operari*

However, this '(Anti-)Copernican revolution' evidently presupposes – against Kant – man's ability to rise to a "point of view" *beyond* that confined to the sensible world. The remainder of fragment 66 reads:

---

20 Schelling 1980, p. 185 (Eighth Letter).
21 Cf. Schelling 1980, p. 180: "It is this intuition which first convinces us that anything *is*, strictly speaking, while everything else merely *appears*, and *is* only inasmuch as we transfer the word *being* to it"; p. 185: "We awaken from intellectual intuition as from a state of death".
22 Kant 1996c, p. 228.
23 Schelling 1980, p. 185 (Eighth Letter).
24 Schelling 1980, p. 185. Cf. Gerhard 2008, pp. 110–111.

> But the ability [*Vermögen*] of one and the same I to become conscious of itself [*sich seiner bewußt zu werden*] (to posit itself [*sich zu sezzen*]) as temporal and spatial or even as non-temporal and non-spatial is *freedom*.[...]²⁵

The same I can "become conscious of itself", i.e. "posit itself", as *temporal and spatial* or as *non-temporal and non-spatial*. This possibility or capacity, for Schopenhauer, constitutes the freedom of the I.

In various passages of Fichte's course "On the Facts of Consciousness", the freedom of the I was determined as the possibility of the "transition [*Uebergang*]" from one determination to the opposite one.²⁶ But especially the expression "to posit oneself" (*sich setzen*), referring to the I, is of Fichtean origin. At the beginning of the *Foundations of the Entire Science of Knowledge* (which Schopenhauer read in 1812), Fichte wrote: "The *self posits itself* [*Das Ich setzt sich selbst*], and by virtue of this mere self-assertion it *exists*; and conversely, the self *exists* and *posits* its own existence by virtue of merely existing."²⁷

It is surprising that Schopenhauer, in the above-mentioned fragment, seems to regard the expressions "becoming conscious of oneself" and "positing oneself" as equivalent. Indeed, if one considers their meaning, they are not equivalent at all. "To posit oneself" means "to posit one's being", which therefore does not pre-exist the act of 'positing' but follows from it. "Becoming conscious of oneself", on the other hand, does not posit the being of this same "self", but only recognizes it, so that it is prior to and independent of the acquisition of this consciousness.

Now, earlier in the same fragment 66, there is only the expression "becoming conscious of oneself" ("if we become conscious of ourselves as not in time and space"). The "positing itself" of the I, on the other hand, appears only once, so that the main meaning of the text seems to be linked to the first expression. Indeed, if the "self-positing" of the I had an ontothetic meaning, then only those who *posit themselves* as a "non-temporal and non-spatial" being would *be* such. But for Schopenhauer, on the contrary, every person is made up of both a sensible (or temporal) nature and a supersensible (or supertemporal) nature – although not everyone is aware of the latter (as can be seen from the above-mentioned fragments 6, 12, 22, 26, 58). Philosophical astonishment, in particular, comes precisely from this awareness (cf. *supra*, 7.10). All this means that the temporal and super-

---

25 MR 1, n. 66, p. 36. Translation modified.
26 MR 2, p. 48. Cf. also p. 46, where the "intuition of reproduction" is defined as "an arbitrary [mental] repetition of perceptions that have been had or a combination from perceptions that have been had"; MR 2, p. 56, in which the I passes from reproduction ("the reproducing I") to acting ("acting I"); MR 2, p. 79, where there is a transition from "factual intuition [*faktische Anschauung*]" to the "higher intuition [*höhere Anschauung*]".
27 Fichte, 2003, p. 97.

temporal nature of the subject are 'realistically' independent of the self-positing act mentioned by Schopenhauer. But then, what is the meaning of the "self-positing" of the I in the text?

Some later fragments make it clear that man's temporal nature is the empirical consciousness, while his supratemporal nature is the better consciousness.[28] Schopenhauer had previously stated that the individual who becomes aware of the duplicity of his being is faced with "the choice whether he wants to be *reason* or *better consciousness*" (cf. *supra*, 7.11).[29] It is likely that the *freedom* mentioned in fragment 66 (the I's ability to "become conscious of itself" and "posit itself" either as temporal and spatial or as non-temporal and non-spatial) consists in the possibility of choosing whether to be a temporal nature or a supertemporal nature.[30] But then the freedom of the I is precisely its capacity to determine its own being, so that the act of "self-positing", in which it consists, inevitably has an ontological character.

This raises the problem of reconciling the non-ontothetic nature of the "self-positing" (which, on the basis of the reasons given above, must necessarily be affirmed) with the identity – which must also necessarily be affirmed – between the "self-positing" and something ontothetic such as the faculty of determining one's own being. Fragment 72, elaborating on the theme of "freedom", helps to settle the question.

> When an anchoret voluntarily renounce all the pleasures of life, deliberately deprives himself, so to speak, of every enjoyment, because there is awakened in him an awareness that he is an extratemporal, supersensible, free and absolutely blissful being and he wants to

---

[28] In fragment 88, "vice" (which, according to fragment 72, is the negation of the individual's extratemporal nature) is defined as the "negation of the extratemporal consciousness" (cf. MR 1, p. 56). In fragment 99, asceticism (which, according to fragment 72, is the negation of temporality) is defined as the "negation of the temporal consciousness" (cf. MR 1, p. 74).
[29] MR 1, n. 35, p. 23. Translation modified.
[30] With regard to the "choice" that every individual has to make between their temporal nature and their eternal nature, R. Heimann finds an initial, implicit reception of the writings of Pseudo-Tauler, in particular of the *Nachfolgung des Armen Lebens Christi* (cf. Heimann 2013, pp. 163–193), even if the first explicit reference to this text appears much later, in a note to a fragment of 1817 (cf. MR 1, n. 666, p. 515). Schopenhauer might very well have been influenced by Pseudo-Taler, but this part of the discourse is already present in the manuscripts of 1812, in the form of the choice between empirical consciousness and better consciousness (cf. *supra*, 7.10–7.11), and is implied in fragment 12 [i] of 1808, in which Schopenhauer speaks of man's possibility of participating in the corporeal and spiritual world (cf. *supra*, 1.5). Therefore, the possible influence of Pseudo-Tauler does not seem to be the decisive element here.

8.3 The Freedom of the I as a Capacity for Self-Positing. *Esse sequitur operari*

act [*handeln will*] in accordance with this cognition [*Erkenntniß*] in order in this way to keep such cognition always alive, – then he does the right thing.[31]

The "awareness [*Bewußtseyn*] that he is an extratemporal [...] being" is a "cognition [*Erkenntniß*]" that neither posits nor produces its own object (being an extratemporal being), but merely recognizes or ascertains it. The extratemporal nature of the subject does not arise from this cognition, but already exists and only becomes cognized. The consequence of this cognition, however, is the *will* to act in accordance with the "extratemporal [...] being": this will is followed by the individual's *actual* behavior – that is, his *operari*, which is *being acting* in a certain way (indeed, like an anchoret). The individual would no longer *be* an anchoret if he stopped "*wanting* [italics mine] to act" as an anchoret; that is, the anchoret *is* such to the extent that he *wants* to be such (just as the "individual" is reason "if he *wants* [italics mine] to be reason", and is better consciousness "if he *wants* [italics mine] to be better consciousness").[32]

Now, if a man wants to act as an anchoret, i.e. in accordance with his supertemporal nature, "he does the right thing". On the other hand, Anacreon and Horace, when they exhort man to the opposite behavior – that is, to enjoy the pleasures of life – also "are right".[33] But then two opposite determinations – asceticism and enjoyment, that is, being a hermit and being a *bon-vivant* – pertain to the same entity (man). How can this antinomy be explained?

> Truth (and at the same time freedom) is *that man can at any moment consider himself* [sich ... betrachten] *as a sensible, a temporal, or even as an eternal being* [Wesen]. As soon as he has entirely done one of the two, the above-described two ways of thinking [*Denkweisen*] follow automatically and each [way of thinking] is perfectly right and perfectly true. If I consider myself as extratemporal, then everything belonging to a different province and dragging me back therein is for me turmoil and hell, even if it were a pleasure. If I consider myself as temporal, then only the present moment is mine (for in time only it is real and past and future are nothing at all); I must use it, for only in it am I real and do I exist.[34]

The above-mentioned antinomy depends on the duplicity of the human being. Although both enjoyment and asceticism are adequate or convenient for man, they are not so in the same respect (*sub eodem*): the former is suitable for man as a temporal being, the latter for man as an eternal being (this is a perfectly 'Kantian'

---

[31] MR 1, n. 72, p. 39. Translation modified.
[32] MR 1, n. 35, p. 23.
[33] MR 1, n. 35, p. 23.
[34] MR 1, n. 72, pp. 39–40.

way of resolving the antimony, referring one thesis to the phenomenal realm and the other thesis, or respective antithesis, to the non-phenomenal one).

But this also means, conversely, that enjoyment does not suit man as an eternal being, and that asceticism does not suit man as a temporal being. The transient (sensuous) pleasures of the world are gratifying to man only insofar as he is a temporal being; but insofar as he is (also) a supertemporal being, they represent for him "turmoil and hell" – young Schopenhauer therefore agrees with Faust that: "this earth's the source of all my joys,/ and this sun shines upon my sorrows".[35]

Human freedom is the ability to "consider [*betrachten*]" oneself as either being – to identify with either one of them – and to act "in accordance" with the chosen one. It is evident that each of these two natures, insofar as it belongs to the original duplicity, pre-exists the individual's act of choice (of identification), because it makes it possible; and yet, insofar as it is invested by this act – that is, insofar as it is placed in synthesis with the individual's "self" – it does *not* pre-exist, but *follows* from this act.

This is the overall sense of the text: originally (i.e. '*de facto*', before any choice is made) man *is* both a temporal and an eternal being; however, once he has become aware of this original duplicity, he is *free* to choose which of the two natures to identify himself with "entirely" – which of the two to *be*. But this univocal being, 'posited' (*gesetzt*) by his freedom, differs from his original twofold being: the latter, unlike the former, exists prior to the choice, representing what the choice itself is about. The meaning of the self-positing" of the I, mentioned in fragment 66, can therefore be determined: it *is not* ontothetic in relation to the original (dual) being of the individual; but it *is* ontothetic in relation to the individual's (univocal) being as the 'result' of the choice, i.e. of the identification with only one of the two beings.

If we understand *esse* as the univocal being that 'results' from freedom, and by *operari* we mean acting in accordance with it (i.e. acting either as an anchorite or as a hedonist), then, based on what has been said above, the principle in force here is *operari sequitur esse*. But if by *operari* we mean the act of freedom itself, through which the individual posits or determines his own *esse* (as univocally temporal or eternal), then the opposite principle applies: *esse sequitur operari*. In sum: an *operari* (the free act of choice or self-positing) is 'followed' by an *esse*, and this in turn is 'followed' by an *operari* (acting in accordance with the posited *esse*).

---

35 MR 1, n. 72, pp. 39–40. Cf. J. W. Goethe, *Faust* I, vv. 1663–1664, Goethe 2014, p. 43. Payne uses Bayard Taylor's translation, which goes "Here, on this earth, my pleasures have their sources; Yon sun beholds my sorrows in his courses."

This does not, however, concern the original twofold *esse*, which constitutes the basic premise of the whole argument. In these reflections, Schopenhauer does not yet ask how the duplicity of the human being arose – that is, how the human being as such came into existence; this decisive question would be the origin of his metaphysics of will (cf. *infra*, 10.7). Here Schopenhauer only means to ask how man can and should act, given the fact of his duplicity. The central role of the "will" in relation to human "freedom" – which consists in man's double possibility of self-determination – would be made explicit in fragment 91 (cf. *infra*, 8.18–8.19).

8.4 Duplicity and the Experience of Contradiction. The "Residue" of Individuality and the Impossibility of Suppressing Original Duplicity

We have seen that, according to Schopenhauer, two completely opposite terms (ascetic renunciation and enjoyment) can only apply to the same entity, namely man, insofar as the latter is essentially twofold. This explanation, however, does not resolve the contradiction at all, but only leads it back to a higher and more original contradiction: the duplicity of the human being. The latter consists in man's two manifestly contradictory predicates: *temporality* and *eternity*. The fact that Schopenhauer openly argues for this contradiction should not come as a surprise, because he did not deduce it from some principle, but rather *experienced* it (or believed he experienced it) directly (cf. the "mysterious connexion" between reason and better consciousness mentioned in fragment 35; man's ability to consider himself temporal or eternal). Schopenhauer's intimate experience was indeed painfully contradictory; this contradiction was the source of his philosophical astonishment, which induced him to philosophize (cf. *supra*, 7.10). The twofold nature of the self is not original in that it would transcend or precede experience: for young Schopenhauer it constituted the original experience itself.

In fragment 66, the opposition between the (contradictory) terms of this duplicity takes on the extreme and radical form of the opposition between "being" and "nothing". Man's two natures are one the nothing of the other, so that he, being one, is necessarily – and tragically – the nothing of himself, since he is (also) the other. Schopenhauer's youthful philosophy represents the exposition of this painful contradiction and, at the same time, the attempt to *practically* remove or obliterate it: "My hope and belief is that this better (supersensible and extratemporal) consciousness will become my only one."[36]

---

[36] MR 1, n. 81, p. 44.

Based on the analysis presented in the previous section, the individual's "choice" of one of the two natures is to be understood as his decision to identify with only one of them. This presupposes that the individual's innermost "self", before and independently of this choice, is *indeterminate:* precisely because it can be determined as either one or the other, it constitutes a mysterious 'residue' which, in itself, is neither one nor the other. Fragment 35 also assumes that, prior to the "choice whether he wants to be *reason* or *better consciousness*", the individual is neither one nor the other; only after the choice (i.e. depending on his *will* to be one or the other) is he determined as one or the other (cf. *supra*, 7.11).

It is clear, however, that the identification with one of the two natures does not remove the other term, that is, it does not eliminate duplicity at all, because the duplicity exists prior to the choice and is independent of it. This means that choosing "entirely" one of the two natures is, in fact, impossible, so that *this duplicity cannot be resolved* – and indeed, the attempt to remove the contradiction produces a further contradiction. In 1814, Schopenhauer would explicitly consider it impossible that there could be "a complete saint or a complete scoundrel", going so far as to hypothesize (as in the note to Fichte's *The Way Towards the Blessed Life:* cf. *supra*, 7.10) that man's duplicity can only be abolished by physical death.[37] We shall return to this point (cf. *infra*, 8. 11).

8.5 The Role of the Concept of "Nothing" within "True Criticism"

In 1812 Schopenhauer argued that cognition of the supersensible can only be expressed in negative form;[38] therefore, of the better consciousness "we speak [...] only negatively [*negativ*]" (cf. *supra*, 7.6 – 7.7).[39] In 1813 he formulated the very foundation of these statements: what is in space and time is the "nothing" of what is outside space and time, and – due to the relativity of the concept of nothingness – vice versa. The discourse on the supersensible must necessarily involve the negation of the terms belonging to the discourse on the sensible world, because the content of the former (the supersensible world) is the nothing of the content of the latter (the sensible world); and vice versa.

---

37 Cf. MR 1, n. 209, pp. 123–124. According to Schopenhauer, it is not possible for man to make a definitive decision for either saintliness or pleasure: "Even if one thing constantly triumphs, the other nevertheless constantly struggles, for it lives *as long as he lives* [italics mine]." Cf. also MR 1, n. 165, p. 101.
38 MR 1, n. 32, p. 20.
39 MR 1, n. 35, p. 24.

But the ability of one and the same I as temporal and spatial or even as non-temporal and non-temporal and non-spatial to become conscious of itself (to posit itself) is *freedom*. It is to be noted here that the I in the last-mentioned connexion can be described only *negatively* – non-temporal, non-spatial. This results from the fact that *language* itself appertains to the temporal and spatial (just as also the *understanding* and its concepts have meaning only in the temporal and spatial). Therefore originally "nothing" also indicates only that which is not in time and space. And if, considering ourselves as non-temporal, we call the temporal *nothing*, then this is done only metaphorically and in a figurative sense and indicates merely for the understanding that there is also a converse relation whose opposite positive quantity can for *it* never be given but only described as an *x*. And it has been granted to it as understanding to call this *x nothing*.[40]

The temporal and spatial realm is the nothing of the non-temporal and non-spatial realm, and vice versa. This reciprocal relationship of perfect symmetry between the two realms does not, however, also apply to the *discourses* concerning them. The discourse on what is beyond time and space is made up of terms that are the negation (the nothing) of the terms making up the discourse on what is in time and space, but not vice versa. It's impossible to speak of what is in time and space by negating the terms belonging to the discourse on what is beyond time and space, since the latter, unlike the former, *do not exist positively* but only in negative form, i.e., as negation of the former. "*Language* itself", as the medium of all discourse, "appertains to the temporal and spatial": that is why "originally 'nothing' also indicates only that which is not in time and space". It follows that the I (like any other entity), as non-temporal and non-spatial, "can be described only *negatively* [negativ]". Thus, with respect to the discourses about them, the two terms, which are symmetrically the nothing of each other, are rather asymmetrical: the positivity of what is in time and space can be translated into a discourse of positive logical form, and thus adequately, whereas the positivity ("the positive quantity [*positive Größe*]") of what is not in time and space, and which young Schopenhauer admits, can only be expressed in negative form, and thus inadequately.

We have seen that Kant, in the *Critique of Pure Reason*, determines the noumenon negatively, as *ens rationis* (cf. *supra*, 8.2). The noumenon is "the object of a concept to which no [empirical or pure] intuition that can be given corresponds"; the concept of noumenon is therefore "the concept of that which cancels everything out, i.e., *none*".[41] Kant, therefore, had already thought of the concept of noumenon as a negative concept, since its object was defined as devoid of a corre-

---

40 MR 1, n. 66, pp. 36–37.
41 Kant 1998, B 347, p. 382.

sponding positive knowledge (intuition). The thing-in-itself, for human reason, is and will always remain an uncognizable x.[42]

But young Schopenhauer, unlike Kant, believed that the supersensible can be cognized positively, through the use of "powers" other than the understanding (cf. *supra*, 7.2–7.4). Again in 1813, commenting on Kant's *Prolegomena*, he wrote: "true criticism [...] teaches us that the understanding is the conditional way of cognition, but that the better consciousness (and not the understanding) is the absolute way of cognition [*der Verstand die bedingte, das beßre Bewußtsein aber (und nicht jener) die absolute Erkenntnißweise ist*]".[43] The better consciousness is precisely that which allows man to go beyond the realm of nature and thus satisfy man's natural predisposition to metaphysics (*Anlage zur Metaphysik*).[44]

The negative form, then, for Schopenhauer only concerns the "communication"[45] of the supersensible (since "every word must denote a concept of the understanding"),[46] not also its cognition or cognizability.

> We can divide al philosophers into (a) those who from the exceedingly varied and opposite elements of life form through syncretism a perfect whole, where of course the bestial, for example, is accommodated after the divine, but in all fairness the divine also comes after the bestial. In the end there emerges a thing about which one asks what it is supposed to be and the nothingness [*Nichtigkeit*] of which is at once apparent[...]. At the head of these stands Aristotle. (b) those who attribute reality and triumph solely to the divine. Here Plato is at the top. Perfection will be true criticism.[47]

In affirming the necessity of such a negative communication, Schopenhauer believes he is being faithful to Kant's criticism. True criticism, by defining the supersensible as the nothing (negation) of the realm of the understanding, must prohibit the transcendent use of the understanding, i.e. any (contradictory) attempt to unify the two worlds:

> The philosophy of nature as a system of identity attempts to find for these two worlds, here described as speaking opposite languages, the point of union where they are only one (iden-

---

[42] Kant 1998, A 109, p. 233.
[43] MR 2, p. 295. Translation modified.
[44] Cf. MR 2, p. 295 (Payne translates as "aptitude for metaphysics"). Schopenhauer refers to Kant's *Prolegomena* (Kant 2012, pp. 102–115). Cf. also MR 2, p. 431: "Can we not then go beyond nature? Yes of course, but then we must leave the understanding behind, since this is only for nature just as nature is only for it. There is a *better consciousness* which shows itself to the understanding merely through its effects, yet the understanding can never see more than the outside."
[45] MR 1, n. 32, p. 20.
[46] MR 2, pp. 371–371.
[47] MR 1, n. 71, p. 39.

tity of the ideal and the real). This just gives us a Babel-like confusion of tongues and is syncretism whose Opposite is criticism and genuine philosophy. For *union* [*Vereinigung*] is already a concept [*Begriff*] from the temporal and spatial world, and the laws of this must be observed for bringing about the union; it is therefore an absurd undertaking.[48]

Yet, Schelling, precisely through his "philosophy of nature", intended to realize "the absolute separation of the phenomenal world from reality-per-se": the former is "nothing" in relation to the latter.[49] Moreover, by mentioning those Chinese sages who place supreme bliss in nothingness (cf. *supra*, 8.2), he intended to present precisely a valid (though rare) alternative to the dogmatism otherwise prevalent in all traditions.[50]

Either way, for Schopenhauer, an essential task of true criticism (as the exhaustive distinction of man's cognitive faculties and their respective realms) was to prevent terms belonging to the realm of the understanding from being illegitimately referred to what for the understanding itself is necessarily "nothing".

8.6 The Impossibility of a Personal God. The Term "God" as a Symbolic Expression of the Better Consciousness

Schopenhauer considered the concept of God to be a "product of the transcendent understanding"[51] (cf. *supra*, 6.5 and 6.9; 7.3). Every theology based on such a concept originated from an attempt to refer to that inexpressible (*das Unnennbare*) which true criticism would have to present, for the first time, in its purity – that is, as distinct from any possible determination of the understanding.[52] What religion calls "God" "is the same as what philosophy cognizes [erkennt] with greater abstraction and purity and irrefutably (as being free from all addition)".[53]

In 1813 Schopenhauer developed these reflections with radical consequentiality, concluding that any possible theism (even the most cultured or philosophical) is in any case in error:

> Gradually, especially during the time of Scholasticism and later, *God* has been dressed in all kinds of qualities; but enlightenment has forced him to take them off again [...]. Now there are two garments that cannot be taken off, in other words two inseparable qualities of God,

---

48 MR 1, n. 66, p. 37.
49 Schelling 2010, p. 38.
50 Schelling 1980, p. 186 (Eighth Letter).
51 MR 2, p. 342. Cf. also MR 2, p. 372.
52 MR 2, p. 337.
53 MR 2, p. 241. Translation modified.

> namely *personality* and *causality*. These must always be found in the concept God and are the most necessary characteristics. [...] But I say that in this temporal and sensible world of our understanding there are indeed personality and causality, in fact they are even necessary. However, the better consciousness in me lifts me into a world where there is no longer personality and causality or subject and object. My hope and belief is that this better (supersensible and extratemporal) consciousness will become my only one, and for that reason I hope that it is no God.[54]

Since personality and causality belong to the realm of the understanding, they cannot be attributed to what, in relation to the understanding and its determinations, is nothing (the supersensible). This attribution achieves precisely the arbitrary and figurative connection between the world of appearance and the real world which, according to fragment 32, is the essence of religion (cf. *supra*, 7.2–7.3).

The extraneousness of the better consciousness to any kind of personality is also to be related to the Kantian categorical imperative, which for Schopenhauer is a mode of manifestation of the better consciousness.[55] The categorical imperative, in fact, prescribes acting according to a universalizable principle, which is valid irrespective of any particular or personal interest. Thus, according to young Schopenhauer, it demands that the agent's individuality (i.e. his "own will") be destroyed (cf. *supra*, 7.9).[56]

Now, if personality and causality are "two inseparable qualities of God [... which], must always be found in the concept God", denying that they can be legitimately attributed to a supersensible reality means denying the legitimacy of the very concept of God – but *not* of what this concept seeks to express (namely, the "inexpressible"). Schopenhauer symmetrically observed that "witches, devil and fate" are nothing more than "the bad, the vacuous [*das Nichtige*] and the fortuitous realized and personified", i.e. presented in a figurative or mythical form.[57]

It is evidently with reference to the attribute of causality that Schopenhauer, after noting that "the idea that there is *a God* is for man [is] specially substantiated by weather phenomena", concludes (with a good dose of irony) that "the most natural proof for the *existence* of God is not the ontological, cosmological or physico-theological, but the ceraunological".[58] The sense of this statement is that man comes to imagine the existence of a God primarily by attributing a specific *personality* to the overwhelming and dreadful *causality* of atmospheric events. This the-

---

54 MR 1, n. 81, p. 44.
55 Kant 1996a, p. 164.
56 MR 2, p. 402.
57 MR 1, n. 46, p. 28.
58 MR 1, n. 76, p. 42.

sis, here only implicit, would be spelled out clearly in *The World as Will and Representation*.[59]

Young Schopenhauer wished that "this better (supersensible and extratemporal) consciousness will become [his] *only* one". But in the "world" into which the latter miraculously lifts him "there is no longer personality and causality"; this world is therefore totally opposite to that of the understanding (in which personality and causality are two necessary determinations). The desire to be only better consciousness implies the desire for a world in which these two attributes – together with all that they entail – are absent. In this sense (and only in this sense), young Arthur wished "that it is no God".

> But if anyone wants to use the expression *God* symbolically for that better consciousness itself or for much that we are unable to separate and to name, so let it be, yet not among philosophers I should have thought.[60]

Strictly speaking (i.e. "among philosophers"), the expression "God" cannot be used to designate the better consciousness, precisely because the latter necessarily excludes any personality and causality.

Similar considerations are made in fragment 119. Here Schopenhauer writes that the term "idea" was used in a radically different way by Kant and Plato, so that when making use of it, one must always specify whether one is referring to the "Platonic Idea" or to the "Kantian idea".[61] In ordinary (non-philosophical) language, the word "idea", without further specification, denotes instead a symbolic or figurative representation of the better consciousness, i.e. "an object, either *concept* or individual object, which we have closely and *indissolubly* connected with the *better consciousness*. Thus to every believer his religion is an Idea [...]. For an Idea [...] men gladly die."[62] Schopenhauer understands "idea" here in the spe-

---

[59] Cf. Schopenhauer 2010b, I 607–608, pp. 541–542: "Kant, as I said, was only concerned with speculative theology in his critique of these proofs, and limited himself to the academy. If, on the other hand, he had kept an eye on life and popular theology as well, he would have had to add a fourth proof to the other three, the proof that really stirs the great masses and, in Kant's technical vocabulary, would most appropriately be called the *ceraunological* proof. It is the proof grounded in the human feeling of helplessness, impotence and dependence in the face of the infinitely superior, inscrutable and mostly ominous powers of nature. Added to this is the natural human tendency to personify everything, and finally also the hope of achieving something with pleas, flattery and even gifts. In every human endeavour there is something outside our power and beyond our calculations: the gods originated in the wish to win this over for ourselves. An old saying of Petronius' is: 'fear first creates gods in the world'. Hume mainly criticizes this proof [...]."
[60] MR 1, n. 81, p. 44.
[61] MR 1, n. 119, p. 83.
[62] MR 1, n. 119, p. 83.

cific sense of "ideal" (with all the practical and ethical meanings that this word entails). In a strictly theoretical sense, Kant had determined the idea of God as "the *ideal* of pure reason [*das* Ideal *der reinen Vernunft*]".[63]

Young Schopenhauer, like Hegel in those same years, posited that religion finds its true fulfillment and overcoming in philosophy: the content of the former is fully resolved in the latter. However, the fact that it is possible (though not desirable) to use the term "God" to denote the better consciousness does not at all mean that the better consciousness *is* God (otherwise the concept of God would still be retained); it means, rather, that what religion and theology inadequately express with the term "God" is properly – in the language of philosophy – the better consciousness.

> The philosopher, the *unraveller* [der Entwirrer] of all the phenomena of life, is like the analytical chemist; he liberates the better consciousness from everything to which it may be tied and keeps it free and pure. Therefore the philosopher cannot have any Ideas (*Ideen*).[64]

8.7 Practical Affirmation and Negation of Temporality or Eternity. The Salvific Power of Pain

In fragment 60 Schopenhauer says that "the motive for a purely moral resolve is a supersensible one".[65] But the realm of the supersensible (according to fragment 66) is the nothing of the understanding. When, therefore, in fragment 67, he defines what determines the will "in its moral expression" as the nothing of the understanding, he is merely drawing the necessary consequence from these premises.[66]

In the remainder of fragment 72, Schopenhauer goes on to define the terms "vice" and "virtue". The former is the "affirmation [*Affirmation*] of temporal existence [*der zeitlichen Existenz*]" *combined* with the "negation [*Negation*] of the eternal" – a denial (*Verleugnung*) and annihilation (*Vernichtung*) of it in us.[67] Virtue, on the other hand, is a pure "affirmation of the extratemporal being [*Affirmation des Außerzeitlichen Seyns*]; indeed it is the direct expression of the awareness [*des Bewußtseyns*] of such a state".[68] In asceticism (*Asketik*), this pure affirmation of the supertemporal is accompanied by "an intentional negation" of what is in time – a

---

63 Kant 1998, B 398, p. 410.
64 MR 1, n. 119, p. 83.
65 MR 1, n. 60, p. 34. Translation modified.
66 MR 1, n. 67, p. 37.
67 MR 1, n. 72, p. 40.
68 MR 1, n. 72, p. 40. Translation modified.

veritable denial (*Verleugnung*) and rejection (*Zurückweisung*) of "everything temporal as such".⁶⁹ Asceticism is thus perfectly opposite and symmetrical to vice.

In a passage from the Gospel according to Matthew, Jesus says: "Whoever wants to be my disciple must deny themselves [ἀπαρνησάσθω ἑαυτόν], and take up their cross and follow me".⁷⁰ The Greek verb ἀπαρνέομαι (which in the English translation is "to deny") is rendered by Luther through the German verb *verleugnen* (*Wil mir jemand nachfolgen, der verleugne sich selbs*).⁷¹ With reference to this passage in the New Testament, Jakob Spener (later followed by the whole pietist tradition) used the term *Verleugnung* (*Verläugnung*) to indicate the mystical renunciation of oneself, i.e. of one's earthly nature, with a view to the heavenly homeland.⁷² Kant had used the same concept to determine what the moral law requires of man (cf. *supra*, 7.9).⁷³ It is thus no coincidence that Schopenhauer refers this same term, charged with all these resonances, to the ascetic, who 'denies himself' as a temporal being and fully identifies with his eternal nature.⁷⁴

Now, since extratemporal being and temporal being are each the nothing of the other, the *affirmation of the one* should be equivalent *eo ipso* to the *negation of the other*. For Schopenhauer, instead, it is possible to affirm one *without* negating the other, so that the negation of one of the two terms seems to add to the affirmation of the other as something distinct and independent. Logical rigor probably gives way here, on the one hand, to the influence of Christian casuistry, according to which there can be a sensible life that is not sinful (which in Schopenhauer becomes the possibility of affirming a temporal existence that is not, at the same time, vice or negation of supertemporal being). On the other hand, another source of influence here is certainly Goethe: in describing the figure of the "beautiful soul", in fact, he had called for the possibility of a moral action that does not mortify, but expresses sensuous inclinations.⁷⁵ In Schopenhauer, this becomes the possibility of an affirmation of supertemporal being or virtue, which does not imply a

---

69 MR 1, n. 72, p. 40.
70 Matthew 16:24.
71 Cf. Luther 1883–2009, vol. 6, p. 77.
72 Cf. e.g. Spener 1708, pp. 228, 247, 255.
73 Kant 1996a, p. 266.
74 Here one could suppose the influence of Pseudo-Tauler (cf. Heimann 2013, p. 166). But this would not be the only possible or decisive influence, since the theme of the annihilation of the self is present not only in the pietist tradition, as we have just seen, but also in authors such as Böhme and Eckhart, whom Schopenhauer certainly read and was familiar with. Arthur addressed this theme as early as 1812, in his commentary on Fichte's *System der Sittenlehre* (cf. *supra*, 7.9).
75 Goethe 1874, Book VI, "Confessions of a Fair Saint". Cf. also F. Schiller, *Grace and Dignity* (Schiller 1988, p. 368).

denial of the individual's temporal nature. Goethe's beautiful soul (*schöne Seele*) is expressly mentioned later in the fragment.[76]

Now, "certain measures and provisions of nature", especially the naturally damaging consequences of vice, "seem to have as their object the furtherance of [man's] morality".[77] Pain, in fact, by annihilating the individual's sensory well-being, can discourage vice, which is the "negation of extratemporal consciousness", and thus indirectly stimulate the latter, that is, the "better consciousness".[78] In this sense, Schopenhauer admits, alongside the "teleology of nature", a "much more mysterious" teleology of morality – in the sense that, in some cases, the events of life seem to secretly conspire to awaken man's morality.[79]

> Just as a man who has fallen into the sea again comes to the surface through striking the bottom, so are men of the better sort brought to conversion often through sin; thus Gretchen in *Faust*. Here sin acts like a horrible dream whose terrors drive away all sleep from us.[80]

Like pain portrayed in tragedy, pain experienced in the first person also helps man to understand that his ultimate destination is not to "thrive and flourish like the plants of the earth" (cf. *supra*, 1.6).[81]

8.8 Freedom in the Negative Sense: "Breaking Away" from the World, i.e. from Empirical Consciousness. Virtue and Asceticism as the Possible "Return Journey"

We have seen that man's positive freedom consists in his ability to posit himself (*sich setzen*) as a temporal or supertemporal being. But Schopenhauer also defines a *negative* freedom of man, consisting in the capacity to deny his (own) temporal nature, i.e. to break away (*sich losreißen*) from it:

> When we compare the moral, ascetic element [*das Moralische, Asketische*] breaking away [*sich losreißende*] from everything earthly [*von allem Irdischen*]— in other words *freedom in man* – with being tied [*Gebunden-seyn*] to the natural laws of animals, then the comparison clearly suggests that the whole of the long graduated series of animals is like the unripe fruits

---

[76] MR 1, n. 72, p. 41. Payne translates it as "fine souls".
[77] MR 1, n. 88, p. 55.
[78] MR 1, n. 88, p. 56.
[79] MR 1, n. 88, p. 55.
[80] MR 1, n. 63, p. 35.
[81] MR 1, n. 12 [v], p. 8.

of the tree which cling to it more or less [...], but man is like the ripe fruits which at the point of highest perfection become detached by themselves [*sich von selbst ablösen*].⁸²

This form of freedom concerns the individual insofar as *he has already determined (or posited) himself as a temporal nature:* "breaking away" is precisely the abandonment of this acquired determination. The properly negative character of this freedom thus consists in the possibility for man to consciously and voluntarily *deny* his temporal or 'earthly' nature.

In Fichte's lectures "On the Facts of Consciousness", the freedom of the I is repeatedly defined as its ability to break away (*sich losreißen*) from a law (*Gesez*) of knowing and acting to which it is bound (*gebunden*).⁸³ The use of the term *Losreißen* (which belongs to the pietistic vocabulary) returns in Schopenhauer's fragment 79:

> [...] this very world (i.e. our empirical, sensible and rational consciousness in space and time) has its origin [*Entstehen*] only through that which, according to the utterance [*Ausspruch*] of our better consciousness, ought not to be [*nicht seyn sollte*], but is the wrong direction from which virtue and asceticism are the return journey [*Rückkehr*] and, in consequence of this, a peaceful death [*ein, in folge dieser, seeliger Tod*] is the release [*Ablösung*] (like that of ripe fruit from the tree and Plato [*Phaedo*] therefore calls the entire life of the sage a long dying, i.e. a breaking away [*Losreißen*] from such a world)[...].⁸⁴

"This world" coincides with "our empirical consciousness" in the sense that the being of this world is nothing but being cognized or represented (cf. *supra*, 8.2), and the correlative cognizing subject is, precisely, empirical consciousness.⁸⁵ But then breaking away from the world is, in the final analysis, *breaking away from empirical consciousness* – hence the remaining of the better consciousness alone.⁸⁶

With respect to the origin of this world (and therefore also to the human being as temporal nature or empirical consciousness), virtue and asceticism are the return journey (*Rückkehr*), but to where? Evidently to the state or condition in which "what ought not to be", i.e. life in time, *was not*. Man is the only ripe fruit on the tree of life in the sense that in him, and only in him, life reaches such a degree of

---

82 MR 1, n. 74, p. 41. Translation modified.
83 Cf. MR 2, pp. 48–52, 77–79 (HN II, pp. 45–49, 71–73).
84 MR 1, n. 79, p. 43. Cf. Langen 1968².
85 The same equivalence between the sensible world and consciousness of the sensible world is set out in the note to Fichte's first lecture "On the Facts of Consciousness" (cf. MR 2, p. 33: the *"philosophical astonishment* at the world, *in other words* [italics mine] at that second consciousness [given] in perception [...]").
86 MR 1, n. 99, p. 74.

development (awareness) that he can decide to fall from the tree of his own accord, i.e. to sever the link between him and life itself. It is clear that Schopenhauer is not referring to suicide: the act of breaking away from this world is not immediate or instantaneous, but prolonged (the life of the sage is a "long dying").

The text examined does not allow for any further clarification. However, its analysis – especially the term "return journey" – shows that, according to Schopenhauer, man was originally only better consciousness. This interpretation is also prompted by the conceptual coherence of the text, since only empirical consciousness, existing in time, can – indeed must – come and go, arise and perish; the better consciousness, being eternal, can neither begin nor cease to be. In fragment 85, the better consciousness is defined as "the true redemption of the world [*Welterlösung*]" – that is, as that which restores man and the Whole to their primeval and pristine state.[87]

These considerations can only be clarified and further explored by examining additional and more explicit texts (cf. *infra*, 8.10, 8.18 and 8.19; 10.5).

8.9 Reason as a Necessary Condition of Negative Freedom: The Difference between Man and Animal

Young Schopenhauer peremptorily denied that reason can be the faculty of moral action: just as in the theoretical sphere (i.e. as theoretical reason) it is the faculty of cognition of the sensible world alone, so in the practical sphere (as practical reason) it is the faculty of acting with a view to a "purpose" that "favours my sensible existence". The moral law, on the other hand, reflects or expresses the supersensible world, with which reason cannot have any kind of relationship (cf. *supra*, 7.4 – 7.6).

> Would *reason* [Vernunft] be the highest and best thing in man?! In the Speculative it is the source of all error, fort tries to endow the fleeting appearance with permanence and to turn time into eternity. [...] It positively aims at making the world of experience into an absolute, into something at rest, complete in itself and existing by and through itself, and at deceptively setting up phantoms as the ultimate and only existence.[88]

Reason, unable to access a sphere beyond that of the senses, induces man to consider the sensible world as the Whole. A proof of this, according to Schopenhauer, comes from Kant's system of antinomies, in which reason tries to rise to the total-

---

[87] MR 1, n. 85, p. 47. Translation modified.
[88] MR 1, n. 85, p. 46. Translation modified.

8.9 Reason as a Necessary Condition of Negative Freedom

ity of things, while remaining *within* the world of experience.[89] The identification of the empirical sphere with the Whole is the characteristic trait of the philistine; indeed, "If [the individual] wants to be reason, then as theoretical reason he will be a philistine"[90] (cf. *supra*, 7.6).

Similarly, in the practical sphere, reason impels the individual to seek – and thus to first consider possible – the fulfillment and perfection of his happiness "in the sphere of this world of experience".[91] For Schopenhauer, practical reason *tout court* coincides with what Kant considers non-pure practical reason: that which produces empirical practical principles, whose ultimate goal is always the self-interest of the acting subject; to derive morality from it is "blasphemy".[92] The "usage of [the German] language" itself confirms the antithesis between reason and moral action:

> Who will foolishly blame the philistine, or deny that he tackles his affairs exceedingly wisely? On the other hand, who will say that it was extremely reasonable of Jesus Christ that he let himself be crucified, of Sir Thomas More that he preferred to give his head to the executioner rather than to the king against his conviction and consent, and of Arnold von Winkelried that he drove the spear into his body?[93]

By staging man's destined unhappiness, tragedy exhibits the inevitable defeat of any possible *practical reason* (understood as the calculation of means in relation to the aim of sensuous happiness), and is therefore "the real antithesis of all philistinism".[94] Goethe's *Faust* also represents the misfiring of all possible human knowledge, that is, of all *theoretical reason*,[95] and is therefore a "unique" work.[96]

All theories concerning a universal order of things, which guarantees the just reward of virtue, are merely poetic inventions, designed to ward off the *tragic* awareness that human reason is doomed to failure. Every possible theodicy and every possible moral theology (even Kant's) are nothing but "philistinism". Moral action is actually something opposite to reason, because it is infinitely superior to it:

---

[89] MR 1, n. 85, p. 46.
[90] MR 1, n. 35, pp. 23–24.
[91] MR 1, n. 85, p. 46.
[92] MR 1, n. 85, p. 47.
[93] MR 1, n. 85, p. 47. Cf. Schopenhauer 2010b, I 611–612, pp. 545–546.
[94] MR 1, n. 85, p. 48.
[95] Cf. J. W. Goethe, *Faust* I, vv. 354–364, Goethe 2014, p. 13: "I've studied now, to my regret / Philosophy, Law, Medicine / and – what is worst – Theology / from end to end with diligence./ [...] and [I] find we can't have certitude!"
[96] MR 1, n. 85, p. 48.

> In this [the moral] element there is expressed the *better consciousness* which lies *far above all reason*, expresses itself in conduct as holiness, and is the true redemption of the world. This same consciousness expresses itself in art as genius, as a consolation for the temporal and earthly state.[97]

Nevertheless, according to Schopenhauer, Kant was not entirely wrong to relate the moral law to reason: the latter is a condition of moral freedom in the negative sense (as the possibility of "breaking away" from temporality: cf. *supra*, 8.8) insofar as, by enabling the consideration of life and the world *in their totality*, it can 're-lease' man from identification with his immediate desires or appetites.[98] In *The World as Will and Representation*, Schopenhauer would give this specific faculty (in any case derived from reason) the name *Besonnenheit* (cf. *supra*, 5.8).

Based on these considerations, Schopenhauer tries to explain the difference between man and animal, and in particular the absence of moral freedom in the latter. Since the "appearance [*Erscheinung*]" of the animal "is in many respects [...] similar to ours" (so much so that the latter is considered "an animal *genus*"), it is unlikely to be something "essentially, intrinsically and utterly different" from man; there must therefore be some "trace [*Spur*]" of the better consciousness even in animals.[99] By assuming that what bears nothing analogous (*kein Analogon*[100]) to the better consciousness is essentially (*wesentlich*) and intrinsically (*innerlich*) different from man, Schopenhauer shows that he understands the better consciousness as the inner essence of man himself.

> However, animals cannot be called free, and this is due to the fact that they lack *reason*, a faculty that is totally subordinated to the loftiest better consciousness [*ein dem höchsten bessern Bewußtseyn tief untergeordnetes Vermögen*]. Reason is the faculty of embracing everything [...].[101]

---

97 MR 1, n. 85, p. 47. Translation modified.
98 MR 1, n. 85, p. 47. Cf. also MR 1, n. 87, pp. 53–54: "If some desire or emotion is stirred in us, we are, and so too is the animal, full of this desire for the moment, full of anger, full of joy, full of fear; at such moments the better consciousness cannot speak, nor can the understanding consider the consequences. But the faculty of reason enables us to see even now life and our actions as an uninterrupted chain, which associates our previous decisions, or even the future consequences of our actions, with the moment of the emotion now filling our entire consciousness. It shows us the identity of our person even when this is under the most varied influences, and we are thus able to act according to maxims."
99 MR 1, n. 87, p. 53.
100 MR 1, n. 87, p. 53.
101 MR 1, n. 87, p. 53. Translation modified.

In the passage just quoted, the expression "better consciousness" is the result of a correction that was not indicated in the German edition: at first Schopenhauer had used the expression "inner essence" (*inneres Wesen*).[102] But this substitution, revealing the identical meaning of the two expressions, only explicates the content of the initial passage of the fragment (on the use of the expression *innerstes Wesen*,[103] cf. *supra*, 6.9).

According to Schopenhauer, the absence of moral freedom in animals is due to their lack of reason. Only the latter, as the faculty of totality, allows man to have a comprehensive view of his life, making him capable of assessing the remote consequences of his actions and thus, if necessary, of ignoring or opposing his immediate appetites.[104] Reason allows man to view his sensible nature from the outside and to suspend identification with it; thus, reason can foster man's identification with "the loftiest better consciousness", and only in this sense is it "totally subordinated" to the latter.

All this means that reason is indeed a necessary condition of morality, but – *contra* Kant – not a sufficient one. Virtue is in fact the expression of what is absolutely opposed to reason, namely the better consciousness.[105] Reason is not in itself capable of producing moral action; indeed, it is only through it that humans can be scoundrels or *Bösewicht* ("which animals can never be").[106] In other words, only through it can one consciously and gratuitously seek the suffering of others as such – which is why Schopenhauer, quoting Goethe, says of humans: "they call it Reason and employ it only / to be more bestial than any beast".[107] The constitutive impossibility of a rational foundation for ethics would be reiterated in the dissertation of 1813 (cf. *infra*, 9.13).

But if animals, despite bearing some trace of the better consciousness, are not capable of moral freedom, then even the better consciousness, just like reason, is only a necessary but not sufficient condition for morality. Schopenhauer does not go so far as to state this; on the contrary, in the remainder of the fragment he

---

102 Cf. Segala 2011, p. 635. Digital copies of Schopenhauer's manuscripts, first editions and personal copies of his works can be found in "Nachlass Arthur Schopenhauer" of the Schopenhauer-Archiv.
103 MR 2, pp. 371–372.
104 MR 1, n. 87, p. 54. In fragment 28, written in 1811, freedom was defined as the "ability voluntarily to face up to every physical pain, to overcome every impression of the present moment" (MR 1, n. 28, p. 18).
105 MR 1, n. 87, p. 54.
106 MR 1, n. 87, p. 54.
107 MR 1, n. 87, p. 54. The quote is from *Faust* I, vv. 285–286, Goethe 2014, p. 10. Payne, as always, uses Bayard Taylor's translation, which reads: "He calls it Reason – thence his power's increased / To be far beastlier than any beast".

seems to argue that morality and virtue can also derive immediately from the better consciousness, independently of reason.[108] The philosopher here does not draw the necessary consequence (which contradicts the terms of the problem posed at the beginning), namely that animals, although deprived of reason, must also be capable of morality. If Schopenhauer lost coherence with the rest of the text in this passage, it is only because of a burst of enthusiasm.

8.10 The Analogy between Man and Animal: The Intelligible Character as a Ground for Existence

In the fragment just quoted, Schopenhauer states that man and animal are two extremely similar beings, so it is unlikely that the latter has a "ground for its existence [*Grund seiner Existenz*]" that is completely different from the former's.[109] *What* this ground is in fact, emerges a few lines below:

> Obviously against this [the hypothesis that humans and animals have a different ground of existence] there are also the thoroughly vicious, evil, and in themselves ominous characters of some animals (crocodiles, hyenas, scorpions and snakes) and the gentle, friendly and contented characters of others (of dogs for instance). Here too, as with man, an extratemporal [*außerzeitlicher*] character must [*muß*] form the basis [*zum Grunde liegen*] of the one that appears [*dem erscheinenden*].[110]

Animals (considered in terms of their species), like humans (considered in terms of their individuality), possess a specific and particular "character". In both cases, the "ground" of the character that appears, i.e. that manifests itself as an appearance (*Erscheinung*) in space and time, must be an extratemporal character – which, of course, does *not* appear (except through the former). Schopenhauer already put forward this thesis in fragment 85, determining (in accordance with Kantian termi-

---

108 MR 1, n. 87, p. 55: "It is also possible to think of a very virtuous man in whom the better consciousness is always so animated that it speaks at all times and never allows the emotions to become so strong that he is wholly filled with them. Thus he is always guided directly by this better consciousness and not through the *medium* of reason by means of maxims and moral principles. Therefore lofty morality and kindness are possible in spite of feeble reason and feeble understanding (whose strength does just as little for the essential thing in man as does bodily strength). Jesus says: 'Blessed are the poor in spirit', and Jacob Boehme says in noble and splendid words: 'He therefore lies in silence in his own will, like a child in the womb and lets his inner mainspring, whence man has emanated, guide and lead him. He is the noblest and richest on earth'".
109 MR 1, n. 87, p. 53.
110 MR 1, n. 87, p. 53.

nology) the temporal character as "empirical" and the extratemporal character as "intelligible".[111]

In his *Philosophical Investigations into the Essence of Human Freedom*, Schelling had admitted that God bears within himself the "ground of his [God's] existence [*Grund seiner Existenz*]", defining it as the "yearning [*Sehnsucht*] the eternal One feels to give birth to itself": a primal and abysmal "will".[112] Schopenhauer refers the same expression (*Grund seiner Existenz*) to the extratemporal or intelligible character: a concept that appears suddenly, without any justification or foundation. In the dissertation of 1813, in the light of Schelling's reflections, Schopenhauer would propose an original reworking of Kant's doctrine of the intelligible character (cf. *infra*, 9.8 – 9.11).

In the passages mentioned above, as well as in the very enigmatic fragment 79 (cf. *supra*, 8.8), Schopenhauer deals with the origin of man as a temporal being or empirical consciousness. The content of these two texts is clearly not self-sufficient, but rests on theoretical assumptions that remain unexpressed; Schopenhauer's considerations presuppose essential premises that he does not make explicit. The problem of the origin of empirical consciousness (and of its content or object: the world) constitutes a decisive point, which only in the fragments of 1814 would reach an explicit and rigorous formulation (precisely in relation to the "intelligible character"). Those later texts will therefore retrospectively shed light on the meaning of the fragments just cited (cf. *infra*, 10.7– 10.9; 11.6 – 11.7), which, for the moment, must remain partially unclear.

8.11 Life and Death, or: The Dream and Awakening of an "Eternal Spirit". More on the Indeterminate Residue of Individuality

The better consciousness represents the immortal part of the individual; however, this is an impersonal immortality, since the better consciousness lies essentially beyond any possible personality.[113]

> My imagination often (especially with music) toys with the idea that the lives of all people and my own life are only *dreams* of an eternal spirit, good and bad dreams, and every *death* is an awakening.[114]

---

111 MR 1, n. 85, p. 48.
112 Schelling 2006, p. 28.
113 MR 1, n. 81, p. 44.
114 MR 1, n. 77, p. 42.

The lives of "*all* [italics mine] people", that is, of all possible finite personalities, are but the kaleidoscopic dreams of a single eternal spirit. The death of each individual is then a (partial?) awakening of that same spirit – the end of the dream.

Schopenhauer identifies the "peaceful death" as breaking away from empirical consciousness.[115] Not every death, but *only* the kind which follows a life of "asceticism and virtue" is blissful.[116]

> An experience, in which the *double nature of our consciousness* becomes clear, are our different attitudes at different times to death. There are moments when we have vivid thoughts about death and it appears in such a frightful form that we do not understand how anyone with such a prospect can have a moment's peace and why everyone does not spend his life lamenting over the necessity of death. At other times we think of death with serene joy, and even with longing. In both cases we are right.[117]

In fact, as we are "wholly imbued with temporal consciousness", we are "nothing but an appearance in time; as such, death is to us destruction and is rightly to be feared as the greatest evil".[118] If instead "the better consciousness is alive" in the individual, then he "rightly looks forward to loosening the mysterious bond [*es freut sich mit Recht auf die Lösung des geheimnißvollen Bandes*] by which with the empirical consciousness it is combined into the identity of *one I*".[119]

Insofar as the individual "wants to be" (cf. fragment 35) empirical consciousness, death – the end of empirical consciousness – is for him total annihilation; if, on the other hand, he "wants to be" better consciousness, death is for him the fullest being. This is because the empirical world is the nothing of the sphere of the better consciousness, so what for the empirical consciousness is annihilation, for the better consciousness is being, and vice versa. It is therefore from the perspective of the better consciousness that Schopenhauer describes "boredom" as the feeling of "the nothingness [*Nichtigkeit*], misery and wretchedness […] which are essential and original to life (i.e. to consciousness that is enslaved by the understanding and sensibility)".[120] Empirical consciousness as such cannot realize its own nothingness: within its point of view, it necessarily considers itself and what it can cognize as "being".

Being the dissolution of the bond which, within a single self, unites the two consciousnesses, death is properly their *separation*. But this separation entails

---

115 MR 1, n. 79, p. 43.
116 MR 1, n. 86, p. 48. Cf. also MR 1, n. 85, p. 48.
117 MR 1, n. 99, pp. 73–74.
118 MR 1, p. 74. Translation modified.
119 MR 1, p. 74.
120 MR 1, n. 109, p. 79. Translation modified.

the *vanishing of the empirical consciousness and the retaining of the better consciousness alone*. Anticipating his future follower Mainländer, young Schopenhauer formulates the wish that all should practice chastity, because in this way "the human race would die out, that is to say there would no longer be the inexplicable co-existence of the temporal with the better consciousness. Thus the better consciousness would clearly affirm itself".[121] If all people died, only ('their') better consciousness would remain.

However, this does not mean that every individual is immortal as such:

> The temporal element in us belongs to time and must suffer and pass away in time, and from this there is no escape, Only the eternal element can save itself through self-affirmation, i.e. virtue (cf. l. c. [i.e. fragment n. 72]). If, on the other hand, we deny [*verläugnen*] it, in other words are vicious and depraved, then for this very reason we are wholly temporal beings and have fallen entirely into evil and death.[122]

The individual can also face total surrender to evil and death. The reference to fragment 72 is very significant: it states that human freedom is that *"man can at any moment consider himself* [sich ... betrachten]" (and therefore "act") as a temporal or as an eternal being. Schopenhauer means: if the individual regards himself as a temporal nature, i.e. if he posits himself (according to fragment 66) as identical with the temporal element in him, he follows the latter's destiny; if, on the other hand, he sees himself as identical with his eternal element, he will escape death. Here, too, the individual's *being* is at stake ("If, on the other hand, we deny it [the eternal element], in other words are vicious and depraved, then for this very reason we *are* [italics mine] wholly temporal beings").

The point, however, is that the individual's temporal element, as such, is destined to perish anyway ("The temporal element in us belongs to time and must [*muß*] suffer and pass away in time"). In the same way, the individual's eternal element is in any case destined not to perish (otherwise it would not be eternal). Schopenhauer, therefore, cannot mean the individual's salvation as the becoming eternal of his temporal element; and he does not and cannot mean the individual's surrender to evil and death as the becoming temporal of his eternal element.

But then, if the eternal element is in any case (necessarily) saved, and the temporal element is in any case (necessarily) lost, *what is it, properly, that can either be saved or lost? The individual, insofar as he is formally distinct from his temporal (and therefore 'personal') being and his eternal being,* i.e. as *indeterminate* in him-

---

121 MR 1, n. 99, p. 74. Cf. Mainländer 1996. On Philipp Mainländer, cf. Müller-Seyfarth 2000; Beiser 2016, pp. 201–228.
122 MR 1, n. 99, p. 74.

self. In this regard, it is worth recalling what Schelling wrote in his *Philosophical Investigations into the Essence of Human Freedom*: taking up and transfiguring a very ancient tradition, celebrated by Pico della Mirandola in his *De hominis dignitate*,[123] he spoke of the "original undecidedness of human being [*die ursprüngliche Unentschiedenheit des menschlichen Wesens*]".[124] If this is so (and this also applies to the definition of freedom as *sich setzen*), Schopenhauer's discourse presupposes once again man's indeterminate residue, irreducible to his two natures: this residue is man's own free individuality, which, precisely because it is originally indeterminate, can "posit itself" as one nature or the other (cf. *supra*, 8.4).

In relation to the concept of freedom as self-position, the individual who freely posits himself *as* something is formally distinct from this something; reciprocally, this something, insofar as it has entered into synthesis with the self of the individual 'after' the positing, is formally distinct from itself insofar as, prior to the positing, it is not yet a term of this synthesis (cf. *supra*, 8.3). This difference is also implicitly found in fragment 99 between the eternal (or temporal) part of the individual, *insofar as* the individual has identified himself with it, and the eternal (or temporal) part of the individual itself, *insofar as* the individual has not identified himself with it. In relation to the better consciousness, this difference arises between the permanence of the better consciousness *as such*, which must in any case be affirmed (if humanity were to become extinct, only the better consciousness would remain), and the permanence of the better consciousness *in synthesis with the individual's self.* This is ultimately the difference between salvation and the surrender to death.

Schopenhauer does not explicitly pose – and therefore cannot solve – the problem of individuality. Nevertheless, the latter is present insofar as, in order to affirm the individual freedom of man, he must presuppose in every person the existence of *an element that can posit itself as empirical or better consciousness* – that is, which can posit itself in synthesis with one or the other – *precisely because it is not necessarily either one or the other.* Consequently, while nominally eliminating the attribute of personality from the "world" of the better consciousness (cf. *supra*, 8.6), Schopenhauer must still presuppose some metaphysical reality of individuality, without which there would be no possibility of a difference between salvation or perdition of the individual.

In relation to Schopenhauer's mature philosophy, too, one might ask

> how deeply the roots of individuality penetrate into the essence in itself of things. To this we can at best answer: they penetrate as deeply as the affirmation of the will-to-life; they come to

---

[123] Cf. Pico della Mirandola 2012, pp. 116–119.
[124] Schelling 2006, p. 48.

an end where negation begins, because they arose with affirmation. But one could even raise the question: "What would I be, if I were not the will-to-life?"[125]

The problem of the *"individual* will [italics mine]" – namely of what it is, properly, that which "is free to be or not the will-to-life"[126] – would accompany Schopenhauer throughout his life (cf. *infra*, 12.10).

8.12 The Aesthetic Phenomenon of the Sublime as a Manifestation of the Duplicity of Human Consciousness

As evidence of Schopenhauer's careful reading of Kant's *Critique of the Power of Judgment* in early 1813, we have notes on individual passages of the work as well as fragment 86 of the manuscripts. His comments on the work, which I am about to analyze, mainly concern the aesthetic phenomenon of the "sublime".

In the *Critique of the Power of Judgment*, Kant divides the sublime into two species: the "mathematical" and the "dynamical". The mathematical sublime concerns that which is *"absolutely great"*, i.e. great compared to anything else (*absolute non comparative magnum*).[127] In this sense, *"That is sublime in comparison with which everything else is small."*[128] But there is no object in nature which, however large, cannot also be considered "infinitely small" in relation to another, larger object of nature; and vice versa, there is no natural object which, however small, cannot also be considered extraordinarily large in relation to even smaller units of measurement.[129] "The telescope has given us rich material for making the former observation, the microscope rich material for the latter."[130] In nature, there is only that which is comparatively great (*comparative magnum*), which means that there is nothing sublime in nature.[131] Yet we believe that we do find the sublime in nature. How can this be?

Faced with an extremely large object, the individual is incapable of unifying all the partial representations of the object he receives through single sensible intuitions and thus of *imagining it* in its entirety.[132] However, in addition to the fac-

---

125 Schopenhauer 2018, II 737, p. 658.
126 Schopenhauer 2018, II 642, p. 576.
127 Kant 2000, pp. 131–132. For the history of this concept, cf. Doran 2015.
128 Kant 2000, p. 134.
129 Kant 2000, p. 134.
130 Kant 2000, p. 134.
131 Kant 2000, pp. 133–134.
132 Cf. Kant 2000, p. 135.

ulties of imagination and understanding, man also possesses the faculty of reason, which allows him to *think* of the infinite in space and time as a whole – that is, as *"given entirely"*.[133] The aforementioned inability of the imagination awakens in the subject precisely the idea of the infinite; compared to the latter, which "is absolutely great", it is that same physical object – as, on the other hand, any other possible object of the senses – that is small.[134] Since infinity *as such* cannot be given to the senses, its concept refers "to a supersensible substratum [*übersinnliches Substrat*]" of nature itself and our faculty for thinking, which, being "great beyond any standard of sense", "allows not so much the object as rather the disposition of the mind in estimating it to be judged sublime".[135] Therefore, "sublimity must be sought [...] not in the object in nature",[136] even though we may believe otherwise, but in our ideas: *"That is sublime which even to be able to think of demonstrates a faculty of the mind that surpasses every measure of the senses."*[137]

> Thus the feeling of the sublime in nature is respect [*Achtung*] for our own vocation, which we show to an object in nature through a certain subreption (substitution of a respect for the object instead of for the idea of humanity in our subject), which as it were makes intuitable the superiority of the rational vocation of our cognitive faculty over the greatest faculty of sensibility.[138]

On the one hand, when confronted with disproportionately large objects, man notes the inadequacy of his imagination and his physical or sensible *inferiority* to the object in question; on the other hand, however, and as a consequence, he discovers in his "soul [*Gemüthe*]" – specifically, in his capacity to conceive of the infinite in the form of the "ideas of reason" – "a *superiority* [italics mine] over nature itself even in its immeasurability".[139] The feeling of respect is due precisely to the fact that in the experience of the sublime, as in the moral domain, the humiliation of sensibility is combined with the awareness of something in man that is superior to sensibility itself.

This argument suggests that, *within the same "we"*, the "we" that experiences inferiority to nature in its immeasurability is not the same "we" that recognizes its own superiority over nature itself: the former is the purely sensible dimension of

---

[133] Kant 2000, p. 138.
[134] Kant 2000, p. 138.
[135] Kant 2000, p. 139.
[136] Kant 2000, p. 139.
[137] Kant 2000, p. 134.
[138] Kant 2000, p. 141.
[139] Kant 2000, p. 145.

man; the latter is his rational essence.[140] Kant's theory of the sublime thus seems to presuppose in the subject – to take up the expression used by Schopenhauer in fragments 66 and 72 (cf. *supra*, 8.2–8.3) – the capacity to consider himself in a twofold way, namely as a sensible finite being, and as a rational being bearing the ideas of reason. In this sense, it was only natural that these pages of Kant should ignite young Arthur's enthusiasm: at the beginning of fragment 86, he defines the Kantian theory of the sublime as "correct and excellent".[141]

For Kant, however, what elevates the individual's soul above any object of the senses is the faculty of reason. On this point Schopenhauer cannot agree; he comments:

> Here the elevation [*Erhebung*] of the mind comes rather from the fact that we see the faculty of reason demand the impossible and consequently something that contradicts what guides us to a consciousness that is superior [*erhabenes*] to all reason [*über alle Vernunft*].[142]

For Schopenhauer, the infinite as such can never be conceived by reason, because "reason" in a broad sense is the faculty of cognition of the finite, i.e. of the sensible world (cf. *supra*, 7.4–7.5); awareness of the infinite therefore belongs to "a consciousness elevated above all reason". Here Schopenhauer is evidently referring to the better consciousness, which is equally "above [*über*]"[143] and "beyond [*jenseits*]"[144] "all reason".

The subject's shift from a feeling of inferiority to one of superiority in relation to nature also occurs, for Kant, in relation to the second kind of sublime – the "dynamical sublime". Given that "*power* is a capacity that is superior to great obstacles", and that a power "is called *dominion* if it is also superior to the resistance" of a further power, then nature is sublime in the dynamical sense when it is "considered in aesthetic judgment as a power that has no dominion over us".[145]

The dynamical sublime occurs when the feeling of our powerlessness in the face of the forces of nature is combined with awareness of our essential *independence* from nature itself, i.e. of the "humanity in our person", which, unlike our physical nature, is not subject to those forces.[146] In this way, nature is regarded

---

140 Kant 2000, p. 141.
141 MR 1, n. 86, p. 48.
142 MR 2, p. 321.
143 MR 1, n. 85, p. 47.
144 MR 1, n. 35, p. 23.
145 Kant 2000, p. 143.
146 Kant 2000, p. 145.

as "fearful [*furchtbar*]", but without feeling fear in the face of it.¹⁴⁷ In other words, nature is dynamically sublime to the extent that

> it calls forth our power (which is not part of nature) to regard those things about which we are concerned (goods, health and life) as trivial, and hence to regard its power (to which we are, to be sure, subjected in regard to these things) as not the sort of dominion over ourselves and our authority to which we would have to bow if it came down to our highest principles and their affirmation or abandonment. Thus nature is here called sublime merely because it raises the imagination to the point of presenting those cases in which the mind can make palpable to itself the sublimity of its own vocation even over nature.¹⁴⁸

Here, too, the subject ("we") that cares for goods, health and life, and is thus subject to natural power, is *not* the same that, regarding these things as insignificant, places itself above all nature. Schopenhauer comments:

> "if it came down to our highest principles" – not merely then, but also without such hypothesis we become aware that our person is subject to such colossal forces as chance can bring against us, and in this way there is awakened a consciousness other than our personal one, and this other consciousness lies outside the sphere of chance and nature.¹⁴⁹

Whereas for Kant the subject's "personality" is not at the mercy of natural events, for Schopenhauer the subject is indeed at their mercy precisely because it's a person. Personality, in fact, belongs to man as a sensible being, not as better consciousness: the latter "lifts [the individual] into a world where there is no longer personality and causality or subject and object" (cf. *supra*, 8.6).¹⁵⁰

8.13 Beauty as Theoretical Affirmation of the Eternal World and Theoretical Negation of the Temporal World. The Contemplation of the Platonic Idea

According to Kant, the feeling of the sublime, consisting in the understanding of the "inadequacy" of sensible nature in relation to the *ideas of reason*, necessarily presupposes the latter. It is only by virtue of these that the individual can experience "sublimity of its own vocation even over nature"; "without the development

---

147 Kant 2000, p. 144.
148 Kant 2000, p. 145.
149 MR 2, p. 321. Translation modified.
150 MR 1, n. 81, p. 44.

of moral ideas, that which we, prepared by culture, call sublime will appear merely repellent to the unrefined person".[151] Consequently, while still requiring a certain degree of "culture [*Kultur*]", the aesthetic judgment of the sublime "has its foundation in human nature", precisely "in the predisposition to the feeling for (practical) ideas, i.e., to that which is moral".[152]

Schopenhauer, instead, believes that the sublime derives from the subject's sudden awakening to a "consciousness other than our personal one": one that "lies outside the sphere of chance and nature" and is "superior to all reason". Indeed, the moral law for Schopenhauer is only a manifestation of the better consciousness (cf. *supra*, 7.5–7.6); that is why, at the beginning of fragment 86, he writes: "Kant's *explanation of the sublime* is correct and excellent; he knows only the *better consciousness* as the sole moral motive and therefore traces everything to this".[153] Kant indicates as the ground of the aesthetic phenomenon of the sublime what, in reality, is only a *manifestation* of its actual ground.

On the other hand, for Schopenhauer, Kant's "explanation of the *beautiful* is wrong":[154] it is insufficient, "as he himself admits, *Critique of Judgment*, pp. 60, 61".[155] Commenting on these pages of the work (in the third edition of 1799), Schopenhauer quotes Kant's statement: "Judgment according to an ideal of beauty is no mere judgment of taste."[156] From it, he deduces that "Kant himself feels the inadequacy of his theory of the beautiful".[157] He probably draws this conclusion because, on the one hand, he implies that Kant proposed to reduce the judgment on beauty to a judgment of taste; on the other hand, he interprets Kant's statement as the admission of a constitutive irreducibility of judgments on beauty to judgments of taste.

Now, Schopenhauer intends to affirm precisely this irreducibility insofar as, for him, any judgment on beauty implies a reference to the metaphysical dimension. Indeed, he attempts to develop his own original theory of beauty based on the distinction between the "temporal world" and the "eternal world" and, correspondingly, between "empirical consciousness" and "better consciousness". The hitherto only hinted at or sketched relationship between better consciousness and the aesthetic sphere is here finally systematized (cf. *supra*, 7.8).

---

[151] Kant 2000, p. 148.
[152] Kant 2000, p. 149.
[153] MR 1, n. 86, p. 48.
[154] MR 1, n. 86, p. 48.
[155] MR 1, n. 86, p. 49.
[156] MR 2, p. 319 (cf. Kant 2000, p. 120).
[157] MR 2, p. 319.

First of all, Schopenhauer disputes that the "beautiful" and the "sublime" are two different kinds of aesthetic phenomenon:

> The *beautiful* is a species [*Gattung*] of the sublime, or better the sublime is a species of the *beautiful*, namely the extreme of the beautiful where the *theoretical negation of the temporal world and affirmation of eternity, these being the very essense of all beauty* (just as the practical negation and affirmation of those two are asceticism and virtue) express themselves most directly and indeed almost palpably. Bordering on the sublime, as described by *Kant*, is first of all something which is usually included with the beautiful [...] although it has all the characteristics of the sublime as described by Kant; I refer to the *tragedy*.[158]

Beauty – together with its "extreme" represented by the sublime – is in the theoretical sphere what asceticism and virtue are, respectively, in the practical sphere: "*negation* [Negation] [...] *of the temporal world and affirmation* [Affirmation] *of eternity*" (cf. *supra*, 8.7). Aesthetic experience presupposes the foreboding of a higher world, namely the eternal (on tragedy, cf. *supra*, 7.10).

The inadequacy of Kant's theory thus concerns the theoretical or cognitive side of aesthetic judgment. It ultimately depends on the fact that *his* criticism, by ignoring those powers other than the understanding that enable man to cognize the supersensible, is not yet true and definitive criticism (cf. *supra*, 7.1–7.3).

> Every painting, every statue, which depicts some human countenance with the expression of the better consciousness, corroborates my explanation of the beautiful, just as, on the other hand, it is not arrived at from Kant's explanation [...]. Likewise every poem which directly or indirectly presents us with that better consciousness in its many different effects (whose sorting out and arrangement for the cognition of our understanding is the business of philosophy).[159]

The better consciousness can shine in a human face; the latter, in turn, can be reproduced in figurative art. It is likely that Schopenhauer was thinking of the expression (of bliss) that a human face assumes when it contemplates the eternal world.

> Kant *knows of nothing but concept and feeling* [...]. He simply does not know what is higher than all faculty of reason and does not realize that the apodictic nature of aesthetic judgement (which to his [Kant's] astonishment rests on no concept) just springs from where the categorical imperative comes. His astonishment at the phenomenon [*Phänomen*] of beauty is like that of a man who discovers by accident the first electric spark, and Kant's hypotheses

---

158 MR 1, n. 86, p. 48.
159 MR 1, n. 86, p. 49. Translation modified.

8.13 Beauty as Theoretical Affirmation of the Eternal World — 249

for explanation are like the attempts that man might make to explain the spark atomistically.[160]

According to this note to the *Critique of the Power of Judgment*, Kant "does not know what is higher than all faculty of reason", namely the better consciousness.[161] The beginning of fragment 86 states instead that Kant "knows only the *better consciousness* as the sole moral motive". These two passages are not contradictory, because "knowing the better consciousness as the moral motive" means knowing an expression of the better consciousness, but *not as such* (i.e. not as an expression of the better consciousness). In this sense, Kant "does not know" the better consciousness, and at the same time knows it only "as the sole moral motive". Schopenhauer can claim that the better consciousness makes the (intersubjective) apodicticity of aesthetic judgment possible only insofar as he assumes – through an unexpressed analogical argument – that it is present in all human beings, not only in himself (cf. *supra*, 7.11).

Now, after laying out the basic principle of his aesthetic theory (namely that "the very essense of all beauty" is the "*theoretical negation of the temporal world and affirmation of eternity*"), Schopenhauer pauses to analyze some cases that would seem to refute it.

Firstly, the subject of art is very often also the non-beautiful, i.e. "the immoral and the ugly and unpleasant (but not the disgusting)", "the vacuous [*das Nichtige*] and everything cursed and damned [...]" (Shakespeare's sycophants and Richard III; along with the crucified Saviour the irritable and evil-minded Pharisee, and so on).[162] But this happens because poets and painters have cognized (*erkannt haben*) "the whole riddle of the world", and therefore also reproduce (or rather reveal) in their work "the very things whereby this world of nothingness [*diese Welt der Nichtigkeit*] has become what ought not to be [*das, was nicht seyn sollte*]"[163] (cf. *supra*, 8.8). It is clear, however, that this mysterious principle of the temporal world, which Schopenhauer does not determine here, does not belong to the temporal world itself. In this case too, therefore, art manifests a metempirical or eternal content: the "object of art" is always "the making known [*Mittheilung*] of that which is outside time and above nature".[164]

Secondly, there are many artworks that, while not focusing on the theme of vice, represent "mere sensuous well-being, life and action which we find in paint-

---

160 MR 2, pp. 319–320.
161 Cf. MR 1, n. 85, p. 47.
162 MR 1, n. 86, p. 49. Translation modified.
163 MR 1, n. 86, p. 49.
164 MR 1, n. 86, p. 49.

ings and poems (Propertius, Tibullus, Catullus, Homer, Anacreon, Horace, Goethe's Elegies, and so forth)".[165] But according to Schopenhauer, not even this circumstance refutes his thesis: here, too, the principle applies that the artist must represent the mystery of the world in its entirety, including sensual pleasure, which is the affirmation of temporal consciousness. Precisely for this reason, art does not merely depict the prevalence of either consciousness in man, but also the struggle between them, which takes place within the human soul (and the outcome of which is the prevalence of one or the other).[166]

Thirdly, art can also represent vice, which is the practical negation of eternity. In this case, the object of art is once again the eternal world, even if it is practically negated. Finally, art often represents "the beauty of nature, of the mere human form without any supersensible expression".[167]

> My explanation is perfectly applicable also to these, when it is borne in mind that, if our temporal consciousness completely dominates us and we are in this way abandoned to desires and thus gravitate towards vice (i.e. negation of the better consciousness), our entire nature is *subjective*, that is to say we see in things nothing but their relation to our individuality and its needs. But on the other hand, as soon as *we objectively consider* [objektiv betrachten], i.e. *contemplate* [kontempliren] the things of the world, then for the moment *subjectivity* and thus the source of all misery has vanished. We are free and the consciousness of the material world of the senses stands before us as something strange and foreign which no longer wears us down. Also we are no longer involved in considering the nexus of space, time and casualty (useful for our individuality), but see the Platonic Idea of the object. [...] This liberation [*Befreiung*] from temporal consciousness leaves the better eternal consciousness behind. [...].[168]

The text, in its intentions, is implicit but clear. The objective depiction of a thing or a human face devoid of "supersensible expression" (Schopenhauer had spoken earlier of the "expression of the better consciousness") does not actually depict the object in question, but rather, through it, the corresponding "Platonic Idea". The content of the beautiful form exhibited by art is, in this case, the *eternal Idea*.[169] This statement was already anticipated in fragment 80, to which Schopenhauer actually refers;[170] indeed, this theoretical acquisition had long been present in his reflections (cf. *supra*, 2.5).

---

165 MR 1, n. 86, p. 50.
166 MR 1, n. 86, p. 50.
167 MR 1, n. 86, p. 50.
168 MR 1, n. 86, p. 50.
169 MR 1, n. 86, p. 52.
170 MR 1, n. 80, p. 43: "Perhaps the reason why common objects in *still life* seem so transfigured and generally everything *painted* appears in a supernatural light is that we then no longer look at things in the flux of time and in the nexus of cause and effect which the understanding grasps and

8.13 Beauty as Theoretical Affirmation of the Eternal World — 251

Since the attribute of personality exists only in the temporal world (cf. fragment 81), the liberation from subjectivity coincides with the "liberation from temporal consciousness". Disinterested observation, i.e. the aesthetic contemplation of an object, results in the "stimulation of our better consciousness":[171] "the consciousness of the material world of the senses stands before us as something strange and foreign which no longer wears us down."[172]

This point seems to recall the dialectic between "factual" or "empirical" consciousness and "higher consciousness" (or consciousness of empirical consciousness) in Fichte's Berlin lectures "On the *Wissenschaftslehre*":[173] the better consciousness here would seem to be the *consciousness* of the "consciousness of the sensible world". Like Fichte, Schopenhauer seems to imply that consciousness is formally distinct from its content, so that the individual can only perceive or glimpse his own consciousness of the sensible world (as such and in its entirety) 'from above' insofar as he is no longer identified with it (the latter appears to him as "something strange and foreign"). This is a theme that Fichte himself also related to the aesthetic sphere.[174]

In Fichte, however, the transition from lower to higher consciousness takes place within the *single*, all-encompassing sphere of knowledge (*Wissen*), so that the *terminus a quo* and the *terminus ad quem* are essentially homogeneous. Empir-

---

makes the condition of all appearances. On the contrary, we are snatched out of that eternal flux of all things and removed into a dead and silent eternity. In its individuality the thing itself was determined by time and by the conditions of the understanding; here we see this connexion abolished and only the *Platonic Idea* is left." Translation modified.
171 MR 1, n. 86, p. 52. In an addition to fragment 86 (cf. MR 1, p. 51), the state of "contemplation [*Kontemplation*] [...] by which [...] the better consciousness becomes free", is defined by Schopenhauer, more precisely, as the activity of the senses and the understanding (directed towards the contemplated object) and the inactivity of discursive reason. "Sensible intuition", in fact, "is not the business of the mere senses, but comes about only through the categories [of the understanding] that are brought to bear at the same time" (MR 1, p. 51). Schopenhauer means: in order to intuit the sensible object, both the activity of the understanding and that of the senses are necessary; on the other hand, the intuition of the single object is the presupposition or starting point to grasp the corresponding Platonic Idea. The latter therefore necessarily requires the activity of both the senses and the understanding; the difference between the contemplative and the active state (of withdrawal and involvement in the world of the senses) must consist respectively in the inactivity or activity of discursive reason. The implicit distinction between the role of reason and that of understanding is akin to that established in the 1813 dissertation *The Fourfold Root of the Principle of Sufficient Reason* (cf. *infra*, 9.3).
172 MR 1, n. 86, p. 50.
173 MR 2, pp. 88–97.
174 Cf. Pareyson 2014, p. 65–67. Cf. the last pages of Fichte's *Wissenschaftslehre nova Methodo*, in Fichte 1992, pp. 472–474. Cf. also Fichte 2005, pp. 333–336 in this regard.

ical consciousness and better consciousness, on the other hand, belong to two absolutely heterogeneous spheres, so that the transition of the same individual from one to the other inevitably implies a mediation or a connection that, strictly speaking (given the absolute opposition of the two terms in question), is impossible. This problem would be discussed in fragments 91 and 96 (cf. *infra*, 8.18 and 8.19).

Now, according to Schopenhauer, not all forms of nature are equally conducive to the contemplative state (liberation from subjectivity or empirical consciousness and stimulation of the better consciousness): in particular, plant forms and the human figure favor it to a greater extent than certain animal species, whose "evil character [*böser Karakter*]" indicates a "a supersensible principle of negation [*ein übersinnliches Princip von Negation*]".[175] Schopenhauer is probably thinking of "crocodiles, hyenas, scorpions, and snakes", which he mentions in the following fragment precisely because of their *böse[r] Karakter* (cf. *supra*, 8.10).[176] Such *negation*, which prevents or hinders the stimulation of the better consciousness, must evidently have as its (negated) 'object' or content the better consciousness itself. The concept of intelligible character is presupposed here; the meaning of this remark will only become clear later (cf. *infra*, 10.7–10.9).

Drawing the conclusions of his discourse, Schopenhauer writes that in the "beautiful" proper, as opposed to its particular species called the "sublime", the better consciousness does not burst forcibly (*gewaltsam*) through a particular temporal reality (the disproportionately large or overpowering object of nature), but, on the contrary, is what simply remains after the suppression of all temporality.[177] This is why, in his view, Kant states: "the feeling of the sublime brings with it as its characteristic mark a *movement* of the mind connected with the judging of the object, whereas the taste for the beautiful presupposes and preserves the mind in *calm* contemplation [*ruhiger Kontemplation*]."[178]

> I think I have established that the beautiful is identical with the sublime and, like this, is not to be found in objects, but in the stimulation [*Anregung*] of our better consciousness; such stimulation, when it arises from the mere contemplation [*Kontemplation*] of objects called beautiful is only the liberation of the better consciousness from all subjectivity.[179]

By overcoming these possible objections, Schopenhauer believes he has demonstrated that the content of art always consists of the eternal or supersensible real-

---

175 MR 1, n. 86, p. 51. Translation modified.
176 MR 1, n. 87, p. 53.
177 MR 1, n. 86, p. 50.
178 Kant 2000, p. 131.
179 MR 1, n. 86, p. 52.

ity. Kant's *aesthetic* '(Anti-)Copernican' revolution ("beauty is nothing by itself, without relation to the feeling of the subject")[180] is thus based by Schopenhauer not on feeling, but on man's better consciousness (or "supersensible consciousness") – which, in spite of Kant's interdiction, has access to cognition of eternal reality. Now, Kant stated that the "determining ground" of the judgment of taste "may lie in the concept of that which can be regarded as the supersensible substratum of humanity [*das übersinnliche Substrat der Menschheit*]".[181] Schopenhauer comments: "Obscure but, as it seems, deviating from his false theory and drawing near to mine."[182]

8.14 The Platonic Idea as an Object of Cognition of the Better Consciousness

The better consciousness is consciousness of metaphenomenal reality (remember the note to the *Prolegomena*, according to which it is "the absolute way of cognition"):[183] it is eternal not only because it is outside of time, but also because it cognizes the eternal world.

Now, in fragment 86, the eternal dimension cognized by the better consciousness seems to coincide with the Platonic Ideas. Indeed, on the one hand, "as soon as we *objectively consider*, i.e. *contemplate*", subjectivity "has vanished", "the consciousness of the material world of the senses stands before us as something strange and foreign which no longer wears us down" and we "see [*sehn*] the Platonic Idea of the object". On the other hand, "this liberation from temporal consciousness leaves the better eternal consciousness behind". Seeing the Platonic Idea of the object and the subsistence of the better consciousness are both indicated as the consequence of liberation from subjectivity, i.e. from the consciousness of the sensible world, so that it would seem legitimate to identify the two terms. In this regard, it can be recalled that, in fragment 80 (to which Schopenhauer explicitly refers in fragment 86),[184] the cognition of the Platonic Idea is opposed to the understanding's cognition;[185] but the cognition alternative to the latter, for

---

180 Kant 2000, p. 103.
181 Kant 2000, p. 216.
182 MR 2, p. 325. He goes on to say: "Yet I must note that *concept* is possible only of objects of sensible intuition for which alone are the categories to be used, – but not of something supersensible." (MR 2, p. 325)
183 MR 2, p. 295. Translation modified.
184 MR 1, n. 86, p. 50.
185 MR 1, n. 80, p. 43.

Schopenhauer, is precisely that which is accessible only to the better consciousness.[186]

On the other hand, precisely in the light of the first of the previous two quotes, the intuition of the Idea certainly cannot belong to the individual as temporal consciousness (the Idea, as eternal, cannot be the object of consciousness confined in time). If, therefore, the Idea were not even the object of the better consciousness, but its intuition simply prepared the individual to *become* a better consciousness, the subject, when seeing the Idea, would be neither temporal nor better consciousness. Yet Schopenhauer seems to imply, in all his fragments, that *tertium non datur*. In this sense, the "double" – and not triple – "nature of our consciousness" necessarily implies that the Platonic Idea is the objective correlate of the better consciousness.[187]

However, it cannot be ignored that Schopenhauer is far from explicit on this point. This missing clarification is probably the sign of a theoretical deadlock. Platonic Ideas can be described (and are described by Plato) *positively*, through a superfetation of the same (positive) qualities found in the world of the understanding (even if, from an ontological point of view, it is rather the latter that are images of Ideas). On the other hand, the eternal and supersensible world, the object of the better consciousness, is the *nothing* of the sensible world according to "true criticism". By not explicitly determining Ideas as the cognitive object of the better consciousness, Schopenhauer avoids openly expressing something that, on the one hand, is required by the coherence of these texts and, on the other, is inconsistent with the discourse developed in other fragments about the absolute opposition of temporal and supertemporal realms.

The tension between the explicit and implicit parts of the fragment 86 manifests the contrast between the two requirements. The object or "world" (cf. *supra*, 8.6) of the better consciousness is in fact described by Schopenhauer only as "supersensible", "unconditioned", "eternal", "devoid of personality and causality". But these attributes are negative (they are equivalent to "non-sensible", "non-conditioned", "non-temporal"), so that Schopenhauer's difficulty in determining the object of the better consciousness in a different way is, in fact, the *impossibility* of determining it positively, since (according to what is stated in fragment 65), "language itself appertains to the temporal and spatial (just as the understanding [...])", and that object is the nothing of the determinations of understanding and language.

---

[186] MR 2, p. 295.
[187] MR 1, n. 99, p. 73.

Based on these considerations, however, it should be noted that fragment 86 attributes to the better consciousness the same determinations that, in the mature system (indeed, already from the manuscripts of 1814 onwards), would characterize the figure of the "pure subject of cognition" – the ability to cognize Platonic Ideas and being beyond any individuality as such (cf. *infra*, 11.11).[188]

Now, provided that the artist and the recipient of art have access to the contemplation of Platonic Ideas, the question arises as to how this is generally possible. Schopenhauer argues in this respect that "the eternal forms of nature are based on a necessity which is impenetrable to our understanding but yet in some mysterious association with our innermost being, and which may well be beyond all explanation".[189] In fragment 15 ("On Plato") from 1810, Schopenhauer understood Ideas as the eternal forms of being, used by the Deity as a model for the creation of finite things (cf. *supra*, 2.4–2.5).[190] In this sense, it was implied that the Creator himself, as such, was the 'medium' between man and the eternal Ideas. This point was perfectly explicit with regard to Ideas with no corresponding object of the sense world: they are communicated to man directly by God.[191] By 1813 this solution was no longer admissible: from the theistic perspective (clearly underlying that solution) Schopenhauer had moved on to explicit philosophical atheism, which denies the legitimacy of the *concept* of "God" (cf. *supra*, 8.6). Consequently, the "association" between Ideas and man's "innermost being" (the connection that makes the cognition of Ideas possible) cannot but remain irretrievably "mysterious" and "beyond all explanation".

8.15 "The Magic of the Past". Memory and Contemplation

In 1808, Schopenhauer wrote that the consolation offered by philosophy consists in the possibility of looking at "the phenomena of the external world" "from an exalted seat", "with the greatest calm and unconcern [*ohne Teilnahme*]".[192] This lack of participation or direct involvement in external events was for Schopenhauer the reason for the "delightful tranquillity" that comes with reminiscing (cf. *supra*, 1.5).[193]

---

188 Cf. Schopenhauer 2010b, I 207–213, § 33–34, pp. 198–204.
189 MR 1, n. 86, p. 52.
190 MR 1, n. 15, pp. 10–12.
191 MR 1, n. 15, p. 11.
192 MR 1, n. 12 [i], p. 8.
193 MR 1, n. 12 [iv], p. 8.

In a note to fragment 86, reflecting further on the contemplative joy that follows liberation from subjectivity, Schopenhauer writes: "The *magic* [Zauber] *of the past* comes from the same source."[194] In fact, "when we picture to ourselves past days", we "recall merely the objects, not the subject with all its woe and misery", so that "we remember merely the objective", we lift ourselves above ourselves "and the better consciousness becomes free".[195] Subjectivity is in fact "the source of all misery".[196] The basis of what in 1808 was called *Teilnahme* (participation) in external events is therefore identified in subjectivity.

> And so it comes that, especially when we are in trouble and afraid, the sudden recollection of a time when there was not this trouble flies past us like a lost paradise, because now only this objective and not the subjective returns, and we imagine that at that time we were as free for that objective as we now are; yet even then the subjective had its troubles.[197]

What is common to contemplation and remembrance is a *purely cognitive relationship* with external events, which, however, in the first case (in contemplation), are current; in the second case (in remembrance or "recollection"), on the contrary, they are no longer so. To remember is to contemplate one's past; and, conversely, to contemplate is akin to remembering, rather than living, one's present. In both cases, this liberation from subjectivity – i.e. "liberation from temporal consciousness" – leads to the stimulation of the better consciousness: the individual experiences, albeit in a different way, his own essential extraneousness and superiority to the sensible world.

The implication of all these considerations is that the individual can pass from empirical consciousness to better consciousness. But such a transition, in turn, presupposes the possibility of some *relation* between the *terminus a quo* and the *terminus ad quem* (cf. *infra*, 18–19).

8.16 The Better Consciousness and Music. The Lost Essay *On the Gradation of the Arts*

In 1806, probably under the influence of Wackenroder, Schopenhauer expressed a marked predilection for "divine music": in a letter to his mother, he described it as

---

[194] MR 1, n. 86, p. 51.
[195] MR 1, n. 86, p. 51.
[196] MR 1, n. 86, p. 50.
[197] MR 1, n. 86, p. 51.

a "heavenly flower" that, though "rooted in the soil of wretchedness", "rises tall in full magnificence".[198] Music is a "direct echo of eternity" (cf. *supra*, 1.4; 2.5).[199]

The immediacy of the relationship between music and the eternal is reasserted in fragment 86:

> Music is a very special and separate species of the beautiful; it knows merely time, this being its immediate condition, but nothing of that which occurs in time. It is not, like other arts, a presentation of the effects of the better consciousness in the material world of the senses, but itself one of these effects. [...]
>
> If we compare the whole of our consciousness to a sphere, then music is perhaps the motion of its shortest radii nearest to the centre [...] Yet this much is certain, that it stimulates most immediately the better consciousness, but also lies farthest from the empirical. See the essay on the gradation of the arts [*den Aufsatz über die Stufenfolge der Künste*].[200]

Unlike the other fine arts, music is not compromised by any condition of the appearance, apart from time. (This assertion, reproposed in *The World*,[201] is obviously inaccurate: originating from the vibration of bodies in the air, sound is also subject to spatial determinations; so much so that, for example, it always and necessarily has a source.) Music therefore seems to be the art form that is most closely related to the metaphysical origin of all art: the better consciousness. It is probably based on this same criterion – namely, the greater or lesser 'proximity' to the better consciousness – that Schopenhauer, in the youthful essay mentioned in the fragment, which is unfortunately lost, tried to establish a veritable "gradation" between the arts.[202]

These considerations lead young Arthur to disagree with what Kant writes about music in the *Critique of the Power of Judgment*. For Kant, in fact, music is nothing but a "beautiful play of sensations" of hearing,[203] that can be compared to games of chance and good conversation insofar as it's a mere source of pleasure or amusement.[204] Music is "more enjoyment than culture (the play of thought that is aroused by it in passing is merely the effect of an as it were mechanical association); and it has, judged by reason, less value than any other of the beautiful

---

198 Cf. Lütkehaus 1991, pp. 125–126. Arthur to Johanna, November 1806. Translation taken from Cartwright 2010, p. 111.
199 Cartwright 2010, p. 111.
200 MR 1, n. 86, pp. 52–53.
201 Cf. Schopenhauer 2010b, I 315, p. 294: "music is perceived [...] entirely and only in and through time, completely excluding space".
202 Cf. what A. Hübscher writes in HN I, p. 505.
203 Kant 2000, pp. 201–202.
204 Kant 2000, pp. 208–209. Cf. MR 2, p. 325.

arts".²⁰⁵ This last statement is found in paragraph 53 of the *Critique of the Power of Judgment*, entitled "Comparison of the aesthetic value of the beautiful arts with each other".²⁰⁶ It is possible that Schopenhauer, in his essay *On the Gradation of the Arts*, intended to propose an alternative and polemical comparison to the Kantian one.

On the other hand, according to Schopenhauer, Kant's aesthetic theory is essentially flawed by the fact that he "does not know what is higher than all faculty of reason",²⁰⁷ i.e. the eternal better consciousness; and music, unlike the other arts, is for Schopenhauer not "a presentation of the effects of the better consciousness in the material world of the senses", but "one of these effects".²⁰⁸ It should be remembered that the close relationship between musical art and the dimension of the eternal had been hinted at in the suggestive fragment 77, already cited:

> My imagination often (especially with music) toys with the idea that the lives of all people and my own life are only *dreams* of an eternal spirit, good and bad dreams, and every *death* is an awakening.²⁰⁹

8.17 The Peak of Humanity: Genius and Sainthood

For Kant, the aesthetic judgment on the sublime can only express a claim of universality insofar as it necessarily presupposes the moral ideas present in every individual.²¹⁰ Schopenhauer notes in this regard: "He [Kant] therefore confirms my statement [...] that the beautiful, like the sublime, is a stimulation [*Anregung*] of the better consciousness which among other things reveals itself as morality".²¹¹ In the relationship posited by Kant between the moral and aesthetic spheres, Schopenhauer finds confirmation of his reflections on the common origin of art and morality: the better consciousness. He takes this as his starting point for a number of considerations on the similarities and differences between *genius* (understood as the highest artistic ability) and *sainthood* (or moral perfection).

In every person there is a "a trace [*Spur*]" of the better consciousness, but in different degrees, distinguishing individuals from one another – even the genius

---

205 Kant 2000, p. 205. Cf. Giordanetti 2001.
206 Kant 2000, p. 203.
207 MR 2, p. 320.
208 MR 1, n. 86, p. 52.
209 MR 1, n. 77, p. 42.
210 Kant 2000, pp. 148–149.
211 MR 2, p. 322.

and the saint.²¹² Although the former can never be "wicked [*boshaft*]" and the latter, for his part, will always be very sensitive to beauty, "perhaps never in one individual is there to be found very great genius with very exalted saintliness".²¹³ In the saint, in fact, "the better consciousness predominates so undisturbed that the world of the senses appears to him only in feeble colours, so to speak; he acts in accordance with that consciousness, is blissful in it, and his appearance [*Erscheinung*] serves only as an example for the elevation of the world".²¹⁴ The genius, instead, must always preserve his relationship with the sensible world, because that is where he must realize his masterpieces. (This point was already central in a 1811 note to Fichte, where Schopenhauer had determined the genius's *hohe Besonnenheit* as his ability to communicate metempirical cognition through empirical objects: cf. *supra*, 3.2–3.4.)²¹⁵

Consequently, the genius must have not only a "vivid [*lebendig*]" or active better consciousness, but also the temporal consciousness, i.e. "awareness of the world of the senses" – and "sensuality" with it.²¹⁶ Precisely the exercise of the latter prevents the genius from attaining the condition of saintliness. While the saint can be content with his own "pure firm will", disregarding the actual success of his good intentions (in morality, in fact, only the will counts: cf. *supra*, 4.1–4.2), the genius has to realize something specific in the world of experience, namely "works of art".²¹⁷ Unlike the saint, he cannot say "my kingdom is not of this world": his kingdom is *also* – though not only or mainly – of this world.²¹⁸ In the genius the "contrast [*Kontrast*]" between the two consciousnesses is always present: "in this constant double nature of his [*Duplicität seiner Natur*] the genius does not enjoy the peace and composure of the saint and his mere existence [*Daseyn*] is already a kind of martyrdom for the benefit of mankind."²¹⁹ The martyrdom of the genius is not the stake or stoning, but his mere existence, while the existence of the saint is, as such, not a martyrdom, but a form of beatitude, because he has eliminated the duplicity of his nature. Consequently, the saint can elevate

---

212 MR 2, p. 322.
213 MR 2, p. 322.
214 MR 2, p. 323. Recall that the metaphor of colors was present in Schopenhauer's commentary on Fichte's second lecture "On the Study of Philosophy": "There comes a moment when the entire world of appearance fades, outshone and eclipsed by the ego or I which cognizes its reality and that of a supersensible world" (MR 2, p. 25, translation modified; cf. *supra*, 3.5).
215 MR 2, p. 19.
216 MR 2, p. 323. Cf. De Cian 2011, pp. 174–178. On Schopenhauer's reception of the Third Kantian Critique, cf. Gebrecht 2021.
217 MR 2, p. 323.
218 MR 2, pp. 323–324.
219 MR 2, p. 323.

the world even if only through his own beatitude (by "example"); the genius, on the other hand, can only serve humanity through his martyrdom.

Finding himself, as it were, midway between the consciousness of the empirical world and that of the metempirical world, the genius represents a particular type of humanity situated between the philistine, who is turned exclusively towards the sensible world, and the saint, who is turned exclusively towards the supersensible world. The inner state of the genius is therefore, in turn, somewhere between the obtuse blissfulness of the former[220] and the transcendent blissfulness of the latter. Precisely this singular borderline position between two *opposing* conditions of happiness condemns the genius to a state of extraordinary and unsuppressable pain.

The text clearly presupposes that man's extreme suffering is due to the dissonance between his two natures, and that true and supreme happiness consists in eliminating the duplicity of being in favor of the better consciousness alone. Here, then, Schopenhauer still affirms possibility of eliminating the aforementioned duplicity *in life* (cf. *supra*, 8.4).

Young Arthur openly admitted the duplicity of his own being ("My *hope* [italics mine] and belief is that this better [...] consciousness *will* [italics mine] become my only one": fragment 81); in those years, therefore, he was already inclined to regard himself more as a genius than as a saint.

8.18 The Mysterious "Connexion" between Empirical Consciousness and Better Consciousness and the Primacy of the Will

In fragment 35 (in which the figure of the better consciousness appears for the first time), Schopenhauer describes as "mysterious" the "connexion [*Verbindung*]" which, in the same individual, exists between reason and better consciousness (in this text, the term "reason" denotes the overall cognitive faculty of man's empirical or finite consciousness: cf. *supra*, 7.6). Fragment 99 also mentions the "mysterious bond" (*Band*) that keeps the better consciousness "combined" with the empirical consciousness in order to form "the identity of *one I or ego*".[221]

This bond or connection, although mysterious, must in any case be necessarily admitted. The same fragment 35 states that because of it "for the individual there

---

[220] MR 1, n. 85, pp. 46–47.
[221] MR 1, n. 99, p. 74.

8.18 The Mysterious "Connexion" between Empirical and Better Consciousness

[...] arises the choice whether he wants to be *reason* or *better consciousness*".[222] If better consciousness and empirical consciousness were not related, the individual could not be (alternately) one or the other – that is, he could not pass from one to the other; their relation constitutes the condition of *possibility* of this transition. Now, the *reality* of the latter is, for Schopenhauer, absolutely indubitable: he believes he experiences it himself. Therefore, such a relation must exist; that is, there must be some connection between these two terms, which are at the same time absolute opposites (cf. *supra*, 8.4).

This problem is first explicitly addressed in fragment 91. The pretext is the circumstance that, "on the days and at the hours when the desire for voluptuousness is strongest", "it is then that the highest powers of the mind, and indeed the better consciousness, are *ready* for the greatest activity, although, at the moment when consciousness has abandoned itself to desire and is wholly preoccupied with it, they are *latent*."[223]

> [...] *Kielmeyer* rightly says that brain and genitals are *opposite poles*; and I add that they are the representatives of the temporal and of the better consciousness that is above and beyond time. [...] At the aforesaid times on the whole *life is really most active and vigorous,* since both poles manifest their polarity with the maximum energy, and so only in exceptionally brilliant men is this seen. In such hours more life is often lived than in years of dullness and apathy. It is merely a question of *what direction* is taken. *One pole* does not understand *the other; the one does not exist for the other* [der eine ist für den andern gar nicht da]. Yet, as the faculty for perceiving the totality of life in its oneness, as the bond [*Band*] between temporal and better consciousness, and in consequence of the synthetic unity of apperception, reason is historically acquainted with both principles. And as its synthetic unity of apperception is never effaced, it can, at the moment when consciousness is absorbed in cupidity, vividly picture to itself the maxim "to take the other direction" – a maxim that has sprung from the better consciousness. However, the faculty of reason holds up such a maxim only as a *lifeless concept* against the *living desire*, but it represents it as such and makes choice [*Wahl*] possible, that is to say *freedom*, whose condition it is. It should therefore be the instrument of that which is infinitely better than itself.[224]

As the "faculty of embracing everything" (cf. *supra*, 8.9) reason ecompasses life and experience as a whole and, therefore, encloses both natures that make up man as such: empirical consciousness and better consciousness. Through the faculty of reason, the individual remains aware of the better consciousness – and thus of the possibility of determining himself, indeed, as better consciousness – even at times when he is determined as empirical consciousness. In the possibility of

---

[222] MR 1, n. 35, p. 23. Translation modified.
[223] MR 1, n. 91, p. 57.
[224] MR 1, n. 91, p. 58.

this transition, that is, in the possibility of choosing between the two consciousnesses, lies man's own *freedom*. By representing the link between the two consciousnesses (in the sense indicated above), reason constitutes the condition of possibility of this choice and, consequently, of human freedom itself.

But empirical consciousness and better consciousness are the absolute opposite – i. e. the nothing – of each other ("*the one does not exist for the other*"); reason is therefore the link that unites what would otherwise never be united. This function of reason is in turn made possible, according to Schopenhauer, by the synthetic unity of apperception.

This last point is extremely interesting. In a famous and controversial passage from the *Critique of Pure Reason*, Kant stated: "The *I think* must *be able* to accompany all my representations".[225] In fact, "all *my* representations in any given intuition must stand under the condition under which alone I can ascribe them to the identical self as *my* representations".[226] For Kant, "pure apperception" is that fundamental and original form of "self-consciousness" which, "because it produces [*indem es ... hervorbringt*] the representation *I think*", makes it possible for each self to be aware of its own numerical identity, even in the extreme variability of empirical situations ('internal' and 'external').[227] Schopenhauer is probably thinking of something similar here, insofar as he understands the synthetic unity of apperception as that which makes the numerical identity of the same self (individual) possible, even in its being, in different times and circumstances, empirical consciousness or better consciousness.

> The change of direction, the transition [*Uebergang*] from the kingdom of darkness, of need, desire, illusion, of that which becomes but never is, to the kingdom of light, repose, joy, amiability, harmony and peace, is *infinitely difficult* and *infinitely easy* [...] To accomplish what is immensely difficult, impossibile, we need only *will*, but *will* we must.[228]

---

[225] Kant 1998, B 132, p. 246. Fichte, in his thirteenth lecture "On the Facts of Consciousness", had briefly taken up Kant's discourse: "[...] But between the represented and the represented there is an absolute bond (as principle and original they cannot exist the one without the other) which cannot be further explained. *Kant* has called this the absolute synthetic unity of apperception, [...] and by his saying that it is the principle of the deduction of the categories and constantly accompanies all thinking, he showed a high degree of reflectiveness [*Besonnenheit*] and came very near to idealism. This *copula* between the I or ego and its representation is therefore the absolute essence of all thinking and knowing." (MR 2, p. 45)
[226] Kant 1998, B 138, pp. 249–250.
[227] Kant 1998, B 132, p. 246.
[228] MR 1, n. 91, p. 58. Translation modified.

8.18 The Mysterious "Connexion" between Empirical and Better Consciousness

Reason connects the two consciousnesses and thus constitutes, for the individual, the condition of possibility of the transition from one to the other. But what makes this passage *real* or effective is the *will*; the latter is therefore infinitely more important than reason.

> *To will!* Great words! They are the tongue on the scales of the Last Judgment, the bridge between heaven and hell! The faculty of reason is not the light shining from heaven, but only a signpost set up by ourselves and directed to the chosen goal, that it may show us the direction when the goal itself is concealed. But we can just as easily point it to hell as to heaven.[229]

Schopenhauer does not specify who or what is that which, in the individual, can pass from being empirical consciousness to being better consciousness (and vice versa). Here he still presupposes an indeterminate and inexplicable residue, which constitutes the innermost core of the individual (cf. *supra*, 8.11).

The brief hymn to the will just quoted clearly presupposes the freedom of the human being (in this respect, too, it is very reminiscent of the hymn to "duty" in the *Critique of Practical Reason*).[230] But it must not be interpreted in the light of the metaphysics of will, which Schopenhauer would only formulate from 1814 onwards (cf. *infra*, 10.7–10.9).[231]

For Schopenhauer "the *way of thinking* [Denkungsart] (in other words the action of the understanding, i.e. of the ability to *think* [Denk*vermögens*]) [...] is quite immaterial but the will is the essential thing, and [...] this obviously in its moral expression is independent of the thinking of the understanding".[232] The choice between better consciousness and empirical consciousness is itself a moral expression of the will: indeed, it is the fundamental choice between "the kingdom of darkness, of need, desire, illusion, of that which becomes but never is" and "the kingdom of light, repose, joy, amiability, harmony and peace". And indeed, as is the case with every moral decision, so here too what is at stake is the individual's eternal destiny (cf. *supra*, 4.1; 4.2).

---

[229] MR 1, n. 91, p. 59.
[230] Cf. Kant 1996a, pp. 209–210. "*Duty!* [Pflicht!] Sublime and mighty name [...] what origin is there worthy of you, and where is to be found the root of your noble descent which proudly rejects all kinship with the inclinations, descent from which is the indispensable condition of that worth which human beings alone can give themselves. It can be nothing less than what elevates a human being above himself (as a part of the sensible world), [...] It is nothing other than *personality*, that is, freedom and independence from the mechanism of the whole of nature [...]."
[231] This circumstance is well underlined by Gjellerup 1919, p. 501. Cf. also App 2011, pp. 68–69. F. Decher (1996, p. 65), instead, interprets the hymn to the will as a prelude to the system of the metaphysics of will.
[232] MR 1, n. 67, p. 37.

This whole section of the discourse implies the *primacy of the will* over man's two modes of cognition (empirical and better consciousness): the latter are only the two choice options of the will. This predominance, however, was already expressed in a nutshell in fragment 35 ("for the individual there then arises the choice whether he wants to be *reason* or *better consciousness*", cf. *supra*, 7.11).

8.19 The "Transcendental Illusion" of the Relationship between Empirical and Better Consciousness and the Dogma of Original Sin as Its Mythical Representation

In the fragments following number 91, Schopenhauer no longer makes use of the "synthetic unity of apperception" to explain the possibility of the relationship between empirical consciousness and better consciousness. This is a failed theoretical attempt, exhausted in the course of the fragment itself – which in fact ends aporetically.

The problem of the relation between empirical consciousness and better consciousness is taken up again in fragment 96, but in a formulation that expressly refutes the solution proposed in fragment 91; indeed, Schopenhauer here denies the very legitimacy of the problem:

> After our clearly indicating and drawing a distinction between the *better consciousness* and the *empirical*, the question now arises concerning the *relation* between the two, *that is to say*, [italics mine] of how could empirical consciousness ever have come about [*nämlich wie es zum empirischen Bewußtseyn je habe kommen können*]? The question is transcendent and this relation is a transcendental illusion.[233]

Schopenhauer identifies the question of the relationship (*Relation*) between the two consciousnesses as the question of how empirical consciousness could ever arise (cf. *supra*, 8.8).

Commenting on Fichte's concept of *absolute Besonnenheit*, Schopenhauer had stated that the individual, depending on his predisposition towards realism or idealism, can ask: "how does there run into my consciousness [given] through perception that which is not in perception?" or "how do I arrive at the consciousness of perception?" (cf. *supra*, 5.5).[234] One might think, then, that in fragment 96, Schopenhauer means that the individual, depending on his predisposition towards philistinism or saintliness (and genius), is asking: "How does my better consciousness

---

233 MR 1, n. 96, p. 72. Translation modified.
234 MR 2, p. 32.

run into my empirical consciousness?" or "How do I arrive at empirical consciousness?"

But, in reality, only one form of the question is possible here – namely, that raised by Schopenhauer, concerning the origin of empirical consciousness. The question as to how one ever arrived at one of the two consciousnesses necessarily presupposes that the consciousness at which one arrived, in earlier times, was not. But the better consciousness is eternal, so that no becoming or attainment can be conceived of it: the adjectives "eternal", "supertemporal", "supersensible", mean not only that it is consciousness of the eternal, the supertemporal, the supersensible, but also and above all that it itself is such. The better consciousness is essentially akin to that which it cognizes (more generally, it can be assumed that, in relation to the duplicity between empirical consciousness and better consciousness, Schopenhauer relies on the Empedoclean principle of knowledge by likeness; cf. *infra*, 12.10). From Schopenhauer's point of view, then, the question about the relation between empirical consciousness and better consciousness can only be asked in the way he frames it, regardless of the philosophical or moral predisposition of the questioner.

Nevertheless, no matter how formulated, this question is "transcendent", and the relationship it implies is a "transcendental illusion".[235]

> For it is assumed here that (i) the empirical consciousness once followed the better consciousness; thus succession and consequently *time* are assumed. But time is only a determination of the empirical consciousness and is conditioned by this; consequently it already assumes such consciousness. (ii) One asks about the relation itself, whether perhaps the empirical consciousness has in the better consciousness a cause [*Ursache*] or some such thing. But all possible relation is only a determination of the empirical consciousness; it has its essential nature only in thinking, and this thinking is a determination of the empirical consciousness that appears as understanding and the faculty of reason.[236]

The question of how empirical consciousness (i.e. the temporal nature of man) ever originated also illegitimately assumes a relation of *succession*, and possibly of *causality*, between the better consciousness and the empirical consciousness; this question therefore (surreptitiously) refers to both terms determinations – such as temporality and causality, but more generally, the category of "relation" – that properly belong to only one of them, namely the empirical consciousness. Similar considerations are made by Schopenhauer in his commentary on Jacobi's *On Things Divine*.[237] Nevertheless, the "transcendental illusion" consisting of the

---

235 MR 2, n. 96, p. 72.
236 MR 2, n. 96, p. 72.
237 MR 2, pp. 428–429.

assumption of a relationship between the two consciousnesses "is inevitable": one cannot help but think of such a relation, which original sin expresses in a mythical form.[238]

The underlying issue is the 'reason' for the passage or 'fall' of man from eternity to temporality, which was one of the decisive points of reflection of young Schopenhauer already in his early annotations (cf. *supra*, 1.3). In fragment 99 he mentions in passing "the inexplicable co-existence [*das unerklärbare Bestehn*] of the empirical consciousness alongside the better consciousness".[239] The "inexplicable" is thus the existence of the empirical consciousness. But does this mean that Schopenhauer's question is: 'Why isn't there only the better consciousness?'; that is, 'Why does empirical consciousness (also) exist'?

In a note from 1811 he admitted: "I wonder how I have become a subject [*wie ich zum Subjekt geworden bin*], and that is why I philosophize: driven by the consciousness that subject-objectivity is not my absolute state or condition, but a state from which I long for redemption [*Erlösung*]."[240] Here Schopenhauer expressly mentions his *becoming* a subject – which would seem to presuppose a kind of 'transition' from the "absolute state" to the state of "subject-objectivity". But *what* exactly has gone through this transition? *What is it* that 'became' a subject? Schopenhauer is silent on this point. In any case, the content of this fragment is only comprehensible in the light of a passage from Schelling's *Philosophical Letters on Dogmatism and Criticism*, which says that the "Fall of man" – understood as the loss of the intuition of eternal reality, that is, of "things-in-themselves" – means "stepping out [*Heraustreten*] of the absolute state".[241] For Schopenhauer, the state of finite subjectivity (in Kantian terms), i.e. of subject-objectivity, coincides precisely with the constitutive *impossibility* of true or absolute knowledge of things. This state, from which young Schopenhauer ardently seeks "redemption", is man's *empirical consciousness* itself, understood as the 'outcome' of what religion calls the "Fall of man".

According to fragment 79, "this very world (i.e. our empirical sensible and rational consciousness in space and time) has its origin only through that which, ac-

---

[238] MR 1, n. 96, p. 72.
[239] MR 1, n. 99, p. 74.
[240] MR 2, pp. 364–365. Translation modified. It should also be remembered that, according to the above-mentioned note on Fichte's *absolute Besonnenheit*, the "*philosophical astonishment* at the world, in other words at that second consciousness [given] in perception", arises when man reaches the point of view "of a consciousness which exists by itself, is not dependent on perception, is not given through this" (cf. MR 2, p. 32).
[241] Schelling 1980, p. 185 (Eighth Letter).

cording to the utterance of our better consciousness, ought not to be."[242] The same idea is strongly reiterated in fragments 99 and 109: "Death is, so to speak, a debt contracted through life",[243] because "life (i.e. to consciousness that is enslaved by the understanding and sensibility)" "exists only through a mistake, a false step, through that which ought not to be [*das, was nicht seyn sollte*]".[244] "The Bible and Christianity through the fall of man *rightly* [italics mine] introduce into the world death and the troubles and miseries of life."[245] The expression used by Schopenhauer ("a false step") seems to echo the original meaning of the Latin verb *peccāre* (to sin), namely, "to put a foot [*pēs*] wrong".

One must consider that, according to the Christian tradition, original sin is the result of man's *free will*.[246] The fundamental implication of these texts thus seems to be, as in fragment 91, the central role of the *will* in the individual's "transition [*Uebergang*]" from the better consciousness to the empirical one – this transition being understood here as the process by which man, from being *only* better consciousness, also became empirical consciousness (cf. *supra*, 8.8; *infra*, 10.9).

According to Schopenhauer, however, the doctrine of original sin expresses the aforementioned transition in a mythical (*mythisch*), non-philosophical way – probably in the sense that it describes it through the *empirical* terms of "time" and "causality": man's act of will, which resulted in that sin, is in fact seen as 'prior' to and the 'cause of' the fall. It should be remembered, in this regard, that for Schopenhauer the essence of religion lies in the position of an arbitrary and "figuratively [*bildlich*] represented [...] connexion of the world of semblance with the true world (of the sensible world with the supersensible)" (cf. *supra*, 7.2).[247] In the dogma of original sin, the same – epistemologically illegitimate – figurative connection is made between the consciousness of the sensible world and the consciousness of the supersensible world.

In itself, i.e. beyond any possible myth, the relationship between empirical consciousness and better consciousness is completely inconceivable, and indeed constitutes a transcendental illusion: something that seems thinkable and knowable, but in reality is not.

> If we want to speak at all about this relation, we can say that it is positively uncognizable to all eternity. For the better consciousness does not think and cognize, since it lies beyond sub-

---

242 MR 1, n. 79, p. 43.
243 MR 1, n. 99, p. 74.
244 MR 1, n. 109, pp. 79–80.
245 MR 1, n. 99, p. 74.
246 Augustine 1998, XIII, 14–15, pp. 555–556; XIII, 21, p. 568.
247 MR 1, n. 32, p. 20. Translation modified.

ject and object. But the empirical consciousness cannot cognize a relation whose one link it itself is. This relation therefore lies beyond the sphere of this consciousness and includes this sphere itself.[248]

The "better consciousness does not think and cognize". Cognition as such is internal – and therefore limited – to *only one* of the two terms of the relation, i.e. to empirical consciousness alone; consequently, the relation itself necessarily falls outside any possible cognition.

However, even to say that the relationship between better consciousness and empirical consciousness "is positively uncognizable to all eternity" means presuming "something as conceived which in itself contradictory and inconceivable" – namely, that relation.[249] Even affirming the unknowability of this relation is in fact contradictory, as it implies that what cannot be conceived is conceived (as the subject of a predication). One must therefore give up talking about this relation altogether.

8.20 The Fundamental Aporia: The Better Consciousness "Does Not Think and Cognize, Since It Lies beyond Subject and Object". Absolute and Non-absolute Opposition

In the final part of the above-mentioned fragment 96, a very important clarification is introduced: "the better consciousness does not think and cognize, since it lies beyond subject and object". In fragment 81 Schopenhauer had already written: "the better consciousness in me lifts me into a world where there is no longer personality and causality or subject and object."[250] These statements are certainly consistent with what young Arthur argued elsewhere: the "falling apart into subjective and objective" is the "basis of our consciousness" in accordance with Reinhold's principle.[251] The duality of subject and object ("subject-objectivity") is not man's absolute state, so much so that Schopenhauer comes to marvel at having become a subject (i.e. no longer being in an absolute state).[252]

---

248 MR 1, n. 96, pp. 72–73. Translation modified.
249 MR 1, p. 73.
250 MR 1, n. 81, p. 44.
251 MR 2, p. 378.
252 MR 2, p. 365.

Nevertheless, the better consciousness is for Schopenhauer "the absolute way of cognition",[253] insofar as it cognize absolute or eternal reality (which in fragment 86 coincides with the Platonic Idea: cf. *supra*, 8.14). How can Schopenhauer assert all these things at once?

If we take the assertion that "the better consciousness does not think and cognize" in a relative (not absolute) sense, then we can say that the thinking and cognizing that do *not* concern the better consciousness are the ones of the *understanding*, whereas the cognition attributed to the better consciousness is antithetical to the latter kind. In this way, the cognition granted to the better consciousness would not be the same as that denied to it, and no contradiction would arise. But Schopenhauer's statement has a peremptory tone: the better consciousness "does not think and cognize" at all, "since it lies beyond subject and object". It is therefore not possible to settle the question in the manner just outlined.

Now, *how can something which does not think and cognize at all, and which is not even the subject of cognition, be nevertheless "consciousness"?* This term inevitably implies a cognitive connotation (and indeed, the better consciousness cognizes "the eternal world"). The contradiction exists between the limitation of cognition as such to the empirical sphere alone – and thus to the consciousness of the latter, which is precisely empirical consciousness – and the affirmation of the possibility of metempirical cognition. This is, once more, the basic opposition between the 'Platonic' vector (epistemic, i.e. positive, knowability of reality in itself) and the 'Kantian' vector (unknowability of reality in itself; cf. *supra*, 2.13).

In this particular point lies the real *fundamental contradiction* of the theory of the better consciousness (cf. *supra*, 7.14). In the final analysis, it consists in the attempt to think and describe *positively* what is at the same time defined as the nothing of all that is (positively) thinkable and cognizable. In fact, on the one hand, the better consciousness is absolutely opposed to empirical consciousness; on the other hand, it is still "consciousness", and therefore *not* absolutely opposed to empirical consciousness, sharing with it (at least) the fact of being a "consciousness". The opposition between the two consciousnesses is explicitly posited as *absolute* (each is the nothing of the other), and implicitly – through the term "consciousness" – as *non-absolute*.

In conclusion: *the relation* – which Schopenhauer calls "transcendental illusion" – *between empirical consciousness and better consciousness is implied precisely by the term "consciousness"*, so that the use of this term is irremediably transcendent, just like the relation it expresses. With respect to this complex contradiction, the only possible solution is (and indeed would be) to determine

---

253 MR 2, p. 295. Translation modified.

what is absolutely opposed to the empirical dimension with a different connotation from the (cognitive) one implied by the term "consciousness". In other words, Schopenhauer was to effectively and radically renounce any *positive* terminology in this regard (cf. *infra*, 11.10 – 11.15).

8.21 Conclusion. The Unfinished Project of a Work on the Better Consciousness

In the annotations of 1813, the properly gnoseological element of the theory of man's twofold consciousness – the distinction between the cognitive sphere of the better consciousness and that of empirical consciousness – remains mostly implicit in the texts (with the exception of the note to the *Prolegomena* and fragment 86; cf. *supra*, 8.5 and 8.13). On the other hand, the relationship of the better consciousness with the aesthetic, moral and religious spheres is made explicit and further developed. Through their common reference to the better consciousness – and thus to the eternal world – they are here thought of as essentially related to each other (it is significant that Schopenhauer feels the need to determine the difference between the saint and the genius).

For this reason, *the figure of the better consciousness is the keystone on which young Schopenhauer sought to build his philosophical system.* The parallelism between the aesthetic and ethical spheres is emblematic in this respect: *"the very essense of all beauty"* is "the *theoretical negation of the temporal world and [theoretical] affirmation of eternity* [...] (just as the practical negation and affirmation of those two are asceticism and virtue)".[254] Asceticism and virtue are also, respectively, the negation *of the consciousness* of the temporal world (the empirical consciousness)[255] and the affirmation or expression *of the consciousness* of the eternal world (the better consciousness).[256] In this sense, there is a systematic connection between the theoretical (cognitive), practical and aesthetic spheres: *virtue* is "the direct expression of the awareness" of "extratemporal being"[257] (cf. *supra*, 8.3 – 8.5, 8.7); *art* is the reproduction of the eternal or true world.

As an indication of the systematic tension running through young Schopenhauer's reflections, fragment 92 reads:

---

[254] MR 1, n. 86, p. 48.
[255] MR 1, n. 99, p. 74.
[256] MR 1, n. 87, p. 54.
[257] MR 1, n. 72, p. 40. Translation modified.

8.21 Conclusion. The Unfinished Project of a Work on the Better Consciousness

> In my hands and perhaps in my mind there is developed a work, a philosophy, which is to be ethics and metaphysics *in one*, for hitherto these were just as falsely separated as was man into body and soul. The work expands and the parts grow together slowly and by degrees like a child in the womb [...].[258]

When mentioning the historical separation of ethics and metaphysics, Schopenhauer is probably thinking specifically of Kant's philosophy – certainly not of Plato's: the word "hitherto" should therefore be taken with a pinch of salt. For Kant, what can be admitted (indeed "postulated") from the moral point of view – the freedom of the human will, the existence of God and the immortality of the soul – can never be admitted, i.e. grounded, from the theoretical point of view. If this interpretation of the text is correct, then here too Schopenhauer means to say that Kant's undertaking, in spite of its momentous value, awaits and indeed requires essential completion. The last word of philosophy, in spite of Kant and Plato, has not yet been spoken; Schopenhauer therefore plans to set it down and speak it *first*, through the work pre-announced in this fragment.

But the work to which Schopenhauer refers here cannot be his masterpiece, *The World as Will and Representation* (even if the latter is about "one thought" that, likewise, comprises and resolves "what has been called metaphysics, what has been called ethics, and what has been called aesthetics"),[259] because the "philosophy" set forth in the latter text is no longer that of the better consciousness.[260] The quoted fragment, written in 1813, evidently refers to ideas he'd already expressed (albeit in an initial and incomplete way): the work in question had already been brought to light, because it "grew" not only inwardly, in the "mind", but already "in [the] hands" of its author. The project mentioned here is to be referred to something that Schopenhauer *had already begun to write*, and consequently can only concern the theory of better consciousness (which, as we have seen, invests both "ethics" and "metaphysics").

The fragments of 1813 analyzed in this chapter – in which, as already noted, there is a clear attempt at developing a philosophical system – are to be regarded as a first, rough draft of the "work" in question. Schopenhauer, however, would not elaborate on it any further. I will return to this point at greater length in the next chapter (cf. *infra*, 9.3; 9.13).

---

258 MR 1, n. 92, p. 50.
259 Schopenhauer 2010b, I VII–VIII, p. 5.
260 Several scholars have misinterpreted the text according to this anachronism; cf. J. Frauenstädt, "Arthur Schopenhauer. Memorabilien, Briefe, und Nachlassstücke", in Lindner and Frauenstädt 1863, p. 244; Döll 1904, p. 9; Kloppe 1972, p. 403; Hübscher 1989, p. 113; Decher 1996, p. 65; Rühl 2001, p. 114. Cf. Novembre 2016b.

The system of the duplicity of consciousness, as we have seen, presents an unsolved issue, indeed a real contradiction, concerning the question of the "relation" between the two consciousnesses. In fact, on the one hand this relation is defined as something *impossible* ("all possible relation is only a determination of the empirical consciousness", and therefore exists only within the latter); on the other hand, it is implied by the fact that both terms are "consciousness". The designation "consciousness" thus acts, so to speak, as a middle term and connects or reconciles two concepts that ought to be absolutely opposed to each other.

This contradiction was pointed out by Schopenhauer himself, albeit at a formally derived level of consequentiality. From his point of view, the problem of the "relation" between better and empirical consciousness concerns the transition from the former to the latter, that is, the problem of how the individual (or, more properly, his 'core'), from being *only* eternal better consciousness, could *also* become empirical or temporal consciousness. For Schopenhauer, this problem is completely unsolvable; indeed, it is even illegitimate to posit it, because "all possible relation", and therefore also any possible "transition" from one condition to another, are determinations of empirical consciousness alone.[261] The process from which the latter originated, expressed mythically in the dogma of original sin, is something that *must* be thought of (as having occurred), but, at the same time, *cannot* be thought of (in its determinateness). At the bottom of the *attempted* system of the theory of twofold consciousness, therefore, lies this aporia – which must be regarded as the main reason why Schopenhauer no longer wrote the work announced in fragment 92.

In the following part of this book, we shall see how the metaphysics of will, developed by Schopenhauer from 1814 onwards, would constitute precisely the overcoming of this aporia – and thus (within certain limits) also the answer to the question of how empirical consciousness could ever have come about.

The reflections that led young philosopher to establish the foundations of his mature system as early as 1814 presupposed some theoretical results of his dissertation, *On the Fourfold Root of the Principle of Sufficient Reason* (1813): in particular, the distinction between "subject of cognition" and "subject of willing" and the doctrine of the "intelligible character". In order to illustrate the genesis of the metaphysics of will, or – according to an expression that Schopenhauer takes, almost literally, from Fichte's lectures[262] – of the "one thought" that would underlie *The*

---

[261] MR 1, n. 91, p. 58.
[262] In the fourth introductory lecture "On the Study of Philosophy", Fichte states that "as a series of many thoughts", the *Wissenschaftslehre* "is then imparted, although it is in fact only one thought [*nur Ein Gedanke*]" (MR 2, p. 28; translation modified). Similarly, in the fourth lecture "On *Wissen-*

8.21 Conclusion. The Unfinished Project of a Work on the Better Consciousness

World as Will and Representation,²⁶³ it is therefore first necessary to analyze the corresponding passages in the dissertation.

---

schaftslehre" (MR 2, p. 98), he says that the task of the disciple is to grasp "the one thought [*der Eine Gedanke*]" in which *Wissenschaftslehre* consists. Translation modified.
263 Cf. Schopenhauer 2010b, I VII–VIII, p. 5; § 71, I 483, p. 435. On this part of the discourse, cf. Malter 1988; Koßler 2006b, 2009b.

Part 4 **The Abandonment of the Theory of the Better Consciousness and the Origin of the Metaphysics of Will**

9 Will and Intelligible Character in the Dissertation of 1813: Between Fichte's *System der Sittenlehre* and Schelling's *Freiheitsschrift*

9.1 Introduction: A Short Biographical Outline

In 1811, young Arthur had moved from Göttingen to Berlin to attend Fichte's courses. On 28 March 1813, Prussia officially declared war on Napoleon. Schopenhauer, who had always been detached from his contemporaries' patriotic sentiment, decided to leave Berlin and fled in the direction of Weimar at the end of May, eventually reaching Rudolstadt.[1] Here, between June and September, he wrote his dissertation *On the Fourfold Root of the Principle of Sufficient Reason*.

In September, however, all connections between Rudolstadt and Berlin were blocked due to the war. Schopenhauer thus decided to defend his dissertation *in absentia* and get his degree from the neighboring University of Jena. On 22 September, he sent the Dean of the Faculty of Philosophy, Professor Heinrich Karl Abraham Eichstädt, 10 gold Fredericks (the graduation fee);[2] two days later, on 24 September, he sent him the dissertation, enclosing a letter in which he wrote:

> When, in the early summer of this year, the noise of war drove the Muses from Berlin, where I was studying philosophy – [...] I, who had sworn allegiance to their colours alone, likewise left the city with their retinue – not so much because, due to a special concatenation of circumstances, I am a stranger everywhere and have no civic duties to discharge anywhere, but because I was most deeply pervaded by the conviction that I was not born to serve mankind with my fist but with my head, and that my fatherland is greater than Germany.[3]

On 2 October, the committee – consisting of Professors Justus Christian Hennings, Friedrich Sigmund Voigt and Heinrich Luden – awarded the work the distinction of *magna cum laude*.[4] On 5 October Schopenhauer received his diploma and wrote again to the Dean to thank him.[5]

---

1 Schopenhauer's movements are also testified by the headings of some of his manuscript fragments: n. 96 was written in Hoyerswerda (cf. MR 1, p. 72), n. 100 in Weimar (cf. MR 1, p. 76), and n. 104 in Rudolstadt (cf. MR 1, p. 78).
2 Cf. Schopenhauer 1978a, p. 3.
3 Cf. Schopenhauer 1978a pp. 4–5; the letter was written in Latin. For the German translation, see Schopenhauer 1978a, p. 643; En. tr. in Safranski 1990, p. 147.
4 Cf. Riedinger 1922, p. 99.
5 Cf. Schopenhauer 1978a, pp. 5–6.

When the book was printed, on 5 November Schopenhauer set off for Weimar, because in the meantime the war had also reached Rudolstadt.[6] From there, he sent two copies of his dissertation to two illustrious professors in Göttingen and Berlin: respectively Gottlob Ernst Schulze and Friedrich Schleiermacher.[7] He also sent a copy to Carl Leonhard Reinhold[8] and (with high hopes) to Goethe,[9] with whom he began to meet regularly soon afterwards to discuss color theory. The outcome of this research, through which Schopenhauer intended to provide a philosophical ground for Goethe's theory (even though he ended up contradicting it on some specific points), would be published about two and a half years later under the title *On Vision and Colours*.[10]

On 20 January 1814, Schopenhauer received Schulze's reply, expressing his warm thanks for the dissertation and voicing a very flattering opinion of the work:

> You have, my dearest Doctor, presented me with a most welcome gift with your work on the principle of sufficient reason, and I offer you my sincerest thanks for it and for the pleasure I have had in reading it. By virtue of our former acquaintance, it was of particular interest to me, and since from that acquaintance I was aware of your talent, I started reading it with no small expectations. But these expectations were far exceeded.
>
> For when I consider, in your work, the importance of the topic for the whole of philosophy, the method that has been followed in the research and in answering the questions concerning the topic, the acumen and correctness of the observations on certain acts of the human spirit and the consequentiality of thinking expressed in the work, the decisiveness and charm of the exposition, the respect for the merits of other philosophers, which is demonstrated in your work, and, finally, the absence of any attempt to merely say something new and original, although much in it is expounded from a new angle – well then, I must regard [your work] as a truly felicitous publication, which makes one expect much more excellence and greatness from its author. You know how little inclination I have to pay you compliments, and therefore I do not need to assure you that the above general judgment of your writing is the genuine voice of my conviction.[11]

---

[6] The heading of fragment 117 reads "Weimar" again (cf. MR 1, p. 82). Cf. also Schopenhauer 1978a, p. 261: "1813 bereitete ich mich zur Promotion in Berlin vor, wurde aber durch den Krieg verdrängt, befand ich mich im Herbst in Thüringen, konnte nicht zurück und sah mich genöhtigt mit meiner Abhandlung über den Satz vom Grunde in Jena zu promovieren. Darauf brachte ich den Winter in Weimar zu [...]". On this stage of Schopenhauer's life, cf. Safranski 1990, pp. 163–164.
[7] Cf. Schopenhauer 1978a, pp. 7–8.
[8] Cf. Schopenhauer 1978a, pp. 8–9.
[9] Cf. Schopenhauer 1978a, p. 9. Cf. Schubbe and Fauth 2016.
[10] Cf. A. Schopenhauer, *On Vision and Colours*, in Schopenhauer 2012, pp. 199–302. For a reconstruction of his meetings with Goethe, see Safranski 1990, pp. 177–190. On color theory, see Grigenti 2005; D'Alfonso 2011; Grigenti 2021.
[11] Schopenhauer 1911–1942, vol. XIV, p. 162.

At the end of the letter, Schulze further emphasized:

> And those who, like you, have chosen Plato, Aristotle and Kant as models for their treatment of philosophy, are on their way to ever greater perfection. I therefore nourish the joyful hope that philosophy, i.e. the clarification of the supreme questions of the human spirit, will still have much to thank your talents and your ardor for, and, with highest esteem and sincere sentiments of friendship, I remain yours [Gottlob Ernst Schulze].[12]

About a year later, Schulze gave an extremely favorable review of the dissertation in the prestigious journal *Göttingische Gelehrte Anzeigen*, publicly acknowledging the value of the work and "the high hopes [...] raised by the author's philosophical talents and his ardor for the supreme achievement in philosophy".[13] Despite these compliments, Schulze did not fail to make a few critical remarks in both his letter and his review (cf. *infra*, 9.3). And, a few years later, he would not comment at all on the work with which his gifted pupil tried to realize "the high hopes" raised by the dissertation.[14]

9.2 Some Preliminary Reflections: The Four Basic Laws of the Understanding and the Principle of the Unalterability of a Concept

The determination of the sensible world as the "nothing" of the supersensible world, theorized in fragments 66 and 72 (but already implicit in fragment 46), implies that the laws that apply to the former cannot also apply to the latter, and vice versa (cf. *supra*, 7.8; 8.2 – 8.5).

In fragment 93, entitled "Hypothetical Essay", Schopenhauer attempts to determine the "basic laws of the understanding".[15] They only apply in the sphere of the understanding – that is, the sensible world – and are: the principle of the excluded third (*principium exclusi medii inter duo contradictoria*), the principle of identity (*principium identitatis*), the principle of contradiction (*principium contradictionis*),

---

12 Schopenhauer 1911–1942, vol. XIV, pp. 162–163.
13 Cf. Schulze 1916. Cf. Hübscher 1966, p. 33.
14 As hypothesized by R. Piper (1916, p. 166), this is perhaps due to Schulze's later resentment at the fact that, in the first edition of his masterpiece, Schopenhauer takes up some of Schulze's criticism of the concept of thing-in-itself, without, however, explicitly naming him. The passage in which Schulze is praised (cf. Schopenhauer 2010b, I, 516, p. 462) is absent from the first edition of the work (cf. Schopenhauer 2020, pp. 310–311), as it only appeared in the second edition (cf. Schopenhauer 1844, henceforth WWV 1844, p. 490).
15 MR 1, n. 93, p. 60.

and the principle of sufficient reason (*principium rationis sufficientis*).[16] According to Schopenhauer, these four laws are all to be traced back to "the one *principle of unalterability of a concept* (*principium immutabilitatis notionis*), which runs: 'a concept is absolutely unalterable'"; that is, in every concept "nothing can be added or taken away" (alteration being any addition or removal).[17]

> To the concept belongs everything that Plato says of the Ideas, which indeed are really concepts. He contrasts them with sensuously given intuitions or individual things, since he repeats that these always change and are transient: the concept, on the other hand, is the ἀεὶ ὡσαύτως ὄν, the unalterable and imperishable. The changeable nature of actual things is due to the fact that they are matter and form and that matter is permanent, whilst form changes. But the concept is nothing but form; if we change this form, then we bring into consciousness a new concept instead of the old; however the old remains what it was and never becomes the same as the new, in other words it is unchangeable.[18]

Interestingly, Schopenhauer here contradicts many of his previous and subsequent statements by asserting the identity between the concepts of understanding and Platonic Ideas.[19] I will to return to the meaning of this theoretical attempt (cf. *infra*, 11.10).

Now, for Schopenhauer, it is only by virtue of the principle of unalterability of the concept that those four basic laws indeed apply to concepts. Being unchangeable, in fact, every concept is *determined*, i.e. it is always "equal to the sum of its attributes" (principle of identity); consequently, "every predicate must be denied or attributed to it" (principle of the excluded third), so that a certain predicate

---

[16] MR 1, p. 62.
[17] MR 1, p. 61.
[18] MR 1, p. 60.
[19] This identity contradicts not only fragment 15 "On Plato", whose theoretical effort consisted precisely in defining the difference between the two terms, but also fragment 86, in which the view of the "Platonic Idea of the object" was opposed to the observation of "the nexus of space, time and causality", i.e., implicitly, to the cognition of the understanding (cf. *supra*, 2.5; 8.13). In this period (before the dissertation, that is), for Schopenhauer, the concept was a product of the understanding: thus the identity between the Platonic Idea and the concept implies that the understanding is the faculty related to the Idea. But Schopenhauer certainly did not mean this. The passage in question stands in contradiction both with the fragments that precede it and with those that follow it: in 1814, as we shall see, Schopenhauer would explicitly identify the Platonic Idea, but absolutely not the concept of understanding, with the thing-in-itself (cf. *infra*, 11.9). In fragment 226 (cf. MR 1, p. 142), Schopenhauer explicitly rules out the identity of Platonic Ideas and general concepts. The above-mentioned passage must therefore be understood as a theoretical experimentation (based on the circumstance that concepts, like Platonic Ideas, are unchanging).

and its negation "cannot exist at the same time" in relation to the same subject (principle of contradiction).[20]

With regard to the principle of sufficient reason, Schopenhauer refers to fragment 55, where it is defined as "the *principium identitatis* applied to – the *copula*".[21] For "'to be', 'is', states: to be given as object (that is to say sensuously perceivable)",[22] *esse est percipi*, so that the *judgment* of perception in which that copula appears can only be thought of as the ground or sufficient reason of *another judgment of perception*, insofar as the judgment that contradicts the first – i. e. the judgment in which, instead of "is", "is not" appears, or vice versa – is thought of as false.[23] But this is only possible, again, if the copula that appears in the first judgment is (thought of as) *identical* to the copula appearing in the judgment that contradicts it.[24] Consequently – Schopenhauer concludes – even the principle of sufficient reason, being nothing more than a particular case of the principle of identity, is to be traced back to the "one principle of the unalterability of a concept".

Since "being" means "being cognized" (cf. *supra*, 8.2), the basic laws of human *cognition* are also the laws of its content, namely *being*. According to Schopenhauer, however, the four basic laws of pure understanding do not exhaust this legislation. In addition to these, he lists "the synthetic principles of pure understanding (everything has a cause; everything is substance or accident)" and "the principles of mathematics which are based on pure intuition", i.e. the two pure intuitions of space and time.[25]

These fragments clearly show the intention to rigorously and comprehensively determine the basic or formal laws of the understanding (and, therefore, of every possible "being" given in experience). The notebooks from this period (and the books he borrowed from the Weimar library)[26] document Schopenhauer's focused and in-depth study of various philosophical texts: Fries' *Neue Kritik der Vernunft*,[27] some of Plato's dialogues,[28] Bacon's *De augmentis scientiarum*[29] and Locke's *Essay Concerning Human Understanding*.[30] It is extremely interesting that Schopenhauer

---

[20] MR 1, p. 62.
[21] MR 1, n. 55, p. 32.
[22] MR 1, n. 55, p. 32. Cf. MR 2, p. 291.
[23] Cf. MR 1, n. 55, p. 32.
[24] MR 1, n. 55, p. 32.
[25] MR 1, n. 94, p. 64. Translation modified.
[26] Cf. App 2006a, pp. 48–49.
[27] Cf. MR 2, pp. 417–425.
[28] Cf. MR 2, pp. 432–437.
[29] Cf. MR 2, pp. 442–443.
[30] Cf. MR 2, pp. 444–446.

interpreted and, indeed, judged all these works from the perspective of Kantian criticism – which, in his eyes, encompassed the most advanced philosophical point of view.

At the same time, however, he sought to improve criticism by amending the errors and inconsistencies he believed he found in it. He devoted much time to studying the *Prolegomena to Any Future Metaphysics*,[31] and he reread both the *Critique of the Power of Judgment*[32] and the *Critique of Pure Reason* – the latter in its fifth edition,[33] which, except for the correction of some printing errors, faithfully reproduced the second edition of 1787.[34] In it, Kant had made considerable changes compared to the first edition (1781); Schopenhauer would later argue for the greater value of the latter work (which he only read for the first time in 1826), so much so that he convinced the publisher Rosenkranz to reprint it.[35]

In his notes on Kant, Schopenhauer pays particular attention to the concepts of "space", "time", "alteration", "movement", "imagination", "substance", "cause", "ground [*Grund*]", "principle", "image", "concept",[36] "understanding" and "reason [*Vernunft*]".[37] He also tries to expose the transcendent use of the category of causality (in line with Schulze's criticism)[38] and, above all, complains about the lack of distinction between the concepts of "ground", "cause" and "motive".[39]

Fragments 92–95 document an early stage of these reflections, which would later find a successful outcome in the dissertation *On the Fourfold Root of the Principle of Sufficient Reason*, which I will now discuss.[40]

---

[31] MR 2, pp. 290–295.
[32] MR 2, pp. 316–328.
[33] I. Kant, *Critik der reinen Vernunft*, Leipzig: Hartknoch, 1799 (cf. HN V, [293], p. 94).
[34] Cf. MR 2, pp. 295–316.
[35] *Immanuel Kant's sämmtliche Werke*, ed. by K. Rosenkranz and F. W. Schubert, 12 vols., Leipzig: Voss, 1838–42. For Schopenhauer's famous letter to Rosenkranz and Schubert, cf. Schopenhauer 1911–1942, vol. XIV, p. 472–477. Cf. also Schopenhauer 2010b, I 514, p. 461.
[36] Cf. MR 2, pp. 267–275, 290–305.
[37] Cf. MR 2, p. 304 305. Cf. also pp. 285–286 (footnote), 328–332.
[38] Cf. MR 2, pp. 292–293, 309. Cf. D'Alfonso 2008, p. 76.
[39] MR 2, pp. 299–302, 310–312, 328. Cf. Schopenhauer 2012 [1813], § 59, pp. 149–152. The distinction between "cause", "reason or ground" and "motive" is drawn in fragment 60 of the manuscripts (cf. MR 1, p. 34.). N. De Cian (cf. De Cian 2011, pp. 172–174) has well documented how Schopenhauer's reflections on Kant's third *Critique* underlie these annotations (cf. MR 2, pp. 316–318).
[40] In a note to fragment 96 Schopenhauer himself wrote: "N. B. Sheets L, M, N [corresponding to fragments 93–95] contain hardly anything but studies and extracts for the purpose of a dissertation on the principle of sufficient reason." (Cf. MR 1, p. 72)

9.3 Purpose and Structure of the Dissertation *On the Fourfold Root of the Principle of Sufficient Reason*. The Identity of "Appearance" and "Representation" and the First Three Forms of the Principle of Reason

In the Preface to the first edition of *The World as Will and Representation* (1818), Schopenhauer states that, in order to fully understand the *"single thought"* expounded in that text,[41] it is necessary that "the introduction be read before the book itself, even though it is not located inside the book but rather appeared five years earlier under the title: *On the Fourfold Root of the Principle of Sufficient Reason: A Philosophical Essay*".[42]

> It is absolutely impossible to truly understand the present work unless the reader is familiar with this introduction and propaedeutic, and the contents of that essay are presupposed here as much as if they had been included in the book. Moreover, if the essay had not preceded the present work by several years, it would be incorporated into the First Book instead of standing in front of it as an introduction; there are gaps in the First Book where the material from that essay would have been, and the resulting incompleteness must be made good by constant appeal to that essay.[43]

The 1813 dissertation is thus regarded by Schopenhauer as "propaedeutic", indeed, as an integral part of his masterpiece – in particular, of the First Book of the work, the title page of which reads: "The world as representation, first consideration. Representation subject to the principle of sufficient reason: the object of experience and science".[44] In relation to the attempt – starting from the Second Book – to establish what the world is, beyond its being a "representation",[45] it is propaedeutic and indeed indispensable to rigorously establish the limits of the representation itself, comprehensively determining the basic (formal) law that governs it. But this law, according to Schopenhauer, is constituted precisely by the principle of sufficient reason: this is why the dissertation should ideally be considered "incorporated into the First Book" of his major work.

In 1847, introducing the second edition of the dissertation, Schopenhauer wrote: "This treatise in elementary philosophy, which first appeared in the year 1813, when I had gained my doctorate with it, has since [*nachmals*] become the un-

---

41 Schopenhauer 2010b, I VIII, p. 5.
42 Schopenhauer 2010b, I X, p. 7.
43 Schopenhauer 2010b, I X, p. 7.
44 Schopenhauer 2010b, I 1, p. 23.
45 Schopenhauer 2010b, I 118–133, § 18–22, pp. 123–137.

derpinnings [*Unterbau*] of my whole system".⁴⁶ The fact that the dissertation only *later* became the basis or "underpinnings" of Schopenhauer's mature system – the very system that is set out in *The World as Will and Representation* – evidently means that in 1813 Schopenhauer did not understand it as such. But this is quite simply because, in 1813, the "system" in question did not yet exist. And in fact, as we shall soon see, it is through the dissertation that the actual ground of the metaphysics of will appears for the first time, albeit only in a nutshell: the doctrine of "intelligible character". Before delving into this point, however, it is necessary to take a look at the work as a whole.

In his dissertation, Schopenhauer primarily sets out to apply to the principle of sufficient reason ("a fundamental principle of all cognition") the two fundamental rules of all philosophizing, equally recommended by "Plato, the divine" and the "amazing Kant": the law of *homogeneity* and the law of *specification*.⁴⁷ Within this single principle, Schopenhauer intends to duly distinguish "among its highly differing applications".⁴⁸ This distinction, according to Schopenhauer, had indeed not yet been fully made;⁴⁹ in the second chapter of the work he expressly mentions and criticizes all the authors who, in his opinion, constitute the most significant precedents in this sense.⁵⁰

Now, the essential or elementary form of the principle of reason is: "*Nihil est sine ratione cur potius sit quam non sit*", i.e.: "Nothing is without a reason why it is".⁵¹ Put in positive form: everything that exists, exists for a reason, without which it would not exist at all. This principle, for Schopenhauer, is the basis (*Grundlage*) "of all science", or rather of every "*system* of findings";⁵² indeed, it is the "fundamental principle [*Grundsatz*] of all cognition" in general.⁵³ The principle of reason cannot be demonstrated, precisely because it is the basis of any demonstration, and constitutes "the conditions of all thinking and knowing [*die Bedingungen alles Denkens und Erkennens*]".⁵⁴ The "root" of the principle is as follows:

---

46 Schopenhauer 2012 [1847], p. 3.
47 Schopenhauer 2012 [1813], § 1–2, pp. 7–8.
48 Schopenhauer 2012 [1813], § 2, p. 8.
49 Schopenhauer 2012 [1813], § 2, p. 8.
50 In particular, Schopenhauer presents and discusses the positions of Descartes, Spinoza, Leibniz, Wolff, Baugmarten, Lambert, Plattner, Reimarus, Kant, Kiesewetter, Maimon and Schulze (cf. Schopenhauer 2012 [1813], pp. 14–28, 153–157). The records of the Weimar library relating to the year 1813 testify that Schopenhauer read these authors (cf. App 2006a, pp. 48–49). Cf. Kamata 2015.
51 Schopenhauer 2012 [1813], § 5, p. 10.
52 Schopenhauer 2012 [1813], § 4, p. 9.
53 Schopenhauer 2012 [1813], § 6, p. 154.
54 Schopenhauer 2012 [1813], § 13, p. 28.

> Our consciousness, as far as it appears as sensibility, understanding, and reason, divides into subject and object, and, so far, comprises nothing else. To be object for the subject and to be our representation are the same. All of our representations are objects for the subject, and all objects for the subject are our representations.[55]

There is a clear consonance here with Reinhold's "principle of representation", according to which subject and object are both internal to human consciousness, because they are nothing more than the terms in which it splits.[56] But the fact that the object is internal to consciousness means that it coincides with the representation of consciousness itself. The Kantian appearance, i.e. the (intersubjective) object of experience, is thus reduced to representation, in accordance with Schulze's exposition (cf. *supra*, 3.7). Schopenhauer expresses this reduction by also stating that "the so-called being of [...] real things *is absolutely nothing else than their being represented*": "the object is absolutely nothing apart from its reference to the subject, and [...] if one takes this away or abstracts from it, absolutely *nothing* else remains, and the *existence in itself* that was attributed to it was an absurdity [*Unding*] and vanishes".[57] A fragment from the same period as the dissertation, written in Rudolstadt in 1813, reads:

> If anyone became deeply absorbed in thought and then said: "Is it possible that I might cease to exist? If I did not exist, what then would there still be?"— then he would be right, if only we understood him.[58]

These considerations are what led Schopenhauer to consider the Kantian concept of the thing-in-itself as illegitimate *qua* contradictory (cf. *infra*, 11.9). Continuing to expound the "root" of the principle of sufficient reason, Schopenhauer goes on to say:

> But nothing existing of itself and independently, likewise nothing existing in isolation and apart, can become an object for us; rather, all of our representations stand in a connection that is governed by laws and of a form determinable a priori.[59]

As "*All of our representations are objects for the subject, and all objects for the subject are our representations*", then if "*all of our representations stand in a connec-*

---

55 Schopenhauer 2012 [1813], § 16, p. 157.
56 On this, cf. Kamata 1988, p. 133–135.
57 Schopenhauer 2012 [1813], § 20, p. 37, 161. See also the note to fragment 93 of the manuscripts (MR 1, n. 93, p. 61). For a comparison between this principle and the Reinholdian principle of representation, cf. Bondeli 2014, pp. 35–53.
58 MR 1, n. 104, p. 78.
59 Schopenhauer 2012 [1813], § 16, p. 157.

tion that is governed by laws and of a form determinable a priori" it means that all cognizable *objects* stand to one another in that same connection. The latter, in its essential form, is expressed precisely by the very general and fundamental formula of the principle of reason: *Nihil est sine ratione cur potius sit quam non sit.*

On the basis of this assumption, and in accordance with the law of specification, Schopenhauer articulates the single root of the principle of reason in four different ways, which constitute the four ramifications of the principle itself and correspond to the four different spheres of human knowledge – or rather, precisely, to the *"four classes* into which everything which can become an object for us [...] break down".[60]

"The first class of possible objects of our faculty of representation [*Vorstellungsvermögens*] is that of *the complete representations that comprise the totality of an experience.*"[61] By "complete representations" Schopenhauer means those that comprehend (in Kantian terms) both the form and the matter of experience (cf. *supra*, 2.6): these are concrete and 'real' empirical objects.[62] "The principle of sufficient reason governs in it as the law of causality",[63] which constitutes the *principium rationis sufficientis fiendi* ("*principle of sufficient reason of becoming*").[64] The special function of the understanding (*Verstand*) lies in the application of the category of causality (cf. *infra*, 9.6).

"The second class of possible objects for our faculty of representation is made up of *representations of representations:* these are concepts".[65] For since intuitive empirical objects are nothing but representations (albeit complete ones), then concepts, being representations of empirical objects, are representations of representations. I have already pointed to a passage in the *Critique of Pure Reason* that could underlie this definition of the term "concept" (cf. *supra*, 4.3).[66] Here it is interesting to note that in the dissertation, the faculty of concepts is no longer the understanding, as in the manuscripts, but reason (*Vernunft*).[67] The operations relating to concepts – forming them, combining them into judgments and finally compounding the judgments themselves into deductive chains – constitute the specific activity of human reason: this is, in a word, "*thinking* [Denken], in the proper

---

60 Schopenhauer 2012 [1813], § 17, p. 158.
61 Schopenhauer 2012 [1813], § 18, p. 159.
62 Schopenhauer 2012 [1813], § 18, p. 159.
63 Schopenhauer 2012 [1813], § 18, p. 159.
64 Schopenhauer 2012 [1813], § 23, p. 38 (corresponding to § 20 in the second edition).
65 Schopenhauer 2012 [1813], § 27, p. 175.
66 Cf. Kant 1998, B 93–94, p. 205.
67 Schopenhauer 2012 [1813], § 27, pp. 175–176.

sense of the word".⁶⁸ Reason is what distinguishes humans from animals, which are devoid of concepts.⁶⁹

Now, concepts are the constituent elements of judgments, and on the other hand "Judgements have no value, except insofar as they are *true*".⁷⁰ "*Truth is thus the relation of a judgement to something beyond it*" which constitutes the ground (*Grund*) or reason of the judgment itself.⁷¹ In other words: the ground of a judgment is that through which the judgment is known or determined to be true. We are therefore dealing here with the *principium rationis sufficientis cognoscendi* (the principle of reason of knowing).⁷²

Schopenhauer lists four kinds of grounds, corresponding respectively to four kinds of truth. If the ground of a judgment is another judgment (according to the formal rules of deduction), there is a *logical truth*.⁷³ This is also the case if the ground is one of the "four well-known principles of thought", namely: the principle of identity, the principle of contradiction, the principle of the excluded third and the principle of sufficient reason of knowing.⁷⁴ These four principles essentially correspond to the four basic laws of the understanding mentioned in fragment 93.⁷⁵ If, on the other hand, the immediate ground of a judgment is experience, there is *empirical truth*.⁷⁶ Judgments based on the *a priori* forms of pure sensibility (space and time) and on the categories of the understanding have *metaphysical truth*.⁷⁷ Finally, judgments whose ground is given by the "formal conditions of

---

68 Schopenhauer 2012 [1813], § 27, p. 176.
69 Schopenhauer 2012 [1813], § 33, p. 179.
70 Schopenhauer 2012 [1813], § 30, p. 178.
71 Schopenhauer 2012 [1813], § 30, p. 178.
72 Schopenhauer 2012 [1813], § 31, p. 178.
73 Schopenhauer 2012 [1813], § 32, p. 101.
74 Schopenhauer 2012 [1813], § 32, p. 101, 179.
75 These four laws are related here to "reason" instead of the "understanding", because in the dissertation it is the former, not the latter, that constitutes the faculty of concepts. Moreover, what in fragment 93 is determined as the principle of sufficient reason *simpliciter*, is here defined as the principle of sufficient reason *of knowing*. On the distinction between "reason" and "understanding" in Schopenhauer and related issues, cf. Bäschlin 1968; Volpi 1982; Koßler 2013a; Wicks 1993; Soliva Soria 2022.
76 Schopenhauer 2012 [1813], § 33, p. 179.
77 Schopenhauer 2012 [1813], § 35, p. 181. In the 1813 dissertation, Schopenhauer does not take an explicit position on Kant's table of categories, defining the issue as "a very troublesome and difficult business, lying far beyond the bounds of my present task" (Schopenhauer 2012 [1813], § 19, p. 160). For Schopenhauer "even Kant's enumeration of the categories is grounded ultimately upon induction", that is, "according to the logical table of judgements", and "as far as his deduction of the categories is concerned, it is by no means a demonstration that there must be such categories and just that many" (Schopenhauer 2012 [1813], § 17, p. 159). In fragment 324 (MR 1, p. 221) the 12

all thought" possess *metalogical truth*;[78] "there are only four such judgements", namely the four "principles of thought" mentioned above.[79]

The "third class of objects for the subject" is represented by the pure intuitions (i.e. given *a priori*) of space and time.[80] The principle of sufficient reason appears here as the law according to which the parts stand in space and time in a reciprocal relation, i.e. as the law of *position* and the law of *succession*, respectively.[81] Schopenhauer determines this law as *principium rationis sufficientis essendi* ("principle of sufficient reason of being"),[82] which is the basis of mathematics (with regard to relations of position, for geometry,[83] with regard to relations of succession, for arithmetic).[84]

Now, the distinction between the second and third form of the principle of reason (specifically, between the ground of a metaphysical truth and *ratio essendi*) is a point on which Schulze expressly raised doubts in his letter to Schopenhauer:

> Several times (especially in the *Critique of Theoretical Philosophy*, examining Kant's deduction of the principle of causality from the form of hypothetical judgements) I have commented on the great and profound difference between ideal and real grounds. So we would certainly agree on the essentials. But I have not been convinced that what you, in § 37, call the "principle of sufficient reason of being" is an intimately different principle from the logical ground principle.[85]

The fourth and final class of objects "is comprised of only *one* object, namely the immediate object of the inner sense [*das unmittelbare Objekt des innern Sinnes*], the subject of willing [*das Subjekt des Willens*]".[86] In his review of the dissertation, Schulze also disputed the necessity of admitting this further class of objects and, therefore, a further form of the principle of reason.[87] The fourth class and the

---

Kantian categories would be reduced to the single category of causality (cf. Schopenhauer 2010b, I 527–535, p. 473–480; Schopenhauer 2020, pp. 318–320). Cf. D'Alfonso 2015.

78 Cf. Schopenhauer 2012 [1813], § 35, pp. 103, 181 (corresponding to § 33 in the second edition).
79 Cf. Schopenhauer 2012 [1813], § 35, pp. 103–104, p. 181: "1) A subject is equal to the sum of its predicates"; "2) A predicate cannot belong to a subject that it contradicts"; "3) Of any two contradictory, opposing predicates, one must belong to every subject"; "4) Truth is the relation of a judgement to something outside it. This latter is precisely the principle of sufficient reason of knowing."
80 Schopenhauer 2012 [1813], § 36, p. 123.
81 Schopenhauer 2012 [1813], § 37, p. 124.
82 Schopenhauer 2012 [1813], § 37, p. 124.
83 Schopenhauer 2012 [1813], § 40, pp. 126–128, 182.
84 Schopenhauer 2012 [1813], § 39, pp. 125–126, 182.
85 Cf. Schopenhauer 1911–1942, vol. XIV, p. 162.
86 Schopenhauer 2012 [1813], § 41, p. 133.
87 Cf. Schulze 1916, pp. 168–169.

form of the principle of reason in it will be treated more analytically and extensively later in this chapter, because they are directly related to the subsequent genesis of the metaphysics of will.

Before tackling this analysis, however, it is necessary to go back in time to 1812 and examine Schopenhauer's notes to Fichte's *System der Sittenlehre*. Indeed, the latter seem to be the necessary prerequisite for Schopenhauer's later considerations in the dissertation.

9.4 First Retrospective Digression: The Study of Fichte's *System der Sittenlehre* in 1812. The Will as the Second Predicate of the I and the Possibility of the Subject's Self-Cognition

Anyone who is acquainted with Schopenhauer's mature philosophy will find what Fichte wrote at the beginning of the *System der Sittenlehre* (1798) surprisingly familiar:

> (1) Theorem. I FIND MYSELF AS MYSELF ONLY AS WILLING. [*Ich finde mich selbst, als mich selbst, nur wollend.*]
>
> [...] What does it mean to say, "I find myself as *willing*, and I can find myself *only* as willing"?
>
> It is here presupposed that one knows what *willing* means. This concept is not capable of a real definition, nor does it require one. Each person has to become aware within himself of what willing means, through intellectual intuition, and everyone will be able to do so without any difficulty. [...]. I said that I become *conscious* of this willing, that I perceive it. Now I also become conscious of this consciousness, of this perceiving, and I also relate it to a substance. To me, this substance that possesses consciousness is the very same as the one that also wills; therefore, I find myself as the willing Me [*als das wollende Mich*], or, I find *myself* as willing.[88]

The "substance that possesses consciousness" of willing is "the very same as the one that also wills": this means that the *willing* substance coincides with the substance that *thinks* of such willing.

> "I find myself *only* as willing." First of all, I do not, as it were, perceive this substance immediately. What is substantial is no object of perception whatsoever but is simply added in thinking to something that has been perceived. I can immediately perceive only what is supposed to be a manifestation of the substance. But there are only two manifestations that are immedi-

---

[88] Fichte 2005, pp. 25–26.

ately ascribed to the substance in question [that is, to the I]: *thinking* [Denken] (in the widest sense of the term, i.e., representing, or consciousness as such) and *willing* [Wollen]. [...]. In short, the sole manifestation [of the substantial I] that I originally ascribe to myself is willing. Only under the condition that I become conscious of willing do I become conscious of myself.[89]

Young Schopenhauer challenged the "intellectual intuition" posited by Fichte and Schelling based on the logical impossibility of the subject's self-cognition (cf. *supra*, 6.7). His arguments can be read in full here.

That the subject itself becomes object is the most monstrous contradiction that was ever concocted, for object and subject are conceivable only as the one in reference to the other, and this reference is their sole characteristic. After the abolition of this characteristic the concept of that reference is empty. Now if the subject is to become object, then it again presupposes a subject as object; where is this to come from?[90]

I myself can never become object and hence never representation [...]: I can therefore, as Kant says, never perceive and cognize myself.[91]

The subject itself can never become an object, and this follows from the simple truth that there would then no longer be anything to which this object would be an object. What one conceives as I is nothing more than the *point of indifference* where thinking and representing cease and *that which* thinks and represents begins.[92]

[T]he subject does not perceive and cognize itself.[93]

[...] It [the I] cannot possibly be thought just because it always thinks.[94]

The underlying assumption of these reflections is that the subject or I, as such, only possesses one predicate, that is, cognition: "Thus the concept *subject* has only one single characteristic, namely that it perceives objects."[95] Based on this assumption, the subject's self-cognition cannot but acquire a contradictory physiognomy, because then the subject would at the same time (in the same respect) hold two contradictory predicates: being both cognizing and cognized (i.e. not-cognizing) *sub eodem*.

Fichte, however, also rules out this circumstance, when he writes that "Originally and immediately, the former [thinking] is, for itself, by no means an object of

---

89 Fichte 2005, p. 26.
90 MR 2, p. 381.
91 MR 2, p. 349. Translation modified.
92 MR 2, p. 383.
93 MR 2, p. 384.
94 MR 2, p. 343.
95 MR 2, p. 379.

9.4 First Retrospective Digression — 291

any particular new consciousness, but is simply consciousness itself."[96] Thinking as such cannot be the object of itself, precisely because, being thinking, it cannot be at the same time (in the same respect) also thought.

Reading the *System der Sittenlehre*, Schopenhauer 'discovered' another characteristic, namely a further predicate of the subject: *willing*. Of the aforementioned theorem ("I find myself as I myself only as willing"), Fichte provides a "Proof" and a "Corollary", which need not be discussed here.[97] What interests us now, rather, is Schopenhauer's commentary:

> Everything so far seems to me to be *in summa:* If I want to conceive myself, I must imagine myself as *that which wills* [*das* Wollende]; for although *thinking* is the second predicate (next to willing) of the I, yet I cannot imagine myself as that which thinks [*als das Denkende*], because *actu* I am then still that which thinks and here subject and object would flow together, whereby the basic condition of all thinking is abolished. But by my thinking I am not at the same time that which wills, hence – —.[98]

If the cognizing subject were to cognize itself as such, i.e. as cognizing, it would be in the same respect – i.e. relative to cognizing – *in actuality* (as cognizing) and not *in actuality* (as cognized). However, in addition to cognizing, perceiving or thinking, the subject is also *willing*. The subject's self-cognition is then possible, insofar as the subject that cognizes (its own) will is the same subject that, in that will, wills; cognizing its own will, the cognizing subject *cognizes itself* as the subject of that same will. Understood in this way, the subject's self-cognition is no longer contradictory, because in it, in relation to cognizing, the subject is in actuality and not in actuality not *sub eodem*, but in different respects: indeed, it is in actuality as *cognizing*, and not in actuality (or cognized) as *willing*.

The I, Schopenhauer continues, is thus divided into "a thing that cognizes [*ein Erkennendes*] and a thing that wills [*ein Wollendes*]".[99] Fichte does not speak of cognizing (*erkennen*), but of thinking (*denken*). Schopenhauer assumes that, in Fichte's text, "cognizing" is identical to "thinking"; this is probably because Fichte says he understands "thinking" "in the widest sense of the term, i.e., representing, or consciousness as such".[100]

In a fragment from 1828, Schopenhauer would note: "The *analysis* of the hitherto simple *ego* into *will* [Willen] and *cognition* [Erkenntnis] [...] is the turning

---

96 Fichte 2005, p. 26.
97 Fichte 2005, pp. 27–29.
98 MR 2, p. 400.
99 MR 2, p. 401. Translation modified.
100 Fichte 2005, p. 26.

point of my philosophy".[101] But there is no trace of this break-down in the fragments prior to 1812; on the basis of the available documents, one must conclude that Schopenhauer elaborated it through his reading of Fichte's *System der Sittenlehre*. Later, analyzing some passages of *The World as Will and Representation*, we will see in what sense therein lies the "turning point" of Schopenhauer's philosophy (cf. *infra*, 12.2).

9.5 The "Miracle *Par Excellence*": The Identity, in One and the Same I, of Subject of Cognition and Subject of Will. Comparison of Some Passages from the *System der Sittenlehre* and the Dissertation

Picking up on the reflections just analyzed, Schopenhauer writes in the dissertation:

> [...] the subject of cognition can never be cognized, never be an object, a representation. [...] 'I cognize' is an *analytic proposition; in contrast, 'I will'* is synthetic and, indeed, *a posteriori; for it is given through experience, here through inner experience (i.e. only in time)*. However it [the proposition 'I will'] is most likely the first of all empirical propositions in each person's consciousness, the one with which knowledge [*Erkennen*] begins. *To that extent, the subject of willing would be an object for us.*
>
> But now the identity of the subject of willing with the cognizing subject, by means of which (and, indeed, necessarily), the word 'I' includes and indicates both, is absolutely inconceivable.[102]

The fourth class of representations, i.e. of objects for the subject, "is comprised of only *one* object", namely "*the subject of will*".[103] The latter constitutes for every cognizing subject "the immediate object of the inner sense": every cognizing subject (every I) cognizes itself *only as willing* (only as the subject of its own willing). In this regard there are striking – not only conceptual, but even terminological – similarities between the dissertation and Fichte's *System der Sittenlehre*. It is now worth giving them a careful look.

A first point concerns the subject's self-cognition. Fichte: "I find myself as myself only as willing [*Ich finde mich selbst, als mich selbst, nur als wollend*]".[104]

---

[101] MR 3, n. 51, p. 493. Translation modified.
[102] Schopenhauer 2012 [1813], § 43, pp. 135–136, p. 185.
[103] Schopenhauer 2012 [1813], § 41, p. 133, 182.
[104] Fichte 2005, p. 25.

Schopenhauer: "The subject is cognized only as *something that wills*, a spontaneity, but not as *something that cognizes* [*Erkannt wird das Subjekt nur als ein Wollendes, nicht aber als ein Erkennendes*]".[105] In the second edition of the dissertation, there is a formulation that recalls the Fichtean theorem even more clearly: "If we introspect, we find ourselves always as *willing* [*finden wir uns immer als* wollend]".[106]

A second point concerns the concept of "will". Fichte: "It is here presupposed that one knows what *willing* means [*Was* wollen *heisse, wird als bekannt vorausgesetzt*]. This concept is not capable of a real definition, nor does it require one. Each person has to become aware within himself of what willing means, through intellectual intuition, and everyone will be able to do so without any difficulty."[107] Schopenhauer: "Precisely because the subject of willing is immediately given in self-consciousness, what willing is cannot be further defined or described": "insofar as what is essential to willing is found nowhere else, willing cannot be subsumed under any other concept. For this reason, what willing is [*was Wollen sei*], we can – even must – presuppose to be known [*als bekannt voraussetzen*]".[108]

A third point concerns the identity between that which cognizes the will and that which wills. Fichte: "I said that I become *conscious* of this willing, that I perceive it. Now I also become conscious of this consciousness, of this perceiving, and I also relate it to a substance. To me, this substance that possesses consciousness is the very same as the one that also wills; therefore, I find myself as the willing Me [*als das wollende Mich*]".[109] Schopenhauer, too, claims that there is "an actual identity of the cognizer with that which is cognized as willing, thus of the subject with the object, [and this identity] is *immediately given*".[110]

Again, in the *System der Sittenlehre*, specifying the meaning of the theorem quoted above ("I find myself as myself only as willing"), Fichte states that "All willing that is actually perceivable, [...] is necessarily a determinate willing, in which

---

105 Schopenhauer 2012 [1813], § 42, p. 182.
106 Schopenhauer 2012 [1847], § 42, p. 136. Metz (2006) relates Fichte's theorem "Ich finde mich selbst, als mich selbst, nur wollend" to the first chapter of the *Prize Essay on the Freedom of the Will* and with paragraph 18 of *The World as Will and Representation*, without pointing out that Schopenhauer knew this theorem as early as 1812. According to R. J. Berg (2003, p. 360) this trait of Schopenhauer's system would be traceable to Schelling's *Treatise Explicatory of the Idealism in the "Science of Knowledge"*; but the theoretically crucial considerations in this regard are to be found, as we have seen, in the notes to Fichte's *System of Ethics*. Haym (1864, p. 60) had stressed the importance of these notes, albeit only in passing. Cf. in this respect also Kamata 1988, pp. 151–166.
107 Fichte 2005, pp. 25–26.
108 Schopenhauer 2012 [1813], § 44, p. 185.
109 Fichte 2005, pp. 25–26.
110 Schopenhauer 2012 [1813], § 43, p. 136.

something is willed. [...] In willing, I am not perceptible for myself as I am in and for myself; instead, I perceive only how I can relate in a certain way to things existing outside me".[111] For Schopenhauer, too, the (cognizing) subject's cognition of itself (as willing) suffers from an important limitation (*Einschränkung*):[112] "the *subject of willing* is cognized just in willing (i.e. in the individual acts of will), but not in any preceding state".[113] That is, the subject cognizes itself as willing always and only *in conjunction with* (its) concrete and individual acts of will – precisely as what wills in them – and never separately or independently of them. The subject of willing is thus not cognized purely or in itself, but always and only as willing *something*.

Finally, a fifth point of affinity concerns the immediate causal relation between will and body. In the *System der Sittenlehre* Fichte writes: "the will is supposed to exercise causality, and indeed, an immediate causality upon my body [*Leib*]";[114] "our will becomes an immediate cause in our body".[115] In the course "On the Facts of Consciousness", attended by Schopenhauer, Fichte had similarly stated that "the body is [...] the matter in which self determination of the I becomes directly known";[116] Schopenhauer wrote in his 1813 dissertation that, among the real objects which the will "causally affects", the body is the "immediate object of willing" – in the sense that the latter's causal action on the body is, indeed, immediate.[117]

Fichte's is likely to have had a decisive influence on Schopenhauer in connection with these five conceptual points, yet this has gone largely unnoticed by the critics so far.[118] In addition to these extraordinary affinities, however, two impor-

---

111 Fichte 2005, pp. 29–30.
112 Cf. Schopenhauer 2012 [1813], § 41, p. 133: the subject of willing "is object for the cognizing subject and indeed is given only to the inner sense; thus, it appears only in time, not in space, and even there, as we will see, with a significant qualification [*Einschränkung*]".
113 Schopenhauer 2012 [1813], § 46, p. 187.
114 Fichte 2005, p. 16.
115 Fichte 2005, p. 204.
116 MR 2, p. 59.
117 Schopenhauer 2012 [1813], § 44, p. 185. "*Acting* is not willing, but the effect of willing when it becomes causal. [...] It is a fact that with respect to what comes after it [*a parte posteriori*] willing falls under the law of causality because it causally affects real objects, one of which is the immediate object of cognition – the body, which is also an immediate object of willing."
118 I have already drawn attention to this important episode in Schopenhauer's reception of Fichte; cf. Novembre 2011; 2012, p. 45–50; 2018b, pp. 234–235. Cf. also De Pascale 2012. Most of the contributions concerning Fichte and Schopenhauer have placed the comparison between the two systems more on a theoretical or speculative level than on a strictly historical or genetic one. Cf. Schwabe 1887; Schöndorf 1982; Guéroult 1946; Penzo 1987; Philonenko 1997; Koßler 2006b; Waibel 2006; Bastian 2009. A surprising affinity has been detected, on various levels, be-

tant differences should also be pointed out. Firstly, the proposition "I find myself as myself only as willing", for Fichte, is subject to demonstration (it is precisely a theorem, *Lehrsatz*). For Schopenhauer, on the other hand, "the identity of the subject of willing with the cognizing subject, by means of which (and, indeed, necessarily), the word 'I' includes and indicates both, is absolutely inconceivable [*schlechthin unbegreiflich*]", so much so that Schopenhauer calls it "the miracle *par excellence*".[119] The positing of this identity has a 'phenomenological', not a demonstrative, foundation in Schopenhauer. Secondly, Schopenhauer does not speak of "substance" (which for Kant constitutes a category of the understanding), but of the "subject" of cognizing and willing.

9.6 The Lived-Body (*Leib*) as the Immediate Object of Cognition and Willing. Echoes of Fichte and Schelling

In the manuscripts prior to 1813, Schopenhauer uses the term *Körper* or the derivative adjective (*körperlich*) to refer to the human body.[120] Schulze, in his Metaphysics course, had used the same term to contest the fallacious "separation of the 'I', i.e. of the soul, from the organ, from the body [*Körper*]".[121] Such a separation not only leaves open the possibility that the I's existence does not also necessarily imply the existence of the material world (so that the latter is seemingly open to doubt), but is also completely divorced from reality: "the consciousness of the I", in fact, is always, "at the same time, consciousness of the body".[122] Fichte, instead, had used the term *Leib* in his lectures "On the Facts of Consciousness".[123]

Schopenhauer used the term *Leib* for the first time in fragment 85 of the manuscripts (1813) to recount the heroic gesture of Arnold von Winkelried (who, in order to allow his comrades to break through the enemy's ranks, embraced and directed the opponents' spears towards his own body).[124] In the dissertation, the "body" as *Leib* ("lived-body", as felt and experienced by the subject) takes on a

---

tween Fichte's *The Vocation of Man* and *The World as Will and Representation* (cf. Seydel 1857, p. 61; Decher 1990, p. 64; Zöller 2006, p. 372; Metz 2006, p. 389). However, there is no documentary evidence that Schopenhauer read this text by Fichte (on the specificity of Schopenhauer's discourse, cf. *infra*, 12.2).
119 Schopenhauer 2012 [1813], § 43, p. 136.
120 MR 1, n. 14, p. 10; n. 28, p. 18; n. 53, p. 30; n. 69, p. 38; MR 2, pp. 4, 34, 38, 65 (footnote).
121 Cf. D'Alfonso 2008, pp. 76–77. Attention was drawn to this point in Schulze's exposition in relation to Schopenhauer's philosophical education by D'Alfonso 2009, pp. 71–72.
122 Cf. D'Alfonso 2008, p. 77.
123 Cf. MR 2, p. 59.
124 MR 1, n. 85, p. 47.

very important role, as it is defined as the "immediate object" of cognition and willing.[125]

The fact that the lived-body is the immediate object of cognition means that the cognition of all other physical objects (which in the dissertation correspond to the first class of representations)[126] takes place through the body itself. "Only *one* object is given to us *immediately:* our own bodies [*der eigne Leib*]"; cognition of the objective, or external, world is instead mediated and results from an *unconscious* act of the representing subject – precisely, from an "inference of understanding" (a peculiar feature of the understanding, *Verstand*), which, starting from the sensations of the body, comes to cognizing external objects as the *cause* of the sensations themselves.[127] In this sense, the expression "immediate object" already refers to the lived-body (*Leib*) in fragments 94, 116 and 121 of the manuscripts.[128]

Similarly, the fact that the body is the immediate object of the will means that the will can act causally on physical objects only by means of the body itself: the latter is in fact the only physical object with which the will has an immediate causal relation, whose effect is acting (the body's movement).[129]

---

[125] Schopenhauer 2012 [1813], § 21, p. 163; Schopenhauer 2012 [1813], § 45, p. 186: "the immediate object of cognition [*das unmittelbare Objekt des Erkennens*] – the body [...] is also an immediate object of willing [*unmittelbares Objekt des Wollens*]".

[126] Schopenhauer 2012 [1813], § 18, p. 159.

[127] Cf. Schopenhauer 2012 [1813], § 24, p. 168: "Only *one* object is given to us *immediately:* our own bodies. Now there is no way to understand how we get beyond this representation to other objects in space, except by means of the application of the category of causality. Without this application we would have no other object than the immediate object, with its succession of states. [...]. The cognition of *mediated* objects [...] begins with the category of causality [...]. A cause is inferred from an alteration in the eye, ear, or any other organ, and the cause is posited at the point in space where its effect proceeds from, as the substrate of this power. Then the categories of subsistence, existence, etc., can first be applied to the effect. The category of causality is thus the actual point of transition, hence, the *condition of all experience*, and as such, precedes experience, and is not first derived from experience. [...]. That we are not conscious of this inference presents no difficulty [...]. Moreover, it is no inference of reason [*Vernunftschluß*], no combining of judgements [*Urtheilen*]: we have nothing to do with the concept of the category, [...] but with the category itself. The category itself leads immediately from the effect to the cause; therefore, we are as little conscious of its function as that of the other categories, since precisely through these categories our consciousness changes from dull sensation to intuition. I would like to give the name of *inference of understanding* [*Verstandesschlusses*] to this inference." Cf. also Schopenhauer 2012 [1847], § 21, p. 163, and Schopenhauer 2018, II 24–27, chap. 2, pp. 234–237.

[128] Cf. MR 1, n. 94, p. 64; n. 116, p. 82 and n. 121, p. 84.

[129] Cf. Schopenhauer 2012 [1813], § 44, p. 185: "*Acting* [Handeln] is not willing, but the effect [*Wirkung*] of willing when it becomes causal [*des kausal gewordenen Wollens*]". In other words, "willing" is the *cause* if "acting".

The subject, therefore, can *cognize* all objects other than his body in a merely mediated way, i. e. through the body itself; and, likewise, he can (causally) *act* on all objects other than his body in a merely mediated way, through the body itself. From Schopenhauer's point of view, the *identity* of the relation that the body has with the subject of cognition and the subject of willing – being the "immediate object" of both – can only be a confirmation of their 'miraculous', inexplicable identity.

In relation to the theme of the body, reading Fichte and Schelling must have played a fundamental role for young Schopenhauer. The definition of the body as the "immediate object of cognition" seems to be taken almost literally from Schelling's *Bruno*.[130] And, as we have seen, the relation of immediate causality between body and will was already clearly stated in Fichte's *System der Sittenlehre*.[131]

In *The World as Will and Representation* (1819), the causal relation between will and body would be explicitly excluded in favor of the even closer relation of "identity"[132] (cf. *infra*, 12.2). For this reason, the corresponding passages in the second edition of the dissertation would be deleted.

---

130 Cf. Schelling 1984, p. 185: "[...] objective cognition [*das objektive Erkennen*] is finite only insofar as it is related to the body [*Leib*], its immediate object [*als sein unmittelbares Objekt*] [...]". The "body" is thus the "immediate object" of "objective cognition". Cf. on this Schöndorf 1982, p. 31.
131 It is therefore odd that, for Schöndorf (1982, p. 106), the possibility of Fichte's influence on Schopenhauer, with regard to the subject of the body, is to be ruled out. Herbart (1820), in his long review of *The World as Will and Representation*, refers to Fichte's *System der Sittenlehre*, and in particular to the very passage in which it is said that the will immediately becomes a cause in the body; however, he implicitly sees this as a point of contention with Schopenhauer, because he only refers to the passage in *The World as Will and Representation* in which the causal relation between will and body is explicitly rejected, unlike in the first edition of the dissertation. On the other hand, Herbart was convinced that Schopenhauer was not familiar with Fichte's work, so much so that he reproached him with having judged Fichte's thought without knowing the *Sittenlehre* (cf. Herbart 1820, pp. 141–143). For a systematic comparison between Schopenhauer and Fichte on the consciousness of the body's voluntary movements, cf. Knappik 2018.
132 Schopenhauer 2010b, I 119, § 18, pp. 124–125: "An act of the will and an act of the body are not two different states cognized objectively, linked together in a causal chain, they do not stand in a relation of cause and effect; they are one and the same thing, only given in two entirely different ways: in one case immediately and in the other case to the understanding in intuition"; Schopenhauer 2010b, I 122, § 18, p. 127: "the identity of the will and the body [...] can never be demonstrated". Cf. Schopenhauer 2020 pp. 83–84.

9.7 The Fourth Form of the Principle of Reason: The *principium rationis sufficientis agendi*. Motive and Determination of the Will

We said that for Schopenhauer the will is the cause of action, i.e. of the movement of the body.[133] This means that, *a parte posteriori* (with respect to what 'follows' the will), willing "falls under the law of causality".[134] "But under what law does willing fall with respect to what comes before it [*a parte priori*]?"[135]

Given a determinate willing, i.e. a willing-something, everything unfolds from here on according to the law of causality (starting with the first and immediate effect of willing, which is the acting of "our own bodies"). But what determines willing as a concrete willing-something? That is, what causes *this* something to be effectively willed as opposed to something else? This, says Schopenhauer, is the "ancient dispute about freedom".[136]

Schopenhauer observes that in relation to any given decision (one's own or someone else's), we always feel entitled to look for some *reason* for it, and thus assume that the decision itself was determined by "something preceding it, from which it followed".[137] At the same time, however, "we have the most vivid and often the most uneasy awareness" that such a decision "only depended immediately on the subject of willing itself".[138]

In other words, every individual always presupposes, on the one hand, an external reason – that is, properly speaking, a "motive" – for his actions; on the other hand, and at the same time, he feels responsible for what he does. But responsibility presupposes the *freedom* to act otherwise than one actually has acted. These two seemingly contradictory aspects – necessity and freedom – exclude the possibility that the law regulating human action is the law of causality, because the latter comprises only necessity.[139] Consequently, Schopenhauer concludes, human action is governed by "a specific form of the principle of sufficient reason" which he calls "*principium rationis sufficientis agendi*, or more briefly put, *law of motivation*".[140]

---

133 Cf. Schopenhauer 2012 [1813], § 44, p. 185.
134 Schopenhauer 2012 [1813], § 45, p. 185.
135 Schopenhauer 2012 [1813], § 45, p. 186.
136 Schopenhauer 2012 [1813], § 45, p. 186.
137 Schopenhauer 2012 [1813], § 45, p. 186.
138 Schopenhauer 2012 [1813], § 45, p. 186.
139 Schopenhauer 2012 [1813], § 45, p. 186.
140 Schopenhauer 2012 [1813], § 45, p. 186.

At this point, in order to solve the contradiction between necessity and freedom which seems to irretrievably affect human action, Schopenhauer formulates the theory of the "intelligible character".

9.8 The Intelligible Character: "A Universal Act of Will Lying Outside of Time", a "Willing, Which by Its Nature Is Free to the Greatest Degree, Indeed, Which Is the Innermost Essence of the Human Being"

The motive of human action, i.e. the *ratio agendi*, always consists of "states of representations";[141] these can be either complete representations (the so-called "real things")[142] or "concatenation[s] of judgements", which, however, in order to *"provide* a motive", must nevertheless have "a reference to some real objects, i.e., ultimately must have material truth".[143] In the final analysis, the motive always contains a reference to objects (or to properties of objects) of experience.

However, the motive itself (whatever it may be), while being a "reason of acting", is insufficient to explain human action as a whole: "at most [motives] motivate [*motivieren*] wishing [*das Wünschen*], but not a decision [*Entschluß*], which is the act of will proper [*der eigentliche Willensakt*]".[144] Wish, as such, "is itself already a willing", of course; but "nothing is explained by saying that of two opposing wishes, the stronger will become a willing through a decision".[145] The problem is indeed why one desire is stronger than another, that is, "just why the willing subject [*das wollende Subjekt*] so strongly wishes this or that".[146]

As we have seen, for Schopenhauer the subject cognizes his own will only insofar as it is already determined as a concrete willing-something (cf. *supra*, 9.5). The will in itself, 'prior' to this determination, cannot be cognized. This means that the subject has limited self-cognition (i.e., a limited cognition of himself as willing): he only cognizes *that* he wills and *what* he wills, but not *why* he wills what he does. Unlike Fichte's and Schelling's "intellectual intuition" (as Schopenhauer himself interpreted it: cf. *supra*, 6.6; 7.13), the subject's self-cognition admitted by Schopenhauer is thus not a form of absolute cognition.

---

141 Schopenhauer 2012 [1813], § 45, § 46, p. 187.
142 Cf. Schopenhauer 2012 [1813], § 20, p. 36 (corresponding to § 19 in the second edition).
143 Schopenhauer 2012 [1813], § 45, § 46, p. 187.
144 Schopenhauer 2012 [1813], § 45, § 46, p. 187.
145 Schopenhauer 2012 [1813], § 45, § 46, p. 187.
146 Schopenhauer 2012 [1813], § 45, § 46, p. 187.

Now, the fact that "the willing subject so strongly wishes this or that" is either purely coincidental, or follows some rule.[147] Yet experience shows that "given the same observable motives, one person acts in one way, another in another way; however, the same person, given exactly the same circumstances, acts in exactly the same way".[148] This regularity of human behavior leads Schopenhauer to reject the casual nature of action and posit "an enduring state of the subject of the will".[149] This "state" explains that regularity and yet is necessarily unknowable to the acting individual himself, since he can only cognize himself as already willing "this or that": after all, "the subject of willing is cognized just in willing (i.e. in the individual acts of will), but not in any preceding state".[150] Such a "state of the subject of willing […] is not an object of inner sense, thus [also] *not something in time* [nichts in der Zeit]".[151]

Assuming this, a decision must be considered as "the point of contact between the unknowable subject of will (lying outside of time [außer der Zeit]) and motives (lying in time)".[152] In the act of decision – in the concrete act of willing and deciding for something determined – that "enduring state of the subject of the will", which in itself is unknowable and timeless, breaks through (manifests itself) in time. This definition of decision as a point of contact between what is in time and what is not is explained by Schopenhauer as follows: "just like the present, a decision [Entschluß] occupies no time [füllt keine Zeit]".[153] That is, it has no real duration, being rather something instantaneous; as such, it represents a kind of middle ground between what is in time and what is not.

Recall that Fichte, in his lectures "On the Facts of Consciousness", had defined decision (Entschluß) as "a blow, a flash, something timeless [ein Zeitloses]",[154] and Schopenhauer had commented: "decision is outside all time in so far as it is an act of the will which, as a thing-in-itself, stands beyond all time" (cf. *supra*, 4.4).[155] Schopenhauer thus seems to have borrowed the definition of "decision" from Fichte.

From the (empirically observable) constancy of human behavior, Schopenhauer deduces the existence of *an enduring, timeless state of the subject of the*

---

147 Cf. Schopenhauer 2012 [1813], § 45, § 46, p. 187.
148 Schopenhauer 2012 [1813], § 45, § 46, p. 187.
149 Schopenhauer 2012 [1813], § 45, § 46, p. 187.
150 Schopenhauer 2012 [1813], § 46, p. 187.
151 Schopenhauer 2012 [1813], § 46, p. 187.
152 Schopenhauer 2012 [1813], § 46, p. 187.
153 Schopenhauer 2012 [1813], § 46, p. 187.
154 MR 2, p. 59.
155 MR 2, p. 60.

will. But he also deduces that this state – from which, given the motives, every decision necessarily follows – consists in *a free and original act of choice*, for which the individual himself is responsible:

> [...] the same person, given exactly the same circumstances, acts in exactly the same way [...] even if he is most vividly aware [*das lebendigste Bewußtseyn hat*], that he could have acted in a completely different way had he so *willed*, i. e., that his will is determined by nothing external – and it is not a question here of *being able* [Können], but only of willing [*Wollen*], which by its nature is free to the greatest degree, indeed, which is the innermost essence of the human being, independent of everything else [*das innerste von allem Andern unabhängige Wesen des Menschen selbst*]. This observation leads to the assumption that there is an enduring state of the subject of the will, one from which his decisions necessarily follow.[156]

The *empirical character* of the individual – understood as the rule that determines how he acts in all possible circumstances, i. e. his peculiar way of reacting to given motives – must be thought of as the appearance (*Erscheinung*) of the "permanent state, as it were, of the subject of the will, lying outside of time".[157]

> I say permanent state, *as it were*, since *state* and *permanent* are only temporal, but there is no expression for the extratemporal. Perhaps I could better indicate what is meant, although also figuratively, if I call it a universal act of will [*einen ... universalen Willensakt*] lying outside of time, of which all temporal acts are only the emergence [*Heraustreten*], the appearance [*Erscheinung*]. Kant has called this the *intelligible character* (perhaps it would more correctly be called unintelligible), and in the *Critique of Pure Reason*, pp. 560–86 he provides a discussion of the difference between it and the *empirical* character, as well as the whole relation of freedom to nature, a discussion I regard as an incomparable, highly admirable masterpiece of human profundity. In the first volume of his [*Philosophical*] *Writings*, pp. 465–73, Schelling provides a very valuable, illustrative exposition of this.[158]

Complete knowledge of the individual's empirical character – that is, of his actions under all possible conditions – is (empirically) impossible.[159] And yet, if one possessed such knowledge, then, knowing beforehand the circumstances (i. e. the motives) in which an individual was to act, one could predict all his actions with absolute certainty;[160] this is because, given the empirical character as the appearance of the intelligible one, the motive determines man's decision and action with the

---

156 Cf. Schopenhauer 2012 [1813], § 46, p. 187.
157 Schopenhauer 2012 [1813], § 46, p. 187.
158 Schopenhauer 2012 [1813], § 46, pp. 187–188.
159 Schopenhauer 2012 [1813], § 46, pp. 187–188.
160 Schopenhauer 2012 [1813], § 46, p. 188.

same necessity as a cause.¹⁶¹ Precisely in this sense, the motive is the "sufficient ground of acting".¹⁶²

The empirical character is what properly constitutes the individuality (or uniqueness) of a person, i.e. his peculiar and 'characteristic' way of responding or (re)acting to the different motives. In humans, unlike animals, character is essentially individual: in the face of the same motives, different people (re)act differently,¹⁶³ since "each subject has a particular empirical character".¹⁶⁴ Schopenhauer therefore states that the *law of causality* is comparable to the action of light on transparent bodies, while the *law of motivation* is similar to the action of light on colored bodies.¹⁶⁵ In this metaphor, light corresponds to a given external reason or ground (cause or motive); colored bodies to *different individuals*; the physical characteristics of each body, by which it absorbs or reflects certain frequencies of light, to the *peculiar character of each individual*; the colors of the bodies (which vary according to those characteristics) to the *different actions of the individuals* under the same motive. This image, already anticipated in fragment 95 of the manuscripts,¹⁶⁶ seems to echo a passage from Goethe's *Theory of Colours*.¹⁶⁷

However, the empirical character – by virtue of which the individual's actions necessarily result from motives – is merely the manifestation in time (appearance, *Erscheinung*) of the intelligible character. For Schopenhauer, the latter coincides with a "permanent state [...] of the subject of the will, lying outside of time": "a universal act of will [*Willensakt*] lying outside of time", a "willing, which by its nature is *free* [italics mine] to the greatest degree, indeed, which is the innermost essence of the human being, independent of everything else". This original act of will

---

161 Schopenhauer 2012 [1813], § 46, p. 188.
162 Schopenhauer 2012 [1813], § 46, p. 189.
163 Schopenhauer 2012 [1813], § 46, p. 189.
164 Schopenhauer 2012 [1813], § 46, p. 190.
165 Schopenhauer 2012 [1813], § 46, p. 189.
166 MR 1, n. 95, p. 70.
167 In his "Preface" to the *Theory of Colours*, Goethe writes: "It may naturally be asked whether, in proposing to treat of colours, light itself should not first engage our attention [...] Indeed, strictly speaking, it is useless to attempt to express the nature of a thing abstractedly. Effects we can perceive, and a complete history of those effects would, in fact, sufficiently define the nature of the thing itself. We should try in vain to describe a man's character, but let his acts be collected and an idea of the character will be presented to us. The colours are acts of light; its active and passive modifications: thus considered we may expect from them some explanation respecting light itself." (Goethe 1840, p. xvii) In this text, light corresponds to character and colors to the individual's actions: just as the essence of light is expressed in colors, so the essence of a man, his character, is expressed in his actions.

is "universal" in the sense that it relates to the individual's single acts of will just as the universal relates to the particular.

Shortly before, Schopenhauer had stated that "the act of will proper [*der eigentliche Willensakt*]" is "decision".[168] But then, the intelligible character, being an "act of will", is a "decision": indeed, the *original* decision (placed outside of time) from which – given the motives – all of the individual's empirical decisions necessarily derive as their single manifestations: "an enduring state of the subject of the will, one from which his decisions necessarily follow [*aus dem seine Entschlüsse mit Nothwendigkeit folgen*] [...]".[169]

Incidentally: by positing this necessary consequentiality between intelligible character and actions in time, Schopenhauer seems to imply – contradictorily – a necessary relation between what is outside the principle of reason (and thus, also, of any necessary relation) and what is within it. The aforementioned relation, however, is ultimately traceable to the 'phenomenalization' or appearing of the intelligible character in individual temporal actions. The point is that Schopenhauer presupposes, but does not define, the meaning of the predicate 'being the appearance of'.

Since a person's individuality (uniqueness) is constituted by his empirical character, and since the latter is the appearance of the intelligible character, a person's individuality is also the appearance of the intelligible character. The act of will in which the latter consists thus determines the very individuality or distinctiveness of the individual; precisely for this reason, this act "constitutes the innermost essence of the human being".

So, taking up and summarizing the meaning of the entire discourse: every decision made by the individual is necessary (necessitated by motives), given his empirical character. But the empirical character of every individual is the manifestation in time of his intelligible character: the latter constitutes a *free* and original metaphysical decision ("a universal act of will lying outside of time"), from which all of the individual's single empirical decisions necessarily (*mit Notwendigkeit*) derive.

In this way, Schopenhauer believes he has solved the initial problem concerning the apparent contradiction between freedom and necessity in human action. These two opposing determinations are inherent in action not *sub eodem*, but in different respects: the first concerns the metaphysical, original act of will (*Willensakt*), which is the intelligible character; the second concerns the single, concrete acts of will, which belong to the empirical character. The *necessity* of human ac-

---

168 Schopenhauer 2012 [1813], § 46, p. 187.
169 Schopenhauer 2012 [1813], § 46, p. 187.

tions derives from an original and timeless act of *freedom*, by which every individual has predetermined, in their essence (i.e., as regards the "rule" of his acting under given circumstances), all of his temporal and contingent decisions. In this sense, that first and original act of will represents the 'prototype' or 'archetype' of all acts of will in time.

9.9 Some Fundamental Differences between Kant's and Schopenhauer's Doctrines of the Intelligible Character. The Meaning of the Explicit Reference to Schelling's *Freiheitsschrift*

As the main and immediate precedent of his reflections, Schopenhauer mentions the Kantian doctrine of the intelligible character set out in the *Critique of Pure Reason*. In his own words, it represents "an incomparable, highly admirable masterpiece of human profundity". Schelling is said to have provided "a very valuable, illustrative exposition" of it: nothing more, therefore, than a useful reformulation, devoid of truly original elements.[170] Schopenhauer is referring here to the *Philosophical Investigations into the Essence of Human Freedom and Matters Connected Therewith*, published in 1809 in the first volume of the *Philosophische Schriften*.[171] This partially flattering reference to Schelling is no longer found in the second edition of the dissertation; here Schopenhauer no longer expounds the doctrine of the intelligible character, but rather refers the reader to his Prize Essay *On the Freedom of the Will*.[172]

In the pages of the *Critique of Pure Reason* which Schopenhauer expressly addresses,[173] Kant writes:

> I call *intelligible* that in an object of sense which is not itself appearance. Accordingly, if that which must be regarded as appearance in the world of sense has in itself a faculty [*ein Vermögen*] which is not an object of intuition through which it can be the cause of appearances, then one can consider the *causality* of this being in two aspects, as *intelligible* in its *action* [*Handlung*] as a thing-in-itself, and as *sensible* in the *effects* of that action as an appearance in the world of sense.[174]

---

170 Schopenhauer 2012 [1813], § 46, p. 188.
171 Schelling 1809, pp. 399–511.
172 Schopenhauer 2012 [1847], § 44, p. 138.
173 Cf. Kant 1998, B 560–586, pp. 532–546.
174 Kant 1998, B566, p. 535.

9.9 Some Fundamental Differences between Kant's and Schopenhauer's Doctrines — 305

Considering a given "being" as an "effective cause", the "character" of the being itself is defined by Kant as the "law of its causality, without which it would not be a cause at all".[175] In accordance with the distinction between appearance and thing-in-itself, Kant therefore distinguishes between an "empirical character" and an "intelligible character" in every acting subject (considered as a "cause of appearances").[176] The intelligible character cannot be known (only appearances are knowable), and yet it must necessarily be *"thought* in conformity with the empirical character, just as in general we must [*müssen*] ground appearances in thought through a transcendental object, even though we know nothing about it as it is in itself".[177]

As an appearance, the acting subject possesses an empirical character, i.e. "a law of its causality", whereby it is the cause of other appearances. The subject's actions, however, are in turn always the effect of a previous appearance, and so forth; they are thus necessarily connected with other appearances under "constant natural laws" and constitute with them "a single series of the natural order".[178] *As a thing-in-itself,* the subject instead has "an intelligible character, through which it is indeed the cause of those actions as appearances, which does not stand under any conditions of sensibility and is not itself appearance".[179]

> In the case of lifeless nature and nature having merely animal life, we find no ground for thinking of any faculty which is other than sensibly conditioned. Yet the human being, who is otherwise acquainted with the whole of nature solely through sense, knows [*erkennt*] himself also through pure apperception, and indeed in actions and inner determinations which cannot be accounted at all among impressions of sense; he obviously is in one part phenomenon [*Phänomen*], but in another part, namely in regard to certain faculties, he is a merely intelligible object, because the actions of this object cannot at all be ascribed to the receptivity of sensibility. We call these faculties understanding and reason [...].
>
> Now that this reason has causality, or that we can at least represent something of the sort in it, is clear from the *imperatives* that we propose as rules to our powers of execution in everything practical. The *ought* [*Das* Sollen] expresses a species of necessity and a connection with grounds which does not occur anywhere else in the whole of nature.[180]

This page from Kant, concerning the double awareness that man has of himself – as a phenomenon and as an intelligible object –, seems to prefigure or prepare one

---

175 Kant 1998, B567, p. 536.
176 Kant 1998, B567, p. 536.
177 Kant 1998, B568, p. 536.
178 Kant 1998, B567, p. 536.
179 Kant 1998, B567, p. 536.
180 Kant 1998, B574–575, p. 540.

of the central themes of Schopenhauer's mature thought, namely the double cognition that every man has of his own body: as "representation", from without, and as "will", from within (cf. *infra*, 12.2).[181]

For Kant, every man has an empirical character, insofar as the causality of his reason occurs according to a certain observable regularity, from which one can deduce the fundamental "principle" by which it itself operates.[182] Once this principle, i.e. the "rule [*Regel*]" of reason whereby the subject acts, is posited, "all the actions of the human being in appearance are determined in accord with the order of nature by his empirical character and the other cooperating causes" that prompt the application of the rule itself.[183] Hence, if it were possible to investigate all of a man's actions down to their fundamental principle, "then there would be no human action that we could not predict with certainty, and recognize as necessary given its preceding conditions".[184] In relation to the empirical character, therefore, man's actions are *not* free.[185]

And yet, man's empirical character – which Kant identifies with the "mode of sense [*Sinnesart*]" – is "determined [*bestimmt*] in the intelligible character (in the mode of thought [*Denkungsart*])": the latter coincides precisely with the specific "rule" of action, or maxim, that each individual *autonomously* gives himself, through his own practical reason.[186] As such, the intelligible character does not fall into experience; therefore it cannot be properly known, but only 'deduced' or hypothesized from its individual manifestations (the person's actions), i.e., "through appearances, which really give only the mode of sense (the empirical character) for immediate cognition".[187]

"Even before it happens", every human action "is determined beforehand in the empirical character of the human being". And yet, "in regard to the intelligible

---

181 Schopenhauer 2010b, I 118–123, § 18, pp. 123–127.
182 Kant 1998, B577, p. 541.
183 Kant 1998, B577, p. 541.
184 Kant 1998, B578, p. 541.
185 Kant 1998, B578, p. 541.
186 Kant 1998, B579, p. 542.
187 Kant 1998, B579, p. 542. Cf. also B 579–580, pp. 542–543. "Now the action, insofar as it is to be attributed to the mode of thought as its cause, nevertheless does not follow [*erfolgt ... nicht*] from it in accord with empirical laws [...]. The causality of reason in the intelligible character *does not arise* or start working at a certain time in producing an effect. For then it would itself be subject to the natural law of appearances, to the extent that this law determines causal series in time, and its causality would then be nature and not freedom. [...] Nevertheless, this very same cause in another relation also belongs to the series of appearances. The human being himself is an appearance. His power of choice has an empirical character, which is the (empirical) cause of all his actions."

character, of which the empirical one is only the sensible schema, no *before* or *after* applies, and every action, irrespective of the temporal relation in which it stands to other appearances, is the immediate effect of the intelligible character of pure reason", which "acts freely" because it is outside and above the chain of natural causes.[188]

To further clarify what he means, Kant gives the example of "a malicious lie, through which a person has brought about a certain confusion in society".[189] Certainly, one can investigate and find the particular "moving causes [*Bewegursachen*]" from which the act originated – namely, possibly, a "bad upbringing", "bad company", a natural temperament (*Naturell*) "insensitive to shame", a certain "carelessness" and "thoughtlessness".[190] And yet, however much one ascribes that action to the influence of these factors, one will still blame the author for it, holding him *responsible* for what he has done; that is, one will regard that same action as absolutely unconditioned (*unbedingt*) in relation to everything that preceded it.[191] Underlying this blame is the assumption that practical reason is "a cause that, regardless of all the empirical conditions just named, could have and ought to [*sollen*] have determined [*bestimmen*] the conduct of the person to be other than it is".[192] The wicked action "is ascribed to the agent's intelligible character: now, in the moment when he lies, it is entirely his fault". In fact, his "reason, regardless of all empirical conditions of the deed, is fully free".[193]

So for Kant, as well as for Schopenhauer, the following statements apply: the empirical character is the manifestation ("sensible schema") of the intelligible character, which is outside of time; given the former, the individual's actions *necessarily* derive from the circumstances in which he operates; if one could thoroughly know the empirical character of a given individual, then, knowing in advance the circumstances in which he was to operate, one could apodictically foresee all his actions; the responsibility and imputability of actions do not concern man's empirical character, but his intelligible character, which (as a maxim of practical reason) derives from an original act of *freedom*.

From all this, however, Kant does not draw any metaphysical consequences: he only intends to explicate and test the fundamental presupposition that underlies any judgment of imputation. And indeed, later in the text, Kant openly declares that he did not wish (and could not) demonstrate either the "*reality*" or "the *pos-*

---

[188] Kant 1998, B582, p. 543.
[189] Kant 1998, B583, p. 544.
[190] Kant 1998, B583, p. 544.
[191] Kant 1998, B583, p. 544.
[192] Kant 1998, B583, p. 544.
[193] Kant 1998, B583, p. 544.

sibility of freedom", but only the fact that freedom itself does not stand in irremediable antinomy to the necessity of the phenomenal world.[194]

Moreover, unlike Schopenhauer, Kant refers the intelligible character to reason, not to will: a man's intelligible character is his peculiar "mode of thought", i.e. the (abstract) rule of action he deliberately assumes – and not, as in Schopenhauer, "an enduring state of the subject of the will", "a universal act of will lying outside of time", a "willing, which by its nature is free to the greatest degree, indeed, which is the innermost essence of the human being, independent of everything else". These expressions, contained in Schopenhauer's dissertation, are not found in Kant's text[195] (nor do they appear in Schopenhauer's notes to the corresponding pages of the *Critique of Pure Reason*).[196] For Schopenhauer "the *way of thinking* [Denkungsart] (in other words the action of the understanding, i.e. the ability to *think* [Denkvermögens]) [...] is quite unessential[,...] the will is the essential thing".[197] In 1816, he would write that in these passages of the *Critique of Pure Reason*, Kant improperly called the will "reason".[198]

Now, it is worth checking whether, in relation to the points just made, it was not rather Schelling – the *other* thinker mentioned by Schopenhauer – who constituted the truly foundational precedent of his system.

9.10 Second Retrospective Digression: The Study of Schelling's *Freiheitsschrift* in 1811. The "Will" as "Original Being" and Young Schopenhauer's Criticism

In *Philosophical Investigations into the Essence of Human Freedom and Matters Connected Therewith* (1809), which Schopenhauer read in Berlin in 1811, Schelling sets out to reconcile the freedom and necessity of human action. To this end, taking up some motifs already tried and tested in *Philosophy and Religion* of 1804 (cf. *supra*, 6.8), he elaborates a complex and articulated 'cosmogony', which is essentially subordinate (consequent) to an original theogony – an eternal and circular

---

194 Kant 1998, B586, p. 546.
195 On the metaphysical twisting imposed by Schopenhauer on the Kantian concept of "intelligible character", cf. Koßler 1995, especially pp. 194–195, 198. Cf. also Cysarz 1981, pp. 94–96; Schulz 1982, p. 36.
196 Cf. MR 2, p. 309; Schopenhauer 1911–1942, vol. XIII, pp. 199–200, in which Schopenhauer, in relation to intelligible causality, i.e. the causality of something that is not an appearance, accuses Kant of a transcendent use of the category of causality.
197 MR 1, n. 67, p. 37. Translation modified.
198 Cf. MR 2, p. 487.

'becoming' *in God*. It is in relation to this last point that the work represents a radical novelty within Schelling's thought: according to some critics, here he arrives at a "metaphysics of will" that prefigures in many respects the system expounded by Schopenhauer some ten years later in *The World as Will and Representation*.[199]

Schelling's reflections start from a careful consideration of the concept of "God": "Since nothing is prior to, or outside of, God, he must have the ground of his existence [*Grund seiner Existenz*] in himself".[200] All philosophers and theologians agree on this; however, they have left the concept of this "ground" undefined, as they have never described its real and actual nature.[201] By referring to the mystical and theosophical tradition, Schelling intends to make his own original contribution in this regard. He determines this ground as *"nature – in God"*, and describes it through a powerful and suggestive analogy: it is to God what gravity is to light.

> Gravity precedes light as its ever dark ground, which itself is not *actu* [actual], and flees into the night as the light (that which exists) dawns. Even light does not fully remove the seal under which gravity lies contained.[202]

This "precedence [*Vorhergehen*]" of the ground with respect to God is not to be understood "as precedence according to time nor as priority of being".[203] Certainly, the ground of existence, as such, precedes God (as existing); however, since it is *essentially* the ground of existence – precisely – *of God*, it cannot exist separately from God himself.[204] Separated or isolated from that of which it is the "ground", the ground would not be such, it would not be what it is – and therefore it would not be at all. The relation between the two terms is therefore circular and eternal: just as God exists only by virtue of his own ground of existence, so too the latter "could not exist if God did not exist *actu*" already from the beginning.[205]

Based on this distinction, *internal* to God, between God as the ground of his own existence and God as existing, Schelling believes he can explain the existence of finite realities – that is, the existence of what is *not* God.

---

199 Cf. Berg 2003, pp. 173–176.
200 Schelling 2006, p. 27.
201 Schelling 2006, p. 27.
202 Schelling 2006, p. 27.
203 Schelling 2006, p. 28.
204 Schelling 2006, p. 28.
205 Schelling 2006, p. 28.

> In order to be divided from God, they [finite things] must become in a ground different from God. Since, however, nothing indeed can be outside of God, this contradiction can only be resolved by things having their ground in that which in God himself is not *He Himself*, that is, in that which is the ground of his existence.[206]

In the preceding pages, introductory to the work proper, Schelling had announced that he wanted to integrate the realist and deterministic one-sidedness of Spinoza's system with the higher "principle of idealism", which elevates freedom to a "genuine system of reason".[207] In this regard, he had expressly stated:

> In the final and highest judgment, there is no other Being than will. Will is primal Being [*Wollen ist Urseyn*] to which alone all predicates of Being apply: groundlessness [*Grundlosigkeit*], eternality [*Ewigkeit*], independence from time [*Unabhängigkeit von der Zeit*], self-affirmation [*Selbstbejahung*].[208]

In accordance with these preliminary statements, Schelling further determines the ground of God's existence as "the yearning [*Sehnsucht*] the eternal One feels to give birth to itself": a "will in which there is no understanding" but which is at the same time "a will of the understanding, namely yearning and desire [*Begierde*] for the latter".[209] It is not a conscious or aware will, but only "a divining will [*ahnender Wille*] whose divining [*Ahndung*] is the understanding".[210] "The understanding", which finally brought the 'light' of knowledge, "is born in the genuine sense from that which is without understanding [*Verstandlosen*]."[211] The latter is the true "base of reality" (Schelling uses the alchemical term *Basis*), as "all birth is birth from darkness into light".[212]

In correspondence with that primordial yearning – Schelling continues – "an inner [...] representation" emerges in God which, however, can have no other object or content than God himself.[213] It "is with God in the beginning and is the God who was begotten *in* God himself": it is the "understanding – the *Word* – of this yearning".[214]

---

206 Schelling 2006, p. 28.
207 Schelling 2006, p. 21.
208 Schelling 2006, p. 21.
209 Schelling 2006, pp. 28–29.
210 Schelling 2006, p. 29.
211 Schelling 2006, p. 29.
212 Schelling 2006, p. 29.
213 Schelling 2006, p. 30.
214 Schelling 2006, p. 30.

9.10 Second Retrospective Digression: The Study of Schelling's *Freiheitsschrift* in 1811

At this point "the eternal spirit", as the *unity* of the two moments (yearning and Word), "impelled by the love that it itself is, proclaims the word": understanding and yearning thus co-operate in the form of "a freely creating and all-powerful will", which gives rise to creation.[215] (Always bear in mind that, according to the New Testament, creation sprang from an act of "will [θέλημα]" on God's part: cf. Rev 4:11). Yearning is that in virtue of which something exists outside of God; understanding is that which brings order to the propulsive and original disorder of yearning. This disorder, however, is never completely eliminated and mastered by the ordering principle – hence everything in the universe that seems to escape the otherwise prevailing regularity and rationality.[216]

The ordering activity of the understanding takes place through a progressive separation and distinction of what in nature (i.e., in the ground) is indistinctly united: "at each point of division of forces a new being emerges from nature whose soul must be that much more complete the more it contains divided what is not divided in other things".[217] The description of this ascending process, in all its degrees, constitutes the particular task of the "philosophy of nature".[218]

As a consequence of all this, every created or finite being bears a "dual principle" within itself: the ground (i.e., the yearning) corresponds to the "self-will [*der Eigenwille*]" of the creature, which tends to make it independent and 'decentralize' it from the Order of the Whole; on the other hand, the "understanding as universal will [*Universalwille*] stands against this self-will of creatures, using and subordinating the latter to itself as a mere instrument".[219]

At the apex of creation – that is to say, at the apex of the distinction, or explication, of what is implicitly and indistinctly contained in the ground – is *man:* in him are found "the whole power of the dark principle and at the same time the whole strength of the light",[220] "the deepest abyss and the loftiest sky or both *centra*".[221] That is, in man, the *whole* essence of the ground is revealed and illuminated by the light of the understanding, so that both principles come to a complete and exhaustive realization in him. "In him (in man) alone God loved the world", because in him alone God fully revealed himself.[222]

---

215 Schelling 2006, p. 30.
216 Schelling 2006, p. 29.
217 Schelling 2006, p. 31.
218 Schelling 2006, p. 31.
219 Schelling 2006, p. 32.
220 Schelling 2006, p. 32.
221 Schelling 2006, p. 32.
222 Schelling 2006, p. 32.

Nevertheless, man is *not* God. This not-being-God – i.e. his difference from God – is expressed through the *separability* of the two principles which, in God, are indissolubly united.²²³ As we have seen, the ground is illuminated and fully realized in man, which means that the principle that emerged from it, man's self-will, becomes in man "selfhood [*Selbstheit*]", i.e. "spirit [*Geist*]".²²⁴ As such, the latter stands essentially *above* the automatic and necessitating unity of the two principles, which prevails in all other levels of creation.²²⁵ In man (and in man alone), the self-will, having reached the supreme level of "spirit", can consciously and intentionally *separate* itself from the principle of light, that is, from the understanding, and "strive to be as a particular will [*Particularwille*] that which it only is through identity with the universal will [*Universalwille*]; to be that which it only is, in so far as it remains in the *centrum* [...], also on the periphery".²²⁶ For Schelling, this "separation of selfhood having become animated by spirit [...] from the light" is what generates "the possibility of good and evil", that is, *human freedom*.²²⁷

Now, in this grand speculative fresco, which is at once theogonic, cosmogonic, anthropogonic and ethical, young Schopenhauer detects an illegitimate use – not figurative (*bildlich*), but crudely materialistic (*krass materialistisch*) and therefore *transcendent* – of phenomenal concepts such as "things [*Dinge*]", "consequence [*Folge*]", "ground [*Grund*]", as well as the use of inherently illegitimate concepts, such as the very concept of "God [*Gott*]".²²⁸ The core of Schelling's theory, for Schopenhauer, can be traced back to the idea, which he certainly shares, that "underlying [*zum Grunde*] the appearance in time of a human being, there is something outside all time as well as outside all the conditions of the appearance".²²⁹ However, despite what Schelling attempts to do, it is not possible to construct a "concept" of that "something" from phenomenal determinations (cf. *supra*, 6.9).²³⁰ In Schelling's reflections, Schopenhauer sees nothing more than a clumsy plagiarism – guided, moreover, by an insufficient comprehension – of Böhme's *Mysterium magnum*.²³¹

Yet, in relation to the question of human *freedom*, Schelling formulated the theory of the "intelligible being", which, as we shall now see, seems to represent

---

223 Schelling 2006, pp. 32–33, 41.
224 Schelling 2006, p. 33.
225 Schelling 2006, p. 33.
226 Schelling 2006, p. 33.
227 Schelling 2006, p. 33.
228 MR 2, p. 352.
229 MR 2, p. 353. Translation modified.
230 MR 2, p. 353.
231 MR 2, p. 353.

the true, fundamental precedent of the doctrine of intelligible character set out by Schopenhauer in the dissertation.

9.11 Schelling: Man's "Intelligible Being" as a Free Act of Self-Position Based on a Primal Willing. Comparison with Some Passages from the Dissertation

In order to explain how the individual's "selfhood", i.e. the "spirit", does or does not implement the separation from the principle of light, Schelling premised that "idealism actually first raised the doctrine of freedom to that very region where it is alone comprehensible. According to idealism, the intelligible being [*Das intelligibile Wesen*] of every thing and especially of man is outside all causal connectedness as it is outside or above all time."[232] At this point Schelling warns: "We are expressing [...] the Kantian concept not exactly in his very words, but indeed in the way, as we believe, that it would have to be expressed in order to be comprehensible."[233] The reference is to the Kantian doctrine of the intelligible character. By man's "intelligible being", Schelling does not mean "an undetermined generality", but rather the "intelligible being of *this* [italics mine] individual": not something identical in all people, but what constitutes the distinctiveness and irreplaceability of every individual as such.[234]

Now, every "being" acts "in accordance with its own inner nature"; this (necessary) conformity of action to nature, i.e. to the inner constitution of being, represents the "inner necessity" of action.[235] But on what does the determinateness of being itself depend?

> Here lies the point at which necessity and freedom must be unified if they are at all capable of unification. Were this being a dead sort of Being [*ein totes Sein*] and a merely given one with respect to man, then, because all action [*Handlung*] resulting from it could do so only with necessity, responsibility [*Zurechnungsfähigkeit*] and all freedom would be abolished. But precisely this inner necessity is itself freedom; the essence of man is fundamentally *his own act* [seine eigne That]; necessity and freedom are in one another as one being [*Ein Wesen*] that appears as one or the other only when considered from different sides, in itself freedom, formally necessity. The I, says Fichte, is its own act; consciousness is self-positing [*Selbstsetzen*]—but the I is nothing different from this self-positing, rather it is precisely

---

232 Schelling 2006, p. 49.
233 Schelling 2006, p. 49.
234 Schelling 2006, p. 50.
235 Schelling 2006, p. 49.

self-positing itself. This consciousness, however, to the extent it is thought merely as self-apprehension or cognition of the I, is not even primary and all along presupposes actual Being, as does all pure cognition. This Being, presumed to be prior to cognition, is, however, not Being, though it is likewise not cognition: it is real self-positing [*reales Selbstsetzen*], it is a primal and fundamental willing [*ein Ur- und Grund-Wollen*], which makes itself into something [*das sich selbst zu etwas macht*] and is the ground of all ways of being.[236]

Given the intelligible being of an individual, his action "can follow [*folgen*] [...] only [...] with absolute necessity [*mit absoluter Nothwendigkeit*]" from it, i.e. in accordance with being itself.[237] This necessity is also "absolute freedom", because being does not come to man from outside, it is not attributed to him or imposed on him by an extraneous entity, but is rather "*his* [man's] *own act*".[238] The "ground of all ways of being" (of each individual) is in fact "a primal and fundamental willing".

Man is in the initial creation, as shown, an undecided being [*ein unentschiedenes Wesen*]—(which may be portrayed mythically [*mytisch*] as a condition of innocence that precedes this life and as an initial blessedness)—only man himself can decide. But this decision [*Entscheidung*] cannot occur within time; it occurs outside of all time [*sie fällt außer aller Zeit*].[239]

In this way, Schelling believed he was able to reconcile the freedom and necessity of will: the act by which man decides or determines his own originally undecided being – the act of "self-position" – is free (in this sense, *esse sequitur operari*); the acts that follow this original act are, on the other hand, necessary in relation to the being thus posited (in this sense, *operari sequitur esse*). But this necessity is subordinate and consequent to a primordial act of freedom: man is essentially *Tat-Handlung*.

Now, the reflections developed by Schopenhauer in the dissertation show clear analogies, from both a theoretical and a terminological point of view, with this part of Schelling's thought. First of all, Schopenhauer also reconciles freedom and necessity of action, referring the former to the original act of will constituting the intelligible character and the latter to man's individual actions that take place in accordance with the character itself.[240] In this regard, Schopenhauer even

---

[236] Schelling 2006, pp. 50–51. For the definition of Schelling's original speculative contribution in these pages compared to Kant and Fichte, cf. Höfele 2019, pp. 136–140. Cf. also Florig 2010; Rivera de Rosales 2012; Binkelmann 2015.
[237] Schelling 2006, p. 50.
[238] Schelling 2006, p. 50.
[239] Schelling 2006, p. 51.
[240] On this issue, cf. Koßler 1995, pp. 198–200. Reading Fries' *Neue Kritik der Vernunft* (Fries 1807), Schopenhauer noted certain affinities with Schelling's doctrine (cf. MR 2, p. 417), which do indeed

uses the same expression as Schelling: *mit Notwendigkeit folgen*.²⁴¹ Secondly, the intelligible character is for Schopenhauer "a universal act of will lying outside of time", a "willing [*Wollen*], [...] which is the innermost essence [*Wesen*] of the human being". It is revealing that he uses the terms *Wollen* and *Wesen*, which are completely absent from Kant's treatment of this issue but central to Schelling's.²⁴²

Thirdly, since for Schopenhauer "the act of will proper [*der eigentliche Willensakt*]" is "decision [*Entschluß*]",²⁴³ the fact that the intelligible character is "a universal act of will lying outside of time" means that it is a universal *decision* lying outside of time – just as in Schelling the original determination of the "intelligible being" is a "decision [*Entscheidung*]" that "occurs outside all time". It can be assumed that Schopenhauer intentionally used the term "act of will" rather than "decision" to avoid an overly open correspondence to Schelling's text.

Insofar as Schelling's position openly presupposes the Fichtean doctrine of the I as *Tathandlung*, and insofar as Schopenhauer was evidently conditioned by Schelling, Fichte's doctrine can also be said to have affected Schopenhauer in this context (albeit indirectly). In *On the Freedom of the Will*, Schopenhauer would determine the wholeness of man's "being and essence (*existentia et essentia*)" as "[man's] free deed [*seine freie That*]".²⁴⁴ Man's being (*Seyn*) and essence (*Wesen*) are thus, for Schopenhauer, a "deed" of man himself (cf. *infra*, 12.10).²⁴⁵

Despite these similarities, there is nevertheless a substantial difference between Schopenhauer's and Schelling's discourse, which must now be considered.

---

exist; this shows that Schopenhauer read Schelling's work first. Cf. also Müller-Lauter 1993; Ruta 2021.
241 Cf. Schopenhauer 2012 [1813], § 46, p. 187.
242 Cf. Berg 2003, pp. 364–367.
243 Schopenhauer 2012 [1813], § 46, p. 187.
244 A. Schopenhauer, *Prize Essay on the Freedom of the Will*, in Schopenhauer 2009, p. 108.
245 Compared to these very close analogies, even in terms of terminology, with Schelling's text, the possible affinities with Pseudo-Tauler's texts, suggested by R. Heimann (2013, pp. 201–202), become of secondary importance. For a systematic comparison of Schelling and Schopenhauer in relation to this point, see also Hühn 1998; Novembre 2019. For Schopenhauer's notes recorded in his personal copy of the work, cf. Höfele and Schwenzfeuer 2021.

9.12 The Immanent Metaphysics Contained *in nuce* in the Dissertation. Difference between Schelling's and Schopenhauer's Metaphysics of Will

In his *Philosophical Investigations into the Essence of Human Freedom*, Schelling builds on primarily theological considerations, i.e. the concept of "God"; from there he develops the discourse on man's intelligible being and freedom. Schopenhauer, on the other hand, builds his doctrine of intelligible character starting from an indubitable fact of consciousness: namely that everyone acts the same way under equal circumstances, yet everyone "is most vividly aware that he could have acted in a completely different way had he so *willed*, i.e., that his will is determined by nothing external".[246] His argument – which leads to the admission of something that lies beyond any possible experience (namely the intelligible character as a free "universal act of will lying outside of time") – can be regarded as a kind of *abductive inference*. Indeed, in Schopenhauer's view, the distinction between empirical and intelligible character provides the best explanation of the fact that human action involves regularity and necessity, on the one hand, and a sense of responsibility and accountability, on the other.

Now, Schelling also observes that, although the idea of man's metaphysical and original self-determination may appear "incomprehensible [...] to conventional ways of thinking, there is indeed in each man a feeling [*Gefühl*] in accord with it": in fact, "anyone, for instance, who in order to excuse a wrong action, says 'that's just the way I am' is surely aware that he is like he is through his guilt, as much as he is right that it was impossible for him to act otherwise."[247] Freedom and necessity thus meet in the acting subject's own self-understanding subsequent to action; consequently, Schelling asserts that some trace of that original act remains in every man's consciousness[248] (something that Schopenhauer, too, must necessarily presuppose with regard to the acting subject's vivid awareness, *lebendigste Bewußtseyn*, of the freedom of his own will: cf. *supra*, 9.8).

However, the recognition of this fact of consciousness has a purely confirmatory or corroborative function in Schelling, and not a *foundational* one as in Schopenhauer. Exactly in the same way, in *On the Freedom of the Will*, the "higher view",[249] which concerns precisely the treatment of the "intelligible character", would be explicitly based on that peculiar "fact of consciousness [*Thatsache des*

---

246 Schopenhauer 2012 [1813], § 46, p. 187.
247 Schelling 2006, pp. 51–52.
248 Schelling 2006, pp. 51–52.
249 Schopenhauer 2009, pp. 110–111.

Bewußtseyns]" which is "the perfectly *clear and certain feeling* [italics mine] of *responsibility* [*Verantwortlichkeit*] for what we do, of *accountability* [*Zurechnungsfähigkeit*] for our actions, resting on the unshakeable certainty that we ourselves are the *doers of our deeds*".[250]

In the dissertation, the Fichtean perspective (according to which "I find myself as myself only as willing") and the Schellingean perspective (according to which man's intelligible being is the result of a free and primal act of will) combine in an original way: the individual finds himself as willing, i.e. in single uniform acts of will; but these acts – as they must be able to be traced back to a rule that does not contradict the individual's awareness of his own self-determination (i.e. of the fact that his will "is determined by nothing external") – must be thought of as the instances in time of a "universal act of will lying outside of time". The concept of intelligible character is necessary in order to subordinate to unity the original datum of self-consciousness, constituted by the single and free (albeit uniform) acts of will.

Moreover, the universalization of that double datum (i.e., the fact that Schopenhauer considers it valid for all people) implies an unexpressed *analogy* between the self-consciousness of the individual Schopenhauer and the self-consciousness of all other human beings, by which Arthur can attribute to the latter the same awareness of self-determination which he can only feel in himself. In this part of the discourse (and, more generally, regarding man's self-cognition as willing), there is already a subterranean recourse to the analogical argument, which will be decisive in the foundation of the mature system (cf. *infra*, 12.2).

In line with the objections to Schelling noted in 1811, Schopenhauer rigorously avoided constructing a 'transcendent' discourse: he did not build on metempirical concepts, but only provided an interpretation, which is also an *explanation*, of experience. In this way, however, he came to theorize something that is not, and cannot in itself be, a content of experience (the "permanent state of the subject of will", i.e. the intelligible character as a "universal act of will lying outside of time"). Bearing all this in mind, it is not surprising that the skeptic Schulze did not agree with these passages in the dissertation (cf. *supra*, 9.3).

The above considerations also concern the difference between Schopenhauer's and Schelling's later metaphysics of will. The *Philosophical Investigations into the Essence of Human Freedom* explicitly deal with the will; and indeed, the same determinations that Schelling attributes to the will as "original being" ("groundless-

---

[250] Schopenhauer 2009, p. 112. Cf. also Schopenhauer 2009, pp. 104–105, where Schelling is explicitly mentioned. On this theme, cf. Koßler 2002a, 2006c.

ness, eternity, independence from time, self-affirmation")[251] are attributed to the will as a thing-in-itself in *The World as Will and Representation*.[252] Schelling's description of the creature's "self-will" ("pure craving [*bloße Sucht*] or desire [*Begierde*], that is, blind will", devoid of understanding or knowledge)[253] also consistently anticipates Schopenhauer's description of the will as a thing-in-itself (a "blind impulse [*blinder Drang*] and striving in the absence of cognition [*erkenntnißloses Streben*]").[254]

In this sense, Schopenhauer would seem to have unilaterally 'absolutized' what in Schelling constituted only *one* of the two principles of every creature.[255] Yet for Schopenhauer, *contra* Schelling, the attribution of these predicates to the will, as well as the determination of the will as the "thing-in-itself" or "innermost essence" of all things, is only made possible by means of a prior analogical argument, based on the determination of the I's essence in itself (as "body [*Leib*]"): this essence in itself, for Schopenhauer, is indeed the will.[256] The ground of this analogical argument is once more the subject's finding itself as willing – namely, the will being an object of inner sense, that which the subject (as body) cognizes, when it cognizes itself (cf. *infra*, 12.2).

Concerning the doctrine of the intelligible character, the dissertation of 1813 already seems to contain *in nuce* the epistemological status of immanent metaphysics,[257] or "immanent dogmatism",[258] which Schopenhauer would consider peculiar to his thought. He would claim this status as the indisputable proof of his allegiance to Kant's criticism and, therefore, as the fundamental merit of his philosophy, in explicit opposition to Fichte, Schelling and Hegel (cf. *supra*, 6.10).[259]

---

[251] Schelling 2006, p. 21.
[252] Cf. Schopenhauer 2010b, § 23, I 134–136, pp. 137–139. Cf. Hühn 2010; Schwenzfeuer 2018.
[253] Schelling 2006, p. 32.
[254] Schopenhauer 2010b, § 27, I 178, p. 174 (translation modified). Cf. Schopenhauer 2020, p. 116.
[255] Cf. Berg 2003, p. 327.
[256] Schopenhauer 2010b, I 123–126, § 19, pp. 127–130.
[257] Cf. Schopenhauer 2018, II 203–204, chap. 17, pp. 192–193.
[258] Schopenhauer 2014, p. 119.
[259] Schopenhauer 2014, p. 119. For a comprehensive interpretation of Schopenhauer's philosophy starting from this theme, cf. Malter 1991.

9.13 The Function of the Dissertation within "True Criticism" and the Announced Project of a "Larger Work". The Hidden References to the Better Consciousness and Some Consequent Changes in the Second Edition

The principle of sufficient reason concerns the connection (*Verbindung*) between representations (cf. *supra*, 9.3). For "nothing existing of itself and independently, likewise nothing existing in isolation and apart, can become an object for us"; we cognize things only in their relation (*Relation*), i.e. precisely in the necessary connection that binds them to one another and that is expressed by the principle of reason (in its four forms).[260] This cognition is therefore only relative, not absolute.

In an addition to fragment 54 (the fragment dates from 1812, but the addition is probably later), Schopenhauer states that "the understanding, thinking in concepts, cognizes only the relation of things and their succession in space and time; but all this is the essence of multiplicity".[261] Against this kind of cognition, Schopenhauer sets "intuition [*die Anschauung*] [that] grasps the innermost essence [*das innerste Wesen*], the *Platonic Idea*, the meaning of the hieroglyphics of the infinitely varied appearance".[262]

Relation as such necessarily implies multiplicity; but the latter is a determination of the appearance, not of the "innermost essence" of things (which for Schopenhauer corresponds, at this stage of his reflections, to the Platonic Idea). Consequently, every relation as such concerns only and exclusively the phenomenal or sensible world. One can thus understand why Schopenhauer, in fragment 96, peremptorily states that "all possible relation is only a determination of the empirical consciousness [...] that appears as understanding and the faculty of reason [*als Vernunft und Verstand erscheinenden*]".[263] Empirical consciousness is in fact the consciousness of the sensible (empirical) world.

Now, if the principle of reason concerns the various types of (necessary) relations between things, and "all possible relation is only a determination of the empirical consciousness", *the principle of reason inevitably concerns the whole sphere of empirical consciousness and only that.* This conclusion is confirmed in several places in the dissertation. Consider first of all what Schopenhauer writes in the last paragraph of the work (§ 59):

---

260 Schopenhauer 2012 [1813], § 16, p. 157.
261 MR 1, fn to n. 54, p. 31. Translation modified.
262 MR 1, fn to n. 54, p. 31. Translation modified.
263 MR 1, n. 96, p. 72.

> In this treatise I have attempted to show that the principle of sufficient reason is a common expression of four completely different relations, each of which is based on a particular law, given *a priori* (since the principle of sufficient reason is synthetic *a priori*); and according to the principle of *homogeneity*, it must be accepted that just as these four laws [...] they also arise from one and the same original constitution of our entire cognitive faculty [...] which, accordingly, must be regarded as the innermost core of all the dependency, relativity [*Relativität*], instability, and finiteness [*Endlichkeit*] of objects of our consciousness, which is confined to sensibility, understanding and reason, subject and object [*unseres in Sinnlichkeit, Verstand und Vernunft, Subjekt und Objekt befangenen Bewußtseyns*], or that very world which the brilliant Plato repeatedly disparaged as 'that which always becomes and passes away, but never truly is', the cognition of which would be only 'opinion amid non-rational perception', and which Christianity, in the correct sense, called *temporality* [Zeitlichkeit] [...].[264]

Kant's *Erscheinung* is clearly identified here with the content of Plato's δόξα. In his *History of Philosophy*, Tennemann renders δόξα with *Vorstellung*[265] and φαινόμενον (which for Plato is the content of the δόξα) with *Erscheinung* (which for Kant is the content of the true or intersubjective *Vorstellung*; cf. *supra*, 2.7; 3.7).

According to Schopenhauer, the split into subject and object is the constituting feature of the empirical consciousness;[266] indeed, the same expression as the one just cited (*unseres in Sinnlichkeit, Verstand und Vernunft ... befangenen Bewußtseyn*) is referred to it in fragment 234, which deals with the "*double nature of our consciousness*".[267] It is clear, therefore, that in this passage of the dissertation Schopenhauer is implicitly and cryptically hinting at what he calls "empirical consciousness" in his manuscripts. In any case, even the term "temporality", which recurs in the text, would suffice to draw this conclusion: the empirical consciousness is indeed temporal consciousness (*zeitliches Bewußtseyn*) – both in the sense that it is the consciousness of what is in time, and in the sense that it is itself in time (in the same way that the better consciousness is beyond time both because it is consciousness of the eternal and because it is itself something eternal: cf. *supra*, 8.14 and 8.19).

---

264 Schopenhauer 2012 [1813], § 59, p. 150. In the German text, Schopenhauer quotes Plato's Greek, which the English edition reports in corresponding footnotes: ἀεὶ γιγνόμενον μὲν καὶ ἀπολλύμενον, ὄντως δὲ οὐδέποτε ὄν and δόξα μετ'αἰσθήσεως ἀλόγου (non-literal quotation from *Timaeus* 27 D – 28 A; cf. Plato 1914 ff., vol. 9, pp. 48–49).
265 Cf. Tennemann 1798–1819, II, p. 286.
266 MR 2, p. 381.
267 MR 1, n. 234, p. 147. Cf. also fragment 109 (MR 1, p. 79) where "life", i.e., properly speaking, the consciousness of life (and thus precisely the "empirical consciousness") is described as the "consciousness that is enslaved by the understanding and sensibility [*in Verstand und Sinnlichkeit befangenen Bewußtsein*]". Cf. De Cian 2002, pp. 229–260.

9.13 The Function of the Dissertation

In 1812, Schopenhauer wrote that the task of true criticism is to clearly separate the better consciousness from empirical consciousness "like gold from ore".[268] In this way, the better consciousness will be achieved in its purity, "without any admixture of sensibility or understanding", and the empirical consciousness itself will be precisely delimited, "classify[ing] it according to its differences".[269] This rigorous distinction will have to forever interdict the transcendent use of the understanding, i.e. the attribution of determinations of the sensible world (the realm of empirical consciousness) to the supersensible world (the realm of the better consciousness). The critical philosopher must rigorously distinguish "better cognition" from "empirical cognition" (cf. *supra*, 7.1 – 7.6).[270]

In 1813 Schopenhauer still set out to achieve true criticism.[271] The dissertation, through the application of the two principles of "homogeneity" and "specification", seems to offer a classification of empirical consciousness "according to its differences" – which is only *one* of the two essential parts of the philosophical project of "true criticism". The *other*, equally essential part, is the treatment of the better consciousness; and indeed, it is to the better consciousness that reference is implicitly made in many places in the original dissertation. These passages would later be deleted in the second edition.[272] Let's have a closer look at them.

First, expounding the "root" of the principle of reason, Schopenhauer writes:

> *Our consciousness, as far as* [so weit] *it appears as sensibility, understanding, and reason* [als Sinnlichkeit, Verstand und Vernunft erscheint], *divides* [zerfällt] *into subject and object, and, so far* [bis dahin], *comprises nothing else.*[273]

The text suggests that our consciousness "divides into subject and object" *only* "as far as it appears as sensibility, understanding, and reason". Correspondingly, the assertion that consciousness "comprises nothing else" than everything that falls under the division into subject and object is limited by the specification "so far [*bis dahin*]" – where "so far" means "as far as it appears as sensibility, understanding, and reason". Based on this formulation, it would thus seem that *another* modality of consciousness, not subject to that division, is possible (as it is not ruled out). In fragment 96 of the manuscripts (1813) Schopenhauer determines empirical

---

[268] MR 2, p. 416.
[269] MR 2, p. 416.
[270] MR 2, p. 376. Translation modified.
[271] MR 2, p. 295; cf. MR 1, nn. 66 (p. 36), 67 (p. 37), 71 (p. 39).
[272] On the overall textual differences between the two editions, cf. Tielsch 1957.
[273] Schopenhauer 2012 [1813], § 16, p. 157.

consciousness precisely as *als Verstand und Vernunft erscheinend*, and states that the better consciousness, unlike it, "lies beyond subject and object".[274]

In the second edition of the dissertation (1847), Schopenhauer would present the "root" of the principle of sufficient reason differently, using a more unambiguous formulation that excludes any other modality of consciousness:

> *Our cognizing consciousness, appearing* [auftretend] *as outer and inner sensibility (receptivity), as understanding and reason, divides into subject and object and comprises nothing else.*[275]

Both the comparative proposition introduced by the expression *so weit* and the limitation *bis dahin* have been expunged. In this formulation of the "root" of the principle, the division into subject and object and the faculties of (internal and external) sensibility, understanding, and reason thus seem to constitute the only possible mode of "our cognizing consciousness". Consequently, the assertion that "our [...] consciousness [...] comprises nothing else" than what falls within that division here concerns the cognizing consciousness as such or *tout court*.

In § 42, in relation to the possible reason "why" our consciousness appears "as subject and object", Schopenhauer writes that such a question is illegitimate because "the principle of sufficient reason", which grounds every possible answer to the question "why?", already "presupposes subject and object".[276] Nevertheless, "a completely different area of philosophy from the one that the present essay belongs to could provide us with, not so much an answer to this question, as something that renders the question superfluous and satisfies us in a completely different way".[277] This statement, not reproduced in the second edition, still seems to allude to a mode of consciousness not affected by the split into subject and object. Even in 1814 Schopenhauer would write that, as "better consciousness", human consciousness "demonstrates that it can appear otherwise than as subject [*anders als ... Subjekt*]".[278]

In § 46 of the first edition (immediately after setting out the doctrine of the intelligible character), as if to justify a degree of incompleteness in his treatment, Schopenhauer states:

> It is generally my intention to exclude from this philosophical monograph everything extraneous, and particularly to exclude everything ethical and aesthetic [*alles Ethische und Aesthetische*], since these would provide no new class of objects and, like so many other topics, are

---

274 MR 1, n. 96, p. 72; cf. also HN I, p. 67.
275 Schopenhauer 2012 [1847], § 16, p. 30.
276 Schopenhauer 2012 [1813], § 42, p. 184.
277 Schopenhauer 2012 [1813], § 42, p. 184. Cf. Chenet 1997, p. 123.
278 MR 1, n. 234, p. 148.

not necessary to our division of classes of objects; considering them would fill a treatise exceeding the present essay in scope as much as in content, one which would read very differently from our division, but be completely in agreement with it.[279]

And, in the penultimate paragraph (§ 58), he reiterates:

> But what, then, is the innermost essence [*das innerste Wesen*] of the artist [*Künstlers*], the innermost essence of the saint [*Heiligen*], if this essence be one and the same – I will not concern myself with this, for to do so would be inconsistent with my intent not to touch upon ethics [*das Ethische*] and aesthetics [*das Aesthetische*] in this treatise. Perhaps, however, at some time this could become the subject of a larger work for me, the subject of which would be related to the present work as waking is to dreaming.[280]

It is perhaps specifically in relation to the promise of this later work that Schulze, in his review, referred to "the high hopes […] raised by the author's philosophical talents" (cf. *supra*, 9.1).[281]

As mentioned, the principle of reason concerns the world of *temporality*. But then, that the ethical and aesthetic realms do not fall within the principle of reason means that they do not fall within the realm of temporality. This implication of the dissertation is perfectly consistent with the coeval fragments of the manuscripts: the essence of beauty is "*the theoretical negation of the temporal world and affirmation of eternity*", just as "the practical negation and affirmation of those two are asceticism and virtue" (cf. *supra*, 8.13).[282] But the consciousness of the eternal world – i.e. of the Platonic Idea – is the better consciousness, whose prevalence over empirical consciousness characterizes the exceptional figures of the genius (or creator of art) and the saint (cf. *supra*, 8.14 and 8.17).

> In this [the moral] element [*Im Moralischen*] there is expressed *the better consciousness* which lies *far above all reason*, expresses itself in conduct as holiness, and is the true redemption of the world. This same consciousness expresses itself in art as genius, as a consolation for the temporal and earthly state.[283]

In the dissertation, Schopenhauer does not name the better consciousness, but he does expressly state that the faculties of the finite consciousness traditionally as-

---

[279] Schopenhauer 2012 [1813], § 46, p. 188.
[280] Schopenhauer 2012 [1813], § 58, p. 196.
[281] Cf. Schulze 1916, p. 167.
[282] MR 1, n. 86, p. 48.
[283] MR 1, n. 85, p. 47.

signed to morality and art, namely *reason* and *imagination*, constitute only the necessary, but not also sufficient, conditions of those two respective spheres.[284]

Now, "Plato, the divine" set the becoming world (ἀεὶ γιγνόμενον μὲν καὶ ἀπολλύμενον) – which for Schopenhauer constitutes the realm of the principle of reason – against the Idea, and the cognition of the becoming world (δόξα μετ'αἰσθήσεως ἀλόγου) – which for Schopenhauer coincides with cognition according to the principle of reason – against cognition of the Idea.[285] The same Greek passage from § 59 of the dissertation's first edition (though quoted more correctly and completely) occurs on the title page of Book III of *The World as Will and Representation*, which deals with "representation independent of the principle of sufficient reason", i.e. with the "Platonic Idea" as the "object of art".[286]

In the manuscripts, the opposition between cognition of the Idea and cognition according to the principle of reason becomes explicit from fragment 210 (cf. *infra*, 10.12).[287] But already in the dissertation, Platonic Ideas are defined as "normal intuitions [*Normalanschauungen*], which, unlike mathematical intuitions, would not only be valid for the formal aspect of complete representations, but also for the material aspect".[288] In other words, Ideas have a normative or constitutive value not only in relation to the formal or subjective (in the transcendental sense) element of experience, but also in relation to the 'material' element, which is extraneous to the subject's faculties and thus to the principle of reason itself (which, on the contrary, concerns the whole formal side of representations and only that).[289]

Moreover, in expounding the allegory of the cave, Plato compares the empirical world to a dream (ὄναρ) from which one should urgently awaken (cf. *supra*, 3.6).[290] Schopenhauer writes that his announced text on ethical and aesthetic themes "would be related to the present work as waking [*Wachen*] is to dreaming [*Traum*]".[291] In paragraph 49 of the dissertation, in another passage no longer present in the second edition, Schopenhauer uses this metaphor once more.

---

284 Schopenhauer 2012 [1813], § 58, pp. 195–196.
285 Schopenhauer 2012 [1813], § 59, p. 150. Cf. Plato, *Timaeus* 27d–28a; Plato 1914 ff., vol. 9, pp. 48–49.
286 Schopenhauer 2010b, I 197, p. 191.
287 MR 1, n. 210, pp. 124–128.
288 Schopenhauer 2012 [1813], § 40, p. 127.
289 The fact that Platonic Ideas also govern the material element of experience in no way means that they can be understood as transcendental functions of the subject (for a different interpretation, cf. Kamata 1988, p. 233).
290 Cf. Plato, *Republic*, 520 c, Plato 1914 ff., vol. 6, pp. 126–127 (cf. also 476 c–d, vol. 5, pp. 550–553).
291 Schopenhauer 2012 [1813], § 58, p. 196.

[...] People [...] talk about moral feeling, religious feeling, aesthetic feeling. Yet I must explain that [...] I find these terms objectionable, and I absolutely cannot accept them as valid. Having proceeded from completely inessential determinations, these terms have come about through a blind *synchronism*, which subsumes the best in humankind – to which indeed the rest of the world bears a relation as does a shadow in a dream [*ein Schatten im Traum*] to real, solid bodies – under a category with all sorts of things very different from it – with that which is completely animalistic in our nature, indeed even with that which is worse than animalistic – and so has called all of this *feeling*. On account of my plan, mentioned above, not to set foot in the realm of ethics and aesthetics in this treatise, I cannot proceed any further with this topic. As in a preparation of a single part of the anatomy, in a monograph, too, one must always note the places where the part is cut off from the other parts of the whole it necessarily belongs to and where a natural connection is arbitrarily and forcefully destroyed.[292]

Feeling (*Gefühl*), being an object for the subject, is fully within the realm of the principle of reason; consequently, expressions such as "moral feeling, religious feeling, aesthetic feeling" – which refer feeling to what is beyond the principle of reason – are necessarily illegitimate. These considerations probably have their main polemical targets in Schleiermacher, for whom the essence of religion is "feeling",[293] and Kant. The latter, in the *Critique of Practical Reason*, defined "respect [*Achtung*]" for the law as the only possible "*moral feeling*" (specifying, however, that it "not the incentive to morality; instead it is morality itself subjectively considered as an incentive")[294] and, in the *Critique of the Power of Judgment*, had traced aesthetic pleasure back to a feeling that is not empirically grounded (Schopenhauer openly objects to this last point).[295]

In any case, the implication of the text is that element of the individual which relates to the spheres of morality, religion and art – and which is illegitimately referred to a "feeling" – represents "the best in humankind [*das Beste im Menschen*]": it relates to "the rest of the world", and to everything else in man himself, like "a shadow in a dream" to "real, solid bodies" (the term "shadow"

---

[292] Schopenhauer 2012 [1813], § 49, pp. 192–193. F. X. Chenet (1997, pp. 120–124) indicates the passages of the dissertation that, in his opinion, would prove that the better consciousness constitutes "the secret reference point" of the text (1997, p. 120). The passages he quotes include some of those cited above, namely those taken from §§ 42, 49, 58 and 59. Alongside them, however, Chenet quotes others, taken from §§ 26, 46 and 52, which concern the subject of cognition and the intelligible character. Chenet posits a relationship between these figures and the better consciousness; however, it is not clear what kind of relationship he implies, since he cites the aforementioned places in the text without analyzing them.
[293] Cf. Schleiermacher 2003, pp. 18–54: 111–112. See also Schopenhauer's notes on Schleiermacher's lectures, MR 2, pp. 240–246.
[294] Cf. Kant 1996a, p. 201.
[295] Cf. Kant 1996a, pp. 12, 123–124; MR 2, pp. 319–320.

certainly recalls the Platonic allegory of the cave). Nevertheless, there is a "natural connection" between those realms and the content of the dissertation, because they both belong to the same "whole"; by virtue of this common belonging – which is also, necessarily, mutual complementarity – the content of the work concerning ethics and aesthetics would fully agree with the content of the dissertation (even though it would "read very differently").[296]

Immediately after presenting the relation between this future work and the dissertation as that between wakefulness and dream, Schopenhauer adds: "We will counter misinterpretation of this last expression in criticism of our account that is now coming to an end, with Seneca's words: 'to narrate dreams is for the wakeful'".[297] Only one who has woken up can know and recount their dreams as such, thus correctly and comprehensively circumscribing the scope of the dream. With this quotation from the *Letters to Lucilius*[298] – absent in the second edition – Schopenhauer means that only one who has 'awakened' to the contents of ethics and aesthetics can consider the empirical world in its entirety, together with its laws, as a dream, and thus grasp the "whole" of which the dissertation is only a *part* (otherwise, this work would count as the whole itself). This means that Schopenhauer, by explicitly mentioning this "whole" and determining the content of the dissertation as a "dream", implicitly presents himself as *already* 'awake'. Kantian criticism, which he intends to bring to perfection in "true criticism", is for him precisely "an attempt to awaken us from the dream of life".[299] In 1814, he would determine the object of empirical consciousness (i.e. the spatio-temporal world, the *Erscheinung*) as a mere "dream" in relation to the object of the better consciousness (the Platonic Idea; cf. *infra*, 11.10).[300]

Clearly, the "whole" mentioned by Schopenhauer, the parts of which consist of the dissertation and the planned work on the realms of ethics and aesthetics, is the system of "true criticism" insofar as it comprises both the treatment of empirical consciousness and the treatment of the better consciousness. In a note to fragment 96, specifically on the question of the presentation (*Aufzeigung*) and distinction (*Unterscheidung*) of the two consciousnesses, Schopenhauer notes: "N. B. Sheets L, M, N [corresponding to fragments 93–95] contain hardly anything but studies

---

[296] Schopenhauer 2012 [1813], § 46, p. 188.
[297] Schopenhauer 2012 [1813], § 58, p. 196.
[298] Schopenhauer quotes the original Latin: *"Somnia narrare vigilantis est"*. Cf. Seneca 1917, pp. 356–357: "only he who is awake can recount his dream".
[299] MR 1, n. 105, p. 78.
[300] Cf. MR 1, n. 234, p. 148.

and extracts for the purpose of a dissertation on the principle of sufficient reason – Grund."[301]

All these considerations lead to the conclusion that the writing mentioned in the first edition of the dissertation was meant to be about the better consciousness, understood as the keystone of the ethical and aesthetic spheres and as the necessary subjective correlate of the Platonic Idea. In the second edition, the passages in which Schopenhauer announces that work are missing; this fact makes it crystal clear that the text formerly announced is *not* the one that actually appeared between the two editions, namely *The World as Will and Representation*. One can see why Schopenhauer, introducing the second edition, states that the treatise on the principle of reason has only since – i.e. after the first edition – become the underpinnings (*Unterbau*) of his entire system (cf. *supra*, 9.3).[302]

In 1813, the dissertation was understood by Schopenhauer as the first part of his system of "true criticism"; following the building of the new system (the metaphysics of will), the dissertation took on a new function, namely that of underpinnings or basis (precisely) of the new system. The work on ethics and aesthetics announced in the first edition of the dissertation is therefore not *The World as Will and Representation*, but the one mentioned in the contemporary fragment 92 (cf. *supra*, 8.21): "In my hands and perhaps in my mind there is developed a work, a philosophy, which is to be ethics and metaphysics *in one* [...]. The work expands and the parts grow together slowly and by degrees like a child in the womb [...]".[303]

Schopenhauer never produced this work, but another one. How and why this happened will become clear in the next two chapters.

9.14 Conclusion: The Treatment of "Will" as a Link between the Discourse on Empirical Consciousness and the Discourse on Better Consciousness

At the beginning of the dissertation, Schopenhauer mentions "Plato, the divine, and the amazing Kant" as both recommending the principles of homogeneity

---

[301] MR 1, n. 96, p. 72.
[302] I depart from the interpretation proposed by Y. Kamata (1988, p. 129–133), according to which the dissertation of 1813 would sanction a total and complete strengthening of Schopenhauer's strict criticist position, leading to the abandonment of any discourse on the transcendent henceforth. On the contrary, the dissertation stands in clear continuity with the project of a "true criticism", which would include the treatment not only of sensible, but also and above all of supersensible cognition, thereby unifying Kant's position with Plato's. Cf. in this regard also Heimann 2013, p. 208.
[303] MR 1, n. 92, p. 59.

and specification.³⁰⁴ The actual guiding spirit of the dissertation, however, is Kant alone, since the text constitutes an attempt to continue and perfect Kant's investigation by exhaustively circumscribing the domain and laws of the *Erscheinung*. The "divine Plato", on the other hand, would have been the guiding spirit of the announced work on ethics and aesthetics – i.e., the realms of the better consciousness: the eternal world, the Ideas. Young Schopenhauer sought to construct a "true criticism", a philosophy that would integrate and reconcile the two opposing and (in his opinion) one-sided points of view of Plato and Kant (cf. *supra*, 2.13).

The point of transition from one discourse to the other is indicated by Schopenhauer himself at the end of § 46 of the dissertation:

> With the forms of the principle of sufficient reason previously presented [the first three], the knowledge of what is grounded [*Begründete*] was given along with the knowledge of the ground [*Grund*] as such, permitting a hypothetical judgement [in which, given the ground, the grounded is also given] that is certain. This is not the case with the present form: we are able to know motives, but we do not thereby know how the subject will subsequently act. [...] Here the rule-governed quality that applies to the other forms of the principle of sufficient reason ceases because in that case we remain in the world governed by laws, but here we encounter a completely different world, bordering on the realm of freedom. If I compare my presentation of the first three forms of our principle with moving images I had cast on the wall with a magic lantern, then now with the fourth form, a trap door has opened, one through which there enters a light before which some of my images disappear, and some become fragmented, unclear, and confused.³⁰⁵

While the dissertation is about empirical consciousness, the essay on ethics and aesthetics would have been about the better consciousness. It can be assumed that, in Schopenhauer's plans, the theme of the "will" was to link the two works because the will is what allows man to determine himself as empirical consciousness or as better consciousness, or to pass from one to the other; for Schopenhauer, man's "freedom" consists precisely in the possibility of choosing between the two consciousnesses (cf. *supra*, 8.18). In other words, it is possible that Schopenhauer thought to use the analysis of the faculty that allows "transition [*Uebergang*]"³⁰⁶ from the empirical consciousness to the better consciousness (and vice versa) as a link or stepping stone between the *discourse* on the former and the *discourse* on the latter.

---

304 Schopenhauer 2012 [1813], § 1, p. 7.
305 Schopenhauer 2012 [1813], § 46, pp. 189–190.
306 MR 1, n. 91, p. 58.

And yet, what was meant to serve as a simple nexus – the treatment of the will – was destined to become Schopenhauer's main focus in 1814, undermining and overshadowing the two discourses that it was only supposed to bring together.

10 The Manuscripts of 1814: The Development of the Doctrine of Intelligible Character. The Prodromes of the Metaphysics of Will

10.1 The Crucial Year

In May 1814, due to a serious quarrel with his mother, Schopenhauer left Weimar and settled in Dresden. Here he was to conceive and write, over the next four years, *The World as Will and Representation*.[1] In 1849, in a note to fragment 207 of the manuscripts (1814), he would note:

> These sheets written in Dresden in the years 1814–1818 show the fermentative process of my thinking, from which at the time my whole philosophy emerged, rising gradually like a beautiful landscape from the morning mist. Here it is worth noting that even in 1814 (in my 27th year) all the dogmas of my system, even the unimportant ones, were established.[2]

Indeed, the annotations of 1814 document the appearance and elaboration of the themes that would characterize his mature system: the "will-to-life [*Wille zum Leben*]" (understood as the "innermost essence" or "thing-in-itself" of all beings), the opposition between the "pure subject of cognition" and the "subject of willing", and the "negation of the will-to-life". As will be seen, the centrality assumed by the "will" is linked to the development of certain thematic cores of the dissertation, analyzed in the previous chapter (cf. *supra*, 9.5–9.14). After 1814, for Schopenhauer it was no longer a question of discovering or introducing new theoretical elements, but of radically expanding and developing those already acquired, bringing them together and reconciling them in a single, grand system.

In March 1818, when presenting *The World as Will and Representation* to the publisher Brockhaus, Schopenhauer himself wrote:

> That chain of thoughts, in its essence, was already in my head four years ago: but it took me four whole years to develop it and make it clear to myself through countless essays and studies, during which time I dealt exclusively with this and the related study of the works of others.[3]

---

[1] Cf. Safranski 1990, pp. 191–197; Siegler 1994.
[2] MR 1, fn. to n. 207, p. 122.
[3] Schopenhauer 1978a, pp. 29–30.

In 1814, the aforementioned "chain of thoughts" finally joined its final links, welding together in the metaphysics of will that forms the heart of Schopenhauer's mature system.

10.2 Identity and Difference between Religion and Philosophy. The Superiority of Philosophy

In 1812, Schopenhauer identified the peculiarity of religious discourse in the figurative (*bildlich*) attribution of empirical determinations to metempirical reality. In this way, and precisely through such determinations, religion posits an arbitrary – i.e., unfounded – "connexion" between "the world of semblance" and "the true world" (cf. *supra*, 7.2).[4] True philosophy, that is, "genuine criticism", has the task of separating and clearly distinguishing the two worlds through separation and distinction between the metempirical and the empirical human cognitive faculty; the philosopher is thus supposed to adopt a rigorous terminology that avoids both the figurative use (typical of religion) and the transcendent use (typical of dogmatic philosophy) of empirical determinations (cf. *supra*, 6.9; 7.3). As we have seen, however, in relation to this specific point, the theory of the better consciousness is inconsistent (cf. *supra*, 7.14; 8.20). In 1814 Schopenhauer would elaborate on these considerations.

> The essential nature of all *religion* generally means inevitably that it rejects and denies [*verleugne*] reason and science as Paul does, I Corinthians i and ii. For what concerns it as religion and what it preached is far above all reason [*hoch über aller Vernunft*]; and yet since it makes use of the concepts of this reason with boundless capriciousness, as is already evident from the way in which the faculty of reason is wrongly used for that which lies outside its limits, it can never agree and be at peace with that faculty. And yet religion was right in so far as it rejects reason and considers itself superior to this.[5]

On the one hand, religion rejects and denies reason in the name of what lies beyond it; on the other hand, in order to speak of what lies beyond reason, it uses reason itself (its "concepts"). Referring to this arbitrary use of concepts, Schopenhauer compares *The Apocalypse of St. John* to a composition of "hieroglyphics".[6] Just as the latter consist in the depiction of sensible determinations, so too the concepts of reason, being formed by abstraction from empirical objects (cf. *supra*, 9.3),

---

4 MR 1, n. 32, p. 20. Translation modified.
5 MR 1, n. 123, p. 84.
6 MR 1, n. 125, p. 85.

can contain nothing but empirical determinations, and are therefore necessarily inadequate to signify or denote the supersensible. It should be remembered that, in the same sense, Wackenroder had compared art to a "hieroglyphic language": in the work of art, in fact, "the spiritual and the sensuous are merged" (cf. *supra*, 2.5).

In order to ground the legitimacy of its own proceeding, religion should first of all show why reason ought to be rejected and denied: it should "criticize reason".[7]

> But [religion] will not agree to do this; on the contrary, it says that all this is null [*nichtig*] and that it feels no obligation to such nothingness [*Nichtigkeit*]. It recognizes no *must* [*Muß*], but simply denies it out of hand [...] But to a religious person who spoke thus one could quite rightly answer: However, you do not ignore eating, drinking, breathing and sleeping, but give these their due, much as they are to be found in the world of nothingness [*Welt der Nichtigkeit*]. Yet if the faculty of reason is indeed no more null [*nichtiger*] than these, why do you not also want to do justice to this? Why do you simply want to consider yourself superior to it? Indeed for convenience and spiritual satisfaction.

And here is where *philosophy* in the last resort wins its case against *religion*.[8]

Philosophy is superior to religion because it demonstrates (grounds) reason's inability to cognize the supersensible, thus realizing, precisely, a 'critique of reason'. But this presupposes that philosophy and religion have the same content: the supersensible, which "is far above all reason". In fragment 188, Schopenhauer states unequivocally that "the gospels" are "in the main [*in der Hauptsache*] quite true [*ganz wahr*]".[9] The difference between religion and philosophy is also found with respect to this identity of content (i.e. with respect to that "main") – which, for Schopenhauer, goes to the advantage of philosophy.

Now, what lies "far above all reason", for Schopenhauer, is the better consciousness;[10] it is precisely the latter that constitutes the content of both philosophy and religion (cf. *supra*, 8.6). Consequently, the true and ultimate critique of reason can only be realized within the theory of the better consciousness; it is in relation to the better consciousness (i.e. as opposed to it) that the philosopher can truly and definitively show why reason – which, together with the understanding and sensibility, constitutes empirical consciousness[11] – is completely incapable of cognizing the supersensible.

---

7 MR 1, n. 123, p. 84.
8 MR 1, pp. 84–85. Translation modified.
9 MR 1, n. 188, p. 112.
10 MR 1, n. 85, p. 46.
11 Cf. MR 1, n. 234, pp. 147–148.

The dissertation of 1813 partially achieved this goal, insofar as it offers an exhaustive treatment of empirical consciousness (cf. *supra*, 9.13). But this is only the first part of Schopenhauer's theoretical project: "genuine criticism" must also include a comprehensive and direct treatment of the better consciousness.

10.3 "The Main Problem of Philosophy": The Origin of Empirical Consciousness

The main problem of philosophy brings every *dogmatics* to one of the three following transcendent statements.

(1) We spirits who have no rest [*Ruhe*] (κατάπαυσις, Hebrews iv, 1) can also never again find rest (Spinoza, Schelling in the World Soul and Ideas on Natural Philosophy) –

(2) We spirits who have no rest have only *lost* it and can find it again (all systems of emanation; Schelling in Philosophy and Religion) –

(3) We spirits who have no rest, have never yet had it, have come into existence and shall attain to it (all theories of creation, rational theism, Schelling on human freedom).[12]

In the Greek version of the Old Testament, the verb καταπαύω indicates God's rest at the end of Creation, on the seventh day (Gen 2:2).[13] The derived noun, κατάπαυσις, is referred in the Psalms to the promised land, i.e. the resting place that God has prepared for his people (cf. Ps 95 (94):11).[14]

Based on these two precedents,[15] the author of the *Epistle to the Hebrews* uses the term κατάπαυσις in a spiritualized sense, referring to the "sabbath" of eternal bliss in God's dwelling, reserved for the chosen ones (Heb 4:1–10). Those who do not conform to the Word shall be excluded from this final rest, just as many Jews were excluded, because of their unbelief, from entering Palestine (Heb 4:8–11). Luther translates κατάπαυσις as *Ruge* (an archaic form of *Ruhe*).[16]

In Schopenhauer's fragment, "the main problem of philosophy" is implicitly placed in relation to the absence of rest, κατάπαυσις, mentioned by the author of the *Epistle to the Hebrews*. Dogmatism seeks to explain how this restlessness or-

---

12 MR 1, n. 126, pp. 85–86. Translation modified.
13 Cf. Swete 1887, p. 3.
14 Swete 1896, p. 342.
15 In fact, two terms with a different root are used in the Hebrew version; however, the Septuagint renders them through two related Greek terms; cf. Brown, Fitzmyer and Murphy 1990. The author of the *Epistle to the Hebrews* therefore refers directly to the Greek text.
16 Cf. Luther 1883–2009, vol. 7, p. 352. Cf. also the entry "Ruhe" in Weigand 1909–1910^5, vol. 2, p. 620.

iginated, and how (and whether) one can get out of it; but, in doing so, according to Schopenhauer, it falls into "transcendent statements" – precisely, into "systems of emanation" and "theories of creation". This is as far as the explicit dimension of the text goes.

That emanatism and creationism are attempts to solve "the main problem of philosophy [*Das Hauptproblem der Philosophie*]" evidently means that the latter concerns the origin of the world (of finite things). It is therefore understandable why Schelling's works *Philosophy and Religion* and *Philosophical Investigations into the Essence of Human Freedom and Matters Connected Therewith* constitute the primary polemical reference point of the fragment itself (cf. *supra*, 6.8; 9.10). In his *Philosophical Letters on Dogmatism and Criticism*, Schelling had stated that "The main task [*Hauptgeschäft*] of all philosophy consists of solving the problem of the existence of the world" and "the very transition from the nonfinite to the finite is the problem of *all* philosophy [*das Problem* aller *Philosophie*]".[17]

Schopenhauer assumes – like the author of the *Epistle to the Hebrews* – that the specific locus of the *absence of rest* is precisely the *world*; so that to look into the origin of the former is *eo ipso* to look into the origin of the latter. By explicitly mentioning man's restlessness (his constitutive and essential unhappiness), unlike Schelling, Schopenhauer shows that he is concerned with the problem of the origin of the world more from an ethical or 'practical' perspective than from a purely theoretical or speculative one.

Since, given the identity between "being" and "being cognized", this sensible, empirical world is none other than our consciousness of it ("this very world [...] i.e. our empirical, sensible and rational consciousness in space and time"),[18] then the problem of the origin of the world ultimately coincides with the problem of the origin of empirical consciousness. Indeed, the latter is precisely the locus of unhappiness and torment (as opposed, also in this respect, to the better consciousness, which is "the source of all true happiness").[19] In fragment 189 Schopenhauer identifies the better consciousness even more explicitly with participation in the "*peace of God*"[20] – which, in his intentions, probably coincides with the κατάπαυσις mentioned in the *Epistle to the Hebrews*.

Now, the question about the origin of empirical consciousness concerns the relationship between the better consciousness and empirical consciousness, i.e. the problem of how we ever got from the exclusive existence of the former to the existence, alongside it, of the latter – what religion expresses mythically through the

---

17 Schelling 1980, p. 177 (Seventh Letter).
18 MR 1, n. 79, p. 43. Translation modified.
19 MR 1, n. 128, p. 86.
20 MR 1, n. 189, p. 113.

dogma of original sin (cf. *supra*, 8.19). But then *this* is, properly speaking, the real "main problem of philosophy", which the philosopher must try to solve in strictly non-mythical terms.

10.4 The "Fall of Adam" and the "Expiatory Death of Jesus": Original Sin and Redemption

In the *Epistle to the Romans* it is said that, "just as sin entered the world through one man", Adam, "and death through sin" (whereby "death came to all people, because all sinned" in Adam and through Adam), "so also one righteous act", carried out by Jesus, "resulted in justification and life for all people" (Rom 5:12–18). "For the wages of sin is death, but the gift of God is eternal life in Christ" (Rom 6:23).

Possibly with reference to these passages from the New Testament, in fragment 99 Schopenhauer states that "with the empirical consciousness we necessarily have not only sinfulness, but also all the evils that follow from this kingdom of error, chance, wickedness and folly, and finally death", so that "the Bible and Christianity through the fall of man rightly introduce into the world death and the troubles and miseries of life".[21] In any case, the verses of *Romans* just quoted are expressly indicated at the end (and then in a footnote) of fragment 145:

> Romans V, 12–21
>
> It is a superlative, exceedingly profound doctrine of *Christianity*, true in the strictest sense, that through the *fall of Adam* the curse has struck us all, sin has come into the world [...] and that, on the other hand, through the *expiatory death of Jesus* we are all purged from guilt, the world is redeemed, guilt is wiped out [...] so that we all participate in the sin of the former and in the expiatory death of the latter.[22]

In fact, Adam and Jesus express, in universal form, the two natures that constitute every human being as such, i.e. the two sides of "the Platonic Idea of Man", which is "related to the succession of human beings as eternity in itself is [related] to eternity that is stretched and extended into time".[23]

> [...] if we consider the Platonic Idea of *Man*, we see that Adam's fall expresses the final, animal and sinful nature of man [...]. On the other hand, the conduct, teaching and death of Jesus Christ express the eternal supernatural side, freedom, the redemption of man [...].

---

21 MR 1, n. 99, p. 74.
22 MR 1, n. 145, p. 93. Translation modified.
23 MR 1, n. 145, p. 94.

> Now whoever is a human being is as such not only Adam but also Jesus; he can consider himself [*kann sich ... betrachten*] as the former but also as the latter. According as he considers himself (not in reflection but in being that is expressed through actions), he is damned [*verdammt*] and doomed to death, or he is redeemed [*erlöst*] and in eternal life.[24]

According to the *Epistle to the Romans*, "all have sinned and fall short of the glory of God, and all are justified freely by his grace through the redemption that came by Christ Jesus" (Rom 3:23–24). Also in the *First Letter to the Corinthians* (to which Schopenhauer refers in a footnote to the same fragment) it is written: "The sting of death is sin". "For as in Adam all die, so in Christ all will be made alive" (1 Co 15:22): Christ "has become for us wisdom [σοφία] from God – that is, our righteousness, holiness and redemption [ἀπολύτρωσις]" (1 Co 1:30).

The Idea of man, according to Schopenhauer, consists of two opposite and incompatible determinations, represented by Adam and Jesus; it is therefore inherently contradictory. But this contradiction is nothing but the original duplicity of the human being: Adam and Jesus respectively correspond, in fact, to the finite (temporal) and eternal nature of man.

Every individual "can consider himself" as Adam or as Jesus, in the same way that, according to fragment 72 from 1813, he "*can at any moment consider himself as a sensible, a temporal, or even as an eternal being*".[25] Consistent with his earlier reflections, Schopenhauer assumes that man is essentially the synthesis of two completely opposite elements: the possibility of considering oneself as one or the other – the choice of *which* of the two to be – is not to be referred to the human individual in his entirety, but only to a mysterious indeterminate residue in him, which can be either one or the other term because, outside or 'before' this act of identification, he is neither one nor the other (cf. *supra*, 8.3, 8.4 and 8.11).

The act of identification with one of the two natures does not, however, happen once and for all: to the extent that he coincides with that indeterminate residue, man is not always Adam or always Jesus, but, "according as he considers himself" and *thus* acts ("not in reflection but in being [*Seyn*] that is expressed [*sich ... ausspricht*] through actions"), he determines himself as one or the other term, and is thus either damned or redeemed. Because of this original duplicity, "two voices speak" in man "by turns";[26] it is therefore "an impossible and essentially self-contradictory demand of almost all philosophers that man should attain [in life] to *an inner unity of his true nature, a harmony with himself*".[27] Man's being is not uni-

---

24 MR 1, n. 145, p. 94.
25 MR 1, n. 72, p. 39. Translation modified.
26 MR 1, n. 165, p. 101.
27 MR 1, n. 209, p. 123.

tary, but irremediably and tragically dual, because it is the union – impossible, yet real – of two mutually contradictory determinations.

10.5 The Better Consciousness as the "Nothing" and "Annihilation" of the Empirical Consciousness. The Extinction of the Self

What is in time is the *nothing* of what is not in time, and vice versa. Since empirical consciousness and better consciousness respectively represent man's temporal and eternal being, each is the nothing of the other. What befits man as a temporal being – sensuous pleasure – does not suit him as an eternal being, and vice versa: what befits man as an eternal being – asceticism – does not suit him as a temporal being (cf. *supra*, 8.2 – 8.3).

Taking up these considerations, Schopenhauer writes that the *better consciousness* is for the *empirical consciousness* total "decline, death and annihilation [*Vernichtung*]"; "consolation" and "happiness", of which the former is the "source", cannot therefore agree with the latter, just as a noun cannot agree with a predicate that contradicts it.[28] Physical death, which is destruction for the empirical consciousness, is highly desirable from the point of view of the better consciousness.[29]

In Plato's *Gorgias*, quoting Euripides, Socrates exclaims: "Who knows if to live is to be dead, / And to be dead, to live?"[30] Schelling, too, had written that the "supreme moment of being", which manifests itself in intellectual intuition, "is, for us, transition to not-being, the moment of annihilation", and for this reason "we awaken from intellectual intuition as from a state of death" (*supra*, 8.2).[31]

> The *better consciousness* is separated from the *empirical* by a boundary without width, by a *mathematical line*. Often we do not want to see this and imagine rather that it is a *physical* boundary over which we can wander midway between the two territories and from which we can look at both. In other words, we want to be worthy of heaven and at the same time pick the flowers of this earth. But it will not work, for as we set foot in the one sphere, to the same extent have we deserted and disowned [*verleugnet*] the other. For every occasion it is not a case of reconciling and uniting, but only of choosing.[32]

---

28 MR 1, n. 128, p. 86. Translation modified.
29 MR 1, n. 99, pp. 73 – 74.
30 Plato, *Gorgias*, 492e, Plato 1914 ff., vol. 3, pp. 414 – 415.
31 Schelling 1980, p. 185 (Eighth Letter).
32 MR 1, n. 204, p. 120.

Everything the better consciousness is, the empirical consciousness is not, and vice versa. There is no possibility of dialectical transition between one and the other; it is a tragic and radical *aut-aut:* "to be faithful to that better consciousness, we must renounce and break away from this empirical consciousness. Self-mortification [*Selbstertödtung*]".[33] The mark of perfection attained by the philosopher and the saint is precisely that "they do not preserve any part of empirical consciousness", in the sense that they completely *separate* the ('their') better consciousness from it – the former "theoretically", the latter "practically".[34]

In 1812 Schopenhauer had written that in order to fulfill the categorical imperative it is necessary to realize the annihilation (*Vernichtung*) of one's own will, i.e. one's individuality (cf. *supra*, 7.9).[35] In 1813, *asceticism* was defined as the intentional negation (*Negation*) of what in us is in time – a true denial (*Verleugnung*) and rejection (*Zurückweisung*) of all temporality as such.[36] Recall that the term *Verleugnung*, in the pietist sphere, indicated the self-denial required by Christ (Mt 16:24; cf. *supra*, 8.7).

Now, the term *Selbstertödtung* in fragment 128 is to be understood in essential continuity with these reflections: not as suicide (already expressly rejected by Schopenhauer: cf. *supra*, 7.10), but as inner *Selbstverleugnung* or *Selbstvernichtung*. It is always and again a matter of repudiating the self as empirical consciousness with the consequent self-determination as better consciousness: it is not about killing oneself, but, much more radically, the 'root' of the self. Here too, then, what is at stake is the free and decisive act of will by which the individual chooses whether to be empirical consciousness or better consciousness (cf. *supra*, 7.11).

In the *Geheime Geschichte des Philosophen Peregrinus Proteus* (History of the philosopher Peregrinus Proteus), Wieland uses the term *Ertödtung* (which the Grimm Dictionary reports as equivalent to the Latin *exstinctio*)[37] in a similar way: "only through the extinction [*Ertödtung*] of the bestial man is the spiritual man born to life".[38] This extinction concerns "all sensible inclinations and [all] selfish passions"; in order to realize this, man must turn against himself and "regard this self [*dieses Selbst*] as the most dangerous, cunning and stubborn of all enemies".[39] Schopenhauer owned this work[40] (he also had the opportunity to meet Wieland: cf. *supra*, 2.12).

---

33 MR 1, n. 128, p. 86.
34 MR 1, n. 249, p. 162.
35 Cf. MR 2, pp. 402–403.
36 MR 1, n. 72, p. 40.
37 Cf. J. Grimm and W. Grimm 1854–1971, vol. 3, pp. 1030–1031.
38 Cf. Wieland 1839–1840, vol. 16, p. 181.
39 Wieland 1839–1840, vol. 16, p. 234.
40 Cf. HN V, p. 439.

10.6 "Willing-Happiness Is the Opposite of Willing-Life". Life in Time as a "Practical Error"

Comparing bliss (*Glückseligkeit*) to a piece of music, Schopenhauer wrote that life is akin to the "confusion of sounds" and "fleeting introductions" that come from orchestra rehearsals; death, instead, is like the actual execution of the work.[41] The locus of true blessedness is death – which, on the other hand, represents the annihilation of empirical consciousness and the affirmation of the better consciousness (cf. *supra*, 8.11). This implies that the better consciousness is the metaphysical 'locus' of bliss, "the source of all true happiness [*Seeligkeit*]".[42] The rare joyful moments of life – the "confusion of sounds" and "fleeting introductions" of the orchestra – are those in which the individual is determined as the better consciousness.[43]

All of this clearly entails that life is a condition of constitutive unhappiness. As early as 1808–1809, Schopenhauer had written: "If we take out of life the *few* [italics mine] moments of religion, art and pure love, what is left except a number of trivial thoughts?"[44] The better consciousness, in fact, covers precisely the areas of "religion, art and pure love".

> It could be said that all our *sinfulness* is nothing but the fundamental error of *trying to measure eternity through time*, is, so to speak, a constant attempt at *squaring the circle*. For it aims solely at prolonging temporal existence partly in the individual (greed, avarice, hatred), and partly in the species (sex drive). To will and to go on willing temporal existence is life [*Zeitliches Daseyn wollen und immerfort wollen ist Leben*].[45]

Once obtained, the objects of lust, greed and sex drive – which can also lead individuals to competition and, therefore, to mutual enmity – do not at all extinguish said lust, greed and sex drive, unlike what their pursuer thinks. Yet the latter seeks them precisely because he believes they would.

Now, "to go on willing temporal existence", for Schopenhauer, is based on the "fundamental error [*Grundirrthum*] of *trying to measure eternity through time*", that is, as the fragment continues, of deluding ourselves (*wähnen*) that we can "catch through succession" (i.e., in time) "that which can be grasped only at one

---

41 MR 1, n. 130, p. 88.
42 MR 1, n. 128, p. 86. Translation modified.
43 Cf. also MR 1, n. 124, p. 85. "Just as the chord of the seventh requires the next full chord, as red demands green and even produces this in the eye, so does every *tragedy* call for another world which can always be given to us only indirectly, here through such a demand."
44 MR 1, n. 12 [viii], p. 9.
45 MR 1, n. 143, p. 92. Translation modified.

stroke by stepping over from time into eternity, from the empirical into the better consciousness".[46]

Every individual, after all, seeks and desires the bliss that only the better consciousness can offer. Wanting to live is like wanting to square the circle, because it means (unconsciously) seeking what belongs to the better consciousness – happiness or bliss – in the domain that is absolutely opposite to it: that of temporality.

> People imagine and insist that *death is not death*, but the beginning of a new *life*. This, however, is simply the greatest of all errors and the abstract expression of that fundamental error, that practical error [*praktischen Irrthum*] (sin, original sin) which is life itself. They will not give up life and they even speak of a happy life, which is a *contradictio in adjecto*. Willing-happiness [*Seeligkeit-wollen*] is the opposite [*das Gegentheil*] of willing-life [*Leben-wollen*].[47]

That willing-happiness is the opposite of willing-life means that – if we remove the equal term "willing" from the two components of the equation – *happiness* is the *opposite of life*. The concept of "happy life" is thus a contradiction (*contradictio in adjecto*). The text suggests that the "practical error" or "original sin" of willing-life is based on the *theoretical* error of identifying life itself with (the possibility of) happiness. In other words, it seems that it is only by virtue of this fallacious identification that life is willed at all.

10.7 Intelligible Character, Temporal Existence and the Body: The Shadow of Schelling. The 'Deduction' of an Individual and Metaphysical "Willing-Life"

Precisely in relation to the problem of the origin of life in time and the sin connected with it, Schopenhauer elaborated the concept of the individual's metaphysical willing-life (*Lebenwollen*). This concept is implicit in fragment 143: "To will and to go on willing temporal existence is life."[48] Since temporal existence is nothing other than life, this statement means: "to will and to go on willing is life itself"; that is, *living is willing to live*.

However, life is essentially pain; willing happiness is therefore equivalent to willing the opposite of life in time, namely the better consciousness. This implies that *willing the better consciousness* is the *opposite of willing-life*:

---

46 MR 1, n. 143, p. 92.
47 MR 1, n. 146, pp. 94–95. Translation modified.
48 MR 1, n. 143, p. 92.

10.7 Intelligible Character, Temporal Existence and the Body

> We must all aspire to the light, to virtue, to the holy spirit, to the *better consciousness;* [...] Only there are *two ways*. Either there arises from within freely and of itself the better will [*der bessre Wille*]; we voluntarily abandon the willing-life [*Lebenwollen*] [...] and are redeemed.
>
> Or we follow the path of darkness, the vehement urge of the willing-life; we go ever more deeply into vice and sin,[...] until gradually the fury of life turns against itself. We become aware of what the path is that we have chosen [*gewählt*], what kind of a world we have willed [*gewollt*], until through torment, terror and horror we come to ourselves and enter into ourselves, and from the pain the better cognition [*die bessre Erkenntniß*] is born.[49]

Man *has willed, has chosen* the world and life in time; the better will in him is the opposite of this willing-life, because it is the will of eternity (objective genitive; cf. *supra*, 7.11; *infra*, 10.11). It is clear that redemption presupposes a *sin* from which to be redeemed; it is therefore on the meaning of that present perfect ("we have willed") that one must focus the greatest attention.

> *Man does not change*, and hence his *moral character* remains the same positively for the whole of his life. [...] Therefore one asks what life is supposed to be. What is the purpose of the farce in which everything essential is irrevocably fixed and enacted? The purpose is that man may cognize himself, may see what it is that he wills to be [*was es sei das er seyn will*], has willed [*gewollt hat*], hence wills [*also will*] and therefore is [*und darum ist*] [...].[50]

Man (every human being) *is* what he "wills" and "has willed" to be; moreover, the term *darum* means that he is what he is, *'because'* he wills and has willed to be it. "Life is to man, that is to the will, precisely what chemical reagents are to the body. Only in these is there revealed [*offenbart sich*] what it [the body] is, and it is only to the extent that it reveals itself. Life is the *intelligible character's* becoming visible [*Sichtbarwerden*]."[51]

Given that life is for man to "see what it is that he wills to be, has willed, hence wills and therefore is", and given that life is "the intelligible character's becoming visible", then *what man is, wills and has willed to be is the intelligible character itself* (as that which becomes visible in life).

But this means that the individual's whole life is the emergence, the appearance of that character – including the individual's own *body*, understood as the 'vehicle' of his temporal existence.[52] According to Schopenhauer, in fact, there is an

---

49 MR 1, n. 158, p. 98. Translation modified.
50 MR 1, n. 159, p. 99. Translation modified.
51 MR 1, n. 159, p. 99.
52 The identity between man's spatio-temporal being and the body is the implication of fragment 121 (cf. MR 1, n. 121, p. 84).

essential "harmony (wholly beyond the reach of our reasoning faculty) between the corporeity and the intelligible character of every living being".[53] From being the "immediate object of willing" (of *temporal* acts of the will),[54] as it is defined in the dissertation, the body thus becomes, in 1814, the visibility or manifestation of the will as intelligible character.

> *The body* (corporeal man) [Der Leib (*der körperliche Mensch*)] *is nothing but the will that has become visible* [der sichtbar gewordene Wille]. The form of all objects is time. The will itself, the intelligible character, stands firm and is not in time, otherwise it itself would be only visibility, not that which has become visible. Therefore man does not change; he does not become better or worse in life. But the life of man is only the development [*die Entwickelung*], so to speak the setting asunder [*Auseinandersetzung*], of the will in time [*in der Zeit*]. [...]. In all the evil that others inflict on us, we suffer only that which in other circumstances we ourselves would be capable of doing, the fruits of our own sinfulness that is assumed with the body. [...] Only for each one of us can life be the mirror of his own sinfulness, of his own will, of the willing-life. Each one is culpable not for what he does, but for what he is capable of doing; and for this he rightly suffers all the evils that are possible in the world.[55]

It is remarkable that here the will is explicitly identified with the intelligible character ("The will itself, the intelligible character, [...]"). According to the 1813 dissertation, the intelligible character is "a universal act of will lying outside of time"; all of the subject's decisions and actions, i.e. all of his individual and temporal acts of will, are the appearance (*Erscheinung*) of this original and timeless act of will (cf. *supra*, 9.8). In the fragment just quoted, Schopenhauer similarly states that "The will itself, the intelligible character [...] is not in time".

Now, however, Schopenhauer argues that the intelligible character manifests itself not only in the individual's actions, but in his entire life. This conception of intelligible character is evidently much broader than the Kantian notion (to which Schopenhauer explicitly refers in the dissertation). For Kant, in fact, the intelligible character exclusively concerns (precisely) the intelligible causality of the acting subject; that is, it manifests itself only in what he *does* (cf. *supra*, 9.9). According to the fragments just quoted, on the other hand, the intelligible character of the individual is revealed not only in everything he does, but also in everything he *undergoes* ("the evil that others inflict on us"), thus in life in its entirety. Precisely for this reason life is only a "farce, in which everything essential is irrevocably fixed and enacted".

---

53 MR 1, n. 188, p. 113.
54 Schopenhauer 2012 [1813], § 45, p. 186.
55 MR 1, n. 191, p. 115. Translation modified.

10.7 Intelligible Character, Temporal Existence and the Body — 343

These statements by Schopenhauer cannot be justified by or based on the doctrine of character set out in the dissertation. There, the intelligible character was deduced from the (empirically observable) constancy of the empirical character of each individual and the feeling of responsibility inherent in us all; this dual empirical grounding made the metaphysical doctrine of the intelligible character legitimate from the standpoint of criticism (cf. *supra*, 9.8 and 9.12). This ground, however, does not justify what Schopenhauer would argue in 1814, namely that "life is the *intelligible character's* becoming visible" and that "*the body* (corporeal man) *is nothing but the will that has become visible*".[56] These developments of the doctrine of the intelligible character thus appear to have no real foundation.

In fact, they indicate once more the effect of Schelling's influence (cf. *supra*, 9.11). In the *Philosophical Investigations into Human Freedom*, Schelling had written that "The act, whereby his [man's] life is determined in time, does not itself belong to time but rather to eternity: it also does not temporally precede life but goes through time (unhampered by it) as an act which is eternal by nature."[57] Through that act, by which man has freely and once and for all decided on his "intelligible being", "even the type and constitution of his [man's] corporeal formation [*seiner Corporisation*] is determined".[58]

Schopenhauer can affirm that human life and the human body are the "visibility" – or appearance, or "mirror" – of the intelligible character (i.e. that there is a mysterious "harmony" between the latter and the individual's "corporeity [*Korporisation*]"), only insofar as he also assumes that, in the timeless act of will in which the intelligible character consists, the individual has decided and determined not only his own actions, but his whole life, i.e. his temporal existence *as a whole*.[59] That Schopenhauer understood the Kantian doctrine of the intelligible character in this way from the outset – i.e. through the mediation of Schelling's thought – is clear from two annotations from the years 1811/1812.

Commenting on the *Philosophical Investigations into the Essence of Human Freedom*, Schopenhauer found agreement between Schelling's doctrine of intelligi-

---

56 This circumstance means that the doctrine of character set out in the manuscripts cannot be traced back to purely physiognomic or phenomenological grounds. On characterology and metaphysics in Schopenhauer, cf. Gurisatti 2001, p. 89. Cf. also Gurisatti 2002.
57 Schelling 2006, p. 51.
58 Schelling 2006, p. 52.
59 M. Koßler has rightly pointed out that the position of this mirror-image relationship between will (intelligible character) and life in the manuscripts constitutes a necessary precondition for the construction of the metaphysics of will (2011a, pp. 445–449). Here I want to show that this element (additional to the doctrine of the intelligible character set out in the dissertation) comes from Schelling.

ble being and the Platonic myth of Er, set forth in the *Republic:* here, in fact, Plato "allows everyone to choose [*wählen*] his own life".[60] And yet, when commenting on this very passage in the *Republic*, Schopenhauer wrote that it agrees rather with the Kantian doctrine of the intelligible character, concerning precisely the "choice [*Wahl*] of life".[61] This clearly shows that Schopenhauer identified the content of Schelling's treatise with Kantian thought – in accordance with what he stated in the 1813 dissertation: Schelling would provide nothing more than "a very valuable, illustrative exposition" of Kant's theory (cf. *supra*, 9.8).[62] With this background in mind, it is clear in what sense Schopenhauer states in fragment 87 (using a Schellingean expression) that the extratemporal character is for man the ground of his existence, *Grund seiner Existenz* (cf. *supra*, 8.10).[63]

In the *Prize Essay On the Freedom of the Will*, written many years later, Schopenhauer would also state: "An elucidatory paraphrase of the highly important doctrine of Kant's [...], concerning the intelligible and empirical character, has been provided by *Schelling*".[64] There, however, he would go so far as to accuse Schelling of plagiarism.[65]

Schopenhauer does not justify the (infinite) leap from invisibility to visibility (i.e. the 'becoming' visible of that which is outside time), but assumes that the act of will in which the intelligible character consists necessarily involves life, i.e., existence in time (with the body as the visibility of will "are necessarily assumed [*gesetzt*] objects and the law of causality").[66] This leap, however, is described through expressions that seem to involve a transcendent use of the principle of reason. In fact, to say that *"the body [...] is nothing but the will that has become visible"* – namely that "Life is the *intelligible character's* becoming visible" – means to refer becoming to that which, being outside time, is also necessarily outside the principle of reason. But this becoming visible (*sichtbar werden*) ultimately means appearing (*erscheinen*); here too, then, as in the relation of necessary consequentiality (affirmed in the dissertation) between intelligible character and individual acts of will, the decisive question concerns the meaning of *erscheinen* (i.e. of the predicate "being the appearance of"), which Schopenhauer presupposes and uses, but does not define (cf. *supra*, 9.8; *infra*, 12.4).

---

60 MR 2, p. 353.
61 MR 2, p. 437.
62 Cf. Schopenhauer 2012 [1813], § 46, p. 188.
63 MR 1, n. 87, p. 53.
64 A. Schopenhauer, *Prize Essay on the Freedom of the Will*, in Schopenhauer 2009, p. 97.
65 Schopenhauer 2009, p. 98.
66 MR 1, n. 191, p. 115 (footnote).

In any case, the intelligible character (the act of will in which it consists) coincides here with willing-life – where "life" means not so much, or not only, existence in time in general, but also and primarily a specific and unrepeatable existence, peculiar to a single individual. This identity between the intelligible character and willing-life is evident from the fact that, for Schopenhauer, the life of every individual is, on the one hand, the manifestation or "the appearance [*Erscheinung*] of willing",[67] and on the other, "the *intelligible character's* becoming visible".[68] The individual's willing-life and "intelligible character" coincide insofar as both are what becomes visible – that is, manifested or phenomenalized – in the life of the individual himself.

Schopenhauer thus seems to derive the concept of an individual and metaphysical willing-life (*Lebenwollen*) by combining the premise that man essentially exists in time (he is a "temporal being", as stated in fragment 72) and the premise, of Schellingean origin, that man is the 'result' or 'outcome' of his own act of will (man is what "he wills to be, has willed, hence wills and *therefore* [italics mine] is"). If man has determined himself as existing in time and space – that is, has 'determined' himself *simpliciter* – through an act of will, then the latter is, evidently, a will to exist in time, a will-to-life.

10.8 The Pure Subject as the Antithesis of Will and Body. *Kshetra* and *Kshetrajna*

At the end of fragment 191, implying the identity between will and intelligible character, Schopenhauer writes:

> But the *subject* is not the will; it is that which merely cognizes [*das bloß Erkennende*], that *to which* the will, the body [*Leib*] and the whole of life become visible, the calm and pure spectator of that entire tragedy of life who lies outside time; that to which the cognition of its own will is to be taught, such instruction being the whole purpose of life. Hence the serenity and bliss of all pure objectivity, i. e. of the state where not one's own will and body are the object, but the indirect objects, the scene of that tragedy; of the state where for a time we are set free from willing, from sinful impulse and again become conscious of ourselves [*wieder... uns unsrer bewußt werden*] as the pure, extratemporal and calm subject [*als das reine außerzeitliche ruhige Subjekt*]. Hence the pleasure of all pure contemplation, of the beauties of nature, of landscape painting, the emotional side of still life.[69]

---

67 MR 1, n. 213, p. 130. Translation modified.
68 MR 1, n. 159, p. 99.
69 MR 1, n. 191, p. 116. Translation modified.

The "subject" is not the will (the intelligible character), nor is it the body or life, which are the appearance of the will itself. Rather, the subject is that which simply *cognizes* all this, that to which all this becomes visible.

It is remarkable that liberation from will coincides for the individual with becoming *again* conscious of himself "as the pure, extratemporal and calm subject". This seems to betray a significant implication of the text, for it entails that the 'state' of the pure subject is what the individual was 'before' he began to exist in time (before becoming an "individual"), but also, at the same time, what he ought to "again [*wieder*]" become by repudiating his own will. The pure subject would thus coincide with man's still uncontaminated nature, 'prior' (in the transcendental sense) to the timeless act of will which generated existence in time as its appearance.

The text also suggests that the pure subject is the *author* of that act of will; it is he, in fact, who must receive the παίδευσις of life (cf. *supra*, 1.5): "the subject […] is that which merely cognizes, that to which the cognition of *its own* [italics mine] will is to be taught, such instruction being the whole purpose of life". Despite being "that which merely cognizes" (and does not will), the *will* on which he is instructed by life is *his own* – which means that life in time, together with all that it implies, is nothing but the manifestation of his own will.[70]

Schopenhauer would never determine 'who' or 'what' is, properly speaking, the author of the original act of will in which intelligible character consists; his mature system would preserve a fundamental ambivalence in this regard.[71] In any case, the "subject" mentioned in fragment 191 was not yet what in *The World as Will and Representation* would be called the "pure subject of cognition". The identification of these two terms would generate a serious anachronism; I shall elaborate on this point later, indicating the specific theoretical reason why Schopenhauer would be forced to modify the concept of the pure subject (cf. *infra*, 11.11).

In fragment 191, "subject" is to be understood as man himself, in his truest and innermost essence: that which he has always been 'above' and 'beyond' his existence in time – in this sense, something very akin to what Schopenhauer calls "better consciousness". The latter, like the pure subject, is also situated outside time, has a purely cognitive relationship with the empirical world (cf. *supra*, 8.13), is opposed to willing-life (cf. *supra*, 10.6) and represents what man, in order to redeem himself, must 'again' become, i.e. go back to being *exclusively* (cf. *supra*, 8.6–8.8,

---

[70] Assuming perhaps such a notion of subject (evidently not reducible to Kant's "transcendental apperception"), in his dissertation Schopenhauer had stated in passing that the subject of cognition is, like the subject of willing, in itself uncognizable (*unerkennbar*) and outside of time (*außer der Zeit liegend*). Cf. Schopenhauer 2012 [1813], § 46, p. 187.
[71] Cf. Birnbacher 2009, pp. 97–99.

8.11). Note also that, with reference to the figure of the pure subject, Schopenhauer uses the expression *sich bewußt werden als* ... (man must "become conscious of himself as ...") – the same expression that, in fragments 66 (cf. *supra*, 8.3) and 189, is referred to the individual's extratemporal nature and better consciousness.[72]

However, there are further elements to take into consideration. In the winter of 1813–1814, in Weimar, Schopenhauer often visited the orientalist Friedrich Majer (Herder's pupil), who initiated him to the study of ancient Indian texts.[73] On 4 December 1813, Schopenhauer borrowed two volumes of the *Asiatisches Magazin* from the Weimar library, in the first of which he found an annotated German translation of the *Bhagavad Gita* redacted by Majer himself.[74] This work belongs to the vast epic poem *Mahabharata* and reports the speech in which Sri Krishna, *avatar* of Vishnu, revealed supreme wisdom to his disciple and cousin Arjuna. The symbolism of this text, whose title means "Song of the Blessed One", is extremely complex; its multiple levels of meaning (also implied by the etymology of the names of the numerous characters who recur in it) cannot even be mentioned here.[75]

What is worth noting, for our purposes, is that in Chapter XIII, Krishna reveals to Arjuna the difference between the body (*Kshetra*) – the 'field' of action of the devotee engaged on the spiritual path – and the Knower of the body itself (*Kshetrajna*), the immaculate and immortal Self dwelling in man's body, untouched by the changes and sufferings the latter is subjected to. Krishna says:

> Learn that the work *Kshetra* means the *body* [*Körper*], and the word *Kshetrajna* the one who *perceives* [erkennt] it. Know that *I* am this *Kshetrajna* in all its mortal forms. The knowledge [*Kenntniß*] of *Kshetra* and *Kshetrajna* I call *Gnan* or wisdom [*Weisheit*].[76]

Schopenhauer must have been very impressed with this distinction: the passage just quoted is transcribed verbatim in one of his notebooks.[77] Assuming that this annotation dates from late 1813 or, at most, early 1814, it can be inferred that the figure of the pure subject – that which is not, but only cognizes (*das*

---

72 Cf. MR 1, n. 189, p. 113.
73 Cf. Schopenhauer 1911–1942, vol. XV, p. 55.
74 Cf. Majer 1802. Cf. MR 2, pp. 262–263. However, Majer did not translate from the Sanskrit, but from a pre-existing English translation (cf. App 2006a, pp. 52–55).
75 An extraordinarily wide commentary, illustrating this text from a more spiritual than 'scientific' (in the Western sense of the term) point of view, is offered by Yogananda 1999².
76 Cf. Klaproth 1802, vol. 2, p. 287 (MR 2, p. 262).
77 Cf. MR 2, p. 262.

bloß Erkennende) the will, the body and life – corresponds in some way, in Schopenhauer's intentions, to the *Kshetrajna* of the *Bhagavad Gita*.[78]

In a note added to fragment 191, Schopenhauer refers to the "subject" in question a quotation from the text of the *Oupnekhat* (a Latin translation of 50 *Upanishads*,[79] based on an earlier Persian translation of the Sanskrit text; cf. *infra*, 11.2), in which it is said that the *atma*, the eternal divine Self that inhabits man's body, is similar to a spectator attending a theater performance, without being involved in it in any way (*is similis spectatori est, quod ab omni separatus factus, spectaculum videt*); in this metaphor, the show corresponds to the world.[80] On the same page, the *atma* is determined again as *purus, sine motu* (i.e. *stabilis*) and *sine desiderio*.[81] These expressions find an almost literal correspondence in Schopenhauer's fragment: the subject is the "pure [*reine*]" and "calm [*ruhige*]" "spectator [*Zuschauer*]" of life, completely foreign to the body and the will.

Implying the identification between pure subject and *atma* (or man's divine Self), such correspondences constitute a further clue in favor of the interpretation proposed above, according to which by pure subject young Schopenhauer meant what man was 'before' falling into time and into the vehicle of temporal existence (the body). Fragment 274 also seems to confirm this hypothesis (cf. *infra*, 11.7 and 11.11).

10.9 The Doctrine of Intelligible Character as the Solution to the "Main Problem of Philosophy". The Fulfillment of the Voluntarist Position: *esse sequitur velle*

It is clear from the previous paragraphs that the concept of *Lebenwollen* ("willing-life") is formally distinct from the concept of a will to self-preservation. *Lebenwollen*, in fact, is not simply a will to maintain or preserve life (the obtainment of

---

[78] U. App (2006a, pp. 59–61) has argued very convincingly and thoroughly for this dating, which differs from the one proposed by Hübscher (according to whom, instead, Schopenhauer's annotations to the *Bhagavad Gita* date from 1815–1816). However, I do not agree with U. App that the "will" Schopenhauer speaks of in the same fragment 191 can be traced back to the universal spirit that, according to the Indian texts, inhabits every finite form (2006a, pp. 71–73). This hypothesis is not supported by the texts; it is rather the figure of the "subject" as pure cognizer – which as such, for Schopenhauer, is *opposed* to will and body – that shows clear affinities with the *Kshetrajna*.
[79] Anquetil-Duperron 1801–1802.
[80] Anquetil-Duperron 1801–1802, I, p. 304.
[81] Anquetil-Duperron 1801–1802, I, p. 304.

which would remain extraneous to it), but primarily a will to *acquire* a life that one does not yet have. This will not only "wills", but also and above all "has willed" life, even before achieving it; indeed, it acquired it precisely 'because' it has willed it (man is what he "wills to be, has willed, hence wills and therefore [*darum*] is"). So, for Schopenhauer the term *Lebenwollen* denotes not only the will to go on living, but, first and foremost, a will to achieve life (and a specific life in particular). For this reason, it is better translated as "willing-life" rather than "willing to live".

This part of the discourse enables Schopenhauer to anchor his philosophical interpretation of the original sin on the concept of *Lebenwollen*. According to Schopenhauer, willing-life is indeed man's original sin.[82] The body (*Leib*), understood as the 'vehicle' of spatio-temporal existence, is the "incarnated sinful propensity which has become visible",[83] or rather the "will that has become visible" – a will that is identified with the intelligible character.[84] This implies that "sinful propensity" and "intelligible character" coincide, as that which man's body makes visible (therefore, Schopenhauer concludes, if one admits that Christ was free of sin, one must also admit that his body was only a phantom one).[85]

The relationship between the concepts of intelligible character and empirical consciousness is not made explicit by Schopenhauer; however, it becomes evident as soon as one considers that man's empirical consciousness is his temporal nature, and that willing-life, i.e. the act of will in which the intelligible character consists, is what lies at the origin of man's temporal existence – in the sense that the latter is the manifestation or appearance of that same willing. Personality, which manifests an individual's unrepeatable individuality (and thus his intelligible character), is an exclusive attribute of the empirical consciousness, not of the better consciousness.[86] One can see why Schopenhauer maintains, on the one hand, that the 'result' of original sin is empirical or temporal consciousness (cf. fragments 79, 96 and 99), and on the other hand, that the individual's temporal existence is the manifestation or appearance of the intelligible character. It is precisely based on these assumptions that Schopenhauer likens the Kantian doctrine of the intelligible character to the Platonic myth of Er (cf. *supra*, 10.7).

In *Philosophy and Religion*, Schelling had traced the meaning of Fichte's *Thathandlung* back to the ancient doctrine of original sin, as well as to Platonic myths concerning the soul's otherworldly destiny (cf. *supra*, 6.8). In his *Freedom* essay, the

---

[82] Cf. MR 1, n. 146, p. 94.
[83] MR 1, n. 188, p. 113.
[84] MR 1, n. 191, p. 115.
[85] MR 1, n. 188, p. 112. This is the central tenet of the heresy of Docetism, which is also maintained, based on the same arguments, in *The World* (cf. Schopenhauer 2010b, I 479–480, § 70, pp. 432–433).
[86] Cf. MR 1, n. 81, p. 44 (*supra*, 8.6); n. 222, p. 140.

same *Thathandlung* is made to correspond to man's metaphysical act of self-determination, by which he has chosen once and for all his own intelligible essence.[87] We have already seen how much Schopenhauer owes to Schelling's concept of the intelligible being (cf. *supra*, 9.11; 10.7); the parallelism between the theory of the intelligible character and the myth of Er – reiterated by Schopenhauer in *The World as Will and Representation* and later extended even to the doctrines of the Egyptians and Indians[88] – thus probably originated from Schelling.[89] But at this point the discourse expands further.

In relation to man's intelligible being, Schelling (again referring to Fichte) speaks of the self-position (*Selbstsetzen*) of consciousness.[90] Schopenhauer certainly does not say that man, through the act of will in which the intelligible character consists, has 'posited himself' as a temporal being; and yet for him too, man is responsible for his being what he is – which is precisely why the theory of the intelligible character is *"the true theodicy"*.[91] Schelling also presents the theory of the intelligible being as the only possible solution to the problem of evil, left fundamentally unsolved by Leibniz as well as all philosophers who dealt with it.[92]

In 1813, in relation to the individual's choice between his temporal being and his eternal being, Schopenhauer defined human freedom as the self's ability to posit itself (*sich zu setzen*) as temporal and spatial or as non-temporal and non-spatial (cf. *supra*, 8.3).[93] This act of choice or self-position does not concern man in his entirety, but only an indeterminate residue in him, which can set itself as temporal or as supertemporal precisely because, originally (or outside of this act), it is neither one nor the other. Here Schopenhauer presupposes the individual as already constituted or existing (in time).

But he also and mainly asks how the individual as such came into being, i.e. what is the origin of man's empirical consciousness (of temporal and finite existence). This, in his opinion, is the main problem of philosophy (cf. *supra*, 10.3). In 1811, he had programmatically written: "I wonder how *I have become* [italics

---

[87] Cf. Schelling 2006, pp. 49–51.
[88] Cf. A. Schopenhauer, *Prize Essay on the Basis of Morals*, in Schopenhauer 2009, p. 228.
[89] For a comparison of Schopenhauer's and Schelling's interpretation of mythology, cf. Auweele 2017.
[90] Cf. Schelling 2006, pp. 50–51. R. Heimann traces these passages in the manuscripts, once more, back to Pseudo-Tauler (Heimann 2013, p. 239). According to the latter, there is certainly a relationship between "body", individual "will" and "sin"; however, there is no mention of all the other conceptual traits that constitute the peculiarity of Schopenhauer's discourse and are indisputably linked to the concept of "intelligible character".
[91] MR 1, n. 191, p. 115.
[92] Schelling 2006, pp. 36–37, 65.
[93] MR 1, n. 66, p. 36.

mine] a subject, and that is why I philosophize: driven by the consciousness that subject-objectivity is not my absolute state" (cf. *supra*, 7.10).[94]

Every individual (already constituted as such), to the extent that he becomes aware of his two natures or consciousnesses, is faced with the "choice" of whether to be one or the other; what enables him to make this choice, and thus to determine or "posit himself" as empirical consciousness or as a better consciousness, is the *will*.[95] Now, the act of will in which the intelligible character consists, for Schopenhauer, is the choice – made, however, 'before' and 'outside' all time – of life or temporal existence as a whole.[96] The individual – or, more precisely, that which would 'become' the individual, but which was originally in an undefined "absolute state", different from temporality and individuality – chose, 'before' and 'outside' all time, to exist in time (precisely as an individual or as empirical consciousness).

Through the doctrine of intelligible character, Schopenhauer thus seems to raise the choice (*Wahl*) of will between empirical consciousness and better consciousness to a primal or absolutely original level, 'prior' to the existence of empirical or temporal consciousness itself. It can be justifiably assumed that, in relation to this original choice, Schopenhauer intentionally avoids using the expression *sich setzen* in order not to attribute temporal and causal determinations to something that necessarily transcends the realm of experience. Commenting on Schelling's *Philosophy and Religion* (in which the latter also refers to Fichte's principle that "the I-ness [*Ichheit*] is *its own deed* [*ihre eigene That*]"),[97] Schopenhauer in fact objected that man's act of self-position should be metaphysical and timeless, and yet, contradictorily, it implies both "time and causality" (cf. *supra*, 6.8).[98] Nevertheless, Schopenhauer agrees that man, insofar as he is what he has willed to be – and is such precisely *because* (*darum*) he has willed to be such –, has evidently placed or determined himself for what he is.

All these elements lead to the conclusion that, through the concepts of "intelligible character" and "willing-life", Schopenhauer sought a way out of the deadlock concerning the origin of empirical consciousness in the theory of double consciousness (cf. *supra*, 8.21).

> Nothing is more absurd than to ridicule the tales of Faust and others *who sold their souls to the devil*. The only thing wrong in this is simply that the story is told from the particular, but

---

94 MR 2, pp. 364–365. Translation modified.
95 MR 1, n. 35, p. 23; n. 91, pp. 57–58.
96 Cf. MR 2, p. 437.
97 Cf. Schelling 2010, pp. 31–32.
98 MR 2, p. 376.

we are all in the same boat and have made a pact with him. We live and make strenuous efforts to preserve life [...], We enjoy life, and for all this we have to die [...].[99]

Having made this pact, we "live", with all that this entails; and, ultimately, we must necessarily die.

> *Procreation* is followed by *life,* and *life* is irrevocably followed by *death.* Now it is worth considering how the *pleasure of procreation* which one individual (the father) enjoys is atoned for not by himself, but by another (his son) [...].

> Procreation is a willing-life [*Lebenwollen*] at an enhanced potential. We ourselves atone for our own life through death, but that willing-life, which in a manner of speaking is raised to the fourth power, has to be atoned for by another individual through life and death.[100]

These considerations – which, according to Schopenhauer, lucidly demonstrate "the unity and oneness of the human race and of its sinfulness"[101] – clearly resonate with the words of the *Epistle to the Romans,* according to which the entire human race sinned and gave itself up to death in Adam's sin (Rom 5:12–19; cf. *supra,* 10.4).

In *The World as Will and Representation,* Schopenhauer would write that the will-to-life is the original sin, symbolized by Adam, and that human beings are not "the work [*Werk*] of someone else", unlike what Judaism claims, "but rather of their own wills [...]: then there does not need to be freedom in the *operari* [acting], because it lies in the *esse* [being]".[102] "The very origin of man himself is the act [*That*] of his free will and thus the same as the fall into sin; so the original sin of which all other sins are consequences had already arisen along with the person's *essentia* and *existentia*".[103] In addition, in On the Freedom of the Will, speaking about the intelligible character, Schopenhauer would state that the "whole

---

99 MR 1, n. 202, p. 119.
100 MR 1, n. 203, p. 120.
101 MR 1, n. 203, p. 120.
102 Schopenhauer 2010b, I 482, § 70, p. 434.
103 Schopenhauer 2018, II 693–694, chap. 48, 619. Schopenhauer attributes "consequences [*Folgen*]" to something that, being outside time, is also outside the principle of sufficient reason and, therefore, outside any possible relationship of consequentiality. However, here, as in the necessary consequentiality set out in the dissertation between intelligible character and actions in time (Schopenhauer uses the expression *mit Nothwendigkeit folgen*: cf. *supra,* 9.8), this relationship of consequentiality can be traced back to the concept of "appearing" (*erscheinen*): all the sins that the individual commits in time are the appearance (*Erscheinung*) of that original act of will by which he determined his own *essentia* and *existentia.* On the issues related to the concept of original sin in Schopenhauer, cf. Koßler 1999, pp. 80–90.

being and essence (*existentia et essentia*) of the human being [...] must be thought of as a free deed [*seine freie That*]".[104]

Man exists in time insofar as he *has willed* to exist in time. Certainly, man's empirical *operari* necessarily follows from his *esse*; in this sense the principle *operari sequitur esse* applies. But for Schopenhauer this very *esse* (existence in time as a determinate individual, with a determinate character: cf. *supra*, 9.8) is the appearance in time of an original *operari*, constituted by a metaphysical and timeless act of will; in this sense the principle *esse sequitur operari* applies. This last *operari* – the primordial *That* or *Akt* – consists in a free act of will (*Willensakt*) and is thus, properly speaking, a *velle*. Therefore, the ultimate principle of the whole discourse is: *esse sequitur velle*. That is to say, man's existence in time, together with all that it entails, 'follows' from his will to exist in time – where, however, this 'following' does not have a temporal or causal value, but simply means being its appearance (*Erscheinung*). Through the doctrine of intelligible character – understood as an individual and metaphysical will-to-life, of which life in time is the *Erscheinung* – Schopenhauer's voluntarist position, which was implicitly formed as early as 1812, is thus radicalized (cf. *supra*, 7.11; *infra*, 10.13).

It is clear that at this point Schopenhauer faces the major problem of coordinating these new theoretical elements, which already belong to a metaphysics of will, with the pre-existing theory of double consciousness. In the manuscripts from 1814, these two perspectives coexist, in a rather unstable equilibrium, until fragment 286; from here on, the theory of double consciousness disappears altogether leaving room for the metaphysics of will alone. The systematization of the latter would engage Schopenhauer over the next four years and would constitute the content of his main work and, in general, of his mature thought. It is therefore a question of determining what reasons led Schopenhauer to definitively drop the theory of double consciousness and concentrate all his speculative efforts on the development of the metaphysics of will.

10.10 "We Are Sanctified Not by Works, But by Faith". Irrelevance of *operari* and Decisiveness of *esse*

According to *Romans*, the righteousness (δικαιοσύνη) or justification of God only comes to man through faith in Jesus Christ.[105] In everything else, there is no difference between Christians and pagans, "for all have sinned and fall short of the glory

---

104 A. Schopenhauer, *Prize Essay on the Freedom of the Will*, in Schopenhauer 2009, p. 108.
105 Romans 3:22.

of God, and all are justified freely by his grace through the redemption that came by Christ Jesus. [...] a person is justified by faith [πίστει] apart from the works [ἔργων] of the law", i.e., from actions, even if they comply with the Commandments.[106] In this sense, the external Law, "written [...] on tablets of stone", in the New Testament is set against inner faith, written on the heart.[107] The latter works by "expressing itself through love [ἀγάπης]"[108] and, according to *Romans*, constitutes "the law of the Spirit",[109] which is what truly matters: "for the letter kills, but the Spirit gives life".[110]

These passages from the New Testament – the same ones that triggered Luther's decisive theological reflections[111] – were Schopenhauer's essential reference, but he sought to strip them of their 'mythical' aspect in order to address their essential content. It must always be borne in mind that Schopenhauer, when taking up terms or expressions from the Bible, never did so with theological or confessional intentions, but rather with the aim of unraveling the authentic (properly *philosophical*) content behind their figurative or improper use (cf. *supra*, 10.2). This attempt is already apparent in fragment 145, in which the content of *Romans* is interpreted in relation to the two different sides of the "Idea of man", represented by Adam and Jesus (cf. *supra*, 10.4).

Picking up on Paul's opposition between faith and works, Schopenhauer notes: "faith, i.e. the Holy Spirit, extirpates death and sin and is the means of grace, but works are always imperfect", and refers to Melanchthon's *Apology of the Augsburg Confession* and Luther's *Smalkadic Articles*.[112] "*Faith* is so much and *works* without it are nothing; also *innocence* is so little but *conversion* [Bekehrung] so much. These two hang together".[113] By following moral teachings, we only improve our actions, not ourselves. This "paradox", with "its objectionable feature", Schopenhauer argues, "disappears, if we consider that we are sanctified not by works, but by faith (i.e. the better consciousness)".[114] Schopenhauer identifies faith with the better consciousness – the same faith that, for him, coincides with the Holy Spirit; and

---

[106] Romans 3:22–28.
[107] 2 Corinthians 3:3.
[108] Galatians 5:6.
[109] Romans 8:2.
[110] 2 Corinthians 3:6.
[111] Cf. Luther's autobiographical account in the Preface to the complete edition of his works (Wittenberg 1545), in Luther 1883–2009, vol. 54, p. 185.
[112] MR 1, fn. to n. 145, p. 93. On Schopenhauer's early encounter with Luther and Melanchthon, cf. Massei 2018.
[113] MR 1, n. 149, p. 96.
[114] MR 1, n. 186, p. 112.

indeed the latter (in its philosophical meaning) also coincides in his opinion with the better consciousness.[115]

The ultimate meaning that Schopenhauer attributes to Paul's texts is as follows: it is not through individual actions, however virtuous they may be, that man can truly redeem himself from his temporal dimension (actions, as such, are in time). To achieve 'salvation' it is not enough simply to determine one's deeds as virtuous or deserving; rather, much more radically, it is necessary to determine *oneself* as a better consciousness ("the source of all virtue").[116] For this reason, innocence (not harming anyone, not acting wickedly) counts for little, and conversion (changing or reversing one's being) is the decisive aspect. What matters is the inner choice – that fundamental choice by which the individual decides whether to be empirical consciousness or better consciousness (cf. *supra*, 7.11).

Consequently, the ethical principles taught by philosophy and religion cannot improve the individual; they can only improve his conduct. *"Ethics* is as little able to help one to *virtue* as is the teaching of a complete system of *aesthetics* to the production of *works of art.* [...] For virtue, like genius, is inborn and cannot be acquired through learning."[117]

Virtue does not consist in what one does; it is not enough to perform virtuous actions to *be* truly virtuous.

> A person without any genuine inclination to do good nevertheless does it, [...] but he does good in order to escape purgatory, for example, or even to live according to Kantian principles that he likes for his own theoretical satisfaction, [...] such a man can be as bad as any criminal and he is exactly like the dull and insipid imitator in art. This is what Luther and the oldest teachers of the Christian Church meant when they taught that only faith makes us blessed, not *opera operata*; but faith is granted solely by the *Holy Ghost.*[118]

The inescapable need of a radical inner change in man to achieve salvation was a characteristic theme of pietist spirituality, which used the expressions "new man [*neuer Mensch*]" (cf. Eph 4:22–24, KJV) and "rebirth [*Wiedergeburt*]" in this regard.[119] Luther himself had spoken with great emphasis of man renewed by faith in Christ – the latter, being God, is more than man (*Übermensch*); some

---

115 Cf. MR 1, n. 158, p. 98.
116 MR 1, n. 215, p. 132.
117 MR 1, n. 244, pp. 159–160. Cf. also MR 1, n. 186, pp. 111–112 and n. 161, p. 100.
118 MR 1, n. 244, p. 160.
119 On this topic cf. Schmidt 1969.

later authors, to indicate the new or spiritually transformed (and therefore Christ-like) man, use the same term *Übermensch*.[120]

By mentioning the opposition between faith and deeds, Schopenhauer also intends to refer to an extreme inner change in the individual – so extreme that he must even *cease to be a human being*. In fact, to attain the "peace of God", it is necessary that "man, this frail, finite and transitory being, be [*sey*] something quite different [*etwas ganz andres*], that he become aware of himself no longer as a human being at all, but as something quite different".[121]

But what is this change and how can it be attained?

10.11 Looking at the Mirror of Life: Pain, Better Cognition and Redemption. The Rejection of the Intelligible Character

According to Schopenhauer, there are two possible ways to arrive at better consciousness (which is "the true redemption of the world [*Welterlösung*]",[122] "the eternal keynote of creation" which we "must [*müssen*]" all reach, sooner or later).[123] Either man's "better will" "arises from within freely and of itself", i.e. spontaneously, causing the extinction of "willing-life [*Lebenwollen*]" and the "illusion" connected to it; or the individual, persevering in willing-life and experiencing the suffering and horror of existence, finally understands "what kind of a world we have willed": "from the pain" then arises the "better cognition [*bessre Erkenntniß*]", by virtue of which man returns to himself, to his innermost essence – which is none other than the "better consciousness" – and, repudiating willing-life, is redeemed (*erlöst*).[124]

The terms "better cognition" and "better will" are opposed to "illusion [*Täuschung*]" and "willing-life" respectively. Just as in the fragments of 1811/1812 (cf. *supra*, 6.9; 7.7 and 7.11), here too better cognition and better will have eternity as their object. More precisely, man ought to *cognize* and *will* (in the sense of: will to determine himself as) his own eternal being, the eternity which he himself is: the better consciousness. Willing-life and illusion, on the other hand, have tempo-

---

120 Cf. entry "Mensch, neuer" in Ritter, Gründer and Gabriel 1971–2007, vol. V, p. 1114.
121 MR 1, n. 189, p. 113.
122 MR 1, n. 85, p. 47. Translation modified.
123 MR 1, n. 158, p. 98.
124 MR 1, n. 158, p. 98. Translation modified.

rality as their object: the individual dominated by them *wills* life in time and *cognizes* himself only as a temporal being.

The better cognition, insofar as it originates from the pain of life, is first and foremost the knowledge of the necessary link between life in time and pain, and therefore, by antithesis, of the equally necessary link between happiness and eternity; for this very reason it is able to awaken the better will, which is the will to eternity itself. The sage *knows* that "on earth we cannot be happy at all, that life is only a constantly prevented dying"; he realizes the "disappearance of the ordinary illusions concerning life".[125] In the fragments following n. 158, Schopenhauer mainly reflects on the second way to attain the better consciousness, namely the path of pain (already mentioned in a fragment of 1813; cf. *supra*, 8.7).

As we have seen, every individual's life is for Schopenhauer the appearance of his intelligible character. Living, man sees "what it is that he wills to be, has willed, hence wills and therefore is";[126] indeed "everyone forges his own fortune".[127] It is no coincidence that Schopenhauer uses two different tenses here. The present perfect ("has willed") denotes, through reference to a kind of 'transcendental past' of the individual, his intelligible character, i.e. the "universal act of will lying outside of time" by which he has chosen his life; in this sense, life itself is precisely a "farce in which everything essential is irrevocably fixed and enacted". The present tense ("wills") denotes instead the individual acts of will insofar as they conform to that original act: that is, it indicates the individual's persistence in that original will.

Willing-to-be what one is, therefore, is formally distinct from *having-willed-to-be* what one is (even though the object of the will is the same in both cases). And indeed Schopenhauer is convinced that man, once he has become aware of his own essence through life, can stop willing to be what he "has willed" to be.

> For in so far as he [man] is alive and is a human being, he is doomed not merely to *sin* and *death*, but also to *delusion* [Wahn] and this *delusion* is as real as life, as real as the world of the senses itself, indeed it is identical with these (Maya of the Indians). On it are based all our desires and cravings, which are again only the expression of life, just as life is only the expression of delusion. To the extent that we live, will to live and are human beings, the delusion is truth; only in reference to the better consciousness is it delusion. If peace, quiet and bliss are to be found, then the delusion must be forsaken [*aufgegeben*], and if this is to be forsaken, then life must be forsaken. This is the serious step, the problem that is insoluble in life and is to be solved only with the help of death, which in itself dissolves not the illusion but only the appearance [*Erscheinung*] thereof, namely the body; this is sanctification.

---

125 MR 1, n. 197, p. 118.
126 MR 1, n. 159, p. 99.
127 MR 1, n. 241, p. 155.

> The evil we suffer in the world (privation and pain) gives us, whenever it presses on us, a momentary cognition of what life is, (namely sin and death as the appearance of delusion). It shatters the delusion with more or less difficulty according as we are deeply involved in it. [...] For just as with life the delusion is infallibly and inevitably set up, so too is life with the delusion. And whoever persists in willing-life will live, although this body dies; for to the extent that there is delusion, its appearance does not fail to come.[128]

As has been duly documented, the mention of the "Maya of the Indians" does not belong to the original fragment, but to a later addition (cf. *infra*, 11.1).[129]

It is not entirely clear what the term delusion (*Wahn*) means in this text. Schopenhauer writes that it is "identical" to the world of the senses, and that life and the body are respectively its expression (*Ausdruck*) and its appearance (*Erscheinung*). But life and the body are the setting asunder (*Auseinandersetzung*) and the *Erscheinung* of willing-life (cf. *supra*, 10.7). The *delusion* in question thus seems to be identified with willing-life – or more precisely, with that *false and fatal knowledge about life, according to which life itself is willed*. If this is so, this delusion cannot be anything other than the theoretical or fundamental error (*Grundirrthum*) of identifying life in time with happiness; in turn, this leads to the "practical error (sin, original sin) which is life itself" (cf. *supra*, 10.6).[130]

One can see why Schopenhauer writes about such a delusion that "on it are based *all* [italics mine] our desires": the latter, being addressed to particular objects of the senses, are nothing more than particular expressions or specifications of willing-life or willing the world (meaning the "world" as the totality of all possible objects of the senses). Life is the exact opposite of happiness, it is *pain*; sin and death, as constitutive characteristics of life, manifest precisely the illusory nature of the identification between life in time and happiness. Recall that "death" and "sin" are the two consequences that Paul, in the *Epistle to the Romans*, expressly ascribes to original sin (Rom 5:12–18; cf. *supra*, 10.4), and that the latter, according to Schopenhauer, coincides with the metaphysical willing-life (cf. *supra*, 10.9).

The overall sense of the text is then as follows: man *has willed* and *wills* life in time due to the delusion that life is a condition of (possible) happiness; consequently, the knowledge (experience) of the fact that life is pain, by destroying this delusion, is able to extinguish the desire for life.

---

128 MR 1, n. 189, pp. 113–114. Translation modified.
129 Cf. App 2011, p. 222. In truth, the Deussen edition, unlike the Hübscher edition, marked the passage in question as an addition: cf. Schopenhauer 1911–1942., vol. XI, p. 101 (here the fragment is numbered § 169).
130 MR 1, n. 146, p. 94.

> [...] the purpose of life (I really make use of this expression only figuratively and could say the essential nature of life or of the world) is that we cognize [*erkennen*] our own evil will, that it becomes for us an object and that we therefore [*demnach*] convert [*uns bekehren*] in our innermost being.[131]

If one bears in mind that the *will*, of which life is the "mirror", coincides with the *intelligible character*, one can well understand that the negation of the former necessarily entails the negation of the latter. At first, Schopenhauer seems to believe that a change in the intelligible character is possible:

> Life is the *intelligible character's* becoming visible; in life this does not change [*ändert sich*], but it does outside life and outside time in consequence [*in Folge*] of the self-cognition [*Selbsterkenntniß*] that is given through life.[132]

But it is clear that the intelligible character, being outside of time, is also outside of any possibility of change.[133] Taking his line of reasoning to its logical conclusion, Schopenhauer states that the individual cannot change his character, i.e. he cannot decide to will anything other than what he "has willed" and "wills"; he can, however, decide *not to will at all* – that is, not to will what, provided he does will, he necessarily must will. Consequently, to deny (one's) character does not mean to modify or abolish (*aufheben*) it in order to possibly acquire another; man can only reject it or deny it (*verleugnen*) as it is, in its entirety.[134]

The repudiation of willing-life, i.e. of one's intelligible character, thus takes on the meaning of self-denial (*Selbsverläugnung*), of self-annihilation (*Selbstvernichtung*; cf. supra, 10.5). Only, at this point, for Schopenhauer it is no longer a question of simply denying or repudiating (one's) temporal being, but, much more radically, what lies at the origin of it: (one's) willing-life.

In contrast to Schelling, who in his treatise on the essence of human freedom did not contemplate the possibility of denying one's intelligible being, Schopenhauer believes that man *can* repudiate or reject his character (the act of will in which it consists) through an equal and opposite act of will. In fact, in 1812 his criticism of Schelling had focused precisely on the irreversibility of the position of the intelligible being: even then, Schopenhauer was concerned with avoiding what (in his view) happens in Schelling, namely that "life becomes a dramatic piece whose

---

[131] MR 1, n. 229, p. 144. Translation modified.
[132] MR 1, n. 159, p. 99. Translation modified.
[133] Cf. MR 1, n. 153, p. 97; n. 159, p. 99.
[134] Cf. MR 1, n. 242, p. 157. Cf. HN II, p. 144: "aufheben kann er [der Mensch] seinen Karakter nie: er kann ihn bloß verleugnen".

scenes and ending are known in advance and whose purpose therefore no one understands", so that "man's moral worth is determined before his birth, [and] all religion and philosophy become as pointless and superfluous as life".[135]

To this conception Schopenhauer opposed "what the mystics call regeneration or rebirth [*Wiedergeburt*] and all conversion [*Bekehren*]".[136] In 1814, Schopenhauer still wanted to preserve the possibility of this conversion, i.e. the *freedom* of the will, even 'after' the timeless act by which each individual determined himself. In truth, Schelling did not exclude that the individual can pass from evil to good (it is here that he mentions man's "better nature": cf. *supra*, 7.7), but he only admitted this possibility insofar as it was already always part of man's original act of self-determination, so that any passage to good is not – and cannot be – a revocation or neutralization of this act, but, on the contrary, only a further realization of it.[137]

In 1808/1809 Schopenhauer stated that the only meaning of the "mockery and sham [*Possenspiel*] of the world" lies in the "changes, which [one's] will undergoes through the παίδευσις of life in its innermost depths whether for good or for evil" (cf. *supra*, 1.9).[138] The core of his discourse, in 1814, remained the same: life and the world have meaning only insofar as they are the mirror in which man, seeing his own abjection, can convert; outside of this, the world "has no reality" (cf. also *supra*, 4.1).[139] The παίδευσις of life is achieved through pain, which produces the *knowledge* that life is pain; and the ultimate outcome of this παίδευσις is not-willing: "He alone is truly happy *who in life does not will life*, in other words does not strive for its good things."[140] If in the years 1811–1812 Schopenhauer primarily attributed to tragedy – understood as the representation of pain – the power to distract the spectator from the sensible world (cf. *supra*, 1.6–1.7; 7.10), in 1813 and 1814 he attributed the same power to personal experience of pain (cf. *supra*, 8.7).

---

135 MR 2, p. 353.
136 MR 2, p. 353.
137 Schelling 2006, p. 54.
138 MR 1, n. 13, p. 10.
139 MR 1, n. 245, p. 160.
140 MR 1, n. 184, p. 11.

10.12 Beyond the Principle of Reason: Art and Philosophy. Knowledge of the "Idea of Being in Time" and the Consequent "Will-Not-to-Be". The Double Nature of Human Consciousness and Will

In the dissertation, Schopenhauer implicitly contrasts cognition according to the principle of reason, which concerns the empirical world, with cognition of the Platonic Idea (cf. *supra*, 9.13). The antithesis between these two forms of cognition becomes explicit in fragment 210.

> [...] The principle of sufficient reason is nothing but the finiteness, or rather nothingness [*Nichtigkeit*], of all objects, always showing itself in the four classes of representations [...] or generally [it is] the bloody transfer of every object to death and non-existence [*Nichtseyn*], which we are aware of when we see how every second exists only in so far as it swallows up the preceding second [...] By virtue of that finiteness every object has only an illusory existence [*scheinbare Existenz*], like a shadow we cannot grasp, for every object exists only to the extent that its non-existence still lies in the future and not in the present [...]. [...] the principle of sufficient reason or ground is only the expression of the nothingness of each and every representations [...].[141]

The nothingness of every object in the world, *that is*, of every representation (since "the world is nothing but a representation of the cognizing subject"),[142] entails the non-existence or non-reality of the objects of the world, as opposed to the existence or reality of the *Idea*:

> Plato discovered the exalted truth; only the *Ideas* are real [*wirklich*], in other words the eternal forms of things, the intuitive [*anschauligen*] adequate representatives of the concepts. Things in time and space are evanescent shadows of nothingness [*nichtige Schatten*]; they and the laws by which they arise and pass away are only the subject of science, as are also mere concepts and their derivation from one another. But the subject of philosophy, [i.e.] of the art whose mere material are concepts, is only the (Platonic) Idea. [...][143]

Only Ideas are eternal and thus truly real: "things in time and space", on the contrary, are but null and void "shadows" (in keeping with the Platonic allegory of the cave), because they are structurally impermanent: their destination, and thus their true nature, is nothingness. In his treatise on the principle of reason, Schopenhauer defines time as the "prototype of all finiteness".[144]

---

[141] MR 1, n. 210, pp. 125–126. Translation modified.
[142] MR 1, p. 125. Translation modified.
[143] MR 1, p. 127. Translation modified.
[144] Schopenhauer 2012 [1813], § 52, p. 143.

Now, since philosophy addresses the supersensible and the eternal (cf. *supra*, 10.2), and since only the Platonic Idea is eternal, *then the latter constitutes the object of philosophy*.[145] But the Platonic Idea is also the object of art (cf. *supra*, 2.3–2.5; 8.13). Probably drawing on some Schellingean suggestions,[146] Schopenhauer argues that the philosopher is an 'artist' who renders the ultimate essence of empirical things – the Platonic Idea – not through marble or canvas, but through the abstract concepts of reason.[147] In other words, the philosopher's special task is to reproduce (*abbilden*) and repeat (*wiederholen*), through concepts (*Begriffe*), the "[Platonic] Ideas of all that which is to be found in consciousness and which appears as an object".[148]

But what is the ultimate essence of all things, which the philosopher must conceptually reproduce? That is, what is the Platonic Idea or eternal form of which the world, in its totality, is the manifestation or appearance?

> When he [the philosopher] has discovered and depicted the (Platonic) Idea of all that *is* and lives, there will arise [*wird ... sich ergeben*] for practical philosophy *a will-not-to-be* [Nicht-seynwollen]. For then it will have been shown how the Idea of *being* in time is the Idea of a luckless and wretched state; how being in time is the world, the kingdom of chance, error and wickedness; how the body is the visible will which always wills and can never be satisfied; [...] how suffering mankind and the suffering animal world are the Idea of life in time; how *willing-life* [Lebenwollen] is the real damnation and virtue and vice are only the weakest and strongest degrees of the willing-life; how foolish it is to fear that death can deprive us of life, for unfortunately the willing-life is already life, and if death and suffering do not kill this willing-life, life itself eternally flows from the inexhaustible spring, from infinite time, and the will-to-life [*Wille zum Leben*] will always have life [...].[149]

"The Idea of *being* in time is the Idea of a luckless and wretched state"; the essence of life is pain ("suffering mankind and the suffering animal world are the Idea of life in time"). Consequently, when this essence is discovered and (conceptually) depicted, the 'result' will be the *rejection of life itself*. The practical consequence of the theoretical solution to the enigma of the world consists in the will-not-to-be (*Nicht-seynwollen*): the exact opposite of willing-life (*Lebenwollen*).

---

145 MR 1, fn. to n. 210, p. 126: "*Cognition thus sent from one thing to another* is only finite, only for the faculty of reason, for science. But philosophical cognition is complete and at rest in itself; it is the *Platonic Idea*, which we obtain through pure, objective, naïve intuition. Everything then presents itself as what it is; it expresses itself clearly and does not send us from one thing to another as does the principle of sufficient reason or ground." Translation modified.
146 Cf. Schelling 1966, Lectures 6 (pp. 60–70), 11 (pp. 115–124) and 14 (pp. 143–152).
147 MR 1, n. 210, pp. 126–127. Cf. also MR 1, n. 239, pp. 151–152.
148 MR 1, n. 210, p. 127.
149 MR 1, p. 128. Translation modified.

Here, too, Schopenhauer assumes that man only wills life in time insofar and as long as he mistakenly believes it to be a (possibly) happy condition. Just as the practical consequence of error and delusion (which consists in the identification of life and happiness) is willing-life (cf. *supra*, 10.6 and 10.11), so the practical consequence of truth (which consists in the identification of life and pain) is not to will life.

Now, if *"nicht"* in *Nichtseynwollen* is to be referred to *Seynwollen* in its entirety, *Nichtseynwollen* means "not willing to be": a negative form of will, in which, since there is no will, there is also no willed. If, on the other hand, the negation expressed by *nicht* is to be referred only to *Seyn* in *Seynwollen* (as Payne renders it), *Nichtseynwollen* means "willing not to be": a positive form of will, where what is willed is the negation (i. e. the opposite) of temporal "being" – eternal being. This second interpretation seems more correct, because young Schopenhauer openly admits, in addition to "being in time", a second object (or basis of determination) of the human will:

> The *double nature of our consciousness* [Duplicität unsers Bewußtseyns] is revealed to some extent practically in the double nature of the will [*Duplicität des Willens*] which has a *twofold* [zwiefaches] supreme good whereof the one cannot be referred, subordinated, or united to the other, and moreover is unattainable unless the other be given up and wholly disregarded.[150]

The duplicity of human consciousness is the opposition, in every individual, between an empirical consciousness, aimed at the temporal world, and a higher consciousness, aimed at the eternal world. The corresponding duplicity of the will therefore consists of a double yearning, respectively for the *temporal world* and the *eternal world.*

In 1812 Schopenhauer distinguished between empirical will and better will (cf. *supra*, 7.11); according to the 1813 fragments, "willing" is what allows man to determine himself as empirical consciousness or better consciousness (cf. *supra*, 8.3 and 8.18). Now, in 1814, the better will is expressly set against willing-life (cf. *supra*, 10.7): the duplicity of human will is expressed in *willing* or *not willing* life (existence in time) – where this "not willing", however, is a positive will, because it is the will to something positively determinable (or cognizable): eternity.

---

150 MR 1, n. 234, p. 147.

10.13 Voluntarism or Intellectualism? The Subordination of the Will-in-Itself to the Law of Motivation

In the fragments analyzed in the previous two paragraphs, Schopenhauer considers a type of cognition to which the human will is essentially subordinated. The expressions he uses emphasize this subordination unambiguously: the intelligible character changes "in consequence [*in Folge*] of the self-cognition that is given [to man] through life";[151] the purpose of life is that "we cognize our own evil will [...] and that we therefore [*demnach*] convert in our innermost being";[152] "through [*durch*]" the knowledge of the essence of life, man's will can retrace its steps and redeem itself;[153] from the intuition of "the Idea of all that *is* and lives, there will arise [*wird ... sich ergeben*] for practical philosophy a *will-not-to-be*".[154] This discourse is clearly discordant with some of Schopenhauer's earlier reflections, and yet also largely consistent with others. Let's first look at the former.

In 1812 Schopenhauer attributed to the individual's will the ability to choose between empirical consciousness and better consciousness (cf. *supra*, 7.11). Since a certain type of cognition is intrinsically connected to each of the two consciousnesses (cognition of the empirical world to the empirical consciousness, cognition of the supersensible world to the better consciousness), then cognition, *falling within the sphere of either the empirical consciousness or the better consciousness*, is necessarily subordinate to the will, which makes the choice between the two consciousnesses in the first place.

The fragments of 1813 concerning the authentic meaning of what religion calls "original sin" (cf. *supra*, 8.19) and those of 1814 concerning the intelligible character as an act of timeless will which is expressed or manifested in temporal existence (cf. *supra*, 10.7–10.9), led to a remarkable development of this point. It is clear, in fact, that the cognition internal to life in time – cognition according to the principle of reason – is inevitably subordinate to the will of which life in time, in its entirety, is the manifestation or appearance (*Erscheinung*). The content of this cognition is in fact the *esse* that coincides with the *appearance* of that metaphysical *velle* (cf. *supra*, 10.9); and on the other hand, *esse* itself is nothing but *percipi*, that is, being perceived or cognized – more precisely, being cognized according to the principle of reason (cf. *supra*, 9.2–9.3). Thus, 'logically' or 'formally' speaking: since *esse*, which is the *Erscheinung* of *velle*, is essentially *percipi*, then this *percipi* itself is the

---

[151] MR 1, n. 159, p. 99.
[152] MR 1, n. 229, p. 144. Translation modified.
[153] MR 1, n. 274, p. 182.
[154] MR 1, n. 210, p. 128.

Erscheinung of *velle*, so as to be – together with the related or respective *percipere* – necessarily subordinate to it.

But also in another, more concrete sense (conceptually following from the one just indicated), cognition on the basis of the principle of reason is subordinate to the will. According to the dissertation of 1813, the lived-body (*Leib*) is everyone's "immediate object" of cognition: all other physical objects in the world are only cognized through their interaction with the body itself (cf. *supra*, 9.6). Now, the latter "*is nothing but the will that has become visible*" (cf. *supra*, 10.7). This implies that cognition according to the first form of the principle of reason, concerning the relation of physical objects to the *body*, ultimately concerns their relation to the *will*. This syllogism is formulated in fragment 218.

> The question concerning the reality of representations (or cognitions) is first settled and set aside by my essay on the principle of sufficient reason. The question concerning the difference between life and the dream is answered in that essay by my saying that the one representation, called by me the immediate object (the body), enters as an integral part into all representations of the first class (real objects), but that this is not the case with phantasms, and so these are distinguished from real objects [...].
>
> Therefore what really gives the world reality is the body, this special representation of the first class. But in these M. S. it is said of the body that it is nothing but the will that has become visible, the imprint [*Abdruck*] of the will in the world of real objects. This substantiates that explanation of mine. It is our will on which everything depends; reality, seriousness and sorrow exist where its imprint is. Willing is the source of all evil; willing is the sole path to salvation [...].
>
> Therefore that world in which a permanent copy of the will appears is the real world.[155]

The so-called real objects (the things of the world) are all and only those that stand in relation to the will (as phenomenalized or objectified in the body). From this point of view, and for this whole section of the discourse, Schopenhauer's position is fully voluntaristic, because it implies the total subordination of cognition to the will.

However, there is also another substantial group of reflections in the manuscripts, in which, on the contrary, the will is subordinate to cognition. Indeed, Schopenhauer believes that the individual is free to choose whether (to want) to be empirical consciousness or better consciousness only insofar as he is aware of both, and not only, like the common man, of the former (cf. *supra*, 7.11). The two distinct natures that make up the human being pre-exist the act of will by which he decides to identify himself totally with one or the other; the task of

---

155 MR 1, n. 218, pp. 135–136.

"true criticism" is precisely to reveal the duplicity of human consciousness, so that the choice for the better consciousness becomes universally possible (cf. *supra*, 7.13).

Insofar as he cognizes both his natures truthfully – i. e. the empirical consciousness as the place of pain and torment, and the better consciousness as the home of "bliss" – the individual cannot but want to be a better consciousness.[156] Conversely, he wills temporality only insofar as he deludes himself (the verb used by Schopenhauer is *wähnen*) that it may be a happy condition (cf. *supra*, 10.5–10.6; 10.11–10.12).[157] (In this regard, it is worth recalling that, according to the *Genesis* account, Eve also ate the forbidden fruit because she mistakenly believed that the consequences would be positive for her; this is precisely where the serpent's deception lies). The cognition of life as pain can effectively defuse the *Lebenwollen* only insofar as the latter has been 'triggered' by the opposite belief or conviction (which for Schopenhauer is fallacious): the "momentary cognition [*Erkenntniß*] of what life is […] shatters [*erschüttert*] the delusion [*Wahn*]".[158]

The use of the terms *wähnen*, *Wahn* and *Grundirrthum* in relation to willing-life is extremely significant. In the dissertation, the term *Irrthum*, "error", is traditionally understood as opposed to the term "truth". The latter is the *"the relation of a judgement to something outside it"*, which constitutes the "ground [*Grund*]" of the judgment itself.[159] Being the denial of truth, error is the absence of the aforementioned relation. And indeed, according to fragment 210, "We err [*irren*] by combining concepts in such a way that a reference corresponding to this combination [expressed by the concepts] is not to be found outside them".[160] But the point is that judgment – understood as the expression (or affirmation) of a certain link between two concepts – also invests the practical sphere:

---

[156] "[…] an anchoret voluntarily renounces all the pleasures of life, deliberately deprives himself, so to speak, of every enjoyment, because [*weil*] there is awakened in him an awareness [*Bewußtseyn*] that he is an extratemporal, supersensible, free and absolutely blissful being and he wants to act in accordance with this cognition [*dieser Erkenntniß gemäß*]" (MR 1, n. 72, p. 39, translation modified). "Virtue is the affirmation [*Affirmation*] of the extratemporal being; indeed it is the direct expression of the awareness of such a state, pure affirmation" (MR 1, p. 40, translation modified). To reach *"the peace of God* (in other words for the appearance of *the better consciousness*) it is necessary that man […] become aware of himself [*sich bewußt werde*] […] as something quite different" to what he think he is when he identifies with his temporal being (MR 1, n. 189, p. 113).
[157] Cf. also MR 1, n. 209, p. 124: "it is best that he [man] cognizes [*erkenne*] which part's [of his consciousness] triumph hurts him most". Translation modified.
[158] MR 1, n. 189, p. 114. Translation modified.
[159] Schopenhauer 2012 [1813], § 35, pp. 104, 181.
[160] MR 1, n. 210, p. 126. Translation modified.

if we have to indicate the motive [*Motiv*] of a decision [*Entschlusses*], then we indicate the states of representations, either of the complete representations comprising the totality of experience, where a motive must be a relation among objects, or the concatenation of judgements [...]. In these connections, error reigns: to avoid this requires good sense [*Klugheit*]. Since good sense is distributed in unequal measure, it occurs that the same conditions of real objects provide very different judgements, and *so* [italics mine] different motives.[161]

Since the decision (*Entschluss*) constitutes the act of the will proper, the motive for a decision is the ground (*Grund*) or reason why the will decides for one thing rather than another (cf. *supra*, 9.7–9.8). Given the empirical character of the individual (which is the appearance of his intelligible character), the decision is determined by motives, which, however, being "states of representations", can also be made up of judgments (so that they are in turn determined, in that case, by the individual's greater or lesser "good sense"). Provided that the motive consists in a judgment or in a concatenation of judgments, the individual's decisions – *given his particular character* – are determined by the judgment itself, even if it is erroneous.

Building on these considerations, starting from 1816 Schopenhauer would admit a third form of character, namely the "acquired character": culture and experience do not modify one's character or will, but rather one's cognition and thus judgments, which, given one's character, necessarily shape one's actions.[162]

Now, the concept of a "happy life" is for Schopenhauer "a *contradictio in adjecto*":[163] the judgment that combines the concepts of "life" and "happiness" is an error, because – in accordance with the definition given in fragment 210 – it arises "by combining [the] concepts [of life and happiness] in such a way that a reference corresponding to this combination [expressed by the concepts] is not to be found outside them". Based on the above considerations, and using the terminology of the dissertation, it can be said that this (fallacious) judgment formally constitutes the *motive* for willing-life. This should not come as a surprise: at this stage of his reflections, Schopenhauer believed that not only man's empirical will, but also his metaphysical will (the intelligible character, which objectifies itself, i.e., appears, as the body) is subject to the law of motivation:

> What distinguishes *theists* from *atheists*, *Spinozists* and *fatalists* is that theists assign to the world an arbitrary principle, the atheists etc. a natural principle; the former represent the world as springing from a will, the latter represent it as arising from a cause. A cause oper-

---

[161] Schopenhauer 2012 [1813], § 46, pp. 186–187.
[162] MR 1, n. 595, p. 443. Cf. Schopenhauer 2010b, I 359, § 55, p. 331. Cf. in this regard Debona 2020.
[163] MR 1, n. 146, pp. 94–95.

ates with necessity, a will with freedom. But a will without a motive [*ein Wille ohne Motiv*] is as inconceivable as an effect without a cause. […].

Both sides of the question can be solved only by our showing how will and causality, freedom and nature are one and the same. The way to this will be shown by my new doctrine, namely that the body is the will that has become an object, and yet the will-in-itself [*der Wille an sich*] is under the dominion of the law of motivation [*dem Gesetz der Motivation ... unterworfen*], but as body is under the dominion of the law of causality.[164]

The "will-in-itself" or metaphysical will "is under the dominion of the law of motivation."[165] But a *motive* is a set of states of representations, that is, properly speaking, a *cognition* (be it truthful or erroneous). Consequently, the will that 'has chosen' (cf. *supra*, 10.7) existence in time is subordinated to some kind of cognition – which, at this point, can only be identified with the "fundamental error" of combining the concepts of "life" and "happiness".

It is clear that insofar as the will-in-itself is subject to the law of motivation, and insofar as the latter necessarily presupposes cognition, Schopenhauer must also presuppose some kind of cognition in relation to the will itself. But what kind of cognition is it? And *who* or *what* is it that cognizes? Is it the "pure subject", who, apart from being the author of the act of will which originated existence in time, is also the one who has to learn from life what life itself and its will really are (cf. *supra*, 10.8)? In any case, here the analysis of the fragments must come to a halt, because it has reached a point that, although logically presupposed by the texts themselves, is confined to their implicit dimension, thus remaining fundamentally unexpressed.

It can, however, be established with certainty that Schopenhauer's position is not contradictory: the *will* subordinated to cognition is not the same *will* that subordinates cognition to itself; and likewise, *cognition* subordinated to will is not the same *cognition* that subordinates will to itself. Schopenhauer does not affirm this double or reciprocal subordination *sub eodem:* the will that chooses between temporality and eternity is subordinated to the (correct or fallacious) cognition of what "temporality" and "eternity" are (this cognition constitutes the "motive" of the decision). Instead, the cognition within the sphere that has been chosen is subordinated to the will that has already made the choice, and has therefore already determined itself as willing-life or willing-eternity. Consequently, *within life and willing-life*, (empirical) cognition is subordinate to will; but *in the original choice*

---

[164] MR 1, n. 232, p. 146.
[165] Cf. also MR 1, n. 220, pp. 137–138: "*in so far as the will is the body* [italics mine], it is under the dominion *not merely* [italics mine] of the law of motivation, *but also* [italics mine] of the law of causality".

between life (temporality) and non-life (eternity), will is rather subordinate to cognition (of temporality and eternity).

It is important to recognize in this part of the discourse the development of the fundamental core of the theory of double consciousness. In fact, the *will's choice between life in time and the denial of life in time corresponds to the choice between the realm of empirical consciousness and the realm of better consciousness* – and thus, ultimately, to the choice between the two consciousnesses. It is precisely through the will that the individual chooses whether to be one or the other.[166] Empirical cognition (within the temporal sphere) and metempirical cognition (within the eternal sphere) are the consequence of this original choice of the will: this is the 'voluntaristic' part of the discourse. But, in making the choice, the will depends in turn on the cognition of the two choice options: this is the 'intellectualistic' part of the discourse.

Insofar as empirical cognition coincides with cognition according to the principle of reason and metempirical cognition with cognition of the Platonic Idea (cf. *supra*, 10.12), Schopenhauer will have to explain in voluntarist terms how the individual can pass from the first to the second form of cognition (i.e. by tracing this transition back to a momentary suspension of the will-to-life: cf. *infra*, 11.11; 12.9).

So, resuming the main thread of the argument and coming to its conclusion: in every decision or choice, for Schopenhauer the will is always subordinated to the law of motivation and thus to cognition. However, where cognition (together with its object) 'arises' as an *Erscheinung* of the will's choice, *this* cognition is (evidently) subordinate to the will that has made the choice. More concretely: the relationship between the metaphysical will and its two choice options (temporality and eternity), as well as the relationship between man's empirical will (the empirical character) and empirical motives, follows an 'intellectualistic' logic. The same applies to the human will insofar as, given the cognition that life is pain, it is restored to its original (metaphysical) choice between temporality and eternity. But since it is only based on the intelligible character that a certain representation takes on the value or meaning of "motive", the relationship between representations as motives and the intelligible character – as well as, in more general terms, the relationship between cognition according to the principle of reason (cognition internal to existence in time) and the metaphysical will that has chosen existence in time – follows a 'voluntarist' logic: here the will is more original than cognition. Schopenhauer does not contradict himself, because his voluntarism and his intellectualism concern different spheres.

---

166 Cf. MR 1, n. 35, p. 23.

From 1815 onwards, Schopenhauer would radically and definitively exclude that the will-in-itself (which is external to the principle of sufficient reason) is subordinate to the law of motivation.[167] Nevertheless, the considerations just made – albeit relating to a phase of his thought that was not yet definitive – are essential to understand why some voluntarist traits and other decidedly intellectualist ones are also present in his mature system (cf. *infra*, 11.13; 12.7–12.8).

10.14 The Vanity of Suicide

The rejection of life, i.e. the will-not-to-be that follows from the cognition of what life itself is, should in no way be understood as *suicide*. The remarks on the irrelevance of external events and, therefore, of all *opera operata* (cf. *supra*, 10.10) are reflected in Schopenhauer's explicit and radical position in relation to this issue. One must always bear in mind that for Schopenhauer life, i.e. temporal existence, is the appearance of the intelligible character (*supra*, 10.7). "The will itself, the intelligible character, stands firm [*steht fest*] and is not in time".[168] Only in the light of these points is it possible to understand what Schopenhauer writes in fragment 189:

> Death is not sanctification [*Heiligung*], but merely furnishes the possibility thereof. For just as delusion is infallibly and inevitably set up [*gesetzt*] with life, so too life is set up with delusion. And whoever persists in willing-life [*Lebenwollen*] will live, although this body dies; for to the extent that there is delusion, its appearance [*Erscheinung*] does not fail to come.[169]

Given the "delusion" that life in time is a happy condition, so too is willing-life – and thus also the appearance of such a will, i.e. life itself. Mere physical death *per se* does not offer true "redemption [*Erlösung*]": it does not realize the "forgiveness" of our "trespassing [*Schuld*]",[170] because it "dissolves not the delusion but [indeed] only the appearance thereof, namely the body".[171]

Man's true original sin is not the mere fact of living or existing, but *having willed* to live or exist (whereby life is only the *Erscheinung* of this will). In order to be redeemed and truly take leave of existence and its pain, man must not stop living, but rather cease to *want* to live – that is, he must deny or annihilate in himself the

---

167 Cf. MR 1, n. 413, pp. 287–289; n. 457, pp. 330–331.
168 MR 1, n. 191, p. 115.
169 MR 1, n. 189, p. 114. Translation modified.
170 MR 1, n. 194, p. 117. Translation modified.
171 MR 1, n. 189, p. 114. Translation modified.

will of which life is the manifestation. Only the extinction of willing-life can truly save one from life; otherwise, if one continues to want life, one will always and again have life, even beyond physical death, because that will shall always manifest itself. Developing an idea from fragment 263,[172] in 1817 Schopenhauer would state that this is precisely the authentic meaning of the "myth" of reincarnation,[173] to which he therefore attributed a very high speculative value ("The *myth of metempsychosis* is far and away the most valuable, most important and nearest to philosophical truth of all the myths ever devised, that I regard it as the *non plus ultra* of mythical description").[174]

Now, the necessary consequence of these premises is the uselessness of suicide for the purposes of salvation. Suicide is "the greatest contradiction": a person who takes their own life does so because they want life – indeed, they want a life that is different from the one they have, free of pain.[175] Through his act, the suicidal person does not cease to want to live, but only to live: one thus "destroys the appearance of willing though willing, instead of abolishing willing itself";[176] this way one exercises, instead of denying, one's own will.

According to Schopenhauer, the only legitimate form of suicide – that is, the only one in which the will-to-life is effectively denied – is the passive form, which consists in death by starvation: it expresses "the highest degree of asceticism".[177] Once the pain connected with existence has been acknowledged, the will can wish to "abolish [*aufheben*] its concrete appearance", i.e. it can decide to extinguish the body by means of "voluntary death by starvation", "whereby it does away with itself and this is freedom, the possibility of redemption".[178] All other modes of suicide betray the "intention to avoid a long agony", and thus do not actually realize the negation of the will-to-life.[179] Concerning these points, fragment 275 already expresses Schopenhauer's definitive position.[180]

---

172 Cf. MR 1, n. 263, p. 213. The doctrine of reincarnation already seems to be hinted at in fragment 122 from 1813: "Just as in our dreams deceased persons appear as living without there being even a thought of their deaths, so after our present life's dream comes to an end through death, there will at once begin a new one which knows nothing of that life and that death" (MR 1, p. 84).
173 Cf. MR 1, n. 646, pp. 487–488.
174 MR 1, n. 686, p. 531.
175 MR 1, n. 275, p. 183.
176 MR 1, n. 275, p. 183. Translation modified.
177 MR 1, n. 275, p. 183.
178 MR 1, n. 220, p. 138. Translation modified.
179 Cf. MR 1, n. 99, pp. 74–75: "the highest degree of asceticism, the total denial of the temporal consciousness, is the *voluntary death by starvation* […] From absolutely pure asceticism we cannot think of any other death than that through starvation, since the intention to avoid a long agony and affliction is already an affirmation of the world of the senses". This part of the text does not belong

Once again, it is a matter of denying not the *appearance* of willing-life (life itself, the body), but *this very will*. True salvation does not come from outward deeds (of which, in the final analysis, suicide is an instance), but from faith, from the inner dimension – that is, from the *will*.

10.15 Will as the Origin of Pain. The Infinity of Will

For Schopenhauer, life is essentially pain; wanting life is therefore equivalent to (unconsciously) wanting pain: "Willing-happiness is the opposite of willing-life".[181] Since existence, apart from the rare times when the better eternal consciousness takes over, is pain (cf. *supra*, 10.6), and since the will-to-life is at the origin of life, then the will-to-life is the true origin of pain, of all pain – i. e. of pain as such.

> That we *will* at all is our misfortune; it does not matter in the least *what* we will. But willing (the fundamental error [*Grundirrthum*]) can never be satisfied [*befriedigt*], and so we never cease to will and life is an abiding state of woe and misery, for it is simply the appearance of willing [*die Erscheinung des Wollens*], is objectified willing [*das objektivirte Wollen*]. We constantly delude ourselves [*Wir wähnen*] that the desired object can put an end to our willing, may rather that only we ourselves can do so, in that we just cease to will [...].[182]

Later, Schopenhauer adds: "For as soon as the desired object is obtained, it merely assumes another form [*Gestalt*] and at once exists again. It is the very devil that always taunts us in different forms [*unter andern Gestalten*]".[183]

The statement "that we will at all [*überhaupt*] is our misfortune" evidently presupposes the determination of the will *tout court* as the will-to-life (or will to exist in time), and thus prefigures the univocalization of the concept of will, which was to be fully realized in the following fragments (cf. *infra*, 11.14). The will is in itself a misfortune, because (as willing-life) it is the condemnation to an eternal, implacable thirst. An object (something willed) that, once obtained, can quench the will forever, *does not exist*.

---

to the original drafting of fragment 99, but was added later; it probably does not date back to 1813, like the rest of the fragment, but to 1814; note, in this respect, the use of the same expression as in fragment 275 to characterize "voluntary death by starvation": "the highest degree of asceticism".
180 Schopenhauer 2010b, I 471–476, § 69, pp. 425–429.
181 MR 1, n. 146, p. 95. Translation modified.
182 MR 1, n. 213, p. 130. Translation modified.
183 MR 1, n. 213, p. 130, fn.

10.15 Will as the Origin of Pain. The Infinity of Will — 373

In the course "On the Facts of Consciousness", Fichte spoke of the infinity of acting according to the drive (*Trieb*): the latter, as the expression of the superfactual being in the I, is "eternal" and "everlasting" like the superfactual being itself, so that it can never be fully satisfied (*befriedigt*) – its satisfaction is necessarily postponed indefinitely.[184] The individual stages of this process of infinite satisfaction lie in attaining the objects of the concepts of purpose which, time after time, provisionally give shape (*Gestalt*) to the drive, which is shapeless (*gestaltos*) in itself.[185] In this regard, Schopenhauer had written that Fichte "gives the soul", i.e., the I as the principle of the world, "a drive which is just as strange and odd" as the world: a drive which "always wills something and, when it has this, again wills something else"[186] (cf. *supra*, 6.4). Schopenhauer understands Fichte's "drive" as "will", but Fichte, in the course "On the Facts of Consciousness" (according to Schopenhauer's transcription), only once mentions the "will", in a context, moreover, that taints the term with the meaning of arbitrariness (*Willkühr*).[187]

Now, in 1814, Schopenhauer personally supported what he previously (wrongly) attributed to Fichte: "willing can never be satisfied", for "as soon as the desired object is obtained, it merely assumes another form". Just as the "drive" for Fichte, so for Schopenhauer the "will" can never reach definitive satisfaction (*Befriedigung*); the object of the will is destined to endlessly take on a new *Gestalt*.

But it should also be noted that here, as later in the mature system, the willed object entertains with the willing subject a relationship analogous to that which, in Fichte's *Wissenschaftslehre*, the thing-in-itself entertains with the finite I: it too, as soon as it is reached, immediately reappears in another form (since each time it is only shifted further: *nur weiter hinausgesetzt*), so that the identity of ideal and real – which represents the ultimate goal of *Streben* – is, from the point of view of the finite I, always and only ideal, never real (cf. *supra*, 6.4).

Referring to the infinity of the will, which is at one with its endless unfulfillment, Schopenhauer mentions again the better cognition:

> We constantly delude ourselves [...] that the desired object can put an end to our willing, may rather that only we ourselves can do so, in that we just cease to will. This (release from willing) occurs through better cognition, and so *Oupnekhat* [...] says: *tempore quo cognitio simul advenit amor e medio supersurrexit;* here by *amor* is meant *maya* which is just that willing, that love (for the object), whose objectification or appearance is the world. As the fundamen-

---

[184] Cf. MR 2, pp. 63–64.
[185] MR 2, p. 63.
[186] MR 2, p. 64. Translation modified.
[187] Cf. MR 2, p. 37. The arbitrariness (*Willkühr*) is mentioned on the same page, just above (MR 2, p. 37: Payne translates it as "arbitrary action"; cf. HN II, p. 34).

tal error [*Grundirrthum*] it is at the same time, so to speak, the origin of evil and of the world (which are really one and the same).[188]

That the object of willing can actually satisfy the will itself is a delusion (*Wahn*) – the fundamental error by virtue of which man *wills* at all. The better cognition (*cognitio*) thus seems to have as its content, once more, the necessary link between life in time and pain (and thus, conversely, between happiness and eternity). The experience from which better cognition can arise is first and foremost the fact that pain remains, even if the desired object is obtained. "Living" and "willing" "are identical", because life (the world) is the manifestation of the will;[189] the unhappiness of life and the unhappiness of willing are thus, likewise, the same thing.

As a result of all this, and, above all, of the identity between "world" and "evil", "it is clear that it is far truer to say that the devil created the world than that God created it. Likewise it is truer to say that the world is identical with the devil than to say that it is identical with God."[190]

If one embraces the creationist hypothesis, then it must be said that the world was created by the devil and not by God; if, on the other hand, one embraces the immanentist hypothesis, then it is more accurate to speak of pandevilism ("the world is identical with the devil") than of pantheism ("the world is identical with God"). Schopenhauer here implicitly admits the theoretical hypothesis that Schelling, in his treatise on freedom, had explicitly discarded: "pandemonism [*Pandämonismus*]".[191] Nietzsche would define Schopenhauer's thought precisely as a form of *Pandiabolismus*.[192] While in the years 1809–1810 young Schopenhauer did not doubt the existence of a benign divine principle as the creator of the world (cf. *supra*, 1.7; 2.3), in 1814 he stated peremptorily that "it is far truer to say that the devil created the world".

In fragment 213 Schopenhauer mentioned the sacred texts of India – but, it seems, only to find in them an authoritative confirmation of what he had already elaborated on his own (his personal reflection is *followed* by: "so [*daher*] Oupnekhat says [...]"). However, at this point it is necessary to address the problem of young Schopenhauer's reception of Indian wisdom, which opened up a new and decisive part of his reflections.

---

[188] MR 1, n. 213, p. 130. Translation modified.
[189] MR 1, fn to n. 263, p. 175.
[190] MR 1, n. 213, p. 130.
[191] Schelling 2006, p. 25.
[192] Cf. Nietzsche 1967 ff., vol. IV, 2, *Menschliches, Allzumenschliches I. Nachgelassene Fragmente 1876 bis Winter 1877–1878*, fragment 23 [27], p. 509.

11 The Study of *Oupnekhat* and the Elaboration of the Concept of a Universal "Will-To-Life". The Abandonment of the Theory of the Better Consciousness and the Birth of the System

11.1 The Encounter with Indian Wisdom

In the manuscripts, the first explicit reference to Oriental texts is in fragment 189, which I already analyzed (see *supra*, 10.11).[1] The "Maya of the Indians" is here identified by Schopenhauer with "life" and the "world of the senses". This mention of "Maya", however, does not belong to the original drafting of the fragment, but to a later addition.[2] In a note to fragment 191, Schopenhauer quotes a passage from the *Oupnekhat*; but the fragment itself has remarkable terminological correspondences with the passage in question and thus already seems to allude to it (cf. *supra*, 10.8).[3] In fragment 192, Indian wisdom is mentioned in relation to the correct method of philosophical inquiry: against "foolish dogmatics", which focuses only on the objects of knowledge, Schopenhauer sets "the wiser Indians", who, in order to understand the world and the universe, "started from the *subject*" (cf. *infra*, 11.5).[4] The first fragment in which Indian wisdom is explicitly related to the metaphysics of will is number 213: here "Maya" is identified with *amor* or "willing [*Wollen*]", of which the "world" is an "appearance" (cf. *supra*, 10.15).[5]

Schopenhauer obtained his first basic information about Indian civilization in 1811, while attending the ethnography lectures of historian Arnold Hermann Ludwig Heeren in Göttingen.[6] In the winter of 1813–1814, in Weimar, he was able to greatly expand his knowledge by frequenting the orientalist Friedrich Majer. In this regard, Schopenhauer recounts in a letter: "At the same time [as his interactions with Goethe], without being asked, Friedrich Majer introduced me to Indian antiquity, which has been an essential influence on me".[7] On 4 December 1813 he borrowed the two volumes of the *Asiatisches Magazin* from the library, in the first

---

1 MR 1, n. 189, pp. 113–114.
2 Cf. App 2011, p. 222.
3 MR 1, fn. to n. 191, p. 115.
4 MR 1, n. 192, p. 116.
5 MR 1, n. 213, p. 130.
6 Cf. App 2003; 2006b; 2006a, pp. 37–40.
7 Schopenhauer 1978a, p. 261 (Letter to Johann Eduard Erdmann, 9 April 1851). En. tr. in Cartwright 2010, p. 239.

of which he could read a German article related to Chinese Buddhism[8] and an annotated translation of the *Bhagavad Gita* by Majer himself (cf. *supra*, 10.8). In the spring of 1814, he immersed himself in the study of the *Mythologie des Indous* by the cousins Polier[9] and, above all, the two volumes of the *Oupnekhat*.[10] In late 1815, he started consulting the volumes of the *Asiatic Researches*;[11] from this point onwards, Schopenhauer became a passionate and habitual reader of Oriental texts.[12]

11.2 The Reading of the *Oupnekhat:* Maya as Universal *voluntas aeterna* and Individual *appetitus existentiae*. *Cognitio, nolitio* and *annihilatio*

The *Oupnekhat* (1801–1802) is the Latin translation of a partial Persian translation of the *Upanishads*. In the Persian translation, authored by Prince Dara Shikoh around 1656, the original text of the *Upanishads* was supplemented, without any indication, with comments and explanations drafted by Dara himself and the team of scholars who collaborated with him.[13] These comments were conditioned by Sankara's commentaries on the Upanishads and the Sufi doctrine of the One-All.[14] The Latin translator, Anquetil-Duperron, translated the work without suspecting this second layer of the text; and even Schopenhauer, who read Duperron's translation directly, understood Dara's comments as an integral part of the text of the *Upanishads* (to the point that, in *Parerga and Paralipomena*, he expressly and passionately defended the reliability of Dara's translation).[15] Moreover, in some notes to the text and in an appendix to both volumes (entitled *Emendationes et an-*

---

8 *Ueber die Fo-Religion in China*, in Klaproth 1802, vol. 1, pp. 149–169. On this text, cf. App 1998b; App 2010a.
9 Polier and Polier 1809.
10 *Oupnek'hat (id est, secretum tegendum)* (Anquetil-Duperron 1801–1802). On the popularity of this text, cf. App 2010b, pp. 363–439; App 2012. Weimar library's register of Schopenhauer's loans is reproduced in App 2006a, pp. 47–51. A German translation of the *Oupnek'hat* was edited by F. Mischel (1882).
11 For Schopenhauer's relative annotations, see MR 2, pp. 459–461, but especially App 1998a.
12 For a general reconstruction of Schopenhauer's relationship with India, see the comprehensive essay by G. Gurisatti, "Schopenhauer e l'India" (Gurisatti 2007). For a systematic comparison between Schopenhauer's mature philosophy and Indian thought, cf. Kapani 2011; Barua 2013; Cross 2013.
13 On Dara, cf. Hasrat 1982. On Dara's translation, cf. Göbel-Gross 1962; Piantelli (1986; reprinted in 2013, pp. 75–121); Gerhard 2008, p. 18; App 2011, pp. 117–136; Gerhard 2013.
14 Cf. Piantelli 2013, p. 79. Cf. Dara Shikoh 1929.
15 Cf. Schopenhauer 2015, p. 356.

notationes), Duperron offers some clarifications, which naturally constitute his interpretation of the texts themselves. The *Oupnekhat* is thus extremely composite, because it has (at least) three levels: the content of the *Upanishads* as selected and translated into Persian by Dara (and translated again by Duperron into Latin), Dara's own comments and Duperron's explanations.

One more premise is needed here. In the *Oupnekhat*, the *Brahman* (which for the Indians is the unmanifest Absolute, devoid of any form or determination) is designated by the term "Brahm" and defined as the Creator of the world;[16] on the other hand, the God *Brahma* (who in Hinduism is properly God the Creator, that is, the Absolute *insofar as it is determined or manifested as Creator*) is designated by the name "Brahma" and is identified with the archangel Gabriel.[17] The relationship between the unmanifest Absolute and the world is thus equivocally determined as "creation";[18] and the distinction between the unmanifest Absolute and God the Creator is equivocally presented as analogous to that which in the Judeo-Christian tradition is found between God the Creator and his (created) 'prime minister'. This anomaly would condition Schopenhauer's interpretation of the terms *Brahm* and *Brahma* for a long time (cf. *infra*, 11.13). In any case, for the sake of greater adherence to the text, I will respect this terminology.

At the end of the *Praefatio*, written by the Persian translator and translated by Duperron into Latin, Schopenhauer found a glossary of the main Sanskrit terms (*Explicatio praecipuorum verborum samskretikorum quae in Oupnek'hat adhibentur*).[19] The term *maïa* is defined here as follows: "*voluntas aeterna; quod causa ostensi sine fuit* (existentiâ) *est*", i.e.: "eternal will; that which is the cause of the manifestation without being (existence)".[20] Next to this definition, Schopenhauer notes a reference to page 17 of the second volume,[21] where the world (*mundus*) is defined as *figura*, i.e. image or 'allegory', of *Brahm*.[22]

Everything is *figura* of *Brahm*; everything is one, and the multiplicity of things is only apparent (*tota figura mundi, figura vestra est:* Brahm, *vos estis; id est, creator, vos estis. Vos unum estis*).[23] In truth, there is but one Being, and, as Duperron explains in a footnote, *maïa* is the *desiderium*, which this one Being experiences, of

---

16 Anquetil-Duperron 1801–1802, I, p. 7.
17 Cf. Anquetil-Duperron 1801–1802, I, pp. 10, 353, 439–440.
18 Cf. Piantelli 2013, pp. 103–104.
19 Cf. Anquetil-Duperron 1801–1802, I, p. 7.
20 Anquetil-Duperron 1801–1802, I, p. 10.
21 The texts of Schopenhauer's library are available online, on the website of the Schopenhauer-Archiv.
22 Cf. Anquetil-Duperron 1801–1802, I, p. 321; II, p. 17.
23 Cf. Anquetil-Duperron 1801–1802, II, p. 17.

coming out of itself and appearing as manifold.²⁴ The *maïa* resides in *Brahm* himself:²⁵ before everything was, "in the beginning", was *maïa* (*Priùs ab omnibus productionibus, maïa fuit*).²⁶ In this sense, *maïa* is the divine and primordial *amor aeternus* that produces the illusory existence of finite realities.²⁷ The passages concerning the identity of "*maïa*" and cosmogonic "Love" (in Persian: *ishq*) belong to Dara's unreported additions.²⁸

> *Maïa* est quod videtur esse, et reverà non est. Sic Ens supremum, in quo est *maïa*, unicum primò fuit, semper est, semper erit; quamvis in eo homines τὸ facere et τὸ fieri, imaginentur : et hoc impossibile, cùm omne ipsum ist.²⁹

According to the text of the *Oupnekhat*, therefore, *maïa* is both the primordial *amor* or *desiderium*, from which the appearance of the manifold originates, and this manifold itself, which only *appears* to be, but in reality is not at all (*quod videtur esse, et reverà non est*). The sage, however, sees or knows everything as a manifestation of *Brahm*, and therefore knows that all things are one:³⁰ "*Causâ amoris aeterni, quòd* maïa (*est*), *et* aoudia (ignorantiae), *duo apparetis*".³¹ The term "aoudia" is here a kind of transliteration of the Sanskrit term *avidyā*, which means precisely "ignorance" (*a-vidyā:* "ne-science").

In relation to *Brahm*, Duperron defines *maïa* as *desiderium ad sese effundendum:* a ludic *volitio*, in which the supreme Being (*Ens summum*), wanting to play with itself, multiplied (or divided) itself into the various entities.³² On p. 215 of the second volume, in a footnote to the text, Duperron made a comment that must have particularly struck Schopenhauer: *Ens supremum maïa dictum, id est amor aeternus, actio aeterna; sed actio apparens tantùm.*³³ In other words: *maïa* – understood as *amor aeternus*, the *voluntas aeterna* from which the appearance of the world originates – is the supreme Being itself.

In relation to man and, in general, to individual beings (*quatenùs in homine, in rebus externis, singularibus*), *maïa* is defined by Duperron as *desiderium, amor, ap-*

---

24 Anquetil-Duperron 1801–1802, II, p. 17.
25 Anquetil-Duperron 1801–1802, I, p. 203.
26 Anquetil-Duperron 1801–1802, I, p. 317.
27 Cf. e.g. Anquetil-Duperron 1801–1802, I, p. 405.
28 Cf. Anquetil-Duperron 1801–1802, I, p. 405. Cf. Piantelli 2013, pp. 95–96.
29 Anquetil-Duperron 1801–1802, I, p. 589.
30 Cf. Anquetil-Duperron 1801–1802, I, pp. 372–374. On this point, cf. Schopenhauer's note in MR 2, p. 263, quoting, however, the text of the *Bhagavad Gita*.
31 Cf. Anquetil-Duperron 1801–1802, II, p. 17.
32 Cf. Anquetil-Duperron 1801–1802, I, p. 640.
33 Cf. Anquetil-Duperron 1801–1802, II, p. 215, footnote.

petitus existentiae, propensio ad apparendum.[34] It blinds the individual because it draws him into an illusion, concealing from him the only truly real Entity and making him perceive as existing that which in truth does not exist, never has existed and never will: *Mundus, pura apparentia; Deus, solus existens.*[35] The dichotomy between *atma* (man's Self, which is one with *Brahm*) and *ostensum* (world) is equivalent in the texts to the dichotomy between *verum* and *mendacium.*[36]

The content of the universal illusion is the existence of the manifold (of a multiplicity of entities). But whoever breaks this illusion dissolves the 'external' or universal *maïa* and, at the same time, also the 'internal' or individual maïa, as *amor* or *desiderium* for the manifold itself.[37] Knowledge of the non-existence or unreality of what is desired extinguishes desire forever. In this sense, in a page of the *Oupnekhat* particularly dear to Schopenhauer (it is quoted in fragment 213 and later in *The World*),[38] it is stated that cognition (*cognitio*) definitively extinguishes *amor*: *Tempore quo cognitio simul advenit, amor é medio supersurrexit* – that is, "The moment cognition arrives, thence desire left the scene."[39] This extinction of *amor* is also called *nolitio* in the texts.[40] One who, by seeing through the illusion, cognizes *Brahm* as the only truly real Being, *ceases to exist* – that is, properly speaking, he ceases to *believe* he exists as an 'individual' entity, distinct and separate from the Whole.[41] The supreme *cognitio* produces *nolitio* – that is, the end of *amor*, or *appetitus existentiae* – and the definitive *annihilatio* of the individual (as such).

The term *ostensum* (literally "that which is manifested", "that which appears": the world) is often treated in the *Oupnekhat* as a synonym for *apparitiones* (*Erscheinungen* in German).[42] And indeed Schopenhauer, in a note to the text, explic-

---

34 Cf. Anquetil-Duperron 1801–1802, I, p. 639.
35 Anquetil-Duperron 1801–1802, I, pp. 639–640.
36 Cf. Anquetil-Duperron 1801–1802, I, pp. 405–406; Anquetil-Duperron 1801–1802, II, p. 351.
37 Cf. Anquetil-Duperron 1801–1802, I, p. 640. Cf. also Anquetil-Duperron 1801–1802, I, p. 391.
38 Cf. the title page of the Fourth and last Book of *The World as Will and Representation* (Schopenhauer 2010b, I 317, p. 297).
39 Cf. Anquetil-Duperron 1801–1802, I, p. 405; cf. also Anquetil-Duperron 1801–1802, II, p. 216. Here I disagree with the translation provided in the Cambridge edition, in which the motto is interpreted in the opposite sense: "When knowledge asserted itself, thence arose desire" (Schopenhauer 2010b, I 317, p. 297). Deussen translates correctly as follows: "Zur Zeit, wo die Erkenntnis sich einstellte, hat die Begierde sich von dannen gehoben" (Schopenhauer 1911–1942, vol. I, p. 717). This also corresponds to Schopenhauer's interpretation in fragment 213 of the manuscripts, cited below.
40 Cf. Anquetil-Duperron 1801–1802, II, pp. 77–92.
41 Anquetil-Duperron 1801–1802, II, p. 10: "*Quisquis omnia animantia et elementa τὸν Brahm (esse) scit; et omnes mundos τὸν Brahm (esse) scit [...], ipse in (se) ipso deletus (annihilatus) fit*".
42 Cf. Anquetil-Duperron 1801–1802, II, p. 217.

itly traces the opposition between *atma* and *mundus* back to the Kantian dualism between *Ding an sich* and *Erscheinung*.[43]

This explains why Schopenhauer, in fragment 213 of the manuscripts, identifies *Maya* with the "willing, love (for the object) whose objectification [*Objektivirung*] or appearance [*Erscheinung*] is the world".[44] In two slightly later annotations, *Maya* is assimilated to the "inner driving force" of the corporeal world, which Giordano Bruno called "God",[45] as well as to the ἔρως that "the poets and philosophers of antiquity" posited as the "principle [*Princip*] of the world".[46] It was only towards the end of 1815 that (on the basis of his study of the "Asiatic Researches") Schopenhauer would modify his understanding of the term *Maya*, identifying it no longer with the metaphysical *voluntas*, but with the "objecthood [*Objektität*]" of the latter – that is, with Kant's "appearance".[47] The addition to fragment 189, in which *Maya* is identified not with *amor*, but with "life" and the "world of the senses", presupposes this correction and is therefore necessarily later than 1814.[48]

In a section at the end of the first volume (*Animadvertenda quaedam in annotationibus*), Anquetil-Duperron invites readers to consider the *Oupnekhat* from a primarily philosophical, not (only) antiquist or philological point of view.[49] In this sense, he also seeks to point out concrete parallels between Eastern and Western philosophy, devoting space especially to the *transcendentalismus* of *Emanuelis Kant*.[50] By focusing not on things, but on the human *consciousness* of things, Kant's philosophy, just like Brahmanism, calls man back to himself (*hominem ad seipsum revocat*).[51]

---

43 Cf. Anquetil-Duperron 1801–1802, I, p. 395. Cf. App 2011, pp. 111–112.
44 MR 1, n. 213, p. 130.
45 MR 1, n. 234, p. 148.
46 MR 1, n. 461, p. 332.
47 MR 1, n. 461, p. 332. Translation modified. This note is later than the first draft of the fragment. The same must therefore be said for the conclusion of fragment 359 (cf. MR 1, p. 247). The first fragment, in which the identification between Maya and Kant's appearance is found in the body of the text, is number 564 from 1816 (cf. MR 1, p. 419).
48 U. App (2011, p. 147) seems to miss this point, although he himself notes these two distinct phases in Schopenhauer's understanding of the term *Maya* (2011, pp. 183–184).
49 Cf. Anquetil-Duperron 1801–1802, I, p. 722.
50 Cf. Anquetil-Duperron 1801–1802, I, p. 711. On this, cf. Halbfass 1988, pp. 66–68.
51 Cf. Anquetil-Duperron 1801–1802, I, p. 711. On Duperron's attempt to establish common ground between Eastern and European philosophy, cf. Gerhard 2008, pp. 124–127; Kurbel 2015, pp. 151–160.

11.3 The First Occurrence of the Term *Maya* in the Manuscripts of 1814 and the New Concept of a Universal Metaphysical Will, of Which the Whole World Is the Appearance

As a consequence of the above, the question arises as to what role the Oriental texts – in particular the *Oupnekhat* – played in the genesis of Schopenhauer's philosophy.

Schopenhauer's retrospective statements do not unambiguously settle the matter. For example, in 1816 Schopenhauer wrote: "I confess that I do not believe my doctrine could have come about before the Upanishads, Plato and Kant could cast their rays simultaneously [*zugleich*] into the mind of one man".[52] In this fragment (much debated among scholars),[53] the precedence given to the *Upanishads* is dampened by the adverb *zugleich*, which seems to exclude any kind of hierarchy between the three terms: the fragment's implication, in fact, is that not only without the *Upanishads*, but also without Plato and Kant the "doctrine" in question could never "have come about". The order in which the three terms are mentioned could be merely chronological – purely relative, that is, to the historical dating of the respective doctrines or texts. And yet, the impression one gets when reading this passage is that Schopenhauer intends to give the Indian texts real priority. Except that elsewhere, in *Parerga and Paralipomena*, Schopenhauer assigns the main role to Kant: "the root of my philosophy already lies in the Kantian philosophy, especially in the doctrine of empirical and intelligible character".[54]

In the Preface to the first edition of *The World as Will and Representation*, Schopenhauer writes that "each of the individual and disconnected remarks that form the *Upanishads* could be derived as a corollary of the thoughts I will be imparting, although conversely my thoughts certainly cannot be found there".[55] And yet, in the 1851 letter quoted above (cf. *supra*, 11.1), Schopenhauer expressly affirms that "Indian antiquity" had been "an essential influence" on him.[56]

---

52 MR 1, n. 623, p. 467. According to B. P. Göcke, this parallel of Kant, Plato and the Indians can be traced back to Schopenhauer's acquaintance with Karl Christian Krause (Göcke 2021). About the main theoretical points on which Göcke assumes Krause's influence on Schopenhauer (i. e., the immediate self-knowledge of the subject as will and the 'analogical' extension of this self-knowledge to entities other than the self), the terminology used by Schopenhauer seems to refer mainly to other sources (Fichte and Indian wisdom respectively: cf. *supra*, 9.4 – 9.5; *infra*, 11.5 – 11.7).
53 Cf. Hübscher 1989, p. 66; App 2006a, p. 57; Safranski 1990, pp. 202 – 203.
54 Schopenhauer 2014, p. 121.
55 Schopenhauer 2010b, I XII – XIII, p. 9.
56 Schopenhauer 1978a, p. 261. En. tr. in Cartwright 2010, p. 239.

Based on these statements, most scholars have taken extreme and opposing positions. Some minimize the question of the Oriental influence on young Schopenhauer;[57] others claim that Indian philosophy supposedly offered him only an authoritative and surprising confirmation of what he had already thought independently and in other ways.[58] On the opposite side of the spectrum, some scholars instead argue that Schopenhauer's metaphysics mainly depends on the Indian texts.[59] Instead of trying at all costs to univocalize the issue and attributing true relevance to only one or the other of those statements (as representatives of the two opposing historiographical parties sometimes do),[60] I think it is preferable to admit the fundamental *ambiguity* of Schopenhauer's position as a fact, and only then try to explain it.

Now, it is clear that any influence that oriental texts may have had on young Schopenhauer can only concern theoretical elements that are *peculiar to those texts* and are only found in the manuscripts *after* their reception by Schopenhauer. The fundamental question is then: do such theoretical elements exist? And, if they do, what are they?

As we have seen, the "will" had been a focal point of Schopenhauer's reflections since 1811. It is through the will (understood as the faculty of choice between good and evil) that man determines his eternal destiny (cf. *supra*, 1.9; 4.1–4.2); the will allows the individual to choose whether to *be* empirical consciousness or better consciousness (cf. *supra*, 7.11; 8.3 and 8.18). Man's very existence in time (as empirical consciousness) is for Schopenhauer the 'consequence' of an act of will, which religion mythically describes as "original sin" (cf. *supra*, 8.19).

In the dissertation of 1813, the will was explicitly thematized and gained extraordinary relevance through the doctrine of the "intelligible character" (cf. *supra*, 9.8). Developing the latter, in 1814 Schopenhauer arrived at the concept of an individual "willing-life [*Lebenwollen*]", of which "life" itself – man's existence in time, as a "body" – is the appearance (cf. *supra*, 10.7). The doctrine of the "negation of the

---

57 Cf. Hecker 1897, pp. 4–11; A. Hübscher 1989, p. 65; Kamata 1988, p. 254; Safranski 1990, pp. 202–203; Maage 1997, p. 15.
58 Cf. Vecchiotti 1969, pp. 372–373, 453–520, and Riconda (1969, p. 215), who takes up the work of H. von Glasenapp (1960). G. Zöller (2013b) also excludes any actual influence of Indian thought, on the basis that all myths from India, like Christian myths, were not passively assimilated by Schopenhauer, but actively reworked with a view to determining their philosophical core. Cf. also Zöller 2013a.
59 Cf. Mockrauer 1928; Meyer 1994; Berger 2004; App 2011; Kurbel 2015.
60 As two extreme interpretations of the 1816 fragment, cf. A. Hübscher, according to whom Schopenhauer "should have mentioned Plato and Kant first" (cf. Hübscher 1989, p. 66), and U. App, who, on the contrary, considers the aforementioned fragment as the key to understanding the influence of India on Schopenhauer (cf. App 2011, p. 154).

will", which would constitute a capital point of the mature system, was formulated for the first time in terms of the negation of the intelligible character (cf. *supra*, 10.11).

We have established that Schopenhauer's understanding of the concept of intelligible character, as well as the very terminology he used, depended heavily on Schelling (cf. *supra*, 9.11; 10.7). Consequently, with regard to the parts of the discourse that appear as a development of the doctrine of intelligible character, the primary role of Indian influence must be ruled out.[61] The same conclusion must be drawn with regard to the themes of *man's self-cognition as will* and the *infinity (unfulfillability) of the will*, for which Schopenhauer uses an overtly Fichtean terminology (cf. *supra*, 9.4–9.5; 10.15).[62]

And yet, in view of all this, it must also be noted that the concept of "willing-life", which Schopenhauer developed from the concept of intelligible character, exclusively concerns the individual: it is an *individual, particular will*. The appearance of this will – that is, of the timeless and original will, which Schopenhauer identifies with the "intelligible character" – is the life (existence in time) *of a single individual* (cf. *supra*, 10.7). However, this is necessary, insofar as the human character – as well as the will with which it is identified – is essentially individual (cf. *supra*, 9.8).

In fragment 213 Schopenhauer speaks instead, for the first time, of a metaphysical will, whose *Erscheinung* is not the existence or life of a single individual, but the existence of the world in its entirety.[63] This will constitutes the "origin of evil and of the world", and is therefore *universal* or 'collective', precisely insofar as it does not (only) manifest itself in a single element of the world (the "body" of a particular individual),[64] but rather in the world itself, which includes *all* things and *all* individuals. Schopenhauer *identifies* this will with the Maya of the Indians; this is the first occurrence of the term "Maya" within the manuscripts (the addition to fragment 189 being necessarily later than 1814: see *supra*, 11.2).

---

[61] This relationship is perhaps underestimated by U. App: the identity (posited by Schopenhauer in fragment 191) between intelligible character and the extratemporal will, of which the body and life are the "visibility", is certainly mentioned by him (cf. App 2011, p. 153), but as something obvious or marginal, not worthy of specific reflection or investigation. The intention here is instead to give due attention to this trait in the text.
[62] To me, the similarities that U. App finds with some passages in the *Bhagavad Gita* regarding the first of these two themes (cf. App 2006a, pp. 68–73) are less evident than those involving Fichte's *System der Sittenlehre*.
[63] MR 1, n. 213, p. 130.
[64] MR 1, n, 191, p. 115.

But this means that *the term "Maya" and the concept of a universal metaphysical will appear together, for the first time, in fragment 213 of the manuscripts, and are moreover explicitly identified here.* (Fragment 210 contains the first appearance of the term *Wille zum Leben*, but not the concept itself.)[65] This circumstance, which is extremely significant, leads to the conclusion that Schopenhauer formulated the concept of a universal metaphysical will on the model of the Maya of the Indians *as described in the Oupnekhat* – and thus on the basis not only of the original texts of the *Upanishads*, but also of Dara's (unreported) additions and Duperron's explanations.

Indeed, the expression *Wille zum Leben*, with which Schopenhauer denotes this universal will, seems to combine two different definitions of Maya given by Dara and Duperron, namely, *"voluntas aeterna"* and *"appetitus existentiae"* respectively (cf. *supra*, 11.2). The *Wille zum Leben* is literally *voluntas existentiae*. This synthesis can be found not only on a terminological and logical level, but also on a conceptual one. In fragment 213, the *Wollen* that Schopenhauer identifies with the "Maya" is, *on the one hand*, that of which the whole "world" is the appearance or objectification; *on the other hand*, that which is extinguished as a result of the "better cognition" – whereby Schopenhauer quotes the maxim of the *Oupnekhat: Tempore quo cognitio simul advenit, amor é medio supersurrexit*. But these two determinations evidently presuppose two distinct and complementary meanings of the term "Maya", corresponding precisely to those two definitions: the *Wollen* of which the world is the appearance is the Maya as the primordial and universal *voluntas aeterna*; the *Wollen* which is extinguished as a consequence of "better cognition" is the Maya as the individual *appetitus existentiae*.

As mentioned above, the first meaning of *Wollen* (the *universal* will-to-life, which is manifested or phenomenalized in the world) would constitute the keystone of Schopenhauer's metaphysical doctrine. It should be remembered, in this regard, that Duperron expressly identifies Maya as *amor aeternus* with the *Ens supremum*, of which the world is the appearance.[66]

The "better cognition", which produces "release from willing [*Befreiung vom Wollen*]",[67] relates instead to *Wollen*'s second meaning, as the *individual's amor* or desire for sense objects and for existence itself as a whole. For Schopenhauer, too, as claimed in the *Oupnekhat*, *cognitio* produces *nolitio*; and yet, beyond this formal analogy, the two positions cannot be likened any further. The content of the *cognitio* mentioned in the *Oupnekhat* does not coincide *sic et simpliciter*

---

65 MR 1, n, 210, p. 128.
66 Cf. Anquetil-Duperron 1801–1802, II, p. 215, footnote.
67 MR 1, n. 213, p. 130.

with the content of the "better cognition" Schopenhauer speaks of: the first is essentially the illusory nature or non-existence of the manifold; the second, on the other hand, is the constitutive nothingness and unhappiness (*das Nichtige und Unseelige*) "of willing or living, which are one".[68] For young Schopenhauer, "release from willing" does not originate from knowledge of the non-reality of what is willed, but from knowledge – more precisely, from *experience* – of the fact that will is essentially and inevitably pain.[69] About the specific content of "better cognition" (pain as the essence of life and the knowledge of this truth as a 'call' to liberation from willing-life), Schopenhauer's discourse seems to be linked back to Buddhism (cf. *supra*, 11.1) and thus to a 'syncretistic' reworking of Indian texts.

However, based on all that has been said so far, it must be concluded that the concept of a universal metaphysical will, which wills the world and therefore appears in the world itself, came to Schopenhauer from his study of the *Oupnekhat*. This concept, in fact, is a theoretical element peculiar to this text and occurred in the manuscripts only after its reception by young Schopenhauer.

> Haec productio mundi, quòd nomen et figura est, et causa ostensum (*esse*) illud, *maïa* est; id est, volitio vera productionis mundi.[70]

11.4 A Few Reasons for Young Schopenhauer's Sensitivity to Oriental Wisdom. The Meaning of His Ambiguous Retrospective Reflections

Despite the above considerations, it is not possible to consider the *Oupnekhat* as the sole source of Schopenhauer's metaphysics. Indeed, Schopenhauer's reflections prior to his knowledge of this text already contained certain theoretical elements, developed in dialogue with other traditions and authors, that could then find a fruitful path of development in the doctrines of the *Oupnekhat*.

In particular, with regard to the concept of a universal metaphysical will that lies at the origin of the world, Schopenhauer ascribed the origin of the individual's empirical consciousness and, therefore, of its content – the temporal or empirical world (cf. *supra*, 8.7 and 8.19) – to "willing" as early as 1813. The intelligible character is the primordial and timeless act of will with which each individual has chosen and determined his life in time (cf. *supra*, 10.7–10.9). The *cognitio – nolitio*

---

68 MR 1, footnote to n. 262, p. 175. Translation modified.
69 On the theme of suffering in Buddhism and Schopenhauer, cf. Ryan 2018.
70 Anquetil-Duperron 1801–1802, II, p. 225.

– *annihilatio* dynamic also finds a strong correspondence in the manuscripts, particularly in the interest in asceticism, which Schopenhauer interprets as the inner annihilation (*Vernichtung*) of oneself as a temporal being, as a consequence of the knowledge of one's eternal nature (cf. *supra*, 8.6 – 8.7; 10.5, 10.10 – 10.13). Also, the theme of the superiority of inner over outer knowledge, i.e., the assumption that man's interiority can open the door to metaphysical cognition, can be found in Schopenhauer's manuscripts well before 1814 (cf. *infra*, 11.5 and 11.7). Finally, with regard to the determination of the *mundus* as *pura apparentia*, one cannot forget Schopenhauer's repeated assertions about the illusory nature of the world of the senses, which has no true reality, but is pure semblance, akin to a "dream" (cf. *supra*, 3.6; 9.13). In the manuscripts, he imagines "that the lives of all people and my own life are only *dreams* of an eternal spirit, good and bad dreams, and every *death* is an awakening".[71]

By virtue of these pre-existing theoretical elements, Schopenhauer could see his own *Weltanschauung* confirmed and, at the same time, considerably enriched in the doctrines of the *Oupnekhat*; he was thus oriented towards certain tenets of the Indian doctrines (those he felt closest to) to the point of appropriating them, albeit in an original or 'creative' way. Even with regard to the theme of "better cognition" (i.e., the knowledge of pain essentially related to life as a 'means' to "redemption"), which in perspective is more connected to the Buddhist readings than to the study of *Oupnekhat*, the manuscripts document some reflections prior to 1814 which certainly oriented young Arthur's attention and sensibility in the study of Buddhist texts (cf. *supra*, 1.6 – 1.7; 7.10; 8.6).

On the other hand, even if one were to argue – for historical reasons that have yet to be determined – that the metaphysics of will came to Schopenhauer exclusively from the Indian texts, one would still have to justify why only certain traits of the latter affected the young philosopher so profoundly, and not others (or all of them) (cf. *infra*, 11.7 and 11.13). Yet, in order to account for this circumstance, one could do no more than refer to the aforementioned pre-existing theoretical elements, which would thus again become the fundamental and unavoidable starting point.

I can anticipate here that, in Schopenhauer's later reflections, the new theoretical acquisition borrowed from the *Oupnekhat* – the concept of a *universal* metaphysical will, which is phenomenalized in the whole world – would constitute an extremely powerful unification pole for all the previous themes (not only those mentioned above), which would gradually become conceptually subordinate to it. It is thus clear why Schopenhauer, in reconstructing the role that knowledge

---

71 MR 1, n. 77, p. 42.

of Oriental philosophy played in the genesis of his system, is extremely ambiguous, acknowledging its "influence" while also claiming the substantial originality and independence of his own thought, as well as his main debt to Kant ("the root of my philosophy already lies in the Kantian philosophy, especially in the doctrine of empirical and intelligible character").[72] In the light of the above considerations, it can be said that *influence* of the *Oupnekhat* concerns the new concept of the metaphysical will; Schopenhauer's *independence*, on the other hand, lies in the previously elaborated themes into which that concept is grafted (cf. *infra,* 11.6–11.7). However, this addition was destined to have repercussions on those same themes, giving rise to their structural rearrangement and unprecedented reformulation, which would then remain almost definitive in Schopenhauer's thought (cf. *infra,* 11.11–11.15).

Still, Schopenhauer's problematic self-understanding of the theoretical and genetic relationship between his philosophy and Indian wisdom is already contained *in nuce* in fragment 213. In quoting the passage from the *Oupnekhat*, Schopenhauer does not intend to refer to or repeat the Indian doctrine, but rather, much more ambitiously, to expand it in a new and radical way, pointing to its true and unexpressed *ground*. This is precisely the meaning of the "so [*daher*]" that introduces the above quotation: "release from willing [...] occurs through better cognition, and so [*daher*] Oupnekhat says [...]". *Daher* here indicates the reduction of the doctrine set out in this passage from *Oupnekhat* to the theme of "better cognition", and thus betrays the attitude that would later become peculiar to mature Schopenhauer, usually unwilling to acknowledge his intellectual debts. In the above-quoted passage from *The World as Will and Representation*, which is worth re-reading at this point, he would indeed state: "each of the individual and disconnected remarks that form the *Upanishads* could be derived [*ableiten*] as a corollary [*Folgesatz*] of the thoughts I will be imparting, although conversely my thoughts certainly cannot be found there."[73]

Now, at the time of fragment 213 of the manuscripts, Schopenhauer had two concepts that could be broadly referred to a metaphysics of will: on the one hand, the concept of an *individual will-to-life* ('deduced', as we have seen, from the concept of intelligible character), the appearance of which is the individual's body; on the other hand, the concept of a *universal will* (equivalent, for Schopenhauer, to the Maya of the Indians), the appearance of which is the entire sensible world or universe. The problem of the relationship between these two concepts is

---

72 Schopenhauer 2014, p. 121.
73 Schopenhauer 2010b, I XII–XIII, p. 9.

addressed and brought to a solution in fragment 242, which constitutes a further, decisive step towards the mature system, and which I will shortly analyze in depth.

11.5 Starting from the Subject: The Method of the "Wiser Indians" as the Only Possible Alternative to Transcendent Dogmatism

As early as 1811 Schopenhauer was searching for a new metaphysics that, while taking account of Kant's fundamental interdictions, would at the same time be capable of overcoming them. That is, he sought an alternative to "dogmatism", both pre-Kantian (all philosophy prior to Kant) and post-Kantian (Fichte and Schelling: cf. *supra*, 6.10).

> In the *theoretical* childish and foolish *dogmatics* has tried to explain everything through the relations of *objects*, especially through the *principle of sufficient reason or ground*; it represented a God as constructing the world, deciding the fate of men, and so forth. The wiser Indians started from the *subject*, from Atma, Jivatma. The essential point is that the subject has representations or mental pictures; it is not the connexion of the representations with one another.[74]

Of course, Fichte and Schelling also intended to start from the subject, but ended up understanding the relationship between subject and object in terms of causality (cf. *supra*, 6.3 and 6.7), and thus according to the principle of sufficient reason, which is the law of "everything [...] that can become an object for us".[75] For Schopenhauer, truly starting from the subject means instead considering only what is essential to the subject itself, i.e. the primary and indubitable fact that it has "representations". The principle of connection within the latter properly concerns the "object", and is therefore something derivative with respect to that first and fundamental determination, constituting a mere specification of it.

Now, if one starts from the object (i.e. from the laws that apply in relation to it), one is bound to the thread of the principle of reason, always and only remaining within it and thus always and only finding the "world".[76] But young Schopenhauer set out to cast a glance at what lies *beyond* the "world". To do this, in his view, one must (and can only) start from the subject:

---

74 MR 1, n. 192, p. 116.
75 Schopenhauer 2012 [1813], § 17, p. 31.
76 Cf. also MR 1, n. 216, p. 133.

> Remaining at the standpoint of reflection and in empirical rational consciousness, we can start from the *subject* instead of from the *object*, as I do in my essay. But as the subject is just as much conditioned by the object as the object is by the subject, it may well be asked whether this method has any advantages. It has the following: The whole problem of empirical consciousness is here seized, as it were, by the hair, for the point where all its parts are united is the subject. To this all four classes of representations refer, and just to have combined these under the concept of *representation* is for reflection a great thing. [...]. Finally, as the transition [*Uebergang*] to the better consciousness annihilates not one class but all classes of objects, so is such a transition best made from the point which all classes of objects have in common, namely from the subject.[77]

The "transition" referred to here is not the individual's self-determination from empirical consciousness to better consciousness; rather, it is the transition from the *philosophical treatment* of empirical consciousness (already achieved in the dissertation) to the *philosophical treatment* of better consciousness, which Schopenhauer still aimed to carry out (cf. *supra*, 9.14).

If one starts correctly from the subject – i.e. stopping at the simple fact that it "has representations" – one encloses or comprehends at once "the world *together* [italics mine] with the principle of sufficient reason ruling in it".[78] Thus, only the subject remains, which, being irreducibly different from the object – "the distinction between subject and object [...] is the most important of all distinctions that we are able to comprehend"[79] – is also "entirely free from the principle of sufficient reason" (as the form of every object).[80] The "subject" thus represents the only gateway to what lies beyond the principle of reason.

These assumptions, as well as the metaphysical ambition connected with them, can be seen in fragment 192 through the reference to the "wiser Indians" and their taking their cue "from Atma, Jivatma". In the *Oupnekhat*, the term *atma* denotes man's individual soul, which in itself is identical with the universal Spirit, the only truly existent reality – *Brahm*. Insofar as it is joined to a body, the *atma* takes the name *djiv atma*.[81]

Now, by virtue of its identity with Brahm, the *atma* constitutes the innermost essence of the human being and, at the same time, of all 'things', which are precisely *one*, beyond their apparent multiplicity: *ipse hic âtmaï tuus, âtmaï omnium*

---

[77] MR 1, n. 234, pp. 148–149.
[78] MR 1, n. 192, p. 116.
[79] Schopenhauer 2012 [1813], § 20, p. 161.
[80] MR 1, n. 240, pp. 153–154. Cf. also MR 1, n. 263, p. 176.
[81] Cf. Anquetil-Duperron 1801–1802, I, p. 93: "*Ipse hic* âtma, *causâ addictionis cum corpore*, djiv âtma *nomen habet*". In the *Explicatio* of the Sanskrit terms (cf. ibid, p. 8), the *djiv âtma* is defined as: *spiritus (*anima*) universale cum corpore (*conjuntus corpori*)*.

*existentium rerum est.*⁸² Conversely: *ipsum illud* (ens) – any 'thing': the earth, water, fire, wind, the sun, the moon, the heavens and stars – *est âtmaï tuus.*⁸³ This is the principle of the *Tat twam asi*, expressly quoted in *The World as Will and Representation.*⁸⁴ By knowing himself and his own ultimate depth, the individual *eo ipso* knows the essence of everything.⁸⁵

Indeed, the "subject" mentioned by Schopenhauer in fragment 191 bears great affinities with the *Kshetrajna* and the *atma* spoken of respectively in the *Bhagavad Gita* and the *Oupnekhat:* the silent, uncontaminated Witness of all that takes place in the body (cf. *supra*, 10.8). But for Schopenhauer, starting from the subject or consciousness also means fulfilling the fundamental criterion of epistemological legitimacy that consists in starting from what is 'first for us' (*priora quoad nos*), i.e., from something that is first and actually *given*, rather than 'pretended' or imagined by thought alone. Precisely for this reason, he explicitly sets his own method (which he sees exemplified in the texts of the "wiser Indians") against the transcendent speculations of "foolish dogmatics".⁸⁶

11.6 The Original Analogical Inference of Manuscripts: From the Concept of Intelligible Character to the Concept of a Universal Will-to-Life

The subject of cognition cannot, *as such*, be cognized (for then it would be the object, and not the subject, of cognition); in this sense, to cognize oneself as a cognizer is contradictory and therefore impossible.⁸⁷ Man, however, can cognize himself as willing, i.e. as the subject of (his own) will, by virtue of that 'miraculous' identity, which constitutes every I, between the "subject of cognition" and the "subject of willing" (cf. *supra*, 9.5).

Now, the essence of man as a willing, for Schopenhauer, is the will as *intelligible character*. The latter was 'deduced' in the dissertation through a kind of abductive inference from internal and external experience and defined as "a universal act of will lying outside of time", "a willing, which by its nature is free to the greatest degree, indeed, which is the innermost essence [*Wesen*] of the human

---

82 Anquetil-Duperron 1801–1802, I, p. 191.
83 Cf. Anquetil-Duperron 1801–1802, I, pp. 196–197.
84 Cf. Schopenhauer 2010b, I 260, § 45, p. 245; I 420, § 63, p. 382.
85 Anquetil-Duperron 1801–1802, I, p. 196. Cf. App 2011, p. 164.
86 On this, cf. also MR 1, n. 210, pp. 124–128 and n. 211, pp. 128–129.
87 Cf. MR 1, n. 171, p. 104.

being" (cf. *supra*, 9.8 and 9.12). In the fragments of 1814 analyzed above, these determinations are consistently maintained and developed (cf. *supra*, 10.7). The intelligible character is for Schopenhauer the essence of the individual as existing in time.

> I have called the *intelligible character* an act of will lying outside t1me [*einen außer der Zeit liegenden Willensakt*], whose development is life in time or the *empirical character*. For practical affairs we all have the one as well as the other, for they are our being [*unser Seyn*]. [...]. It certainly seems to us as if our lot were assigned to us almost entirely from without and imparted to us, so to speak, like an unfamiliar melody through the ear. But on looking back over our past, we see at once that our life consists merely of variations on one and the same theme (which is the character) and that everywhere the same fundamental bass can be heard. *Everyone can and must experience this in himself* [italics mine].[88]

Since one can only cognize oneself as willing, starting from the "subject" means starting from this self-cognition and from what can be deduced from it: the intelligible character.

In fragment 87 from 1813, based on the many similarities between man and animal, Schopenhauer had asserted, without any systematicity, that even with animals "as with man, an extratemporal character must form the basis of the one that appears" (cf. *supra*, 8.10).[89] In fragment 242, he argues and develops this thesis, going so far as to extend the concept of intelligible character to the plant kingdom as well.

> Man's body and the animal's are nothing but their will in the appearance [Der Leib des Menschen und des Thieres ist nichts als sein Wille in der Erscheinung], their will that has become an object in space. Man's life is the development of this will in time [...], variations on the extratemporal theme that is his intelligible character, the mirror in which he ought to see himself (i.e. his will) and be dismayed. [...]. Like man and the animal, the plant must [*muß*] be the appearance of a will, an embodied will [*verkörperter Wille*]; for all growth, vegetation and reproduction are conceivable only as the appearance of a will. This will must have a character which must also be empirical and intelligible.[90]

The intelligible character is an extratemporal act of will, a decision by which every individual has chosen his life in time. Man's life is therefore the temporal or diachronic manifestation of this timeless willing-life or will-to-life. However, man exists in time specifically as a body (*Leib*); that is, the body is the 'vehicle' of his temporal existence, the peculiar mode of his being in time. Insofar as he exists and

---

88 MR 1, n. 241, p. 155.
89 MR 1, n. 87, p. 53.
90 MR 1, n. 242, pp. 156–157. Translation modified.

lives in time, man is essentially a body. Consequently, the body, like life itself, *"is nothing but the will that has become visible"*, the manifestation in time of the intelligible character.[91] Just as life in time is "objectified willing [*das objektivirte Wollen*]",[92] so the body is "the appearance [*Erscheinung*], the objectification [*Objektivirung*] of the subject of willing".[93] Assuming all this, Schopenhauer writes in the above-mentioned fragment that *"Man's body and the animal's is nothing but their will in the appearance"*.

Now, plants show an intrinsic dynamism, which can only be the same thing that we all experience *in ourselves* (and only in ourselves) as "will";[94] *consequently*, plants, like human beings and animals, must also be considered as the manifestation or expression, in time, of a will placed outside of time – that is, of an "intelligible character". The positing of this analogy does not, however, imply the identity of man, plant and animal: the relationship that exists in them between the intelligible character and its manifestation in time (the empirical character) is in fact markedly different, indeed even specific to each of them. This is the ground of the observable diversity between them – which nevertheless constitutes, in the discourse that follows, the *priora quoad nos*, i.e. that from which that first, fundamental difference is inferred.

By virtue of the freedom deriving from reason, man is able to restrain or deny (*verleugnen*) his own character, preventing it from manifesting itself in his actions.[95] The animal, on the other hand, "without the faculty of reason […] is not free", and thus its character (which is the character of the species to which it belongs)[96] invariably manifests itself in its behavior.[97] Underlying these considerations is the assumption that an animal's behavior never differs significantly from that of other individuals of the same species. (On reason as a condition of 'negative' freedom, cf. *supra*, 8.9.)

Nevertheless, in both man and animal, the *empirical* and *intelligible character* are distinct: the former is "a single extratemporal act of will"; the latter is "a series of actions" in time, in which the former manifests itself.[98] In the plant kingdom, on

---

[91] MR 1, n. 191, p. 115.
[92] MR 1, n. 213, p. 130.
[93] MR 1, n. 206, p. 121.
[94] Cf. Schopenhauer 2012 [1813], § 44, p. 185: "Precisely because the subject of willing is immediately given in inner sense, what willing is cannot be further defined or described […] insofar as what is essential to willing is found nowhere else, willing cannot be subsumed under any other concept. For this reason, what willing is, we can – even must – presuppose to be known."
[95] MR 1, n. 242, pp. 156–157.
[96] Cf. Schopenhauer 2012 [1813], § 46, p. 188; MR 1, n. 371, p. 256.
[97] MR 1, n. 242, p. 157.
[98] MR 1, n. 242, p. 157.

the other hand, the two terms "coincide [*fallen ... zusammen*]", because a plant, properly speaking, *does not act*, i.e. it does not express its nature in a series of actions (potentially different from one another); it only grows and develops, along a uniform and therefore predictable direction.[99] Its life in time thus presents itself as "a single act [*ein einziger Akt*]": its mere form or figure (*Gestalt*) "exhausts the sum and substance of its will", so that it reveals its whole essence (*Wesen*) at once, already "to our first glance".[100]

> Finally mineralogy shows us more and more that all rock is crystal and everything uncrystalline is merely shattered crystal, fragments. But crystallization itself is evidently a striving [*Streben*], a polarization, and every individual striving or tendency is a will, and thus the stone is also to be regarded as the expression [*Ausdruck*] of a will.[101]

In a note to the fragment, Schopenhauer critically reconsiders the reduction of every possible "rock" to a "crystal", which constitutes the specific or 'material' presupposition of his reasoning (in particular, of the attribution of a *Streben* also to minerals).[102] But here it is mainly the formal structure of his argument that is of interest: *since* an intrinsic dynamism (a *Streben*) also appears (is observable) in the mineral kingdom, and *since* such a *Streben* can only be a "willing", *then* stones too – like the human body, animals and plants – must be thought of as the "expression of a will". And yet, Schopenhauer continues, a rock knows no development comparable to the growth of a plant or the actions of an animal or human; it is therefore devoid of any real "temporal life", so that "life and death coincide with it. Crystallization is its sole act [*sein einziger Akt*] *in as well as outside* time [*in wie außer der* Zeit]".[103]

From the mineral kingdom to man, therefore, there is an increasing complexity in the relationship between the sole timeless act (*Akt*) of will, in which the intelligible character consists, and its manifestation in time. In *human beings*, this complexity is at its greatest, to the point that it can even result in a relationship of negation: in addition to dissimulating their intentions (so that their actions can appear as arising from a character other than their own), individuals are free to deny their character, i.e. to prevent it from manifesting itself in time (cf. *supra*, 10.11).

---

99 MR 1, n. 242, p. 157.
100 MR 1, n. 242, p. 157.
101 MR 1, n. 242, p. 158.
102 MR 1, n. 242, p. 158.
103 MR 1, n. 242, p. 158.

Animals, like humans, express their intelligible character – which coincides with the character of the species to which they belong – through a series of actions, which never completely exhaust the manifestation of the character itself; unlike humans, however, they cannot conceal or deny (in the sense indicated above) their character. *Plants* manifest their character – i.e. the will, of which their bodies are the appearances in time – through their growth and development; these, however, unlike the actions of humans and animals, follow a rigidly uniform and invariant course. Finally, *minerals* do not even undergo growth and development (which involve an intrinsic differentiation marked out in various stages), but only one sole "act", which is crystallization.

The ultimate conclusion that Schopenhauer draws from this whole analogical reasoning is this: "generally we see that everything that exists is only appearance of *will* [*Erscheinung von* Willen], embodied *will* [*verkörperter* Wille]."[104]

The term *Willen* could also be understood as dative plural, rather than singular; in fragment 321 Schopenhauer says unequivocally: "The individuals are the appearance [*Erscheinung*] of separate individual wills [*einzelner Willen*]".[105] In analogy with the human body (*Leib*), every physical body (*Körper*) is conceivable as the *Erscheinung* of a will, i.e. an intelligible character.

> However, we know that all our pain and anguish come only from our will [fragment 220]. Only in the will are we wretched; on the other hand, in pure cognition and freed from the will, we are happy. The will therefore is *the origin of the bad* and also of *evil*, which exists only for its appearance, namely the body; the will is also the *origin of the world* [Ursprung der Welt].[106]

In relation to the term *Wille*, the use of the singular and plural forms, as well as the indeterminative and determinative articles, is revealing here. All things in the world, all natural bodies are the appearances of metaphysical *wills:* the human and the animal body are "their will", i.e. man's will and animal's will respectively (*sein Wille*), "in the appearance"; every plant and every mineral are the appearance of *a* will (*eines Willens*). Accordingly, it can be concluded that *the* will in general (*der Wille*) is "the origin of the world". In fragment 246, this universal will, "whose appearance is this null [*nichtige*], unsatisfactory and dismal world", is called the "will-to-life".[107]

By extending the concept of the intelligible character – understood as the individual and metaphysical willing-life (*Lebenwollen*), of which the individual's body

---

104 MR 1, n. 242, p. 158. Translation modified.
105 MR 1, n. 321, p. 219. Translation modified
106 MR 1, n. 242, p. 158. Translation modified
107 MR 1, n. 246, p. 161. Translation modified.

and life are the appearance in time – to all entities, in analogy with man, Schopenhauer thus arrives at the concept of a general or universal will-to-life (*Wille zum Leben*), whose appearance is the world in its entirety. In this way, a true equality of relations is realized: the *will-to-life* is to the *world as a whole* what the *intelligible character* is to the *body of the individual*. That is, the will-to-life is to life or existence in general what the intelligible character is to the life or existence of the individual. The world and existence are in fact the *Erscheinung* of the will-to-life, just as the individual's body and temporal existence are the *Erscheinung* of his intelligible character. In the fragments analyzed here, *the concept of "will-to-life" is thus introduced as a universalization of the concept of "intelligible character"*.[108]

To the metaphysical question *par excellence:* "Why does what exists, i.e. the world, exist?" Schopenhauer answers by theorizing the concept of a metaphysical and universal (impersonal) will to existence. The will of the world (objective genitive) is "the origin of the world", in the sense that the world is nothing but the manifestation or appearance of this will. On a universal level, just as in relation to the individual, *esse sequitur velle* (cf. *supra*, 10.9).

11.7 Meaning and Consequences of the Analogical Argument. Fidelity to "True Criticism" and Following Differences between the Will-to-Life and the Maya of the *Oupnekhat*

To complete the considerations just made, it must be acknowledged that Schopenhauer, when drafting fragment 242, knew very well what he was getting at, so to speak, because he already had what he sought to formally 'deduce' through his reasoning. In fact, the concept of a universal will, whose appearance (*Erscheinung*) is the whole world, occurs in the manuscripts well before fragment 242, and precisely in fragment 213; this concept is there explicitly identified with the Indian concept of "Maya". It has been noted that the expression *Wille zum Leben* (corresponding to the Latin *voluntas existentiae*) seems to translate and combine into a single term two definitions of Maya given by Dara and Duperron respectively, namely: *voluntas aeterna* and *appetitus existentiae* (cf. *supra*, 11.3). And yet, the way Schopenhauer intended to deduce the concept of the "will-to-life" is not indifferent to the *content* of this concept.

---

[108] This point seems to escape U. App (2011, pp. 165–166), who traces the argumentation of fragment 242 back to the concept of Maya, despite the explicit centrality of the concept of "intelligible character" in the text. More generally, however, this is a circumstance that has not been noted in the literature on Schopenhauer.

First of all, his main methodological – or rather, epistemological – concern was to avoid a dogmatic or transcendent discourse, based on terms that are completely unrelated to "experience". Starting from the subject (in the manner of the "wiser Indians") was, in his view, the only possible way to avoid falling into the transcendent speculations of "foolish dogmatics".[109]

> *My philosophy* is to be distinguished from all previous systems (Plato's *to a certain extent* being an exception) by the fact that, in its inner essence, it is not, like all those, a mere application of the principle of sufficient reason or ground [...], and so it should not be a science but an art. On the contrary, it will keep not to what *must be* [*an dem ... seyn muß*] in consequence of a demonstration, but solely to what *is* [*an dem was* ist]. From the welter and confusion [*Gewirre*] of our consciousness it will bring out every individual fact and describe and name it, just as from the great shapeless mass of marble the sculptor causes definite forms to emerge. It will, therefore, [...] set to work detaching and separating throughout; for it will not create anything new, but will show how to differentiate only what actually exists. For this reason it will be given the name of *criticism* in the original sense of the word.[110]

Schopenhauer could not admit *sic et simpliciter*, or by authority, a universal metaphysical will; for this reason he sought to *philosophically* or conceptually deduce what in the *Oupnekhat* is only presented or expounded. However, in order to be epistemologically legitimate (according to Schopenhauer's understanding of "criticism"), such a deduction cannot take place on a purely conceptual or speculative level; rather, it must start from "what *is* [*an dem was* ist]", i.e. from what *is given* to "our consciousness" (since *esse est percipi*). In fragment 240, shortly before writing fragment 242, Schopenhauer had attempted another analogical argument, which, however, did not fulfill this 'epistemological imperative':

> Every organism shows a clear analogue of polarity. It seems as if every body [*Körper*], to the extent that it polarizes, is in a small degree an immediate object [of cognition] [...] The entire globe exhibits magnetic and electrical polarity. Finally, where is there matter which would not be in some degree an immediate object?
>
> Every immediate object of cognition is also the object of a will, indeed only the material appearance of a will. Therefore it seems that there could not be an object unless it were the expression of a will. Is then the whole globe also such an expression?[111]

The structure of the reasoning is as follows: *since* the "immediate object of cognition", i.e. the human body (cf. *supra*, 9.6), is the appearance of a will, *then* every

---

109 MR 1, n. 192, p. 116.
110 MR 1, n. 220, p. 136.
111 MR 1, n. 240, p. 153. Translation modified.

other object, insofar as it can also be considered as an "immediate object", is likewise thinkable as the appearance of a will. But the premise of this argument – namely, that every being is an immediate object of cognition – is evidently hypothetical or 'speculative': its content does not, and cannot, belong to experience, because the cognition with respect to which every thing (every being) other than the body (*Leib*) is, or can be, an immediate object is not and cannot be given. This ultimately depends on the fact that the different subjects of cognition, of which the different things of the world would be the immediate object (i.e., properly speaking, the body), are, by hypothesis, *other* than the consciousness that constructs and formulates the aforementioned reasoning, so that they can in no way be given *as such* (as subjects of cognition). No subject of cognition can be given as such (as the subject of cognition) to *another* subject of cognition. This first deduction therefore necessarily misses the mark.

In fragment 242, on the other hand, the assumptions of the reasoning are 'phenomenological' or observational. The basis for the extension of the concept of intelligible character to the animal kingdom is the great similarity that exists, in many areas, between animals and humans; similarly, the basis for the extension of the same concept to the plant and mineral kingdoms is the fact that both plants and stones *manifest* a certain intrinsic dynamism – the former as growth and development, the latter as crystallization – which, as such, can be subsumed under the concept of "will". This second form of analogical inference satisfies the epistemological requirement that Schopenhauer cared about, because it takes something actually and indisputably given (in experience) as its starting point. In §§ 18–21 of *The World as Will and Representation*, Schopenhauer would present a third variant of this deduction, based on even more 'phenomenological' premises (cf. *infra*, 12.2).

Now, this strict method by which Schopenhauer sought to stay true to criticism inevitably and remarkably conditioned the very determination of the concept of "will-to-life" – also and especially in its difference from the concept of "Maya".

First of all, consistent with his earlier reflections on the philosophical illegitimacy of the concept of God (cf. *supra*, 8.6), Schopenhauer strongly rejected all the elements of theism that he believed he found in the *Oupnekhat*, even going so far as to strike out the word *Deus* from some pages of the book.[112] Dara defines Maya as the *voluntas aeterna* that *caused* the appearance of the world (i.e., the appearance of what does not actually exist); Duperron, in turn, refers Maya expressly to Brahm, God the Creator (cf. *supra*, 11.2). These two (by no means secondary) features of the concept of Maya – being the cause of the world and inherent in a Cre-

---

[112] On this cf. App 2011, pp. 149–150.

ator – were completely expunged by Schopenhauer. The "will-to-life" of which he spoke is in no way the will of a God. Even more radically, it is not even, in general, the 'attribute' of some individuality or personality (even if divine), but an entirely *impersonal* will, which, far from having a relationship of inherence in (and therefore subordination to) some 'subject' or 'substance', is *itself* the absolute metaphysical Essence, the *primum* with respect to which all else – including every possible subjectivity or individuality – is only something derivative or secondary.

Similarly, and secondly, Schopenhauer excluded from the outset that the will-to-life can be the cause of the world, because causality is a determination of phenomena alone (cf. *infra*, 11.12)[113] – even though, in two fragments of 1814, he wrote that the will "creates [*schafft*]" the world,[114] so as to be *das Weltschaffende*.[115] These two slips of the tongue (the second even repeated in *The World as Will and Representation*)[116] further confirm that the concept of will-to-life was derived from the concept of Maya. However, this derivation came with a *transformation* on the basis of what Schopenhauer had already established in 1813: the attributes of personality and causality exist only within the world of experience (cf. *supra*, 8.6), whereas the aforementioned will is something essentially metempirical.

Thirdly, for Schopenhauer the intelligible character is the individual willing-life, i.e. the original "sinful propensity" from which man must redeem himself (cf. *supra*, 10.9 and 10.11). Therefore, the universal will-to-life, understood as the intelligible character of the Whole or the world, unlike *Brahm*'s Maya, is an essentially sinful, "evil" will (cf. *infra*, 11.13).

The method of the wiser Indians, who started from the innermost essence of the Self (the *atma*) in order to know the one essence of all things, certainly provided Schopenhauer – as he himself admits – with the fundamental model for his analogical argument. However, in some fragments from 1809 and 1810, he had already stated very clearly that only inner knowledge can provide the key to access supersensible reality (cf. *supra*, 1.5 and 1.8; 2.2 and 2.13). This is why he was initially so interested in the Fichtean-Schellingean concept of intellectual intuition (cf. *supra*, 3.2 and 3.5). Indeed, in 1814, he did not hesitate to compare the *Oupnekhat* to Schelling's and even Kant's philosophy, as three imperfect attempts to construct a philosophy of the subject.

> [...] *Objective infinity* is the result of the philosophies of the *Eleatics*, of *Bruno* (see in particular the account of his One in Jakobi on Spinoza p. 294), of *Spinoza*; it is related to *subjective*

---

[113] MR 1, n. 305, p. 205.
[114] MR 1, n. 260, p. 170.
[115] MR 1, n. 278, p. 185.
[116] Cf. Schopenhauer 2010b, I 597, p. 533 ("the will as world-creator, as thing-in-itself").

infinity as the illuminated body is to the sun. The latter is discussed especially in the *Oupnekhat*, in Kant, and in Schelling's absolute ego. I hope to present it clearly for the first time.[117]

But it should also be remembered that the theory of the better consciousness itself, concerning the possibility of man's cognition of the supersensible, was from the very beginning intimately related to the theme of man's "supersensible" or "supreme" self-consciousness (cf. *supra*, 7.6 and 7.13). This point – cognition of the supersensible through inner self-consciousness – must therefore be regarded as a further theoretical element that, prior to the study of the *Oupnekhat*, helped to focus Schopenhauer's attention and interest on certain passages of the work.

Now, the fact that Schopenhauer adopted the method of the Indians and yet universalized the concept of *intelligible character* in place of the *atma* does not imply that he identified these two terms. In this respect, the following considerations can be made (which, however, remain hypothetical, as the analysis or interpretation of the manuscripts can shed no further light on the matter at this point).

In fragment 191 Schopenhauer refers to the subject in itself (which is absolutely opposed to the will and its appearance, the body) the same predicates that the *Oupnekhat* refers to the *atma* (*purus, sine motu, stabilis* and *sine desiderio*).[118] We have seen that by "subject" Schopenhauer seems to mean here the eternal, uncontaminated element of the individual (what man was 'before' he existed in time as a body), which, however, is also the *author* of what religion calls "original sin" – that is, properly speaking, of the timeless act of will from which existence in time arose (cf. *supra*, 10.8). Fragment 274 would also seem to point in this direction:

> [...] *the identity of the subject of willing with the subject of cognition* [...] is just the union of heaven and hell within us, and men have falsely tried to explain this union by a transcendent use of time and of the principle of sufficient reason in general, first through fall [*Abfall*] and emanation, and then (like Schelling "on the essence of freedom") through absolute eternal becoming.[119]

The term "fall" refers to the dogma or myth of original sin; and the reference to Schelling evidently relates to the doctrine of man's "intelligible being", according to which every individual, by an act of will placed outside of time, has chosen to be what he is (in Schopenhauer this same notion is expressed by the doctrine of the intelligible character).

---

117 MR 1, n. 240, p. 154.
118 MR 1, n. 191, p. 116.
119 MR 1, n. 274, p. 183. Translation modified.

In fragment 242, the extension of the concept of will to *all* entities essentially means attributing to them *the timeless act of will* in which the intelligible character consists (the term used by Schopenhauer for humans, animals, plants and minerals is precisely *Akt*). The universalization of the latter would seem to imply the universalization of that which accomplished it, namely the *pure subject* mentioned in fragment 191. In this sense, assuming that Schopenhauer presupposes the affinity between the pure subject (thus understood) and the *atma*, the intention to follow "the wiser Indians" – who, in order to know the essence of the Whole, universalized the *atma* – would already prefigure, in essence, the analogical argument of fragment 242. Even the failed analogical argument of fragment 240, by extending the determination of "immediate object" to all entities, necessarily implies the universalization of the correlated "subject" – that same subject which, in man, *is not* the body, but only *cognizes* the body (as its own immediate object).[120]

In any case, in 1814 Schopenhauer still openly admitted a human dimension that is completely alien to "this world":

> As individuals, as persons, or for empirical consciousness, we are in time, in a finite state, in death. That which is from this world comes to an end and dies. That which is not of this world shoots through it with almighty force like a flash of lightning that strikes upwards and knows neither time nor death.[121]

The problematic nature of the considerations just made does not entail their insignificance or arbitrariness; they concern a fundamental, and yet effectively aporetic, point of Schopenhauer's discourse: he would never determine 'who' or 'what' is, properly speaking, the 'author' of the original act of will in which intelligible character consists (cf. *infra*, 12.10).

As a result of the above considerations, it is now of the utmost importance to follow the theoretical developments undergone by the figure of the pure subject in the fragments following number 191, not least because they directly and decisively affected the fate of the concept of the "better consciousness".

11.8 The Pure Subject of Cognition: Suspension of the Will and Intuition of the Idea. The *Besonnenheit* of Genius

Beyond the affinity – whether presupposed by Schopenhauer or not – between the pure subject and the *atma* of the Indians, the unequivocal sense of fragment 191 is

---

120 MR 1, n. 191, p. 116.
121 MR 1, n. 222, p. 140.

the radical opposition between *cognizing* and *willing:* as "that which merely cognizes [*das bloß Erkennende*]", the subject is neither the will nor the body, but their mere spectator, the serene witness of life.[122] This extreme heterogeneity of cognizing and willing – and, consequently, of their respective "subjects" – is taken up and developed in the later annotations.

> Whoever contemplates really *objectively* and with the eyes of an artist knows merely that someone perceives [*auffaßt*] this object with his senses and understanding, but he does not know *who* it is and *in what point of time* his perception falls. In other words, he is the pure subject of cognition [*reines Subjekt des Erkennens*], free from individuality and its principle.[123]

The individual is the "pure subject of cognition" insofar as he has a purely – i.e. exclusively – cognitive relationship with the object: the attribute "pure" means that he is *only* the subject of cognition. Since (according to the dissertation) every I is both subject of cognition and subject of willing, that the individual is only subject of cognition means that, at those rare junctures, he is *not also* subject of willing. The principle of individuality – from which the pure subject of cognition is essentially free – is precisely the *will:* indeed, man's individuality consists in his empirical character, i.e. in the manifestation (in time) of that "universal act of will", lying outside time, which is his intelligible character (cf. *supra*, 9.8).

In the same fragment in which he characterizes his own philosophical project as "*criticism* in the original sense of the word" – being the analysis of what is *given* in the "welter and confusion of our consciousness" – Schopenhauer proudly states:

> An exceedingly important distinction already made by me, which at first will give much offence, is that between the *subject of cognition* and the *subject of willing.*
>
> As the *subject of willing* I am an exceedingly wretched being and all our suffering consists in willing. Willing, desiring, striving [*Streben*] and aspiring are simply the state of being finite, simply death and distress.
>
> On the other hand, as soon as I am wholly and entirely the *subject of cognition,* in other words am absorbed in cognition, I am blissfully happy, wholly contented, and nothing can assail me. Whatever object I contemplate, I am that object. If I see a mountain with blue sky behind it and the sun's rays on its summit, then I am nothing but this mountain, this sky, these rays of the sun; and, purely apprehended, the object appears in infinite beauty [...].[124]

---

122 MR 1, n. 191, p. 116. Translation modified.
123 MR 1, n. 217, p. 134. Translation modified.
124 MR 1, n. 220, p. 137. Translation modified.

In his treatise on the principle of reason, Schopenhauer had written that "the distinction between subject and object, [between] that which cognizes and is never cognized and that which is cognized but never cognizes, is the most important of all distinctions that we are able to comprehend".[125] Nevertheless, the subject can *cognize himself*, not as cognizing, but as willing – so that, in this case, there is indeed a 'miraculous' identity between that which is cognizing and that which is cognized.[126] This identity, given immediately in internal experience (thus falling within the "welter and confusion of our consciousness"), represents something absolutely "inexplicable", "the miracle *par excellence*".[127] In fact, the subject of cognition and the subject of willing are *identical* – because the former, cognizing the latter, cognizes himself – and at the same time *different*, precisely because they are the subject and object of cognition: two terms that, for Schopenhauer, can never coincide (cf. *supra*, 6.6). This relation of identity-difference, i.e. the fundamental *duplicity* of the human subject – which is precisely subject of both cognition and willing – is expressed by the word 'I', which simultaneously includes and denotes both terms (cf. *supra*, 9.5).[128]

It is probably in relation to this dual nature of the I that Schopenhauer thought he had made "an exceedingly important distinction". *In addition* to the tenets of the dissertation, however, the above-mentioned fragment presents the connection between will and pain. All pain derives from the will ("all our suffering consists in willing"; cf. *supra*, 10.15), so that the individual, when he is purely a subject of cognition (i.e. when he is not also a subject of willing), is completely immune to pain. "All things are so charming and delightful to be from outside (i.e. to contemplate)" or to cognize, "but so painful and worrying to be from within (i.e. simply to be)".[129]

The inexplicable identity between subject of cognition and subject of willing in the same I is reflected in their respective "immediate object", the body, which is therefore, in an equally inexplicable way, the "immediate object of blessed cognition" and at the same time the "appearance of the unblessed will" (i.e. will appearing as the object of the first class of representations).[130]

But *what* does the pure subject of cognition cognize? The answer in fragment 221 is unequivocal: the *Platonic Idea*.

---

125 Schopenhauer 2012 [1813], § 20, p. 161.
126 Schopenhauer 2012 [1813], § 43, p. 136.
127 Schopenhauer 2012 [1813], § 43, p. 136.
128 Schopenhauer 2012 [1813], § 43, p. 136.
129 MR 1, n. 206, p. 121.
130 MR 1, n. 220, pp. 137–138. Translation modified.

> In *contemplation* [Kontemplation] a man forgets his own self and through this he merely knows that here someone is contemplating, but he does not know *who it is*, in other words he knows about himself only to the extent that he knows about objects. He is thereby elevated [*erhebt ... sich*] to the *pure subject of cognition* and is no longer a *subject of willing* (always limited and individual [*einzelnes*]).
>
> Furthermore, by not being aware of the point of time in which he now finds himself in common with the object, he raises [*erhebt*] this object to the *Platonic Idea*. In this way he is released from the final and most firmly adhering form of the principle of sufficient reason (time).[131]

Subject and object are necessarily related; consequently, if the former changes, the latter changes as well. This symmetry is expressed in the text by the use of the verb *erheben:* by divesting himself of his individuality (and thus his being the subject of willing), man raises or elevates (*erhebt*) *himself* to being the *pure subject of cognition* and, at the same time, the *object* he contemplates to the *Platonic Idea*.

The Idea is the ὄντως ὄν, "the true being of the world" (*das wahrhaft Seyende der Welt*), i.e., its "true essence" (*Wesen*); it is also "the adequate representative of the concept", because, like the latter and unlike empirical (individual and changeable) entities, it is universal and immutable.[132]

Therefore, the correlate (the object of cognition) of the empirical subject lies in individual becoming things, devoid of true being, whereas the correlate of the pure, timeless subject is the Platonic Idea. A double, specular affinity is thus found within these two pairs of terms: just as the empirical subject and the empirical object are both *individual* and *temporal*, so the pure subject and the Platonic Idea are both non-individual (*universal*) and *eternal*.[133]

For Schopenhauer, the *genius*, whether artistic or philosophical, is characterized by this capacity to contemplate the Platonic Idea – that is, to cognize the one true being of the world, beyond the plurality and impermanence of empirical reality. Unlike the artist, however, the philosopher reproduces the Idea not through objects of the senses, but through concepts (cf. also *supra*, 10.12).[134] Ordinary people

---

131 MR 1, n. 221, pp. 138–139. Translation modified.
132 MR 1, n. 221, pp. 139–140. Translation modified.
133 This point, still inexplicit here, would be clarified in 1815: "Just as the *individual thing* is related to the (Platonic) *Idea* expressing itself in that thing, so is an *individual cognizing being* related to the *pure subject of cognition*. [...] The individual person as such always perceives only the individual thing, but the pure subject of cognition perceives the (Platonic) Idea" (MR 1, n. 436, pp. 313–314).
134 Cf. MR 1, n. 261, p. 174.

"are subjective, not objective, but thoroughly subjective";[135] instead, "all *creative genius* is *objectivity* and all *objectivity* is *creative genius.*"[136]

> There are *two ways of considering life*, one according to the *principle of sufficient reason or ground*, according to *ratio*, λόγος, reason, *Vernunft*; the other considers the (Platonic) *Idea*.[137]

> The eternal contrast between a consideration according to the principle of sufficient reason, namely science and the faculty of reason, and a consideration of the (Platonic) *Idea*, namely art and genius, was first clearly expressed by Aristotle and Plato.[138]

Now, in order to know what lies *beyond* representation (beyond the world of experience), the individual must first of all grasp or comprehend at once, in his consciousness, all that is "representation"; that is, he must grasp it in its entirety and *as such*. This capacity is identified by Schopenhauer with the peculiar *Besonnenheit* of genius (cf. *supra*, 3.4; 5.8).[139]

As can be seen, in these annotations Schopenhauer refers to the pure subject of cognition what in 1813 he referred to the *better consciousness:* non-individuality, the capacity of cognizing the Idea and the essence of genius (cf. *supra*, 8.13, 8.14 and 8.17). In fragment 234, however, he still attributed knowledge of the Platonic Idea to the better consciousness.[140] Therefore, there is a certain 'competitiveness' between the concept of "better consciousness" and "pure subject of cognition"; in relation to this part of the discourse, such a conflict is resolved in favor of the latter concept (cf. *infra*, 11.10 – 11.11).

11.9 The Secret Concordance between Plato and Kant: The Identity of Plato's Idea and the Thing-in-Itself

After some brief annotations from 1811 (cf. *supra*, 3.2; 4.4), Schopenhauer almost completely dismissed the concept of "thing-in-itself", considering it contradictory and thus illegitimate. Indeed, provided that the verb 'to be', conjugated in the second and third person, means 'to be represented' or 'to be cognized' (cf. *supra*, 4.3; 6.5; 8.2; 9.3), the concept of something that *is*, without ever being able to *be cog-*

---

[135] MR 1, n. 103, p. 77.
[136] MR 1, n. 206, p. 121.
[137] MR 1, n. 256, p. 167.
[138] MR 1, n. 330, p. 226.
[139] MR 1, fn. to n. 266, p. 179. The reference to Jean Paul's terminology, here still implicit, would become clear in fragment 352 (MR 1, p. 240).
[140] MR 1, n. 234, p. 148.

nized, constitutes a contradiction in terms,[141] "a ghost that springs from a total inability to think clearly".[142] Indeed, "a being of things that is independent of our representations (thing-in-itself) is something that is quite inconceivable".[143] For Schopenhauer, the concept of thing-in-itself represents "the weak side of Kant's teaching",[144] also because (even apart from its contradictory content) it originates from a "transcendent conclusion [*trascendenter Schluß*]", based on an illegitimate – indeed, transcendent – use of the category of causality.[145] The admission of the thing-in-itself constitutes a "fundamental error [*Grundirrthum*]".[146] In these reflections Schopenhauer made clear use of the results of the post-Kantian debate, especially the lesson of his professor Schulze (cf. *supra*, 3.7–3.9). In the dissertation of 1813, he had expressly warned the reader: "our investigation does not rigidify in a thing-in-itself".[147]

However, in 1814 Schopenhauer recovered the concept of thing-in-itself, interpreting it in a radically different way. As we have seen, Platonic Ideas ("the eternal forms of things") constitute, in his view, the true and ultimate reality; "things in time and space", on the other hand, "are empty evanescent shadows".[148] Therefore, Ideas constitute the object of philosophy, while empirical realities are the object of the natural sciences. These considerations led Schopenhauer to identify Plato's Idea with Kant's thing-in-itself.

> *Plato's* doctrine that not visible and palpable things, but only the *Ideas*, the eternal forms, *really* [wirklich] *exist*, is only another expression of *Kant's* doctrine that *time* and *space* do not appertain to *things-in-themselves*, but are merely the form of my intuition [...].
>
> An animal stands before me [...]. Plato says that the animal does not exist [*ist nicht*], but merely its *Idea*; it is immaterial whether the animal exists now or existed a thousand years ago, whether here or in distant places, [...]. Only the (Platonic) *Idea* of the animal *exists* [*ist*]. And Kant says that time and space are forms of my intuition; they do not adhere to that animal, but I perceive it in time and space; *in itself* [an sich] the animal is free [*frei*] from these determinations.[149]

---

[141] MR 2, pp. 290–291.
[142] MR 2, p. 421.
[143] MR 1, fn. to n. 93, p. 61.
[144] MR 2, pp. 290–291.
[145] MR 2, p. 293.
[146] MR 2, p. 421.
[147] Schopenhauer 2012 [1813], § 42, p. 184.
[148] MR 1, n. 210, p. 127.
[149] MR 1, n. 228, pp. 143–144. Translation modified.

The ground of the identification of Platonic Idea and thing-in-itself is thus their common foreignness to time and space: "the *Platonic Idea* is *Kant's thing-in-itself* [...] in other words is free from time and space, and thus from plurality, change, beginning and end. It alone is the ὄντως ὄν or *thing-in-itself*."[150] In fact, "diversity, multiplicity and change are only through time and space": it is in virtue of these that "the one Idea [is] indeed divided into many separate individuals".[151]

The use of the plural form (*Ideen, Dingen an sich*) in fragment 228, while implying a plurality of things-in-themselves – i.e. of Ideas – does not contradict the previous statement. The Platonic Idea is outside the plurality that characterizes individuals *of the same species*; however, for Schopenhauer different species necessarily imply different Ideas, and therefore Ideas also constitute a plural reality which corresponds (precisely) to the plurality of existing species. The difference or diversity of Ideas, on which the diversity of species depends, is referred to by Schopenhauer as "transcendental diversity [*transscendentale Diversität*]".[152] The use of the plural form is to be attributed to this specific consideration.

Being situated outside of time and space, the Platonic Idea and thing-in-itself are completely foreign to becoming, the process of birth (or beginning), change and death (or end) that characterizes the transient things of the world. The Platonic Idea or thing-in-itself consequently constitutes the only true reality eternally identical with itself; it alone is the ὄντως ὄν, *das wahrhaft Seyende der Welt*.[153]

Schopenhauer seems to be particularly proud of this theoretical 'discovery', which reconciles two great philosophical doctrines – Platonic metaphysics and Kantian criticism – that are apparently antithetical.

> The identity of these two most famous paradoxes of those two great philosophers has never yet been noticed, a proof that, since the appearance of Kant, neither he nor Plato has been properly understood by anyone. But the two paradoxes themselves are [...] the one [...] the best commentary of the other. The identity of these two great and puzzling doctrines is an infinitely fruitful thought which is to become a mainstay of my philosophy.[154]

Recall that the identification of the Platonic Idea and thing-in-itself was already implicit in a fragment from 1810, written at the same time as Tennemann's *Geschichte der Philosophie*. In his work, Tennemann explicitly identifies the two terms; this identification, however, has a purely expository, non-speculative or theoretical function for him: in other words, he does not intend to argue that Plato's Idea is

---

150 MR 1, n. 250, p. 163.
151 MR 1, n. 228, pp. 143.
152 MR 1, n. 287, p. 193.
153 MR 1, n. 221, p. 139.
154 MR 1, n. 228, p. 143.

Kant's thing-in-itself, but that Plato mistakenly considered "Ideas" as "things-in-themselves" (cf. *supra*, 2.7). The – rather singular – circumstance that Schopenhauer does not mention Tennemann's precedent in any way can perhaps be explained by the properly speculative value that this identification assumes in his thought, as opposed to Tennemann's.

The position of the identity between Idea and thing-in-itself conditioned Schopenhauer's understanding of the second term in a crucial way. This identification, in fact, does not mean that the Platonic Idea must be understood in the light of Kant's thing-in-itself, but, conversely, that the latter must be understood in the light of what Plato called "Idea" (οὐσία, *Wesen*, "essence"). That is to say, Schopenhauer used the Platonic Idea as an interpretative key for Kant's thing-in-itself. In this sense, and limited to this point, if Tennemann expounded and interpreted Plato in the light of Kantian philosophy, Schopenhauer interpreted and explained Kant in the light of Plato's.

On the other hand, Schopenhauer was no stranger to the daring juxtaposition of Kantian and Platonic doctrines: suffice it to think of the identity he asserted between the theory of intelligible character and the meaning of the Platonic myth of Er (cf. *supra*, 10.7). For Schopenhauer, Plato's doctrine of anamnesis (as expounded in the *Phaedo*), contains *in nuce* the Kantian doctrine of the *apriori* nature of geometrical knowledge.[155]

Certainly, even more than having discovered a secret affinity between Plato and Kant, Schopenhauer was proud to have deciphered the obscure and controversial meaning of the expression "thing-in-itself" (beyond, and indeed against, the meaning that Kant himself intended to attribute to it in the letter of his texts). Even Fichte, in the Berlin course "On the Facts of Consciousness" attended by Schopenhauer, had confessed: "In addition to *appearance* Kant assumed things-in-themselves, and no one knows what he meant by these".[156]

So, in Schopenhauer's thought, *insofar as it is interpreted as a Platonic Idea, the thing-in-itself necessarily acquires its characteristics and determinations.*

First of all, not being affected by time and space, and therefore not even by becoming, the thing-in-itself is understood, like the Platonic Idea ("only the *Ideas*, the eternal forms, *really* [wirklich] *exist*"), as what is real (*wirklich*) – perfectly in line, incidentally, with Schulze's teaching (cf. *supra*, 3.7–3.8). This obviously implies that everything that is not a thing-in-itself – the phenomenon or appearance (in the example chosen by Schopenhauer, a specific animal) – is not real and does not *really exist*. Kant's *Erscheinung* is also understood here as Plato's

---

155 MR 2, p. 353.
156 MR 2, p. 38. Translation modified.

φαινόμενον (cf. *supra*, 2.7); which means, again, that knowledge of the *Erscheinung* is identified with the δόξα (knowledge of the φαινόμενον) of which Plato speaks. On the other hand, this identity was already affirmed in the dissertation (cf. *supra*, 9.13).[157]

Secondly, not being affected by the plurality (*Vielheit, Mannigfaltigkeit*) that characterizes individuals, the thing-in-itself constitutes, like the Platonic Idea, the identity of the different within the same species:

> The principle of diversity [*Das* Princip der Diversität], that whereby things are *different* [verschieden], is *time* and *space*. On the other hand, that whereby things (of *one* species of course) are identical [*identisch*], is their (*Platonic*) *Idea* or the *thing-in-itself* [*ihre Idee* oder das *Ding an sich*].[158]

Thirdly, and consequently, between thing-in-itself and appearance there is a relationship of similarity or resemblance, such that the latter is the 'image' or 'copy' of the former. In 1815 Schopenhauer would state:

> As soon as a person, abandoning the ordinary mode of cognition [*Erkenntniβart*] according to the principle of sufficient reason, passes over to the contemplation of a thing and therefore intuits [*anschaut*] only the (Platonic) *Idea* whose copy [*Abbild*] is the thing (according to Plato), or [*oder*] the thing-in-itself (according to Kant), such a person is at once also the *pure subject of cognition.*[159]

Finally (as is clear from the text just quoted), like Plato's Idea, the thing-in-itself can be cognized (intuited). In speaking of the latter, Schopenhauer does not in any way refer to something that *exists* whilst being absolutely *uncognizable*; the synthesis of these two determinations – being (or existence) and uncognizability – constitutes a contradiction for him, again and again:

> Things-in-themselves which existed *without being represented* and which were therefore something different from representations – *to represent* such things to us is the greatest possible contradiction.[160]

> It is a *fundamental* error, as pitiable as it is universally current and deep-rooted, that we think there can be in objects and in ourselves all kinds of things which indeed might generally be cognizable, (in other words really *might exist* again, for to be is to be cognizable [*Seyn ist er-*

---

157 Schopenhauer 2012 [1813], § 59, pp. 149–152.
158 MR 1, n. 287, p. 192.
159 MR 1, n. 436, p. 313. Translation modified.
160 MR 1, n. 171, p. 104.

kennbar-seyn]), but which could never be cognized *by us* on account of the restricted nature of our mental powers.¹⁶¹

Schopenhauer certainly does not set out to achieve "the greatest possible contradiction" or to commit the "pitiable" "fundamental error" that he denounces. Consequently, when speaking of the thing-in-itself or Platonic Idea, he means to refer to something that *can be cognized* by man. One could even conclude – even if the text does not explicitly say so – that, if "to be" means nothing but "to be cognizable", the thing-in-itself, as ὄντως ὄν (truly being), represents what is truly or absolutely cognizable: the object of perfect or epistemic cognition, just like the Platonic Idea.

> Whoever is incapable of discovering anything other than the connexion of representations, that is to say the combining of grounds and consequents, may become a great scholar [*ein großer Gelehrter*], but he will as little become a philosopher as he will a painter, a poet, or a musician. For all such men must cognize [*erkennen*] things-in-themselves, the Platonic Ideas; the scholar cognizes merely the appearance [*Erscheinung*] [...].¹⁶²

The Idea or thing-in-itself is the object of cognition for the genius, who is able to momentarily suspend the whirlwind of his will and thus elevate himself to the condition of "pure subject of cognition".

But what has become of the "better consciousness" in all this?

11.10 Coincidence and Opposition of Better Consciousness and Cognition of the Idea. The Better Consciousness Is Not "Consciousness": The Breaking Point of the Theory and the Abandonment of the Expression "Better Consciousness"

We have seen that the theory of double consciousness implies a fundamental contradiction from the outset. On the one hand, the eternal better consciousness can only be spoken of negatively (*negativ*),¹⁶³ because words, denoting "concepts", are

---

161 MR 1, n. 223, pp. 140–141. Cf. also n. 210, pp. 124–128.
162 MR 1, n. 301, p. 204. Translation modified. The identification of Platonic Idea and thing-in-itself and the reception of Indian wisdom mean that the genesis of Schopenhauer's concept of thing-in-itself cannot be explained solely by reference to the debate of post-Kantian idealism. One such attempt is conducted with considerable theoretical effort by Kisner 2016.
163 MR 1, n. 35, p. 24.

based on the activity of reason and the understanding, and thus can only refer to what belongs to the empirical realm; on the other hand, the determination "consciousness" is positive, and thus cannot legitimately refer to what Schopenhauer intends to denote with the expression "better consciousness".

This contradiction produces another: on the one hand, empirical consciousness and better consciousness are *absolutely opposed*, so that all determinations of the former are completely foreign to the latter, and vice versa; on the other hand, they are still *united* by the determination "consciousness", which implies cognition (empirical consciousness cognizes the empirical world, the better consciousness cognizes the supersensible world: cf. *supra*, 7.6; 8.5). The use of the comparative adjective "better" only makes sense with the assumption of such a commonality (cf. *supra*, 7.14; 8.20). In 1813, Schopenhauer had come one step away from pointing out this contradiction, when he wrote that the better consciousness, unlike empirical consciousness, "does not think and cognize, since it lies beyond subject and object".[164] In the fragments of 1814, this part of the discourse was addressed in much greater depth, ultimately engendering the final crisis of the system of the double consciousness.

Developing some reflections from 1813 concerning the essentially relative nature of the concept of "nothing" (cf. *supra*, 8.2–8.5), in 1814 Schopenhauer wrote that man, by virtue of the "double nature of [his] consciousness", can assume two different and antithetical points of view.[165] In the first, the true and only reality is matter and the empirical world, so that then "everything is for us null [*nichtig*] which does not fill space and is not matter, and so too are the Platonic Ideas, the eternal forms of things".[166] From the second point of view, that of the better consciousness, "that entire world vanishes like a light morning dream or optical illusion", so that the only true reality is represented by the "Platonic Ideas".[167] For empirical consciousness, only the world in time is real, while the eternal realm is nothing; reciprocally, for the better consciousness, the empirical world is nothing, only the eternal world is real.

These two different perspectives would seem to recall the two positions that Kant called respectively "empirical realism" and "transcendental idealism" – which, however, in Kant's intentions, are not opposite or antithetical, but complementary (cf. *supra*, 2.6); moreover, "transcendental idealism" in no way includes positive cognition of the *thing-in-itself*, whereas the second view mentioned by

---

164 MR 1, n. 96, p. 72. Translation modified.
165 MR 1, n. 234, p. 147.
166 MR 1, n. 234, p. 148. Translation modified.
167 MR 1, n. 234, p. 148.

11.10 Coincidence and Opposition of Better Consciousness and Cognition of the Idea — 411

Schopenhauer consists of perfect and complete intuition of *Ideas* (i.e., for Schopenhauer, of things-in-themselves).

The point, however, is that:

> [...] even the Platonic Ideas ultimately disappear as consciousness withdraws into the eternal peace and serene bliss, Plato's spiritual sun (*Rep.* VII). It now becomes clear that the reality of matter, till now eternal, immovable and infinite, was nevertheless only relative, namely a reality dependent on the appearing of consciousness as subject [*daß das Bewußtsein als Subjekt auftrat*] for which alone objects exist. But consciousness now demonstrates that it can appear [*auftreten*] otherwise than as subject, and here is freedom, the possibility of annihilating [*vernichten*] the world even theoretically.[168]

Transcending the Platonic Ideas themselves (which are the object of cognition), consciousness presents itself as something different from being-a-subject (*anders als Subjekt*); nevertheless, it remains "consciousness". The problematic nature of this point is evident.

But again: on the one hand, *the better consciousness cognizes Ideas*; on the other hand, *it lies beyond them, as well as beyond all possible cognition*, and is thus on the level of what is beyond essence (ἐπέκεινα τῆς οὐσίας): the Good,[169] or, for Plotinus, the One.[170] Lying beyond the split into subject and object, the better consciousness is not distinct from that of which is (or would be) "consciousness", and is therefore in *absolute unity* with its 'object' – which therefore, contrary to the Platonic Idea, is not really such. Insofar as the better consciousness is not a cognizing "subject", its 'sphere' (that to which it is addressed, the 'place' it inhabits) cannot be properly an "object" of cognition.

A few pages earlier, Schopenhauer had attempted to trace the cognition of the Platonic Idea (i.e. the Platonic Idea not in itself, but as an object for a subject) to the faculty of empirical consciousness:

> The *Platonic Idea* is really a phantasm in the presence of the faculty of reason. It is a phantasm to which the reasoning faculty has set the seal of its universal nature; a phantasm to which it says: "thus are they all", in other words, "that wherein this representative is not adequate, is not essential to its concept." Therefore the Platonic Idea comes about through the combined activity of the imagination [*Phantasie*] and of the faculty of reason.[171]

---

[168] MR 1, n. 234, p. 148. Translation modified.
[169] Cf. Plato, *Republic,* 509 b–516 c, Plato 1914 ff., vol. 6, pp. 92–113.
[170] Cf. Plotinus, *Ennead* I 7, 1, in Plotinus 2018, p. 105.
[171] MR 1, n. 226, p. 142.

Through recourse to two faculties of the mind, namely reason and imagination, Schopenhauer sets out to explain the dual nature – respectively: *universal*, like concepts, and *intuitive*, like phantasms – of the Idea.[172] (On the difference between "concept" and "phantasm", cf. *supra*, 4.3). This attempt to explain knowledge of the Platonic Idea through the faculties of empirical consciousness is due to the fact that here Schopenhauer attributes such knowledge to the empirical subject, rather than to the better consciousness or – as will be the case in his later reflections – to the pure subject of cognition. This theoretical experiment, even if it was quickly abandoned, betrays a decisive theoretical deadlock fraught with consequences (cf. *supra*, 9.2; *infra*, 12.9): how can the Platonic Idea be outside the sphere of the principle of reason and, at the same time, be an object for a subject?

The contradiction between the *identity* and *difference* of the better consciousness and cognition of Platonic Ideas fully comes out in fragment 250. Here the two possible points of view of man correspond, respectively, to the rational individual and the genius: for the former, the true and only reality is the empirical world; for the latter, it is the Platonic Idea.[173] This contrast takes the form of a radical and insoluble "antinomy":

> This *antinomy* does not reside in the faculty of reason, but it is the turning point on which the world is balanced. It is one of the expressions of the contrast [*des Gegensatzes*] between the empirical and the better consciousness; each of its antitheses is true and false, according as we take up this or that point of view.[174]

The first point of view characterizes "empiricism" and "rationalism", which are enclosed within cognition according to the principle of reason; the second point of view characterizes "genuine criticism [*der ächte Kriticismus*]".[175] Schopenhauer evidently implies that the opposition between *cognition according to the principle of reason* and *cognition of the Platonic Idea* corresponds to the opposition between *empirical consciousness* and *better consciousness*. However, the end of the fragment severely limits the value of this correspondence:

> But the better consciousness knows [*kennt*] neither object nor subject; it is therefore not to be found at either point of view, for even the Platonic Idea is an object. Its expression [*Aeußerung*] as genius, however, is at the second standpoint; its other expression as holiness consists in intuiting [*daß man ... anschaut*] the (Platonic) Idea of the world and in *not willing* it.[176]

---

172 Cf. MR 1. Cf. also n. 261, pp. 171–174.
173 MR 1, n. 250, p. 163.
174 MR 1, n. 250, pp. 163–164.
175 MR 1, n. 250, p. 164.
176 MR 1, n. 250, p. 164. Translation modified.

11.10 Coincidence and Opposition of Better Consciousness and Cognition of the Idea

In itself, the better consciousness is neither subject nor object; it therefore stands at a higher level than the Platonic Idea, which, being an object of cognition in any case, always presupposes a subject. Consequently, the point of view from which the Platonic Idea is contemplated does not belong to the better consciousness itself, but to one of its two possible manifestations, namely *genius*. Its other manifestation or "expression", namely *holiness*, combines the cognition of the "Idea of the world" with the *rejection* or repudiation of it.

We have seen that, in fragment 86 from 1813, the internal coherence of the text requires that the Platonic Idea be the object of cognition of the better consciousness; nevertheless, Schopenhauer does not state this explicitly, and this lack of clarity can be interpreted as a sign of his reservations in this regard (cf. *supra*, 8.14). If this is so, those reservations would find their grounding in 1814, when their content was finally made explicit: the Platonic Idea cannot be the correlate of the better consciousness because, unlike the latter, it opposes the empirical world in a non-absolute manner.

The eternal better consciousness is the "nothing" of temporal consciousness and its realm (cf. *supra*, 8.2–8.6; 10.5); and indeed it is the theoretical and practical annihilation of the world (the withdrawal of the better consciousness into Plato's spiritual sun realizes the possibility of "annihilating the world even theoretically"; not willing "the Idea of the world" annihilates the world practically). *The Platonic Idea, on the other hand, though eternal, is not the "nothing", but the true being of the empirical world*, "the innermost essence [*das innerste Wesen*]" of the latter,[177] its ὄντως ὄν.[178] This substantial difference between two terms that are both *eternal* implies two different and opposing concepts of eternity, which will have to be analyzed later (cf. *infra*, 12.9). What interests us here is to note that while the Idea is an "object", the better consciousness is not a "subject"; the difference between them therefore ultimately coincides with the difference between *non-absolute* and *absolute opposition* to the "world".

In fragment 253, Schopenhauer finally draws the radical consequence of the difference between "better consciousness" and "being-subject": *the better consciousness is not, and cannot be, a "consciousness"*.

> *To know* [Wissen] really means to have *concepts* and their combinations in practice and use, i.e. dependence on the will for their visualization; it is therefore conditioned by the *faculty of reason*. Accordingly *to be conscious* [bewußt seyn] of a thing means to have set it down and practised in concepts […].

---

[177] MR 1, fn. to n. 54, p. 31.
[178] MR 1, n. 250, p. 163.

> According to all this, *consciousness* [Bewußtseyn] would have to be restricted to the *faculty of reason*, but this won't do; for we need this word (there being no other) not only to denote the whole of being-subject as the correlative of *all* classes of representations, but even to include under it the *better consciousness* as well, which is no longer a being-subject at all.[179]

This fragment can be seen as the decisive point of crisis for the theory of the double consciousness. From here on, the figure of the better consciousness would make three fleeting appearances of little theoretical relevance (fragments 256, 274, 286), before disappearing for good.[180]

In fragments 290, 291 and 319, Schopenhauer would still use the adjective "better" in a 'metaphysical' sense (in an attempt to denote an absolute opposition to the empirical world), though no longer referring to the noun "consciousness", but rather to the terms "genius",[181] "man",[182] and "nature" respectively.[183] The use of these words clearly indicates Schopenhauer's reservations about the noun being replaced. These qualms essentially depend on the rejection of the transcendent use of the understanding, namely the illegitimacy of using a term belonging to the empirical realm ("consciousness") to denote something that necessarily transcends that realm, and is indeed its "nothing".

11.11 Affinities and Differences between Better Consciousness and the Pure Subject of Cognition. Cognition of the Idea as a Result of "Disengaging Oneself" from the Will

The disappearance of the term "better consciousness" does not at all indicate the disappearance of the basic traits of the concept. The determination that is no longer referable to it – being consciousness or the subject of cognition of metempirical reality, i.e. the Platonic Idea – is 'taken over' by the figure of the pure subject of cognition. This first and fundamental commonality – *the ability to cognize the Platonic Idea* – generates all the other determinations shared by these two figures, which I will now consider.

---

[179] MR 1, n. 253, p. 165. Translation modified.
[180] In fragment 281 Schopenhauer only *implicitly* refers to the better consciousness, when he writes that "in him [man] there lives yet another consciousness [than the natural one] that admittedly he is not, but can be, something different from nature, the moment he wants to [*sobald er will*]" (cf. MR 1, p. 188).
[181] MR 1, n. 290, p. 195.
[182] MR 1, n. 291, p. 196.
[183] MR 1, n. 319, p. 217.

First of all, *the opposition to the will-to-life*. As we have seen, it is through the will that the individual can choose to be empirical consciousness or better consciousness (cf. *supra*, 7.11). Willing-life (*Lebenwollen*), or willing existence in time, is absolutely opposed to the better will (*der bessre Wille*, the will of the better consciousness as an objective genitive: cf. *supra*, 10.11). In fact, temporal life is the absolute opposite realm to the better consciousness:[184] each is the nothing or opposite (*Gegensatz*) of the other.[185] If and insofar as he *wills* life, the individual *is* empirical temporal consciousness and thus *cognizes* the empirical world; conversely, if and insofar as he does not want life, i.e. he *wills* better consciousness, the individual *is* eternal better consciousness and thus *cognizes* the metempirical realm. Holding firm the assumption that the cognition of empirical consciousness is governed by the principle of sufficient reason, up to fragment 234 Schopenhauer assumed that the better consciousness cognizes the Platonic Idea. Precisely in this sense, the two forms of cognition are the opposite (*Gegensatz*) of each other,[186] as are the two respective realms and, ultimately, the two respective consciousnesses.

Whether the individual cognizes empirical reality or the Platonic Idea therefore depends on his self-determination as empirical consciousness or better consciousness; but this self-determination in turn depends on the individual's *will*. Those two forms of cognition (of which the first for Schopenhauer is absolutized by dogmatism, while the second corresponds to the viewpoint of genuine criticism) are therefore subordinate to the will that chooses between empirical consciousness and better consciousness (i.e. between life in time and its negation); they take over by virtue of a practical decision, rather than as a consequence of a theoretical demonstration. This is the voluntarist feature of Schopenhauer's discourse (cf. *supra*, 10.13). Recall that Fichte too – albeit in a profoundly different theoretical context – traced the choice between "dogmatism" and "criticism" back to a practical dimension, namely the inclination (*Neigung*) and interest (*Interesse*) of the individual.[187]

Following fragment 250, Schopenhauer attributed cognition of the Platonic Idea to the pure subject of cognition, no longer to the better consciousness; but the voluntaristic dynamic highlighted above would persist. In order to gain access to intuition of the Platonic Idea, it is necessary to first deactivate or abandon cognition according to the principle of reason; and this is possible only through a momentary suspension of the will-to-life, by virtue of which the individual – who is

---

184 MR 1, n. 158, p. 98.
185 MR 1, n. 46, p. 27.
186 MR 1, n. 330, p. 226.
187 Cf. J. G. Fichte, *[First] Introduction to the* Wissenschaftslehre, in Fichte 1994, p. 18. Cf. also F. W. Schelling, 1980 pp. 173–147 (Sixth Letter).

normally the subject of both cognition and willing – ceases to be the subject of willing, becoming *only* the subject of cognition (hence the adjective "pure"):

> Man's most blissful state is the one in which, having disengaged himself from willing [*vom Wollen losgerissen*], he has become the *pure subject of cognition* and in which the body is his object only in so far as it conveys cognition of indirect objects and consequently is not by itself perceived as an object of the will.[188]

A little earlier, Schopenhauer had written that the aim of philosophy, in the theoretical sphere, is cognition of the Platonic Idea; in the practical sphere, it is the realization of "happiness", for which it is necessary to "disengage ourselves from willing [*vom Wollen uns loszureißen*], and abide in the better consciousness".[189] Detaching oneself from the will thus produces, *in the theoretical sphere*, the elevation of the individual to the pure subject of cognition (and the consequent intuition of the Platonic Idea) and, *in the practical sphere*, the self-determination of the individual himself as better consciousness. This circumstance indicates very clearly that the figure of the pure subject of cognition took over the theoretical or cognitive sphere previously attributed to the better consciousness (and thus also the underlying voluntarist trait of discourse, indicated above). All this would have extremely relevant consequences for the structure of Schopenhauer's mature system (cf. *infra*, 12.9).

The detachment from all possible will in relation to objects leads to *the purely contemplative* (cognitive) *attitude* of the pure subject of cognition, which constitutes a third element in common with the better consciousness (in addition to the ability to intuit the Platonic Idea and the opposition to the will). Just as the better consciousness considers things *"objectively"* (cf. *supra*, 8.13), so as to relate to the world as an Olympian god,[190] so too the pure subject of cognition "contem-

---

188 MR 1, n. 257, p. 168. Translation modified.
189 MR 1, n. 256, p. 168.
190 Cf. MR 1, n. 187, p. 112. Schopenhauer raised the problem of the relationship between the philosophy of the better consciousness and ancient Greek culture: "With the Greeks, and in particular with *Homer*, the *better consciousness* was still quite unknown to their faculty of reason, and therefore in their language no expression for it was yet to be found. [...] At that time it still reposed entirely in the interior of the mind, like a God in the Holy of Holies, and it made no effort to enter the rational empirical consciousness [...]." In this sense, "Homer uniquely and resolutely keeps within the world of the senses", which is the world of empirical consciousness, "and is so purely *objective*" (MR 1, n. 162, p. 100). Later, however, Schopenhauer would change his opinion: Homer represented "the scrambling, scampering, bickering and roaring of the world, as they are the subject of our empirical rational consciousness" – that is, the unhappiness of willing. "But the better consciousness in us, untouched and unshaken by all those things, is enthroned deep within us and is objectified by him and just like the separate forces of nature) personified

plates truly *objectively* and with the eyes of an artist",[191] as the quiet spectator of the whole tragedy of life (cf. *supra*, 10.8).[192]

Fourthly, the pure subject inherits its *foreignness to time and space* from the better consciousness. Just as the better consciousness is eternal, so the subject of cognition, the correlate of the Platonic Idea, "lies outside time".[193]

Finally, the pure subject of cognition and the better consciousness share *non-individuality*. Lying beyond time and space, which constitute the principle of individuation, the pure subject, like the better consciousness (cf. *supra*, 8.8), is "free from individuality and its principle".[194] Its correlate, the Platonic Idea, is likewise universal, not individual (unlike empirical objects, which constitute the objective correlate of the empirical individual subject).

As a consequence of the displacement of the purely contemplative or cognitive attitude, previously attributed to the better consciousness, onto the pure subject, Schopenhauer brings the experience of the sublime back no longer to the better consciousness (cf. *supra*, 8.12), but to the pure subject of cognition.[195]

As a pure cognizer, the subject of cognition is a figure akin to the Witness described in the Indian texts (cf. *supra*, 10.8). This affinity is recognized by Schopenhauer in the second edition of the dissertation:

> [...] For the I that represents, the subject of cognition, can never itself become a representation or object, since, as the necessary correlate of all representations, it is their condition, however, the beautiful passage of the sacred Upanishad applies to it: "that which sees all is not to be seen; that which hears all is not to be heard; that which knows all is not to be

---

in the blissful immortal gods who from Olympus calmly watch the tumult and for whom all this is only a jest" (MR 1, n. 187, p. 112).

191 MR 1, n. 217, p. 134.
192 MR 1, n. 191, p. 116.
193 MR 1, n. 191, p. 116.
194 MR 1, n. 217, p. 134.
195 "My *I as body, as will*, loses itself in infinite time and vanishes in infinite space, and so, looking back on my I, I think with a shudder at the succession of thousands of years and behold with a shudder the innumerable worlds in the heavens. But by reflecting and becoming aware of myself as *the eternal subject of cognition*, I express with pride and confidence the undeniable truth that those worlds are my representation or mental picture and that therefore I, the eternal subject, am the bearer of this universe, whose entire existence is nothing but a relation to me. Where now is the shudder, where the alarm? I am, nothing else exists; supported on me the world rests in the peace that emanates from me. How could it terrify me, how could I be frightened by its size which is always only the measure of my own greatness that always surpasses it? This cognition is the feeling of the *sublime*." (MR 1, n. 337, p. 229, translation modified)

known; that which discerns all is not to be discerned. Beyond it, seeing, and knowing, and hearing, discerning, there is nothing." – *Oupnekhat*, Vol I, p. 202.[196]

This passage confirms the influence exerted by the *Oupnekhat*. But once again, one must not forget some important precedents in the manuscripts: as early as 1809, Schopenhauer ascribed contemplation to a point of view foreign to the world of experience and becoming (i.e. to a "spiritual world": cf. *supra*, 1.5–1.7), so much so that "the best way to express Kant's defects [*Mangel*]" – since he excluded the metempirical world from his theoretical investigation – is perhaps "if we say that he was not acquainted with contemplation" (cf. *supra*, 2.7).[197] In 1813, well before Schopenhauer studied the *Oupnekhat*, he referred the contemplative attitude to the better consciousness (cf. *supra*, 8.13–8.15). Fragment 121 reads:

> By mistaking himself for his immediate object, man sees himself as a temporal being [*Zeitwesen*] and believes he has come into existence and must pass away. He is like one who, standing on the shore, follows the waves with his eyes and imagines himself to be swimming away whilst the waves are stationary. But it is he who is at rest and only the waves that move.[198]

Only in the light of these pre-existing interests and reflections could the texts of the *Oupnekhat* offer a privileged source and a fundamental term of comparison for young Schopenhauer. It is significant that, as already mentioned, he sought to find a further precedent for his considerations in Kant's philosophy: for Schopenhauer, Kant demonstrated that everything that belongs to experience (the *Erscheinung*) exists only as an *object* in relation to the *subject*, which, being specular and opposed to the object itself, is necessarily foreign to all objective or phenomenal determinations.[199] Schopenhauer thus likened Kant's criticism and Schelling's philosophy to the texts of the *Oupnekhat*, as unfinished attempts to expound "subjective infinity".[200] On the other hand, in the appendix to the first volume of the *Oupnekhat*, Duperron himself had stated that Kant's transcendental philosophy, like the Indian sacred texts, calls man back to himself (cf. *supra*, 11.2).[201]

---

196 Schopenhauer 2012 [1847], § 41, pp. 133–134. The text from the *Oupnekhat* (which Schopenhauer quotes in Latin) reads: "*Id videndum non est: omnia videt; et id audiendum non est: omnia audit; sciendum non est: omnia scit; et intelligendum non est: omnia intelligit. Praeter id, videns, et sciens, et audiens, et intelligens ens aliud non est*".
197 MR 1, n. 17, p. 13.
198 MR 1, n. 121, p. 84.
199 MR 1, n. 227, p. 142.
200 MR 1, n. 240, p. 154.
201 Cf. Anquetil-Duperron 1801–1802, I, p. 711.

Now, the ability to cognize the Platonic Idea, which – given the specific way in which Schopenhauer understands cognition of the Idea – generates all the other common determinations between the figure of the pure subject of cognition and the better consciousness, does not fully cover the meaning Schopenhauer ascribed (or had ascribed) to the latter expression ("better consciousness"), but only cognition of the eternal, which is now expressly expunged from the aforementioned expression (together with the term "consciousness") and referred to the pure subject. Part of that meaning is unaccounted for: namely the *absolute opposition to the empirical world and, consequently, to cognition as such* (since the so-called "being" of things in the world is nothing but "being cognized": cf. *supra*, 9.3).

> In these sheets [...] I have often stated and shown how when we are *willing* we are *wretched* [*unseelig*] and when we are *cognizing* we are *blessed* [seelig] [...]. Here it is still puzzling that the *better consciousness* (bliss [*Seeligkeit*]) in the real sense) is nevertheless not divided into subject and object and therefore being-subject belongs to the empirical consciousness that is to the state of wretchedness (or at any rate to the possibility of wretchedness) [...].

> Were we merely willing and not cognizing beings, we should be abandoned to eternal damnation and perdition. Therefore life is a blessing only in so far as we are *cognizing* beings, for to the extent that we are *willing* beings it is an affliction. *Cognition* is the promise of redemption, the true gospel; willing, on the other hand, is hell itself. Thus we now have our bliss to the extent that we find ourselves as the pure subject of cognition; for although cognition is still not supreme bliss [*Seeligkeit*], is not yet the better consciousness itself, yet it is the condition of and the path to this, the promise of this.[202]

Cognition, in itself, does not yet constitute true and proper redemption, but only its promise, its announcement (that is why it is the "gospel"). Rather, supreme bliss and authentic redemption are found with the better consciousness, which "does not think and cognize, since it lies beyond subject and object".[203] Cognition is in essential relation to the world (even and especially when its content consists of the Platonic Ideas, which constitute the *essence* of the world itself). For this reason, while retaining a partial affinity with the *atma* of the *Oupnekhat*, the pure subject of cognition can no longer represent, unlike the better consciousness, what man was 'before' he willed the world and thus 'fell' into time – that is, what he should "again" become, redeeming himself (cf. *supra*, 10.8). This irreducible surplus of the better consciousness compared to the pure subject of cognition would soon be taken over by another theoretical figure, destined to enter the scene as the true

---

[202] MR 1, n. 274, pp. 181–182. Translation modified. On the opposition between better consciousness and will-to-life, cf. Segala 2017.
[203] MR 1, n. 96, p. 72. Translation modified.

and final protagonist of Schopenhauer's reflections: the negation of the will-to-life (cf. *infra*, 11.13–11.15).

11.12 "The World as Thing-in-Itself Is a Great Will". The Identification of Thing-in-Itself, Platonic Idea and Will

In fragment 210, Schopenhauer wrote that the task of philosophy is to faithfully reproduce, through the concepts of reason, the "Ideas of all that which is to be found in consciousness" and, ultimately, "the Idea of all that *is* and lives", i.e. "the Idea of *being* in time" in general (cf. *supra*, 10.12).[204] But "being in time" is nothing other than "the world [*die Welt*]".[205] The actual object of philosophy is consequently "the Idea of the world".[206]

In his subsequent notes, Schopenhauer elaborates and deduces by analogy – through the universalization of the intelligible character – the concept of a *universal* will-to-life, the appearance of which is precisely "this null, unsatisfactory and dismal world" (cf. *supra*, 11.6–11.7).[207]

If we now add to all these premises the identification of Platonic Idea and thing-in-itself (cf. *supra*, 11.9), the conclusion can only be the following: *"The world as thing-in-itself* [Die Welt als Ding an sich] is a great will which knows not what it wills; for it does not *know* but merely *wills* just because it is a will and nothing else."[208]

This "great will", of which the world is the appearance, cannot know or cognize anything, precisely because it is "a will and nothing else"; willing and cogniz-

---

[204] MR 1, n. 210, pp. 127–128.
[205] MR 1, n. 210, p. 128.
[206] MR 1, n. 250, p. 164.
[207] MR 1, n. 246, p. 161. Translation modified.
[208] MR 1, n. 278, pp. 184–185. While accepting the general thesis proposed by Y. Kamata (1988), according to which the development of Schopenhauer's thought up to 1814 is to be read as a progressive strengthening of his criticism, I do not agree with the radical consequence he draws (cf. Kamata 1988, pp. 235–236), namely that the "will" as "thing-in-itself" is the transcendental condition of experience (so that "in itself" would be equivalent to "*a priori*": cf. Kamata 1988, p. 240). Without discussing the reasoning behind this thesis, which is based on a speculative consideration of certain passages in the dissertation (cf. Kamata 1988, pp. 171–172, 209–210), I would only observe that, if this interpretative hypothesis were true, Schopenhauer would be using Kant's terminology in a completely distorted way, identifying what for Kant is absolutely *external* to consciousness, namely the "thing-in-itself", with the formal and transcendental structure of consciousness itself – something that, far from being "in itself", is rather *in consciousness*.

ing are two antithetical determinations (cf. *supra*, 11.8). As pure and simple "will", it simply *wills*, without *knowing* what it wills.

In general, the thing-in-itself or Platonic Idea represents the *identity of the different* within the same species (cf. *supra*, 11.9). Since "everything that exists is only appearance [*Erscheinung*] of *will*, embodied *will*",[209] the Idea or thing-in-itself of a single thing is ultimately the "will" of which that single thing is the "objecthood [*Objektität*]".[210]

But then, the fact that the will is the "thing-in-itself" in relation to which the entire world is an appearance means that the will is the identity of the different in relation to *all* the objects in the world, so that it relates to them just as, within the same species, the Platonic Idea relates to individuals. That is, the will as a thing-in-itself represents the supreme identity of the different – the 'transcendental' identity of all species (just as "transcendental diversity" is the difference or diversity that exists between the various Platonic Ideas, corresponding to the diversity of the existing species, cf. *supra*, 11.9).

It can also be said that the entire empirical sphere, i.e. the Kantian phenomenon as such and in its entirety, constitutes the *genus* with respect to which the will is the Platonic Idea or the thing-in-itself. And indeed, in fragment 577, the relation between the will as *Ding an sich* and the *Erscheinung* is thought of, like that which exists between Platonic Idea and thing-in-itself, in terms of the opposition between "universal [*Allgemeines*]" and "particular [*Einzlenes*]".[211]

But how should the relationship between will and world, i.e. between thing-in-itself and appearance, be properly conceived of?

> The Platonic *Idea*, the *thing-in-itself*, the *will* (for they are all the same) is in no way the *ground* of the appearance [Grund der Erscheinung], for it (the Idea) would thus be the *cause* [Ursach] and as such a *force* [Kraft], but as such *capable of being exhausted*. [...]
>
> As cause and effect (generally as ground and consequent) only appearances mutually hang together, not the Idea or the thing-in-itself with the appearance. Rather is the appearance nothing but the Idea itself in so far as this is *cognized*.
>
> The will is the Idea [*Der Wille ist die Idee*]; if it is to be *cognized*, it appears as a body and therefore generally as substance [...].[212]

As a thing-in-itself or Idea, the will is foreign to the determinations of the appearance (such as being "cause", "reason" or "ground"). In a comment on the *Timaeus*,

---

209 MR 1, n. 242, p. 158. Translation modified.
210 MR 1, n. 287, p. 194. Translation modified.
211 MR 1, n. 577, p. 433.
212 MR 1, n. 305, pp. 205–206. Translation modified.

Schopenhauer wrote that only "Everything that is not *Idea*, [or] thing-in-itself, but appearance, comes under the law of causality".[213] Conversely, all this implies that the world (understood as the totality of appearances) cannot be a consequence or effect of the will (understood as thing-in-itself); it is nothing but the will – the Platonic Idea, the thing-in-itself – *as cognized.* The absence of a causal relation between thing-in-itself and appearance implies that the relation between will and world cannot be defined in terms of creation (unlike what is posited in the *Oupnekhat* with reference to the concept of Maya: cf. *supra*, 11.2).

From fragment 321 onwards, Schopenhauer began to differentiate between the will as a thing-in-itself and the Platonic Idea, tending to interpret the latter – i.e. the Platonic Ideas as a whole – as a first degree of phenomenalization of the former.[214] For if Ideas are the archetypal and universal models of the individual things in the world, and if the world as a whole is the appearance of the will, then Ideas are not the will itself, but (precisely) the eternal prototypes of its appearance. The reflections on this point can be found in the manuscripts up to 1817 and cannot be analyzed in detail here.[215] However, the final result of these considerations, as formulated in *The World as Will and Representation*, must be mentioned: Platonic Ideas, for the reasons given above, constitute the first degree of objectification or phenomenalization of the thing-in-itself, and are therefore the "immediate objecthood" of the will; in them the will (thing-in-itself) becomes an *object*, or representation, 'for the first time'.[216] Consequently, "Kant's thing-in-itself and Plato's Idea" – "these two great, obscure paradoxes of the two greatest philosophers of the West" – are not really "identical", but "very closely related and distinct in only one respect": the latter, unlike the former, is an "object for a subject" (although this subject is not the empirical individual, but the pure subject of cognition).[217]

Nevertheless, the identification of Platonic Idea and thing-in-itself, even after being abandoned, would leave a significant trace in the manuscripts: *the relationship between will and appearance would be understood as analogous to that between Idea and individual thing.* Still in 1817, Schopenhauer would write:

---

[213] MR 2, p. 438.
[214] MR 1, n. 321, pp. 218–219.
[215] Despite the difference already asserted in fragment 321 and consistently developed in fragments 442 and 479 (cf. MR 1, pp. 319, 354), Schopenhauer's position oscillated on this topic, and for a long time he would tend to regard the Platonic Idea and the thing-in-itself as identical (e.g. in fragments 486 and 510–511, written in 1815 and 1816 respectively: cf. MR 1, pp. 357–358; 376–377).
[216] Schopenhauer 2010b, I 201, § 31, p. 192.
[217] Schopenhauer 2010b, I 201, § 31, p. 193.

> Just as a *laterna magica* or a theatre of optical performances shows many different pictures [*Bilder*], and yet it is one and the same flame that illuminates all of them, so are all the appearances [*Erscheinungen*] and events ever seen by the world only the copy and image [*Abbild*] of the one will-to-life which appears in them all and itself remains unmoved, in spite of all their change and variation.[218]

The metaphor of the magic lantern (already present in the dissertation of 1813: cf. *supra*, 9.14),[219] by implicitly equating the objects of the world with mere shadows, seems to offer a variant of the Platonic allegory of the cave. Just as the single thing is the image (εἰκών) of the Idea,[220] so for Schopenhauer the appearance is the copy or image (*Abbild*) of the thing-in-itself. This relevant and heterodox assumption would be retained in the mature system (cf. *infra*, 12.4–12.6).

11.13 Self-Cognition and Self-Denial of the Will-to-Life

According to Schopenhauer, man, through life, sees "what it is that he wills to be, has willed, hence wills and therefore is".[221] Man *is* what he has *willed* to be because his life in time is nothing but the appearance or manifestation in time of his intelligible character. In his life, each individual sees himself as in a "mirror", which enables him to achieve self-cognition (*Selbsterkenntniß*) (cf. *supra*, 10.7–10.9).[222]

However, as a consequence (*in Folge*) of this knowledge – the content of which also and mainly includes pain as the essence of life itself – man comes to reject or deny (*verleugnen*) his own character, and is thus redeemed (cf. *supra*, 10.11–10.13). Knowledge of (one's) own will, insofar as it constitutes the necessary condition of redemption, represents "the whole purpose [*Zweck*] of life".[223]

Furthermore, Schopenhauer deduces the concept of the will-to-life by universalizing the concept of intelligible character (understood as the individual willing-life): the universal will-to-life is to the world and existence in general what the intelligible character is to the body and existence of the individual (cf. *supra*, 11.6).

If all these premises are taken into account, it won't be surprising that the very 'dialectic' between the *knowledge (experience) of life as pain* and the *negation*

---

[218] MR 1, n. 687, p. 531. Translation modified.
[219] Schopenhauer 2012 [1813], § 46, pp. 189–190.
[220] Cf. Plato, *Phaedrus*, 250 b, Plato 1914 ff., vol. 9, pp. 426–427.
[221] MR 1, n. 159, p. 99.
[222] MR 1, n. 159, p. 99.
[223] MR 1, n. 191, p. 116.

of the will, originally referred only to the intelligible character, is now also attributed by Schopenhauer to the universal will-to-life. Just as the life of the individual is the "mirror" of his intelligible character,[224] so life in its totality is the "mirror" of the universal will-to-life: through (*durch*) such self-cognition, the will-to-life "can convert [*sich wenden*] and redemption is possible".[225]

> *The world as appearance* is the cognition of itself which is imparted to this will and in which it cognizes what it wills. In so far as this cognition is brought about, it destroys the will which then no longer *wills*, because what it wills contradicts itself and it now cognizes what it wills.[226]

"Pain, suffering and hard toil", which characterize life and the world, "kill the will-to-life";[227] "*If we are unhappy*, then precisely in this way is the will-to-life killed [*getödt*] more and more and we are brought nearer to redemption".[228]

The will-to-life, for Schopenhauer, is the universal "wicked will", of which the world is the appearance.[229] This point marks a fundamental divergence from the doctrines of the *Oupnekhat*, according to which the world in itself – insofar as it is recognized as a *figure* of Brahm, the Creator god – is not evil, because it is indeed God's sacred cosmic *ludus* (*līlā* in Sanskrit), with which he has wished to delight himself by dividing (or multiplying) himself in the various entities.[230] Nor is Brahm an evil God. For Schopenhauer, rather, the world is evil in itself, and therefore the metaphysical will that willed and wills it is essentially *wicked*. This (broadly speaking) 'gnostic' assumption contributes to further differentiating the concept of "will-to-life" from the concept of Maya as Brahm's *voluntas aeterna*. The underlying presupposition here, namely that what the world originated from is wicked, makes it clear again that Schopenhauer's reception of the Indian texts was oriented and determined by his previous reflections (cf. *supra*, 1.7; 8.8; 10.15).[231]

By virtue of this difference between the concept of *Wille zum Leben* and that of Brahm's *voluntas aeterna*, it is not even possible to simply identify the *nolitio* of

---

224 MR 1, n. 159, p. 99.
225 MR 1, n. 274, p. 182. Translation modified. Cf. also n. 273, p. 181.
226 MR 1, n. 278, p. 185. Translation modified.
227 MR 1, n. 246, p. 161. Translation modified.
228 MR 1, n. 293, p. 197. Translation modified.
229 MR 1, n. 326, p. 22.
230 Cf. Anquetil-Duperron 1801–1802, I, p. 203 (Duperron's note), pp. 315–317, 640; II, p. 17 (Duperron's note), 157.
231 Duperron himself, however, had proposed a comparison between the Indian doctrines and the Gnostic sect of the Valentinians. Cf. Anquetil-Duperron 1801–1802, I, pp. 562–566. On the Schopenhauerian reception of these passages, cf. Regehly 2008.

the *Oupnekhat* – which is man's return to, or annihilation in, Brahm[232] – with the negation or denial of the *Wille zum Leben*. On the other hand, even if one were to assume the complete conceptual identity between the "will-to-life" and Brahm's *voluntas aeterna*, then the negation of the will-to-life should rather be made to correspond to the annihilation (or self-denial) of Brahm himself – and thus, again, to something different from what is meant by *nolitio* in the *Oupnekhat*.

The only way to maintain the correspondence of the negation of the will-to-life mentioned by Schopenhauer and the *nolitio* of the *Oupnekhat* (man's return to Brahm) would be to attribute to Schopenhauer, as early as 1814, an indologically correct understanding of Brahm as the unmanifest Absolute (*Brahman*), rather than, in accordance with the *Oupnekhat*, as God the Creator of the world (cf. *supra*, 11.2). Such an attribution would be anachronistic: only in § 71 of the third edition of *The World* (1859) would Schopenhauer definitively identify Brahm with the "negation of the will-to-life", as opposed to *Brahma*, which would instead represent its affirmation. The philosopher would thus implicitly refute a passage from *Parerga and Paralipomena* (1851), in which Brahm and *Brahma* were seen as conceptually equivalent in their being both symbols of the procreation and birth of beings.[233]

In short: while the *nolitio* that follows from the *cognitio* of the supreme Being, in the *Oupnekhat*, is the definitive return or reabsorption of the individual into this very Being, for Schopenhauer the *nolitio*, which follows from the *cognitio* of the will-to-life as the sole essence of the whole, is instead the definitive 'escape' from this essence, its radical *negation*.

---

232 Cf. Anquetil-Duperron 1801–1802, II, pp. 10, 73–74.
233 Cf. Schopenhauer 2014, p. 116. In fragment 603 of 1816 (cf. MR 1, p. 449) Schopenhauer traces the Indian Trimurti, i.e. the gods *Brahma* (God of creation), *Vishnu* (God of self-preservation) and *Shiva* (God of destruction-palingenesis), which are manifestations of Brahm, back to the concept of "will-to-life'". The variants of § 71 of *The World as Will and Representation* in the first three editions of the work are very significant in this regard. In the first edition (1819), the negation of the will-to-life is juxtaposed with *"Resorbtion in den Urgeist, oder Nieban der Buddhaisten"* (cf. Schopenhauer 2020, p. 297); in the second (1844), with the *"Resorbtion in den Urgeist, oder Nirwana der Buddhaisten"* (cf. WWV 1844, vol. 1, p. 464), and finally, in the third (1859), with the *"Resorbtion in das Brahm, oder Nirwana der Buddhaisten"* (cf. Schopenhauer 1859, henceforth quoted as WWV 1859, vol. 1, p. 487). Compared to the first two editions, in the third the term *Brahm* takes the place of the term *Urgeist* as equivalent to the Buddhist *"Nirwana"* or *"Nieban"*. Already in Chapter 48 of the second edition, however, the negation of the will-to-life was described as *"Absorbtion in das Brahm"* (cf. WWV 1844, p. 606). Yet, in the above-mentioned passage from *Parerga and Paralipomena*, Schopenhauer regards *Brahma* as merely a "popular personification" of Brahm and links the latter to the *affirmation* of the will-to-life. These oscillations reveal Schopenhauer's enduring uncertainty about the meaning of the term Brahm. Cf. HN IV/1, Pandectae 1 [123], p. 125.

> It is not the purpose of the world to be a vapid fool's paradise, but to be a tragedy, in which the will-to-live cognizes itself [*sich erkenne*] and reverses course [*sich wende*] […].
>
> The difference between the one who causes suffering and the one who endures it is only in the appearance. All this is the one will-to-live which is identical with great suffering, and through a cognition of this it can turn [*sich wenden*] and come to an end.[234]

As soon as he cognizes his own essence in itself (which is also the world's essence in itself), man denies it. That is to say: as soon as it comes to cognize itself in man, the world's essence in itself (the will-to-life) comes to self-denial.

> In this endless drama [of the world] we see only occasionally how the will comes to cognize itself and reverses course [*sich wendet*]; instead of concern for our own individuality there now appear as love mercy and pity for others. The cognition of another's misery and distress causes us to forget our own, a denial of life [*Verneinung des Lebens*] shows itself as self-denial [*Selbstverläugung*].[235]

Since the will-to-life constitutes the individual's innermost essence, by denying or suppressing it the individual *denies himself*. In other words, the denial (*Verleugnung*) of the will-to-life *in* oneself is ultimately a repudiation or denial *of* oneself (*Selbstverleugnung*). The self-denial of the will-to-life, which for Schopenhauer can only be realized in the human individual, therefore coincides with the self-denial of the individual itself. The term used by Schopenhauer refers once again to the verb *verleugnen* (or *verläugnen*), the same with which Luther renders Jesus' invitation to deny oneself (ἀπαρνησάσθω ἑαυτόν) in Matthew 16:24 (cf. *supra*, 8.7). In *The World as Will and Representation*, the reference to this New Testament passage would be made explicit.[236]

The "denial of life" is not to be understood as mere death or suicide, i. e. as the negation of the mere 'fact' of life and the body, but, much more radically, as the denial or suppression of that of which life and the body itself are the *Erscheinung* (cf. *supra*, 10.14).

> To the *will-to-life* [*Willen zum Leben*] life is always sure and certain, for it is simply nothing but that will itself, or rather only *its mirror.* That will does not have to fear death […]. Only an individual can die; life cannot die […]. To will or not to will to live [*Leben wollen oder nicht leben wollen*] is the only question that is answered in eternity; and time is the mirror of the answer "I will to live" [*ich will leben*].[237]

---

234 MR 1, n. 326, p. 22. Translation modified.
235 MR 1, n. 357, pp. 244–245. Translation modified.
236 Cf. Schopenhauer 2010b, I 457, § 68, p. 413.
237 MR 1, n. 273, p. 181. Translation modified.

This relationship between cognition and will strongly limits Schopenhauer's voluntarist position. We have seen that the will in itself, in his view, is subject to the law of motivation, i.e. to the cognition of options for choice (cf. *supra*, 10.13). In 1815, for the sake of internal consistency, Schopenhauer would deny this assumption, definitively removing the will in itself (which is outside the principle of sufficient reason) from the realm of the law of motivation.[238] Nevertheless, he would continue to maintain the possibility of a (self)negation of the will as a consequence of cognition:

> *Apart from the abolition of the will generally through cognition as a tranquillizer* [italics mine], the will itself, that is to say *what* a man wills, his goal and purpose, can never be changed through cognition [...].[239]

I shall return to the relationship between cognition and will in Schopenhauer's mature system in the final chapter (cf. *infra*, 12.7–12.8). Now it is necessary to ask a different question: how can one describe or define the negation of the will-to-life?

11.14 Univocity of Human Consciousness, Cognition and Will. 'Positivity' of Pain and 'Negativity' of Pleasure. Turning Back from Existence: Nothing and Nirvana

Initially, Schopenhauer contrasted the will-to-life or willing-life (*Lebenwollen*) with a *positive* form of will: the "better will". By this expression, which already occurs in some fragments of 1812, he indicated the will of the eternal, which is antithetical to the will of temporality (objective genitives; cf. *supra*, 10.11–10.12). Later, however, the antithesis of willing-life – meaning the latter both in an individual sense, as "intelligible character", and in a universal sense, as the "will-to-life" – would have taken on a negative logical and linguistic form, becoming identical with *not-willing* temporality as such, i.e. with the negation or denial of the will-to-life. Henceforth, the "better will" would no longer be mentioned in the manuscripts.

---

[238] MR 1, n. 413, p. 288, n. 457, pp. 330–331.
[239] MR 1, n. 497, p. 368. Translation modified. German Text: "Abgesehn von der Aufhebung des Willens überhaupt durch die Erkenntniß als Quietiv, kann der Wille selbst, d.h. das was der Mensch will, sein Ziel und Zweck, nie durch die Erkenntniß also von Außen geändert werden" (HN I, p. 334).

This is similar to the case involving the figure of the better consciousness. The latter expression, from the point of view of Schopenhauer's 'criticism', is necessarily illegitimate, because it refers a *positive* determination – "consciousness" – to something that, being absolutely opposed to the empirical world, can only be described negatively, by the negation of all the predicates of what is cognizable for us (including cognizability itself). In order to be consistent with his assumptions, Schopenhauer was forced to renounce any positive description of what is totally other (*ganz anders*) than the world,[240] and consequently also the expression "better consciousness" (cf. *supra*, 11.10).

But the "better will" *wills* this totally Other: it is in fact the will of the better consciousness (objective genitive). Being a positive willing-something, the "better will" presupposes the (terminological and logical) positivity of what is willed by it – the positivity of something that for Schopenhauer can only be described negatively. Taking the consequentiality of his own discourse to the end, Schopenhauer was thus also forced to drop the expression "better will". Since the 'object' of such a will is, from a linguistic and logical point of view, necessarily negative, it is not and cannot be a positive willing-something; rather, it is a willing-not – that is, in the final analysis, a *not-willing* that which otherwise is or would be willed.

It should be borne in mind, in this regard, that the "double nature of [...] [our] will" for young Schopenhauer was the practical manifestation of the *"double nature of our consciousness"*.[241] In fact, the same dualism between the world and the totally Other than the world, which from a gnoseological or theoretical point of view grounds the duplicity of human consciousness and cognition (empirical/ better *consciousness*; empirical/better *cognition*), from a practical point of view likewise grounds "the double nature of the will", which "has a *twofold* supreme good" (cf. *supra*, 10.12). Indeed, from 1811/1812 onwards, for Schopenhauer, the (theoretical) task of the true philosopher was in fact to separate or divide (*ablösen*,[242] *trennen*,[243] *sondern*[244]) the better consciousness and cognition from the empirical consciousness and cognition. Similarly, but in the practical sphere, the task of the virtuous was to separate or divide the better will from the empirical will (cf. *supra* 7.11; 10.7 and 10.11). In fragment 249 Schopenhauer wrote again (for the last time) that "the perfect philosopher theoretically [*theoretisch*] presents the *better con-*

---

240 Cf. MR 1, n. 189, pp. 113–114; but also MR 2, pp. 411–412.
241 MR 1, n. 234, p. 147.
242 Cf. HN II, p. 329.
243 HN II, p. 360.
244 HN II, p. 329.

sciousness in all its purity by separating it accurately and entirely from the empirical. The saint does the same thing practically".²⁴⁵

However, given the impossibility of positively expressing what is totally other than the empirically given world (and its essence), the previous dualisms must disappear, or, more appropriately, take on the form of pure logical oppositions, in which what served as the second 'positive' term (better consciousness, better cognition and better will) is transformed into the logical and terminological *negation* of the first term. In other words, the rigorous distinction or separation of the world from what is totally other than the world itself has an important implication: the concepts of human "consciousness", "cognition" and "will" must lose the duplicity that was peculiar to them, henceforth taking on a largely univocal meaning.

Man's *consciousness* is always and only empirical, in the sense that it is always and only consciousness of the world; consequently, its absolute opposite – that which addresses the absolutely Other than the world – is not and cannot be another ("better") consciousness, but is simply *non-consciousness*.²⁴⁶

In the same way, human *cognition* is likewise always and only cognition of the world (or, in the case of Ideas or the will as a thing-in-itself, of the essence of the world itself), so that its absolute opposite is not and cannot be another ("better") cognition, but is simply *non-cognition* (just as the absolute opposite of its content, i.e. of the world, is simply non-world, i.e. negation of the world and its essence).

Finally, man's *will* is always and only the will (desire) of empirical things, i.e., on a metaphysical level, of the world or life (temporal existence) in its entirety; its absolute opposite, consequently, cannot be another, different kind of will, but is simply *non-will*. The freedom of man thus no longer consists in the choice between two positive options (to be *empirical consciousness* or *better consciousness*), but rather in the choice between a positive option and its negation: to *be* will-to-life or *not*. The alternative which allows man's redemption passes from a positive characterization to a negative one.

> And so I will attempt [...] to show that what appears as several when considered from several points of view, often only because we make several concepts of it through abstraction, is one. Thus if only we should gain the right point of view, the entire world should gradually appear

---

245 MR 1, n. 249, p. 162.
246 In *Parerga and Paralipomena*, Schopenhauer admits the possibility of a post-death state that is devoid of cognition (*erkenntnißlos*) (cognition according to the principle of reason), and yet not devoid of consciousness (*nicht bewußtlos*); this, however, relates to the transcendent sphere, which, as such, falls outside the realm of philosophy properly and rigorously understood (cf. Schopenhauer 2015, § 139, pp. 247). Here, the possibility of a consciousness outside the scope of the principle of reason seems to be admitted. See also the passage from the letter to Fraunstädt in which Schopenhauer paraphrases this point from the *Parerga* (in Schopenhauer 1911–1942, vol. XV, p. 76).

as one and this one only as the visibility of the will [*Sichtbarkeit des Willens*]: from all this what is neither world nor will is to be kept separate.[247]

What philosophy must keep strictly distinct or separate (*getrennt*) from the world is determined no longer positively, but negatively: it is "neither world nor will". In 1815, Schopenhauer wrote:

> Man as such is the appearance of the willing-life [*Erscheinung des Leben-wollens*]. The wicked man is the concentrated appearance of this willing-life [...].
>
> His opposite is the saint who is the appearance of *not* willing-life [*Erscheinung des Nicht-leben-wollens*], of a will that is *not* concerned with life. It is true that his body as such is the appearance of willing-life; but through death this body comes to an end. His [the saint's] character, however, that is to say the common element in the whole series of his actions, is appearance of the will which is not concerned with life, in other words has turned [*sich gewendet hat*], so that it is not the [same] will whose appearance is the body as such.[248]

The saint is no longer one who determines himself as a better consciousness; rather, he is the "appearance of *not* willing-life". The terminology used by Schopenhauer should not be misleading: the saint's "character", the 'holy will', is not determined here as a positive willing-something, but rather as a *not-willing* what the will as such wills: *life*, existence in time and, therefore, the world. This becomes clear in the remainder of the fragment:

> Here, of course, we can *express ourselves only negatively* [negativ], just because the material in which philosophy works, namely concepts, are representations and are therefore conditioned by life and belong to this. And so for our point of view the turning [*Wenden*] of the will, holiness, salvation, bliss [*Seligkeit*] are certainly a transition into *nothing* [*ein Uebergang ins Nichts*]. But closely connected with this is the view that the concept *nothing* expresses a mere relation, is a mere boundary-stone, and this is discussed on sheet E. p. 1 [fragment n.66].[249]

The place or 'home' of bliss is no longer described positively, as "better consciousness" (cf. *supra*, 10.3, 10.6 and 10.14), but negatively, as "turning of the will" and even as "nothing". What is positive (positively knowable) for us, i.e. the world as *Erscheinung* of the will, is essentially *evil* and *pain*; the absolutely other than pain (bliss) thus necessarily becomes for us something *negative*. The determinations of positive and negative, or of "being" and "nothing", are not to be understood

---

[247] MR 1, n. 280, pp. 186–187. Translation modified.
[248] MR 1, n. 389, p. 269. Translation modified.
[249] MR 1, n. 389, pp. 269–270. Translation modified.

here in an ontological (or absolute) sense, but in a gnoseological (or relative) sense, i.e. as dependent on our particular "point of view".

Schopenhauer's mature doctrine, according to which all pleasure is merely the negation or cessation of a pre-existing painful state, is already contained here in its core (a first explicit development of it is found in fragment 396).[250] That is to say, it is not only based on empirical considerations (the *experience* of the fact that "every satisfaction is only the removal of a pain"),[251] but also in consequence of his own fundamental gnoseological assumptions that Schopenhauer argues for the essentially *negative* nature of pleasure (or, more generally, of happiness), as opposed to the 'positivity' or reality of pain alone.[252] In fact, just as bliss, as the nothing of pain, is also, consequently (given the identity between being and pain), the nothing of all that we call "being" (as that which we can cognize), so, *within what we call "being"*, all empirical pleasure is merely the annulment (or cessation) of a pre-existing and 'positive' condition of pain. By virtue of this specific consequentiality, Schopenhauer's position presents an entirely peculiar physiognomy with respect to the considerations on the negativity of pleasure made by Pietro Verri and Giacomo Leopardi.[253]

It should be remembered that Schelling, in his *Philosophical Letters on Dogmatism and Criticism*, had mentioned some "Chinese sages" for whom "the supreme good" and "the absolute bliss [*Seligkeit*], consist of nothingness [*Nichts*]"; in this regard he also speaks of a "transition to non-being [*Uebergang zum Nicht-Seyn*]".[254] The term "nothing", Schelling pointed out, indicates here what for us is an absolute non-object (cf. *supra*, 8.2 and 8.5). In relation to the 'negativity' of the holy will, Schopenhauer uses the verb *sich ausdrücken*. This indicates precisely that the

---

250 MR 1, n. 396, p. 273; cf. also MR 1, fn to n. 445, p. 322.
251 Schopenhauer 2010b, I 443, § 67, p. 402.
252 Cf. Schopenhauer 2010b, I 376, § 58, p. 345: "All satisfaction, or what is generally called happiness, is actually and essentially only ever *negative* and absolutely never positive".
253 Cf. Verri 2001; Leopardi 1991. For the proposition of a certain affinity between Schopenhauer's thought and Leopardi's, see De Sanctis 1858. See also De Lorenzo 1923. M. Losacco, while emphasizing the specificity of Schopenhauer's metaphysics, considers his doctrine of pleasure and pain as a "continuation of the Italian hedonistic theory" (1903, pp. 240–241). It is true that Schopenhauer himself emphasized the affinity of his own philosophy with Leopardi's thought (cf. Schopenhauer 2018, II 675, chap. 46, p. 603). The most recent studies that have addressed the issue, however, have focused more on the differences between the two; cf. E. Severino (1990, pp. 344–345), who, precisely in relation to the concept of "nothing", notes that Leopardi's nothing, unlike that of which Schopenhauer speaks, is to be understood as absolute, not relative. See also, for more general considerations (which cannot be addressed here), Negri 1987, pp. 13, 268–269, 333–334, 351–352; Donà 2013, pp. 300–305.
254 Schelling 1980, p. 185 (Eighth Letter).

holy will *is not* 'negative' in itself; it is only *expressed* (described, determined) negatively, since it does not constitute any real object of cognition for us. In fragment 66 Schopenhauer also made abundant use of declarative verbs, such as *nennen*, "to call", and *sagen*, "to say".[255] An addition to fragment 389 reads:

> Therefore on this main point [the turning of the will] philosophy can only give negative pronouncements, that is, it can only speak of negation [*Verneinung*] [,] abolition [*Aufhebung*] of the will: if we were to ask for a positive presentation of what we express only negatively, then there would be nothing left for us but to refer to the state which all holy ascetics among Indians and Christians have experienced and which is called ecstasy, rapture, withdrawal within oneself, illumination, union with God, and so on. But a cognition of that state is possible only from one's own experience [...].[256]

The negation of the will-to-life is the repudiation of that of which the world and existence are the manifestation or appearance; it is therefore also, and necessarily, repudiation or denial of the world itself. It is an equal and opposite act of will to that from which life in time has arisen as its appearance: "our will [can] seriously set itself in opposition to the world, can deny [*verleugnen*] and annihilate [*vernichten*] it; for the world exists only in so far as the will creates [*schafft*] it".[257]

The world and life in time are what should not be (*das, was nicht seyn sollte*; cf. *supra*, 8.8 and 8.19). The will, therefore, can – and indeed ought to, *soll* – 'undo' what it has 'done' (on the meaning to be attributed here to the use of the verb "create", *schaffen*, cf. *supra*, 11.7). Insofar as the will-to-life corresponds for Schopenhauer to what religion calls "original sin" (which, according to Christian doctrine, is also the origin of this world), and insofar as the *negation* of the will-to-life corresponds to redemption from that same sin, the negation of the will-to-life is a kind of transcendental – or rather metaphorical – 'turning back' (*zurückkommen*) from the world and existence, towards what is totally other than them.[258] But this 'totally Other', which until 1814 Schopenhauer had called "better consciousness", can only be described negatively, precisely as the *negation* of all that is world and will of the world (objective genitive).

---

255 MR 1, n. 66, p. 36.
256 MR 1, n. 389, p. 270. Translation modified.
257 MR 1, n. 260, p. 170. Translation modified.
258 Cf. MR 3, p. 360 (Foliant II [198]): "the whole of life and existence itself are an aberration from which we have to turn back [*das ganze Leben und Daseyn selbst eine Verirrung ist, von der wir zurückzukommen haben*]". Cf. also MR 1, n. 79, p. 43, where morality and asceticism constitute the "return journey [*Rückkehr*]" from the world (which is precisely what "ought not to be") to the condition of better consciousness.

In 1816, when furthering his study of Oriental wisdom, Schopenhauer would identify the nirvana of Buddhism with the negation of the will-to-life – and, by way of a backlash, would begin to reinterpret and reformulate his own discourse also in the light of Buddhist doctrines.[259]

11.15 Conclusion. Absolute and Non-absolute Opposition: The Splitting of Contradictory Determinations That Constituted the Figure of the Better Consciousness

From all the above, it is clear that the two contradictory sides that made up the figure of the better consciousness – the side of *absolute* opposition and the side of *non-absolute* opposition to the world – in 1814 split into two different figures: the negation of the will-to-life and the pure subject of cognition.

Insofar as the better consciousness, *on the side of non-absolute opposition* (which consists in being either consciousness or subject of cognition), is resolved in the figure of the pure subject, the duplicity of human consciousness is resolved in the opposition between *the empirical individual* and *the pure subject of cognition, free of will:* the former is the subject both of willing and of cognition (according to the forms of the principle of reason); the pure subject, on the other hand, is only the subject of cognition (and its object of cognition are Platonic Ideas). In the final analysis, then, the duplicity of human consciousness is resolved here in the dualism between subject of cognition and subject of willing, which constitutes of every I.

This is also evident in the fact that fragment 86 (from 1813) defines lyrical poetry as the expression of the "mixture of eternity and temporality of which our consciousness consists"[260] and then, in fragment 266 (from 1814), as "the poetical presentation" of the astonishing and 'miraculous' "identity of the subject of willing with the subject of cognition".[261] Moreover, precisely in relation to the opposition between the subject of cognition and the will, Schopenhauer mentioned twice, again in 1815, the "twofold nature of our very essence [*Duplicität unsres Wesens*]".[262] This expression would have the same reference in *The World as Will and Representation*.[263] In his masterpiece, when describing the feeling of the sub-

---

[259] Cf. MR 1, n. 612, p. 470. Cf. Atzert 2007.
[260] MR 1, n. 86, p. 49.
[261] MR 1, n. 266, p. 179. Translation modified.
[262] MR 1, n. 404, p. 279. Cf. also n. 570, p. 425.
[263] Schopenhauer 2010b, I 328, § 54, p. 304.

lime that arises by the contemplation of overwhelming natural forces, Schopenhauer would expressly speak of the "twofold character of his [the spectator's] consciousness [*die Duplizität seines Bewußtseyns*]": "he feels himself to be both an individual, a frail appearance of the will that can be crushed by the slightest blow of those forces [...]; and yet at the same time the eternal, tranquil subject of cognition".[264] It is also worth mentioning that the polarity of brain and genitals, which in the juvenile system corresponds to that of better consciousness and empirical consciousness (*supra*, 8.18), in the mature system corresponds to the duplicity of every human being as subject of cognition and subject of will.[265]

On the other hand, the figure of the better consciousness, *on the side of its absolute opposition to the empirical consciousness* (which consists in its lying beyond subject and object and, in general, beyond all determinations that are positive for us), is resolved in the figure of the negation of the will. Therefore, the duplicity between better consciousness and empirical consciousness is resolved in the opposition between *affirmation* and *negation of the will-to-life*. The negation of the will represents the absolutely other from all that man, as such, *is* and *cognizes*; it is the true redemption from (and of) the world.

In the first fragments of 1814, the better consciousness is expressly set against the will-to-life (cf. *supra*, 10.11 – 10.12); it is then understandable why Schopenhauer describes the conversion of the individual (necessary for metaphysical "salvation") *both* as a transition to the better consciousness *and* as a negation of the will.[266] In fragment 186, Paul's saying that "we are sanctified not by works, but by faith" is interpreted by identifying faith – the salvific inner disposition – with the better consciousness.[267] In fragment 265, instead, Schopenhauer interprets the same maxim as an indication that man, in order to save himself, has "no way out other than his completely throwing off that very will of which his entire being [*Wesen*] now consists and the becoming visible of which is his own body, and willing and becoming the very opposite [*Gegentheil*] of all that he now wills and is".[268] In the latter text, the negation of the will-to-life takes the place of the better consciousness as what corresponds to the term "faith" in the interpretation of Paul's teaching. Finally, just as the better consciousness (cf. *supra*, 8.6), so too the negation

---

[264] Schopenhauer 2010b, I 242, § 39, p. 229. Cf. Novembre 2016a. The use of the expression "twofold character of [...] consciousness" is particularly significant and confirms the considerations made by M. Segala (cf. Segala 2011, p. 644). Cf. also Ruffing 2005. On the concept of the sublime in Schopenhauer, cf. Shapshay 2012; Vandenabeele 2015.
[265] Cf. Schopenhauer 2010b, I 239, § 39, p. 227.
[266] MR 1, n. 158, p. 98; n. 213, p. 130; n. 256, p. 167.
[267] MR 1, n. 186, p. 112.
[268] MR 1, n. 265, p. 177.

of the will-to-life can be made to correspond, according to Schopenhauer, to what religions call "God".[269]

Through this dual resolution and dissolution, the figure of the better consciousness was doomed to disappear. But the two different sides that constituted it were destined to remain: what vanished was only their (contradictory) union in the same figure. The next chapter, in conclusion, will highlight some relevant traces that the theory of better consciousness, together with other – later abandoned – reflections from the manuscripts, has left in the more distinctive features of Schopenhauer's mature system.

---

[269] Cf. HN IV/1, Cholera-Buch [52], p. 103. Cf. also HN III, pp. 343–344.

12 From the Early Manuscripts to *The World as Will and Representation*. Origin and Meaning of the Aporias in Schopenhauer's Mature System

12.1 Introduction

In this last chapter, I will examine some of the problematic passages in Schopenhauer's masterpiece, in respect of which the genetic reconstruction carried out so far can provide a particularly valuable interpretative key. Of course, I cannot deal with the complex issues mentioned here in exhaustive detail, but I can point to a possibly decisive direction of analysis.

More precisely, I will show that the most relevant aporias of the mature system originate from the permanence of certain theoretical traits that were no longer compatible with the 'criticistically correct' physiognomy that Schopenhauer, from 1814 onwards, endeavored to imprint on his reflections. As we shall see, these are specific points that, having constituted the basis and core of the proto-system, could not be dropped without dragging the entire theoretical edifice down with them.

Moreover, the way Schopenhauer grounds his metaphysics of will in his published works is essentially different from the way he originally conceived and deduced it. That is, the reasons with which Schopenhauer justifies his fundamental theses to the reader *are not the same* as the reasons by which he actually devised and formulated them. This *discrepancy* between the actual genesis of the doctrine and its subsequent foundation in the printed works is the result of extensive formalization and coherentization (carried out in the years 1815–1818), which, on the one hand, made the exposition of the system more elegant and structured, but, on the other hand, also obscured some of its essential features, which I shall bring to light in what follows.

As already exposed in the Preface, my purpose is not to eliminate the aporias of Schopenhauer's system; on the contrary, I will argue that they are indeed present, while trying to *explain* them from both a genetic and a theoretical point of view.

12.2 The Analogical Argument in *The World as Will and Representation:* The Silent Foundational Role of the Doctrine of the Intelligible Character

In the manuscripts from 1814, Schopenhauer arrived at the concept of a universal "will-to-life" – the appearance of which is the world as a whole – by extending and universalizing the concept of "intelligible character", which he originally referred only to the human being (cf. *supra*, 11.6). In his major work, the deduction of the will as the thing-in-itself follows a different path: the starting point is no longer the concept of intelligible character, but the lived-body (*Leib*), as each (in Schopenhauer's opinion) experiences it.

The indisputable fact, to which Schopenhauer refers here, is that every individual cognizes his own body not only as a *representation* like any other, but also as *will*. For every person, what constitutes the difference between their own body and all other representations – that is, all other objects that they perceive in space and time – is this further cognition of their body as will. It consists precisely in the cognition of the identity between *act of will* and *movement of the body*.

In themselves, they are "one and the same thing", but we cognize them in two completely different ways: once immediately (from within, i.e. only in time), as will, and another time mediately (from without, i.e. also in space), as body movement.[1]

> An action of the body is nothing but an objectified act of will, i.e. an act of will that has entered intuition. [...] And thus we can also say, in a sense: the will is *a priori* cognition of the body, and the body is *a posteriori* cognition of the will. – Resolutions of the will concerning events in the future are really just rational deliberations over things that will be willed later, they are not true acts of will: a decision is stamped only in the execution, and until that time it remains an unsettled design and exists only in reason, abstractly. Willing and doing are different only for reflection: in actuality they are one. Every true, genuine and immediate act of will is instantly and immediately also an appearing act of the body [*erscheinender Akt des Leibes*]: correspondingly, any effect on the body is instantly and immediately an effect on the will as well [...].[2]

---

[1] Cf. Schopenhauer 2010b, I 119, § 18, pp. 124–125: "An act of the will and an act of the body are not two different states cognized objectively, linked together in a causal chain, they do not stand in a relation of cause and effect; they are one and the same thing, only given in two entirely different ways: in one case immediately and in the other case to the understanding in intuition".
[2] Schopenhauer 2010b, I 119–120, § 18, p. 125. Translation modified.

So far, this is what Schopenhauer considers the 'original datum'. Henceforth begins his argumentation or deduction, the outcome of which he anticipates right away:

> We now clearly understand our double cognition [*Erkenntniß*] of the essence and operation of our own body, a cognition that we are given in two completely different ways; and we will go on to use this cognition as a key to the essence of every appearance in nature; and when it comes to objects other than our own body, [...] we will judge them on the analogy with our body [*nach Analogie jenes Leibes*], assuming that, since they are on the one hand representations just like the body and are in this respect homogeneous with it, then on the other hand, what remains after disregarding their existence as representation of a subject must have the same inner essence as what we call *will*.[3]

First of all, Schopenhauer cares to remove the will from the realm of the principle of reason:

> These acts of will continue to have a ground outside themselves, in motives. But these motives do not determine anything more than what I will at *this* time, in *this* place, under *these* circumstances; not *that* or *what* I will in general, i.e. the maxims that characterize the whole of my willing. [...]. The motive provides sufficient grounds for explaining my actions only when my empirical character is taken into account; when I abstract away from my character and ask why in general I will this and not that, there can be no answer, because the principle of sufficient reason governs only the *appearance* of the will, not the will itself, which should accordingly be considered *groundless*. I am, in part, presupposing Kant's doctrine of empirical and intelligible character here, as well as the relevant discussions from my *Fundamental Problems of Ethics*, pp. 48–58, and again on pp. 178 ff. of the first edition. But [...] this is a theme that we will need to discuss more thoroughly in the Fourth Book.[4]

The sense of this preliminary argument is clear. Schopenhauer wrote earlier that each individual's cognition of his body *as will* is different from the cognition he has of it *as representation*. This entails that "will" (as such) is something essentially different from "representation". But if it were subject to the principle of sufficient reason (in particular to the law of motivation), the will would be nothing more than, precisely, a representation. By affirming that not the will itself, but only its manifestation is subject to the principle of sufficient reason, Schopenhauer grounds the heterogeneity of the terms "will" and "representation", thus preparing the possibility of a metaphysical, yet immanent, use of man's self-cognition as will.

Before taking this last, decisive step, however, he still had to formally deduce that not only the action of the body, but also and above all the body itself, in its entirety, is an appearance or objectification of the will:

---

3 Schopenhauer 2010b, I 125, § 19, p. 129.
4 Schopenhauer 2010b, I 127, § 20, p. 131.

> Every action of my body, then, is the appearance of an act of will: and this act is just my will itself [*mein Wille selbst*], in general and in its entirety [*im Ganzen*] (and therefore also my character) expressing itself again in the presence of certain motives. But if this is so, then the indispensable condition and presupposition of my body's action would have to be the appearance of the will. This is because only what exists directly and solely through the will can condition the will's appearance; otherwise the condition would be merely accidental and make the will's appearance a mere accident: but this condition is the entire body itself [*der ganze Leib selbst*]. Therefore the entire body must itself be an appearance of the will, and must be related to my will as a whole [*meinem Willen im Ganzen*], i.e. to my intelligible character (whose appearance in time is my empirical character) in the same way that an individual action of the body is related to an individual act of the will. So the entire body must be nothing other than my will made visible [*mein sichtbar gewordener Wille*], it must be my will itself to the extent that my will is an intuitive object, a representation of the first class.[5]

We have seen that "An act of the will and an act of the body [...] are one and the same thing [*Eines und das Selbe*], only given in two entirely different ways: in one case immediately and in the other case to the understanding in intuition".[6] On the other hand, every single and temporal act of will manifests the *intelligible character*, which lies outside of time. The individual acts of will, which coincide with the actions of the body, therefore belong to the *empirical character*. (On the probable Kantian ancestry of the theme of man's double self-awareness, precisely in relation to the distinction between empirical and intelligible character, cf. *supra*, 9.9.)

Now, the first "condition" of the *actions of the body* is evidently the *body itself* as such and in its entirety: if there were no body, there would be no actions of the body either. Since the latter (in accordance with the "philosophical truth *par excellence*") are nothing more than an "appearance" of the temporal acts of the will that belong to the empirical character, and since the empirical character itself is in turn the "appearance" of the intelligible character, then the body in its entirety, being the *condition of the actions of the body*, constitutes the *condition of the appearing of the intelligible character*. As such, Schopenhauer argues, the body itself must likewise, and indeed in the first instance, be the appearance of the intelligible character.

This argument implies that in the opposite case – that is, if the body, which is the condition of the appearance of the intelligible character, were not itself such an appearance – the *appearance* of the intelligible character, depending on the body, would depend on something extrinsic to the character itself and would therefore be completely "accidental" in relation to it. Schopenhauer peremptorily excludes

---

5 Schopenhauer 2010b, I 127–128, pp. 131–132.
6 Schopenhauer 2010b, I 119, § 18, pp. 124–125.

such accidentality, but does not specify the ground for this conclusion (so that it constitutes an unjustified presupposition within his argument).

One can only hypothesize the principle that would ground the exclusion of the aforementioned accidentality: namely, that the appearance (*Erscheinung*) of *x* (in this case, of the intelligible character) cannot be "accidental" with respect to *x* (the intelligible character). But this principle would in turn, and ultimately, presuppose the assertion of a necessary (non-accidental) connection between what (as *Erscheinung*) is internal to the principle of reason and what is outside of it (that of which, or with respect to which, the *Erscheinung* is such: the intelligible character). In other words, it would presuppose a transcendent application of the notion of necessity, already effectively detected in the way Schopenhauer shows he understands the terms *erscheinen* and *Erscheinung* (cf. *supra*, 9.8; 10.7–10.9).

In any case, Schopenhauer believes he has thus demonstrated that the entire *body* relates to the *intelligible character* as the *action of the body* relates to the *individual temporal act of will:* the third term is the "appearance" (in time and space) of the fourth (which is only in time), just as the first term is the "appearance" (in time and space) of the second (which is outside time and space). But it is clear that the word "appearance" (*Erscheinung*) is understood here in a sense that is not univocal but, indeed, analogous: in one case it means the *manifestation in space and time of that which is only in time*, in the other case it means the *manifestation in space and time of that which is neither in space nor in time*. Moreover, the first meaning of *Erscheinung* seems to overlap with that of identity since, as we have seen, the two terms in question (the act of will and the movement of the body) for Schopenhauer are "one and the same thing". The problematic nature (i.e. the insufficient foundation) of all these passages is evident.[7]

At this point, however, the analogical argument, with the full wealth of its consequences, can finally be drawn:

> These considerations should give rise to a clear and certain recognition in the abstract of what everyone immediately feels concretely, namely that the essence in itself of our own appearance is *will*, and this is presented to us as a representation by our actions as well as by their permanent substrate, the body. [...] Anyone who has reached these conclusions with me will automatically have the key to knowledge [*Erkenntniß*] of the innermost essence of nature as a whole; all that needs to be done is to apply this insight to appearances that are not given in an immediate as well as mediated way (as is the case with our own appearance), but are only given in a mediated and one-sided form, as *representation*. [...]. Because we are using reflection in this manner we do not have to remain with appearances but can pass over to

---

[7] On the insufficient foundation of these passages (based on a different analysis of the text from the one conducted here), cf. Welsen 2016, p. 164.

the *thing-in-itself*. [...] Only the will is *thing-in-itself*: as such, the will is by no means a representation, it is quite different in kind from representation [...].[8]

Schopenhauer asks the reader to consider every object in the world, and thus the world itself as a whole, as an *analogon* of the lived-body (*Leib*): like the latter, every object in the world and the world as a whole can be considered not only *as representation*, but also, in their innermost essence, *as will*. Hence the title of his masterpiece.

Compared to the analogical inference carried out in fragment 242 of the manuscripts (cf. *supra*, 11.6), in his major work Schopenhauer seems to generalize not the concept of intelligible character, but rather the content of the particular and, indeed, unique form of cognition, whereby the body is *also* given to everyone as will. In other words, it would seem that the only necessary presupposition for the deduction is the aforementioned cognition, which, unlike the intelligible character, does not need to be deduced or demonstrated, because it is essentially immediate.

But this is not the case. Without the assumption of the intelligible character (to which Schopenhauer, in fact, explicitly refers), the analogical argument of *The World as Will and Representation* could not succeed at all. As we have seen, in order to show that the will is capable of opening up access to a sphere that is truly other than representation (i.e. other than the sphere of the principle of sufficient reason), Schopenhauer must first recall that the will is not subject to the law of motivation. However, the latter thesis is based on the distinction between empirical character and intelligible character, and thus, properly speaking, on the deduction of the latter conducted in the dissertation, because *only the will as intelligible character is released from the principle of reason.*

> In the essay *On the Principle of Sufficient Reason*, the will, or rather the subject of willing, is indeed treated as a special class of representations or objects: but even there we saw that this object coincides with the subject, i.e. ceases to be an object; there we called this coinciding the miracle *par excellence:* the entirety of the present work is, to some degree, an explanation of this.[9]

According to the 1813 dissertation, the content of the subject's self-cognition as willing consists, on the one hand, *in the single, uniform acts of will determined by motives* and, on the other hand (in apparent contradiction to the first), in *the aware-*

---

[8] Schopenhauer 2010b, I 130–131, § 21, pp. 134–135.
[9] Schopenhauer 2010b, I 121, § 18, p. 126.

ness of the freedom of one's own will.[10] Schopenhauer theorizes the distinction between empirical character and intelligible character through a kind of abductive inference, to explain the coexistence of those two different sides in the self-consciousness of each individual, referring the first (necessity) to the empirical character and the second (freedom) to the intelligible character (cf. *supra*, 9.8 and 9.12).

Compared to the first edition of the dissertation, in *The World* Schopenhauer takes a step further. As we have seen, he identifies the individual acts of will, through which the subject cognizes his own will as "empirical character", with the individual movements of the body (which in the dissertation were seen instead as the effect, *Wirkung*, of the former: cf. *supra*, 9.6).

> [...] the cognition I have of my will, although it is immediate, cannot be separated from that of my body. I do not have cognition of my will as a whole, in its unity, in perfect accordance with its essence; rather I cognize it only in its individual acts, which is to say in time, time being the form in which my body (like every other object) appears: this is why the body is the condition of cognition of my will. Consequently, I cannot truly imagine my will without my body. [...].

> [...] the identity of the will and the body [...] can only really be established [...]; On the other hand, by its nature it can never be demonstrated, i.e. derived as mediate cognition from some other immediate source, precisely because it is itself the most immediate cognition there is [...]. I would therefore like to distinguish this truth above all others, and call it *philosophical truth par excellence*.[11]

The will, whose individual acts are identical to the individual acts (or actions) of the body, is identical to the body itself. That is, insofar as the single acts *of will* are identical to the single acts *of the body*, the "will" is identical to the "body". Cognition of the identity of the will and the body, which Schopenhauer determines as "the most immediate" type of cognition, is not deduced from the cognition of the identity between individual act of will and individual action of the body (if it were deduced, it would not be "immediate"), but strictly speaking *coincides* with it. By immediately cognizing the identity between single act of will and single movement of the body, the subject cognizes *eo ipso* – in an equally immediate manner – the identity between his will and his body. That is to say, the immediate cognition of the identity between will and body (the "philosophical truth *par excellence*") is the *same* as the immediate cognition of the identity between individual act of will and individual act of the body.

By virtue of this identification, "I do not have cognition of my will as a whole [*Ich erkenne meinen Willen nicht im Ganzen*]", but only "in its individual acts", i.e.

---

[10] Schopenhauer 2010b, I 121, § 18, p. 126.
[11] Schopenhauer 2010b, I 121–122, § 18, pp. 126–127.

precisely in the single acts of the body. Consequently, the body, defined in the dissertation as "the immediate object of willing", is determined in *The World* as "the *objecthood* of my [...] will".[12]

In the manuscripts of 1814, the assertion that the body is the *Erscheinung* of the intelligible character is not founded on the identity between the single act of will and the single movement of the body, but on the general assertion that man's whole temporal existence (which also includes being-a-body) is the *Erscheinung* of the intelligible character (cf. *supra*, 10.7). Despite the emphasis with which Schopenhauer expounds it, that identity emerged long after the construction of the whole system; it constitutes the foundation that Schopenhauer, in his masterpiece, provides the reader with, but it does not belong to the original conception and foundation of his metaphysics of will.[13]

Now, *the analogical inference is necessary because the will that every subject immediately cognizes in himself is an appearance, not a thing-in-itself.* If, on the contrary, it were a thing-in-itself, any analogical inference would be either futile or impossible. For if the immediately cognized will were *the universal thing-in-itself*, the latter would already be cognized to begin with, so that analogical inference would be pointless. If, on the other hand, the immediately cognized will were *the thing-in-itself of the body, but not of the other objects*, the thing-in-itself of the latter would certainly still have to be deduced. This hypothesis, however, would imply a substantial inhomogeneity of objects as to their essence – because otherwise, cognizing the will as the thing-in-itself of his own body, the subject would also cognize it *eo ipso* as the thing-in-itself of all other objects, and we would fall back into the first case – so that the analogical argument, resting precisely on the exclusion of this inhomogeneity, would be impossible.

More generally, given the all-encompassing nature of the distinction between "appearance" and "thing-in-itself", the human will mentioned in the texts must always be understood, necessarily, either as appearance or as thing-in-itself (*tertium non datur*). But the individual will as appearance is the *empirical character*; the individual will as a thing-in-itself, on the other hand, is the *intelligible character*.[14] It follows that whenever Schopenhauer speaks indeterminately of the (individual) human will, the latter is always to be understood either as empirical character or

---

12 Schopenhauer 2010b, I 121–122, § 18, p. 127.
13 The first complete formulation of the identity between a single act of will and the body's movement occurs in fragment 650 of the manuscripts from 1817 (cf. MR 1, pp. 490–491). The two notes added to fragment 425 (MR 1, pp. 302–303) are certainly much later than the fragment because they correct and amend it in several parts.
14 Cf. Schopenhauer 2010b, I 185, § 28, p. 180; I 341, § 55, p. 315.

as intelligible character. Unless each occurrence of the term is traced back to one of these two concepts, it is not possible to understand the texts concretely and fully.

In the passages we are considering, the human or individual will has three different connotations: it occurs as *that which is identical to the body*, as *that which constitutes the essence of the body itself* and, finally, as *that with respect to which the analogy between the body and other objects is posited*. In relation to each of these three aspects, it is necessary to determine whether it is empirical character or intelligible character.

The will that every subject immediately cognizes in himself in the single actions of the body, and whose single acts in time coincide precisely with the latter, is evidently the *empirical character*, not the intelligible character (which is outside of time). Identifying itself with the body (in the sense indicated above), this will cannot constitute the "essence" of the body itself, i.e. that of which the body and, therefore, it too (insofar as it is identical with the body) are the appearance.

The will as essence of the body is the will "as a whole", i.e. the "intelligible character"; it is in relation to this connotation of the term that Schopenhauer writes: "the entire body must be nothing other than my will made visible [*mein sichtbar gewordener Wille*]".[15] Fragment 191 of the manuscripts also reads: "*the body* (corporeal man) *is nothing but the will that has become visible* [der sichtbar gewordene Wille]", and the will in question was there expressly identified with the intelligible character (cf. *supra*, 10.7).[16]

Now, the will that is identical with the body, since it does not constitute the essence of the body itself, cannot be considered, by analogy, as the essence or thing-in-itself of all other objects either, so that the analogical inference cannot be drawn in relation to it.[17] *The will universalized in the analogical argument is that which constitutes the "essence" of the body, i.e. that of which the body as a whole is the appearance: the intelligible character*. This implies that the concept of will as the thing-in-itself of all beings, which Schopenhauer arrives at through his analogical argument, is nothing but the universalization or generalization of the concept of intelligible character, in accordance with fragment 242 of the manuscripts (cf. *supra*, 11.6). In § 28 of the major work, the extension of the concept of intelligible character to the mineral, plant and animal kingdoms, as well as its coincidence with the will as thing-in-itself, become fully explicit (cf. *infra*, 12.7).

---

15 Schopenhauer 2010b, I 127–128, pp. 131–132.
16 MR 1, n. 191, p. 115.
17 J. Atwell discusses this matter, but tries to solve it by recalling the fact that Schopenhauer distinguishes between two senses of the term "will": a will as appearance, and a will as thing-in-itself (cf. Atwell 1995, p. 127). But the problem is precisely the foundation of this distinction.

The will as the thing-in-itself thus is to the "world" what the intelligible character is to the individual as "body"; this is precisely the analogy or equality of relations that Schopenhauer posits in his analogical argument. And indeed, the intelligible character of each man is *"his* [italics mine] will as a thing-in-itself".[18] If and insofar as the will as a thing-in-itself is, by analogy, the intelligible character of the world, the intelligible character is reciprocally the will as a thing-in-itself of the individual.[19]

The *will* (essence of the body), which is universalized in the analogical argument, is thus not the same *will* (coinciding with the body itself) that each cognizes in himself immediately, although it is 'deducible' from the latter, as shown in the dissertation. On the basis of the pure and simple self-cognition of the subject (the mere internal experience of the lived-body), Schopenhauer could never have drawn the analogical inference, because he would have lacked the fundamental term, namely the will as the essence of the body in itself: "I do not have cognition of my will as a whole, in its unity, in perfect accordance with its essence; rather I cognize it only in its individual acts", i.e. in its appearance.[20]

Of course, the subject also feels or 'senses' the *freedom* of his will (this is the 'vivid awareness' mentioned in the dissertation); but the datum of self-consciousness inexorably stops there.[21] *The distinction between the will, insofar as it is subject to the law of motivation, and the will, insofar as it is not subject to the same law, does not pertain to the immediate content of self-consciousness*, because its second term is entirely unknowable. In order to be affirmed, this distinction must rather

---

18 A. Schopenhauer, *Prize Essay on the Freedom of the Will*, in Schopenhauer 2009, p. 107.
19 Cf. MR 1, n. 659 (1817), pp. 508–509: "Every being in nature, indeed the whole of nature, is the objectification [*Objektivirung*] of the will, precisely as [*grade so wie*] my actions are the objectification of my will and my empirical character is the objectification of my intelligible". Translation modified.
20 I therefore cannot agree with the fine observations made by R. Malter (1991, pp. 186–187), according to which the experience of one's own body would *in itself* suffice to open the door to the discourse concerning the "essence" of the world.
21 Cf. Schopenhauer 2012 [1813], § 46, p. 187: "[...] the same person, given exactly the same circumstances, acts in exactly the same way [...] even if he is most vividly aware [*das lebendigste Bewußtseyn hat*], that he could have acted in a completely different way had he so *willed*, i.e., that his will is determined by nothing external – and it is not a question here of being able [*Können*], but only of willing [*Wollen*], which by its nature is free to the greatest degree, indeed, which is the innermost essence of the human being, independent of everything else [*das innerste von allem Andern unabhängige Wesen des Menschen selbst*]". This is how one should understand the passage in § 23, in which Schopenhauer writes: "because in self-consciousness [*im Selbstbewußtseyn*] the will is known immediately and in itself, this consciousness is also a consciousness of freedom" (Schopenhauer 2010b, I 135, p. 138).

be deduced from that datum; but this deduction, which is carried out in full in the dissertation of 1813, is not repeated in the major work.

In sum, the analogical inference of *The World as Will and Representation* is articulated in these six steps:

1. *Defining the content of the subject's self-cognition as the identity between a single act of will and a single act (or movement) of the lived-body*, and thus, in this sense, between will and lived-body. This, for Schopenhauer, is the "most immediate cognition" there is; it is therefore an intuitive or purely 'phenomenological' truth.
2. *Determining each single (temporal) act of will as an appearance of the intelligible character*, according to the distinction between empirical and intelligible character, i.e. between will as appearance (subject to the law of motivation) and will in itself (which is "groundless", and thus free). In his 1813 dissertation (and, later, in his *Essay on the Freedom of the Will*) Schopenhauer justifies this distinction through a kind of abductive inference (cf. *supra*, 9.12).
3. *Determining each single movement of the lived-body as an appearance of the intelligible character.* This is a logical consequence of points 1 and 2.
4. *Determining the lived-body in its entirety as an appearance of the intelligible character, i.e. of the individual's will in itself.* This point can be considered the result of a kind of meta-abductive deduction. Indeed, as we have seen, the proposition that the body as a whole is the appearance of the intelligible character seems to constitute for Schopenhauer the best explanation of point 3 (which in turn presupposes an abductive and a logical conclusion).
5. *Setting up an analogy between the lived-body and every other object of the world.* This constitutes the (broadly speaking) hermeneutic instance of the discourse, according to which the 'inside' (the content of the subject's self-cognition) can provide the interpretative key for the 'outside' (the 'foreign'). Consequently, every object in the world – and thus *the world itself in its totality* – can be interpreted as an *analogon* of the lived-body. This point is neither the content of an immediate cognition nor the result of any deduction; in conformity with its 'hermeneutic' character, it is formally and explicitly problematic, i.e., hypothetical.[22]

---

[22] Schopenhauer's metaphor of the world as a mysterious "text" that the philosopher has to interpret is to be understood in this way: the analogy between the lived-body and the world is precisely the interpretive key to the "text" of the world (cf. Schopenhauer 2018, II 204–205, chap. 17, pp. 193–194). Cf. on this Hallich 2002. I believe that only in this very general sense can a hermeneutic character of Schopenhauer's philosophy be legitimately admitted. On the more strictly hermeneutic or existentialist interpretations of Schopenhauer's thought, cf. *infra*, 12.6.

6. *Extending the determination 'being the appearance of a will in itself' to every possible object in the world – and thus to the totality of possible objects, the world.* This extension is a logical consequence of points 4 and 5.

The problematic character of point 5, due to its hermeneutic status (in the sense specified above), is exacerbated by the fact that Schopenhauer presents the analogy between the lived-body and the world as the only possible alternative to solipsism, which for him is an entirely irrefutable hypothesis.[23] The analogy is thus based on a theoretically unfounded rejection of solipsism, and this lack of foundation inevitably propagates to the conclusion expressed in point 6, further undermining the cogency of the entire argument.

The epistemological status of Schopenhauer's analogical inference is, therefore, very complex and multi-layered. Only considering these passages as a whole makes it possible to concretely and thoroughly understand the title of Schopenhauer's masterpiece, particularly the determination of the "world" in its entirety "as will".[24]

It is especially noteworthy that point 2, although indispensable to the development of the deduction, is not justified or substantiated. The foundation of the distinction between will as appearance (empirical character) and will in itself (intelligible character) was *programmatically* omitted in Schopenhauer's masterpiece since its first edition (1819), because it had already been explained in § 46 of the 1813 dissertation.

Schopenhauer glosses over this essential conceptual dependence or non-self-sufficiency of the text; but he does so probably only for expository purposes, i.e. to avoid raising issues and questions that, to be resolved, would require a full restatement of the doctrine of intelligible character. In § 20, however, he warned the reader expressly and once and for all: "I am, in part, *presupposing* [italics mine] Kant's doctrine of empirical and intelligible character here, as well as the relevant

---

23 Cf. Schopenhauer 2010b, I 124–125, § 19, pp. 128–129. On the theoretical ground of the irrefutability of solipsism within Schopenhauer's system, cf. Novembre 2010.
24 I have already indicated elsewhere the formal and overall structure of Schopenhauer's analogical argument, the outcome of which is expressed by the title of his masterpiece (cf. Novembre 2016a, pp. 317–318). However, the concrete articulation of that structure, and thus the precise meaning of the title "The World as Will and Representation", can only emerge through the detailed analysis of the decisive passages considered here; it is therefore impossible to decipher the title based on purely theoretical or 'logical' considerations. The fine considerations made by E. Eschmann (2022b), which cannot be discussed here analytically, prescind from those decisive passages of the work and consequently do not address a genuinely central question: namely, how the term "will" in the title is to be understood and, therefore, what it concretely means that "the world" can or should be considered "as will".

discussions from my *Fundamental Problems of Ethics* [...]".[25] In the first edition of *The World*, in contrast to the third, Schopenhauer did not refer to the *Fundamental Problems of Ethics* (specifically, to the *Essay on the Freedom of Will*, written many years later), but rather to § 46 of the dissertation, in which the "intelligible character" is deduced in the manner mentioned above.[26]

After all, in the Preface to the first edition, Schopenhauer clearly and more generally states that the dissertation is an indispensable "introduction and propaedeutic" to the discourse developed in *The World*; without being familiar with it, "It is absolutely impossible to truly understand the present work" and indeed "the contents of that essay are presupposed here as much as if they had been included in the book".[27] An explicit reference to the doctrine of intelligible character set out in the 1813 dissertation is contained in § 55 of the third edition of *The World*.[28]

The central aporia of the system – namely the question: how is it possible to deduce the will as *thing-in-itself* (first of all of the lived-body and then, by analogy, of all other objects) from the will as *appearance?* – can only be explained, within Schopenhauer's thought, by noting the quietly *foundational* role taken in these passages of the major work by the doctrine of intelligible character set out in the dissertation.[29]

Going through these underlying folds of the major work – and, precisely, its most crucial part – one can understand very concretely why Schopenhauer stated in *Parerga and Paralipomena:* "the root of my philosophy already lies in the Kantian philosophy, especially in the doctrine of empirical and intelligible character".[30]

---

25 Schopenhauer 2010b, I 127, § 20, p. 131.
26 Cf. Schopenhauer 2020, p. 87. Cf. also Schopenhauer 2020, pp. 215–216 (this passage, expunged from the second and third editions of *The World*, has an almost literal correspondence in Schopenhauer 2017–2021, vol. 4, pp. 34–35). I therefore cannot agree with T. Bohinc that the doctrine of intelligible character only gained prominence within the Schopenhauerian system after the first edition of the major work (cf. Bohinc 1989, pp. 149–151).
27 Schopenhauer 2010b, I X–XI, p. 7.
28 Cf. Schopenhauer 2010b, I 341, § 55, p. 569. See also Schopenhauer 2020, p. 214.
29 Scholars who have dealt with this delicate point in Schopenhauer's thought have not pointed out the strictly foundational function of the doctrine of intelligible character. Cf. e. g. Haym 1864, pp. 19–21; Zimmermann 1970; Spierling 1998, pp. 228–231; Atwell 1995, pp. 86–93; Booms 2003, pp. 295–298; Schubbe 2010, pp. 117–122; Kurbel 2015, pp. 230–236; Noveanu 2016. R. Haym, emphasizing the aporetic aspect, considers Schopenhauer's discourse to properly fall under literature, not philosophy (Haym 1864, p. 113). Cf. also Seydel 1857.
30 Schopenhauer 2014, p. 121. I therefore agree (while substantiating and articulating it differently) with M. Koßler's general core thesis (cf. Koßler 2002a), according to which, for Schopenhauer, it is the experience of character that grounds the metaphysics of will. Cf. Novembre 2022. The foundational role of the theory of intelligible character essentially differentiates the analogical argument

12.3 Denomination from the Superior Term, Genus and Species. Observational or 'Inductive' Confirmation of the Analogical Inference and the Difference between Science and Philosophy

After conducting the analogical argument in § 18–21, in § 22 Schopenhauer specifies in what sense the identification of "will" and "thing-in-itself" is to be understood.

> This *thing-in-itself* (we will retain the Kantian expression as a standing formula) can never be an object, because an object is only its appearance and not what it really is. If we are to think objectively about this thing-in-itself, it must borrow its name and concept from an object, from something that is somehow objectively given, and thus from one of its appearances: but if this is to further our understanding, it can be nothing other than the most complete of all its appearances, i.e. the clearest, most highly developed appearance, the one that is illuminated immediately by knowledge: but this is just the human *will*. It is nonetheless fair to say that we are only using a denomination from the superior term [*denominatio a potiori*] that gives the concept of will a broader scope than it has had before. As Plato has so often remarked, recognizing the identical in different appearances and the different in similar appearances is the precondition for philosophy. But until now, people have not recognized the identity that obtains between the will and the essence of all the striving and acting forces in nature, and have therefore failed to notice that the many and varied kinds of appearances are only different species of the same genus; instead, people have seen them as heterogeneous: this is why there could be no word to designate the concept of this genus. Accordingly, I will name the genus after its most important species; the more intimate and immediate cognition we have of this species leads to the mediated cognition we have of all the others.[31]

First of all, Schopenhauer evidently likens the relationship between *will* as a thing-in-itself and *appearance* to the relationship between *genus* and *species:* "the many and varied kinds of appearances [*Erscheinungen*]" (that is, the different classes of phenomena) "are only different species of the same genus" (that is, of the "will"). The latter seems to constitute the supreme and universal essence of which all the individual things of the world – single appearances – are specifications or, rather, individuations. The reference to Plato is not accidental, because, just as the Idea with respect to all individuals of the same species, so the thing-in-itself with respect to all possible appearances represents the one and identical essence

---

of *The World as Will and Representation* from the discourse developed by Fichte in *Die Bestimmung des Menschen*, notwithstanding the similarities noted by F. Decher (1990).

31 Schopenhauer 2010b, I 132, § 22, pp. 135–136.

(*Wesen*) that shines in them. We shall soon see (cf. *infra*, 12.4–12.5) that this fundamental commonality necessarily gives rise to other and no less remarkable ones.

Already at this point, however, it is clear that Schopenhauer's notion of "thing-in-itself" cannot be superimposed on Kant's, and Schopenhauer is perfectly aware of this, for he warns from the outset: "we will retain the Kantian expression as a standing formula". "We will": the use of the expression "thing-in-itself" is not the result of a strictly conceptual necessity. This passage already appears in the first edition of the work and thus belongs to the original dimension of the discourse (it is not the result of a later addition due to the objections Schopenhauer received later).[32]

Referring to knowledge of "the identical in different appearances and the different in similar appearances", Schopenhauer intends to pay homage, once again, to the principles of *homogeneity* and *specification*, celebrated in the 1813 dissertation as the two fundamental rules of all philosophizing (cf. *supra*, 9.3). At the same time, however, he implicitly foreshadows what he is about to do, namely to ascertain – through the analysis of the (in his opinion) most prominent features of the various 'things' – that the different species of objects are indeed all *Erscheinungen* of the *one and the same universal will*, but each *to a different degree.*

Now, the human will as such, as each individual finds and experiences it in himself, is not the will as a thing-in-itself, but only one of its many *Erscheinungen*, albeit the most clear and accomplished – that is, the one in which the one universal essence, which is manifest in everything, shines through the most.

> But anyone incapable of broadening the concept in the way we require will remain in a state of perpetual misunderstanding, using the word *will* to mean just the one species that has borne the name so far, the will that is accompanied by cognition and is expressed exclusively in accordance with motives – and indeed only through abstract motives, under the guidance of reason; however, as we have said, this is only the most distinct appearance of the will.[33]

The human will, insofar it is "accompanied by cognition and is expressed exclusively in accordance with motives", coincides with the *empirical character* – something that always belongs to the "appearance", being nothing but the manifestation of the intelligible character (which, with respect to the empirical character, is precisely the "thing-in-itself" or "essence"). This will, as such, is not the thing-in-itself. But it cannot be concluded, then, that it is indifferent to use the human will or any other determination of the world to determine or denominate the thing-in-itself: the term *will*, unlike all other terms, indicates "something so thoroughly familiar

---

32 Cf. Schopenhauer 2020, p. 90.
33 Schopenhauer 2010b, I 132, § 22, p. 136.

that we know and understand what will is much better than anything else, whatever it may be".[34] In the *denominatio a potiori* of the thing-in-itself as "will", the very particular and determinate *species* of the thing-in-itself (or of the essence of the whole) that is the human will therefore rightly takes on the value of *specimen*.

Note, however, that Schopenhauer's discourse is perfectly circular: he states that the thing-in-itself, in order to be determined or 'objectified', must necessarily "borrow its name and concept" from the "most complete of all its appearances", i.e. from the human will. But only insofar as the thing-in-itself has *already* been deduced by analogy with the human will, the latter can *now* be considered, 'retroactively', as the most perfect appearance – or, in Goethean terms, as the *Urphänomen* – of the thing-in-itself. The definition of the *human will* as the most perfect *Erscheinung* of the *thing-in-itself* and the consequent designation (or determination) of the latter on the basis of the former is thus only a further development of the analogical argument, which started precisely from what is immediately or best known to us – our will – and always remains the ultimate condition of validity or ground of all of Schopenhauer's subsequent statements.

The choice of the term "will" for the thing-in-itself is thus not arbitrary (something Schopenhauer has often been accused of),[35] but is a direct consequence of the analogical inference. Without it, strictly speaking, one could not even talk about a thing-in-itself of the world or of objects other than the body (*Leib*), since the latter are merely representations, regardless of that inference. In fact, for Schopenhauer, analogical argument constitutes the only valid alternative to "theoretical egoism" (or solipsistic idealism): the position of those who deny the "reality of the external world" and consider "all appearances outside of the individual to be phantoms".[36] It is simply impossible to name the thing-in-itself of the world in any other way or by any other term, because without the analogical argument – necessarily conducted starting from the human will (as the latter represents the reality best known to us) and thus necessarily implying, as its outcome, the determination of the thing-in-itself as "will" – it is not possible to admit any "thing-in-itself" of the world in general.[37] The internal coherence of this crucial section of the discourse must not be called into question.

---

[34] Schopenhauer 2010b, I 133, p. 136.
[35] This objection was already raised by R. Haym (1864, pp. 23–24) and was later taken up by Nietzsche (cf. the fragment "On Schopenhauer", Nietzsche 1998, pp. 258–265). Cf. Barbera 2010, p. 127.
[36] Cf. Schopenhauer 2010b, I 124–125, § 19, p. 129.
[37] Cf. Schopenhauer 2010b, I 133–134, § 22, pp. 136–137.

Now, Schopenhauer would seem to presuppose here only the content of the subject's self-cognition. But this is not the case. The distinction between *the will as subject to the law of motivation* and *the will as not subject to that law*, while not belonging to the immediate content of self-consciousness (since its second term is not knowable *per se*), is once again foundational: only on the basis of it can Schopenhauer distinguish between "will" as "appearance" or *species* and "will" as "thing-in-itself" or *genus* of all things, thus achieving his decisive denomination from the superior term: the *will* "as we have said, [...] is only the most distinct appearance of the *will* [italics mine]". This is because, in the final analysis, it is only from the model of the human will as unrelated to the principle of reason – the intelligible character – that Schopenhauer can 'infer' or 'deduce', by analogy, the will as a thing-in-itself of all beings. On the basis of the pure and simple self-cognition of the subject, i.e. disregarding the doctrine of intelligible character, the analogical inference could not be drawn, the consequent denomination from the superior term could not be justified, and Schopenhauer's mature system, which is based on both, could not be built.

After all these deductive and preparatory steps, in § 23 Schopenhauer finally begins to speak of the will as a thing-in-itself.

> As thing-in-itself, the *will* is completely different from its appearance, and entirely free of all forms of appearance. The will only takes on these forms when it appears, which is why these forms concern only its *objecthood* and are foreign to the will itself. The will has nothing to do with even the most general form of all representation, that of being an object for a subject, and it has even less to do with the subordinate forms that are collectively expressed in the principle of sufficient reason. As we know, space and time belong to the principle of sufficient reason, and so, in consequence, does multiplicity, which exists and is made possible only through these. With respect to this last point, I would borrow an old scholastic expression and call time and space the *principium individuationis* and I ask the reader always to bear this in mind. It is only by virtue of time and space that something that is one and the same in essence and concept can nonetheless appear as different, as a multiplicity of coexistent and successive things: time and space are thus the *principium individuationis*, the object of so much hair-splitting and controversy among the scholastics, which you can find collected together in Suarez (*Disputatio* 5, section 3).[38]

Unlike "its" appearance, the will as a thing-in-itself lies completely outside the principle of sufficient reason – even its very general form, the determination of "being an object for a subject" (the division into subject and object is the "root" of the principle: cf. *supra*, 9.3). This implies that the will itself is also outside time and space.

---

38 Schopenhauer 2010b, I 134, § 23, p. 137.

Time and *space* constitute the fundamental conditions of the multiplicity of entities: the former is the condition of succession, and therefore of the diachronic plurality or otherness of things (but also of the same thing with respect to itself); the latter is the condition of coexistence, and therefore of the synchronic plurality or otherness of things. Time and space are therefore the *principium individuationis*, that by which a single, identical essence is multiplied and refracted in several individuals. The will as a thing-in-itself, being outside the principle of reason and, consequently, the *principium individuationis*, "has absolutely no ground [*ist ... schlechthin grundlos*]" – that is, it has no "sufficient reason" and is "free of all *multiplicity*".[39]

At this point, Schopenhauer tries to show that the attribution of "will" to all things – thus not only to the human sphere, but also to the animal, plant and mineral kingdoms – is intuitively very plausible, as it is surprisingly in line with what can be observed of 'things' themselves. But for this purpose, as a preliminary step, it is necessary to abandon the usual concept of will as something that, being always and in any case guided by cognition ("motives"), can only exist in connection with the latter. That is to say, it is necessary to bear in mind that the will in itself is completely extraneous to the law of motivation.[40] Only with this indispensable premise – which, as Schopenhauer points out here once again, presupposes the doctrine of the intelligible character[41] – is it possible to subsume animal instinct, as well as all the physiological and vegetative functions of living bodies, under the concept of "will".

> The one-year-old bird has no representation of the eggs it builds its nest for; the young spider has no representation of the prey it spins its web for; nor is the antlion thinking of ants when it digs a hole for the first time; the larva of the stag beetle chews a hole into the wood where its metamorphosis will take place, and the hole is twice as big if it is going to be male than if it is going to be female, in order to accommodate the horns it has no idea it will acquire. The will is clearly at work in this kind of animal behaviour as it is in the rest of their behaviour: but it is in blind activity, which, although accompanied by cognition, is not guided by it.[42]

On the other hand, the will operates in this way in the human body itself.

> The same will often acts blindly in us as well: in all our bodily functions that are not guided by cognition, in all the body's vital and vegetative processes, digestion, circulation of the blood, secretion, growth, reproduction. Not only actions of the body but the whole body itself,

---

39 Schopenhauer 2010b, I 134, p. 138.
40 Schopenhauer 2010b, I 136, p. 139.
41 Schopenhauer 2010b, I, 135, p. 138.
42 Schopenhauer 2010b, I, 136, p. 139.

as we established above, is appearance of the will, objectified will, concrete will: everything that occurs in it must therefore occur through will, although this will is not guided by cognition here, not determined by motives, but rather acts blindly, according to causes that in this case are called *stimuli* [Reize].[43]

Understood as an irresistible and blind "striving" or impulse, according to Schopenhauer the "will" can also be attributed to plants[44] and inorganic bodies.[45]

These descriptions of the various natural entities must serve to clarify and corroborate, from an observational point of view, the outcome of the analogical argument, according to which everything in the world is – or can be considered as – the appearance of a will. Indeed, the corroboration is offered by the (observable) fact that all entities manifest an intrinsic striving, a peculiar endogenous *Streben*, which for Schopenhauer is assimilable to what in ourselves we call "will". This congenital "striving" represents the common element of all entities, the (phenomenal) trait shared by all world-phenomena, so that from it it is possible to (inductively) hypothesize what is the one and identical "essence [*Wesen*]", the one and identical "being in itself [*Seyn an sich*] of every thing in the world". Observation of things,

---

[43] Schopenhauer 2010b, I, 136–137, p. 140.
[44] Schopenhauer 2010b, I 140, p. 142: "Thus what appears in representation as plant, as mere vegetation and blindly driving force, we will treat, as regards its essence in itself, as will, and recognize it as what constitutes the basis of our own appearance as it expresses itself in our deeds as well as in the entire existence of our body itself".
[45] Cf. Schopenhauer 2010b, I 140–141, p. 143: "[...] let us look at the violent, inexorable impulse of masses of water rushing down to the depths, the perseverance of the magnet that always returns to the North Pole, the longing with which iron flies to the magnet, the vehemence of two poles in an electric current striving [*streben*] to reunite (as with human desires, this striving is only intensified by obstacles). Let us look at how the crystal suddenly and rapidly forms with such regularity in its development, a development that is clearly only a striving [*Bestrebung*] in different directions (albeit an exceptionally staunch and precisely determined striving) that is constrained and held fast in the grip of rigidity. Let us notice the selectivity with which bodies attract and repel, unite and separate when they are in a fluid state and freed from the bonds of rigidity. Finally, let us feel immediately how encumbered our bodies are when some burden is striving [*Streben*] towards the earth, incessantly pushing and pressing our bodies in pursuit of its only endeavour. [*Bestrebung*] – Once we have seen all this it will not take any great stretch of the imagination to recognize (despite its distance from our own essence [*Wesen*]) the very same thing that in us pursues its goal illuminated by cognition while here, in the weakest of its appearances, it is blind, dull, one-sided and unalterable in its striving. Nonetheless, because it is everywhere one and the same [*Eines und das Selbe*], – just as the first light of dawn shares the name sunlight with the bright rays of noon, – it must be called *will* here as well as there, a name signifying the being in itself [*das Seyn an sich*] of every thing in the world and the sole kernel of every appearance."

i.e. experience (in the broad sense), is thus perfectly in line with the conclusion of the analogical syllogism.[46]

As a result of these considerations, Schopenhauer pinpoints the difference between science and philosophy in § 24. The natural sciences, which cognize the world according to the principle of sufficient reason, explain phenomena by tracing them back (aetiologically) to the *fundamental qualities* of things or elements, but they do not account for the latter, which remain an eternal, unexplained presupposition.[47] In the same way, knowing the "motives", one can certainly account for a person's actions by tracing them back to their *character*; but the latter, from the point of view of the principle of reason, also remains an eternal, unexplained presupposition:

> What a person considers to be his unfathomable character, a character that is presupposed in every explanation of his deeds from motives; just this is the essential quality of every inorganic body, its manner of operation whose manifestations arise due to some external influence, while it itself [the essential quality] is not determined – and therefore not explained – by any external source [...].[48]

Philosophy, unlike the sciences, turns to what the principle of reason leaves unexplained, namely the ultimate "essence" of things. This intent necessarily determines its method of investigation, namely the analogical argument and the consequent *denominatio a potiori*, the meaning of which Schopenhauer further clarifies here:

> [...] we who are pursuing philosophy and not aetiology, i.e. not relative, but unconditioned cognition of the essence of the world, we [...] start from what we know immediately and most perfectly [...], from what is closest to us, in order to understand what we know only distantly, in a one-sided and indirect manner: from the most powerful, most meaningful, and clearest appearance we will come to understand the less complete and weaker ones. [...] Only by comparison with what happens in myself when, swayed by a motive, my body performs an action [...], can I gain insight into the manner in which those inanimate bodies alter themselves according to causes, and thus understand their inner essence. Knowing the cause of the inner essence's appearance only gives me the rule for how it enters time and space, nothing more. [...] This means: the fourth class of representations that I treated in the essay *On the Principle of Sufficient Reason* must be my key to the knowledge of the inner essence of the first class, and I must use the law of motivation to understand the inner meaning of the law of causality.[49]

---

[46] On the general epistemological status of Schopenhauer's metaphysics, cf. Birnbacher 2020; Morgenstern 2022.
[47] Schopenhauer 2010b, I 144–152, § 24, pp. 146–151.
[48] Schopenhauer 2010b, I 148, p. 149.
[49] Schopenhauer 2010b, I 149–150, p. 150. Translation modified.

Given the 'analogical' determination of everything's being in itself from the human will, it must be said, retroactively or circularly, that the one and the same being in itself, which appears in all things in the world, reaches in the human being, and only in the human being, "the strongest degree of manifestation".[50]

12.4 Terminological Analysis: The 'Platonizing' Description of the Distinction between Appearance and Thing-in-Itself

In the first volume of *The World as Will and Representation*, the "will" being the will-to-life is not justified or argued for in any way. The term *Wille zum Leben* is introduced for the first time, without any explicit foundation, in paragraph 27, which describes the universal struggle for life and survival engaged in by all beings. Schopenhauer implies that the metaphysical will, of which life (existence) as a whole is the appearance, wills life: in other words, he implies that insofar as life is the appearance of this will, this will must be the will-to-life. The specification "to life [*zum Leben*]" is not expressly referred to the immediate content of self-consciousness; it seems rather to be a consequence of the analogical inference (starting from that content), according to which the world and life are the appearance (*Erscheinung*) of a will in itself, just as the body and life of each individual are the appearance of his intelligible character.[51] Apart from this implicit consequentiality, the reason why the human will is to be thought of both as the *object of inner sense* and as the will-*to-life* – that is, the ground of the relationship between these two distinct determinations of the will – is left entirely undetermined in the first volume of the major work.[52]

But what is the relationship between the will as a "thing-in-itself" and the *world* or *life* as its overall "appearance"? Here the question concerns the meaning of the predicate "being the appearance of", which Schopenhauer does not define (cf. *supra*, 9.8; 10.7). In fact, it is strictly speaking inappropriate to speak of a relationship or relation, because relations exist only within the principle of sufficient reason, from which the will as a thing-in-itself, as we have seen, is free. And indeed, in the first edition of the work, in a passage that was later expunged in subsequent editions (I will try to explain the reason for this choice later: cf. *infra*, 12.6), Schopenhauer had written that the "relation [*Verhältniß*] between the will and its

---

50 Schopenhauer 2010b, I 150–151, p. 151.
51 Cf. Schopenhauer 2010b, I 341, § 55, p. 315.
52 In Chapter 19 of the second volume (cf. Schopenhauer 2018, II, 227–228) Schopenhauer states explicitly that the will that is the object of the inner sense is the will-to-life.

appearance (i.e. between the intelligible character and the empirical one)" can be considered such "only metaphorically [*nur gleichnißweise*]".⁵³

However, this does not detract from the fact that Schopenhauer – even in the editions following the first – does use terms that identify or imply a kind of relationship or relation between thing-in-itself and appearance.

> If then, as I believe I have adequately proven and made abundantly clear, this thing-in-itself is *the will*, then as such and considered apart from its appearance [*seine Erscheinung*], it lies outside of time and space, and thus knows no multiplicity, and is consequently *one* [...]. Thus, the multiplicity of things in space and time, which together constitute the *objecthood* of the will [*seine Objektität*], fails to affect the will itself, and it remains indivisible in spite of them. It is not as if there is a smaller part of the will in a stone and a larger part in a person, since the relation between part and whole belongs exclusively to space and no longer makes sense apart from this form of intuition. Rather, even more and less are relevant only for appearance, i.e. manifestation [*Sichtbarkeit*], objectivation [*Objektivation*]. There is a higher degree of objectivation in plants than in rocks, a higher degree in animals than in plants: indeed, the will becomes manifest [*sein Hervortreten in die Sichtbarkeit*], it enters into objectivation [*seine Objektivation*] in as infinite a number of gradations [*Abstufungen*] as can be found between the weakest twilight and the brightest sunshine, between the loudest sound and the most distant echo. We will return later to consider the degrees of manifestation that belong to its objectivation, to the image [*Abbilde*] of its essence. [...]. It [the will] reveals itself [*offenbart sich*] just as fully and completely in a single oak tree as in millions [...], it itself is present [*gegenwärtig*] whole and undivided in every single thing in nature, in all of life [....].⁵⁴

The terms through which Schopenhauer describes the relationship between things in the world – or the world as a whole – and the will as a thing-in-itself are as follows: *Objektität, Objektivation, Sichtbarkeit, Abbild* and the expressions *sich offenbaren* and *gegenwärtig sein*. However, even just the use of the possessive adjective *sein* – "its [the thing-in-itself's] appearance", *its* "objecthood", *its* "objectivation" – implies some relation between thing-in-itself and appearance.

Now, since the world is the appearance (*Erscheinung*) of the will as a *thing-in-itself*, the aforementioned terms illustrate or specify the relationship that exists between the appearance and the thing-in-itself. But this means that the terms *Objektität, Objektivation, Sichtbarkeit, Abbild* are used by Schopenhauer as synonyms of *Erscheinung*; indeed, it can be argued that they ultimately clarify precisely the meaning of that term. At the end of Book II, Schopenhauer writes: "the only self-cognition of the will as a whole is representation as a whole, the entire intui-

---

53 Cf. Schopenhauer 2020, p. 348. Cf. Koßler 2013b, p. 202.
54 Schopenhauer 2010b, I 152–153, § 25, pp. 153–154.

tive world. This is its objecthood [*Objektität*], its revelation [*Offenbarung*], its mirror [*Spiegel*]."[55] *Offenbarung* and *Spiegel* also specify the meaning of *Erscheinung*.[56]

Of course, given that one can only speak of a relation (*Verhältniß*) between *Ding an sich* and *Erscheinung* in a metaphorical sense (*nur gleichnißweise*), all those terms, insofar as they illustrate or specify that relationship, must likewise only be understood in a metaphorical sense. This, however, in no way authorizes us to underestimate their relevance. Firstly, they do not occur only at this point in the text, or only here, but consistently recur throughout Schopenhauer's work. Secondly, those terms yield considerable theoretical consequences in the system, which will have to be considered in a moment.

Thirdly, insofar as the thing-in-itself is (or should be), as such, completely unknowable and unobjectivizable, the discourse concerning it must necessarily entail kind of linguistic stretch; and conversely, for this very reason, no kind of discourse about the thing-in-itself is possible beyond or outside of such a stretch (always remember that the determination of the thing-in-itself as will took place through a denomination from the superior term).[57] Consequently, it is impossible to isolate the Schopenhauerian *doctrine* of the thing-in-itself from the *terminology* with which it is in fact formulated, claiming that the aforementioned terms, being metaphorical, are contingent or inessential to the doctrine *per se*. On the contrary: *the latter, without them, would not exist at all*. Their analysis is thus of primary importance, because it does not concern the specific or accidental way in which Schopenhauer speaks of the thing-in-itself here or elsewhere, but rather his doctrine of the thing-in-itself as a whole.

More generally, it is not at all possible to distinguish Schopenhauer's thought from the terminology (and thus conceptuality) with which he expounds it in his writings. Since his thought, separate from that terminology, is not given in any way, such a distinction is arbitrary, i.e., strictly speaking, unfounded. Attempts (however sophisticated and ingenious)[58] to explain or resolve the inherent aporias within Schopenhauer's system by changing or supplementing its terminology seem to presuppose that the interpreter's task is to formulate Schopenhauer's thought better than Schopenhauer himself (i.e., non-metaphorically and non-aporetically). However, the conceptuality or content of a text cannot emerge independently of the terms used: these two levels are so inseparable and interdependent that any change in the latter necessarily entails a corresponding change in the former. Con-

---

55 Schopenhauer 2010b, I 196 § 29, p. 189.
56 Cf. also Schopenhauer 2010b, I 423, § 64, p. 385.
57 On this issue, cf. Shapshay 2009.
58 In this respect, very noteworthy examples include the experiments by Malter 1991; Kamata 1988; Spierling 1998; Schubbe 2010.

sequently, the analysis of Schopenhauer's terminology is by no means a pedantic or idle occupation; on the contrary, it represents the fundamental hermeneutical task.

Now, the lexicon used by Schopenhauer to express the distinction between appearance and thing-in-itself has, in some places, an unmistakably Platonic feel to it. Consider first of all the term *Abbild:* the "appearance, i.e. manifestation, objectivation" of the thing-in-itself is nothing but the "image [*Abbilde*] of its essence"; the "world as representation", in its totality, is the *Abbild* of the thing-in-itself.[59] Schleiermacher used *Abbild* to render the Greek εἴδωλον ("image", "copy"), which in Plato's dialogues determined the relation between the thing and the Idea that constitutes its form (εἶδος) or essence (οὐσία).[60] This term clearly entails some relation of 'resemblance' or 'similarity' (in the broad sense); only by implying this can Schopenhauer state that the appearance is the "mirror" of the thing-in-itself, i.e. that the "essence" of the will "is mirrored [*sich ... abspiegelt*] in the whole world".[61] It is no coincidence that Plotinus used the term mirror (κάτοπτρον) to illustrate the relationship between the sensible and intelligible realms.[62]

In the passage quoted above, Schopenhauer goes on to write that the will, as the thing-in-itself or essence of every entity, "is present [*gegenwärtig*] whole and undivided in every single thing in nature, in all of life".[63] In fact, "none of the differences in the forms of nature and none of the variations among individuals belong to the will but rather only to its objecthood'" so that "the will is indivisible and wholly present [*ganz gegenwärtig*] in every appearance".[64] The presence (παρουσία) of the Idea in the individual thing is mentioned, for example, in Plato's *Phaedo* and *Sophist* (Schleiermacher renders it with *Anwesenheit* and *Einwohnung*).[65]

On the other hand, the predicates that Schopenhauer refers to the thing-in-itself – despite his claim that the latter is constitutively non-objectifiable – are extraordinarily similar to those that Plato attributes to the Idea: the thing-in-itself is unity (τὸ ἕν),[66] because it is untouched by the dispersion and plurality of the things of the world; it is extraneous to becoming, i.e. it neither comes to be nor perishes (οὔτε γιγνόμενον οὔτε ἀπολλύμενον),[67] and constitutes the essence

---

59 Schopenhauer 2010b, I 179, § 27, p. 175.
60 Cf. Plato, *Theaetetus*, 191 d, Plato 1804ff., II.1, p. 284; *Symposium* 212 a, Plato 1804ff., II.2, p. 433.
61 Schopenhauer 2010b, I 339, § 55, p. 314.
62 Cf. Plotinus, *Ennead* III 6, 13, in Plotinus 2018, p. 325.
63 Schopenhauer 2010b, I 153, § 25, p. 154.
64 Schopenhauer 2010b, I 184, § 28, p. 179.
65 Cf. Plato, *Phaedo*, 100 c–d, Plato 1804ff., II.3, p. 94; *Sophist* 247 a, Plato 1804ff., II.2, p. 198.
66 Cf. Plato, *Philebus*, 15 a-c, Plato 1914ff., vol. 9, pp. 214–215.
67 Cf. Plato, *Symposium*, 211 a, Plato 1914ff., vol. 3, pp. 272–273.

(οὐσία,[68] *Wesen*) of phenomenal things. In his exposition of Plato's philosophy, Tennemann wrote that the Idea or thing-in-itself, unlike the appearance, is not in space (*nicht im Raum*), is not composed (*nicht zusammengesetzt*), is not mutable (*nicht veränderlich*) and is not destructible (*nicht zerstörbar*), because it possesses unity, totality (*Totalität*) and "absolute being in all time [*absolutes Seyn zu aller Zeit*]".[69] Schopenhauer, as we have seen, states that the thing-in-itself "lies outside of time and space, and thus knows no multiplicity, and is consequently *one*"; it is also "indivisible", in that "gradations [...] do not directly concern the will itself", which is present in everything "whole and undivided".[70]

Just as the Platonic Idea is the one and identical "essence" of all things belonging to the same species (which are an "image" of it), so the thing-in-itself is the one and identical "essence" of all things belonging to the *Erscheinung* species, i.e. the *Erscheinung* in its totality (which is its "image" and "mirror"): "since everything in the world is the objecthood of one and the same will", they are "identical with respect to [their] inner essence".[71] The *principium individuationis* – with which the Scholastics sought to explain the transition from universal essence to individual realities – is thus related by Schopenhauer to the difference between thing-in-itself and individual *Erscheinungen*.

Only on the basis of these major and relevant assumptions (with which Kant, of course, would never have agreed) can Schopenhauer compare the relationship between the *thing-in-itself* and individual *appearances* to the relationship between *genus* and *species* ("the many and varied [...] appearances are only different species of the same genus").[72] Only in this way can he refer to the thing-in-itself what Plato said of the knowledge of the Idea, namely that it can only be accessed by synoptically grasping the identity underlying different things.[73]

> [...] the knowledge of the unity of the will (as thing-in-itself) through the infinite variety and multiplicity of appearances is the only thing that really sheds light on that remarkable, un-

---

[68] Cf. Plato, *Philebus*, 53 c, Plato 1914 ff., vol. 9, pp. 350–351.
[69] Cf. Tennemann 1798–1819, II, pp. 366–367.
[70] Schopenhauer 2010b, I 153, § 25, pp. 153–154.
[71] Schopenhauer 2010b, I 171, p. 168. H. G. Ingenkamp (cf. Ingenkamp 1991) has rightly pointed out that in Schopenhauer the dualism between appearance and thing-in-itself has a Platonic character, insofar as it corresponds to that between semblance (*Schein*) and being (*Sein*). On this, cf. also Giametta 2008.
[72] Schopenhauer 2010b, I 132, § 22, p. 135.
[73] Schopenhauer 2010b, I 132, § 22, p. 135. Cf. Plato, *Republic*, 537 c7, Plato 1914 ff., vol. 6, pp. 188–189: "he who can view things in their connection [ὁ συνοπτικὸς] is a dialectician [διαλεκτικός]; he who cannot, is not."

mistakable analogy between all the productions of nature, the family resemblance that can be regarded as variations on the same, un-given theme [...].[74]

And again, it is only by understanding the relationship between appearance and thing-in-itself in this way that Schopenhauer can consider the observation of the universal *Streben*, inherent in every appearance, as an actual empirical corroboration of the analogical syllogism, i.e. of the "will" being the "thing-in-itself" of the world, the inner essence of all entities (cf. *supra*, 12.3).

In his *Bruno*, Schelling repeatedly defines finite realities as the *Abbild* and *Spiegel* of the metempirical world.[75] His influence on Schopenhauer appears more direct, however, in relation to the use of the terms *Objektität* and *Objektivation*, with which Schopenhauer further describes the relationship between thing-in-itself and appearance (the world is "objecthood", "objectivation" of the will), as well as the use of the reflexive verb *sich objektiviren* (the will in itself, "which is one and the same in all beings [...] objectif[ies] itself [*sich objektivirt*] as life, as existence").[76] In the *Ideas for a Philosophy of Nature* – a text read extensively by Schopenhauer in the years 1810–1811 (cf. *supra*, 6.5–6.6) – Schelling in fact uses the term *Objektivirung* to denote the becoming-finite of the Infinite, i.e. its becoming an object.[77] Schopenhauer sometimes uses *Objektivirung* as a synonym for *Objektivation* and *Objektität:* the "will [...] is the in-itself of all things and whose gradual [*stufenweise*] objectivation [*Objektivirung*] is this whole visible world."[78] The centrality of these expressions – and the content they convey – can be seen in the very title of Book II of the major work (from which the above quotations are taken), which reads: "The world as will, first consideration. The objectivation [*Objektivation*] of the will".[79] The world is will insofar as it is, indeed, the "objectivation of will" itself – that is, will itself as object or appearance.

But the term *Offenbarung*, "revelation", also belongs to the lexicon with which Schelling described the relationship between the phenomenal and extra-phenomenal realms.[80] In the *Philosophical Investigations into the Essence of Human Freedom*, the cosmic Creation is determined by Schelling as the gradual and progressive "revelation" and "manifestation [*Manifestation*]" of God, culminating in

---

74 Schopenhauer 2010b, I 183, § 28, p. 179.
75 Cf. Schelling 1984, pp. 125, 137, 151.
76 Cf. Schopenhauer 2010b, I 259, § 44, p. 441.
77 Cf. Schelling 1803, part 1, p. 260.
78 Schopenhauer 2010b, I 164, § 26, p. 162.
79 Schopenhauer 2010b, p. 119.
80 Schelling 2001, pp. 209–214.

man,[81] so that the primordial will, which constitutes the "ground" of God and initiates the genesis of finite realities, is properly a will to revelation (*Wille zur Offenbarung*).[82] Fichte had already described the finite sphere as the *Offenbarung* of the infinite or metempirical one.[83] He also used the term *Sichtbarkeit* ("visibility") in a similar sense: in the lectures "On the *Wissenschaftslehre*" attended by Schopenhauer, he stated that "the factual world" is the "*visibility*" of an "invisible spiritual being", i.e. God.[84]

For Schopenhauer, the "world" is the revelation (*Offenbarung*) of the will in itself, its visibility (*Sichtbarkeit*), manifestation (*Manifestation*)[85] and expression (*Ausdruck*):[86] the natural phenomena as a whole constitute the different manifestations or expressions of the will (*Willensäußerungen*) to varying degrees.[87] All these terms are once again synonymous with *Erscheinung* for Schopenhauer. But it is clear that, like *Abbild* and *Spiegel*, they imply a relationship – albeit only allusive and imperfect – of 'similarity' or 'semblance' between appearance and thing-in-itself; so much so that the various entities (or species of entity) in nature are classified by Schopenhauer according to the degree of clarity (*Deutlichkeit*) and perfection (*Vollendung*) with which they manifest, or reveal, the essence in itself. At the apex of this long scale – *given* the analogical determination of the essence in itself from the human will – is man.[88]

Moreover, Schopenhauer makes this feature of his discourse completely explicit, and even consciously uses it – as he had already done for the empirical or inductive corroboration of the analogical inference – to make his arguments more powerful and suggestive. The expressions *Objektivation*, *Objektität*, *Abbild*, *Ausdruck* and *sichtbar werden* (in addition, of course, to *Erscheinung*) are all integral in denoting the similarity between the thing-in-itself and "its" appearance.[89]

---

81 Schelling 2006, p. 42.
82 Schelling 2006, p. 45.
83 Cf. Fichte 1849, p. 69.
84 MR 2, p. 184.
85 Cf. Schopenhauer 2010b, I 259, § 44, p. 245.
86 Cf. Schopenhauer 2010b, I 142, § 24, p. 144 (if the objects of the world "are not just empty phantoms, that is, if they are to be significant, then they need to signify or express something [*so müßten sie ... der Ausdruck von etwas seyn*] that is not just another object or representation (as they are), something whose existence is not just relative to a subject, something that can exist without an external support as its essential condition, i.e. something that is not a *representation* but rather a *thing-in-itself*").
87 Cf. Schopenhauer 2010b, I 180–181, § 27, p. 176.
88 Cf. Schopenhauer 2010b, I 199, § 30, p. 191.
89 Cf. Schopenhauer 2010b, I 174–176, § 27, pp. 171–173.

The point, however, is that these same terms are also referred by Schopenhauer to *the relationship between the empirical character,* or the "body" as a whole (as the condition of the individual and temporal acts of will that constitute the empirical character), *and the intelligible character*[90] – which only reaffirms the value of the analogical inference – as well as to *the relationship between the individual thing and the Platonic Idea*.[91] That is, Schopenhauer uses the same terminology to describe the relationship (the distinction) between empirical and intelligible character, between appearance and thing-in-itself, as well as between single object and Platonic Idea. This is an unmistakable sign that he conceives of these three oppositions as akin (beyond the legitimacy or otherwise of his interpretation of Plato, which I cannot go into here).[92] And indeed, the intelligible character, which is the will as a thing-in-itself of the individual (cf. *supra*, 12.2), is also the Platonic Idea of the individual himself (cf. *infra*, 12.7). In *Parerga and Paralipomena*, Schopenhauer explicitly identifies (like Tennemann) the opposition φαινόμενον / ὄντως ὄν of the ancient Greek philosophers with the opposition *Erscheinung/Ding an sich*.[93]

Now, given the analogy between the *individual thing/Idea* opposition and the *appearance/thing-in-itself* opposition, the structural affinity or homogeneity of the first terms – the *individual thing*, or single appearance, and the set of all appearances, i.e. the *appearance* as a whole (the world) – necessarily implies the affinity of the respective counterterms: the *Platonic Idea* and the *thing-in-itself*. Schopenhauer does not avoid this delicate question, but rather tackles it openly at the beginning of Book III of the work – and he does so with the flair of one who is sure he is the first to understand how things really are.

---

90 For *Erscheinung*, cf. e.g. Schopenhauer 2010b, I 128, § 20, p. 132; for *Abbild*, I 189, § 28, p. 183; for *sich offenbaren*, I 339, § 55, p. 313; for *Aeußerung*, I 127, § 20, p. 131; for *Ausdruck*, I 187, § 28, p. 181; for *objektiviert* and *Objektität*, I 119–120, § 18, pp. 124–125.
91 For *Erscheinung*, cf. e.g. Schopenhauer 2010b, I 190, § 28, p. 184; for *Abbild*, I 174, § 27, p. 171; for *Offenbarung* and *sich offenbaren*, I 246, § 41, p. 233; I 175, § 27, p. 309; for *Aeußerung*, I 173, § 27, p. 172; I 184–187, § 28, pp. 179–182; for *Ausdruck*, I 174, § 27, p. 171; for *Objektivation*, I 206, § 33, pp. 197–198: "The individual thing that appears in conformity with the principle of sufficient reason is [...] only an *indirect* [italics mine] objectivation [*Objektivation*] of the thing-in-itself (which is the will), and the Idea stands between this individual and the will as the only immediate objecthood [*Objektität*] of the will".
92 On this issue, cf. Mann 2018; Sattar 2022. On this topic cf. also Asmuth 2006.
93 Schopenhauer 2014, pp. 32–33.

12.5 Platonic Idea and Thing-in-Itself

> I hope that my argument in the previous Book was convincing: what Kant's philosophy calls the *thing-in-itself* [...] is nothing other than the *will*, given our determination of the expanded scope of this concept. I hope further that after what has been said, there will be no reservations about recognizing what Plato calls the *eternal Ideas* or the unchanging forms (εἰδῆ) in the particular levels of the objectivation of the will that constitutes the in-itself of the world [...].

> Now if we consider the will to be the *thing-in-itself*, and the *Idea* to be the immediate objecthood of that will on a specific level, then we see that Kant's thing-in-itself and Plato's Idea, which for him is the only thing that truly is, these two great, obscure paradoxes of the two greatest philosophers of the West, – are certainly not identical, but are nonetheless very closely related [...].[94]

Kant limited the validity of the determinations of "time, space and causality" – together with what they make possible, i.e. multiplicity and becoming – to our cognition of things, i.e. to things as cognized (appearances); and "given that our cognition is conditioned by these forms", he showed that "the whole of experience is only cognition of appearance, not of the thing-in-itself".[95] Plato, in his own way and in his own peculiar terminology, said the same thing, namely that "the things of this world, which our senses perceive, have absolutely no true being: *they always become and never are:* they have only relative being [*ein relatives Seyn*] [...] which is why their entire existence [*Daseyn*] can just as well be called a non-existence [*Nichtseyn*]".[96]

Consequently, for Plato as well as (according to Schopenhauer) for Kant, sensible knowledge is not "genuine cognition (ἐπιστήμη)", but "mere opinion arising from sensation (δόξα μετ' αἰσθήσεως ἀλόγου)".[97] That is what Plato admirably depicted in the famous allegory of the cave, whose authentic, or speculative, meaning is as follows:

> [...] the only things deserving the name of truly being (ὄντως ὄν), because *they always are and never become or pass out of existence*, are the real archetypes [*die realen Urbilder*] of those shadow images: they are the eternal Ideas, the primordial forms [*Urformen*] of all things. *Multiplicity* does not apply to them, because each is, in its essence, only one, being the archetype itself whose copies or shadows are all the particular, transitory things of the same sort and with the same name. Neither does *arising or passing away* apply to them because they truly

---

94 Schopenhauer 2010b, I 200–201, § 31, pp. 192–193.
95 Schopenhauer 2010b, I 201, p. 193.
96 Schopenhauer 2010b, I 201, p. 193.
97 Schopenhauer 2010b, I 201, p. 193.

exist [*sie sind wahrhaft seiend*], never becoming nor passing away, like their vanishing copies [...]. So there can be genuine cognition [*eigentliche Erkenntniß*] only of the Ideas [...].⁹⁸

Having thus set out the essential lines of the doctrines of the "two greatest philosophers of the West", Schopenhauer summarizes them in a formula that can (in his view) be legitimately applied to both and reveals their substantial and unacknowledged consonance:

> It is obvious and requires no further proof that both doctrines have precisely the same inner sense, that both explain the visible world as an appearance that is null [*nichtig*] in itself, and that has meaning and borrowed reality only by virtue of what is expressed in it [*das in ihr sich Ausdrückende*] (the thing-in-itself for the one, the Idea for the other); but this reality, true existence [*welchem letzteren, wahrhaft Seienden*], is, according to both doctrines, utterly foreign to all appearance, even the most universal and essential forms of that appearance [*alle, auch die allgemeinsten und wesentlichsten Formen jener Erscheinung durchaus fremd sind*][...]. To bring Kant's language even closer to Plato's, we could also say: time, space and causality are the structure of our intellect by means of which the *one* essence that genuinely exists [*das eigentlich allein vorhandene* eine *Wesen*] [...] presents itself to us as a multiplicity of similar beings in endless succession, beings that are always arising anew and passing away again.⁹⁹

Like the Platonic Idea, Kant's thing-in-itself is foreign to the fundamental determinations of the "visible world" (space, time and causality) and represents at the same time "what is expressed in it"; unlike the world of the senses, which, as becoming, "is null in itself", the thing-in-itself constitutes, like the Idea, what truly is (*das wahrhaft Seyende*), "the one essence that genuinely exists" (with the expression *wahrhaft seyend* Schleiermacher renders the Platonic locution ὄντως ὄν: cf. *supra*, 4.1).

As a consequence of all this, "the inner sense" of Kant's and Plato's doctrine is "precisely the same". Schopenhauer tries to show this concretely, by imagining what Kant and Plato would say when confronted with the sight of an animal (the example is taken from fragment 228 of the manuscripts; cf. *supra*, 11.9).¹⁰⁰ This thesis is also reiterated in the Appendix, in a passage that I have already analyzed (cf. *supra*, 3.6).

The passages considered are already present in the first edition of *The World as Will and Representation*.¹⁰¹ In the second edition (in § 24, to be exact), Schopenhauer adds that what in the phenomena is not ascribable to the forms of the prin-

---

98 Schopenhauer 2010b, I 202, pp. 193–194.
99 Schopenhauer 2010b, I, 203–204, pp. 194–195.
100 Schopenhauer 2010b, I 203, § 31, p. 353.
101 Cf. Schopenhauer 2020, pp. 131–134.

ciple of reason – and is therefore referable to the thing-in-itself – constitutes their genuine reality (*wahrhaft Reales*); which implies that this latter determination is attributed properly to the thing-in-itself,[102] in perfect continuity with its characterization as *wahrhaft seyend*, already present in the first edition.

Nevertheless, the Platonic Idea and Kant's thing-in-itself are not entirely identical. Unlike the thing-in-itself, which is extraneous to all forms of the appearance, the Platonic Idea retains the very general determination of the appearance, namely that it is an object for a subject (remember that the "root of the principle of reason", which then branches off in four directions, is the division of consciousness into the two poles of subject and object).[103] The Platonic Idea "is necessarily an object, something cognized [*ein Erkanntes*], a representation and, for precisely this reason (*but for only this reason*) [italics mine], distinct from the thing-in-itself".[104] It follows that, apart from this difference, they are completely identical.

As an object for a subject, Platonic Ideas represent the "immediate objecthood of the will" as a thing-in-itself, while every individual thing is only an "an indirect objectivation of the thing-in-itself";[105] through Ideas, or *as* Ideas, "the essence of the will enters representation" and 'becomes' "object".[106] Ideas therefore constitute an intermediate level of phenomenalization between the thing-in-itself and individual entities. But this means that *the relation between Platonic Ideas and single entities is nothing but a specification of the relation between thing-in-itself and appearance* – which is therefore, once again, implicitly assimilated to the former. That each Platonic Idea constitutes a certain "*degree* [italics mine] of objectivation" of the will means precisely that the relation between Idea and individual thing is not qualitatively different from that between the *Ding an sich* and the individual thing itself.

And in fact, just as the thing-in-itself is the "inner essence" of all phenomena, "the essential" of the world in its entirety,[107] so each Platonic Idea represents "the essential" within a given species of entity.[108] This implies that, although Platonic Ideas lie outside the *principium individuationis*, as a whole they nevertheless constitute a *multiplicity*, which corresponds to the multiplicity of the different species of entity – the different species of the genus "appearance". The thing-in-itself is outside multiplicity *simpliciter*; the Platonic Idea, on the other hand, is outside multi-

---

102 WWV 1844, p. 139; Schopenhauer 2010b, I 145, § 24, p. 147.
103 Schopenhauer 2012 [1813], § 16, p. 157.
104 Schopenhauer 2010b, I 205–206, § 32, p. 197.
105 Schopenhauer 2010b, I 206, p. 198.
106 Schopenhauer 2010b, I 199, p. 191.
107 Cf. Schopenhauer 2010b, I 324, p. 301.
108 Cf. Schopenhauer 2010b, I 214–219, §§ 35–36, pp. 204–209.

plicity only *secundum quid*, i.e. only with respect to the corresponding species (cf. *supra*, 11.12).

This multiplicity, however, still implies "the identity of the will that is objectified in all Ideas [*die Identität des in allen Ideen objektivirten Willens*]", namely "the identity of the appearing will in all the Ideas".[109] The will is objectified in Ideas and, through them, in the individual objects of the world. "The will is the in-itself [*Ansich*] of the Idea, which completely objectifies it; it is also the in-itself of the particular thing, and of the individual cognizing it".[110] Being the archetypes of the individual appearances of the will, Ideas manifest the will in a primal or original way, and according to an ascending scale: the lowest rung of this ladder is represented by natural forces, the highest (*given the analogical inference*) is represented by man, precisely insofar as the intelligible character – the individual will as a thing-in-itself – is for Schopenhauer the Platonic Idea of the individual (cf. *infra*, 12.7).

12.6 Cognizability and Uncognizability of the Thing-in-Itself. The Original Identification of Platonic Idea and Thing-in-Itself and the Subsequent Correction in the Light of Criticism

By distinguishing the thing-in-itself from the Platonic Idea solely on the basis of the predicate of being an object, or of knowability in general (which would belong only to the Idea), Schopenhauer evidently assumes that he can separate this predicate from all the other 'predicates' that Idea and thing-in-itself have in common (cf. *supra*, 12.4). That is, he clearly implies that the latter predicates do not necessarily imply the former, so that they can also coexist with *uncognizability*.

We have thus come to the heart of the matter, namely the fact that the thing-in-itself is, *on the one hand*, absolutely unknowable and non-objectifiable; *on the other hand*, it is the universal (genus) of which all the entities of the world are the particular (species, individuation), the one and identical essence, of which everything that exists is – to varying degrees – the "expression", "manifestation", "revelation", "image" and "mirror". It is evident that the thing-in-itself, *insofar as it has these determinations, is cognizable*; and on the other hand, *insofar as it is uncognizable, it cannot have those determinations*. The two sides of the argument are incompatible. So how is it possible for Schopenhauer to admit both?

---

[109] Schopenhauer 2010b, I 172, § 27, p. 169.
[110] Schopenhauer 2010b, I 212, § 34, p. 203.

In a letter from 1852, Schopenhauer would write to his pupil Frauenstädt:

> My philosophy never speaks of the realm of the nephelococcygia, but of *this* world, i.e. it is *immanent*, not transcendent. It reads the given world like a hieroglyphic table (the key to which I have found, in the will) and shows its coherence everywhere. It teaches what the appearance is and what the thing-in-itself is. But the latter is a thing-in-itself only relatively [*relativ*], that is, in its relationship [*Verhältniß*] to the appearance – and the latter is an appearance only in its relation [*Relation*] to the thing-in-itself. For the rest, it is a brain-phenomenon [*Gehirnphänomen*]. But what the thing-in-itself is outside of that relation, I have never said, because I do not know – within it, it is will-to-life.[111]

These reflections, however, were formulated well after the publication of *The World*, and in fact have no correspondence in the manuscripts until 1818. From a philological point of view, it would not be properly correct to interpret the system (in its entirety) in the light of the author's retrospective considerations, which are subsequent to the system itself and, above all, extremely different from the assumptions that accompanied and underpinned its construction. Rather, they are to be seen as the sign of a partial rethinking on Schopenhauer's part. In this letter, as well as in the *Epiphilosophy* of the second and third editions of *The World*, he attempts to soften the otherwise sharp and peremptory tone of his statements.[112] On the other hand, there are also several passages in the *Parerga* and in the second volume of *The World* in which all these epistemological reservations seem to decidedly take a back seat.[113]

In the first edition of *The World*, the double meaning of the expression "thing-in-itself" and the metaphilosophical clarifications of the *Epiphilosophy* are completely absent; at the beginning of a long paragraph, later expunged from the following editions, Schopenhauer wrote indeed:

> The true *thing-in-itself* [*das eigentliche* Ding an sich] [...], if we summarise in general terms Kant's purest statements about it, is that which appears in time and space and in all forms of cognition, i.e., that whose becoming visible are these appearances, but which in itself is not subject to those forms. Thus conceived, it leads to something that is not at all object or

---

111 Cf. Schopenhauer 1911–1942, vol. XV, pp. 155–156 (letter dated 24 August 1852). On Schopenhauer's epistolary, cf. Invernizzi 1986.
112 On the three editions of *The World as Will and Representation* published in Schopenhauer's lifetime, cf. Morini 2017.
113 Cf. e.g. Schopenhauer 2018, II, 22, chap. 1, p. 22, where the will as "thing-in-itself" is determined as "the purely metaphysical [*das rein Metaphysische*]". Cf. also Schopenhauer 2018, II 198–199, chap. 17, pp. 187–188; II 209, p. 197 (the "obligation" of the metaphysics is "to be true"); Schopenhauer 2018, II 294, chap. 20, p. 273 ("will is the real substrate [*das reale Substrat*] of the whole of appearance"); Schopenhauer 2014, pp. 21–22 (the will as thing-in-itself is "the absolutely real [*das absolut Reale*]"). On this issue, cf. Baum 1982; Cartwright 2001.

representation but that constitutes the essence of the world, insofar as it [the world] is not representation; this, according to my exposition, is the *will*. Also, Kant's thing-in-itself, when conceived in this pure and general way – as that to which all *plurality* must be extraneous, since it is outside time and space, and which determines, on the contrary, the peculiar essence of everything – leads quite close to Plato's Ideas, which we have recognised as the different levels of the adequate objecthood of the will [...].[114]

Here "the true thing-in-itself", i.e. the thing-in-itself *as such*, coincides with the *will*.

Elsewhere in the first edition, Schopenhauer stated that the "relation [*Verhältniß*] of the will to its [*seiner*] appearance (or of the intelligible character to the empirical)" can "really be called a relation only metaphorically [*nur gleichnißweise*]".[115] This means it is the thing-in-itself *as will* that, properly speaking, has no "relation" to the appearance; which implies that the thing-in-itself is "will" even *outside* of such (actually inexistent) relation – in other words, that *the will* is the non-relative thing-in-itself (foreign to any possible relation).

The implicit dimension of these passages is incompatible with the statements added in the second and third editions of the work, according to which the thing-in-itself is "will" only "relatively", i.e. only *within* its relation (*Beziehung*) to the appearance.[116] This is probably why Schopenhauer decided to expunge the quoted passages from the editions following the first. However, the third edition of the work also bears a trace (perhaps missed by Schopenhauer's scrutiny) of the original peremptoriness: in § 29 of all three editions, it is reiterated that the *will* is "the true *thing-in-itself* [*das eigentliche* Ding an sich]".[117]

But even leaving aside purely philological or historical considerations, Schopenhauer's answer to Frauenstädt and the related reflections in the *Epiphilosophy*

---

114 Schopenhauer 2020, p. 316. WWV 1819, p. 625. The passage is missing in WWV 1844 (cf. pp. 499–504) and WWV 1859 (cf. pp. 526–531).
115 Cf. Schopenhauer 2020, p. 348.
116 Cf. Schopenhauer 2018, II 203, chap. 17, p. 192: here Schopenhauer states that his philosophy "never speaks of the thing-in-itself other than in its relation [*Beziehung*] to appearance". Cf. also Schopenhauer 2018, II 738, chap. 50, p. 659: "The essence of things before or beyond the world, and consequently beyond the will, is closed to all investigation because cognition in general is itself only phenomenon [*Phänomen*] and therefore takes place only in the world, just as the world takes place only in it": here Schopenhauer even assumes an essence (*Wesen*) of things that is "beyond the will", i.e. *different* from the will as the thing-in-itself. He is likely referring here to the negation of the will-to-life (cf. *infra*, 12.10).
117 Cf. Schopenhauer 2010b, I 193, § 29, p. 187. Cf. Schopenhauer 2020, p. 125; WWV 1859, p. 193.

(taken up by some interpreters)[118] are by no means decisive from a theoretical point of view.

First of all, it is very difficult to convince oneself that Schopenhauer's discourse is really only about the relative thing-in-itself (the thing-in-itself as it is in relation to the appearance). For, given that every possible relation is internal to the principle of reason, the thing-in-itself of which Schopenhauer speaks, reduced to its relation to the appearance, would necessarily fall within the principle of reason, and then would no longer be distinguished from the appearance itself. By asserting that the *will* as the thing-in-itself "lies outside the province of the principle of sufficient reason" (and thus also outside any possible relation), Schopenhauer betrays that he understands it as (also) *external* to any relation to the appearance – that is, as "the true thing-in-itself".[119]

Secondly, the considerations put forward by Schopenhauer in his letter to Frauenstädt and in the *Epiphilosophy* do not manage to avoid the formation or emergence of the aporia. The *uncognizability* of the thing-in-itself, in fact, is not only external, but already internal to the appearance-thing-in-itself "relation": the reason for the distinction between these two terms is precisely the knowability of the former, as opposed to the unknowability of the latter. But the *cognizability* of the thing-in-itself is also internal to this relation, because it is implied by all the positive determinations (indicated above) that specify said relation. Consequently, *the contradiction between cognizability and uncognizability of the thing-in-itself, originating the aporia, already exists within the relation between appearance and thing-in-itself*, and thus *within Schopenhauer's discourse* (even assuming that the latter only concerns the 'relative' thing-in-itself).

Thirdly, Schopenhauer's 'epiphilosophical' considerations also fail to resolve the aporia. Having made the distinction between the "thing-in-itself" as such (the "thing-in-itself" *in itself*, so to speak) and the "thing-in-itself" as the object of discourse (the "thing-in-itself" *for us*), it is clear that everything Schopenhauer says about the thing-in-itself – starting from the analogical inference and the resulting *denominatio a potiori* – necessarily falls into the second set. So, without the latter, his *whole* doctrine of the thing-in-itself falls too, bringing his whole metaphysics of will down with it. As the "thing-in-itself" *for us* (i.e. considered as the "essence" of the appearance), the thing-in-itself necessarily has all the positive, i.e. ultimately 'phenomenal', determinations specified above (which, strictly speaking, would also include those of "thing", "in" and "itself"). On the other hand, as a

---

118 A. Hübscher (1989, p. 382) judges the aporia irrelevant and basically dismisses it by repeating Schopenhauer's response to Frauenstädt. Other critics have also based their analysis of the aporia on such considerations: cf. Spierling 1998, pp. 233–234; Schubbe 2010, pp. 54–55.
119 Schopenhauer 2010b, I 134, § 23, pp. 137–138. Cf. also Schopenhauer 2010b, I 194, § 29, p. 188.

"thing-in-itself" *in itself*, it cannot be the object of any kind of discourse (not even one that intends to only distinguish it from 'its' appearance).

In other words, the distinction between the two senses of the expression "thing-in-itself" is not properly internal to Schopenhauer's discourse, because it is rather the latter – as the metaphysics of will – that is completely realized within the second sense (the thing-in-itself for us, i.e. in its "relation" to the appearance). Consequently, the aforementioned (supposed) solution to the aporia, which is based on that distinction, cannot legitimately be included therein. That is to say, *whereas the aporia is internal to the system* (i.e. it rightfully belongs to Schopenhauer's philosophy, because it involves the thing-in-itself as the object of discourse), *the distinction of the two senses of the expression "thing-in-itself" is external to the system* (and in fact falls within considerations of epi- or metaphilosophy), so that it cannot serve to solve it.

But at this point it must be considered that, in the manuscripts of 1814, the genesis of the metaphysics of will is chronologically and theoretically contextual to the identification between Platonic Idea and thing-in-itself. Indeed, only as a consequence of this identification did young Schopenhauer recover the Kantian concept of the "thing-in-itself", which he otherwise considered illegitimate (cf. *supra*, 11.9). Understood as something absolutely unthinkable and unknowable, Kant's thing-in-itself, for Schopenhauer, was "a ghost [*Gespenst*] that springs from a total inability to think clearly".[120]

On the other hand, insofar as it is identified with the Platonic Idea, it acquires all the characteristics of the latter (given the way Schopenhauer interprets the doctrine of Ideas), namely: extraneousness to multiplicity and becoming, being in the full sense (ὄντως ὄν, *wahrhaft Seyend*),[121] constituting the essence of the things of the world (which in turn represent the image, *Abbild*, of it) and, above all, knowability (cf. again *supra*, 11.9). For Schopenhauer, the Idea of an object – properly speaking, the Idea of the species to which it belongs – is nothing but the object as a thing-in-itself.[122] Since the Idea or thing-in-itself of an object coincides with the metaphysical will of which the object is "objecthood [*Objektität*]",[123] then "the Platonic *Idea*, the *thing-in-itself*, the *will*" are "all the same" (cf. *supra*, 11.12).[124] The will-to-life is the Platonic Idea or thing-in-itself of the whole world (i.e. it represents that of which the world, as such and as a whole, is the object-

---

120 MR 2, p. 421.
121 MR 1, n. 250, p. 163.
122 MR 1, n. 250, p. 163. Cf. also n. 400, p. 275: "in each appearance [*Erscheinung*] a thing-in-itself and hence a (Platonic) Idea appears". Translation modified.
123 MR 1, n. 287, p. 194.
124 MR 1, n. 305, p. 205.

hood); it relates to each individual appearance as the universal, *das Allgemeine*, relates to the particular, *das Einzelne* (in the same way as the Idea relates to the individual thing).[125]

The definitive distinction between Idea and thing-in-itself (the former is not the will *simpliciter*, but "the will as object", i.e, as cognized)[126] and the decisive removal of the predicate of cognizability from the thing-in-itself were *subsequent* to the foundation of the system, and indeed came relatively late, at a time when its construction was already at an advanced stage. In fragment 511 (1816), the thing-in-itself and the Platonic Idea are still considered "one and the same thing";[127] and in fragment 620 (one of the last from 1816), Schopenhauer contrasts cognition of the appearance with "cognition [*Erkenntniß*] of the (Platonic) Idea of life [*Idee des Lebens*], of the will [*des Willens*], i. e. of the thing-in-itself [*des Dings an sich*]".[128] The different degrees of objectification of the will, i. e. the individual Ideas, are referred to in fragment 627 as *speciellen Ideen:* the different 'species' of the one 'genus', the all-encompassing Idea of the world or life, which is the will.[129] All this occurred less than two years before the publication of *The World as Will and Representation* (the drafting of which, however, was already complete by March 1818).[130] In fragment 684 of 1817 Schopenhauer still mentions "the (Platonic) Idea of life".[131]

However, in line with his 'criticism', Schopenhauer must necessarily exclude the possibility of all cognition transcending the principle of reason, and so he is forced, on the one hand, *to include cognition of the Idea within the principle of reason itself* (even if only within its most general form, being an object for a subject), and on the other hand, *to peremptorily deny the cognizability of the thing-in-itself.* The difference between Idea and thing-in-itself results from these two distinct, but converging, moments of reflection.[132]

---

125 Cf. MR 1, n. 577, p. 433.
126 MR 1, n. 442, p. 319.
127 MR 1, n. 511, p. 377.
128 MR 1, n. 620, p. 465.
129 MR 1, n. 627, p. 470.
130 Cf. the letter to the publisher Brockhaus from 28 March 1818, in Schopenhauer 1911–1942, vol. XIV, pp. 221–224.
131 MR 1, n. 684, p. 530. The long text "Against Kant" (MR 2, pp. 463–493) implies the definitive distinction between Platonic Idea and thing-in-itself on the one hand, and the identity between a single act of will and body movement (cf. *supra*, 12.2) on the other. Consequently, it must date back to the period between 1817 and 1818.
132 I therefore cannot agree with R. Malter, who argues for the priority of the transcendental point of view in Schopenhauer's metaphysics (cf. Malter 1991). Rather, the early manuscripts testify that the structuring of the system in the 'transcendental' sense came later, as a formalization or 'coherentization' of an already established content. Y. Kamata also endeavors to subordinate Scho-

Nevertheless, and in a anomalous way from the standpoint of 'criticism', *the thing-in-itself still retains all the other characteristics of the Platonic Idea* ("the Platonic Idea is necessarily an object, something cognized [*ein Erkanntes*], a representation and, for precisely this reason (*but for only this reason* [italics mine]), distinct from the thing-in-itself").[133] This was inevitable, however, insofar as the suppression of the aforementioned characteristics would have irretrievably jeopardized the very possibility of a metaphysics of will (a doctrine that seeks to speak of the will as the "thing-in-itself", or "essence", that appears in all the individual phenomena of the world).[134] Indeed, their suppression would ultimately have entailed the breakdown of the entire system. Still, it is clear that they necessarily imply some form, albeit weakened and imperfect, of knowability of the thing-in-itself – wherein lies the contradiction most frequently imputed to Schopenhauer. The latter, in reality, is only the most relevant trait of the 'residue' that his juvenile identification of Platonic Idea and thing-in-itself leaves in the mature system – a residue that cannot be renounced, on pain of renouncing the system itself. In this respect, it should not be overlooked that, for Schopenhauer, even the thing-in-itself, like the Platonic Idea, can be intuitively cognized in exceptional cases (cf. *infra*, 12.7).

This Platonic understanding of the term "thing-in-itself" explains why Schopenhauer describes the relationship (the difference) between thing-in-itself and appearance with the same terminology with which he describes the relationship between Idea and single thing (cf. *supra*, 12.4). Schopenhauer certainly repeats several times that the thing-in-itself is "completely different [*gänzlich verschieden*]" from its appearance.[135] Yet this diversity does not concern the 'content', but rather the 'form', and precisely the *a priori* forms (*Formen*) of the appearance (space, time and causality), which are not inherent in the thing-in-itself[136] – so much so that the latter constitutes the content (*Gehalt*) and the essential aspect (*das Wesentliche*) of the appearance itself,[137] just like Platonic Ideas.[138]

---

penhauer's metaphysics of the will to the transcendental point of view, elaborating the concept of "transcendental will" for this purpose (cf. Kamata 1988, p. 171). This concept, however, has no terminological or theoretical counterpart in Schopenhauer's texts. Cf. *supra*, 11.12.
133 Cf. Schopenhauer 2010b, I 205–206, § 32, p. 197.
134 On the epistemological ambiguity of Schopenhauer's metaphysics, cf. Welchman 2018.
135 Cf. e.g. Schopenhauer 2010b, I 134, § 23, p. 245.
136 Schopenhauer 2010b, I 134, § 23, p. 245.
137 Cf. Schopenhauer 2010b, I 324, § 54, p. 301; Schopenhauer 2020, p. 204.
138 Cf. Schopenhauer 2010b, I 217, § 36, p. 207; Schopenhauer 2020, p. 141. Many passages of the third edition of the work unequivocally document the actual *metaphysical* meaning that Schopenhauer attributes to the Ideas even in the last years of his life. Cf. Schopenhauer 2018, II 415–419,

All this explains why Schopenhauer, while strongly asserting the value of the Kantian distinction between appearance and thing-in-itself, ends up describing the former in terms similar to those used by Fichte[139] and Schelling (i.e. as "manifestation [*Manifestation*]" or "revelation [*Offenbarung*]"), whose aim was rather to eliminate or attenuate that distinction.[140] The *Erscheinung* is understood by Schopenhauer not only as φαινόμενον (that *which* appears to the senses and, more generally, to human consciousness) but also, problematically, as ἐπιφάνεια (that *in which* what in itself or as such does not appear appears, manifests or reveals itself, even if only partially and imperfectly). In this sense, Schopenhauer considers the "appearance", as it were, not only from the side of man (φαινόμενον), but also from that of the thing-in-itself (ἐπιφάνεια).[141]

The significant and numerous affinities between Schelling's philosophy of nature and Schopenhauer's system are conceptually subordinate to this fundamental commonality.[142] Only in this way, and based on these assumptions, does Schopenhahuer's philosophy of nature tend to become, in fact, a (non-exhaustive) 'phenomenology' of the will as a thing-in-itself – or even, in the final analysis, its (non-exhaustive) self-phenomenology: "the world is the self-cognition [*Selbsterkenntniß*] of the will".[143]

In the second volume of *The World*, Schopenhauer would write:

> I have absolutely no objections to Kant's doctrine that the world of experience is mere appearance and that *a priori* cognition is valid only with respect to this: but I *add* [italics mine] that this world, precisely as appearance, is the manifestation [*Manifestation*] of what appears, and with Kant I call this the thing-in-itself. The thing-in-itself must therefore express [*ausdrücken*] its essence and its character within the world of experience, and it must therefore be possible

---

chap 29, pp. 380–383; cf. also Schopenhauer 2018, II 466, chap. 24, p. 425, where he states: "the Platonic sense [...] is the only meaning I acknowledge for the word *Idea*".
139 Cf. Ivaldo 1983.
140 Within the system, the "relation" between thing-in-itself and appearance (according to which the latter is a mirror or objectification of the former) contradicts the radicality of their difference, which is otherwise affirmed (cf. Booms 2003, p. 280). This aporia, which Booms sees as one of the places where the system 'rebels against itself', only becomes comprehensible in the light of the genetic considerations just made.
141 On the complex history of the German noun *Erscheinung*, cf. Novembre 2021a.
142 More precisely, the affinities concerning the *Abstufungen*, i.e. the degrees of phenomenalization of the *in-itself*, are conceptually subordinate to the affinity of the way the relationship between "appearance" and "in-itself" is understood. For the detection of such affinities, cf. Barbera 2009. Cf. also: Grigenti 2000; Segala 2001; Segala 2006; Ulrichs 2012; Invernizzi 2013; Eschmann 2022a. On the relationship between philosophical pessimism and epistemology in Schopenhauer, see Cavallini 2018.
143 Cf. Schopenhauer 2010b, I 485, § 71, p. 437.

to interpret this essence and character from experience, and indeed from the material, not from the mere form of experience. Accordingly, philosophy is nothing other than the accurate, universal understanding of experience itself, the true interpretation of its sense and content [*Gehalt*]. This is what is metaphysical, ie. what is merely clothed in appearance and wrapped in its form; it is to appearance what a thought is to the words.[144]

But it is clear that the interpretation of the Kantian *Erscheinung* as *Manifestation* – or *Offenbarung, Ausdruck, Abbild, Spiegel* – of the thing-in-itself is no small 'addition'.

Some interpretations of Schopenhauer's philosophy attempt to make it consistent – i. e., to resolve the aporias concerning the compatibility of the *theory of cognition* with the *metaphysics of will* – by drastically downplaying the literal significance of the latter and shifting the axis of the system on the former (variously understood, reformulated, implemented or, sometimes, hypertrophied). Such interpretations are then forced to disregard the terminological and historical-genetic issues addressed here. Furthermore, and more generally, to support such interpretations, one must dismiss too many passages from Schopenhauer's works, in which the metaphysical claim (in the traditional sense of the term) is unequivocally expressed.[145]

---

[144] Schopenhauer 2018, II 204, chap. 17, p. 193.

[145] Cf. e. g. Schopenhauer 2010b, I 149, § 24, p. 150 ("philosophy", as opposed to the science of nature, is "not relative, but unconditioned cognition of the essence of the world [*nicht relative, sondern unbedingte Erkenntniß vom Wesen der Welt*]"; translation modified). In this respect, the recent hermeneutic, existentialist, and perspectivist interpretations of Schopenhauer's system seem to be emblematic. They are indeed almost all characterized by the disregard for or underestimation of the following elements of Schopenhauer's system: the doctrine of the intelligible character; the coincidence of the individual's will as thing-in-itself with his intelligible character; the metaphysical (i. e., 'Platonic', in Schopenhauer's view) significance of the Platonic Idea; the affinity between the Platonic Idea and the thing-in-itself; the correspondence of the intelligible character (and thus of the individual will in itself) with the Platonic Idea of the individual; the intuitive cognizability of the thing-in-itself (which Schopenhauer refers to the saints and mystics of all religions: cf. *infra*, 12.7); the identity between man's indestructible essence (that which remains after his death) and his will as thing-in-itself (cf. Schopenhauer 2015, pp. 244, 248–250; cf. also *supra*, 10.14); the relationship between philosophy and mysticism (cf. *infra*, 12.12). See the essays collected in Regehly and Schubbe 2016, in which these points are little considered or, for the most part, not even mentioned. Cf. also Schubbe 2013. For a perspectivist interpretation, cf. Eschmann 2021. Particularly valuable for its complexity and systematic nature is the attempt of D. Schubbe (2010), according to whom Schopenhauer's distinction between "appearance" and "thing-in-itself" has nothing to do with a metaphysical or ontological dualism (Schubbe 2010, p. 45), nor with the question of the difference between "ideal" and "real" (Schubbe 2010, p. 106); rather, it denotes two different ways of considering or 'experiencing' the "world". The use of Kantian terminology would therefore constitute a serious inaccuracy on Schopenhauer's part, which must be amended (cf. Schubbe 2010,

12.7 The Intelligible Character as a Platonic Idea of the Individual. The Intuitive Cognition of the Thing-in-Itself and the 'Consequent' Denial of the Will-to-Life

The body of every individual is the appearance of his intelligible character (cf. supra, 12.2), i.e. of "an extra-temporal and thus indivisible and unchanging act of will".[146] The analogical inference drawn in §§ 18–20 of *The World* extended the concept of intelligible character to all entities (as considered in analogy with the human body). That every physical object is the appearance of a will thus

---

pp. 47, 54). The term "thing-in-itself" would properly indicate a peculiar openness of the world (*Welterschloßenheit*), which is different from "representative" openness in the strict sense (cf. Schubbe 2010, p. 56). Schubbe thus interprets Schopenhauer's philosophy as an unwitting exercise in hermeneutic philosophy *ante litteram*, and reformulates it in a terminology foreign to the texts (*doppelter Verweisungshorizont*, p. 54; *situative Eingebundenheit*, p. 79; *Bedeutungshorizont*, p. 106; *situative Bedeutung*, p. 107). Now, while recognizing the ingenuity of this interpretation, I cannot agree with it, not so much or not only from a genetic or philological point of view, but also and above all from a theoretical one. First of all, if the distinction between appearance and thing-in-itself were a pure distinction between two ways of considering the world, the *thing-in-itself* as such would be reduced to the *consideration of the world as a thing-in-itself*; but Schopenhauer very often reminds the reader that the thing-in-itself is never an "object" for philosophy (so that its determination as will is the result of a denomination from the superior term). The world as thing-in-itself is not exhausted in the discourse or consideration of the world as thing-in-itself; this difference makes it impossible to reduce the distinction between appearance and thing-in-itself to the distinction of two possible points of view. Secondly, as we have seen, Schopenhauer understands the relation between appearance and thing-in-itself in unequivocally Platonizing terms; he traces these two terms back to the φαινόμενον and the ὄντως ὄν of the Greek philosophers (cf. Schopenhauer 2014, pp. 32–33), as well as to the "ideal" and the "real" of the world (cf. Schopenhauer 2014, pp. 21–22). Schubbe considers all these statements inessential as well (cf. Schubbe 2010, pp. 54–59), with the result that a truly relevant dimension of Schopenhauer's texts is sacrificed to the interpretative hypothesis. Thirdly – and this applies, more generally, to any attempt to conceive of Schopenhauer's thought as a hermeneutic philosophy *ante litteram* – it must be borne in mind that the 'situationality' possibly referable to the ground of Schopenhauer's philosophy is profoundly different from that theorized by hermeneutic philosophy, because it is not at all *historical*, but 'physical': it consists in the fact that every individual has, or rather is, a "body [*Leib*]" in the "world", regardless of the historicity of the world itself (and even of the *concepts* of "body", "will" and "world"). Schopenhauer never historicizes either the content of his statements or the result of his investigations; on the contrary, he considers them as valid *regardless of any historical-linguistic coordinates or traditions* (so much so that the recognition of the "essence of the world" as "will" can also be attributed to saints and mystics of all epochs and religions: cf. *infra*, 12.7–12.8, 12.10). With respect to the constitutive limits of human knowledge, Schopenhauer presents his investigation in terms of explicit and decisive *definitiveness*; in this sense, his methodological, or metaphilosophical, self-understanding is anything but 'situational' or 'hermeneutical' or 'perspectivist'.

146 Schopenhauer 2010b, I 341, § 55, p. 316.

means that it is the appearance of an intelligible character, i.e. ultimately of a similar timeless "act of will".

> [...] the will is indivisible and wholly present in every appearance, although the degrees of its objectivation, the (Platonic) Ideas, are very different. To make this easier to grasp, we can view these different Ideas as separate [*einzelne*] and intrinsically simple [*an sich einfache*] acts of the will [*Willensakte*], in which its essence expresses itself to a greater or lesser extent: but the individuals are themselves appearances of Ideas [*Erscheinungen der Ideen*] (and thus of these acts), in time, space and multiplicity. [...]. In humans, each individual already has a distinctive empirical character (indeed, as we will see in the Fourth Book, to the point of abolishing the character of the species completely, namely through the self-abolition of the whole of willing). What is recognized as the empirical character through the individual's necessary development in time and temporally conditioned division into individual actions, is, abstracting from its temporal form of appearance, the *intelligible character* [...]. The intelligible character coincides with the Idea, or more specifically with the original act of will revealed in the Idea: to this extent, not only the empirical character of every person but also of every species of animal, indeed every species of plant, and even every original force of inorganic nature, can be seen as the appearance of an intelligible character, i.e. of an extra-temporal [*eines außerzeitchen*], indivisible act of will [*Willensaktes*].[147]

Every Platonic Idea represents a particular act of objectivation of the universal will, "a single act of will [*ein einziger Willensakt*]",[148] and therefore coincides with an "intelligible character".[149] This universal identity of Idea and intelligible character does not, however, suppress the differences between the various species of entities – first and foremost, in very general terms, between the inorganic and organic realms. Minerals have no growth or development comparable to that of living organisms, so their empirical character expresses the intelligible character instantaneously or simultaneously, as it were; in plants, animals and humans, on the other hand, the intelligible character manifests itself through the empirical character in a necessarily diachronic manner.[150] These considerations take up and develop those formulated in fragment 242 of the manuscripts, in which the analogical inference was first formulated (cf. *supra*, 11.6).

Now, since in the mineral, plant and animal kingdoms there is no individuality, but only individuation (of the species) – i.e. only the individual *de facto*, and not also, so to speak, *de jure* – the character or Idea of single things, plants and animals coincides with the character of their species.[151] In humans, on the other hand,

---

147 Schopenhauer 2010b, I 185–186, § 28, pp. 179–181.
148 Schopenhauer 2010b, I 186, p. 181.
149 Cf. also Schopenhauer 2018, II 416, chap. 29, p. 318.
150 Cf. Schopenhauer 2010b, I 186–187, pp. 180–181.
151 Cf. Schopenhauer 2010b, I 260, § 45, p. 246.

character is essentially and markedly individual, so that "every human being is a particularly determined and characteristic appearance of the will, and can even be viewed as his or her own individual Idea [*eine eigene Idee*]".[152]

> Since the character of any particular person is thoroughly individual and not entirely subsumed under that of the species, it can be seen as a specific Idea [*eine besondere Idee*] corresponding to a distinctive [*eigentümlichen*] act of the will's objectivation [*Objektivationsakt des Willens*]. This act itself would then be the person's intelligible character, and the empirical character would be its appearance.[153]

Insofar as every Platonic Idea (every degree of the will's objectivation) coincides with a distinctive intelligible character, the intelligible character of every person is "a specific Idea", a "distinctive act of the will's objectivation". That is, the *intelligible character* of the individual – "his [the individual's] will as a thing-in-itself"[154] – is the *Idea* of the individual itself.

Incidentally: since every person's intelligible character is their will as a thing-in-itself, the identity of intelligible character and Platonic Idea ultimately entails the identity between *the individual will as a thing-in-itself* and *the Platonic Idea of the individual*. Since the will-to-life as the thing-in-itself of the world has been deduced, by analogy, precisely from the individual's will-in-itself, the thing-in-itself and the Platonic Idea of the world end up implicitly coinciding on this side of the discourse as well. One can thus understand even more concretely why Schopenhauer uses the same terminology to describe the relation (distinction) between the *Platonic Idea* and the *individual thing*, between *intelligible* and *empirical* character and between *thing-in-itself* and *appearance* (cf. *supra*, 12.4).

It should also be noted that Schopenhauer's discourse continues to be perfectly (virtuously) circular: insofar as the will-to-life has been preliminarily deduced through the *universalization* of the intelligible character, each intelligible character can now be considered, reciprocally, as "a *distinctive* [italics mine] act of the [universal] will's objectivation". Here too, as in the case of the denomination from the superior term (cf. *supra*, 12.3), Schopenhauer is merely carrying out the consequentiality of the analogical inference, which always constitutes the ultimate ground of the whole discourse.

Since the uniqueness or unrepeatability of each human being is due, according to Schopenhauer, to the peculiarity and uniqueness of his character, the coincidence of intelligible character and Idea implies that each individual corresponds

---

152 Schopenhauer 2010b, I 156, § 26, pp. 156–157.
153 Schopenhauer 2010b, I 188–189, § 28, p. 183.
154 A. Schopenhauer, *Prize Essay on the Freedom of the Will*, in Schopenhauer 2009, p. 107.

to a Platonic Idea. This means that the determinations that constitute the Idea of the human species do not exhaust the "essence" of the human individual: the latter also includes, in no small measure, the traits of the individual's unique and unrepeatable character. Precisely by virtue of this constitutive surplus or irreducibility of individual character with respect to the character of the species, man, unlike all other entities, is *free* to *deny*, along with his own character, the character of the species itself, thus achieving the "self-abolition of the whole of willing" (again in accordance with fragment 242 of the manuscripts: cf. *supra*, 11.6). The "negation of the will-to-life" constitutes the object of Book IV of Schopenhauer's masterpiece, and indeed represents the ideal epilogue of his entire discourse – but also, at the same time, a problematic and surprising opening to 'something' that, in his view, no discourse is or will ever be able to communicate (cf. *infra*, 12.10).

In 1814 Schopenhauer claimed that the negation of the will-to-life occurs "in consequence [*in Folge*]" of the cognition of life (or its essence: cf. *supra*, 10.11–10.13; 11.13). This point, which seems to significantly undermine the radicality of his 'voluntarist' position, is also present in the mature system. In *The World as Will and Representation*, Schopenhauer makes egoism – i. e. the attitude of considering one's own individuality as an end, and all others only as a means – depend on the subjection of cognition to the *principium individuationis*, by virtue of which one and the same essence appears as multiplied and differentiated in innumerable individuals. On the other hand, altruism, love for others and compassion depend on the "seeing through [*Durchschauung*] the *principium individuationis*", i. e. the ability to look beyond the apparent "distinction between [one's] person and that of others". The "immediate cognition [*unmittelbare Erkenntniß*]" of the unique essence of all things – and thus of their noumenal *identity* – inhibits the self-assertion of the individual will.[155]

---

[155] Schopenhauer 2010b, I 447–448, § 68, pp. 405–406. "But if this seeing through the *principium individuationis*, this immediate cognition [*unmittelbare Erkenntniß*] of the identity of the will in all of its appearances, is present at a high degree of clarity, then it will at once show an even greater influence [*Einfluß*] on the will. If the veil of *māyā*, the *principium individuationis*, is lifted from a human being's eyes to such an extent that he no longer makes the egoistic distinction between his person and that of others, but rather takes as much interest in the sufferings of other individuals as he does in his own [...] then it clearly follows [*dann folgt von selbst*] that such a human being, who recognizes [*erkennt*] himself, his innermost and true self in all beings, must also regard the endless suffering of all living things as his own, and take upon himself the pain of the whole world. [...] He no longer bears in mind the changing well-being and woe of his own person, as is the case with the human being still trapped in egoism; as he sees through the *principium individuationis* [*da er das* principium individutationis *durchschaut*], everything is equally close to him. He recognizes [*erkennt*] the whole, comprehends [*faßt... auf*] its essence, and finds that it is constantly passing away, caught up in vain strivings, inner conflict, and perpetual suffering. Wherever he looks, he

Schopenhauer emphasizes the intuitive or immediate (non-conceptual) character of this cognition through the verbs *durchschauen* and *auffassen*, and the subordination of the will to this cognition through the (unambiguous) terms *Einfluß* and *folgen*. By means of a rhetorical question, he even seems to exclude the possibility that, in the presence of such "cognition", the will-to-life perseveres in its self-affirmation (cf. *infra*, 12.8): "Given what he knows about the world, how could he [*Wie sollte er nun*] affirm this very life by constant acts of will, binding himself ever closer to it, embracing it ever more tightly?"[156]

Schopenhauer considers an "immediate cognition" of the "essence of things-in-themselves", i.e. of the "will-to-life", to be possible.[157] It becomes clear later in the text that Schopenhauer here uses the term "cognition [*Erkenntniß*]" not lightly, but in its proper sense and with full 'epistemological' awareness.

> And what I have described here with a feeble tongue and general terms is not some philosophical fable I invented about the present: no, it was the enviable life of a great many saints and beautiful souls among the Christians, and even more among the Hindus and Buddhists, as well as among practitioners of other faiths. Despite the vast differences in the dogmas imprinted on their reason, these people conducted their lives in ways that gave identical expression to the inner, immediate, intuitive cognition [*innere, unmittelbare, intuitive Erkenntniß*] from which all virtue and holiness spring. Because here too, we see the distinction between intuitive and abstract cognition, a distinction that has been so important, and that has extended to all aspects of our discussion, but that has received too little attention so far.[158]

This cognition of the being in itself of the world is essentially different from that resulting from the analogical argument of §§ 18–21 – even though the *content* of the two kinds of cognition (namely the essence of the world, the will-to-life) is the same. There Schopenhauer stated that the will can only be cognized insofar as it is manifested in the individual movements of the body (*Leib*).[159] In order to be able to conclude that the "will" is the "thing-in-itself" of the world it was therefore necessary to first presuppose the concept of intelligible character (which is not part of the subject's self-cognition, although it can be deduced from it); and second, to universalize it (cf. *supra*, 12.2). The cognition resulting from all these deduc-

---

sees the sufferings of humanity, the sufferings of the animal kingdom, and a fleeting, fading world."
156 Schopenhauer 2010b, I 448, p. 406.
157 Schopenhauer 2010b, I 448, p. 406.
158 Schopenhauer 2010b, I 452, p. 409.
159 Schopenhauer 2010b, I 121, § 18, p. 126: "the cognition I have of my will, although it is immediate, cannot be separated from that of my body. I do not have cognition of my will as a whole, in its unity, in perfect accordance with its essence; rather I cognize it only in its individual acts […]. Consequently, I cannot truly imagine my will without my body."

tive steps was thus not immediate, but "mediated [*mittelbare*]", and was presented there as the *only* possible route to the thing-in-itself.[160]

Now, on the other hand, Schopenhauer surprisingly admits the possibility of an "inner", "immediate" and "intuitive" cognition of the thing-in-itself. Only this cognition, and not the philosophical or conceptual kind (which can be traced back to analogical inference), is able to determine the will of the individual, inducing it to self-denial:

> A saint can be full of the most absurd superstitions, or conversely he can be a philosopher: it makes no difference. Only his deeds confirm him to be a saint: because morally, his deeds do not come from abstract cognition, but from an intuitively grasped [*intuitiv aufgefaßten*], direct cognition of the world and its essence, and he filters this through some dogma only to satisfy his reason. That is why it is just as unnecessary for the saint to be a philosopher as it is for a philosopher to be a saint [...]. [...] the cognition that gives rise [*hervorgeht*] to the negation of the will is intuitive [*eine intuitive*] and not abstract [*keine abstrakte*] [...].[161]

The philosopher does not attain intuitive cognition of the essence of the world, which is only proper to the saint; he stops at abstract knowledge of it. The limitation posed in §§ 18–21, according to which analogical argument is the only way to 'infer' the essence of things in itself, therefore only concerns the philosopher. The *philosophical doctrine* of the negation of the will-to-life does not originate from intuitive cognition (which rather leads to the *practical realization* of it), but from the attempt to explain conceptually (or abstractly) the very special phenomena of "saintliness" and "asceticism".[162]

On the other hand, if he were to only admit the possibility of abstract cognition of the essence of the world, i.e. the cognition resulting from his analogical syllogism, Schopenhauer could not claim priority over the latter and, at the same time, attribute cognition of the *content* of his conclusion – the will as the essence of the world – to the saints of all traditions as well (thereby claiming to explain the phenomena of holiness and asceticism). In other words, if the determination of the thing-in-itself as will-to-life were possible by analogical inference alone, then Schopenhauer would have to ascribe the formulation of that inference to all saints of all traditions and renounce that priority.

But this is not the case: what he claims priority over is, properly speaking, the abstract or conceptual formalization of the intuitive cognition possessed by saints

---

160 Schopenhauer 2010b, I 132, § 22, p. 136.
161 Schopenhauer 2010b, I 453, § 68, pp. 410–411.
162 Cf. Schopenhauer 2010b, p. 411.

and mystics of all ages and latitudes.¹⁶³ Unlike the philosopher, the saint has no need to formulate and draw the analogical inference, because he cognizes the essence of things (the will-to-life) in a direct and immediate way. Referring to the saint, Schopenhauer speaks unequivocally of a "different mode of cognition [*veränderten Erkenntnißweise*]" and of an "alteration in cognition [*Veränderung der Erkenntniß*]".¹⁶⁴

In the possibility of a "complete abolition of the character" as a result of such exceptional cognition lies the *freedom of the will*, which belongs to man alone and coincides with what religion calls the "effect by divine grace" and "being born again [*Wiedergeburt*]".¹⁶⁵ This, in fact, is not an action attributable to the individual (and thus explicable as the effect of certain motives on his character), because it is rather the radical negation or suppression of individuality itself (i. e. character), as such and as a whole.

12.8 Intuitive Cognition or Uncognizability of the Thing-in-Itself? Primacy of the Will or Primacy of Cognition? Explanation of These Aporias in the Light of the Genetic Perspective

This part of the discourse gives the system an extremely problematic physiognomy.¹⁶⁶ Firstly, the intuitive or immediate cognition of the thing-in-itself – which for Schopenhauer is the necessary condition for saintliness and asceticism – evidently contradicts the presupposed uncognizability of the thing-in-itself. Secondly, the subordination of the will to cognition contradicts another fundamental as-

---

163 Cf. MR 1, n. 684, p. 530, in which Schopenhauer justifies the originality of his theory precisely by virtue of the distinction between intuitive and abstract cognition.

164 Cf. Schopenhauer 2010b, I 477–478, § 70, pp. 430–431: "the state in which the character is removed from the power of the motive does not proceed immediately from the will, but rather from an altered mode of cognition. As long as we are only dealing with cognition that is caught up in the *principium individuationis* and follows the principle of sufficient reason, the motive has an irresistible force; but when we see through the *principium individuationis*, we immediately recognize the Ideas, indeed the essence of things-in-themselves [*die Ideen, ja das Wesen der Dinge an sich, als der selbe Wille in Allem, unmittelbar erkannt wird*], as [*als*] being in everything the same will, and from this cognition comes a universal tranquillizer of willing; individual motives become ineffective, because the mode of cognition that corresponds to them retreats, obscured by an entirely different mode [*ganz andre*] of cognition."

165 Schopenhauer 2010b, I 478, p. 431.

166 For an examination of the theoretical problems implied by this feature of the system, cf. Invernizzi 2011; Shapshay 2019.

sumption of the system, according to which cognition is only a "means [*Mittel*] (μηχανή)" of the will.¹⁶⁷ "The will is first and primordial; cognition only comes in later, since it belongs to the appearance of the will as its instrument."¹⁶⁸

But one must consider, even here, the theoretical context within which the doctrine of the negation of the will was born and developed. This theory originated in 1814 based on a number of assumptions later disavowed by Schopenhauer, namely: 1) the admission of a cognition that completely transcends the principle of reason; 2) the determination of the proper object or content of this cognition as the Platonic Idea; 3) the identity of "Platonic Idea", "thing-in-itself" and "will"; 4) the consequent cognizability of the thing-in-itself; 5) the subordination of the will in itself to the law of motivation (cf. *supra*, 10.11–10.13).

In the manuscripts from 1814, cognition "in consequence" of which the will repudiates the world and life – the cognition to which will is subordinate – had as its content the "Idea of the world", the "Idea of *being* in time" (cf. *supra*, 10.12), i.e. the will as a "thing-in-itself" (cf. *supra*, 11.13). "Holiness consists in our intuiting [*daß man ... anschaut*] the (Platonic) Idea of the world [*die Idee der Welt*] and in *not willing* it."¹⁶⁹ This intuitive cognition was understood by Schopenhauer as absolutely antithetical to cognition according to the principle of reason.¹⁷⁰ In fragment 675 of 1817, he wrote that the negation of the will-to-life arises (*erfolgt*) precisely from the "cognition of the (Platonic) Idea of life [*Erkenntniß der Idee des Lebens*], which involves a cognition of the nothingness of the *principium individuationis*" and represents "true cognition [*die wahre Erkenntniß*]".¹⁷¹

Compared to fragments 673–675 (which seem to constitute an early draft of these passages in the major work), § 68 of *The World as Will and Representation* presents only one theoretically relevant difference, namely the replacement of the term "Idea of life" with the expressions "thing-in-itself" and "essence of the world"; as for the rest, the doctrine expounded is the same (even, at times, in its terminology).¹⁷²

Schopenhauer abandoned those five assumptions only after formulating, on their basis, the doctrine of the negation of the will. In the absence of this theoretical framework, the doctrine of the negation of the will through cognition is necessarily aporetic in the mature system; conversely, if it were still in force, the aforementioned aporias would not arise.

---

167 Schopenhauer 2010b, I 208, § 33, p. 199.
168 Schopenhauer 2010b, I 345, § 55, p. 319.
169 MR 1, n. 250, p. 164. Translation modified.
170 MR 1, n. 547, p. 402.
171 MR 1, n. 675, p. 523. Translation modified.
172 MR 1, n. 675, pp. 522–523.

First of all, immediate or intuitive cognition of the thing-in-itself is only admissible if the latter is understood – in accordance with the manuscripts from 1814 – as a *Platonic Idea*. And indeed, since the only difference between them is that the thing-in-itself, unlike the Idea, cannot be cognized,[173] then if this difference also disappears – insofar as the thing-in-itself, just like the Idea, can be grasped intuitively (*intuitiv aufgefaßt*)[174] – they *no longer differ:* the will-to-life thus becomes once again the Platonic Idea of the whole *Erscheinung*, or "the Idea of life", in accordance with fragment 620 from 1816.[175]

Secondly, in *The World* Schopenhauer seems to assume that the intuitive cognition of the will-to-life transcends the principle of reason (he speaks of a "different mode of cognition" and an "alteration in cognition"). In this way, he seems to ultimately admit the possibility of cognition that goes beyond "representation" as such – which is in clear contradiction to his criticism.

Provided that cognition of the Platonic Idea is understood to be qualitatively different from cognition according to the principle of reason, and provided that cognition of the thing-in-itself is identified with cognition of the overall Idea or life (which presupposes the identity of Platonic Idea and thing-in-itself), the intuitive cognizability of the thing-in-itself does not produce any aporia or inconsistency. Still, in the manuscripts, *the reduction of the cognition of the Idea to the principle of reason*, the definitive *distinction between Platonic Idea and thing-in-itself* and the concomitant affirmation of the absolute *uncognizability of the thing-in-itself* came relatively late, at a time when the doctrine of the negation of the will had already been fully theorized and fixed. The resulting specific contradictions therefore affected the mature system, but not its original formulation.

There is, however, one more element to consider: outside or beyond the law of motivation, the will is completely indifferent to cognition, so that the latter should represent neither a "motive" nor an anti-motive or "tranquillizer" for it. Indeed, even as a tranquillizer, cognition still exerts an "influence [*Einfluß*] on the will";[176] and such an influence is only possible under the law of motivation. Speaking of one who "has seen through the *principium individuationis* and recognizes [*erkennt*] the essence of things-in-themselves, and thus the whole", Schopenhauer

---

[173] Schopenhauer 2010b, I 206, § 32, p. 197.
[174] On the Idea cf. Schopenhauer 2010b, I 250, § 42, p. 237. Moreover, this expression – as well as the other one, which also refers to the thing-in-itself in § 68, i.e. *unmittelbar erkannt* – belongs to the lexicon with which Schopenhauer describes the intuitive cognition of the "understanding", which consists in going from the effect to the cause (cf. e.g. Schopenhauer 2010b, I 25, § 6, p. 43).
[175] MR 1, n. 620, pp. 463–465.
[176] Schopenhauer 2010b, I 447, § 68, p. 405.

writes: "His will reverses course, and no longer affirms his own being, mirrored in appearance, but negates it instead."[177]

I have already noted that whenever Schopenhauer speaks generically or ambiguously of the human (individual) will, it is essential to determine, for the purposes of an adequate understanding of the text, whether we are dealing with the will as appearance or the will as thing-in-itself – that is, ultimately, the empirical or the intelligible character (cf. *supra*, 12.2). The question must therefore be asked: the individual will ("*his* [italics mine] will") which, under the influence of the intuitive cognition of the thing-in-itself, "reverses course", going so far as to negate or abolish itself – is this the empirical character or the intelligible character?

In the passages under consideration, Schopenhauer is not explicit on this point; it is clear, however, that it is necessarily the latter of the two: freedom "applies only to the thing-in-itself",[178] and the self-abolition of the will is "the only act of the freedom of the will that emerges into appearance", "the immediate expression of the *freedom of the will*", so that it can only be fulfilled by the individual's will in itself – that is, precisely, by his intelligible character.[179] Schopenhauer seems to state this in the manuscripts.[180] The empirical character is only the manifestation in time of the intelligible character, so that it cannot be denied or abolished, except insofar as the latter is denied or abolished. The abolition of the empirical character is therefore, strictly speaking, only the appearance of the self-abolition of the intelligible character[181] (and indeed this self-abolition gives rise to an "alteration" in man that is not merely empirical, but precisely "transcendental"). Alternatively, one could understand the "abolition of the character" as accomplished by an unfathomable, *indeterminate* dimension of the individual, which would itself have been the 'author' of the "act" (of self-determination) in which the intelligible character consists. But such a deeper dimension of individuality is not made explicit in Schopenhauer's discourse: it only seems to be implied by it (cf. *supra*, 10.7–10.9; *infra*, 12.10).[182]

Insofar as the negation of the will in the individual is equivalent to the negation of the intelligible character, and insofar as the latter is not the universal will-

---

177 Schopenhauer 2010b, I 449, pp. 406–407.
178 Schopenhauer 2010b, I 339, § 55, p. 314.
179 Schopenhauer 2010b, I 471, § 69, p. 425; I 478, § 70, p. 431.
180 MR 1, n. 496, pp. 363–365.
181 Cf. in this regard also Schopenhauer 2010b, I 338–339, § 55, pp. 312–314; I 449, § 68, p. 407; I 452, § 68, p. 409 (the saint does not simply deny his own empirical will, but first and foremost "the expression of the will that is his own person [*den in seiner Person erscheinenden Willen*]", which is nothing other than his intelligible character).
182 Cf. Schopenhauer 2010b, I 467, § 68, p. 422; I 471, § 69, p. 425; I 477, § 70, p. 430.

to-life, but only "a distinctive act of the will's objectivation" (the individual's character is *"his* [italics mine] will as a thing-in-itself"), the negation of the will-to-life in the individual *cannot* automatically entail the negation of the universal will as a thing-in-itself of all entities (and thus neither can it entail the abolition of the entire world as appearance of this will). In this sense, the question as to why the redemption of an individual is not *eo ipso* equivalent to universal redemption can only be answered "when we know how deep the root of individuality goes".[183]

Now, if the will that denies itself in the individual is his will as a thing-in-itself, and if this denial occurs as a consequence of the intuitive cognition of the essence of the world, then the will in itself – although it is eternally free from the principle of reason (and therefore free *tout court*, given that the sense of necessity is exhausted in the principle of reason itself) – seems to be subject to the conditioning of cognition, specifically the intuitive cognition of the essence of the world. In the mature system, therefore, these two contrasting positions coexist: on the one hand, *the will in itself is outside the principle of reason*, and thus also outside the law of motivation, so as to be completely indifferent to cognition (*velle non discitur*);[184] on the other hand, *the will in itself is under the influence of cognition.*

But at this point the question must be asked: why does the negation (or self-negation) of the essence of the world derive (*ausgeht*) from the cognition (or self-cognition) of this same essence? In the final analysis: why does the influence of such cognition on the will result in a *negation*, rather than a conscious and empowered reaffirmation, of what is cognized? Schopenhauer's answer is clear and simple: because the essence of the world and of life is *pain*. He who sees through the *principium individuationis* is led to "regard the endless suffering of all living things as his own, and take upon himself the pain of the whole world". Looking into the "essence" of the whole, he "finds that it is constantly passing away, caught up in vain strivings [*nichtigem Streben*], inner conflict, and perpetual suffering. Wherever he looks, he sees the sufferings of humanity, the sufferings of the animal kingdom".[185] The content of the cognition in question is not indifferent to the kind of conditioning that such cognition exerts on the will; the 'nature' or 'character' of the essence of the world (which constitutes that content), on the contrary, is diri-

---

[183] Letter to Adam von Doß of 22 July 1852, in Schopenhauer 1911–1942, vol. XV, p. 148 (this is a reply to von Doß's own letter of 12 July 1852; cf. ibid., pp. 139–146). This theoretical problem immediately attracted the attention and criticism of Schopenhauer's pupils, in particular von Doß and Frauenstädt. Cf. J. Frauenstädt, "Meine erste Bekanntschaft mit Schopenhauer", in Lindner and Frauenstädt 1863, pp. 133–156, here: 153. See also Schopenhauer 2015, p. 300; Schopenhauer 2018, II 736–738, chap. 50, "Epiphilosophy", pp. 657–659.
[184] Schopenhauer 2010b, I 359, § 55, p. 331; I 435, § 66, p. 395.
[185] Schopenhauer 2010b, I 448, § 68, pp. 405–406.

ment: the will-to-life is rejected and denied *insofar as it is cognized as the origin of pain.* It is mainly by virtue of this overall and central feature of the discourse that Schopenhauer can liken his thought to the Buddhist doctrine (cf. *supra*, 11.3 and 11.15).[186]

The denial of the will-to-life thus represents the most radical form of rejection of pain, as it is the denial of that from which pain metaphysically originates.[187] What seems to underlie the effectiveness of the law of motivation is, in the final analysis, the aforementioned link between the *content* of the cognition in question and the nature of its *influence* on the will. Recall the rhetorical question Schopenhauer asked earlier: "Given what he knows about the world, how could [anyone] affirm this very life?"[188] What this question means is: How could anyone still want life, knowing that the essence of life is pain? How could anyone ever want pain *as such?*

Conversely, those who want life, want it insofar as and to the extent that they ignore its essential nature as pain.

> But for those of us who are still caught in the veil of māyā, we sometimes gain a very intimate cognition [*Erkenntniß*] of the nothingness and bitterness of life in the form of our own painful sufferings or our vivid recognition of the sufferings of others, and we would like to take the sting out of desire and prevent any suffering from coming in, to cleanse and sanctify ourselves through complete and lasting renunciation – but then we are quickly enmeshed in the illusion [*Täuschung*] of appearance once more, and its motives put the will back into motion: we cannot tear ourselves away. The temptations of hope, the flatteries of the present, the sweetness of pleasure, the well-being that falls to our personal lot amid the distress [*Jammer*] of a suffering world [*einer leidenden Welt*] ruled by chance and error, all this pulls us back and fastens our bonds once more.[189]

Knowledge of the "nothingness and bitterness of life", which induces the will to deny itself, is set against the "illusion [*Täuschung*] of appearance", which consists of the brief and deceptive gratification of the senses "amid the distress of a suffering world". The ordinary individual sometimes attains that cognition and, *in the fleeting moments when he possesses it,* he too, just like the saint, wishes to negate

---

186 Cf. Schopenhauer 2010b, I 450–451, pp. 407–408.
187 The saint, or more appropriately the ascetic, abolishes the will-to-life in himself because he proposes to definitively abolish all pain in himself: "he takes to fasting, he takes to castigation and self-torture in order to keep breaking and deadening the will through constant deprivation and suffering, since he recognizes [*erkennt*] and abhors [*verabscheut*] the will as the source [*Quelle*] of his own suffering existence [*des... leidenden Daseyns*] and that of the world." (Schopenhauer 2010b, I 451, p. 409)
188 Schopenhauer 2010b, I 448, p. 406.
189 Schopenhauer 2010b, I 448, p. 406. Translation modified.

his will-to-life, in order to "take the sting out of desire" and "prevent any suffering from coming in" – even if he is then soon sucked back into the vortex of desires and the "delusion [*Wahn*]" of the *principium individuationis*.[190] In fact, only those who fall victim to the latter delusion (*Wahn*) can also – by virtue of their own transient happiness – fall into the illusion (*Täuschung*) that life can be happy, mistakenly believing that the connection between life and pain is only contingent, and not necessary or essential.[191]

In contrast to the will-to-life, the "negation of the will-to-life" is true bliss – that which, insofar as it is cognized or foreshadowed, can only be yearned for:

> it is an imperturbable peace, a profound calm and inner serenity; and when we behold this person with our eyes or in our imagination, we cannot help feeling [*nicht ... können*] the greatest longing [*Sehnsucht*], since we acknowledge that this alone is in the right and infinitely superior to everything else, and our better spirit [*unser besserer Geist*] calls to us the great 'Dare to know' [*sapere aude*].[192]

At the sight of the 'state' in which the denial of the will-to-life consists, man *cannot help feeling longing or 'nostalgia' for it*.

Now, precisely because the tranquillizer (*Quietiv*) of the will is the cognition of pain as the essence of the world, "suffering in general, as it is meted out by fate", experienced in the first person, is for Schopenhauer "a second way (δεύτερος πλοῦς)" of achieving the "negation of the will".[193] However, it is not pain as such that represents a second way towards the negation of the will, but rather *pain insofar as it produces cognition that pain itself is the essence of the world* ("the whole of life" is "seen [*aufgefaßt*]" or understood "essentially as suffering").[194] The two paths mentioned by Schopenhauer are thus, properly speaking, *two different ways of arriving at the same cognition* (which represents the will's only possible tranquillizer): one path is immediate and direct, the other, on the other hand, passes through personal experience.[195]

---

190 Cf. Schopenhauer 2010b, I 448–449, pp. 406–407.
191 Cf. Schopenhauer 2010b, I 374, § 57, p. 343.
192 Schopenhauer 2010b, I 461, § 68, p. 417.
193 Schopenhauer 2010b, I 463–464, p. 419.
194 Schopenhauer 2010b, I 468, p. 423.
195 Schopenhauer 2010b, I 469–470, p. 424: "Only when suffering assumes the form of absolute and pure cognition, so that, astranquillizerof *the will*, it leads to [*herbeiführt*] true resignation, – only then is it the path to redemption [...] the negation of the will-to-life, which is what people call utter resignation or holiness, always comes from [*geht... hervor*] the tranquillizer of the will, and this is recognition of the will's inner conflict and its essential nothingness, which expresses itself in the suffering of all living things. The difference that we have presented by means of two paths is whether this recognition is called into existence by suffering that is merely and purely

12.8 Intuitive Cognition or Uncognizability of the Thing-in-Itself? — 489

These two different paths to redemption had already been theorized in fragment 158 (1814) of the manuscripts, which, however, instead of the negation of the will-to-life referred to the "better consciousness" and, instead of the cognition of pain as the essence of the world, the "better cognition" (cf. *supra*, 10.11). The latter expression (*bessere Erkenntniß*) also appears in the major work and stands for a cognition of things that differs from that according to the *principium individuationis*.[196] The sentence from the *Oupnekhat* – "*tempore quo cognitio simul advenit, amor e medio supersurrexit*" – which expresses the subordination of will or love (*amor*) to cognition and which in the manuscripts is referred precisely to the "better cognition" (cf. *supra*, 10.15; 11.3), is emblematically placed by Schopenhauer on the title page of the Fourth Book of *The World as Will and Representation*, as if to indicate and anticipate its essential content.[197] The same title page reads: "With the achievement of self-cognition [*Selbsterkenntniß*], affirmation and negation of the will-to-life".[198] The will-to-life is a "blind impulse", a "striving in the absence of cognition [*erkenntnißloses Streben*]":[199] in fact, it wants life (it is the will *to live*) only insofar as it does not know what life itself is; instead, as soon as it is enlightened by cognition, it rejects life, negating itself.

The negation of the will, even if it has come "through [*durch*]" the aforementioned cognition, is certainly not "inherited property", but "it must constantly be regained by steady struggle" – which produces the violent "spiritual struggles" typical of all saints.[200] However, this episodic reoccurrence of the will-to-life coincides for Schopenhauer with "the desertion of grace, *i.e.* [italics mine] of that mode of cognition that renders all motives ineffective, that serves as a universal tranquillizer to quell all willing".[201] Even if one has traveled the second path, that of personally experienced pain, it may happen that "the will-to-life can re-emerge together with the previous character". However, this can only occur because "Cognition of the nature of this existence [...] can nonetheless recede again with whatever oc-

---

cognized, and which is freely approached by our seeing through the *principium individuationis*, or whether, on the other hand, recognition comes from one's own immediate *feeling* of suffering."
196 Schopenhauer 2010b, I 417, § 63, p. 379: "The boundless world, everywhere full of suffering, with its infinite past and infinite future, is alien to him – in fact, it is a fairy tale: his vanishing little person, his unextended present, his momentary comfort, these alone have reality for him: and he does everything he can to maintain these as long as a more adequate cognition [*eine bessere Erkenntniß*] does not open his eyes".
197 Cf. Schopenhauer 2010b, I 317, p. 297.
198 Schopenhauer 2010b, I 317, p. 297. Translation modified.
199 Schopenhauer 2010b, I 178, § 27, p. 174 (cf. Schopenhauer 2020, p. 116). Translation modified.
200 Schopenhauer 2010b, I 463, § 69, p. 418 (cf. also MR 1, n. 673, pp. 518–521.).
201 Schopenhauer 2010b, I 463, § 69, p. 418.

casioned its arrival [*Anlaß*]", namely with the painful experience that produced it.[202]

It would thus seem that the self-affirmation of the will cannot coexist with that cognition: the self-negation of the will unfailingly flows from it, just as every specific, individual act of will belonging to the empirical character follows unfailingly from its corresponding motive. It is extremely interesting, in this regard, that Schopenhauer describes the relationship between cognition of the essence of the world and the will itself using the same terminology with which he describes the action of "motives" on the empirical character – namely the noun "influence [*Einfluß*]" and the verbs *herbeiführen* and *ausgehen*, as well as the phrases *in Folge*, *durch Erkenntniß* and *von außen*.[203]

What I observed above in relation to the thing-in-itself (cf. *supra*, 12.4) also applies here: it is not possible to distinguish the *doctrine* of the negation of the will by cognition from the *terminology* with which it is formulated. In other words, it is impossible to state that the anomalies do not concern the former, but only the latter (so that the task of the interpreter would be to devise a proper, non-metaphorical and non-aporetic terminology). Such a distinction would be completely unfounded: for Schopenhauer's readers – and perhaps for anyone, *possibly* apart from Schopenhauer himself – the doctrine, as separate and distinct from the terminology used in the texts, is not given in any way.[204] The analysis of the terminology is therefore also indispensable here.

---

[202] Schopenhauer 2010b, I 467, p. 422. Cf. also MR 1, n. 673, pp. 518–521.
[203] The saint comes to "negate the will-to-life that fills all things and drives and strives in all things" in consequence (*in Folge*) of the intuitive cognition of the essence of the world (Schopenhauer 2010b, I 456, § 68, p. 412); the "will-to-life", as "the sole metaphysical entity or thing-in-itself", "cannot be suppressed by anything except *cognition* [*kann durch nichts aufgehoben werden, als durch Erkenntniß*]" (Schopenhauer 2010b, I 474, § 69, p. 427); the "immediate cognition of the identity of the will in all its appearances", where it is acquired, exerts a fundamental "influence [*Einfluß*] on the will" of the individual (Schopenhauer 2010b, I 447, p. 405); such cognition "as tranquillizer of the will, [...] leads to [*herbeiführt*] true resignation" (Schopenhauer 2010b, I 470, § 68, p. 424); "the *self-abolition* of the will derives [*ausgeht*] from cognition [*von der Erkenntniß*], but cognition and insight are as such independent of free choice; consequently, that negation of the will, that entrance into freedom [...] comes [*kommt*] suddenly, as if flying from outside [*von außen*]" (Schopenhauer 2010b, I 478, § 70, p. 431. Translation modified.). For the use of these same expressions with reference to empirical character and motives, cf. Schopenhauer 2010b, I 350, § 55, p. 323; I 88, § 15, p. 99; I 31, § 7, p. 48; I 347, § 55, p. 320.
[204] I thus cannot agree with R. Malter's considerations, which are essentially based on this distinction (cf. Malter 1991, pp. 399–400, 414–415). Malter is inclined to drastically underestimate the theoretical relevance of the terminology used by Schopenhauer (also in relation to the saint's "intuitive cognition" of the thing-in-itself: cf. Malter 1991, pp. 382, 399). The inconsistencies produced by the aforementioned terminology are easily mitigated by him in this way. In the essay *Er-*

As we have seen, in 1814 Schopenhauer believed that the will in itself is subject to the law of motivation:[205] it was precisely as part of this conviction that he developed the doctrine of the negation of the will. He started from the assumption that the metaphysical willing-life follows from the delusion (*Wahn*) that life itself might be happy; therefore, it can only be broken through the demolition of that illusion, by the true cognition of the Idea or essence of life. The latter is in truth "the Idea of a luckless and wretched state", as "suffering mankind and the suffering animal world [*die leidende Menschheit und die leidende Thierheit*] are the Idea of life in time"[206] (the same expression in § 68 of *The World* is referred to as the "essence" of the whole).[207] On the other hand, and conversely, the individual cannot but want to be a better consciousness, insofar as he *knows* this to be the condition of supreme happiness or bliss, *Seeligkeit* (cf. *supra*, 10.3, 10.6 and 10.13). An annotation from 1815 reads:

> For the moral worth of a man first consists [...] in the maxim of his conduct according to *previous* [italics mine] cognition of the world as representation. [*nach vorhergegangner Erkenntniß der Welt als Vorstellung*] [...]. From the intuition of the world which everyone as there follows [*geht ... hervor*] as a result a maxim for his whole conduct which he does not express and cognize in the abstract, but states through all his actions, first cognizing himself in these, and this is his intelligible character. From the motives the maxim itself does not flow, but only the manner of its expression which is unessential.[208]

The intelligible character is here the "maxim" of action that stems from a previous cognition or intuition (*Anschauung*) of the world. In another note from the same year (in which one can clearly sense the effort of conceptualization and the search for an adequate terminology), Schopenhauer states even more clearly:

> The *animal* [...] can never disavow [*verleugnen*] and deny [*verneinen*] its nature. Man can do this. [...]. By combining fantasy with his faculty of reason he cognizes (Platonic) *Ideas*, that is to say life and his will whose expression it is. Now in these Ideas he may have dissatisfaction and satisfaction [*er kann nun Mißfallen und Wohlgefallen an den Ideen haben*]; through his faculty of reason he can determine his actions according to that dissatisfaction and satisfaction and with annihilation of the natural character he can create for himself an artificial one. This is an empirical character, but an expression of the intelligible, in other words of the de-

---

lösung durch Erkenntnis (1982, pp. 56–57), Malter had already attempted to settle the issue, starting with the definition of the Platonic Idea as the *"a priori* synthesis of cognition and will"; this definition, however, is terminologically and conceptually foreign to Schopenhauer's texts.
205 MR 1, n. 232, p. 146.
206 MR 1, n. 210, p. 125.
207 Cf. Schopenhauer 2010b, I 448, § 68, pp. 405–406.
208 MR 1, n. 377, pp. 262–263. Translation modified.

termination [*Bestimmung*] of his will in consequence [*in Folge*] of cognized ideas and in reference to these, just as [*so wie*] the empirical character is the determination of his will in consequence [*in Folge*] of cognized individual things and in reference to these.[209]

Just as the empirical character is the determination of the individual's empirical will in consequence of the cognized empirical things, so the intelligible character is the determination of the individual's will in itself in consequence of the cognized Ideas (or, more appropriately, in consequence of the "satisfaction" or "dissatisfaction" related to the intuited Ideas).[210]

From these two fragments, which affirm the dependency or derivation of the intelligible character from the cognition of Platonic Ideas (and thus presuppose the subordination of the will-in-itself to the law of motivation), one can see how true cognition of the essence of life and the world – and therefore of *pain* as inseparable from them – can cause the individual's will-in-itself (his intelligible character) to reject life and the world, thus negating *itself* as the will-to-life and the will of the world.

In later fragments, Schopenhauer detached the will in itself from the law of motivation;[211] at the same time, however, he continued to understand cognition of the essence of the world as the *motive* for the conversion of the will: "Virtue is not exactly a positive weakness of the will. It is, on the contrary, a turning [*Wendung*], an inhibition of the will (violent in itself) motivated [*motivierte*] through cognition of the inner essence of the will in its appearance, the world."[212]

In an addition to fragment 470 (1815), he wrote: "The consciousness *in concreto* of the nothingness of the *principium individuationis* [...], in so far as it is permanent, profound, and serious and therefore determines conduct, gives us holiness."[213] But the cognition that *determines* action is, properly speaking, a "motive".[214] Fragment 618 from 1816 reads:

> Just as the motive, which reveals the appearance of the will in that it brings about [*indem es ... herbeiführt*] with necessity an individual act of will, is an individual representation, a cognition according to the principle of sufficient reason, so is the cognition that precedes the turn-

---

209 MR 1, n. 403, p. 277. Translation modified.
210 Cf. also Schopenhauer's addition to fragment n. 438, p. 317: "The true character does not consist in abstract maxims, but is the intelligible character which is determined and really developed through the intuitive cognition of life, that is to say through the (Platonic) Ideas". Translation modified.
211 MR 1, n. 413, p. 288; n. 457, pp. 330–331.
212 MR 1, n. 420, p. 296. Translation modified.
213 MR 1, n. 470, p. 342. Translation modified.
214 MR 1, n. 697, p. 536.

ing of the will a cognition of the (Platonic) Idea, of the totality of the world, i. e. self-cognition of the will.[215]

Cognition of the Platonic Idea of the world, that is, of the essence of the world in its entirety, *coincides* with the "self-cognition of the will", because the will itself is the Idea of the world. Such cognition relates to that extraordinary act of "turning" of the will in itself just as empirical motive relates to a particular (empirical) act of will.

The point is, however, that the will in itself, as mentioned above, is not subject to the law of motivation. The term "tranquillizer [*Quietiv*]", which is intended to resolve this conceptual and terminological dyscrasia, occurs relatively late in the manuscripts: it appears for the first time in fragment 673 from 1817.[216] What was hitherto thought of as the *motive* of *non-willing*, from this fragment onwards is determined as the tranquillizer (counter-motive) of *willing*: the negation is transferred to the first term. This terminological solution avoids determining as a "motive" a cognition (such as that of the Idea of the world) that is constitutively external to the principle of reason; at the same time – assuming that only something 'positive' can be properly 'motivated' – this solution avoids implying the positivity of what is described (and describable) only in negative terms, precisely as *non-willing* (cf. *supra*, 11.14 – 11.15).

Nevertheless, the relationship between cognition of the Idea or essence of the world and the will in itself remains essentially the same as that established by the law of motivation. In the aforementioned fragment 675 (1817), Schopenhauer states that "as soon as this cognition has actually come to pass, the will-to-life cannot [*kann ... nicht*] hold on any longer".[217] That is to say: although it is outside all necessity (principle of reason), the will in itself, in the presence of that cognition, "cannot" continue to assert itself, it is not free *not* to convert – just as, given a determined motive, the individual's empirical will cannot avoid committing the ensuing act. From the "cognition of the (Platonic) Idea of life", which is "true cognition", "there result [*erfolgt*] on the one hand, love [...] and, on the other, a giving up of the

---

215 MR 1, n. 618, p. 462. Translation modified.
216 The term "*Quietiv*" also appears in additions to earlier fragments (cf. MR 1, n. 445, p. 323; n. 497, p. 368), but only in fragment 673 does it occur in the body of the text. That this word appears here for the first time is clear from the fact that Schopenhauer tries to justify or motivate its appropriateness: "When everything that usually determines the will to actions is a *motive*, that occurrence of the genuine disposition may be called a *tranquilizer*" (MR 1, n. 673, p. 518). Translation modified.
217 MR 1, n. 675, p. 522. Translation modified.

will-to-life".[218] According to fragment 684 from 1817, the "tranquillizer" of willing – namely the exceptional cognition that consists in the "the intuition of the (Platonic) Idea of life [*Anschauung der Idee des Lebens*]" – is nothing but "the ethical motive [*das Ethische Motiv*]".[219]

From all these antecedents of the system, unequivocally documented in the manuscripts, one can see why Schopenhauer, in the printed works, makes the non-willing of life dependent on the cognition of life in its entirety, adopting the same terminology in this regard as in the law of motivation. In the major work, just as in the manuscripts, the intuitive cognition of the essence of the world ("tranquiliser of the will") is in fact understood as the *motive for the negation of the will* – more precisely, as the motive for the exceptional act of the will which consists in the self-negation of the will itself ("Dare to know!").

Except that all this implies, first of all, the intuitive cognizability of the thing-in-itself; or, more analytically, the possibility of an intuitive cognition that transcends the principle of reason (to the point that Schopenhauer speaks of a "different mode of cognition", "alteration in cognition")[220] and whose content is the thing-in-itself. In turn, since (as already noted) for Schopenhauer the Platonic Idea and the thing-in-itself differ only in virtue of the cognizability of the former as opposed to the cognizability of the latter, the intuitive cognizability of the thing-in-itself implies the identity between the thing-in-itself and the Platonic Idea of life or the world (cf. *supra*, 12.6). Finally, the statement about the "influence" of the aforementioned cognition on the will in itself implies that the individual's will in itself is subordinate to this cognition and thus to the law of motivation (in its most general formulation).

As we can see, these are the same assumptions indicated above as the theoretical context within which the doctrine of the negation of the will through cognition originated in the 1814 manuscripts. *The aporetic implications of this doctrine, as set*

---

[218] MR 1, n. 675, p. 523. Translation modified. In fragment 682 Schopenhauer determines the difference between "genius" and "holiness" by noting that "cognition of the (Platonic) Idea of life" becomes a "tranquilizer of the will" only in the former; the genius, on the other hand, merely reproduces the "Idea of life" in works of art, without relating it to his own will (cf. MR 1, n. 682, pp. 528–529, translation modified). However, Schopenhauer seems to believe that this latter circumstance is only temporary, and that even in genius, the will is nevertheless destined, sooner or later, to deny itself by virtue of the aforementioned cognition: "That pure, true and profound cognition of the inner nature of the world now becomes for him [the genius] an end in itself [...], *until* [italics mine] his power, enhanced by contemplation, is finally weary of the game and seizes the serious side of things" (MR 1, n. 682, pp. 528–529).
[219] MR 1, n. 684, p. 530. Translation modified.
[220] Schopenhauer 2010b, I 477, § 70, pp. 430–431.

12.8 Intuitive Cognition or Uncognizability of the Thing-in-Itself? — 495

forth in the mature system, coincide with the theoretical coordinates within which this doctrine actually came into being.[221]

An episode in the layering of *The World as Will and Representation* in the three editions published in Schopenhauer's lifetime offers an important confirmation of these considerations. In § 70 Schopenhauer states that the negation of the will-to-life "emerges from [*geht aus ... hervor*] the innermost relation [*Verhältniß*] of cognition to willing in human beings, and thus arrives suddenly, as if flying in from outside. That is precisely why the church calls it the *effect of divine grace*".[222] This "relation" between cognition and will consists precisely in the fact that "the *self-abolition* of the will proceeds from cognition [*von der Erkenntniß ausgeht*]."[223] The immediately following passage, which would seem to suddenly – and rather vaguely – disprove the primacy of *cognition* represented by "grace" over the *will*, is only found in the third edition of the work ("but just as the church thinks that this is still dependent on the acceptance of grace, the effect [*Wirkung*] of the tranquillizer is also ultimately an act of the freedom of the will").[224] The content of this addition, in any case, is somehow aporetic, because such "effect" on the will is difficult to reconcile with the absolute freedom of the will itself (insofar as it lies outside the principle of reason and, therefore, outside all possible relationships with or conditioning by external 'factors').

In Chapter 49 of the Supplements to *The World* Schopenhauer states:

> There is only *one* innate error [*angeborenen Irrtum*], and it is that we exist to be happy. It is innate in us because it coincides with our existence [*Daseyn*] itself, and our whole being [*Wesen*] is really only a paraphrase of it, indeed our body is its monogram: we are in fact nothing but will-to-life, and what we think of under the concept of happiness is the successive satisfaction of all our willing.[225]

That such an error (believing that life, i.e. existence in time, is a happy condition) is innate, that it coincides with our life or existence in time, that our essence (*Wesen*) is its "paraphrase" and our body its "monogram" (i.e. unitary sign or symbol), are all conceptually significant elements. In fact, they consistently allude to the fact that we exist as a body, i.e. as *appearance of the will-to-life*, only insofar as we *will* and *"have willed"* life (cf. supra, 10.7–10.9). What's more, we will and

---

[221] From the point of view of the mature system alone, the doctrine of the negation of will through cognition inevitably represents an inexplicable aporia (cf. e.g. Booms 2003, p. 298).
[222] Schopenhauer 2010b, I 478–479, § 70, p. 432.
[223] Schopenhauer 2010b, I 478–479, § 70, p. 432. Translation modified.
[224] Schopenhauer 2010b, I 478–479, § 70, p. 432. Cf. Schopenhauer 2020, p. 293; WWV 1844, p. 456. The passage only appears in WWV 1859, p. 479.
[225] Schopenhauer 2018, II 729, chap. 49, p. 650.

have willed it by virtue of an "innate" or originary error that precedes life itself. Later in the text Schopenhauer determines it, even more clearly, as *"a priori* inherent error" and the "πρῶτον ψεῦδος", i.e, false premise, "of our existence".[226] This is the same "fundamental error [*Grundirrthum*]" that, according to the fragments from 1814, is at the origin of the will-to-life or existence in time, thus constituting the *motive* of the will-to-life in relation to the individual's will in itself (cf. *supra*, 10.13). In the mature system, the opposite cognition – the correct identification of existence and pain – constitutes, as a perfect mirror image, the *tranquillizer* of the will-to-life.

Now, the fact that intuitive cognition of the essence of life or the world exerts an influence (*Einfluß, Wirkung*) on the will in itself contradicts two fundamental assumptions of the mature system (the impossibility of cognition transcending the principle of reason and the absolute extraneousness of the will in itself to the principle of reason itself). On the other hand, however, it avoids a contradiction that would arise *anyway* with respect to the overall 'voluntarist' structure of the system. In fact, for Schopenhauer "The will is first and primordial; cognition only comes in later, since it belongs to the appearance of the will as its instrument".[227] Still, this statement relates exclusively to phenomenal or empirical cognition (that which, precisely, "belongs to the appearance of the will"), so that intuitive cognition of the essence of the world (that which, as a tranquillizer, subordinates the will to itself), insofar as it transcends the principle of reason, is in no way involved.[228]

Cognition that exerts no influence on the individual's will in itself (*velle non discitur*) is internal to the principle of reason and to the world itself; on the

---

226 Schopenhauer 2018, II 729, chap. 49, p. 651.
227 Schopenhauer 2010b, I 345, § 55, p. 319.
228 This is stated very clearly in § 66 of *The World*. Cognition that does not affect the will is cognition according to the principle of reason; in particular, Schopenhauer refers to abstract or conceptual cognition: "Virtue does indeed come [*geht hervor*] from cognition, but not from abstract cognition that can be communicated through words. […] The only value dogmas have for morality is that they provide a schema or formula for virtuous people whose cognition is already derived from elsewhere […]; such people can then use this formula to articulate a (mostly fictitious) account of their own non-egoistic deeds for the benefit of their own reason. They do not *comprehend* the true essence of their non-egoistic deeds […] Thus, a truly good disposition, disinterested virtue, and nobility of mind do not begin [*gehn... aus*] with abstract cognition, but do nonetheless begin with cognition – namely, an immediate and intuitive cognition that cannot be reasoned for or reasoned away, a cognition that cannot be communicated precisely because it is not abstract. […] We, who are looking to virtue for a theory and must express abstractly the essence of the cognition that grounds it, we, nonetheless, will not be able to provide the cognition itself in this expression, but rather only the concept of it." (Schopenhauer 2010b, I 435–437, § 66, pp. 395–397) Cf. also Schopenhauer 2010b, I 347–348, § 55, pp. 320–321.

other hand, the cognition to which the will is subordinate (which, by exerting an "influence" on the will, acts on it as a "tranquillizer") is the intuitive cognition of the *essence* of "life" or the "world".[229] If, on the other hand, in keeping with the explicit grounds of the system, there were no cognition other than that which is based on the principle of reason (which is irretrievably subordinate to the will), then the same cognition would be both subordinate and subordinating to the will – that is, the will would be both subordinate and not subordinate to cognition.

More generally, Schopenhauer's 'voluntarism' concerns the relationship between the *will-to-life* and *cognition according to the principle of reason* – at the individual level, between the intelligible character and the representation that, by virtue of it, takes on the value or meaning of "motive" (thus determining the individual and temporal actions of the subject, which belong to his empirical character). Schopenhauer's 'intellectualism', on the other hand, concerns the relationship between *intuitive cognition of the essence of the world or of life* and *the will that decides between affirmation and negation of life* (insofar as this relationship is analogous to that which, according to the law of motivation, exists between motive and individual act of will).

Within life and the will-to-life, cognition (which in this case is knowledge according to the principle of reason) is subordinate to the will in itself, of which life is the appearance (even if this cognition then subordinates to itself, through the law of motivation, the phenomenal will, i.e. the empirical character of the individual). Instead, *in the choice between affirmation and negation of life*, the will-in-itself is subordinated to cognition (as intuitive cognition of the essence of the world). The cognition that is subordinated to the will is thus not the same as that which subordinates the will and, vice versa, the will subordinated to cognition is not the same as that which subordinates cognition. In this context, cognition of the Platonic Idea takes on a remarkably ambiguous physiognomy, which will be examined in the next section.

Conclusions can now be drawn from all that has been said so far. The doctrine of the negation of the will through cognition, as it is set out in the mature system, implies certain assumptions which, although nominally denied or absent, represent the conditions of its possibility – and in fact formed the ground on which it was conceived and formulated. In the absence of these, the aforementioned doctrine is untenable; and conversely (or as a consequence), insofar as it is professed and maintained, it cannot help implying them.

---

[229] In 1815, Schopenhauer himself explicitly distinguished between these two different levels of the relation between will and cognition: *"Cognition according to the principle of sufficient reason is a servant of the will; cognition of the (Platonic) Idea, when it is perfect and complete, abolishes the will"* (cf. MR 1, n. 369, p. 253, translation modified). Cf. Novembre 2021b.

Again, as with the doctrine of the will as a thing-in-itself (cf. *supra*, 12.6), on the one hand Schopenhauer abandoned certain theoretical assumptions that were incompatible with the rigorous 'criticism' he set out to implement; on the other hand, he had to retain their most decisive theoretical consequences, in order to save the fundamental features of his own system – that is, not to have to abandon it in its entirety.[230]

12.9 From the Youthful Dualism between Time and Eternity to the Mature Dualism between Appearance and Thing-in-Itself: The Paradigm Shift and Ambiguity of the Platonic Idea

The theory of the better consciousness centers on the opposition between the temporal and eternal realms. In contrast, the metaphysics of will and Schopenhauer's mature system revolve around the opposition between appearance and thing-in-itself. The question then arises: what is the relationship between these two oppositions in the genesis of Schopenhauer's thought? What kind of relation exists between the pairs of terms that constitute them?

The dualism between the "sensible world" and the "supersensible world", i.e. between the "world of appearance" and the "real world" (fragment 32), corresponds for young Schopenhauer to the dualism between the realm of empirical consciousness and the realm of better consciousness (cf. *supra*, 7.2 and 7.6). Since the better consciousness is absolutely opposed to empirical consciousness, the sphere of the former is absolutely opposed to the sphere of the latter; they are therefore each the "nothing" of the other (cf. *supra*, 7.8 – 7.9).

The concept of nothing is purely relative, i.e. it is a concept of relation (*Verhältnißbegriff*), because it is just the determinate negation of what is contextually understood as "being"; but the terms that are the "nothing" of each other – namely the temporal (*zeitlich*) and the eternal (*ewig*), or supertemporal (*außerzeitlich*) – are opposed not 'relatively', but absolutely: all that the one is, the other is *not*,

---

[230] Criticistic coherentization was carried out in the manuscripts *after* the system had been built, and was thus applied by Schopenhauer to a pre-existing and already established content. I therefore believe that the "changes of perspective" characteristic of his philosophy (cf. Spierling 1998, p. 223) can be traced back primarily to this circumstance, and only secondarily to the application of a conscious philosophical or epistemological methodology, which would justify them in an even programmatic way. Being subsequent to the system and to the first edition of *The World*, the 'epiphilosophical' reflection (as it is formulated in the second and third editions of *The World*) cannot have had any truly foundational role in relation to the *content* of the system.

and vice versa (cf. *supra*, 8.2–8.5). For this part of the discourse, the relationship between the sensible and the supersensible is interpreted by Schopenhauer in radically oppositional terms (along the lines of what Kant posited between appearance and thing-in-itself).

Platonic Ideas are an exception to this paradigm: though eternal, they constitute the model or archetype of temporal realities produced by nature or art (cf. *supra*, 1.7; 2.3–2.5; 8.13). Schopenhauer here interprets the relationship between the sensible and the supersensible in terms that are not completely oppositional, but 'mimetic' or 'analogical' (along the lines of the relationship that in Plato's dialogues occurs between the Idea and the individual thing).

Two different ways of understanding the 'relationship' between temporal and eternal reality, as well as two distinct and incompatible concepts of 'eternal', thus coexist in young Schopenhauer's reflections: as a *term absolutely opposed to the temporal sphere* (the better consciousness of eternity is the "nothing" of empirical consciousness and the world) and as a *paradigm or archetype of the temporal sphere itself* (Platonic Ideas are the "essence" of the world). It can be said that this double meaning of the concept of eternity embodies the contrast between a (broadly speaking) Kantian and a (broadly speaking) Platonic interpretation of the relationship between sensible and supersensible reality.

The matter becomes considerably more complicated because Schopenhauer superimposes these two levels, showing that he understands Platonic Ideas as the object of knowledge of the better consciousness (cf. *supra*, 8.14). Insofar as they belong to the sphere of the better consciousness, Platonic Ideas inevitably *also* express a moment of negation or annihilation of the world – the same world of which they constitute the "essence" or model. This point emerges clearly in fragment 86: beauty is the "theoretical negation of the temporal world", and the content of the beautiful form, exhibited by art, is precisely the Platonic Idea (cf. *supra*, 8.13).

The 'Platonic' or 'mimetic' understanding of the relationship between the eternal and the temporal underlies the doctrine of character set forth in the dissertation. Empirical character and intelligible character, though the former is in time and the latter outside time, are by no means the nothing of the other: the first is the appearance of the second, in the sense that it expresses or manifests it in time (cf. *supra*, 9.8). They have a homogeneity or uniformity of 'content', beyond the phenomenal forms that are inherent only in the empirical and not in the intelligible character.

When philosophically elaborating on the dogma of original sin based on the (Kantian-Schellingean) concept of intelligible character, in 1814 Schopenhauer posited a metaphysical and individual willing-life (*Lebenwollen*) at the origin of empirical consciousness and life in time (cf. *supra*, 10.7–10.9). That is how, still within the theory of double consciousness, he began to build his metaphysics of will. The intelligible character (understood as the will in itself of the individual) is extratemporal, and the entire life of the individual is this will becoming visible. The temporal life of the individual is to the intelligible character what the reflected image is to the person standing in front of the mirror, or what the many variations of a single musical theme are to the theme itself.[231] At the same time, the extratemporal better consciousness continues to be understood as the "nothing" of empirical temporal consciousness (cf. *supra*, 10.5).

But at this point Schopenhauer further and decisively overlaps the two paradigms of the relationship between empirical and metempirical spheres, because he identifies Plato's Idea with Kant's thing-in-itself (cf. *supra*, 11.9). Insofar as the thing-in-itself is understood as the Idea, and not the other way around, the 'Platonic' paradigm is, so to speak, set to prevail over the 'Kantian' paradigm: the appearance/thing-in-itself distinction is traced back to the empirical thing/Idea distinction. The Platonic Idea or thing-in-itself, though eternal, is not the nothing of empirical things, but their "innermost essence [*Wesen*]",[232] the ὄντως ὄν.[233] Individual things, in turn, are not the nothing, but the copy (*Abbild*) of the former.

By universalizing the concept of intelligible character, viewed as individual and metaphysical will-to-life (i.e. by extending the latter to all things in the world and to the world itself in its entirety), Schopenhauer finally arrives at the concept of a universal and metaphysical "will-to-life", of which the whole world is the appearance (cf. *supra*, 11.5–11.7). This will constitutes the Idea, or the thing-in-itself, of the world (cf. *supra*, 11.12); it is not the nothing, but the essence of the entire empirical world. Here, too, Schopenhauer uses the simile of a single musical theme expressed in different variations (which would correspond to the individual objects and events of the world).[234] The will-to-life is the "thing-in-itself" of the world and the latter is, reciprocally, the "appearance" of the former. This is the cardinal thought of Schopenhauer's system.

Well, in view of all these circumstances, the sensible or temporal world ("the world of appearance"), which young Schopenhauer refers to empirical consciousness, is rearticulated in the mature system into a properly temporal side (*appearance*) and a supertemporal side, understood as the "essence" of the former (*thing-in-itself*).

Consequently, the term that is absolutely opposite to the sensible world – the "real" or supersensible world to which, as a correlate of better consciousness,

---

231 Cf. MR 1, n. 241, p. 155; n. 242, pp. 157–158.
232 MR 1, fn. to n. 54, p. 33.
233 MR 1, n. 250, p. 163.
234 MR 1, n. 547, p. 402.

Schopenhauer refers the other meaning of eternity (absolute opposition to the empirical or temporal world) – becomes in the mature system a purely *negative* figure of the two sides into which the other term is split. This is the "negation of the will-to-life", which is also the negation of the world (or appearance) and of the essence of the world (or thing-in-itself): "The negation, abolition, and turning around of the will is also an abolition and disappearance of the world, its mirror. [...]. No will: no representation, no world."[235]

The appearance/thing-in-itself opposition, on which the mature system is based, is thus not absolute – that is, such that each of the two terms is the nothing of the other. Rather, *the nothing of the appearance* coincides with *the nothing of the thing-in-itself*. The relation of absolute opposition, which existed between the temporal sphere and the eternal sphere (i. e. between empirical consciousness and better consciousness) in the manuscripts up to 1814, in the mature system arises between *the combination of appearance and thing-in-itself* and *the negation of the thing-in-itself*.

This rearticulation, with the resulting change in the meaning of the concept of "eternal", emerges with particular clarity in relation to the concepts of "asceticism" and "virtue". In 1813, in the context of the theory of better consciousness, Schopenhauer defined virtue as a practical affirmation (*Affirmation*) of the "extratemporal being" (cf. *supra*, 8.7). According to *The World as Will and Representation*, instead, "the final goal, indeed the innermost essence of all virtue and holiness" is the negation (*Verneinung*) of the "will-to-life", which, as a thing-in-itself, is something supersensible and extratemporal.[236] Similarly, in 1813, asceticism was the practical negation of the temporal or sensible dimension of man (cf. again *supra*, 8.7). In the mature system, instead, asceticism is defined as the negation of the extratemporal "will-to-life" as "thing-in-itself".

The continuity and coherence of Schopenhauer's discourse need not be questioned here. The eternal, of which asceticism and virtue represented the practical affirmation in 1813, is *the absolute opposite of the empirical world* (and as such corresponds to the "negation of the will-to-life" in the mature system). The eternal, of which in the mature system asceticism and virtue express the practical negation, is instead *the essence of the empirical world itself* (and as such corresponds to the essence of what in 1813 was called "temporality"). There is therefore no real contradiction between the definitions of "virtue" and "asceticism" found in the youthful reflections and those of the mature system.

---

235 Schopenhauer 2010b, I 485–486, § 71, pp. 437–438.
236 Schopenhauer 2010b, I 182, § 28, p. 177. Cf. Novembre 2016a.

In this overall reconfiguration of the discourse, the *Platonic Idea* occupies an extremely ambiguous position. Indeed, on the one hand, it is formally included within the principle of reason (i.e. within its fundamental determination, being an object for a subject); on the other hand, it constitutes the content of a cognition that is totally freed from service to the will (and thus, in this sense, is opposed to knowledge according to the principle of reason).

> As we have said, it is possible – although only in exceptional cases – to go from the ordinary cognition of particular things to cognition of the Idea. This transition occurs suddenly when cognition tears itself free [*sich ... losreißt*] from the service [*vom Dienste*] of the will [...].[237]

> [...] when some occasion from the outside or a disposition from within suddenly lifts us out of the endless stream of willing, tearing [*entreißt*] cognition from its slavery [*dem Sklavendienste*] to the will, our attention is no longer directed to the motives of willing but instead grasps things freed from their relation to the will, and hence considers them without interests, without subjectivity, purely objectively [...]. the particular intuited thing is at once and inseparably raised to the Idea of its type, and the cognizing individual is raised to the pure subject of will-less cognition.[238]

In the fragments of 1813 and some fragments from 1814, cognition of the Platonic Idea is attributed to the better consciousness and represents a completely opposite cognition to that according to the principle of reason, which belongs to empirical consciousness. Cognition of the Idea and cognition according to the principle of reason arise as a consequence of the individual's self-determination as better consciousness or empirical consciousness, respectively. But this very self-determination depends in turn on the *will* of the individual himself: it is in fact through the will that he chooses whether to be empirical consciousness or better consciousness. This implies that those two forms of cognition are subordinate to the will, which chooses between empirical and better consciousness in the first place. In order to gain access to the cognition of the Platonic Idea, the individual determined as empirical consciousness must first determine himself as better consciousness, tearing himself away from the will-to-life (i.e. ceasing to will existence in time; cf. *supra*, 10.13; 11.11).

When, in 1814, the side of temporality became split or articulated into a properly temporal side and a supertemporal side, of which the former is the "appearance", the Platonic Idea stopped referring to the better consciousness (which is absolutely opposed to the world) and was interpreted more as an *internal* moment in

---

237 Schopenhauer 2010b, I 209–210, § 34, p. 200.
238 Schopenhauer 2010b, I 221–232, § 38, p. 220. On the classicist elements of Schopenhauer's aesthetics, cf. Benchimol Barros 2014.

the distinction between appearance and thing-in-itself – a distinction that Schopenhauer understood in Platonic or Platonizing terms (cf. *supra*, 12.4). The point of transition is represented by fragments 234 and 250 of the manuscripts, in which the Idea is ambiguously interpreted both as the essence of the world and as that which expresses the negation of the world itself; the Idea is here attributed both the (incompatible) meanings of eternity defined above. Namely, the Idea is still referred to the better consciousness, but at the same time the latter is placed 'beyond' the Idea itself (cf. *supra*, 11.10).

In the following fragments, Schopenhauer would expunge the determination "consciousness" from the *content* of the expression "better consciousness", thus definitively separating it from the Platonic Idea; henceforth, the Idea would only be referred to the figure of the "pure subject of cognition" (cf. *supra*, 11.11). The expression "better consciousness" thus disappeared from the manuscripts and the Platonic Ideas were subsumed under the second concept of eternity (the only one that properly remained in the mature system), thereby becoming specifications of the relationship between the single and overall "Idea of life" or thing-in-itself (the will-to-life) and its appearance (the world; cf. *supra*, 12.5 – 12.6). The disappearance of the figure of the better consciousness entailed the disappearance of the concept of "eternal" related to it.

All these developments and reconsiderations, however, left some conspicuous residues in the mature system, giving rise to an aporetic situation. Indeed, on the one hand, the Platonic Idea (as "immediate objecthood" of the thing-in-itself)[239] is an *internal moment of the objectification or phenomenalization of the will-to-life*; on the other hand, it is related to a temporary negation or *suspension of the will-to-life* in the individual. That is to say, it is subordinate and at the same time opposed to the will-to-life. Or again, on the one hand cognition of the Platonic Idea is *internal to the principle of sufficient reason*, since it presupposes its fundamental form (being an object for a subject); on the other hand, unlike cognition according to the principle of reason, it is *freed from subordination to the will*. The second sides of these two aporias belong to the primitive conception of the Idea as the object or sphere of the better consciousness (which is absolutely opposed to the will-to-life); the first, on the other hand, are due to its later interpretation, as an internal moment in the phenomenalization 'process' of the of the will-to-life.

The basic ambiguity that envelops the figure of the Platonic Idea in the mature system is thus ultimately a residue of the ambiguity that affected the concept of "eternal" in the manuscripts up to 1814. The disappearance of the figure of the better consciousness and the consequent univocalization (in a 'mimetic' or 'Platonic'

---

[239] Schopenhauer 2010b, I 201, § 31, p. 192.

sense) of the relationship between the temporal and supertemporal realms produced a corresponding transformation in the way Schopenhauer understood the Platonic Idea: the latter was *shifted from the sphere of the better consciousness* (which is *außerzeitlich* in the sense of being absolutely opposed to the world)[240] *to the sphere of the will-to-life* (which is *außerzeitlich* in the sense of being the essence of the world itself).[241] The aporias noted above betray precisely this shift.

Moreover, this shift involved a long phase (1814–1817) in which Schopenhauer identified the will as thing-in-itself with the overall Idea of the world. The identification of these two terms was dropped in the final year of drafting *The World as Will and Representation* (cf. *supra*, 12.6). All these structural and conceptual changes concerning the Platonic Idea left further traces in the mature system, particularly about the philosophy of music and the notion of aesthetic pleasure – two topics that can only be touched on here.

The possibility of aesthetic pleasure in the mature system is very problematic.[242] In general, pleasure (like pain) exists only in relation to the will; how can it, therefore, occur in relation to aesthetic contemplation, which is "pure, will-less cognition"?[243] In the manuscripts up to 1814, Schopenhauer states that the human will, like human consciousness, is twofold because it has a "twofold supreme good":[244] *temporality* and *eternity* as absolutely opposite terms (cf. *supra*, 7.11; 8.4; 10.7 and 10.12). Aesthetic pleasure derives from the fulfillment of man's will-to-eternity, which has a positive, i.e., positively determinable object, namely the 'sphere' of the eternal better consciousness (to which the Platonic Idea is related until 1814). In the mature system, this "better will"[245] disappears, i.e., it becomes a pure *negation* of the only will that remains (the will-to-temporality, or "will-to-life": cf. *supra*, 11.14); the possibility of aesthetic pleasure thus constitutes an aporetic moment which can only be explained from a genetical point of view.[246] Here, again, Schopenhauer developed his theory based on some fundamental assumptions he later disavowed while retaining their theoretical consequences.

On the other hand, Schopenhauer's philosophy of music betrays the original identification of thing-in-itself as the overall Platonic Idea of the world. He states in his masterpiece that music mysteriously relates to the thing-in-itself (the will) as

---

240 Cf. e.g. MR 1, n. 81, p. 44; n. 88, p. 56.
241 Cf. e.g. MR 1, n. 242, pp. 155–158; n. 413, p. 288. Cf. also Schopenhauer 2010b, I 186, § 28, p. 181; I 314, § 52, pp. 293–294.
242 Cf. Schopenhauer 2010b, I 229, § 37, pp. 218–219.
243 Schopenhauer 2010b, I 246, § 41, p. 233.
244 MR 1, n. 234, p. 147.
245 Cf. MR 1, n. 158, p. 98; MR 2, pp. 376–377.
246 On the problem of aesthetic pleasure in Schopenhauer, cf. Guyer 2008. Cf. also Janaway 1996.

all other arts relate to the Ideas they express: "Music is an *unmediated* objectivation and copy of the entire *will* [...]. Therefore, unlike the other arts, music is in no way a copy of the Ideas [*Abbild der Ideen*]; instead, it is *a copy of the will itself* [Abbild des Willens selbst]".[247] Schopenhauer's philosophy of music rests on an *explicitly* paradoxical assumption: "it assumes and lays down a relationship between music as a representation and something that can fundamentally never be a representation; it claims to regard music as the copy [*Nachbild*] of an original [*eines Vorbildes*] that cannot itself ever be directly presented [*vorgestellt*]".[248]

Now, insofar as music is an image (*Abbild*) or a copy (*Nachbild*) of the thing-in-itself, the latter constitutes a representable model (*Vorbild*); at the same time, it cannot ever be such precisely because it is a thing-in-itself and not a Platonic Idea. In other words, the musical art is a copy or representation of what cannot be copied or represented, so that the thing-in-itself *is a model* (insofar as music is its copy) and at the same time *cannot be a model*. This implies that the thing-in-itself *is* and *cannot be* a Platonic Idea. Such implication betrays the ambiguity noted above (cf. *supra*, 12.4 – 12.8), namely that, in the mature system, the term thing-in-itself, on the one hand, is nominally differentiated from the Platonic Idea; on the other hand, it is *de facto* understood as the Platonic Idea of the entire world, the 'genus' of which all other Ideas are 'specifications' (according to the manuscripts up to 1817). Music is the supreme and most universal of all arts precisely because it (aporetically) 'represents' the thing-in-itself meant as the supreme or most universal Platonic Idea, i.e., the Idea of the Whole.[249]

We can now return to the main thread of the discourse. In the mature system, the set of determinations that constituted the sphere of empirical consciousness is rearticulated into *appearance* and *thing-in-itself* – at the level of the individual, into the "body" and the "intelligible character" as the essence in itself of the former; at the universal level (in 'analogy' with the first level), into the "world" and the "will-to-life". The two contradictory sides that made up the figure of the better consciousness split instead into the *pure subject of cognition* and the *negation of the will-to-life*.

The duplicity of empirical consciousness and better consciousness is thus converted, on the side of the non-absolute opposition (constituted by their both being "consciousness", albeit in relation to two different spheres), into the opposition between the *individual* (subject of empirical cognition and of willing-life) and the *pure subject of cognition* (free of will and correlated with the Platonic Idea); this

---

247 Schopenhauer 2010b, I 304, § 52, p. 285.
248 Schopenhauer 2010b, I 303, p. 284.
249 On Schopenhauer's philosophy of music, cf. Ingenkamp 1989; Goehr 1996; Asmuth 1999; Zöller 2003; Koßler 2011b.

is why Schopenhauer mentions "the twofold character of [...] consciousness" again in his major work.[250] On the other hand, on the side of absolute opposition, the duplicity of empirical consciousness and better consciousness is converted into the opposition between *affirmation* and *negation of the will-to-life* (cf. *supra*, 11.15).

This overall rearticulation of the terms of the discourse is the *ground* for the fact that (as has been rightly noted)[251] the content of the First and Second Books of the major work – respectively: "The world as representation, first consideration. Representation subject to the principle of sufficient reason: the object of experience and science";[252] "The world as will, first consideration. The objectivation of the will"[253] – concerns what in the fragments written up to 1814 referred to *empirical consciousness*. Instead, the content of the Third and Fourth Books – respectively: "The world as representation, second consideration. Representation independent of the principle of sufficient reason: the Platonic Idea: the object of art";[254] "The world as will, second consideration. With the achievement of self-cognition, affirmation and negation of the will-to-life"[255] – concerns what in the fragments written up to 1814 referred to *the better consciousness*.

In 1814, willing-life (*Lebenwollen*), constituting the origin of empirical consciousness and the temporal world, represented the absolute opposite term to better consciousness; later, the term "better consciousness" disappeared and the fundamental metaphysical concept became that of "will" (cf. *supra*, 11.14). *The main figure of the mature system is thus the perfectly antagonistic term to the main figure of the juvenile system* (in its last formulations of 1814). A decisive 'paradigm shift' thus took place within the genetic process of Schopenhauer's philosophy: in the theory of the better consciousness, the keystone of the system is that which is absolutely opposed to the world; in the metaphysics of will, on the other hand, the keystone of the system is that which constitutes the innermost essence of the world itself. Through this change of perspective (which enables the construction of a metaphysics that is no longer "transcendent", but "immanent"),[256] Schopen-

---

250 Schopenhauer 2010b, I 242, § 39, p. 229: "Then the untroubled spectator will experience the twofold character of his consciousness [*die Duplicität seines Bewußtseyns*] most clearly: he feels himself to be both an individual, a frail appearance of the will [...]; and yet at the same time the eternal, tranquil subject of cognition".
251 Cf. Zint 1921, p. 44.
252 Schopenhauer 2010b, I 1, p. 23.
253 Schopenhauer 2010b, I 111, p. 119.
254 Schopenhauer 2010b, I 197, p. 191.
255 Schopenhauer 2010b, I 317, p. 297. Translation modified.
256 Cf. Schopenhauer 2018, II 203, chap. 17, pp. 192–193; Schopenhauer 2014, p. 119. On this, cf. Malter 1991; Spierling 1984; Cacciola 1994; Koßler 2002a; Brianese 2013; Caldeira Ramos 2018.

hauer believes he remains faithful to Kant's criticism: the system of the will, as opposed to that of the double consciousness, revolves around a figure that is one (*Eines, Eins*) with "life" or existence in the world of experience.[257] In this way, Schopenhauer seems to try to fulfill his initial project of a definitive "true criticism" (i.e., an epistemologically legitimate metaphysics that would correct and complete Kantian criticism: cf. *supra*, 6.9; 7.1).

Consequently, whereas the keystone of the youthful reflections cannot in any way be positively named or determined (the very designation "consciousness" is illegitimate: cf. *supra*, 11.10), the keystone of the mature system is instead positively named and determined as "will". Of course, even the latter term can be said, on the one hand, to be 'borrowed' from the phenomenal world and, on the other, to denote that which lies 'beyond' the phenomenal world itself – and in fact Schopenhauer makes it clear that the determination of the thing-in-itself as will is, properly speaking, a denomination from the superior term (cf. *supra*, 12.2–12.4).[258]

But there is a fundamental difference: in the first case, a term belonging to the empirical realm ("consciousness") was used to denote that which is absolutely opposed to this realm; in the second case, on the other hand, a term belonging to the phenomenal world ("will") is used to denote not the "nothing", but rather the "inner essence [*das innere Wesen*]" of the world itself.[259] The denomination from the superior term is justifiable only in this second circumstance ("I will name the genus after its most important species").[260] In relation to the 'content' or 'meaning' of the expression "better consciousness", a denomination from the superior term is quite impossible: if practiced, it would be illegitimate.

However, the main figure of the youthful fragments – the absolute opposite of the world – does not disappear from Schopenhauer's reflections at all, but assumes, for the reasons just stated, a strictly *negative* conceptual and terminological physiognomy, taking the form of "nothing".[261] I will now deal with this very interesting and poignant "nothing" in the conclusion of this work.

---

257 Cf. MR 1, n. 210, p. 128; n. 275, p. 183. Cf. Schopenhauer 2018, II 702–703, chap. 48, p. 626; II 739–740, chap. 50, pp. 659–661.
258 Schopenhauer 2010b, I 132, § 22, p. 135.
259 Schopenhauer 2010b, I 193, § 29, p. 187.
260 Schopenhauer 2010b, I 132, § 22, p. 136.
261 Cf. Koßler 2013b, p. 201.

12.10 Man's Transcendental Freedom and the Summit of Philosophy: Epilogue into "Nothing"

The affirmation and negation of life are for Schopenhauer the two possible and opposite expressions of the *freedom* of the will.[262] The affirmation of the will-to-life, insofar as it constitutes that from which the world 'resulted' (as its appearance), represents man's "original sin"; the negation of the will, being the revocation or extinction of that sin, represents instead man's "redemption".[263]

Now, "the negation and abandonment of all willing" "will seem [*uns ... erscheint*]" necessarily "like a transition into an empty *nothing*", because it is the absolute opposite of everything we know and can know: "world" and "will".[264] The "nothing" thus understood is constituted by virtue of this negative or oppositional relation to everything that for us is, or can be, 'positive'.

Schopenhauer starts here with some general considerations on the concept of "nothing", the first formulation of which dates back to fragment 66 of the manuscripts (cf. *supra*, 8.2).

> [...] the concept of *nothing* is an essentially relative [*relative*] one, and always refers [*sich ... bezieht*] to something particular that it negates. People (namely Kant) have ascribed this quality only to the *nihil privativum*, which is indicated by a '–' in contrast [*im Gegensatz*] to a '+', where the '–' can be made into a '+' by looking at things from the opposite perspective; they oppose the *nihil privativum* to the *nihil negativum*, which would be nothing in every respect, and is illustrated with the example of a logical contradiction that cancels itself out. But considered more closely, an absolute nothing, a true *nihil negativum* is not even conceivable; instead, everything of this sort, when regarded from a higher standpoint or subsumed under a broader concept, is always just another *nihil privativum*. Every nothing is a nothing only in

---

262 Schopenhauer 2010b, I 363, § 56, p. 334; I 355, § 55, p. 327.
263 Cf. Schopenhauer 2010b, I 479–480, § 70, pp. 432–433: "Christian doctrine symbolizes *nature*, the *affirmation of the will-to-life*, using *Adam*, because it focuses on the Idea of human beings in their unity [...] Conversely, Christian doctrine symbolizes *grace*, the *negation of the will, redemption*, in the form of God become man [...]. the original sin is both sin and punishment. It is already present in new-born infants, but only shows itself when they have grown. Nonetheless, the origin of this sin can be derived from the will of the sinner. This sinner was Adam, but we all existed in him: Adam became unhappy, and in him we have all become unhappy. – The doctrine of original sin (the affirmation of the will) and redemption (negation of the will) is really the great truth that makes up the core of Christianity; the rest of it is mostly only wrapping, coverings and appendages. Accordingly, we should always interpret Jesus Christ universally, as the symbol or personification of the negation of the will-to-life, not as an individual, according to either his mythological history in the Gospels or the presumably true history that grounds it." On this, cf. Riconda 2009; Koßler 1999, pp. 80–90. On the affirmation of the will, cf. Blondin 2019.
264 Schopenhauer 2010b, I 483–484, p. 436. L. Hühn found interesting parallels between this section of Schopenhauer's discourse and some passages from Schelling's *Weltalter* (cf. Hühn 2006).

relation [*im Verhältniß*] to something else and presupposes this relation, and thus presupposes the 'something else'. Even a logical contradiction is only a relative nothing. [...]. Thus, when subordinated to a higher concept, the *nihil negativum* or absolute nothing will appear as a mere *nihil privativum* or relative nothing which could always change signs with what it is negating, so that the former could be thought as negation [*Negation*], while it itself could be thought as position [*Position*].²⁶⁵

To support his reflections, Schopenhauer quotes a passage from Plato's *Sophist*, in which the Stranger from Elea, transgressing the firm prohibition of his fellow citizen Parmenides ("Never shall this thought prevail, that not-being [μὴ ἐόντα] is; Nay, keep your mind from this path of investigation"),²⁶⁶ says:

> But we have not only pointed out that things which are not [τὰ μὴ ὄντα] exist, but we have even shown what the form or class of not-being is; for we have pointed out that the nature of the other [θατέρου] exists and is distributed in small bits throughout all existing things in their relations to one another, and we have ventured to say that each part of the other which is contrasted with being, really is exactly not-being.²⁶⁷

Previously, in fact, the Stranger had distinguished between two senses of not-being: not-being as the "opposite [ἐναντίον] of being" and not-being as "different [ἕτερον]" from being.²⁶⁸ The former is defined as that which, in all respects, *is not* (the absolute nothing which, in accordance with Parmenides' prohibition, can neither be thought of nor spoken of); the latter, on the other hand, is defined as that which, although it is not absolute being, nevertheless *is*. The not-being which, against Parmenides' prohibition, can be spoken and thought of, is the not-being that is: it is "different" from being. In this text, Plato therefore agrees with Parmenides that absolute not-being is neither thinkable nor utterable.

Schopenhauer also believes that "an absolute nothing, a true *nihil negativum* is not even conceivable [*denkbar*]", so that every nothing that is actually thought of is, necessarily, only a "relative" nothing. But the agreement between Schopenhauer and Plato ends there, because the inconceivability of absolute nothing, for Schopenhauer, entails the relativity, and thus the potential interchangeability, of the terms "being" and "nothing", which Plato would never have subscribed to.

> What is generally accepted as positive, which we call *what is* [*das Seiende*] and whose negation [*Negation*] has its most general meaning in the concept we express as *nothing*, is precise-

---

265 Schopenhauer 2010b, I 484, pp. 436–437.
266 Parmenides, Fr. 7 (verse 1) as translated in Plato, *Sophist*, 258 d, Plato 1914 ff., vol. 7, p. 421.
267 Plato, *Sophist*, 258 d-e, Plato 1914 ff., vol. 7, pp. 420–423.
268 Plato, *Sophist*, 257 b, Plato 1914 ff., vol. 7, pp. 418–419.

> ly the world of representation, which I have established to be the objecthood of the will, its mirror. This will and this world are what we ourselves are [...].
>
> If the opposite point of view [*Ein umgekehrter Standpunkt*] were possible for us, it would involve reversing the signs and showing that what is being for us is nothing, and what is nothing for us is being. But as long as we are ourselves the will-to-life, we can only recognize and indicate that last thing negatively [...].[269]

For each cognizing subject, "being" means what constitutes the object or content of his *cognition* or *representation*. For "being [*Seyn*]" is nothing other than "being represented [*Vorgestelltwerden*]": "apart from its reference to the subject" the object is "absolutely nothing" (cf. *supra*, 9.3).[270] In his personal copy of *Parerga and Paralipomena* Schopenhauer noted: "The *Critique of Pure Reason* has transformed ontology into dianoiology", i.e., in general, the doctrine of being into a doctrine of cognition (or of the human cognitive faculty).[271] The object of cognition is conditioned by the subject's cognitive apparatus, and the latter coincides, in fact, with the nature or constitution of the subject itself (as cognizing being).

The determination of the concept of being therefore depends on the subject's point of view, and that point of view in turn depends on the essence or nature of the subject himself. In the final analysis, *the subject determines as "being" what he himself is and, consequently, can cognize; he determines as "nothing" or "not-being" what he is not and, consequently, cannot cognize.* Imparting a transcendental twist to Empedocles' principle, Schopenhauer therefore states that "like can only recognize like" (this principle was already at work in the theory of man's double consciousness: cf. *supra*, 8.14 and 8.19).[272]

Since we, like the world as a whole, are the will-to-life ("this will and this world are what we ourselves are"), the world and the will constitute being or what is (*das Seiende*) for us. An inverse viewpoint would only be accessible to us if we ceased to be all that, *negating* the will-to-life in us (and, with it, also ourselves as its appearance): the will and the world would then appear to us as "nothing", and their negation, instead, as "being".

The concept of "nothing" of which Schopenhauer speaks, although relative, is *absolutely opposed* to the concept of "being": it is its negation in "its most general meaning", so that it relates to it like the negative to the positive, or like the sign − to the sign +. *Given the concept of being, the concept of nothing is its total negation*, in the sense that it is opposed to it in every respect. The positing (*Position*) of the con-

---

[269] Schopenhauer 2010b, I 485, p. 437.
[270] Schopenhauer 2012 [1813], § 20, p. 37, 161.
[271] Schopenhauer 2014, p. 77 (footnote).
[272] Schopenhauer 2010b, I 485, p. 437.

cept of being, however, is not necessary or absolute, because it depends on the subject's point of view; it is precisely this essential dependence that makes the concept of nothing relative, as the absolute or total negation (*Negation*) of the content thus posited (which, precisely because it is posited, has a 'positive' value).

On the contrary, Plato's relative nothing – not-being as *different* from being – is not opposed to being in all respects or in an absolute way: it is not its total negation. That is why it is only "different", not contrary or "opposite" to it. In Plato, relative nothing and being do not lie in the same relation as the sign – and the sign +, because they are both of sign +. It is rather absolute nothing – the opposite of being – that constitutes the total negation of being for Plato.

Underlying the difference between these two concepts of relative nothing is the difference in the way the two philosophers understand "being": Schopenhauer as a relative (gnoseological) determination, Plato as an absolute (ontological) determination. It is from totally divergent assumptions that they develop their reflections: Plato's relative nothing is *relative* because *it opposes the absolute being in a non-absolute way*; Schopenhauer's relative nothing is *relative* because *it opposes non-absolute (relative) being in an absolute way.* These are two non-overlapping senses of 'relativity': the first concerns the type of oppositional relation of the nothing in question to being (it is precisely a non-absolute opposition); the second concerns the positive term of the aforementioned opposition (the relative concept of being), in relation to which the concept of nothing is constituted as an absolute negation. For Schopenhauer, the relative nothing thus refers to relative being, as, for Plato, the absolute nothing refers to absolute being.

Now, the positing of the concept of being mentioned by Schopenhauer, while not necessary or absolute, is not arbitrary, because it is conditioned by what the subject is: *given the subject* (*his* nature, or *his* being), the position or determination of the concept of being necessarily follows.

The point is, however, that *the being of the subject is not necessary:* in fact, he "is free to be or not the will-to-life".[273] As was already made very clear in fragment 281 of the manuscripts, "in him [man] there lives yet another consciousness [compared to the natural one] that admittedly he is not, but *can be,* something different from nature, *the moment he wants to* [italics mine]".[274] Freedom lies in *esse*, not in *operari*, because "the human being is not the work [*Werk*] of someone else's will, but rather of his own will".[275] "In truth, the very origin [*Entstehn*] of man himself is the deed [*That*] of his free will and thus the same as the fall into sin";[276] "the

---

273 Schopenhauer 2018, II 641, chap. 44, p. 576.
274 MR 1, n. 281, p. 188.
275 Schopenhauer 2010b, I 481–482, § 70, p. 434. Translation modified.
276 Schopenhauer 2018, II 693–694, chap. 48, p. 619. Translation modified.

whole being [*Seyn*] and essence [*Wesen*] (*existentia et essentia*) of the human being himself" must be seen as "his [man's] free deed [*seine freie That*]".[277] He who denies the will-to-life in himself, by this act of negation changes "his whole being [*sein ganzes Wesen*]".[278]

The non-necessity or non-absoluteness of the concept of being and the consequent relativity of the concept of nothing therefore ultimately depend on man's "*transcendental freedom*" – which would seem to consist in the original determination or 'position' by man himself (i.e. the free will in which he consists) of his own being, or essence, which correspondingly gives rise to the *Position* of the concept of being.[279]

For Schopenhauer, freedom, thus understood, is a profound mystery,[280] "something metaphysical".[281] He never defines 'what' is the part of man that is *free* to *will* or *not to will* life and, therefore, to *be* or *not to be* will-to-life[282] – just as, in his youthful notes, he leaves it completely undetermined 'what' within the individual may *want to be* empirical consciousness or better consciousness (cf. *supra*, 7.11; 8.3–8.4, 8.11, 8.18–8.19; 10.4, 10.7–10.12).[283] This is the really decisive, yet programmatically unexpressed point of his thought, from his youthful phase to his maturity.[284] The 'postulate' of such "transcendental" or "metaphysical" freedom, far from

---

[277] A. Schopenhauer, *Prize Essay On the Freedom of the Will*, in Schopenhauer 2009, p. 108. Translation modified.
[278] Schopenhauer 2010b, I 464, § 68, p. 419.
[279] Cf. Schopenhauer 2009, p. 107; cf. also Schopenhauer 2009, pp. 108–109: "*freedom resides in the esse alone*; but from it and the motives the *operari* follows with necessity [...]. In one word: a human being does at all times only what he wills, and yet does it necessarily. But that rests on the fact that he *is* what he *wills* [...]. Thus *freedom* is not removed by my presentation, but merely pushed out, that is out of the realm of individual actions where it is demonstrably not to be encountered, up into a higher region which is yet not so easily accessible for our cognition: i.e. it is transcendental". Cf. Hühn 1998. The denial of the will-to-life, which is an expression of human freedom, produces precisely a "transcendental alteration" of man (cf. *supra*, 12.8).
[280] Cf. Schopenhauer 2009, p. 109.
[281] Cf. Schopenhauer 2015, pp. 206–207, 212–214.
[282] Cf. Invernizzi 2011, pp. 417–420.
[283] In this regard, it should be recalled that in fragment 66 of the manuscripts, immediately after arguing for the relativity of the concept of "nothing", Schopenhauer states, in Fichtean terminology: "the ability of one and the same I [*des einigen und selben Ichs*] as temporal and spatial or even as non-temporal and non-spatial to become conscious of itself (to posit itself [*sich zu sezzen*]) is freedom." (MR 1, n. 66, p. 36)
[284] Cf. Schopenhauer 2018, II 736–738, chap. 50, pp. 657–659; Schopenhauer 2015, p. 206. For Schopenhauer's discussion of this point with von Doß and Frauenstädt, see *supra*, 12.8.

12.10 Man's Transcendental Freedom and the Summit of Philosophy — 513

being foreign to the system, is on the contrary the very core of Schopenhauer's entire philosophizing.[285]

The relativity of the concepts "being" and "nothing" gains a more weighty significance in light of these considerations. Indeed, if the extension of the concept of being depends on the being of the subject, the latter (the being of the subject) ultimately depends in turn on the will. By determining his own *being* through his *will*, the subject – that is, that which in the subject makes the choice – therefore determines the sphere of his own *cognition* (a sphere that then coincides, for him, with "being"). It follows that the negation of the will-to-life is *first and foremost a practical*, and *consequently theoretical*, negation of the world: only insofar as it is practically annihilated or annulled, i.e. only insofar as it is not willed, does the world appear as "nothing". And the other way around: only insofar as it is willed does it constitute the object or content of cognition and is determined, therefore, as "being". "Behind our existence lies something else and it only becomes accessible to us when we shake off the world", abolishing our will of the world itself and of life.[286]

All of this implies a primacy of man's practical faculty (the will) over the theoretical or cognitive one. This primacy corresponds to the voluntarist trait of Schopenhauer's discourse: the cognition that comes, so to speak, *after* the will's choice between affirmation and negation of life – the cognition within the chosen sphere and whose (possible) content constitutes the extension of the concept of "being" – is subordinate or 'consequent' to the will, insofar as it has already determined itself as one of the two choice options. This part of the discourse is counterbalanced by the other, intellectualistic one, whereby *in* the choice between affirmation and negation of life, the will is subordinate to the cognition of what life itself is in its entirety or essence (cf. *supra*, 10.13; 12.8).

Those who want the world and life, i.e. those who are will-to-life, can only cognize the world and life – and therefore consider them as "being" –, so that they can in no way access a "positive cognition [*positive Erkenntniß*]" of what is absolutely opposite to all this: the negation of the will-to-life.[287] Mystics of every age and tradition, however, have always offered a universal and unanimous testimony to this: it is what they have directly experienced (*erfahren*) and described – in a necessarily inadequate way – through the terms "ecstasy, rapture, enlightenment, unity with God etc.".[288]

---

[285] On Schopenhauer's theory of freedom, cf. Ebeling 1978, pp. VII–XXII; Janaway 2012; Birnbacher 2010; López de Santa María 2020; Zöller 2018.
[286] Schopenhauer 2010b, I 479, § 70, p. 432.
[287] Schopenhauer 2010b, I 485, § 71, p. 438.
[288] Schopenhauer 2010b, I 485, § 71, p. 438.

> But we who are firmly entrenched in the standpoint of philosophy must content ourselves here with negative cognition [*negativer Erkenntniß*], satisfied in having reached the final boundary stone of the positive. [...]. Only nothing remains before us. But our nature, which resists this melting away into nothing, is really only the will-to-life which we ourselves are, as it is our world. The fact that we hate nothing so much is nothing more than another expression of the fact that we will life so much [...]. But if we turn our eyes away from our own petty concerns and limitations and look instead at those who have overcome the world, those in whom the will, achieving full self-cognition rediscovers itself in everything and then freely negates itself [...] – then, instead of the restless impulses and drives, instead of the constant transition from desire to fear and from joy to suffering, instead of the never-satisfied and never-dying hope which are the elements that make up the life-dream of the human being who wills – instead of all this, we are shown the peace that is higher than all reason, we are shown that completely calm sea of the mind, that profound tranquillity, imperturbable confidence and cheerfulness, whose mere glint in a countenance such as those portrayed by Raphael or Correggio is a complete and reliable gospel [...]. But then we look with deep and painful longing at this state which puts the miserable and incurable nature of our own condition into sharp relief.[289]

The nothing of "being" – given the equation between being and pain – is also the nothing of pain. Thus ends Schopenhauer's masterpiece:

> [...] we confess quite freely: for everyone who is still filled with the will, what remains after it is completely abolished is certainly nothing. But conversely, for those in whom the will has turned and negated itself, this world of ours which is so very real with all its suns and galaxies is – nothing.[290]

Philosophy must stop at the abstract (purely conceptual) theorization of this opposite point of view, from which our whole world, which seems "so very real" to us, is "nothing". In this sense – as Schopenhauer wrote, perhaps programmatically, in a fragment from 1810 – "Philosophy is a high mountain road", an "isolated road" that "becomes ever more desolate, the higher we ascend": whoever takes this path "soon sees the world beneath him; its sandy deserts and morasses vanish from his view" (cf. *supra*, 2.10).[291]

Schopenhauer does not, however, intend to relegate that second viewpoint to the realm of mere theoretical *possibility*. Insofar as those who negate the will-to-life actually reach that point of view, and insofar as the historical *reality* of such a negation is explicitly recognized (with reference to the saints and mystics of

---

[289] Schopenhauer 2010b, I 486, pp. 438–439. Cf. Faggin 1951; Riconda 1972; Schirmacher 1988; Koßler 2008; Lemanski 2011, 2013.
[290] Schopenhauer 2010b, I 487, § 71, p. 439. On the theme of "nothing" in Romanticism in relation to Schopenhauer, cf. Fauth 2018, pp. 252–257. Cf. also the seminal essay by Lütkehaus 2014.
[291] MR 1, n. 20, p. 14.

all religions), that point of view is implicitly admitted as real; only for us, who have not (yet) denied the will-to-life, does it remain merely possible.

By admitting the reality of such a viewpoint, Schopenhauer inevitably admitted the reality of a "state" in which the absolutely opposite of the world appears or presents itself as something *positive*.[292] He thus managed *in extremis* to include in his mature system what as a young man he enthusiastically called "better consciousness", and which he now only describes negatively, as the nothing of all that we (as will-to-life) can ever experience, cognize and communicate. The opening to nothing thus understood constitutes the properly conclusive act, the last *possible* word of his philosophical discourse.

It is the faint and distant glow of this "nothing" that Schopenhauer, having reached the summit of philosophy, silently points out to those who have ascended with him, while almost everyone else, immersed in the gorge of "being" and its root (the will-to-life), is "still engulfed in dead of night".[293]

---

292 Cf. Schopenhauer 2018, II 702–703, chap. 48, pp. 626–627: "mystics proceed from their inner, positive, individual experience, in which they discover themselves to be the eternal, unique being, etc. […] when my teaching reaches its highest point, it assumes a negative character, and thus ends with a negation. It can, to be exact, speak only of what is denied, surrendered: it needs (at the end of the Fourth Book) to describe as nothing what is thereby gained and grasped, and can merely add the consolation that this is only a relative nothing, not an absolute one. For if something is nothing of all that we know, then it is certainly nothing at all for us. But this still does not mean that it is absolutely nothing, that it has to be nothing from every possible perspective and in every possible sense; but only that we are restricted to a wholly negative cognition of it, due very probably to the restrictions of our standpoint. – But this is precisely where the mystic proceeds positively [*positiv*]; from this point onwards, nothing remains but mysticism".
293 MR 1, n. 20, p. 14.

Bibliography of Works Cited

1 Schopenhauer's Works

D'Alfonso, Matteo Vincenzo, ed. 2008. *Schopenhauers Kollegnachschriften der Metaphysik-und Psychologievorlesungen von G. E. Schulze (Göttingen 1810–11)*. Würzburg: Ergon.
Lütkehaus, Ludger, ed. 1988. *Arthur Schopenhauers Reisetagebücher*. Zürich: Haffmans.
Lütkehaus, Ludger, ed. 1991. *Die Schopenhauers. Der Familien-Briefwechsel von Adele, Arthur, Heinrich Floris und Johanna Schopenhauer*. Zürich: Haffmans.
Schopenhauer-Archiv, https://sammlungen.ub.uni-frankfurt.de/schopenhauer
Schopenhauer, Arthur. 1819. *Die Welt als Wille und Vorstellung: vier Bücher, nebst einem Anhange, der die Kritik der Kantischen Philosophie enthält*. Leipzig: Brockhaus.
Schopenhauer, Arthur. 1844. *Die Welt als Wille und Vorstellung. Zweite, durchgängig verbesserte und sehr vermehrte Auflage*, 2 vols. Leipzig: Brockhaus.
Schopenhauer, Arthur. 1859. *Die Welt als Wille und Vorstellung. Dritte, verbesserte und beträchtlich vermehrte Auflage*, 2 vols. Leipzig: Brockhaus.
Schopenhauer, Arthur. 1911–1942. *Arthur Schopenhauers sämtliche Werke*, edited by Paul Deussen, vol. I–VI, IX–XI, XIII–XVI. Munich: R. Piper.
Schopenhauer, Arthur. 1978a. *Gesammelte Briefe*, edited by Arthur Hübscher. Bonn: Bouvier.
Schopenhauer, Arthur. 1978b. *Preisschrift über die Freiheit des Willens*, edited by Hans Ebeling. Hamburg: Meiner.
Schopenhauer, Arthur. 1985. *Der handschriftliche Nachlaß*, edited by Arthur Hübscher, 5 vols. Munich: Deutscher Taschenbuch Verlag.
Schopenhauer, Arthur. 1988. *Sämtliche Werke. Nach der ersten, von Julius Frauenstädt besorgten Gesamtausgabe neu bearbeitet*, 7 vols., edited by Arthur Hübscher. Mannheim: Brockhaus.
Schopenhauer, Arthur. 2017–2021. *Vorlesung über Die gesamte Philosophie*, 4 vols., edited by Daniel Schubbe. Hamburg: Meiner.
Schopenhauer, Arthur. 2020. *Die Welt als Wille und Vorstellung. Kritische Jubiläumsausgabe der ersten Auflage von 1819 mit den Zusätzen von Arthur Schopenhauer aus seinem Handexemplar*, edited by Matthias Koßler and William Massei Junior. Hamburg: Meiner.
Stollberg, Jochen and Wolfgang Böker, eds. 2013. *"… die Kunst zu sehn". Arthur Schopenhauers Mitschriften der Vorlesungen Johann Friedrich Blumenbachs (1809–1811)*. Göttingen: Universitätsverlag.

2 English Translations of Schopenhauer's Works

Schopenhauer, Arthur. 1988a. *Manuscript Remains*, vol. 1: *Early Manuscripts (1804–1818)*, edited by Arthur Hübscher, translated by E. F. J. Payne. Oxford/New York/Hamburg: Berg.
Schopenhauer, Arthur. 1988b. *Manuscript Remains*, vol. 2: *Critical Debates (1809–1818)*, edited by Arthur Hübscher, translated by E. F. J. Payne. Oxford/New York/Hamburg: Berg.
Schopenhauer, Arthur. 1989. *Manuscript Remains*, vol. 3: *Berlin Manuscripts (1818–1830)*, edited by Arthur Hübscher, translated by E. F. J. Payne. Oxford/New York/Munich: Berg.

Schopenhauer, Arthur. 1990. *Manuscript Remains*, vol. 4: *The Manuscript Books of 1830–1852 and Last Manuscripts*, edited by Arthur Hübscher, translated by E. F. J. Payne. Oxford, New York and Munich: Berg.
Schopenhauer, Arthur. 2009. *The Two Fundamental Problems of Ethics*, edited by Christopher Janaway. Cambridge: Cambridge University Press.
Schopenhauer, Arthur. 2010a. *On Vision and Colors*. New York: Princeton Architectural Press.
Schopenhauer, Arthur. 2010b. *The World as Will and Representation*, vol. 1, translated and edited by Judith Norman, Alistair Welchman, and Christopher Janaway. Cambridge: Cambridge University Press.
Schopenhauer, Arthur. 2012. *On the Fourfold Root of the Principle of Sufficient Reason and Other Writings*, translated and edited by David E. Cartwright, Edward E. Erdmann, and Christopher Janaway. Cambridge: Cambridge University Press.
Schopenhauer, Arthur. 2014. *Parerga and Paralipomena. Short Philosophical Essays*, vol. 1, translated and edited by Sabine Roehr and Christopher Janaway. Cambridge: Cambridge University Press.
Schopenhauer, Arthur. 2015. *Parerga and Paralipomena. Short Philosophical Essays*, vol. 2, translated and edited by A. Del Caro and Christopher Janaway. Cambridge: Cambridge University Press.
Schopenhauer, Arthur. 2018. *The World as Will and Representation*, vol. 2, translated and edited by Judith Norman, Alistair Welchman, and Christopher Janaway. Cambridge: Cambridge University Press.

3 Primary Literature

Anonymous. 1797. *Herzensergießungen eines kunstliebenden Klosterbruders*. Berlin: Unger.
Anonymous. 1799. *An meinen Sohn H.* Hamburg: Friedrich Perthes.
Anquetil-Duperron, Abraham Hyacinth. 1801–1802. *Oupnek'hat (id est, secretum tegendum)*, 2 vols. Argentorati: Levrault.
Aristotle. 1926 ff. *Aristotle in 23 Volumes*. Cambridge (MA): Harvard University Press; London: William Heinemann.
Arnim, Hans von, ed. 2016. *Stoicorum veterum fragmenta*, III. Eugene (OR): Wipf and Stock.
Augustine. 1964. *Of True Religion*, translated by John H. S. Burleigh. Chicago: Henry Regnery.
Augustine. 1975. *De diversis quaestionibus octoginta tribus: De octo dulcitii quaestionibus*. Turnhout: Brepols.
Augustine. 1998. *The City of God Against the Pagans*, edited by Robert W. Dyson. Cambridge: Cambridge University Press.
Brucker, Johann Jakob. 1723. *Historia Philosophica Doctrinae de Ideis*. Augusta: Dav. Raym Mertz et I. Iac. Mayer.
Cicero, Marcus Tullius. 1927. *Tusculan Disputations*, translated by John E. King. Cambridge (MA): Harvard University Press.
Claudius, Matthias. 1990. *Ausgewählte Werke*, edited by Wilhelm Münz. Stuttgart: Reclam.
Dara Shikoh, Muhammad. 1929. *Majma 'Ul-Bahrain: The Mingling of the Two Oceans*, edited in the original Persian with English Translations, Notes and Variants by Mahfuz-Ul-Haq. Calcutta: The Asiatic Society.
Di Giovanni, George and Henry S. Harris, eds. 2000. *Between Kant and Hegel: Texts in the Development of Post-Kantian Idealism*. Indianapolis: Hackett.

Eckhart, Meister. 2009. *The Complete Mystical Works by Meister Eckhart*, translated by Maurice O'C Walshe. New York: Crossroad.
Euripides. 1994. *Euripides, with an English Translation by David Kovacs*. Cambridge (MA): Harvard University Press.
Fichte, Johann Gottlieb. 1794. *Grundlage der gesammten Wissenschaftslehre*. Leipzig: Gabler.
Fichte, Johann Gottlieb. 1798. *Das System der Sittenlehre nach den Principien der Wissenschaftslehre*. Jena/Leipzig: Gabler.
Fichte, Johann Gottlieb. 1806a. *Die Anweisung zum seeligen Leben oder auch die Religionslehre*. Berlin: Reimer.
Fichte, Johann Gottlieb. 1806b. *Die Grundzüge des gegenwärtigen Zeitalters*. Berlin: Realschulbuchhandlung.
Fichte, Johann Gottlieb. 1849. *The Way Towards the Blessed Life; or, The Doctrine of Religion*, translated by William Smith. London: John Chapman.
Fichte, Johann Gottlieb. 1962 ff. *Gesamtausgabe der Bayerischen Akademie der Wissenschaften*, 42 vols., edited by Reinhard Lauth, Hans Gliwitzky, Hans Jacob, Erich Fuchs, Peter K. Schneider and Günter Zöller. Stuttgart-Bad Cannstatt: Frommann-Holzboog.
Fichte, Johann Gottlieb. 1992. *Foundations of Transcendental Philosophy*, translated and edited by Daniel Breazeale. Ithaca/London: Cornell University Press.
Fichte, Johann Gottlieb. 1994. *Introductions to Wissenschaftslehre and Other Writings (1797–1800)*, edited by Daniel Breazeale. Indianapolis/Cambridge: Hackett.
Fichte, Johann Gottlieb. 2003. *The Science of Knowledge*, translated and edited by Peter Heath and John Lachs. Cambridge: Cambridge University Press.
Fichte, Johann Gottlieb. 2005. *The System of Ethics: According to the Principles of the Wissenschaftslehre*, edited by Daniel Breazeale and Günter Zöller. Cambridge: Cambridge University Press.
Fries, Johann Friedrich. 1807. *Neue Kritik der Vernunft*, 3 vols. Heidelberg: Mohr und Zimmer.
Goethe, Johann Wolfgang von. 1840. *Theory of Colours*, translated by Charles Lock Eastlake. London: John Murray.
Goethe, Johann Wolfgang von. 1874. *Wilhelm Meister's Apprenticeship and Travels*, translated from the German of Goethe by Thomas Carlyle, Book VI. Frankfurt a. M.: Insel.
Goethe, Johann Wolfgang von. 1989. *Sämtliche Werke nach Epochen seines Schaffens*, Münchner Ausgabe, 21 parts in 33 vols. Munich/Vienna: Hanser.
Goethe, Johann Wolfgang von. 2014. *Faust I and II*, edited and translated by Stuart Atkins. Princeton and Oxford: Princeton University Press.
Hamann, Johann Georg. 1762. *Kreuzzüge der Philologen*. Königsberg: Kanter.
Hamann, Johann Georg. 2002. "Aesthetica in nuce: A Rhapsody in Cabbalistic Prose". In *Classic and Romantic German Aesthetics*, edited by Jay M. Bernstein. 1–24. Cambridge: Cambridge University Press.
Hoffmann, Ernst Theodor Amadeus. 1810. "Rezension. Sinfonie pour 2 Violons, 2 Violes, Violoncelle et Contre- Violon, 2 Flûtes, petite Flûte, 2 Hautbois, 2 Clarinettes, 2 Bassons, Contrebasson, 2 Cors, 2 Trompettes, Timbales et 5 Trompes, composée et dediée etc. par Louis van Beethoven. à Leipsic, chez Breitkopf et Härtel, Oeuvre 67. No. 5. des Sinfonies". *Allgemeine musikalische Zeitung* 12(40): 630–642 and (41): 652–659.
Hoffmann, Ernst Theodor Amadeus. 1989. *Musical Writings: Kreisleriana, The Poet and the Composer. Music Criticism*, edited by David Charlton. Cambridge: Cambridge University Press.
Huber, Therese. 1800. *Die Frau von vierzig Jahren*. Vienna: Pichler.

Huber, Viktor Aimé, ed. 1830–1833. *Erzählungen von Therese Huber*, 6 vols. Leipzig: Brockhaus.
Jacobi, Friedrich Heinrich. 1787. *David Hume über den Glauben, oder Idealismus und Realismus*. Breslau: Loewe.
Jacobi, Friedrich Heinrich. 1811. *Von den göttlichen Dingen und ihrer Offenbarung*. Leipzig: Fleischer.
Jacobi, Friedrich Heinrich. 1998 ff. *Werke. Gesamtausgabe*, edited by Klaus Hammacher and Walter Jaeschke. Hamburg/Stuttgart: Meiner.
Kant, Immanuel. 1799. *Critik der reinen Vernunft*. Leipzig: Hartknoch.
Kant, Immanuel. 1838–42. *Sämmtliche Werke*, edited by Karl Rosenkranz and Friedrich Wilhelm Schubert, 12 vols., Leipzig: Voss.
Kant, Immanuel. 1900 ff. *Gesammelte Schriften*, edited by Königlich Preußische Akademie der Wissenschaften (vol. 1–16), Preußische Akademie der Wissenschaften (vol. 17–22), Deutsche Akademie der Wissenschaften zu Berlin and/or Akademie der Wissenschaften zu Göttingen (vol. 23–25 and 27–29), and Berlin-Brandenburgische Akademie der Wissenschaften (vol. 26). Berlin: Reimer and De Gruyter.
Kant, Immanuel. 1996a. *Critique of Practical Reason*. In Immanuel Kant: *Practical Philosophy*, edited by Mary J. Gregor. Cambridge: Cambridge University Press.
Kant, Immanuel. 1996b. *Groundwork of the Metaphysics of Morals*. In Immanuel Kant: *Practical Philosophy*, edited by Mary J. Gregor. Cambridge: Cambridge University Press.
Kant, Immanuel. 1996c. "The End of All Things". In Immanuel Kant: *Religion and Rational Theology*, translated and edited by Allen W. Wood, George Di Giovanni. 217–232. Cambridge: Cambridge University Press.
Kant, Immanuel. 1998. *Critique of Pure Reason*, translated and edited by Paul Guyer and Allen W. Wood. Cambridge: Cambridge University Press.
Kant, Immanuel. 2000. *Critique of the Power of Judgment*, edited by Paul Guyer, translated by Eric Matthews. Cambridge: Cambridge University Press.
Kant, Immanuel. 2012. *Prolegomena to Any Future Metaphysics*, edited by Gary Hatfield. Cambridge: Cambridge University Press.
Klaproth Julius, ed. 1802. *Asiatisches Magazin*. Weimar: Verlag des Industrie-Comptoirs.
Lafontaine, August H. J. 1798. *Quinctius Heymeran von Flaming*. Berlin: Vossische Buchhandlung.
Laks, André and Glenn W. Most, eds. 2016. *Early Greek Philosophy*, vol. IX. Cambridge (MA): Harvard University Press.
Leopardi, Giacomo. 1991. *Zibaldone di pensieri*, critical and annotated edition by Giuseppe Pacella, 3 vols. Milan: Garzanti.
Locke, John. 1975. *An Essay Concerning Human Understanding* (1690). Oxford: Clarendon Press.
Luther, Martin. 1883–2009. *D. Martin Luthers Werke. Kritische Gesamtausgabe*, edited by Joachim Karl Friedrich Knaake et al., 120 vols. Weimar: H. Bölhaus Nachfolger.
Mainländer, Philipp. 1996. "Philosophie der Erlösung (1876)". In Philipp Mainländer: *Schriften*, vol. 1, edited by Winfried H. Müller-Seyfarth, 4 vols. Hildesheim/Zürich/New York: Olms.
Majer, Friedrich, ed. 1802. "Der Bhaguat-Geeta, oder Gespräche zwischen Kreeshna und Arjoon". In *Asiatisches Magazin*, edited by Julius Klaproth, vol. 1, 406–453; vol. 2, 105–135, 229–255, 273–293, and 454–490. Weimar: Verlag des Industrie-Comptoirs.
Milton, John. 1731. *Poetical Works*, 2 vols. London.
Mischel, Friedrich, ed. 1882. *Das Oupnek'hat. Die aus den Veden zusammengefaßte Lehre von dem Brahm*. Dresden: Heinrich.
Naubert, Benedikte. 1793–1797. *Almé oder Ägyptische Märchen*, 5 parts. Leipzig: Beygang (published anonymously).

Nietzsche, Friedrich. 1967 ff. *Werke*. Kritische Gesamtausgabe, edited by Giorgio Colli and Mazzino Montinari. Berlin/New York: De Gruyter.
Nietzsche, Friedrich. 1998. "On Schopenhauer". In *Willing and Nothingness: Schopenhauer as Nietzsche's Educator*, edited by Chritopher Janaway. 258–265. New York: Oxford University Press.
Novalis (Georg Philipp Friedrich Freiherr von Hardenberg). 1842. *Henry of Ofterdingen: A Romance*, translated by Frederick S. Stallknecht and Edward C. Sprague. Cambridge (MA): John Owen.
Novalis (Georg Philipp Friedrich Freiherr von Hardenberg). 1996. "Pollen". In *The Early Political Writings of the German Romantics*, edited by Frederick C. Beiser. Cambridge: Cambridge University Press.
Ovid. 1998. *Metamorphoses*, translated by A. D. Melville and edited, with introduction and notes by E. J. Kenney. Oxford: Oxford University Press.
Paul, Jean. 1801–1804. *Friedrich Richters Geist, oder Chrestomathie der vorzüglichen Stellen aus seinen Schriften*. Weimar/Erfurt: G. J. Cotta.
Paul, Jean. 1990 [1804]. *Vorschule der Ästhetik*, edited by Wolfhart Henckmann. Hamburg: Meiner.
Pico della Mirandola. 2012. *Oration on the Dignity of Man*, edited by Francesco Borghesi, Micheal Papio and Massimo Riva. Cambridge: Cambridge University Press.
Plato. 1781–1787. *Platonis philosophi quae exstant Graece ed editionem Henrici Stephani accurate expressa cum Marsilii Ficini interpretatione. Praemittitur L. III Laertii de vita et dogmatibus Platonis cum notitia literaria. Accedit varietas lectionis*, Stud. Soc. Bip. Biponti, ex Typographia Societatis, I–XII.
Plato. 1804 ff. *Platons Werke*, edited by Friedrich Schleiermacher, Part I, 2 vols. 1804–1805. Berlin: Realschulbuchhandlung; Part II, 3 vols. 1804–1809. Berlin: Realschulbuchhandlung; Dritter Theil, 1828. Berlin: Reimer.
Plato. 1914 ff. *Plato in Twelve Volumes*. vol. 1, 2017; vol. 3, 1924; vol. 5, 2013; vol. 6, 2013; vol. 7, 1921; vol. 8, 1927; vol. 9, 2022; vol. 11, 1926; vol. 12, 1921. Cambridge: (MA): Harvard University Press; London: William Heinemann.
Plotinus. 1969. *Porphyry on the Life of Plotinus and the Order of His Books. Enneads I*, translated by Arthur Hilary Armstrong. Cambridge (MA): Harvard University Press.
Plotinus. 2018. *The Enneads*, edited by Lloyd P. Gerson. Cambridge: Cambridge University Press.
Polier, Marie-Elisabeth de and Antoine-Louis-Henri (colonel de) Polier. 1809. *Mythologie des Indous*, vol. 1. Roudolstadt/Paris: Schoell.
Rätze, Johann Gottlieb. 1820. *Was der Wille des Menschen in moralischen und göttlichen Dingen aus eigener Kraft vermag und was er nicht vermag mit Rücksicht auf die Schopenhauerische Schrifft: Die Welt als Wille und Vorstellung*. Leipzig: Hartmann.
Reinhold, Karl Leonhard. 1790–1794. *Beyträge zur Berichtigung bisheriger Missverständnisse der Philosophen*, 2 vols. Jena: Mauke.
Reinhold, Karl Leonhard. 2013. "Versuch einer neuen Theorie des menschlichen Vorstellungsvermögens" (1789). In *Karl Leonhard Reinhold: Gesammelte Schriften*, vol. 1, edited by Martin Bondeli and Silvan Imhof. Basel: Schwabe.
Schelling, Friedrich Wilhelm Joseph von. 1798. *Von der Weltseele. Eine Hypothese der höheren Physik zur Erklärung des allgemeinen Organismus*. Hamburg: Perthes.
Schelling, Friedrich Wilhelm Joseph von. 1800. *System des transzendentalen Idealismus*. Tübingen: Cotta.
Schelling, Friedrich Wilhelm Joseph von. 1802. *Bruno oder über das göttliche und natürliche Princip der Dinge. Ein Gespräch*. Berlin: Unger.

Schelling, Friedrich Wilhelm Joseph von. 1803. *Ideen zu einer Philosophie der Natur.* Landshut: Krüll.
Schelling, Friedrich Wilhelm Joseph von. 1804. *Philosophie und Religion.* Tübingen: Cotta.
Schelling, Friedrich Wilhelm Joseph von. 1809. *Philosophische Schriften.* Landshut: Krüll.
Schelling, Friedrich Wilhelm Joseph von. 1856–1861. *Sämtliche Werke*, edited by Karl Friedrich August Schelling. Stuttgart: Cotta.
Schelling, Friedrich Wilhelm Joseph von. 1966. *On University Studies*, edited by Norbert Guterman, translated by Ella S. Morgan. Athens (OH): Ohio University Press.
Schelling, Friedrich Wilhelm Joseph von. 1976 ff. *Historisch-Kritische Ausgabe*, edited by Thomas Buchheim, Jochem Hennigfeld, Wilhelm G. Jacobs, Jörg Jantzen and Siegbert Peetz. Stuttgart-Bad Cannstatt: Frommann-Holzboog.
Schelling, Friedrich Wilhelm Joseph von. 1980. "Philosophical Letters on Dogmatism and Criticism". In *The Unconditional in Human Knowledge: Four Early Essays 1794–96*, translation and commentary by Fritz Marti. Lewisburg: Bucknell University Press.
Schelling, Friedrich Wilhelm Joseph von. 1984. *Bruno, or On the Natural and the Divine Principle of Things*, edited by Michael G. Vater. New York: SUNY Press.
Schelling, Friedrich Wilhelm Joseph von. 2001. *System of Transcendental Idealism*, translated by Peter Heath, with an Introduction by Michael G. Vater. Charlottesville: University Press of Virginia.
Schelling, Friedrich Wilhelm Joseph von. 2006. *Philosophical Investigations into the Essence of Human Freedom*, edited by Jeff Love and Johannes Schmidt. New York: SUNY Press.
Schelling, Friedrich Wilhelm Joseph von. 2010. *Philosophy and Religion*, edited by Klaus Ottmann. Putnam: Spring.
Schiller, Friedrich. 1988. "Grace and Dignity". In *Friedrich Schiller: Poet of Freedom*. 337–395. Washington, DC: Schiller Institute.
Schleiermacher, Friedrich. 2003. *On Religion: Speeches to Its Cultured Despisers*, edited by Richard Crouter. Cambridge: Cambridge University Press.
Schulze, Gottlob Ernst. 1792. *Aenesidemus, oder über die Fundamente der von dem Herrn Professor Reinhold in Jena gelieferten Elementar-Philosophie. Nebst einer Vertheidigung des Skeptizismus gegen die Anmaßungen der Vernunftkritik.* No location [partially translated in *Between Kant and Hegel: Texts in the Development of Post-Kantian Idealism*, edited by George di Giovanni and H. S. Harris. 104–135. Indianapolis: Hackett, 2000].
Schulze, Gottlob Ernst. 1801–1802. *Kritik der theoretischen Philosophie*, 2 vols. Hamburg: Bohm.
Schulze, Gottlob Ernst. 1916. "Über die vierfache Wurzel des Satzes vom zureichenden Grunde von A. Schopenhauer, Doctor der Philosophie. 1813. 8. 148 S". In *Göttingische Gelehrte Anzeigen*, 70. Stück, den 30 April 1814, 701–703, reprinted in *Schopenhauer-Jahrbuch* 5: 167–169.
Seneca, Lucius Annaeus. 1917. *Ad Lucilium Epistulae Morales*, vol. 1, translated by Richard M. Gummere. Cambridge (MA): Harvard University Press; London: William Heinemann.
Spener, Philipp Jacob. 1708. *Natur und Gnade.* Frankfurt a. M.: Zunner.
Sulzer, Johann Georg. 1778–1779. *Allgemeine Theorie der schönen Künste in einzeln, nach alphabetischer Ordnung der Kunstwörter auf einander folgenden Artikeln abgehandelt.* Leipzig: Weidmanns Erben und Reich.
Swete, Henry Barclay, ed. 1887. *The Old Testament in Greek According to the Septuagint*, vol. 1. Cambridge: Cambridge University Press.
Swete, Henry Barclay, ed. 1896. *The Old Testament in Greek According to the Septuagint*, vol. 2. Cambridge: Cambridge University Press.
Tennemann, Wilhelm Gottlieb. 1798–1819. *Geschichte der Philosophie*, vol. I–XI. Leipzig: Barth.

Tennemann, Wilhelm Gottlieb. 1825. *Grundriße der Geschichte der Philosophie für den akademischen Unterricht.* Leipzig: Barth.
Thomas Aquinas. 2019. *Thomas Aquinas's Quodlibetal Questions*, translated and introduced by Turner Nevitt and Brian Davies. New York: Oxford University Press.
Tieck, Ludwig. 1795–1796. *William Lovell.* 3 vols. Berlin/Leipzig: Nicolai.
Tieck, Ludwig, ed. 1799. *Phantasien über die Kunst, für Freunde der Kunst.* Hamburg: Perthes.
Verri, Pietro. 2001. *Discorso sull'indole del piacere e del dolore (1781)*, edited by Silvia Contarini. Rome: Carocci.
Wackenroder, Wilhelm Heinrich. 1799. *Phantasien über die Kunst für Freunde der Kunst*, edited by. Ludwig Tieck. Hamburg: Perthes.
Wackenroder, Wilhelm Heinrich. 1971a. *Wilhelm Heinrich Wackenroder's Confessions and Fantasies*, edited by Mary Hurst Schubert. University Park (PA): Pennsylvania State University Press.
Wackenroder, Wilhelm Heinrich. 1971b. "Fantasies on Art for Friends of Art". In *Wilhelm Heinrich Wackenroder's Confessions and Fantasies*, edited by Mary Hurst Schubert. 161–197. University Park (PA): Pennsylvania State University Press.
Wackenroder, Wilhelm Heinrich. 1975. *Outpourings of an Art Loving Friar*, edited by Edward Mornin. New York: Ungar.
Wackenroder, Wilhelm Heinrich. 1984. *Werke und Briefe*, edited by Gerda Heinrich. Munich: Hanser.
Werner, Zacharias. 1807. *Martin Luther, oder Die Weihe der Kraft.* Berlin: Sander.
Wieland, Christoph Martin. 1839–1840. *Sämmtliche Werke.* Leipzig: Göschen.

4 Secondary Literature

Adickes, Erich. 1924. *Kant und das Ding an sich.* Berlin: R. Heise.
Agar, Herbert. 1928. *Milton and Plato.* Princeton: Princeton University Press.
Aler, Jan. 1970. "Krise der Kunst – Kunst der Krise". *Schopenhauer-Jahrbuch* 51: 50–73.
Apollonio, Simona and Alessandro Novembre, eds. 2015. *Schopenhauer. Pensiero e fortuna.* Lecce: Pensa MultiMedia.
App, Urs. 1998a. "Notes and Excerpts by Schopenhauer Related to Volumes 1–9 of the Asiatick Researches". *Schopenhauer-Jahrbuch* 79: 11–33.
App, Urs. 1998b. "Schopenhauers Begegnung mit dem Buddhismus". *Schopenhauer-Jahrbuch* 79: 35–58.
App, Urs. 2003. "Notizen Schopenhauers zu Ost-, Nord- und Südostasien vom Sommersemester 1811". *Schopenhauer-Jahrbuch* 84: 13–39.
App, Urs. 2006a. "Schopenhauer's Initial Encounter with Indian Thought". *Schopenhauer-Jahrbuch* 87: 35–76.
App, Urs. 2006b. "Schopenhauer's India Notes of 1811". *Schopenhauer-Jahrbuch* 87: 15–31.
App, Urs. 2010a. "Arthur Schopenhauer und China: A Sino-Platonic Love Affair". *Sino-Platonic Papers* 200: 1–160
App, Urs. 2010b. *The Birth of Orientalism.* Philadelphia: University of Pennsylvania Press.
App, Urs. 2011. *Schopenhauers Kompass.* Rorschach/Kyoto: University Media.
App, Urs. 2012. "Required Reading: Schopenhauer's Favourite Book". *Schopenhauer-Jahrbuch* 93: 65–85.
Asmuth, Christoph. 1999. "Musik als Metaphysik. Platonische Idee, Kunst und Musik bei Arthur Schopenhauer". In *Philosophischer Gedanke und musikalischer Klang. Zum Wechselverhältnis von*

Musik und Philosophie, edited by Christoph Asmuth, Gunter Scholtz and Franz-Bernhard. 111–125. Frankfurt a. M./New York: Stammkötter Campus.

Asmuth, Christoph. 2006. *Interpretation-Transformation: Das Platonbild bei Fichte, Schelling, Hegel, Schleiermacher und Schopenhauer und das Legitimationsproblem der Philosophiegeschichte.* Göttingen: Vandenhoeck & Ruprecht.

Atwell, John E. 1995. *Schopenhauer. On the Character of the World. The Metaphysics of Will.* Berkeley/Los Angeles/London: University of California Press.

Atzert, Stephan. 2007. "Schopenhauer und seine Quellen. Zum Buddhismusbild in den frühen Asiatic Researches". *Schopenhauer-Jahrbuch* 88: 15–28.

Auweele, Dennis Vanden. 2017. "Schopenhauer and the Later Schelling in Dialogue on Mythology and Religion". *Journal of Religion* 97(4): 451–474.

Barbera, Sandro. 1998. *Il mondo come volontà e rappresentazione. Introduzione alla lettura.* Rome: Carocci.

Barbera, Sandro. 2004. *Une Philosophie du Conflit. Études sur Schopenhauer.* Paris: PUF.

Barbera, Sandro. 2009. "Schopenhauer und Schelling. Aufzeichnungen über den Begriff der Entzweiung des Willens". In *Schopenhauer und die Schopenhauer-Schule*, edited by Fabio Ciracì, Domenico M. Fazio, and Matthias Koßler. 73–87. Würzburg: Königshausen & Neumann.

Barbera, Sandro. 2010. "La prima critica di Nietzsche a Schopenhauer: una fonte", in S. Barbera, "Guarigioni, rinascite e metamorfosi. Studi su Goethe, Schopenhauer e Nietzsche". *Quaderni del Giornale Critico della Filosofia* 18: 119–134.

Barua, Arati. 2012. "Schopenhauer in the Light of Indian Philosophy: With a Special Reference to Sankara's Advaita Vedanta". *Schopenhauer-Jahrbuch* 93: 101–114.

Barua, Arati, Michael Gerhard, and Matthias Koßler, eds. 2013. *Understanding Schopenhauer through the Prism of Indian Culture.* Berlin/Boston: De Gruyter.

Bäschlin, Daniel Lukas. 1968. *Schopenhauers Einwand gegen Kants transzendentale Deduktion der Kategorien.* Meisenheim a. Glan: Hain.

Bastian, Michael. 2009. "Kritik der ruhenden Vernunft. Fichte, Schopenhauer und die Herausforderung der Gelassenheit". *Schopenhauer-Jahrbuch* 90: 117–145.

Baum, Günther. 1982. "Ding an sich und Erscheinung". In *Zeit der Ernte. Studien zum Stand der Schopenhauer-Forschung. Festschrift für Arthur Hübscher zum 85*, edited by Wolfgang Schirmacher. 201–211. Stuttgart: Bad Cannstatt.

Beiser, Frederick C. 2016. *Weltschmerz. Pessimism in German Philosophy.* Oxford: Oxford University Press.

Benchimol Barros, Márcio. 2014. "Classicismo e forma no pensamento estético de Schopenhauer". *Voluntas: Revista Internacional de Filosofia* 5(2): 3–20.

Benz, Richard. 1939. "Schopenhauer und die Romantik". *Deutscher Almanach für das Jahr 1939*: 113–131.

Beretta, Piergiorgio, ed. 1998. *Nuovo Testamento Interlineare Greco-Latino-Italiano.* Cinisello Balsamo: San Paolo.

Berg, Robert. 2003. *Objektiver Idealismus und Voluntarismus in der Metaphysik Schellings und Schopenhauers.* Würzburg: Königshausen & Neumann.

Berger, Douglas Leo. 2004. *The Veil of Maya: Schopenhauer's Theory of Falsification: The Key to Schopenhauer's Appropriation of Pre-Systematic Indian Philosophical Thought.* New York: Global Academic.

Bianco, Bruno, Mario Longo, Giuseppe Micheli, Giovanni Santinello, and Larry Steindler, eds. 1995. *Storia delle storie generali della filosofia.* 4. *L'età hegeliana.* I. *La storiografia filosofica tedesca.* Padua: Editrice Antenore.
Binkelmann, Christoph. 2015. "Derivierte Absolutheit. Die Bedeutung des transzendentalen Idealismus Fichtes für Schellings Freiheitsschrift". *Schelling-Studien* 3: 115–131.
Birnbacher, Dieter. 2009. "Ambivalenzen in Schopenhauers Freiheitslehre". In *Schopenhauer und die Schopenhauer-Schule*, edited by Fabio Ciracì, Domenico M. Fazio, and Matthias Koßler. 89–99. Würzburg: Königshausen & Neumann.
Birnbacher, Dieter. 2010. "Arthur Schopenhauer – Freiheit und Unfreiheit des Willens". In *Klassiker der Philosophie heute*, edited by Ansgar Beckermann and Dominik Perler. 478–496. Stuttgart: Reclam.
Birnbacher, Dieter. 2020. "Schopenhauers Metaphysik: Von der Intuition zur Induktion". In *Das Hauptwerk. 200 Jahre Arthur Schopenhauers* Die Welt als Wille und Vorstellung, edited by Dieter Birnbacher and Matthias Koßler. 119–136. Würzburg: Königshausen & Neumann.
Birnbacher, Dieter and Günther Baum, eds. 2005. *Schopenhauer und die Künste.* Göttingen: Wallstein.
Birnbacher, Dieter and Matthias Koßler, eds. 2022. *Das Hauptwerk. 200 Jahre Arthur Schopenhauers* Die Welt als Wille und Vorstellung. Würzburg: Königshausen & Neumann.
Blondin, Marie-Michèle. 2019. *Vivre et vivre encore: La notion de vie chez Arthur Schopenhauer.* Hildesheim: Olms.
Bohinc, Thomas. 1989. *Die Entfesselung des Intellekts: eine Untersuchung über die Möglichkeit der An-sich-Erkenntnis in der Philosophie Arthur Schopenhauers unter besonderer Berücksichtigung des Nachlasses und entwicklungsgeschichtlicher Aspekte.* Frankfurt a. M.: Lang.
Bondeli, Martin. 2014. *Reinhold und Schopenhauer. Zwei Denkwelten im Banne von Vorstellung und Wille.* Basel: Schwabe.
Bonheim, Günther and Thomas Regehly, eds. 2008. *Philosophien des Willens. Böhme, Schelling, Schopenhauer.* Berlin: Weißensee.
Booms, Martin. 2003. *Aporie und Subjekt. Die erkenntnistheoretische Entfaltungslogik der Philosophie Schopenhauers.* Würzburg: Königshausen & Neumann.
Bottin, Francesco, Mario Longo, and Gregorio Piaia, eds. 1979. *Storia delle storie generali della filosofia*, vol. 2: *Dall'età cartesiana a Brucker.* Brescia: La Scuola.
Brianese, Giorgio. 2013. "Dire di no al mondo. La metafisica immanente di Schopenhauer". In *Arthur Schopenhauer: Supplementi a "Il mondo come volontà e rappresentazione"*, edited by Giorgio Brianese. VII–XXXIII. Turin: Einaudi.
Brown, Raymon E., Joseph A. Fitzmyer, and Roland E. Murphy, eds. 1990. *The New Jerome Biblical Commentary*, Englewood Cliffs (NJ): Longman.
Cacciola, Maria Lucia. 1994. *Schopenhauer e a questão do dogmatismo.* São Paulo: Edusp.
Caldeira Ramos, Flamarion. 2018. "Filosofia transcendental e metafísica da vontade: a crítica de Schopenhauer ao conceito kantiano de metafísica". *Revista de Filosofia Aurora* 30(49): 111–130.
Campioni, Giuliano, Leonardo Pica Ciamarra, and Marco Segala, eds. 2011. *Goethe, Schopenhauer, Nietzsche. Saggi in memoria di Sandro Barbera.* Pisa: ETS.
Carl, Wolfgang. 2013. "Kants kopernikanische Wende". In *Kant und die Philosophie in Weltbürgerlicher Absicht: Akten des* XI. *Kant-Kongresses 2010*, edited by Stefano Bacin, Alfredo Ferrarin, Claudio La Rocca, Margit Ruffing. 163–178. Berlin/Boston: De Gruyter.
Cartwright, David E. 2001. "Two Senses of 'Thing-in-Itself' in Schopenhauer's Philosophy". *Idealistic Studies* 31(1): 31–54.
Cartwright, David E. 2010. *Schopenhauer: A Biography.* Cambridge: Cambridge University Press.

Cartwright, David E. 2018. "Becoming the Author of *World as Will and Representation*: Schopenhauer's Life and Education 1788–1818". In *The Palgrave Schopenhauer Handbook*, edited by Sandra Shapshay. 11–41. London: Palgrave Macmillan.

Cavallini, Simone. 2018. "Der epistemologische Wert von Schopenhauers Pessimismus und seine Bedeutung für die Gegenwart". *Schopenhaueriana. Revista española de estudios sobre Schopenhauer* 3: 67–104.

Chenet, François-Xavier. 1997. "Conscience empirique et conscience meilleure chez le jeune Schopenhauer". *Les Cahiers de l'Herne* 69: 103–130.

Ciracì, Fabio, Domenico Fazio, and Matthias Koßler, eds. 2009. *Schopenhauer und die Schopenhauer-Schule*. Würzburg: Königshausen & Neumann.

Cross, Stephen. 2013. *Schopenhauer's Encounter with Indian Thought. Representation and Will and Their Indian Parallels*. Honolulu: University of Hawai'i Press.

Cysarz, Herbert. 1981. "Schopenhauers 'Intelligibler Charakter' und die Individualitätsproblematik der Folgezeit". *Schopenhauer-Jahrbuch* 62: 91–107.

D'Alfonso, Matteo Vincenzo. 2006. "Schopenhauer als Schüler Fichtes". *Fichte-Studien* 30(3): 201–211.

D'Alfonso, Matteo Vincenzo. 2008. "Schopenhauer als Schüler Schulzes: Die Vorlesungen zur Metaphysik und Psychologie in Göttingen 1810–11". In *Schopenhauers Kollegnachschriften der Metaphysik- und Psychologievorlesungen von G. E. Schulze (Göttingen 1810–11)*, edited by Matteo Vincenzo d'Alfonso. 7–34. Würzburg: Ergon.

D'Alfonso, Matteo Vincenzo. 2009. "Schopenhauer als Schüler Schulzes: Die Vorlesungen zur Metaphysik". In *Schopenhauer und die Schopenhauer-Schule*, edited by Fabio Ciracì, Domenico M. Fazio, and Matthias Koßler. 61–72. Würzburg: Königshausen & Neumann.

D'Alfonso, Matteo Vincenzo. 2011. "Schopenhauer e Goethe. Il battesimo di un inattuale". In *Goethe, Schopenhauer, Nietzsche. Saggi in memoria di Sandro Barbera*, edited by Giuliano Campioni, Leonardo Pica Ciamarra, and Marco Segala. 143–156. Pisa: ETS.

D'Alfonso, Matteo Vincenzo. 2015. "Erfahrung und Erkenntnis. Die Rolle der Kategorien in Schopenhauers Dissertation von 1813". In *Schopenhauers Wissenschaftstheorie: "Der Satz vom Grund"*, edited by Dieter Birnbacher. 29–44. Würzburg: Königshausen & Neumann.

D'Alfonso, Matteo Vincenzo. 2020. "Die 'Zerstörung' der praktischen Vernunft in den frühen Notizen Arthur Schopenhauers". In *Das Transzendentale und die praktische Philosophie*, edited by Giovanni Cogliandro, Carla De Pascale, and Ives Radrizzani. 173–183. Hildesheim/Zürich/New York: Olms.

Debona, Vilmar. 2020. *A outra face do pessimismo: Caráter, ação e sabedoria de vida em Schopenhauer*. São Paulo: Edições Loyola.

Decher, Friedhelm. 1996. "Das 'beßre Bewußtsein': Zur Funktion eines Begriffs in der Genese der Schopenhauerschen Philosophie". *Schopenhauer-Jahrbuch* 77: 65–83.

Decher, Friedhelm. 1990. "Schopenhauer und Fichtes Schrift 'Die Bestimmung des Menschen'". *Schopenhauer-Jahrbuch* 71: 45–67.

De Cian, Nicoletta. 2002. *Redenzione, colpa, salvezza. All'origine della filosofia di Schopenhauer*. Trento: Verifiche.

De Cian, Nicoletta. 2009. "Introduzione". In *G. E. Schulze: Vorlesung über Metaphysik, nach der Nachschrift von A. Schopenhauer/Corso di Metafisica secondo il manoscritto di A. Schopenhauer*. Transcription of the manuscript by N. de Cian and J. Stollberg, Introduction, translation and notes by N. De Cian. VII-LXVII. Trento: Ass. Trentina di Scienze Umane.

De Cian, Nicoletta. 2011. "Il ruolo della Critica del giudizio nell'elaborazione della filosofia schopenhaueriana della redenzione". In *Goethe, Schopenhauer, Nietzsche. Saggi in memoria di*

Sandro Barbera, edited by Giuliano Campioni, Leonardo Pica Ciamarra, and Marco Segala. 167–179. Pisa: ETS.
De Cian, Nicoletta and Marco Segala. 2002. "What Is Will?" *Schopenhauer-Jahrbuch* 83: 13–42.
Deligne, Alain. 1991. "Système et éthique chez Schopenhauer et Schleiermacher". *Schopenhauer-Jahrbuch* 72: 28–36.
De Lorenzo, Giuseppe. 1923. *Leopardi e Schopenhauer*. Naples: Riccardi.
De Pascale, Carla. 1994, "Die Trieblehre bei Fichte". *Fichte-Studien* 6(1): 229–251.
De Pascale, Carla. 2012. "Fichtes Einfluß auf Schopenhauer". *Fichte-Studien* 36(1): 45–59.
De Sanctis, Francesco. 1858. "Schopenhauer e Leopardi. Dialogo fra A e D". *Rivista Contemporanea* 15(2): 369–408.
Deussen, Paul. 1915. "Schopenhauer und die Religion". *Schopenhauer-Jahrbuch* 4: 8–16.
Dobrzański, Michał. 2017. *Begriff und Methode bei Arthur Schopenhauer*. Würzburg: Königshausen & Neumann.
Döll, Heinrich. 1904. *Goethe und Schopenhauer. Ein Beitrag zur Entwicklungsgeschichte der Schopenhauerschen Philosophie*. Berlin: Hofmann.
Donà, Massimo. 2013. *Misterio grande. Filosofia di Giacomo Leopardi*. Milan: Bompiani.
Doran, Robert. 2015. *The Theory of the Sublime from Longinus to Kant*. Cambridge: Cambridge University Press.
Durante, Felipe. 2014. "*La formulazione delle dottrine dello Stato e del diritto del giovane Schopenhauer*". In *Schopenhauer. Pensiero e Fortuna*, edited by Simona Apollonio and Alessandro Novembre. 85–96. Lecce: Pensa MultiMedia.
Dürr, Thomas. 2003. "Schopenhauers Grundlegung der Metaphysik". *Schopenhauer-Jahrbuch* 84: 91–119.
Ebeling, Hans. 1978. "Schopenhauers Theorie der Freiheit". In Arthur Schopenhauer: *Preisschrift über die Freiheit des Willens*, edited by Hans Ebeling. VII–XXII. Hamburg: Meiner.
Elon, Daniel. 2018. "Gottlob Ernst Schulzes skeptizistische Kant-Kritik in ihrer Relevanz für Arthur Schopenhauers Systemkonstitution". *Kant-Studien* 109(1): 124–146.
Eschmann, Erik. 2021. "'Von Innen oder von Außen, vom Centro oder von der Peripherie aus'. Schopenhauers Philosophie von Standpunkt aus einer perspektivistischen Lesart". *Schopenhauer-Jahrbuch* 102: 67–86.
Eschmann, Erik. 2022a. *Die Natur als Produktivität und Wille: Zur Naturphilosophie Schellings und Naturmetaphysik Schopenhauers aus prozessphilosophischer Perspektive*. Würzburg: Königshausen & Neumann.
Eschmann, Erik. 2022b. "Was meint 'Die Welt als Wille und Vorstellung'? Zur Bedeutung des Titels aus Perspektive der Schopenhauerschen Logik". In *Das neue Jahrhundert Schopenhauers: Akten des Internationalen Forschungsprojekts anlässlich des 200. Jubiläums von* Die Welt als Wille und Vorstellung *2018–2020*, edited by Yoichiro Takahashi, Takao Ito, and Tsunafumi Takeuchi. 251–261. Würzburg: Königshausen & Neumann.
Faggin, Giuseppe. 1951. *Schopenhauer: il mistico senza Dio*. Florence: La Nuova Italia.
Fauth, Søren R. 2018. "Romantik". In *Schopenhauer-Handbuch. Leben – Werk – Wirkung*, edited by Daniel Schubbe and Matthias Koßler. 256–261. Stuttgart: Metzler.
Fincham, Richard. 2000. "The Impact of Aenesidemus upon Fichte and Schopenhauer". In *The Warwick Journal of Philosophy* 10: 96–126.
Fischer, Ernst. 1901. *Von G. E. Schulze zu A. Schopenhauer. Ein Beitrag zur Geschichte der Kantischen Erkenntnistheorie*. Aarau: Saulerländer.
Florig, Oliver. 2010. *Schellings Theorie menschlicher Selbstformierung*. Freiburg im Breisgau: Karl Alber.

Fortlage, Carl. 1852. *Genetische Geschichte der Philosophie seit Kant*. Leipzig: Brockhaus.
Furlani, Simone. 2004. *L'ultimo Fichte. Il sistema della dottrina della scienza negli anni 1810–1814*. Milan: Guerini e Associati.
Garewicz, Jan. 1987. "Schopenhauer und Böhme". In *Schopenhauer im Denken der Gegenwart. 23 Beiträge zu seiner Aktualität*, edited by Volker Spierling. 71–80. Munich/Zürich: Piper.
Gebrecht, Raphael. 2021. "Ästhetische Subjektivität als Übergang von der Natur zur Freiheit. Schopenhauers Verhältnis zu Kants Kritik der Urteilskraft". *Schopenhauer-Jahrbuch* 102: 87–112.
Gerhard, Michael. 2008. "Im Spiegelkabinett des Nichts. Wille, Ungrund, fanā, brahman und nirvāṇa". In *Philosophien des Willens. Böhme, Schelling, Schopenhauer*, edited by Günther Bonheim and Thomas Regehly. 105–140. Berlin: Weißensee.
Gerhard, Michael. 2013. "Suspected of Buddhism. Śaṅkara, Dārāṣekoh and Schopenhauer". In *Understanding Schopenhauer through the Prism of Indian Culture*, edited by Arati Barua, Michael Gerhard, and Matthias Koßler. 31–62. Berlin/Boston: De Gruyter.
Gerhardt, Volker, 1988. "Die kopernikanische Wende bei Kant und Nietzsche". In *Kant und Nietzsche – Vorspiel einer künftigen Weltauslegung?*, edited by Jörg Albertz. 157–182. Wiesbaden: Freie Akademie.
Giacoia Junior, Oswaldo. 2011. "La fiaba della libertà intelligibile e l'innocenza del divenire". In *Goethe, Schopenhauer, Nietzsche. Saggi in memoria di Sandro Barbera*, edited by Giuliano Campioni, Leonardo Pica Ciamarra, and Marco Segala. 349–369. Pisa: ETS.
Giametta, Sossio. 2008. "Introduzione". In Arthur Schopenhauer: *I due problemi fondamentali dell'etica*, edited by S. Giametta. XXI–LXII. Milan: Mondadori.
Giametta, Sossio. 2012. *Il bue squartato*. Milan: Mursia.
Giametta, Sossio. 2013. *L'oro prezioso dell'essere*. Milan: Mursia.
Giordanetti, Piero. 2001. *Kant e la musica*. Milan: CUEM.
Giordanetti, Piero, Riccardo Pozzo, and Marco Sgarbi, eds. 2012. *Kant's Philosophy of the Unconscious*. Berlin/New York: De Gruyter.
Gjellerup, Karl. 1919. "Zur Entwicklungsgeschichte der Schopenhauerschen Philosophie. Eine Studie über den elften Band der neueren Gesamtausgabe der Werke Schopenhauers ('Genesis des Systems')". *Annalen der Philosophie* 1: 495–517.
Glasenapp, Helmuth von. 1960. *Das Indienbild deutscher Denker*. Stuttgart: Koehler.
Göbel-Gross, Erhard. 1962. *Sirri akbar. Die persische Upaniṣadenübersetzung des Moġulprinzen Dārā Šukoh*. PhD diss., Marburg.
Göcke, Benedikt Paul. 2021. "Karl Christian Friedrich Krause Einfluss auf Arthur Schopenhauers 'Die Welt als Wille und Vorstellung'". In *Archiv für Geschichte der Philosophie* 103 (1): 148–168.
Goehr, Lydia. 1996. "Schopenhauer and the Musicians: An Inquiry into the Sounds of Silence and the Limits of Philosophizing about Music". In *Schopenhauer, Philosophy and the Arts*, edited by Dale Jacquette. 200–228. Cambridge: Cambridge University Press.
Grigenti, Fabio. 2000. *Natura e rappresentazione. Genesi e struttura della natura in Arthur Schopenhauer*. Naples: La Città del Sole.
Grigenti, Fabio. 2005. "Goethe, Schopenhauer e Wittgenstein: i colori e la filosofia". In *Arte, Scienza e natura in Goethe*, edited by Gian Franco Frigo, Raffaella Simili, Federico Vercellone, and Dietrich von Engelhardt. 205–236. Turin: Traube.
Grigenti, Fabio. 2021. "Goethe, Schopenhauer und Schelling Über die Farben". In *Schopenhauer liest Schelling. Freiheits- und Naturphilosophie im Ausgang der klassischen deutschen Philosophie. Mit einer Edition von Schopenhauers handschriftlichen Kommentaren zu Schellings "Freiheitsschrift"*,

edited by Philipp Höfele and Lore Hühn. 197–216. Stuttgart-Bad Cannstatt: Frommann-Holzboog.

Grimm, Jacob and Wilhelm Grimm (founders). 1854–1971. *Das Deutsche Wörterbuch*, 33 vols. Leipzig: Hirzel.

Guéroult, Martial. 1946. *Schopenhauer et Fichte*. Paris: Les Belles-Lettres.

Gurisatti, Giovanni. 2001. "Schopenhauer e la fisiognomica. Sul fondamento caratteriologico della sua metafisica". *Intersezioni* 21(1): 79–108.

Gurisatti, Giovanni. 2002. *Caratterologia, metafisica e saggezza. Lettura fisiognomica di Schopenhauer*. Padua: Il Poligrafo.

Gurisatti, Giovanni. 2007. "Schopenhauer e l'India". In Arthur Schopenhauer: *Il mio Oriente*, edited by Giovanni Gurisatti. 185–222. Milan: Adelphi.

Guyer, Paul. 2008. "Back to Truth: Knowledge and Pleasure in the Asthetics of Schopenhauer". *European Journal of Philosophy* 16: 164–178.

Gwinner, Wilhelm. 1878. *Schopenhauer's Leben. Zweite umgearbeitete und vielfach vermehrte Auflage der Schrift: Arthur Schopenhauer aus persönlichem Umgange dargestellt*. Leipzig: Brockhaus.

Halbfass, Wilhelm. 1988. *India and Europe: an Essay in Understanding*. New York: State University of New York Press.

Hallich, Oliver. 2002. "Die Entzifferung der Welt. Schopenhauer und die mittelalterliche Allegorese". In *Schopenhauer im Kontext. Deutsch-polnisches Schopenhauer-Symposion 2000*, edited by Dieter Birnbacher, Andreas Lorenz, and Leon Miodonski. 163–189. Würzburg: Königshausen & Neumann.

Hammacher, Klaus. 1994. "Jacobis Schrift 'Von den Göttlichen Dingen'". In *Religionsphilosophie und spekulative Theologie. Der Streit um die Göttlichen Dinge (1799–1812)*, edited by Walter Jaeschke. 129–141. Hamburg: Meiner.

Hasrat, Bikrama Jit. 1982. *Dārā Shikūh: Life and Works*. New Delhi: Munshiram Manoharlal.

Haym, Rudolf. 1864. *Arthur Schopenhauer*. Berlin: Reimer.

Hecker, Max F. 1897. *Schopenhauer und die indische Philosophie*. Cologne: Hübscher u. Teufel.

Heimann, Robert. 2013. *Die Genese der Philosophie Schopenhauers vor dem Hintergrund seiner Pseudo-Taulerrezeption*. Würzburg: Königshausen & Neumann.

Herbart, Johann Friedrich. 1820. "Die Welt als Wille und Vorstellung". In *Hermes oder Kritisches Jahrbuch der Literatur*. Drittes Stück für das Jahr 1820, n. 7: 131–147.

Höfele, Philipp. 2019. *Wollen und Lassen. Zur Ausdifferenzierung, Kritik und Rezeption des Willensparadigmas in der Philosophie Schellings*. Freiburg im Breisgau/Munich: Alber.

Höfele, Philipp and Lore Hühn, eds. 2021. *Schopenhauer liest Schelling. Freiheits- und Naturphilosophie im Ausgang der klassischen deutschen Philosophie. Mit einer Edition von Schopenhauers handschriftlichen Kommentaren zu Schellings "Freiheitsschrift"*. Stuttgart-Bad Cannstatt: Frommann-Holzboog.

Höfele, Philipp and Sebastian Schwenzfeuer. 2021. "Arthur Schopenhauers handschriftliche Kommentare zu F. W. J. Schelling: *Philosophische Untersuchungen über das Wesen der menschlichen Freyheit und die damit zusammenhängenden Gegenstände* – Textkritisch ediert, mit erklärenden Anmerkungen und editorischem Bericht". In *Schopenhauer liest Schelling. Freiheits- und Naturphilosophie im Ausgang der klassischen deutschen Philosophie*, edited by Philipp Höfele and Lore Hühn. 373–410. Stuttgart-Bad Cannstatt: Frommann-Holzboog.

Hoyos, Luis E. 2008. *Der Skeptizismus und die Transzendentalphilosophie. Deutsche Philosophie am Ende des 18. Jahrhunderts*. Freiburg/Munich: Alber.

Hübscher, Arthur. 1952. "Der Philosoph der Romantik". *Schopenhauer-Jahrbuch* 34: 1–26.

Hübscher, Arthur. 1965. "Ein vergessener Schulfreund Schopenhauers". *Schopenhauer-Jahrbuch* 46: 130–152.
Hübscher, Arthur. 1966. "Schopenhauer in der philosophischen Kritik". *Schopenhauer-Jahrbuch* 47: 29–71.
Hübscher, Arthur. 1969. "Vom Pietismus zur Mystik". *Schopenhauer-Jahrbuch* 50: 1–32.
Hübscher, Arthur. 1973. *Denker gegen den Strom*. Bonn: Bouvier.
Hübscher, Arthur. 1989. *The Philosophy of Schopenhauer in Its Intellectual Context: Thinker Against the Tide*, translated by Joachim T. Baer and David E. Humphrey. Lewiston (NY): Edwin Mellen Press.
Hühn, Lore. 1998. "Die intelligible Tat. Zu einer Gemeinsamkeit Schellings und Schopenhauers". In *Selbstbesinnung der philosophischen Moderne: Beiträge zur kritischen Hermeneutik ihrer Grundbegriffe*, edited by Christian Iber, and Romano Pocai. 55–94. Cuxhaven: Traude Junghans.
Hühn, Lore, ed. 2006. *Die Ethik Arthur Schopenhauers im Ausgang vom Deutschen Idealismus (Fichte/Schelling)*. Beiträge des Internationalen Kongresses der Schopenhauer-Gesellschaft e.V. (Frankfurt a. M.), Freiburg im Breisgau 5. bis 8. Mai 2005. Würzburg: Ergon.
Hühn, Lore. 2006. "Der Wille, der Nichts will. Zum Paradox negativer Freiheit bei Schelling und Schopenhauer". In *Die Ethik Arthur Schopenhauers im Ausgang vom Deutschen Idealismus (Fichte/Schelling)*, edited by Lore Hühn. 149–160. Würzburg: Ergon.
Hühn, Lore. 2010. "Schellings Abhandlung Über das Wesen der menschlichen Freiheit (1809) – ein 'Vorspuk' der Willensmetaphysik Schopenhauers?" In *Das Böse und sein Grund. Zur Rezeptionsgeschichte von Schellings Freiheitsschrift 1809*, edited by Gunther Wenz. 61–74. Munich: Beck.
Ingenkamp, Heinz Gerd. 1989. "Traum oder Idee – Wagner oder Rossini? Zu Schopenhauers Metaphysik des Komponierens". *Studi Italo-Tedeschi. Deutsch-Italienische Studien* 11: 23–48.
Ingenkamp, Heinz Gerd. 1991. "Platonismus in Schopenhauers Erkenntnislehre und Metaphysik". *Schopenhauer-Jahrbuch* 72: 45–66.
Invernizzi, Giuseppe. 1986. "Schopenhauer attraverso il suo epistolario". *Rivista di Storia della Filosofia* 41(2): 245–264.
Invernizzi, Giuseppe. 2011. "Osservazioni sulla negazione del volere in Schopenhauer". In *Goethe, Schopenhauer, Nietzsche. Saggi in memoria di Sandro Barbera*, edited by Giuliano Campioni, Leonardo Pica Ciamarra, and Marco Segala. 409–420. Pisa: ETS.
Invernizzi, Giuseppe. 2013. "Schopenhauers Naturphilosophie, metaphorisch gelesen". *Schopenhauer-Jahrbuch* 93: 399–408.
Ito, Takao. 2016. "Zur Genese der Schopenhauerschen Rechtsphilosophie: Die Naturrechtslehre". *Schopenhauer-Jahrbuch* 97: 147–159.
Ivaldo, Marco. 1983. *Fichte. L'assoluto e l'immagine*. Rome: Studium.
Jacobs, Wilhelm G. 2021. "Das Wesen der Freiheit in der Auseinandersetzung zwischen Jacobi und Schelling". In *Friedrich Heinrich Jacobi (1743–1819): Romancier – Philosoph – Politiker*, edited by Cornelia Ortlieb and Friedrich Vollhardt. 207–220. Berlin/Boston: De Gruyter.
Jacquette, Dale, ed. 1996. *Schopenhauer, Philosophy, and the Arts*. Cambridge: Cambridge University Press.
Janaway, Christopher. 1996. "Knowledge and Tranquility: Schopenhauer on the Value of Art". In *Schopenhauer, Philosophy and the Arts*, edited by Dale Jacquette. 39–61. Cambridge: Cambridge University Press.
Janaway, Christopher and Alex Neill, eds. 2009. *Better Consciousness. Schopenhauer's Philosophy of Value*. Malden/Oxford: Wiley-Blackwell.

Janaway, Christopher. 2012. "Necessity, Responsibility and Character: Schopenhauer on Freedom of the Will". *Kantian Review* 17(3): 431–457.
Janke, Wolfgang. 2000. "Besonnenheit. Der philosophiegeschichtliche Ort von Fichtes Spätphilosophie". *Fichte-Studien* 17: 1–15.
Jens, Walter, ed. 1988–1992. *Kindlers neues Literatur-Lexikon*. 20 vols. München: Kindler Verlag.
Kamata, Yasuo. 1988. *Der junge Schopenhauer. Genese des Grundgedankens der Welt als Wille und Vorstellung*, Freiburg/Munich: Alber.
Kamata, Yasuo. 2006. *Der Einfluß von G. E. Schulze und Schelling auf Schopenhauers Theorie der Willensverneinung. Zur Standortbestimmung von Schopenhauers Philosophie*. In *Die Ethik Arthur Schopenhauers im Ausgang vom Deutschen Idealismus (Fichte/Schelling)*, edited by Lore Hühn. 203–212. Würzburg: Ergon.
Kamata, Yasuo. 2015. "Die Kant-Rezeption des jungen Schopenhauer in *Ueber die vierfache Wurzel des Satzes vom zureichenden Grund*". In *Schopenhauers Wissenschaftstheorie: "Der Satz vom Grund"*, edited by Dieter Birnbacher. 45–58. Würzburg: Königshausen & Neumann.
Kapani, Lakshmi 2011. *Schopenhauer et la pensée indienne*. Paris: Hermann.
Kerkmann, Jan. 2021. "Das bessere Bewusstsein und das Absolute – Schopenhauers Lektüre von Schellings Philosophie und Religion". In *Schopenhauer liest Schelling. Freiheits- und Naturphilosophie im Ausgang der klassischen deutschen Philosophie. Mit einer Edition von Schopenhauers handschriftlichen Kommentaren zu Schellings "Freiheitsschrift"*, edited by Philipp Höfele and Lore Hühn. 285–308. Stuttgart-Bad Cannstatt: Frommann-Holzboog.
Kisner, Manja. 2016. *Der Wille als Ding an sich. Schopenhauers Willensmetaphysik in ihrem Bezug zu Kants kritischer Philosophie und dem nachkantischen Idealismus*. Würzburg: Königshausen & Neumann.
Kloppe, Wolfgang. 1972. "Schopenhauer und die Welt des Arztes". *Schopenhauer-Jahrbuch* 53: 402–425.
Knappik, Franz. 2018. "Kant, Schopenhauer und Fichte über unser Wissen von körperlichen Handlungen". *Fichte-Studien* 45: 200–220.
Koßler, Matthias. 1990. *Substantielles Wissen und subjektives Handeln, dargestellt in einem Vergleich von Hegel und Schopenhauer*. Frankfurt a M./Bern/New York/Paris: Peter Lang.
Koßler, Matthias. 1995. "Empirischer und intelligibler Charakter. Von Kant über Fries und Schelling zu Schopenhauer". *Schopenhauer-Jahrbuch* 76: 195–201.
Koßler, Matthias. 1999. *Empirische Ethik und christliche Moral: Zur Differenz einer areligiösen und einer religiösen Grundlegung der Ethik am Beispiel der Gegenüberstellung Schopenhauer mit Augustinus, der Scholastik und Luther*. Würzburg: Königshausen & Neumann.
Koßler, Matthias. 2002a. "Schopenhauers Philosophie als Erfahrung des Charakters". In *Schopenhauer im Kontext. Deutsch-polnisches Schopenhauer-Symposion 2000*, edited by Dieter Birnbacher, Andreas Lorenz, and Leon Miodonski. 91–110. Würzburg: Königshausen & Neumann.
Koßler, Matthias. 2002b. "Zur Rolle der Besonnenheit in der Ästhetik Arthur Schopenhauers". *Schopenhauer-Jahrbuch* 83: 119–133.
Koßler, Matthias. 2006a. "'Der Gipfel der Aufklärung'. Aufklärung und Besonnenheit beim jungen Schopenhauer". In *Vernunft der Aufklärung – Aufklärung der Vernunft. Festschrift für Hans Martin Gerlach*, edited by Konstantin Broese, Andreas Hütig, Oliver Immel, and Renate Reschke. 207–216. Berlin: Akademie Verlag.
Koßler, Matthias. 2006b. "Die eine Anschauung – der eine Gedanke. Zur Systemfrage bei Fichte und Schopenhauer". In *Die Ethik Arthur Schopenhauers im Ausgang vom Deutschen Idealismus (Fichte/Schelling)*, edited by Lore Hühn. 350–364. Würzburg: Ergon.

Koßler, Matthias. 2006c. "Verantwortung als Grundlage der Metaphysik bei Schopenhauer". In *Verantwortung für die Zukunft. Zum 60. Geburtstag von Dieter Birnbacher*, edited by Carmen Kaminsky and Oliver Hallich. 331–344. Berlin: LIT.

Koßler, Matthias. 2008. "'Nichts' zwischen Mystik und Philosophie bei Schopenhauer". In *Philosophien des Willens. Böhme, Schelling, Schopenhauer*, edited by Günther Bonheim and Thomas Regehly. 65–80. Berlin: Weißensee.

Koßler, Matthias. 2009a."'Eine höchst überraschende Übereinstimmung' – Zur Augustinus-Rezeption bei Schopenhauer". In *Augustinus. Spuren und Spiegelungen seines Denkens*, vol. 2: *Von Descartes bis in die Gegenwart*, edited by N. Fischer. 111–125. Hamburg: Meiner.

Koßler, Matthias. 2009b. "'Standpunktwechsel' – Zur Systematik und zur philosophiegeschichtlichen Stellung der Philosophie Schopenhauers". In: *Schopenhauer und die Schopenhauer-Schule*, edited by Fabio Ciracì, Domenico M. Fazio, and Matthias Koßler. 45–60. Würzburg: Königshausen & Neumann.

Koßler, Matthias. 2011a. "Die Entstehung von Schopenhauers Willensmetaphysik". In *Goethe, Schopenhauer, Nietzsche. Saggi in memoria di Sandro Barbera*, edited by Giuliano Campioni, Leonardo Pica Ciamarra, and Marco Segala. 441–449. Pisa: ETS.

Koßler, Matthias, ed. 2011b. *Musik als Wille und Welt. Schopenhauers Philosophie der Musik*. Würzburg: Königshausen & Neumann.

Koßler, Matthias. 2012. "The 'Perfected System of Criticism'. Schopenhauer's Initial Disagreements with Kant". *Kantian Review* 17(3): 459–478.

Koßler, Matthias. 2013a. "'Ein kühner Unsinn' – Anschauung und Begriff in Schopenhauers Kant-Kritik". In *Kant und die Philosophie in Weltbürgerlicher Absicht: Akten des XI. Kant-Kongresses 2010*, vol. 5, edited by Stefano Bacin, Alfredo Ferrarin, Claudio La Rocca, and Margit Ruffing. 569–578. Berlin/Boston: De Gruyter.

Koßler, Matthias. 2013b. "Lieber gar nichts als Etwas. Die Frage unter pessimistischen Vorzeichen bei Schopenhauer". In *Warum ist überhaupt etwas und nicht vielmehr nichts?*, edited by Daniel Schubbe, Jens Lemanski, and Rico Hauswald. 189–204. Hamburg: Meiner.

Koßler, Matthias. 2016. "Die Welt als inintelligibler und empirischer Charakter". *Schopenhauer-Jahrbuch* 97: 93–103.

Koßler, Matthias and Margit Ruffing. 2018. "Immanuel Kant". In *Schopenhauer-Handbuch. Leben – Werk – Wirkung. Aktualisierte und erweiterte Auflage*, edited by Daniel Schubbe and Matthias Koßler. 215–220. Stuttgart: Metzler.

Kurbel, Martina. 2015. *Jenseits des Satzes vom Grund: Schopenhauers Lehre von der Wesenserkenntnis im Kontext seiner Oupnek'hat-Rezeption*. Würzburg: Königshausen & Neumann.

Langen, A. 1968². *Der Wortschatz des deutschen Pietismus*. Tübingen: Niemeyer.

Lauth, Reinhard. 1999. *Il sistema di Fichte nelle sue tarde lezioni berlinesi*, in Johann Gottlieb Fichte: *Dottrina della scienza. Esposizione del 1811*, edited by Gaetano Rametta. 11–50. Milan: Guerini e Associati.

Lemanski, Jens. 2009–2011. *Christentum im Atheismus. Spuren der mystischen Imitatio Christi-Lehre in der Ethik Schopenhauers*, 2 vols. London: Turnshare.

Lemanski, Jens. 2012. "Die Königin der Revolution. Zur Rettung und Erhaltung der Kopernikanischen Wende". *Kant-Studien* 103(4): 448–471.

Lemanski, Jens. 2013. "The Denial of the Will-to-Live in Schopenhauer's World and His Association of Buddhist and Christian Saints". In *Understanding Schopenhauer through the Prism of Indian Culture*, edited by Arati Barua, Michael Gerhard, and Matthias Koßler. 149–183, Berlin/Boston: De Gruyter.

Lemanski, Jens and Daniel Schubbe. 2018. "Konzeptionelle Probleme und Interpretationsansätze der Welt als Wille und Vorstellung". In *Schopenhauer-Handbuch. Leben – Werk – Wirkung. Aktualisierte und erweiterte Auflage*, edited by Daniel Schubbe and Matthias Koßler. 43–51. Stuttgart: Metzler.

Léon, Xavier. 1922–1924. *Fichte et son temps*, 2 vols. Paris: Colin.

Lindner, Ernst Otto and Julius Frauenstädt. 1863. *Arthur Schopenhauer. Von ihm, über ihn*. Berlin: Hayn.

Loer, Barbara. 1974. *Das Absolute und die Wirklichkeit in Schellings Philosophie: Mit der Erstedition einer Handschrift aus dem Berliner Schelling-Nachlass*. Berlin/Boston: De Gruyter.

López de Santa María, Pilar. 2020. "The Mystery of Freedom". In *The Oxford Handbook of Schopenhauer*, edited by Robert L. Wicks. 193–206. Oxford: Oxford University Press.

Losacco, Michele. 1903. "Le dottrine edonistiche italiane del sec. XVIII". *Atti dell'Accademia di Scienze morali e politiche di Napoli* 34: 181–307.

Lütkehaus, Ludger. 1984. "Die Zeit: der Moloch, der sich selbst verzehrt. Zur Textkritik und Interpretation der Übertragung Schopenhauers von John Miltons 'On Time'". *Schopenhauer-Jahrbuch* 65: 260–264.

Lütkehaus, Ludger. 2014. *Nichts. Abschied vom Sein-Ende der Angst*, revised edition. Leipzig: Zweitausendeins.

Magee, Bryan. 1997. *The Philosophy of Schopenhauer*. Oxford: Clarendon Press.

Malter, Rudolf. 1982. "Erlösung durch Erkenntnis. Über die Bedingung der Möglichkeit der Schopenhauerschen Lehre von der Willensverneinung". In *Zeit der Ernte. Studien zum Stand der Schopenhauer-Forschung. Festschrift für Arthur Hübscher zum 85. Geburtstag*, edited by Wolfgang Schirmacher. 41–59. Stuttgart-Bad Cannstatt: Frommann-Holzboog.

Malter, Rudolf. 1988. *Der eine Gedanke. Hinführung zur Philosophie Arthur Schopenhauers*. Darmstadt: Wissenschaftliche Buchgesellschaft.

Malter, Rudolf. 1991. *Arthur Schopenhauer. Transzendentalphilosophie und Metaphysik des Willens*. Stuttgart-Bad Cannstatt: Frommann-Holzboog.

Malter, Rudolf. 1996. "Was ist heute an Schopenhauers Philosophie aktuell?" In *Schopenhauer in der Philosophie der Gegenwart*, edited by Dieter Birnbacher. 9–17. Würzburg: Königshausen & Neumann.

Mann, Wolfgang-Reiner. 2018. "How Platonic Are Schopenhauer's Platonic Ideas?" In *The Palgrave Schopenhauer Handbook*, edited by Sandra Shapshay. 43–63. London: Palgrave Macmillan.

Marchtaler, Hildegard von. 1968. "Lorenz Meyers Tagebücher". *Schopenhauer-Jahrbuch* 49: 95–111.

Massei Jr., William. 2018. "Der Mann, 'der noch beim Träumen den bösen Engel bekämpfte'. Zu Schopenhauers früher Begegnung mit Luther". *Schopenhauer-Jahrbuch* 99: 127–136.

Meattini, Valerio. 2013. "In margine al 'Ding an sich'. Schopenhauer 'discepolo' di Kant". In *Kant und die Philosophie in weltbürgerlicher Absicht: Akten des XI. Kant-Kongresses 2010*, vol. 5, edited by Stefano Bacin, Alfredo Ferrarin, Claudio La Rocca, and Margit Ruffing. 579–589. Berlin/Boston: De Gruyter.

Metz, Wilhelm. 2006. "Der Begriff des Willens bei Fichte und Schopenhauer". In *Die Ethik Arthur Schopenhauers im Ausgang vom Deutschen Idealismus (Fichte/Schelling)*, edited by Lore Hühn. 386–398. Würzburg: Ergon.

Meyer, Urs Walter. 1994. *Europäische Rezeption indischer Philosophie und Religion*. Bern: Lang.

Mittner, Ladislao. 2002. *Storia della letteratura tedesca*, vol. 2: *Dal pietismo al romanticismo*. 3 vols. Turin. Einaudi.

Mockrauer, Franz. 1928. "Schopenhauer und Indien". *Schopenhauer-Jahrbuch* 15: 3–28.

Morgenstern, Martin. 2022. "Schopenhauers Metaphysik – zwischen Forschungsprogramm and Pseudo-Erklärungen". In *Das Hauptwerk. 200 Jahre Arthur Schopenhauers Die Welt als Wille und Vorstellung*, edited by Dieter Birnbacher and Matthias Koßler. 119–136. Würzburg: Königshausen & Neumann.

Morini, Maurizio. 2017. *Trascendentalismo e immanentismo nelle tre edizioni del Mondo come volontà e rappresentazione di Arthur Schopenhauer*. Macerata: Eum.

Müller-Lauter, Wolfgang. 1993. "Das Verhältnis des intelligiblen zum empirischen Charakter bei Kant, Schelling und Schopenhauer". In *Kategorien der Existenz. Festschrift für Wolfgang Janke*, edited by Klaus Held and Jochem Hennigfeld. 31–60. Würzburg: Königshausen & Neumann.

Müller-Seyfarth, Winfried H. 2000. *Metaphysik der Entropie. Philipp Mainländers transzendentale Analyse und ihre ethisch-metaphysische Relevanz*. With a preface by Franco Volpi. Berlin: VanBremen.

Negri, Antonio. 1987. *Lenta ginestra. Saggio sull'ontologia di Giacomo Leopardi*. Milan: SugarCo Edizioni.

Neidert, Rudolf. 2018. "Schopenhauers und Luthers frühe Begegnung mit der 'Deutschen Theologie'". *Schopenhauer-Jahrbuch* 99: 137–159.

Norman, Judith and Alistair Welchman. 2020. "Schopenhauer's Understanding of Schelling". In *The Oxford Handbook of Schopenhauer*, edited by Robert L. Wicks. 49–66. Oxford: Oxford University Press.

Noveanu, Alina. 2016. "'Das Wunder schlechthin'. Vom Leibverständnis Schopenhauers zur analogischen Apperzeption in Husserls 'V. Cartesianische Meditation' – ein Gedankensprung". In *Schopenhauer und die Deutung der Existenz*, edited by Thomas Regehly and Daniel Schubbe. 46–65. Stuttgart: Metzler.

Novembre, Alessandro. 2010. "Schopenhauer tra l'analogia e il solipsismo". *Revista Voluntas: estudos sobre Schopenhauer* 1(2): 98–136. DOI: 10.5902/2179378634128.

Novembre, Alessandro. 2011. *Il giovane Schopenhauer e Fichte. La duplicità della coscienza*. PhD diss., University of Salento/University of Mainz.

Novembre, Alessandro. 2012. "Die Vorgeschichte der Schopenhauer'schen Theorie des Willens als Ding an sich". *Schopenhauer Kenkyu/Schopenhauer Studies* 17: 19–76.

Novembre, Alessandro. 2013. "Schopenhauers Verständnis der Fichte'schen 'absoluten Besonnenheit'". *Schopenhauer-Jahrbuch* 93: 53–62.

Novembre, Alessandro. 2016a. "Das 'Losreißen' des Wissens: Von der Schopenhauer'schen Nachschrift der Vorlesungen Fichtes 'Ueber die Tatsachen der Bewusstseins' und 'Ueber die Wissenschaftslehre' (1811/12) zur Ästhetik von Die Welt als Wille und Vorstellung". *Fichte-Studien* 43: 315–336.

Novembre, Alessandro. 2016b. "Die Dissertation 1813 als Einleitung zu einer geplanten 'größeren Schrift' über das 'bessere Bewußtseyn'". *Schopenhauer-Jahrbuch* 97: 133–146.

Novembre, Alessandro. 2018a. *Invito alla libertà: il principio della filosofia. Il corso di Fichte "Sui fatti della coscienza" 1811–1812*. Rome: Vivarium Novum.

Novembre, Alessandro. 2018b. "Johann Gottlieb Fichte". In *Schopenhauer-Handbuch. Leben – Werk – Wirkung. Aktualisierte und erweiterte Auflage*, edited by Daniel Schubbe and Matthias Koßler. 231–236. Stuttgart: Metzler.

Novembre, Alessandro. 2019. "Autoposizione dell'io e metafisica della volontà. Da Schelling a Schopenhauer". *Schelling-Studien* 7: 69–87.

Novembre, Alessandro. 2021a. "'Erscheinung': ἐπιφάνεια oder phaenomenon? Überlegungen zum semantisch-traduktologischen Fundament der Naturphilosophie". In *Schopenhauer liest Schelling. Freiheits- und Naturphilosophie im Ausgang der klassischen deutschen Philosophie. Mit einer Edition von Schopenhauers handschriftlichen Kommentaren zu Schellings "Freiheitsschrift"*, edited by Philipp Höfele and Lore Hühn. 31–51. Stuttgart-Bad Cannstatt: Frommann-Holzboog.

Novembre, Alessandro. 2021b. "Wille und Erkenntnis: Synthese, Dualismus oder Aporie? Ein konzeptionelles Grundproblem der Philosophie Schopenhauers". *Voluntas: Revista Internacional De Filosofia* 12. DOI: 10.5902/2179378667477.

Novembre, Alessandro. 2022. "Die Zentralaporie des Systems und die Ambivalenz der Metaphysik Schopenhauers". In *Das Hauptwerk. 200 Jahre Arthur Schopenhauers* Die Welt als Wille und Vorstellung, edited by Dieter Birnbacher and Matthias Koßler. 137–151. Würzburg: Königshausen & Neumann.

Pareyson, Luigi. 2014. *Estetica dell'Idealismo tedesco, II. Fichte e Novalis*, edited by Gianluca Garelli and Federico Vercellone. Milan: Mursia.

Penzo, Giorgio. 1987. "Fichte e Schopenhauer e il problema del nulla come dimensione del sacro". In *Schopenhauer e il sacro. Atti del seminario tenuto a Trento il 26–28 aprile 1984*, edited by Giorgio Penzo. 48–58. Bologna: EDB.

Pfeiffer-Belli. 1948. Wolfgang. "Schopenhauer und die deutsche Frühromantik". *Philosophisches Jahrbuch* 58: 277–281.

Philonenko, Alexis. 1997. "Fichte et Schopenhauer". In Alexis Philonenko: *Métaphysique et Politique chez Kant et Fichte*. 437–451. Paris: Vrin.

Piantelli, Mario. 1986. "La Mâjâ nelle Upaniṣad di Schopenhauer". *Annuario Filosofico* 2: 163–207.

Piantelli, Mario. 2013. *Scritti scelti*, edited by Pinuccia Caracchi, Antonella Serena Comba, Alessandra Consolaro, Alberto Pelissero, Gianni Pellegrini, and Stefano Piano. Alessandria: Edizioni dell'Orso.

Pikulik, Lothar. 2005. "Schopenhauer und die Romantik". In *Schopenhauer und die Künste*, edited by Günther Baum and Dieter Birnbacher. 57–77. Göttingen: Wallstein.

Piper, Reinhard, ed. 1916. "Die zeitgenössischen Rezensionen der Werke Schopenhauers. Erster Teil: 1814–1817". *Schopenhauer-Jahrbuch* 5: 161–192.

Piper, Reinhard, ed. 1917. "Die zeitgenössischen Rezensionen der Werke Schopenhauers. Zweiter Teil: 1819–1825". *Schopenhauer-Jahrbuch* 6: 47–178.

Poggi, Stefano. 2000. *Il genio e l'unità della natura. La scienza nella Germania romantica (1790–1850)*. Bologna: Il Mulino.

Pohlenz, Max. 1959. *Die Stoa. Geschichte einer geistigen Bewegung*, 2 vols. Göttingen: Vandenhoeck & Ruprecht.

Pohlenz, Max. 1992[7]. *Der hellenische Mensch*. Göttingen: Vandenhoeck & Ruprecht.

Radrizzani, Ives. 2012. "Einleitung". In Johann Gottlieb Fichte: *Die späten wissenschaftlichen Vorlesungen*, vol. 3 (1811–1812), edited by Hans Georg von Manz, Ives Radrizzani, Martin Siegel, and Erich Fuchs. XV–XXXIV. Stuttgart-Bad Cannstatt: Fromman-Holzboog.

Regehly, Thomas. 1990. "Der 'Atheist' und der 'Theologe'. Schopenhauer als Hörer Schleiermachers". *Schopenhauer-Jahrbuch* 71: 7–16.

Regehly, Thomas. 2008. "Fabula docet. Vom Oupnek'hat über Irenäus zu Böhme, Schelling und Schopenhauer". In *Philosophien des Willens. Böhme, Schelling, Schopenhauer*, edited by Günther Bonheim and Thomas Regehly. 81–104. Berlin: Weißensee.

Regehly, Thomas and Daniel Schubbe, eds. 2016. *Schopenhauer und die Deutung der Existenz: Perspektiven auf Phänomenologie, Existenzphilosophie und Hermeneutik*. Stuttgart: Metzler.

Riconda, Giuseppe. 1969. *Schopenhauer interprete dell'Occidente*. Milan: Mursia.

Riconda, Giuseppe. 1972. "La 'Noluntas' e la riscoperta della mistica nella filosofia di Schopenhauer". *Schopenhauer-Jahrbuch* 53: 80–87.

Riconda, Giuseppe. 2009. "Arthur Schopenhauer (1788–1860)". In *Il peccato originale nel pensiero moderno*, edited by in Claudio Ciancio, Gianluca Cuozzo, Marco Ravera, and Giuseppe Riconda. 773–787. Brescia: Morcelliana.

Riedinger, F. 1922. "Die Akten über Schopenhauers Doktorpromotion" *Schopenhauer-Jahrbuch* 11: 96–103.

Ritter, Joachim, Karlfried Gründer, and Gottfried Gabriel, eds. 1971–2007. *Historisches Wörterbuch der Philosophie*, 13 vols. Basel: Schwabe.

Rivera de Rosales, Jacinto. 2012. "Wollen ist Ursein. Schelling und die Freiheitsschrift". In *Schellings Philosophie der Freiheit. Studien zu den Philosophischen Untersuchungen über das Wesen der menschlichen Freiheit*, edited by Diogo Ferrer and Teresa Pedro. 155–173. Würzburg: Ergon.

Ruffing, Margit. 2005. "Die Duplizitätsstruktur des Bewußtseins bei Schopenhauer und C. G. Jung, oder: 1+1=1". *Schopenhauer-Jahrbuch* 86: 195–212.

Rühl, Matthias. 2001. *Schopenhauers existentielle Metaphern im Kontext seiner Philosophie*. Münster: LIT.

Russell, Bertrand. 1948. *Human Knowledge. Its Scope and Limits*. London: George Allen and Unwin.

Ruta, Marcello. 2021. "Befreiung von der Zeit versus Befreiung der Zeit. Die zweifache Rezeption der kantischen Lehre der Freiheit bei Schopenhauer und Schelling". In *Schopenhauer liest Schelling. Freiheits- und Naturphilosophie im Ausgang der klassischen deutschen Philosophie. Mit einer Edition von Schopenhauers handschriftlichen Kommentaren zu Schellings "Freiheitsschrift"*, edited by Philipp Höfele and Lore Hühn. 309–330. Stuttgart-Bad Cannstatt: Frommann-Holzboog.

Ryan, Christopher John David. 2018. "Schopenhauer and Gotama on Life's Suffering". In *The Palgrave Schopenhauer Handbook*, edited by Sandra Shapshay. 373–394. London: Palgrave Macmillan.

Safranski, Rüdiger. 1987. *Schopenhauer und die wilden Jahre der Philosophie. Eine Biographie*. Munich/Vienna: Carl Hanser.

Safranski, Rüdiger. 1990. *Schopenhauer and the Wild Years of Philosophy*, translated by Ewald Osers. Cambridge (MA): Harvard University Press.

Samuel, Irene. 1947. *Plato and Milton*. Ithaca: Cornell University Press.

Sandkaulen, Birgit. 2000. *Grund und Ursache. Die Vernunftkritik Jacobis*. Munich: Fink.

Sattar, Alexander. 2016. "Schopenhauers 'Systemchen' und Herders Idee zur Philosophie der Geschichte der Menschheit". *Schopenhauer-Jahrbuch* 97: 71–79.

Sattar, Alexander. 2019. "'Some Brought to Us the Truth': A Source of Schopenhauer's View of Plato, Philosophy, the 'Platonic Ideas' and 'Thing in Itself' in W. G. Tennemann's History of Philosophy". *Schopenhauer-Jahrbuch* 100: 29–54.

Sattar, Alexander. 2022. "Kantian vs. Platonic: The Ambiguity of Schopenhauer's Notion of Ideas Explained via Its Origins". *Journal of Transcendental Philosophy* 3(2): 213–234.

Schirmacher, Wolfgang. 1988. "Der Heilige als Lebensform. Überlegungen zu Schopenhauers ungeschriebener Lehre". In *Schopenhauers Aktualität. Ein Philosoph wird neu gelesen*, edited by Wolfgang Schirmacher. 181–199. Vienna: Passagen.

Schmidt, Alfred. 1986. *Die Wahrheit im Gewande der Lüge. Schopenhauers Religionsphilosophie*. Munich/Zürich: Piper.

Schmidt, Martin. 1969. *Wiedergeburt und neuer Mensch. Gesammelte Studien zur Geschichte des Pietismus*. Witten: Luther-Verlag.

Schöndorf, Harald. 1982. *Der Leib im Denken Schopenhauers und Fichtes*. Munich: Berchmans.

Schröder, Wilhelm. 1911. *Beiträge zur Entwicklungsgeschichte der Philosophie Schopenhauers, mit besonderer Berücksichtigung einiger wichtiger frühnachkantischer Philosophen (Maimon, Beck, G. E. Schulze, Bouterwek und Jacobi)*. Rostock: Bold.

Schubbe, Daniel. 2010. *Philosophie des Zwischen. Hermeneutik und Aporetik bei Schopenhauer.* Würzburg: Königshausen & Neumann.

Schubbe, Daniel. 2013. "Schopenhauers Hermeneutik – Metaphysische Entzifferung oder Explikation intuitiver' Erkenntnis?". In: *Schopenhauer-Jahrbuch* 93: 404–424

Schubbe, Daniel, Jens Lemanski, and Rico Hauswald, eds. 2013. *Warum ist überhaupt etwas und nicht vielmehr nichts?* Hamburg: Meiner.

Schubbe, Daniel and Søren R. Fauth, eds. 2016. *Schopenhauer und Goethe. Biographische und philosophische Perspektiven.* Hamburg: Meiner.

Schubbe, Daniel and Matthias Koßler, eds. 2018. *Schopenhauer-Handbuch. Leben – Werk – Wirkung*, 2nd, enlarged edition. Stuttgart: Metzler.

Schulz, Walter. 1982. "Philosophie des Übergangs". In *Zeit der Ernte. Studien zum Stand der Schopenhauer-Forschung. Festschrift für Arthur Hübscher zum 85. Geburtstag*, edited by Wolfgang Schirmacher. 30–40. Stuttgart-Bad Cannstatt: Frommann-Holzboog.

Schwabe, Gerhard. 1887. *Fichtes und Schopenhauers Lehre vom Willen mit ihren Konsequenzen für Weltbegreifung und Lebensführung.* Jena: Frommansche Buchdruckerei.

Schwenzfeuer, Sebastian. 2018. "Friedrich Wilhelm Joseph Schelling". In *Schopenhauer-Handbuch. Leben – Werk – Wirkung. Aktualisierte und erweiterte Auflage*, edited by Daniel Schubbe and Matthias Koßler. 242–247. Stuttgart: Metzler.

Segala, Marco. 2000. "Beethoven, Hoffman e la musica assoluta". In *Musica e filosofia*, edited by Ferdinando Abbri and Elio Matassi. 33–68. Cosenza: Pellegrini.

Segala, Marco. 2001. "Schopenhauer è anti-schellinghiano?" *Rivista di Filosofia* 92(2): 235–265.

Segala, Marco. 2006. "Willensverneinung, Philosophy of Nature, Sciences. Schopenhauer versus Schelling". In *Die Ethik Arthur Schopenhauers im Ausgang vom Deutschen Idealismus (Fichte/Schelling)*, edited by Lore Hühn. 213–221. Würzburg: Ergon.

Segala, Marco. 2009. *Schopenhauer, la filosofia, le scienze.* Pisa: Edizioni della Normale.

Segala, Marco. 2011. "Tracce della coscienza migliore nelle opere di Schopenhauer". In *Goethe, Schopenhauer, Nietzsche. Saggi in memoria di Sandro Barbera*, edited by Giuliano Campioni, Leonardo Pica Ciamarra, and Marco Segala. 635–647. Pisa: ETS.

Segala, Marco. 2017. "The Path to Redemption between Better Consciousness and Metaphysics of Will". *Schopenhauer-Jahrbuch* 98: 71–98.

Sengler, Jakob. 1834. *Über das Wesen und die Bedeutung der spekulativen Philosophie und Theologie in der gegenwärtigen Zeit, mit besonderer Rücksicht auf die Religionsphilosophie.* I: *Allgemeine Einleitung.* Mainz: Kupferberg.

Sengler, Jakob. 1837. *Über das Wesen und die Bedeutung der spekulativen Philosophie und Theologie in der gegenwärtigen Zeit, mit besonderer Rücksicht auf die Religionsphilosophie.* II: *Spezielle Einleitung in die spekulative Philosophie und Theologie.* Heidelberg: Mohr.

Severino, Emanuele. 1990. *Il nulla e la poesia. Alla fine dell'età della tecnica: Leopardi.* Milan: Rizzoli.

Severino, Emanuele. 1992. *Oltre il linguaggio.* Milan: Adelphi.

Seydel, Rudolf. 1857. *Schopenhauers philosophisches System, dargestellt und beurteilt.* Leipzig: Breitkopf & Härtel.

Shapshay, Sandra. 2009. "Poetic Intuition and the Bounds of Sense: Metaphor and Metonymy in Schopenhauer's Philosophy". In *Better Consciousness. Schopenhauer's Philosophy of Value*, edited by Alex Neill and Christopher Janaway. 58–76. Malden/Oxford: Wiley-Blackwell.

Shapshay, Sandra. 2012. "Schopenhauer's Transformation of the Kantian Sublime". *Kantian Review* 17(3): 479–511.

Shapshay, Sandra, ed. 2018. *The Palgrave Schopenhauer Handbook.* London: Palgrave Macmillan.

Shapshay, Sandra. 2019. *Reconstructing Schopenhauer's Ethics: Hope, Compassion and Animal Welfare.* Oxford: Oxford University Press.
Siani, Alberto L. 2007. *Kant e Platone.* Pisa: ETS.
Siebke, Rolf. 1970. "Arthur Schopenhauer und Matthias Claudius". *Schopenhauer-Jahrbuch* 51: 22–31.
Siegler, Hans Georg. 1994. *Der heimatlose Arthur Schopenhauer. Jugendjahre zwischen Danzig, Hamburg, Weimar.* Düsseldorf: Droste.
Soliva Soria, Ana Carolina. 2022. "Die Philosophie und die Abspiegelung der Welt in abstrakten Begriffen". In *Das Hauptwerk. 200 Jahre Arthur Schopenhauers* Die Welt als Wille und Vorstellung, edited by Dieter Birnbacher and Matthias Koßler. 105–118. Würzburg: Königshausen & Neumann.
Spierling, Volker. 1984. "Die Drehwende der Moderne. Schopenhauer zwischen Skeptizismus und Dogmatismus". In *Materialien zu Schopenhauers "Die Welt als Wille und Vorstellung"*, edited by Volker Spierling. 14–83. Frankfurt a. M.: Suhrkamp.
Spierling, Volker, ed. 1987. *Schopenhauer im Denken der Gegenwart. 23 Beiträge zu seiner Aktualität.* Munich/Zürich: Piper.
Spierling, Volker. 1998. *Arthur Schopenhauer. Eine Einführung in Leben und Werk.* Leipzig: Reclam.
Stollberg, Jochen, ed. 2006. *"Das Tier, das du jetzt tötest, bist du selbst ...". Arthur Schopenhauer und Indien.* Frankfurt a. M.: Klostermann.
Takahashi, Yoichiro, Takao Ito, and Tsunafumi Takeuchi, eds. 2022. *Das neue Jahrhundert Schopenhauers: Akten des Internationalen Forschungsprojekts anlässlich des 200. Jubiläums von* Die Welt als Wille und Vorstellung *2018–2020.* Würzburg: Königshausen & Neumann.
Tielsch, Elfriede. 1957. "Vergleich der ersten mit der zweiten Auflage". In Arthur Schopenhauer: *Über die vierfache Wurzel des Satzes vom zureichenden Grunde*, edited by Michael Landmann and Elfriede Tielsch. XXXV–XLIII. Hamburg: Meiner.
Ulrichs, Lars-Thade. 2012. "Das Ganze der Erfahrung. Metaphysik und Wissenschaften bei Schopenhauer und Schelling". *International Yearbook of German Idealism/Internationales Jahrbuch des deutschen Idealismus* 8: 251–281.
Vandenabeele, Bart, ed. 2012. *A Companion to Schopenhauer.* New York: Wiley.
Vandenabeele, Bart. 2015. *The Sublime in Schopenhauer's Philosophy.* New York: Palgrave Macmillan.
Vecchiotti, Icilio. 1969. *La dottrina di Schopenhauer. Le teorie schopenhaueriane considerate nella loro genesi e nei loro rapporti con la filosofia indiana.* Rome: Ubaldini.
Vecchiotti, Icilio. 1987. "Schopenhauer e Schelling: problemi metodologici e problemi di contenuto". *Schopenhauer-Jahrbuch* 68: 82–108.
Vecchiotti, Icilio. 1988. "Sviluppo e senso delle annotazioni schopenhaueriane a Schelling". First part. *Schopenhauer-Jahrbuch* 69: 425–437.
Vecchiotti, Icilio. 1989. "Sviluppo e senso delle annotazioni schopenhaueriane a Schelling". Second part. *Schopenhauer-Jahrbuch* 70: 161–173.
Vercellone, Federico. 1999. *L'estetica dell'Ottocento.* Bologna: Il Mulino.
Volpi, Franco. 1982. "Schopenhauers Unterscheidung von Vernunft und Verstand und ihre begriffsgeschichtliche Relevanz". In *Zeit der Ernte. Studien zum Stand der Schopenhauer-Forschung. Festschrift für Arthur Hübscher zum 85. Geburtstag*, edited by Wolfgang Schirmacher. 279–297. Stuttgart-Bad Cannstatt: Frommann-Holzboog.
Waibel, Violetta L. 2006. "Die Natur des Wollens. Zu einer Grundfigur Fichtes im Ausblick auf Schopenhauer". In *Die Ethik Arthur Schopenhauers im Ausgang vom Deutschen Idealismus (Fichte/Schelling)*, edited by Lore Hühn. 402–422. Würzburg: Ergon.
Weeks, Andrew. 1992. "Schopenhauer und Böhme". *Schopenhauer-Jahrbuch* 73: 7–17.

Weigand, Friedrich Ludwig Karl. 1909–1910⁵. *Deutsches Wörterbuch*, edited by Herman Hirt, 2 vols. Gießen: Töpelmann.
Welchman, Alistair. 2018. "Schopenhauer's Two Metaphysics: Transcendental and Transcendent". In *The Palgrave Schopenhauer Handbook*, edited by Sandra Shapshay. 129–149. London: Palgrave Macmillan.
Welsen, Peter. 1995. *Schopenhauers Theorie des Subjekts*. Würzburg: Königshausen & Neumann.
Welsen, Peter. 2016. "Schopenhauers Hermeneutik des Willens". In *Schopenhauer und die Deutung der Existenz*, edited by Thomas Regehly and Daniel Schubbe. 157–170. Stuttgart: Metzler.
Wetzel, James. 2010. *Augustine: A Guide for the Perplexed*. New York: Wetzel.
Wicks, Robert L. 1993. "Schopenhauer's Naturalization of Kant's A Priori Forms of Empirical Knowledge". *History of Philosophy Quarterly* 10: 181–196.
Wicks, Robert L., ed. 2020. *The Oxford Handbook of Schopenhauer*. Oxford: Oxford University Press.
Yogananda, Paramahansa. 1999². *God Talks with Arjuna. The Bhagavad Gita*, 2 vols. Los Angeles: Self Realization Fellowship.
Zimmermann, Ekkehard. 1970. *Der Analogieschluss in der Lehre von der Ich-Welt-Identität bei Arthur Schopenhauer*. PhD diss., Munich.
Zint, Hans. 1921. "Schopenhauers Philosophie des doppelten Bewußtseins". *Schopenhauer-Jahrbuch* 10: 3–45.
Zint, Hans. 1930. "Das Religiöse bei Schopenhauer". *Schopenhauer-Jahrbuch* 17: 3–75.
Zöller, Günter. 2003. "Schopenhauer". In *Musik in der deutschen Philosophie. Eine Einführung*, edited by S. L. Sorgner and O. Fürbeth. 99–114. Stuttgart/Weimar: Metzler.
Zöller, Günter. 2006. "Kichtenhauer. Der Ursprung von Schopenhauers Welt als Wille und Vorstellung in Fichtes Wissenschaftslehre 1812 und System der Sittenlehre". In *Die Ethik Arthur Schopenhauers im Ausgang vom Deutschen Idealismus (Fichte/Schelling)*, edited by Lore Hühn. 365–386. Würzburg: Ergon.
Zöller, Günter. 2013a. "Anerkennung. Der außerindische Ursprung von Schopenhauers Auffassung des 'tat twam asi'". *Schopenhauer-Jahrbuch* 93: 87–100.
Zöller, Günter. 2013b. "Philosophizing under the Influence – Schopenhauer's Indian Thought". In *Understanding Schopenhauer through the Prism of Indian Culture*, edited by Arati Barua, Michael Gerhard, and Matthias Koßler. 9–17. Berlin/Boston: De Gruyter.
Zöller, Günter. 2016. "Fichte's Later Presentations of the *Wissenschaftslehre*". In *The Cambridge Companion to Fichte*, edited by David James and Günter Zöller. 139–167. Cambridge: Cambridge University Press.
Zöller, Günter. 2018. "Schopenhauer's System of Freedom". In *The Palgrave Schopenhauer Handbook*, edited by Sandra Shapshay. 65–84. London: Palgrave Macmillan.

Index

Abolition of the Will   195, 427, 432, 477, 479, 482, 485–487, 490, 495, 497, 501
Absolute, Absoluteness   35, 39, 53, 56–61, 65, 74, 76–78, 82, 93f., 97, 101, 114–116, 118f., 121–124, 128f., 139, 145–150, 152–155, 157–161, 164–167, 172, 178, 180, 182, 189f., 199–202, 205, 208, 211, 213–216, 218, 226f., 234, 243, 252–254, 261f., 264, 266, 268f., 299, 301, 314, 319, 351, 377, 398f., 411, 413–415, 419, 425, 429, 431, 433f., 460, 484, 488, 495f., 501, 505–509, 511, 515
Accountability (*Zurechnungsfähigkeit*)   316f.
Adam   335f., 352, 354, 486, 508
Aesthetics, Aesthetic Sphere   14, 44, 76, 130–132, 145, 192f., 212, 217, 243, 245, 247–249, 251, 253, 258, 270f., 322–328, 355, 502, 504
Affirmation (of the Will)   110, 196, 310, 318, 425, 434, 480, 489f., 497, 501, 506, 508, 513
Affirmation (of Temporal Existence)   230f., 242f.,, 250, 371
Affirmation (of Extratemporal Being)   230f., 241, 246–250, 270, 323, 339, 366,
Agar, H.   11
Aler, J.   19
Alteration (in cognition)   482, 484f., 494, 512
Alteration (transcendental, of Man)   485, 512
Anacreon   221, 250
Analogical Argument or Inference   203f., 249, 317f., 390–400, 437, 439–441, 443–449, 451f., 454–456, 461–463, 467, 470, 476–478, 480–482, 499
Analogy   38, 43, 86, 92, 126, 238, 309, 317, 384, 392, 394f., 420, 438, 444–448, 451f., 461, 463, 476, 478, 505
Animals   77, 130f., 179–181, 184, 187, 194, 232, 236–238, 287, 302, 391–394, 397, 400, 457, 477
Annihilation (*Vernichtung*)   19, 193–195, 197, 218, 230f., 240, 337–339, 359, 386, 413, 425, 491, 499
Anquetil-Duperron, A. H.   348, 376–380, 384f., 389f., 418, 424f.

Antinomy   82, 140, 221, 308, 412
Antiphon   116
Aporias (within Schopenhauer's philosophizing)   4f., 211, 268f., 272, 436, 448, 458, 470f., 474f., 482–484, 495, 503f.
Appearance (*Erscheinung*)   45, 47–49, 51, 53–55, 57f., 60, 69–72, 74, 80, 82–84, 86–94, 110, 133, 136–138, 148, 162f., 171, 174, 180, 186, 192, 196, 211, 214, 228, 234, 236, 238, 240, 251, 257, 259, 283, 285, 301–308, 312, 319, 330, 341–346, 349, 352f., 357f., 362, 364, 366f., 370–373, 375, 378, 380–384, 387, 391f., 394–397, 399, 402, 406–409, 414, 420–424, 426, 430, 432, 434, 437–440, 443–452, 454–457, 459–479, 483, 485–487, 490, 492, 495–503, 505f., 508, 510
Apperception, Synthetic Unity of   48, 261f., 264, 305, 346
App, U.   5, 14, 28, 34, 190, 197, 263, 281, 284, 347f., 358, 375f., 380–383, 390, 395, 397
Aristarchus   85
Aristotle   6, 31f., 58, 71, 90, 123, 226, 279, 404
Arjuna   347
Arnim, H. v.   32
Art   3, 14f., 25, 27–29, 34f., 40–44, 56, 72, 74–77, 134f., 147, 173f., 181f., 191–193, 200, 214, 236, 248–250, 252, 255–259, 270, 323–325, 332, 339, 355, 361f., 396, 404, 408, 494, 499, 505f.
Asceticism   220–222, 230–233, 240, 248, 270, 323, 337f., 371f., 386, 432, 481f., 501
Ascetics   432
Asmuth, C.   463, 505
Astonishment (philosophical)   26, 122, 197–199, 201, 219, 223, 233, 248, 266
Atheism/Atheists   255, 367
Atma   348, 379f., 388–390, 398–400, 419
Atwell, J.   97, 444, 448
Atzert, S.   433
Augustin, Saint   16, 26, 32, 41, 267
Auweele D. V.   350

Bacon, F.   281
Barbera, S.   190, 451, 474
Barua, A.   376
Bäschlin, D. L.   287
Bastian, M.   294
Baum, G.   468
Beauty, the Beautiful   29, 44, 75, 246–250, 253, 259, 270, 323, 401, 499
Beethoven, L. v.   76f., 79
Being (*Seyn*), concept of   84, 92f., 99, 101, 113, 122, 129, 139, 142f., 147f., 151, 162, 166, 205, 211, 213–218, 223, 230, 240, 281, 334, 336, 341, 408, 419, 430f., 454, 460, 464, 498, 509–515
Being (*Wesen*), intelligible (of Man)   312–317, 343, 350, 359, 399
Being born again, s. Rebirth,   482
Beiser, F.   241
Benz, R.   14
Beretta, P.   13
Berger, D.   382
Berg, R. J.   19, 33, 43, 55, 152, 161, 197, 293, 309, 315, 318
Berkeley, G.   87f., 128
Besonnenheit   72, 76–79, 112, 114, 116, 118f., 122–124, 126–132, 173, 189, 194, 199, 236, 259, 262, 264, 266, 400, 404
Bhagavad Gita   367f., 396, 398, 403, 410
Bianco, B.   51
Bible   267, 335, 354
Birnbacher, D.   346, 455, 513
Blessedness   314, 339
Bliss/Blissfulness   10f., 179, 202, 218, 220, 227, 240, 248, 259f., 333, 339f., 345, 357, 366, 401, 411, 413, 417, 419, 430f., 488, 491
Blondin M.-M.   508
Blumenbach, J. F.   34
Body or Lived-Body (*Leib*)   126, 160, 294–297, 318, 342, 345, 349, 365, 391, 394, 397, 437–439, 441, 445–448, 451, 476, 480,
Bohinc, T.   448
Böhme, J.   196f., 231, 312
Boileau, N.   14
Böker, W.   34
Bondeli, M.   285
Bonheim, G.   197
Booms, M.   5, 448, 474, 495

Brahm   377–379, 389, 397f., 424f.
Brahma   377, 425
Brahman   377, 425
Brahmanism   380
Brain   140, 261, 434, 468
Breaking Away, Tearing Free (*Sich-Losreißen*)   232–234, 236, 240, 416, 502
Brianese, G.   506
Brown, R. E.   333
Brucker, J. J.   41f.
Bruno, G.   39, 44, 74, 81, 146, 297, 380, 398, 461
Buchheim, T.   43
Buddha   24
Buddhism/Buddhists   376, 385f., 425, 433, 480, 487

Carl, W.   46
Carracci, A.   25
Cartwright, D. E.   2, 10, 15f., 36, 62, 257, 375, 381, 468
Categorical Imperative   172, 182, 186, 188, 204f., 228, 248, 338
Categories (of understanding)   45, 51, 87, 99–102, 105f., 120, 134f., 148, 155f., 161, 165f., 214, 251, 253, 262, 287f., 296
Catullus   250
Cause, Causality, Category of   45, 80, 82, 92f., 100, 134–141, 148, 152, 155f., 160, 163, 179f., 250, 265, 267, 281f., 294, 296–298, 302, 304–307, 367f., 397f., 421, 437, 454f., 484
Cavallini, S.   474
Ceraunological Proof for God   228f.,
Character (empirical /intelligible)   111, 161, 238f., 252, 272, 277, 284, 299–308, 313–318, 322, 325, 330, 341–346, 348–354, 356–359, 364, 367–370, 381–383, 385, 387, 390–395, 397–401, 407, 420, 423f., 427, 437–448, 450, 452f., 456f., 463, 467, 469, 475–480, 485, 491f., 497, 499f., 505
Chenet, F. X.   188, 190, 322, 325
China/Chinese   218, 227, 376, 431
Choice, oft he will   107, 111, 124, 185, 191, 194f., 202f., 209, 220, 222, 224, 261–264, 301, 306, 336, 344, 350f., 355, 364, 366, 368f., 382, 427, 429, 490, 497, 513

Choice of the temporal Life   344, 351
Christianity   176, 182, 207, 209, 267, 320, 335, 508
Cicero, Marcus, Tullius   17, 32
Claudius, M.   9
Cognition   4, 25f., 33, 45–49, 51f., 54, 57f., 60, 62, 73f., 81, 84f., 87, 90–93, 99, 105, 108f., 116, 118, 122, 127, 130f., 136, 147f., 155–157, 161, 164f., 171–177, 179–181, 184, 186f., 192f., 195, 200–203, 205, 207–212, 214, 217, 221, 224, 226, 234, 245, 248, 253, 255, 259, 264, 268f., 280f., 284, 289–292, 294–297, 299, 306, 314, 317–321, 324, 327, 341, 345f., 356–359, 361f., 364–370, 373f., 379, 383–387, 390f., 394, 396f., 399, 401–403, 408–417, 419, 423f., 426–429, 432f., 437f., 441f., 445f., 449f., 452–455, 457, 464f., 468f., 472, 474–476, 479–497, 502–506, 510, 512–515
Color   99, 101, 103f., 106, 109, 259, 278, 302
Compassion   479
Concepts, theory of   37–41, 44, 51f., 71, 99–107, 119–122, 130, 134–136, 146–154, 161–166, 173, 180f., 183, 185f., 189, 191, 199f., 209f., 224–227, 279–282, 312, 319, 331, 361f., 366, 409–414, 429–431, 451f.
Consciousness, of Man (s. also Duplicity)   14, 19, 22, 41, 48, 59, 69, 71f., 77, 81, 84f., 87f., 92, 97, 99f., 110, 112–116, 119–125, 127–131, 139, 141f., 144, 147, 153–157, 159, 165, 171, 181, 184–193, 198f., 201–204, 207–213, 219–221, 223f., 226–230, 232–234, 236–243, 245–272, 280, 285, 289–297, 300, 313f., 316f., 319–323, 325–328, 331–335, 337–341, 346f., 349–351, 353–357, 361–366, 369, 371–373, 375, 380, 382, 385, 389f., 396f., 399–402, 404, 407, 409–420, 427–430, 432–435, 442, 445, 452, 456, 466, 474, 489, 491f., 498–507, 510–512, 515
Contemplation, Contemplate   16, 18, 50, 54f., 76, 246, 251f., 255f., 345, 403, 408, 418, 434, 494, 504
Contradiction, Principle of   28, 49f., 55, 91f., 126, 130, 151f., 154, 156f., 161–164, 202, 205, 211, 223f., 269, 272, 279–281, 287, 290, 299, 303, 310, 336, 340, 371, 405, 408–410, 412, 441, 470, 473, 484, 496, 501, 508f.
Conversion (*Bekehrung, Bekehren*)   232, 354f., 360, 434, 492
Copernican (or Anti-Copernican) Revolution   45f., 49, 85, 90, 218, 253
Copernicus, N.   46f., 85
Correggio, A. Allegri da   25, 29, 514
Cosmogony   157, 308
Creation, Creator   28, 37f., 40f., 43, 78, 147, 149, 255, 311f., 314, 333f., 356, 377, 422, 425, 461
Critias   117f.
Criticism   46, 52, 56, 64, 69, 73, 85, 89–92, 112, 133, 134, 137, 166, 171, 177, 226, 248, 282, 318, 326, 343, 397, 406, 415, 418, 420, 428, 472f., 484, 498, 507
Criticism, genuine, true or pure   56, 161, 164f., 171f., 174–178, 181f., 186f., 201f., 207, 209, 212, 224, 226f., 319, 321, 326–328, 331, 333, 366, 395f., 401, 412, 415, 507
Cross, S.   5, 231, 376
Crystals/Crystallization   393f., 397, 454
Cysarz, H.   308

D'Alfonso, M.   35f., 39, 44, 51, 60–63, 71, 74, 87–90, 92, 108, 110, 134, 147, 155, 167, 181, 217, 278, 282, 288, 295
Damnation   362, 419
Dara Shikoh   376
Death   1, 3, 9–11, 18, 20f., 24, 27, 54, 126, 202, 215, 218, 224, 233, 239–242, 258, 267, 335–337, 339f., 352, 354, 357f., 361f., 370–372, 386, 393, 400f., 406, 426, 429f., 475
Debona, V.   367
Decher, F.   198, 263, 271, 295, 449
De Cian, N.   9, 14, 19, 24, 36, 57, 89, 92, 167, 190, 202, 259, 282, 320
Decision   15, 32, 61, 96, 106, 110f., 224, 236, 263, 298–301, 303f., 314f., 342, 367–369, 391, 415, 437
Deed (*Thathandlung*) of I   30f., 159f., 196, 307, 315, 317, 351, 353, 355f., 372, 454f., 481, 496, 511f.
Deity, Divine: s. God   37f., 40–42, 255
Deligne, A.   206

De Lorenzo, G.   431
Delusion (*Täuschung, Wahn*)   18, 21, 58, 84–86, 357f., 363, 366, 370, 374, 488, 491
Denial (*Verleugnung, Verläugnung*), Deny (*verleugnen, verläugnen*)   46, 196, 230–232, 338, 359, 366, 369, 371, 423, 425–427, 432, 476, 481, 486–488, 512
Denomination from the superior term or *Denominatio a potiori*,   74, 449, 451–453, 455, 458, 470, 476, 478, 507,
De Pascale, C.   140, 294
De Sanctis, F.   431
Descartes, R.   87f., 116, 128, 130, 284
Deussen, P.   176, 358, 379
Devil   24, 37, 228, 351, 372, 374
Dianoiology   201, 510
Di Giovanni, G.   35
Dobrzański, M.   106
Dogmatism/Dogmatists   124, 162–164, 176, 227, 318, 333, 338, 415
Döll, H.   271
Donà, M.   431
Doß, A. v.   486, 512
Dream   15, 20, 26, 78, 82–86, 153, 232, 239f., 258, 324–326, 365, 371, 386, 410, 514
Drive (*Trieb*)   20, 27f., 37, 75, 139–143, 145f., 187, 194, 199, 232, 266, 351, 373, 490, 514
Dualism, metaphysical/critical   9, 11f., 24f., 57, 92–94, 125f., 133, 147, 193, 197f., 200, 205, 213, 380, 428f., 433, 460, 475, 498
Duplicity of Man's Nature or Being or Consciousness   11, 123, 125, 191, 197f., 200–205, 213, 220–224, 243, 245, 259f., 265, 270, 272, 336, 363, 366, 402, 428f., 433f., 504–506

Earth, Spirit of the   143f.
Ebeling, H.   513
Effort (*Streben*; s. also Striving)   4, 12f., 123f., 352
Egoism, theoretical   451, 479
Ego (s. also I)   80, 259
Egypt/Egyptians   350
Eichstädt, H. C.   277
Eleatics, Eleatic School   398
Elon, D.   86
Empedocles   510
Empiricism   199, 412
Ens   100–102, 104, 214, 216f., 225, 378, 384, 390, 418
Enthusiasm   15, 34, 64, 133, 182, 190, 238, 245
Epicurus   50, 56
Erdmann, J. E.   375
Erman, P.   69
Eros   150
Error   30, 58, 76, 80, 82, 85f., 90f., 96f., 99, 171, 177–180, 195, 205, 227, 234, 282, 335, 339f., 358, 362f., 366–368, 372, 374, 405, 408f., 487, 495f.
Eschmann, E.   447, 474f.
Essence (*Wesen*)   22, 26, 38f., 52, 71, 96, 102, 109–111, 142f., 147, 161f., 164f., 173–175, 178, 182, 188, 192, 197, 199, 207, 211, 213f., 228, 236f., 239, 242, 245, 262, 267, 299, 301–304, 308, 311, 313, 315–319, 323, 325, 330, 334, 343, 346, 350, 353, 356f., 359, 362, 364, 385, 389–391, 393, 396, 398–400, 403f., 407, 411, 413, 419, 423, 425f., 429, 433, 438, 440–445, 449–455, 457, 459–462, 464–467, 469–471, 473–477, 479–484, 486–497, 499–501, 503–507, 510, 512f.
Eternity   9–16, 21f., 24, 26–28, 36, 38, 57f., 153, 199, 213, 223, 230, 234, 248–251, 257, 266–268, 270, 323, 335, 339–341, 343, 356f., 363, 368f., 374, 413, 426, 433, 498f., 501, 503f.
Euclid   128
Euripides   31f., 337
Evil   11, 21–24, 27, 29–33, 40, 59, 98, 111, 201, 213, 238, 240f., 249, 252, 312, 335, 342, 350, 358–360, 364f., 374, 382f., 394, 398, 424, 430
Existence (*Existenz, Daseyn*)   2, 12, 19f., 23–25, 30, 36–39, 60, 62, 88f., 91–93, 98f., 125, 132, 143, 147f., 150, 153, 157, 162, 171f., 178, 182–184, 186, 198f., 202, 219, 223, 228, 230f., 234, 238f., 241f., 259, 266, 271, 285, 295f., 300, 309f., 333f., 339–341, 343–346, 348–351, 353, 356, 361, 363f., 368–372, 374, 377–379, 382–385, 391, 395, 399, 408, 415, 417f., 423, 427, 429f., 432, 438, 443, 454, 456, 461f., 464f., 487–489, 495f., 502, 507, 513

Index —— 545

Faculties, cognitive   49, 78, 101, 164, 181, 227, 244, 305, 322–324, 412
Faith   3, 19, 353–356, 372, 434, 480
Fall (metaphysical)   13, 157–161, 241, 266f., 335f., 348, 352f., 399, 511
Fatalists   367
Faust   2f., 37, 144, 188, 203, 222, 232, 235, 237, 351
Fauth, S. R.   14, 28, 278, 514
Feeling   18f., 21, 30, 37, 63f., 75, 125, 129, 139, 229, 240, 244–248, 252f., 316f., 325, 343, 417, 433, 488f.
Fichte, J. G.   3, 35, 58, 60f., 63, 65, 69–71, 73–75, 78–83, 86, 90f., 99f., 103–106, 108–116, 118–130, 132–147, 150, 153, 156, 159–161, 163–167, 171–173, 175, 177, 179, 187–191, 193f., 197, 199, 201f., 208f., 212, 215, 219, 224, 231, 233, 251, 259, 262, 264, 266, 272, 277, 289–295, 297, 299f., 313–315, 318, 349–351, 373, 381, 388, 407, 415, 449, 462, 474
Fincham, R.   86
Fischer, N.   86
Fitzmyer, J. A.   333
Flash of Evidence   79–81, 83, 93, 138, 165
Force (of Nature)   46, 96, 135f., 245f., 311, 380, 416, 421, 434, 449, 454, 467, 477
Fortlage, C.   144
Frauenstädt, J.   3f., 468–470, 486, 512
Freedom of Man   62, 96, 98, 110f., 131, 158f., 178, 180, 185, 194f., 195, 218–223, 225, 232–237, 241f., 261–263, 271, 298f., 301, 303, 304, 306–316, 328, 333, 335, 349–353, 359f., 368, 371, 374, 392, 399, 411, 429, 442, 445f., 482, 485, 490, 495, 508, 511–513
Fries, J. F.   281, 314

Gabriel Archangel   377
Gay, J.   10
Genitals   261, 434
Genius   56, 69–78, 91, 93, 108, 125, 131, 134, 173–175, 191f., 212, 236, 258–260, 264, 270, 323, 355, 400, 403f., 409, 412–414, 494
Gerhardt, V.   527
Gerhard, M.   16, 218, 376, 380

Gabriel, G.   332, 356
Giametta, S.   123, 460
Giordanetti, P.   47, 258
Giordano, F.   380
Gjellerup, K.   98, 263
Glasenapp, H. v.   382
Göbel-Gross, E.   376
Göcke, B. P.   381
God   10, 19, 23f., 29, 38–43, 48, 51, 55–57, 61–63, 75, 83, 96, 98, 144, 147, 149f., 153, 160, 163–165, 176, 178, 180, 182, 187, 195, 197, 207f., 227–230, 239, 255, 271, 309–312, 316, 333, 335f., 353–355, 374, 377, 380, 388, 397f., 416f., 424f., 432, 435, 461f., 508, 513
Goehr, L.   505
Goethe, J. W. v.   2f., 25, 37, 56, 73, 131, 144, 188, 203, 222, 231f., 235, 237, 250, 278, 302, 375
Good, Supreme   62, 179, 218, 363, 428, 431, 504
Grace (religious concept)   231, 336, 354, 482, 489, 495, 508
Gravity   100, 135, 163, 179, 192, 309
Greek Philosophers   463, 476
Grigenti, F.   278, 474
Grisebach, E.   10
Grimm, J. and Grimm, W.   107, 109, 338
Ground (*Grund*)   29f., 36, 63, 79f., 100, 113, 135–138, 157, 178, 182, 185, 211, 238f., 247, 253, 278, 281f., 284, 287f., 302, 305, 309–312, 314, 318, 322, 328, 343f., 361f., 366f., 387f., 392, 396, 404, 409, 421, 438, 453, 462, 478
Gründer, K.   32, 356
Guéroult, M.   294
Gurisatti, G.   343, 376
Guyer, P.   504
Gwinner, W.   59

Halbfass, W.   380
Hallich, O.   446
Hamann, J. G.   42
Hamlet   25, 200
Hammacher, K.   138

Happiness   58 f., 61–63, 182, 235, 260, 334, 337, 339 f., 357 f., 363, 367 f., 372, 374, 416, 431, 488, 491, 495
Harris, H. S.   35
Hasrat, J.   376
Haydn, F. J.   76
Haym, R.   293, 448, 451
Heaven   12 f., 15, 26 f., 42, 46, 263, 337, 390, 399, 417
Hecker, M. F.   382
Heeren, H. L.   34, 375
Hegel, G. W. F.   86, 166, 230, 318
Heimann, R.   220, 231, 315, 327, 350
Hennigfeld, J.   43
Hennings, J. C.   277
Henry, P.   26
Herbart, J. F.   297
Herder, J. G. v.   188, 204, 347
Hicetas   85
Hieroglyphics   319, 331
Hinduism/Hindus   377, 480
Hippias   17
History, Historical Knowledge   34, 68–70, 79, 135,
Höfele, Ph.   314 f.
Hoffmann, Ernst Theodor Amadeus   76–79
Holiness, Holy Man s. Saint   62, 236, 323, 336, 412 f., 430, 480 f., 483, 488, 492, 494, 501
Holy Spirit   341, 354
Homer   250, 416
Horace   221, 250
Huber, T.   189
Huber, V. A.   189
Hübscher, A.   4, 9 f., 12, 14, 19 f., 25, 42, 51, 59, 64, 78, 92, 119, 176, 192, 197, 257, 271, 348, 358, 381 f., 470
Hühn, L.   318, 508
Hume, D.   87, 211, 229

Idealism, Idealist   48 f., 74, 87 f., 90, 97, 101 f., 122–124, 137 f., 140–142, 146 f., 150 f., 155 f., 192, 262, 264, 293, 310, 313, 409 f., 451
Ideas of Reason (Kant)   55, 161, 163, 180 f., 200, 230, 244–247
Ideas, Platonic   21–22, 37–43, 51–55, 71, 74 f., 82, 100, 108, 111, 131, 133, 158, 213, 215, 229, 246, 250 f., 253–255, 269, 280, 319, 323 f., 326–328, 361 f., 369, 402–417, 419–422, 429, 433, 460 f., 463–467, 469, 471–473, 475–479, 482–484, 491–494, 497, 499–506
Identity, Principle of   151, 154, 279–281, 287
I (*Ich*), Concept of   70 f., 73, 80, 161, 219, 259, 291–292, 479, 519
Illusion, transcendental   264 f., 267, 269
Image, mental (*Phantasma*)   105 f.
Immortality   19, 62, 99, 178, 239, 271
India/Indians   3, 34, 84 f., 128, 347 f., 350, 357 f., 374–377, 381–390, 395 f., 398–400, 409, 417 f., 424 f., 432
Individuality   161, 182, 195–197, 223, 228, 238 f., 242, 250 f., 255, 302 f., 338, 349, 351, 398, 401, 403 f., 417, 426, 477, 479, 482, 485 f.
Individuation, Principle of, s. *Principium Individuationis*   417, 449, 467, 477
I-ness (*Ichheit*)   160, 351
Inexpressible, the (*das Unnennbare*)   43, 182, 186, 192, 195 f., 210, 212, 227 f.
Infinite   15, 60, 62, 75, 82, 98 f., 143–146, 152–154, 199, 244 f., 344, 362, 373, 401, 411, 417, 457, 460–462
Ingenkamp, H. G.   460, 505
Instinct   131, 183–187, 191, 453
Intellectualism, s. Voluntarism/Intellectualism
Intention (*Gesinnung, Absicht*)   96 f., 99, 213, 259, 371, 393, 410
Interiority   19, 25–27, 36, 41, 64, 81, 386
Intuition   13, 18 f., 21 f., 27, 60 f., 69, 72–75, 81 f., 86, 91, 93, 103–105, 127, 134, 150–157, 165, 177, 181, 190, 207–209, 216–219, 225 f., 243, 251, 253 f., 262, 266, 280 f., 288–290, 293, 296 f., 299, 304, 319, 324, 337, 362, 364, 398, 400, 405, 411, 415 f., 437, 439, 457, 491, 494
Invernizzi, G.   468, 474, 482, 512

Jacob, H.   197, 207, 238
Jacobi, F. H.   92, 137, 186–188, 211 f., 265
Jacobs, W. G.   43, 138
Janaway, Ch.   504, 513
Janke, W.   116
Jantzen, J.   43

Jean Paul 25, 76–79, 131, 404
Jesus Christ 29, 32, 231, 235, 238, 335f., 338, 349, 353–355, 426, 508
Jivatma 388f.
John (the Apostle) 10, 331
Julius Caesar 198

Kabbala 42
Kamata, Y. 19, 39, 86, 190, 284f., 293, 324, 327, 382, 420, 458, 472f.
Kant, Immanuel 17, 34–36, 44–50, 52–58, 61–64, 73, 80, 82, 84–94, 97, 100f., 104, 106, 108, 110, 116, 128f., 133f., 136–138, 140f., 144, 150f., 153, 155, 163–167, 171f., 174, 177–185, 188, 192, 194–197, 199, 201, 203f., 208f., 213f., 216–218, 225f., 228–231, 234–237, 239, 243–249, 252f., 257f., 262f., 271, 279, 282, 284, 286–288, 290, 295, 301, 304–308, 314f., 318, 320, 325, 327f., 342, 344, 346, 380–382, 387f., 398f., 404–408, 410, 418, 420, 422, 438, 447, 450, 460, 464–466, 468f., 471f., 474, 499f., 507f.
Kapani, L. 376
Kielmeyer, C. F. 261
Kiesewetter, J. G. 284
Kisner, M. 409
Klaproth, H. J. 347, 376
Klaproth, M. H. 69
Kloppe, W. 271
Knappik, F. 297
Knowledge of Knowledge 112–114, 116, 118
Knowledge (*Wissen*) 2f., 6, 22, 26–28, 33–36, 39, 41, 44, 46, 48f., 53–58, 61f., 69f., 72–74, 76, 78–80, 82–87, 89–91, 93, 112–118, 120, 128f., 133, 135f., 138, 140f., 144, 149–151, 154f., 157, 166, 171, 173, 176, 179f., 182f., 187, 190, 208, 226, 235, 251, 265f., 286, 292, 301, 310, 318, 328, 347, 357f., 360f., 364, 375, 379, 381, 385f., 398, 404, 407f., 412, 423, 440, 449f., 455, 460, 464, 476, 481, 487, 497, 499, 502
Koßler, M. 32, 79, 179, 273, 287, 294, 308, 314, 317, 343, 352, 448, 457, 505–508, 514
Krishna 347
Kshetra and *Kshetrajna* 345, 347
Kurbel, M. 380, 382, 448

Lafontaine, A. H. J. 25
Laks, A. 116
Lambert, J. H. 284
Langen, A. 233
Language, theory of 15, 37, 40–43, 164, 173, 210, 225f., 254
Language, figurative use of 119–121, 158, 173–175, 177, 199, 211, 225, 228f., 267, 301, 312, 331, 354, 359
Laocoon (sculptural group) 25
Lao-Tzu 218
Last Judgment 263
Lauth, R. 113
Law 30f., 45f., 62, 79, 96–99, 125, 135f., 139, 154f., 156, 161, 163, 166, 172, 178–180, 182–187, 190–197, 203, 212, 214, 227, 231–236, 247, 279–281, 283–288, 294, 298, 302, 305f., 320, 325f., 328, 344, 354, 361, 368, 388, 422, 445, 452, 455
Leibniz, G. W. 42, 284, 350
Lemanski, J. 5, 46, 514
Léon, X. 144
Leopardi, G. 431
Lessing, G. E. 109
Lichtenstein, M.H. 69
Life (*Leben*) 2, 9, 13, 15–17, 19, 24, 27–30, 36, 39, 50, 54, 58f., 61f., 64, 71, 82f., 85, 97f., 130f., 138, 143f., 164, 166, 171, 179, 196f., 200–202, 204–206, 208, 220f., 224, 226, 229–234, 236f., 239f., 242f., 246, 249, 258, 260f., 267, 278, 305, 314, 320, 326, 330, 335f., 338–346, 348f., 351–354, 356–360, 362–372, 374f., 380, 382–387, 391–395, 397f., 401, 404, 415, 417, 419f., 423–427, 429f., 432–435, 437, 456f., 459, 461, 468f., 471–473, 478–484, 486–497, 499–508, 510–515
Lindner, E. O. 271, 486
Locke, J. 41f., 87f., 281
Loer, B. 155
Longo, M. 42, 51
López de Santa María, P. 513
Lorenz, A. 9
Losacco, M. 431
Love 10–13, 27f., 114, 131, 150, 311, 339, 354, 373, 378, 380, 426, 479, 489, 493
Luden, H. 277

Luther, M.   25, 32, 231, 333, 354 f., 426
Lütkehaus, L.   10, 12 f., 15 f., 24 f., 29, 36, 57, 59, 257, 514
Lyric/Lyrical Poetry   433

Maage, B.   382
Madness (*Wahnsinn*), Madman (*Wahnsinnige*)   69–73, 78, 164, 179
Magic Lantern   328, 423
Magnet, Magnetic Polarity   454
Maimon, S.   284
Mainländer, P.   241
Maya, Maïa   84, 357 f., 373, 375 f., 377–381, 383–385, 387, 395, 397 f., 422, 424, 479, 487
Majer, F.   347, 375 f.
Malter, R.   1, 203, 273, 318, 445, 458, 472, 490 f., 506
Manichees   23, 29
Manifold of Sensibility   101
Mann, W. R.   463
Marchtaler, H. v.   9
Marti, F.   25, 61, 69
Massei Junior, W.   354
Materialism/Materialists   122 f., 312
Mathematics   45, 80, 281, 288
Matthew (Apostle)   83, 231, 426
Meattini, V.   93
Medea   31
Meister Eckhart   197
Melanchthon, Ph.   354
Memory   18, 59, 100–104, 160, 255
Metaphysics   4, 6, 14, 18, 34–36, 44, 48–50, 60–62, 64, 71, 85, 87, 90, 92, 98, 123, 133 f., 140–142, 147, 161, 188, 208, 217, 223, 226, 263, 271 f., 282, 284, 289, 295, 309, 316–318, 327, 330 f., 343, 353, 375, 382, 385–388, 406, 431, 436, 443, 448, 455, 468, 470–473, 475, 498, 500, 506 f.
Metempsychosis, s. Reincarnation   371
Metz, W.   293, 295
Meyer, L.   9
Meyer, U. W.   382
Michelangelo   29
Micheli, G.   51
Milton, J.   10–13, 18, 21, 57
Minerals, Mineral Kingdom   393 f., 400, 477

Mirror   77, 342 f., 356, 359 f., 391, 423 f., 426, 458–460, 467, 474, 496, 500 f., 510
Mischel, F.   376
Moral   9, 61–64, 70, 96–98, 117, 124, 177–180, 182–186, 188, 190 f., 193, 195–197, 203 f., 208, 212 f., 230–232, 234–238, 244, 247, 249, 258, 263, 265, 270 f., 323, 325, 341, 350, 354, 360, 491
More, Th.   235.
Morini, M.   468
Moses   29
Most, G. W   119
Motivation, Law of   298, 302, 364, 367–370, 427, 438, 441, 445 f., 452 f., 455, 483 f., 486 f., 491–494, 497
Mozart, W. A.   76
Müller-Lauter, W.   315
Müller-Seyfarth, W. H.   241
Multiplicity, s. Plurality   108, 319, 377, 379, 389, 406, 452 f., 457, 460, 464–467, 471, 477
Music   14–16, 42, 44, 76 f., 79, 239, 256–258, 339, 504 f.
Mysticism/Mystics   61, 83, 153, 192, 197, 199, 203, 209, 231, 309, 360, 475 f., 482, 513–515
Myth   83, 160, 267, 344, 349 f., 371, 382, 399, 407

Napoleon Buonaparte   277
Nature   2, 5, 9, 11, 13 f., 17, 25–27, 37–46, 48, 57, 62, 74, 103, 116, 124–127, 140, 147, 149, 151 f., 155, 157 f., 163–165, 167, 175, 178, 183, 185, 188, 199, 201 f., 204–209, 213, 216 f., 219–224, 226, 229, 231–233, 237, 240–250, 252, 254 f., 259–261, 263, 265, 280, 299–302, 305 f., 308 f., 311, 313, 320, 325, 331, 335 f., 343, 345–347, 349, 351, 358–361, 363, 365 f., 368, 385 f., 390, 393, 400, 402, 407, 409–412, 414, 416, 428, 431, 433, 438, 440, 442 f., 445, 449, 457, 459, 461 f., 475, 477, 486 f., 489, 491, 494, 499, 508–511, 514
Naubert, B.   189
Negation of the Will   194, 196 f., 206, 330, 371, 420, 425, 427, 429, 432–434, 469, 479, 481, 483–486, 488–491, 494 f., 497, 501, 503, 505 f., 508, 513

Negative Theology   190
Negri, A.   431
New Testament   13, 29, 32, 36, 231, 311, 335, 354, 426
Newton, Sir Isaac   45
Nieban   425
Nietzsche, F. W.   374, 451
Nirvana   427, 433
Norman, J.   154
Nothingness (*Nichtigkeit*)   20, 27, 53, 58, 80, 82, 93 f., 96, 110, 133, 160, 162, 164, 190, 193, 201, 212 f., 215, 218, 224, 226 f., 240, 249, 332, 361, 385, 431, 483, 487 f., 492
Nothing (*Nichts*), concept of   194, 215 – 218, 223 – 225, 230 f., 240, 254, 269, 337, 430 f., 498 – 501, 508, 510 – 515
Noumenon   51, 53, 208, 225
Novalis   26, 59, 144
Noveanu, A.   448
Novembre, A.   69, 119, 141, 271, 294, 315, 434, 447 f., 474, 497, 501

Object   s. Subject-Objectivity
Objecthood (*Objectität*) of the Will   380, 421 f., 443, 452, 457 – 461, 463 f., 466, 469, 471 f., 503, 510
Old Testament   29, 333
Olympia   17, 416
Olympus   417
Ontology   510
Ontotheology   166
Opera operata   355, 370
Ought (*Sollen, Soll*)   33, 98, 180, 190 f., 195, 200, 204, 233, 249, 267, 305, 307, 346, 356, 391, 432
Oupnekhat   348, 373 – 382, 384 – 387, 389 – 390, 395 – 399, 418 – 420, 422, 424 f., 489
Ovid   31 f.

Pain   15, 21, 24, 143, 200 f., 230, 232, 237, 260, 340 f., 356 – 358, 360, 362 f., 366, 369 – 372, 374, 385 f., 394, 402, 423 f., 427, 430 f., 473, 479, 486 – 489, 492, 496, 504, 514
Pantheism   374
Paradise, s. Heaven   203, 256, 426
Pareyson, L.   144 f., 251
Parmenides   90, 192 f., 509

Past, transcendental   1, 18, 26, 99, 130, 198 f., 221, 255 f., 357, 391, 489
Paul, Saint   13, 25, 36, 54, 57, 69, 331, 354 f., 358, 434
Payne, E. F. J.   35, 37, 222, 226, 232, 237, 363, 373
Peace of God   36, 334, 356, 366
Peetz, S.   43
Penzo, G.   294
Perception of Perception   114 – 116, 118 – 121, 165
Perception (*Wahrnehmung*)   48, 53, 70, 77, 79 f., 85, 87 – 90, 100 – 102, 113, 115 f., 119 – 126, 128 f., 135 – 137, 173, 189, 199 f., 214, 219, 233, 264, 266, 281, 289, 320, 401
Personality   4, 132, 228 f., 239, 242, 246, 251, 254, 263, 268, 349, 398
Pfeiffer-Belli, W.   14
Phenomenon, s. Appearance   47, 81, 113 f., 135 f., 172, 208, 243, 247 f., 305, 407, 421, 468 f.
Philistine, Philistinism   58 f., 186, 191 f., 235, 260
Philolaus   85
Philosophy   1 – 6, 9, 16 f., 22, 33 – 36, 40 – 45, 49 – 62, 64, 69, 75, 79, 81 f., 85 – 87, 89, 92, 94, 99, 101, 108, 112 – 114, 116, 119, 123, 125 – 130, 133 – 135, 145 – 150, 153, 155, 157, 160 f., 164, 166 f., 171 – 177, 181 f., 188, 191, 197 f., 201, 203 – 205, 207, 210, 214, 223, 227, 230, 235, 242, 248, 255, 259, 271 f., 277 – 279, 283, 288 f., 292, 308, 318, 320, 322, 327 f., 330 – 335, 348 – 351, 355, 360 – 362, 364, 376, 380 – 382, 387 f., 396, 398, 405 – 407, 416, 418, 420, 429 – 432, 446, 448 f., 455, 460, 464, 468 f., 471, 475 f., 498, 504 – 506, 508, 514 f.
Philosophy of Nature (*Naturphilosophie*)   34, 39, 60, 129, 146, 149, 151 – 153, 155, 208, 214, 226 f., 311, 461, 474
Piantelli, M.   376 – 378
Pico della Mirandola   242
Pietism/Pietists   9, 12, 16, 28, 57, 231, 233, 338, 355
Piper, R.   279
Plants, Plant Kingdom   20, 64, 206, 232, 392 – 394, 397, 400, 454, 457, 477

Plato 2, 17, 22, 30f., 34, 36–38, 40f., 43f., 49–55, 57f., 64, 72, 74–76, 80, 82–85, 90, 94, 97, 99, 116–118, 123, 130, 150, 160, 165, 172, 182f., 192f., 195, 201–203, 213, 215–217, 226, 229, 233, 254f., 271, 279–281, 284, 320, 324, 327f., 337, 344, 361, 381f., 396, 404–408, 411, 413, 422f., 449, 459f., 463–465, 469, 499f., 509, 511
Plattner, E. 284
Pleasure 20, 59, 116, 194, 200, 203, 220–222, 224, 250, 257, 278, 325, 337, 345, 352, 366, 427, 431, 487, 504
Plotinus 43, 190, 200, 202, 207, 411, 459
Poetry, Poet 21, 25, 27, 40f., 43f., 70, 75f., 134, 433
Poggi, S. 34
Pohlenz, M. 32
Point of view, Common / Philosophical 115f., 121, 126.
Polier M. E. de/Polier A. L. H. (colonel de) 376
Postulates of Practical Reason 172, 195
Powers (*Kräfte*) of Cognition 23, 71, 175, 178f., 187, 226, 229, 248, 261, 305, 409
Pozzo, R. 47
Plurality 94, 108, 111, 147, 403, 406, 408, 453, 459, 469
Primacy 62f., 260, 264, 482, 495, 513
Principium Individuationis 108, 452f., 460, 466, 479, 482–484, 486, 488f., 492
Procreation 352, 425
Propertius, Sextus 250
Pythagoras 17

Racine, J. 14
Radrizzani, I. 113
Raphael 29, 514
Rätze, J. G. 19
Realism/Realist 46, 122–126, 264, 310
Realism, empirical 48, 87, 410
Reality 17, 30, 42, 45f., 49, 51, 54, 57, 60f., 64f., 73f., 76, 80–82, 84, 87–90, 93f., 96f., 101, 116, 121, 126f., 129, 133, 138, 151f., 158f., 161–165, 167, 171–174, 180, 186, 188, 200, 205, 209f., 213f., 218, 226–228, 242, 247, 252f., 259, 261, 265–267, 269, 295, 307, 310, 331, 360f., 365, 378, 385f., 389, 398, 403, 405f., 410–412, 414f., 431, 451, 465f., 473, 489, 499, 514f.
Reason, Principle of Sufficient 69, 91, 99, 104, 138, 251, 272, 277f., 280–288, 298, 303, 319f., 321–325, 327f., 344, 352, 361f., 364f., 369f., 388f., 396, 399, 402–404, 408, 412, 415, 427, 429, 433, 438, 440f., 452f., 455f., 463, 466, 470, 472, 482–484, 486, 492–497, 502f., 506
Reason (*Vernunft*) 21, 33, 36–38, 49–52, 54f., 60, 62f., 90, 105f., 127, 130–132, 140, 149, 161–166, 171, 177–186, 189–192, 194, 198, 200, 202f., 209f., 216, 220f., 223–226, 230, 234–238, 244–251, 257f., 260–265, 282, 285–287, 296, 305–308, 310, 319–325, 331f., 342, 346, 362, 392, 404, 410–416, 420, 437, 470, 480f., 491, 514
Rebirth (*Wiedergeburt*), spiritual 355, 360, 482
Recollection 18, 22, 25, 183, 256
Redemption (*Erlösung*) 199, 234, 236, 266, 323, 335f., 341, 354, 356, 370f., 386, 419, 423f., 429, 432, 434, 486, 488f., 508
Regehly, T. 176, 197, 424, 475
Reimarus, H. S. 284
Reincarnation 371
Reinhold, K. L. 35, 89, 156f., 268, 278, 285
Religion 2, 16, 25–28, 34, 75, 101, 147f., 157, 161, 164, 172–177, 197, 210, 214, 227–230, 266f., 308, 325, 331–334, 339, 349, 351, 355, 360, 364, 376, 382, 399, 432, 435, 475f., 482, 515
Remembrance 16, 18, 256
Renunciation 223, 231, 487
Representation (*Vorstellung*) 4f., 18, 22, 25, 29, 33, 42, 45–47, 49, 51, 57, 71, 74, 78, 81, 84–92, 94f., 97, 102–106, 108, 126–128, 130f., 134, 140, 142f., 145, 155f., 180f., 192, 196, 212, 216f., 229, 236, 243, 262, 264, 271, 273, 283–286, 290, 292f., 295–297, 299, 306, 309f., 318f., 324, 327, 330, 346, 350, 352, 360f., 365, 367–369, 379, 381, 387–390, 397f., 402, 404f., 408f., 414, 417, 422, 425f., 430, 433, 436–441, 446f., 449, 451–457, 459, 462, 465f., 468f., 472f., 479, 483f., 489, 491f., 495, 497, 501, 504–506, 510
Reproduction 103–106, 219, 270

Index —— 551

Resignation 163, 488, 490
Responsibility (*Verantwortlichkeit*) 63, 298, 307, 313, 316 f., 343
Riconda, G. 22, 382, 508, 514
Ritter, J. 32, 356
Rivera de Rosales, J. 314
Rosenkranz, J. K. F. 282
Rousseau, J. J. 14, 198
Ruffing, M. 179, 434
Rühl, M. 271
Runge, J. H. C. 9
Russell, B. 49
Ryan, C. 385

Safranski, R. 9 f., 14, 28, 188, 277 f., 330, 381 f.
Sainthood, Saintliness, Saints 224, 258 f., 264, 270, 323, 338, 429 f., 475 f., 480 – 482, 485, 487, 489 f, 514
Salvation 241 f., 355, 365, 371 f., 430, 434
Samuel, I. 11
Sandkaulen, B. 137
Sankara 376
Santinello, G. 51
Sattar, A. S. 51, 204, 463
Schelling, F. W. J. v. 2 f., 34, 37, 39, 43 f., 55, 60 f., 64, 74 – 76, 81 f., 86, 90, 94, 96 f., 101, 105, 110 f., 122, 124, 129, 132 – 134, 137 f., 142 – 144, 146 – 167, 171 f., 177, 188 f., 191 f., 196 f., 200, 208 – 210, 212, 214, 217 f., 227, 239, 242, 266, 277, 290, 293, 295, 297, 299, 301, 304, 308 – 318, 333 f., 337, 340, 343 f., 349 – 351, 359 f., 362, 374, 383, 388, 398 f., 415, 418, 431, 461 f., 474, 508
Schema 61, 103 f., 307, 496
Schiller, J. C. F. 14, 26, 231
Schirmacher, W. 514
Schlegel, F. 144
Schleiermacher, F. D. E. 17, 34, 69, 94, 97, 116, 118, 176 f., 190, 207 f., 278, 325, 459, 465
Schmidt, A. 176 f.,
Schmidt, M. 355
Scholasticism/Scholastics 117, 227, 452, 460,
Schöndorf, H. 294, 297
Schopenhauer, H. F. 9 f.
Schopenhauer, J. Trosiener 13, 15, 256 f., 330
Schubbe, D. 5, 278, 448, 458, 470, 475 f.
Schubert, F. W. 282

Schulze, G. E. 34
Schulz, W. 3, 9, 35 – 37, 39, 44, 49, 51, 54 f., 57, 60 – 64, 73, 85 – 90, 92 – 94, 108, 114, 133 f., 137, 147, 156, 166 f., 171, 177, 195, 217, 278 f., 282, 284 f., 288, 295, 308, 317, 323, 405, 407
Schwabe, G. 294
Schwenzfeuer, S. 315, 318
Science of Knowledge (*Wissenschaftslehre*) 35, 60 f., 69, 114, 119, 137 – 139, 141 f., 144 – 147, 153, 156 f., 166, 177, 190, 192, 219, 251, 272 f., 293, 373, 415, 462,
Science, Scientific Knowledge 1 – 3, 27, 34 f., 44 – 46, 48 – 50, 53, 69, 75, 79, 90, 113, 117 f., 135 – 137, 141, 149, 283 f., 331, 361 f., 378, 396, 404 f., 449, 455, 475, 506
Segala, M. 34, 69, 77, 92, 147, 237, 419, 434, 474
Self, Better 200, 208, 210
Self-Cognition/Self-Knowledge 122, 117, 147, 155 – 157, 207 – 209, 289 – 292, 299, 317, 359, 364, 381, 383, 391, 423 f., 438, 441, 445 f., 452, 457, 474, 480, 406, 489, 486, 493, 506, 514
Self-Consciousness 207
Self-Mortification (*Selbsttödtung*) 338
Self-Denial 196, 231, 338, 359, 423, 425 f., 481, 486,
Self-Positing, Self-Position (of I) 159 – 161, 218 – 220, 222, 232, 242, 313 – 315, 349 – 351, 511 f.
Semblance (*Schein*) 70, 84 – 86, 173 f., 201, 205, 213, 267, 331, 386, 460, 462
Seneca 32, 71, 326
Sengler, J. 146
Sensation 15, 92 f., 118, 128, 134, 180, 257, 296, 464
Sensibility (*Sinnlichkeit*) 44, 100 f., 106, 155, 161, 165 f., 185, 187, 240, 244, 267, 285, 287, 305, 320 – 322, 332, 386
Severino, E. 32, 431
Sex Drive 339
Seydel, R. 295, 448
Sgarbi, M. 47
Shakespeare, W. 25, 76, 198, 249
Shapshay, S. 434, 458, 482
Shiva 425

Siani, A. L. 54
Siebke, R. 9
Simili, R. 348
Sin 32, 71, 160, 232, 264, 266f., 272, 284, 286, 335f., 340f., 348–350, 352, 354, 357f., 364, 370, 377, 382, 399, 432, 499, 508, 511
Skepticism 37, 57, 86f., 89, 91f.
Socrates 30–32, 53f., 83, 116–118, 198, 337
Solipsism, s. Egoism, theoretical 447, 451
Soliva Soria, A. C. 287
Soul 10, 13, 15, 22, 29, 34, 48, 55, 62, 75, 79, 99, 116, 135, 140f., 146, 159f., 163, 178, 180, 188, 200–203, 210, 231f., 244f., 250, 271, 295, 311, 333, 349, 351, 373, 389, 480
Space 44–46, 51, 57f., 71, 80, 82, 88, 93f., 100, 108, 133, 135, 139, 198, 213, 215–217, 219, 224f., 233, 238, 244, 250, 257, 266, 280–282, 287f., 294, 296, 319, 334, 345, 361, 380, 391, 405–408, 410, 417, 437, 440, 452f., 455, 457, 460, 464f., 468f., 473, 477
Species 37–41, 44, 58, 102–104, 106f., 204, 238, 243, 248, 252, 257, 305, 339, 392, 394, 406, 408, 421, 449–452, 460, 462, 466f., 471f., 477–479, 507
Spener, Ph. J. 231
Spierling, V. 448, 458, 470, 498, 506
Spinoza, B. 284, 310, 333, 398
Spiritual world (*Geisterwelt*) 16–18, 26, 55, 60, 197, 220, 418
Steindler, L. 51
Still Life 250, 345
Stoics/Stoicism 21f., 32,
Stollberg, J. 34
Striving (*Streben*) 33, 143–146, 200, 318, 393, 401, 449, 454, 479, 486, 489
Suárez, Francisco 452
Subject-Object Polarity, Subject-Objectivity 154–156, 199, 266, 268, 351
Subject of Cognition 255, 269, 272, 292, 297, 325, 330, 346, 390, 397, 399–404, 408f., 412, 414–417, 419, 422, 433f., 503, 505f.
Sublime/Sublimity 243–248, 252, 258, 417, 434,
Substance 45, 100–102, 104, 214, 281f., 289f., 293, 295, 393, 398, 421

Suffering, s. Pain 142, 237, 260, 347, 356, 362, 385, 401f., 424, 426, 479f., 486–489, 491, 514
Suicide 10, 50, 54, 80, 90, 171, 200, 234, 338, 370–372, 426
Sulzer, J. G. 14
Supersensible (*Übersinnlich*) 25–27, 36f., 41–44, 56, 61, 64, 73f., 76, 79–81, 83f., 86, 93, 133, 135–138, 161f., 164f., 167, 171, 173–178, 181, 183, 185–188, 191–193, 195, 197, 200, 202, 205–213, 217, 219f., 223f., 226, 228–230, 234, 244, 248, 250, 252–254, 259f., 265, 267, 279, 321, 327, 332, 362, 364, 366, 398f., 410, 498–501
Swete, H. B. 333

Tantalus 143, 146
Tat twam asi 390
Tauler (Pseudo-) 197, 220, 231, 315, 350
Taylor, B. 37, 222, 237
Teleology 204, 232
Tennemann, W. G. 3, 49, 51f., 55, 58, 64, 86, 94, 111, 213, 320, 406f., 460, 463
Tersteegen, G. 16
Theism 227, 333, 397
Theodicy 235, 350
Theology, Theologians 9, 69, 147, 153, 166, 180, 182, 190, 227–230, 235, 309, 316, 354
Thing-in-Itself 33, 45, 47–55, 57, 61, 69, 73f., 81, 84, 86–94, 99, 106–111, 127, 133f., 137, 144f., 171, 196, 208, 226, 279f., 285, 300, 304f., 318, 330, 373, 398, 404–410, 420–423, 429, 437, 441, 443–445, 448–453, 456–476, 478, 480–486, 490, 494, 498–501, 503–505, 507
Thomas Aquinas 197
Thought, the One (of *The World as Will and Representation*) 4, 261, 272f.
Tibullus Albius 250
Tieck, J. L. 14, 28, 59
Tielsch, E. 321
Time 9–13, 15–22, 27f., 44–46, 52, 57–59, 71, 80, 82, 93f., 99f., 106, 108–111, 133, 144, 153, 157, 159, 161f., 164, 194, 198f., 209, 213, 215–217, 219, 221, 224f., 230f., 233f., 238, 240f., 244, 249–251, 253f., 257, 261, 265–267, 280–282, 287f., 292, 294, 299–

Index — 553

304, 306–320, 334f., 337–346, 348, 350–353, 355, 357–359, 361–364, 368–370, 372, 374, 382f., 385, 390–395, 399–403, 405–408, 410, 412, 415, 417, 419f., 423, 426, 430, 432, 437–440, 442, 444, 452f., 455, 457, 460, 464f., 468f., 473, 477, 483, 485, 491, 495f., 498f., 502
Tragedy   20–22, 27, 31, 59, 96f., 200f., 206f., 232, 235, 248, 339, 345, 360, 417, 426
Tranquillizer (*Quietiv*)   427, 482, 484, 488–490, 493–497
Trimurti   425
Truth   9–13, 17, 21, 24, 26–28, 34, 36, 39, 41, 44, 46, 50, 53–61, 64, 75, 79–86, 89–94, 99, 127f., 150, 153, 159, 171, 175f., 202, 221, 287f., 290, 299, 357f., 360f., 363, 366, 371, 377, 379, 385, 417, 439, 442, 446, 491, 508, 511

Ulrichs, L.-T.   474
Unconditional, Uncoditioned   21, 36, 44, 48f., 55, 57, 60, 74, 164, 180, 192f., 254, 307,
Understanding (*Verstand*)   29, 36–39, 46, 50, 53, 54–55, 60, 71, 73, 80, 90f., 100f., 103, 105f., 119–121, 129, 133f., 136f., 146–149, 151f., 154f., 156, 161–166, 171–184, 186–189, 193, 200f., 204, 209–212, 214, 218, 225–230, 236, 238, 240, 244, 246, 248, 250f., 253–255, 263, 265, 267, 269, 279–282, 285–287, 295–297, 305, 308, 310–312, 316, 318–322, 332, 401, 410, 414, 437, 439, 484
Upanishads   381, 387

Vecchiotti, I.   164, 382
Vedas   84
Vegetation   391, 454
Vercellone, F.   144
Verri, P.   431
Vice   150, 155, 159, 193, 195, 200f., 216, 220, 224f., 230–232, 240, 243, 249f., 263, 279, 281, 328, 337f., 341, 362, 410, 497, 499
Virtue   5, 17, 62f., 71f., 77f., 87, 107, 116f., 146, 150, 185, 191, 193, 195, 198, 219, 230–233, 235, 237f., 240f., 246, 248, 270, 278, 280, 302, 309, 311, 323, 326, 340f., 355f., 361f., 366, 374, 386, 389f., 392, 406, 410, 415,
424, 431, 442, 452, 465, 479f., 482, 487f., 492, 494, 496f., 501, 508
Vishnu   347, 425
Voigt, F. S.   277
Volpi, F.   287
Voltaire   14
Voluntarism/Intellectualism   30, 32f., 202f., 348, 353, 364f., 369f., 415f., 427, 479, 496f., 513
Voluptuousness, Voluptuous Pleasure   12f., 261

Wackenroder, W. H.   14f., 27–29, 42–44, 74, 256, 332
Waibel, V. L.   294
Weigand, K. L.   333
Welchman, A.   154, 473
Well-Being   63f., 204–206, 249, 479, 487
Welsen, P.   440
Werner, Z.   25, 197
Wetzel, J.   32
Why (question)   80, 82, 113, 135f., 322
Wicks, R. L.   24, 287
Wieland, C. M.   2, 61, 338
Will (*Wille*)   19, 23–26, 29–33, 96–99, 106–111, 143–146, 182, 185, 194–197, 202–206, 213, 221, 230, 235f., 238f., 259f., 260, 263f., 267, 289, 291–304, 306–312, 314–318, 328f., 330, 339–346, 348–353, 356–375, 381–388, 390–402, 412–417s
Will, better   202f., 212, 341, 356f., 363, 415, 427f., 429, 504
Willing-Life (*Lebenwollen*)   339–342, 345f., 349, 351f., 356, 358f., 362f, 367f., 370–372, 382, 385, 391, 394, 415, 427, 430, 491, 499, 505f.
Will-not-to-Be   361f., 364, 370
Will-to-Life (*Wille zum Leben*)   164, 196f., 206, 242, 243, 330, 345, 352f., 362, 369, 371f., 384, 386, 390f., 394f., 397f., 415, 419f., 423–427, 432–435, 437, 456, 468f., 471, 476, 478–484, 486–490, 492–497, 500–505, 508, 510–515
Winkelried, A. v.   235, 295
Wolf, F. A.   69
Wolff, Ch.   161, 166, 284
Wood, A. W.   453

World   1–5, 9, 13 f., 16–18, 22–27, 29 f., 33–36, 38, 40–43, 47–49, 51–60, 62, 64, 70–74, 77 f., 80–86, 90 f., 93, 95–99, 101, 104, 108, 114 f., 119–123, 125–134, 136 f., 140–143, 145 f., 151 f., 160 f., 163 f., 166 f., 172–176, 178–184, 186–189, 191–193, 196–201, 203, 205–207, 210–218, 222, 224, 226–229, 232–236, 239 f., 242, 245–251, 253–260, 263, 266–271, 273, 279, 283 f., 292 f., 295–297, 304, 308 f., 311, 318–321, 323–328, 330–335, 339, 341 f., 346, 348–350, 352, 356–365, 367, 371, 373–375, 377–381, 383–390, 394 f., 397 f., 400, 403 f., 406, 410–426, 428–430, 432–434, 436 f., 441–443, 445–451, 454–469, 471–476, 478–481, 483, 486–508, 510, 513–515

Yearning (*Sehnsucht*)   9, 13, 36, 44, 57, 64, 199, 203, 239, 310 f., 363
Yearning (*Streben*), s. Striving   143, 154,
Yogananda, Paramahansa   347

Zimmermann, E.   448
Zint, H.   19, 176, 198, 506
Zinzendorf, N. L. Graf v.   16
Zöller, G.   113, 142, 196, 505, 513

www.ingramcontent.com/pod-product-compliance
Lightning Source LLC
Chambersburg PA
CBHW051532230426
43669CB00015B/2571